EVOLUTION
of
LANGUAGE

THE

EVOLUTION

THE

of

LANGUAGE

Proceedings of the
8th International Conference (EVOLANG8)

Utrecht, Netherlands   14 – 17 April 2010

Editors

Andrew D M Smith
University of Edinburgh, UK

Marieke Schouwstra
Utrecht University, Netherlands

Bart de Boer
Universiteit van Amsterdam, Netherlands

Kenny Smith
Northumbria University, UK

 **World Scientific**

NEW JERSEY · LONDON · SINGAPORE · BEIJING · SHANGHAI · HONG KONG · TAIPEI · CHENNAI

Published by

World Scientific Publishing Co. Pte. Ltd.

5 Toh Tuck Link, Singapore 596224

USA office: 27 Warren Street, Suite 401-402, Hackensack, NJ 07601

UK office: 57 Shelton Street, Covent Garden, London WC2H 9HE

British Library Cataloguing-in-Publication Data
A catalogue record for this book is available from the British Library.

THE EVOLUTION OF LANGUAGE
Proceedings of the 8th International Conference (EVOLANG8)

ISBN-13 978-981-4295-21-5
ISBN-10 981-4295-21-3

Printed in Singapore by B & JO Enterprise

Preface

This volume collects the refereed papers and abstracts of the 8th International Conference on the Evolution of Language (EVOLANG 8), held in Utrecht on 14-17 April 2010. Submissions to the conference were solicited in two forms, papers and abstracts, and this is reflected in the structure of this volume.

The biennial EVOLANG conference is characterised by an invigorating, multi-disciplinary approach to the origins and evolution of human language, and brings together researchers from many fields including anthropology, archaeology, artificial life, biology, cognitive science, computer science, ethology, genetics, linguistics, neuroscience, palaeontology, primatology, psychology and statistical physics.

The multi-disciplinary nature of the field makes the refereeing process for EVOLANG very challenging, and we are indebted to our panel of reviewers for their very conscientious and valuable efforts. A full list of the reviewers in the panel can be found on the following page. Further thanks are also due to:

- The EVOLANG committee: Angelo Cangelosi, Jean-Louis Dessalles, Tecumseh Fitch, Jim Hurford, Chris Knight and Maggie Tallerman.
- The local organising committee: Rudie Botha (Stellenbosch University, Utrecht University), Bart de Boer (University of Amsterdam), Martin Everaert (Utrecht University), Marieke Schouwstra (Utrecht University), Henriëtte de Swart (Utrecht University), Willem Zuidema (University of Amsterdam)
- The plenary speakers: Stephen Anderson (Yale), Morten Christiansen (Cornell), Terrence Deacon (Berkeley),Peter Gärdenfors (Lund), Marc Hauser (Harvard), Wil Roebroeks (Leiden), Eörs Szathmáry (Budapest), Maggie Tallerman (Newcastle)
- The invited speakers: Ian Barnard (Edinburgh), Robert Berwick (MIT), Rebecca Cann (Hawaii) & Karl Diller (Hawaii), Julia Fischer (Göttingen), Kathleen Gibson (Texas at Houston), Patricia Greenfield (UCLA), Eva Jablonka (Tel Aviv) & Daniel Dor (Tel Aviv), Gerhard Jäger (Tübingen), Constance Scharff (FU Berlin), Ann Senghas (Columbia) & Asli Özyurek (MPI, Nijmegen), Marilyn Vihman (York), Thomas Wynn (Colorado at Colorado Springs) & Frederick Coolidge (Colorado at Colorado Springs)
- Finally, and most importantly, the authors of all the contributions collected here.

Andrew Smith, Marieke Schouwstra, Bart de Boer, Kenny Smith
December 2009

Panel of Reviewers

Christian Abry
Michael Arbib
Kate Arnold
Andrea Baronchelli
Mark Bartlett
Teresa Bejarano
Tony Belpaeme
Derek Bickerton
Joris Bleys
Richard Blythe
Jean-Louis Boë
Henry Brighton
Ted Briscoe
Joanna Bryson
Christine Caldwell
Angelo Cangelosi
Ronnie Cann
Andrew Carstairs-McCarthy
Erica Cartmill
Camilo Cela Conde
Morten Christiansen
Louise Connell
Fred Coolidge
Michael Corballis
Hannah Cornish
Wayne Cowart
Tim Crow
Francesco d'Errico
Robert Damper
Joachim de Beule
Bart de Boer
Dan Dediu
Didier Demolin
Jean-Louis Dessalles
Benoît Dubreuil
Shimon Edelman
Mark Ellison
Caleb Everett
Nicolas Fay
Olga Feher
Ramon Ferrer i Cancho
Tecumseh Fitch
Molly Flaherty
Bruno Galantucci
Peter Gärdenfors
Simon Garrod
Les Gasser
Laleh Ghadakpour
Kathleen Gibson

David Gil
Tao Gong
Nathalie Gontier
Tom Griffiths
Rebecca Harrison
Takashi Hashimoto
John Hawks
Bernd Heine
Carlos Hernández-Sacristán
Stefan Hoefler
Jean-Marie Hombert
Carmel Houston-Price
Jim Hurford
Takashi Ikegami
Aritz Irurtzun
Gerhard Jäger
Sverker Johansson
Anne Kandler
Harish Karnick
Judy Kegl
Simon Kirby
Chris Knight
Kiran Lakkaraju
Marion Laporte
Cyprian Laskowski
Simon Levy
Katja Liebal
Phil Lieberman
Elena Lieven
David Lightfoot
John Locke
Erkki Luuk
Dermot Lynott
Davide Marocco
April McMahon
Adrien Meguerditchian
Alexander Mehler
James Minett
Marco Mirolli
Juan-Carlos Moreno
Cabrera
Enric Munar
Makoto Nakamura
Chrystopher Nehaniv
Fritz Newmeyer
Jason Noble
Timothy O'Donnell
Mieko Ogura
Kazuo Okanoya

Asli Özyürek
Irene Pepperberg
Simone Pika
Alessio Plebe
Joseph Poulshock
Camilla Power
Ljiljana Progovac
Greg Radick
Sonia Ragir
Anne Reboul
Luke Rendell
Debi Roberson
Gareth Roberts
Wendy Sandler
Anne-Marijke Schel
Marieke Schouwstra
Ruth Schulz
Thom Scott-Phillips
Robert Seyfarth
Katie Slocombe
Andrew Smith
Kenny Smith
Alona Soschen
James Steele
Samarth Swarup
Maggie Tallerman
Mónica Tamariz
Ian Tattersall
Carel ten Cate
Peter Todd
Huck Turner
Ryoko Uno
Natalie Uomini
Remi van Trijp
Jacques Vauclair
Arie Verhagen
Marilyn Vihman
Paul Vogt
Sławomir Wacewicz
Bill Wang
Andrew Wedel
Pieter Wellens
Mike Wheeler
Liz Wonnacott
Hajime Yamauchi
Henk Zeevat
Jordan Zlatev
Jelle Zuidema

Contents

Part II:Abstracts

Papers

IS GRAMMATICALIZATION GLOSSOGENETIC?

GIORGOS P. ARGYROPOULOS

Language Evolution and Computation Research Unit,
University of Edinburgh, EH8 9LL, United Kingdom

It has recently been suggested that grammaticalization can be fruitfully explained by the glossogenetic mechanisms for language evolution and historical change. Contrary to this position, it is here argued that the incorporation of grammaticalization processes in the glossogenetic ontology is far from unproblematic.

1. Introduction: The Glossogenetic Framework

In glossogenetic models of cultural transmission, language changes through misconvergences between the hypothesis generated by Agent 2 and the one based on which Agent 1 outputs the data that Agent 2 eventually observes (e.g., Brighton *et al.*, 2005). The role of learning/processing biases is here catalytic: linguistic input challenging such constraints does not propagate through the bottleneck, and is marginalized/ regularized by more learnable/ processible schemata, instances of which gradually dominate in *'the arena of use'* (Hurford, 1987). In this respect, *'it is languages, not language users that are adapting'*, since the emergence of more functional forms of communication is *'merely a happy byproduct of the adaptive mechanism at work'* (Kirby *et al.*, 2004), or, as an instance of language adapting to the human brain, and not the reverse (Christiansen & Chater, 2008). Glossogenesis thus provides a radical alternative to (strong versions of) generativist evolutionary considerations, according to which language evolution is principally explicable with respect to the biological evolution of a Language Acquisition Device.

2. Grammaticalization beyond Glossogenesis

Among others, Christiansen and Chater (2008) have recently suggested that the same mechanism can explain grammaticalization phenomena. Contrary to this, I would like to argue that the basic glossogenetic premise of language adaptively changing according to learnability and processibility constraints of the human brain is problematic when employed for the explanation of grammaticalization. In particular, it is susceptible to the same arguments addressed against generativist accounts of grammaticalization (see below for references).

2.1. *The latent generativist premise*

Such accounts have been of paradigmatic value for equivalent evolutionary modeling attempts: Brighton *et al.*, (2005), suggestively, reference simulations of changes resulting *"directly from missconvergences arising during language acquisition"*, such as Clark&Roberts (1993), Niyogi&Berwick (1997), Briscoe (2002), studies explicitly assuming the Principles and Parameters (Chomsky, 1981) framework. Here, the language processor meets significant costs in assigning a particular structure to certain instances of ambiguous input, and reanalyzes them according to a considerably more acquirable/ processible structure, as in Robert's (1993: 228-9) *"Least Effort Strategy"* in the changes of the future tense in Romance (see also Lightfoot (1979) on English modals).

Characteristically, Hashimoto and Nakatsuka (2006) assume Campbell's (2001) heavily criticized position that reanalysis (for Langacker(1977, p. 59), *'change in the structure of an expression or class of expressions that does not involve any immediate or intrinsic modification of its surface manifestation'*) and analogy (according to Hopper and Traugott (1993, p. 56), *'the attraction of extant forms to already existing constructions'*) underlie grammaticalization, and instantiate them in the operations that linguistic agents perform in learning and generalizing their grammar in Kirby's (2002) compositionality model. However, reanalysis has been argued to be dissociable from grammaticalization: reanalysis is an abrupt phenomenon, does not involve the loss of autonomy of linguistic signs, is not inherently unidirectional, and presupposes ambiguity and mis-processing/ mislearning of the input; Reanalysis occurs without the necessary accompaniment of grammaticalization, and, conversely, grammaticalization may occur without reanalysis. Reanalysis involves contracting new syntactic relations with sentence elements not related before, whereas grammaticalization does not involve any real change in constituent structure. Grammaticalization may lead to structures and categories that have not existed, while reanalysis, acting on an analogical basis, only operates on already available categories (see Haspelmath(1998) and Lehmann (2004) for a discussion of the above points) and thus may not suffice as an explanation for the development of a new grammatical category. In this sense, input ambiguity and the interaction of misconvergences with capacity limitations are explicitly considered irrelevant with grammaticalization processes. The argument remains the same if one is to employ *'processing preferences'*-based explanations, (such as Hawkins' (2004), explicitly distinguishes grammaticalization processes from the ones in his work) to account for grammaticalization operations: The derivation of a new grammatical category is not explicable by the adoption of a more preferable template (already there) for the analysis of a given input string.

It has similarly been suggested that semantic miscovergence in historical change might provide a glossogenetic insight into grammaticalization. However, what has been termed *'semantic reanalysis'* (Hoefler and Smith (2009) use the term *'reanalysis'* to denote what Heine (2003) has called *'context-induced reinterpretation'*) is far from intrinsic to grammaticalization, as it pertains to a radically broader range of lexical items, only a minority of which acquires grammatical functions. Despite allowing expressions to increase in frequency of occurrence and acquire basic discourse status, it does not explain the core transition from lexical-conceptual to grammatical-procedural status that grammaticalizing expressions undergo (Nicolle, 1998; Bybee et al., 1994; Haspelmath, 1999).

Thus, despite its emphasis on E-language properties, glossogenesis crucially remains, like the generativist explanation of grammaticalization, a *"competence-based"* (Haspelmath, 1998) one: it is committed to viewing E-language properties as explanatorily significant only for the negotiation of I-language representations, and not for the introduction of *'performance changes'* (*ibid.*), the results of which macroscopically provide grammaticalized variants.

2.2. *Ontological dissociation: Reducing and Conserving*

In delimiting the ontology of grammaticalization and glossogenetic mechanisms, it is valuable to consider the distinction between the *'Conserving'* and the *'Reducing effects'* of linguistic repetition in historical language change (Bybee & Thompson, 2000): Glossogenesis is best construable as studying the *'Storage effects'* (*ibid.*) of repetition (conservation of irregularity, analogical leveling-generalization-regularization, reanalysis), not the *'Processing effects'* (*ibid.*). In their brief discussion of grammaticalization processes, suggestively, Christiansen and Chater (2008) reference Hare and Elman's (1995) simulation as an example of historical language change studied on the basis of learning/processing constraints. Yet the phenomenon described is one of analogical leveling and conservation phenomena in the acquisition of verbal morphology, and is far from relevant with grammaticalization processes to encourage a similar approach to the latter. Hawkins' (2004) processing principles, or even Batali's (2002) work on exemplar competition provide characteristic cases (the ones consistent with observations become liable for re-usage and creation of new S-M mappings, while others are used less often and are overtaken by the most prominent ones).

Grammaticalization, on the other hand, precisely represents a multilevel *"reducing effect"* (Bybee & Thompson, 2000) of repetition. Automatization of performance in language processing, the most widely supported cognitive core of grammaticalization (e.g., Givòn, 1979; Bybee, 1998; Haspelmath, 1999; Lehmann, 2004), represents an instance of domain-general, non-species-specific adaptive responses against repeated behavioral repertoires, and involves particular neurocognitive mechanisms (see Argyropoulos (2008) for neurolinguistic reflections). Here, linguistic change does not involve misprocessing of ambiguous input, but is the result of the user's adaptive minimization of cognitive and attentional/motoric costs, and hence of the freedom in the manipulation of linguistic signs (Lehmann, 2004). A clear example of the dissociation of those two kinds of change (summarized in **Figure 1**) is shown in Hooper (1976), where sound change is demonstrated to affect high-frequency items first, and analogical leveling to affect low-frequency items first.

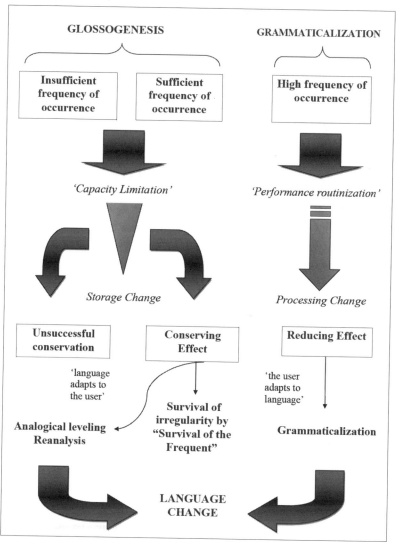

Figure 1: Dissociation between the ontology of glossogenesis and the one of grammaticalization, following Bybee & Thompson's (2000) distinction between the conserving and reducing effects of linguistic repetition; despite the rich interactions between the two effects (not portrayed here), both the changes and their corresponding triggers are clearly dissociable.

3. Functionalist Criticism and Directionality of Language Transmission

Functionalist criticism (Croft, 2004) on glossogenesis has failed to address this topic, rather emphasizing the need to abandon vertical (language acquisition-based) models of transmission for the simulation of historical change; but this premise has been identified as only a methodologically justified simplification (Smith *et al.*, 2003). Yet even in a horizontal transmission model, change is introduced with agents misattributing an underlying representation to linguistic strings because of processing limitations encountered. In Batali (2002, p. 115), for example, where the sender transmits a signal S to express a meaning M1, following a particular analysis A1 of the mapping from the structure of M1 to the signal S, with the receiver deriving an interpretation M2 according to analysis A2 of the mapping from the signal structure to M2, language change is initiated by a discrepancy between A1 and A2, where A2 is more optimal with respect to the processing constraints of the language agent than A1. This is the case in reanalysis and analogical leveling, or in the conservation of irregular frequent patterns- not in grammaticalization, unless one adheres to heavily criticized generativist constraint-based modeling.

4. Concluding remarks

The issue addressed here apparently does not refer to the feasibility of computational simulations of grammaticalization processes, but questions the compatibility of glossogenesis with the explanandum of grammaticalization. Thus, the eventual convergence of grammaticalization theory and evolutionary computational modeling (Hurford, 2003) still deserves encouragement; however, according to the strongest version of the argument, such convergence is impossible in the glossogenetic framework, as its ontology is by definition distinct from grammaticalization phenomena; in its weakest version, the argument instructs that such contradictory assumptions be identified and disposed of in this interdisciplinary discourse.

Acknowledgments

The author warmly acknowledges the financial support from the Pavlos and Elissavet Papagiannopoulou Foundation.

References

Argyropoulos, G. (2008). The subcortical foundations of grammaticalization. In A. D. M. Smith, K. Smith, & R. Ferrer i Cancho (Eds.), *The Evolution of Language: Proceedings of the 7th International Conference on the Evolution of Language*. (pp. 10-17). Singapore: World Scientific Press.

Batali, J. (2002). The negotiation and acquisition of recursive grammars as a result of competition among exemplars. In E. Briscoe (Ed.) *Linguistic Evolution through Language Acquisition: Formal and Computational Models* (pp. 111-172). Cambridge: Cambridge University Press.

Brighton, H., Kirby, S., & Smith, K. (2005). Cultural selection for learnability: Three hypotheses underlying the view that language adapts to be learnable. In Tallerman, M. (Ed.) *Language Origins: Perspective on evolution*. Oxford University Press, Oxford.

Briscoe, E. (Ed.) (2002). Linguistic Evolution through Language Acquisition: Formal and Computational Models. *Cambridge: Cambridge University Press.*

Bybee, J. L. (1998). A functionalist approach to grammar and its evolution. *Evolution of Communication, 2, 249-278.*

Bybee, J.L., Perkins, R., & Pagliuca, W. (1994). *The evolution of grammar. Tense, Aspect, and Modality in the Languages of the World.* Chicago and London.

Bybee, J. L. & Thompson, S. (2000). *Three frequency effects in syntax.* Berkeley Linguistic Society, 23, *65-85.*

Campbell, L. (2001). What's wrong with grammaticalization? *Language Sciences*, 23, *113-161.*

Chomsky, N. (1981). Principles and parameters in syntactic theory. In N. Hornstein & D. Lightfoot (Eds.), *Explanations in Linguistics.* London: Longman.

Christiansen, M.H., & Chater, N. (2008). Language as shaped by the brain. *Behavioral and Brain Sciences, 31(5)*, 489-509.

Clark, R., & Roberts, I. (1993). A computational model of language learnability and language change. *Linguistic Inquiry*, 24, *299-345.*

Croft, W. (2004). Form, meaning and speakers in the evolution of language. *Studies in Language*, 28(3), *608-611.*

Givòn, T. (1979). *On Understanding Grammar.* New York: Academic Press. Structure. Chicago: University of Chicago.

Hare, M., & Elman, J.L. (1995). Learning and morphological change. *Cognition*, 56, 61-98.

Hashimoto, T., & Nakatsuka, M. (2006), Reconsidering Kirby's compositionality model toward modeling grammaticalization. In A. Cangelosi et al. (Eds.), *The Evolution of Language, Proceedings of the 6th International Conference (EvoLang6)*, (pp. 415-416). World Scientific.

Haspelmath, M. (1998). Does grammaticalization need reanalysis? *Studies in Language*, 22, 315-51.

Haspelmath, M. (1999). Why is grammaticalization irreversible? *Linguistics* 37(6), 1043-1068.

Hawkins, J. A. (2004*). Efficiency and complexity in Grammars.* Oxford: Oxford University Press.

Heine, B. (2003). Grammaticalization. In B. D. Joseph, & R. D. Janda (Eds.) *The Handbook of Historical Linguistics.* (pp. 575-601) Oxford: Blackwell.

Hoefler, S., & Smith, A.D.M. (2009). The Pre-linguistic Basis of Grammaticalisation: A Unified Approach to Metaphor and Reanalysis. *Studies in Language* 33(4), 883-906.

Hooper, J. B. (1976). Word frequency in lexical diffusion and the source of morphophonological change. In W. Christie (Ed.). *Current progress in historical linguistics* (pp. 95-105). Amsterdam: North Holland.

Hopper, P., & Traugott, E.C. (1993). *Grammaticalization.* Cambridge: Cambridge University Press.

Hurford, J. (1987). *Language and Number: The Emergence of a Cognitive System.* Oxford: Basil Blackwell.

Hurford, J. (2003). The Language Mosaic and its Evolution. In M.H. Christiansen and S. Kirby, (Eds.), *Language Evolution: The States of the Art.* Oxford University Press.

Kirby, S. (2002). Learning, bottlenecks, and the evolution of recursive syntax. In E. J. Briscoe (Ed.), *Linguistic Evolution through Language Acquisition.* Cambridge: Cambridge University Press.

Kirby, S., Smith, K., and Brighton, H. (2004). From UG to Universals: Linguistic adaptation through iterated learning. *Studies in Language*, 28(3), pp. 587- 607.

Langacker, R. (1977). Syntactic reanalysis. In C. Li (Ed.) *Mechanisms of Syntactic Change* (pp. 57–139). Austin, TX: University of Texas Press.

Lehmann, C. (2004). Theory and method in grammaticalization. *Zeitschrift fur Germanistische Linguistik,* 32(2), 152-187.

Lightfoot, D. (1979). *Principles of Diachronic Syntax.* New York: Cambridge University Press.

Nicolle, S. (1998), A relevance theory perspective on grammaticalization. *Cognitive Linguistics,* 9(1), 1-35.

Niyogi, P., & Berwick, R. (1997), Evolutionary consequences of language learning. *Linguistics and Philosophy,* 20, 697-719.

Roberts, I. (1993). A formal account of grammaticalization in the history of Romance futures. *Folia Linguistica Historica* ,13(1-2), 219-258.

Smith, K., Kirby, S. Brighton, H. (2003). Iterated Learning: A framework for the emergence of language. *Artifical Life,* 9(4), 371-386.

MYTHOLOGY AND THE EVOLUTION OF LANGUAGE

ALAN BARNARD

Social Anthropology, University of Edinburgh,
CMB, 15A George Square, Edinburgh EH8 9LD, UK
a.barnard@ed.ac.uk

Languages are far more complex than they need to be for one-to-one communication. This paper attempts to answer the question as to why that should be. The answer, it is suggested, lies in the evolution of story-telling, legend and myth as culturally-important means of expression. Myth may not mark the dawn of proto- or rudimentary language, or even the beginnings of full language, but its existence accounts at least in part for the evolution of linguistic complexity. Language co-evolved with mythology in symbolic frameworks which extended, to the limits of cognition, the capacity for verbal expression.

1. Introduction

As an undergraduate some 40 years ago, I studied anthropology in an American four-field department. Archaeology and physical anthropology were taught within an evolutionist framework, but cultural anthropology and anthropological linguistics were taught within a relativist framework. The exercises we did in linguistics showed us that Navajo has eleven classificatory verb stems, Swahili has eighteen noun classes, and Inuktitut has, *not* five words for 'snow', but an uncountable number of such words—each as long as a complex English sentence. No-one asked why. Nor were these apparent facts considered relevant to issues in any other branch of four-field anthropology, except in that comparisons in technology and in social organization showed us that supposedly 'primitive' peoples most certainly did not speak 'primitive' languages.

This paper *does* ask why. Why is language often over-determined (and sometimes underdetermined)? Take an example from my early fieldwork in Botswana. Depending on how one counts them, my primary fieldwork language, Naro (Nharo), has something like 86 person-number-gender markers. One could count many more, up to 204 I believe, or rather fewer, depending on how one defines case function, whether changes in tone according to case should count, and how one deals with duplicates, that is, the same form with different meanings (cf. D. F. Bleek 1928: 53-56; Barnard 1985: 15-19; Visser 2001: 238-

11

239). The same applies, more or less, to all other Khoe (Central Khoisan) languages. My practical question, at the time, was: why should these semi-hunter-gatherers, who live in groups of no more than a few dozen, have *so damned many pronouns* (and how am I going to remember them all)?

English has no future. By this I mean that English, like other Germanic languages, is missing a future tense. Of course, in the absence of one, 'will' or 'shall', or 'is about to', and so on, may be inserted before the verb to give future meaning. But why should English have to do this? Languages seem to be put together in ways that makes no practical sense. Most languages are more complicated than they have to be. And very few of them are quite as perfect in ability to express anything as Whorf (1956: 84-85) imagined Hopi to be. And Hopi, according to Whorf (1956: 57-64), is tense-less.

In short, language is both over-determined and under-determined. This might be explainable partly with reference to the cognitive capabilities of the human mind, and if I were a neuroscientist I would certainly look there for explanations. But as a social anthropologist I require social and cultural explanations as well. It troubles me that there is no correspondence between social structure and linguistic structure, but I do have a tentative answer. The answer, I suggest in this paper, lies in the evolutionary power of myth, and in the complexity of language required to meet the semiotic and social requirements for myth-telling.

2. The Language of Myth

'Hé tíkẹn ē, /kǔammaṅ-a há /ne kúi: "Ṅ kaṅ ka, a ≠kákka !kõïṅ, tssá ra χá ā, !kõïṅ ta /kǔ /ê //ě !k'é ē /χárra?'' (Then /kǔammaṅ-a said: 'I desire thee to say to grandfather, Why is it that grandfather continues to go among strangers [literally, people who are different]?') (Bleek & Lloyd 1911: 32-33).

Hé	*tíkẹn*	*ē*	*/kǔammaṅ-a*	*há*	*/ne*	*kúi: 'Ṅ*	*kaṅ*	*ka,*
Then	thing	which	/Kuamman-a	this	(imperative)	say : 'I	(stress)	say

a	*≠kákka*	*!kõïṅ,*	*tssá ra*	*χá*	*ā,*	*!kõïṅ*
(to) thee	say/ask	grandfather,	why	(interrogative)	it is	grandfather

ta	*/kǔ*	*/ê*	*//ě*	*!k'é*	*ē*	*/χárra?*
(habitual action)	(continuous action)	among	go	people	who	(be) different?'

In this /Xam sentence, the now-famous phrase, *!k'é ē /xárra* (*!ke e: /xarra*), 'people who are different', is the object of a complex, and specifically narrative-form, verb *ha /kŭ /ē //ĕ*, (roughly, 'to continue habitually to go among'). A description of habitually continuous action, within an interrogative sentence, within an imperative sentence, within another imperative sentence, within an indicative sentence, within a myth or fable in which animals act as people, told to an English woman by a /Xam man, who had learned it from his mother, who presumably had learned it from someone else, who had put it together with culturally-significant social action, with metaphor and with complex syntax, for a reason well beyond the requirements of ordinary communication.

I say 'now-famous', because by a peculiar twist of fate, the phrase *!ke e: /xarra*, uttered in the telling of the myth to Lucy Lloyd in 1878, found its way into Dorothea Bleek's posthumous *Bushman dictionary* of 1956 (D. F. Bleek 1956: 363), and ended up as the grammatical subject of South Africa's motto in the year 2000. The motto is *!Ke e: /xarra //ke*, officially 'Diverse people unite' or 'People who are different come together'. I think it is both more accurately and more interestingly rendered as 'People of different origins, joining together', or even 'People who differ in opinion, talking with one another'. The complexity of that translation hints at the complexity which lies behind this phrase, as indeed does the verb of the motto, *//ke*, which usually means 'to come together' but can also mean 'to talk with one another' (see Barnard 2003). *//Ke* was added to the phrase by rock-art expert David Lewis-Williams to make up an approximation of the English words 'Diverse people unite', which President Thabo Mbeki had asked him to translate into /Xam.

The myth is called *!Gãúnu-tsaxãú, /hú/hú, he /kággen* (or 'The son of Mantis, the baboons, and the Mantis'). In the version recorded by Lucy Lloyd, it is about 3,000 words long. It tells of the killing of a child by baboons. The child turns out to be one of Mantis's grandsons. The baboons take the child's eye out and use it as a ball, and grandfather Mantis plays ball with the baboons: hence /Kuamman-a's question. Later, Mantis secretly steals the eye and puts it into water. This, apparently, restores life to the child.

3. Myth in Mythological Context

Myths are never just stories. They always occur in the context of a mythological system, which is specific to a given 'society' or 'culture'. I place 'society' and 'culture' in inverted commas because these are contested abstractions. What is not contested, I hope, is the systematic nature of a mythology—a set of myths peculiar to a socio-cultural context. Myths are not only shared within a speech community. They are related to each other. The same deities, the same mythological beasts, the same themes of trickery, death, hunting, sex, kinship and so on, will occur in many myths within the same speech community, and beyond it. Myths occur in sequence, and they are cross-referential. They impart cultural knowledge, and they also draw on prior cultural knowledge, as well as on meaning derived more directly from the words in the myths.

The narrator of this myth remarks in an aside, placed by Lucy Lloyd in a footnote (Bleek & Lloyd 1911: 16-17), that when quoting baboons he speaks in his own style of language –on the grounds that 'the speech of the baboons is not easy'. In other myths, it is revealed that non-human creatures have different ways of speaking than humans, or insects: in the context of these myths, insects *are* to be taken as if human. Baboons are neither insects nor human, but they look like humans, and according to the /Xam they once were human. They speak 'Bushman', but as the informant suggests, speak it in a funny and difficult way. They look like people, and they imitate human behaviour. Baboons also eat like humans, but they violate meat-sharing practices. They are ritually potent, but behave badly in many ways: in one myth, for example, seducing a menstruating girl, and in another, beating Mantis to death (see Hollmann 2004: 7-29).

/Xam mythology comprises a system of knowledge, composed of elements of natural history, Bushman-world prehistory, ethical guidance, kinship structure, narrative composition, metaphor, and of course, language. There are in fact many myths about language, specifically about the languages of animals—both individual deity-animals and collective species of animal. Of Wilhelm Bleek and Lucy Lloyd's three main informants, it is estimated that //Kabbo provided 3,100 pages of material, /Han≠ass'ō 2,800 pages, and Dia!kwāĩn 2,400 pages (Lewis-Williams 1981: 27-28). /Han≠ass'ō (/hañ≠ass'ō), is the narrator of the myth under consideration here. That system of knowledge obviously requires order, which is provided through the narrative structure of myths. Naro, the group among whom I have worked, make no distinction between stories of what happened on the day, legends about exploits of the past, animal fables, and myths—calling them all *huwa-ne*. The situation in the long-extinct /Xam language is actually not clear to me, but judging by the texts themselves, I suspect that much the same is true here as well.

4. Myth in Social Context

In the /Xam myth 'The son of Mantis, the baboons, and the Mantis', there are two social contexts: the social context in which the myth is told, and the social context within the myth. Let me take the latter first.

4.1. *Social Context within the Myth*

The social context within the myth is also part of the mythological context, but it is worth thinking about it as part of a larger (human) societal context too. The characters of this myth are not humans, but insects and baboons. The characters named individually are all insects, although their relatives include Blue Crane, Porcupine, and All-devourer—whose power (in other myths) is related to untamed fire (see Fig. 1). /Kuammang-a is a unique name. The reason he speaks through his son Ichneumon in the /Xam sentence above, is that direct address to one's father-in-law, in this case Mantis, is taboo for the /Xam.

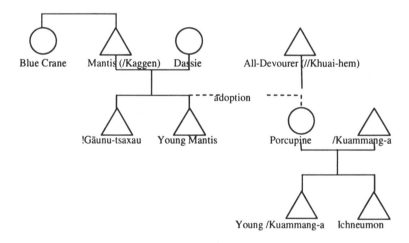

Figure 1. Mantis's family (adapted from Hewitt 1986: 146)

4.2. *Social Contexts in which Myths are Told*

Myths are told in a social context. The duration of a myth-telling is very variable, worldwide. In my own early (and later) fieldwork, I was extremely poor at recording myths, partly because Naro assume that everyone present already knows the myth, and thus it is often abbreviated to a minute or two. At the other extreme, I have heard anthropologists who work in South America speak of a single myth taking up to three days to tell. Myths in South America, and elsewhere, may include narrative elaboration and the telling of myths within myths, interspersed with ritual, consumption of food and drugs, and sleep.

Lucy Lloyd recorded this /Xam myth from Han≠ass'ō, who had heard it from his mother /Xabbi-an. After the sentence quoted above, /Han≠ass'ō continues: 'Then the Mantis answered: "Thou dost appear to think that yearning was not that on account of which I went among the baboons;" while he did not tell /kuaṁmaṅ-a and the others that he came (and) put the child's eye into the water' (Bleek & Lloyd 1911: 33). In other words, /Kaggen the Mantis is implying that he yearned for the life (and as the myth tells later, also the welfare) of the child, and his secret action of putting the eye into the water shows this. It is not clear to me whether this was Mantis being good (as he could be) or Mantis acting as a trickster or in deceit (as often he did), but I suspect the former. Either way, the myth imparts in the present social information about a mythical past.

5. Myth in World Context

Myths occur in a larger inter-societal or cross-cultural mythological context, as well as in the context of specific speech communities. I mean by this that the same themes, and virtually identical beings, occur throughout the world. Jackals, foxes and coyotes are tricksters, in Africa, Europe and North America respectively. Throughout the southern hemisphere, the moon is a benevolent and male being, and the sun is harmful and female. In the northern hemisphere it is the reverse.

Radcliffe-Brown drew our attention to such cross-cultural similarities in his famous essay on 'The comparative method in social anthropology' (1952), and Lévi-Strauss followed suit in 'The structural study of myth' (1955) and in numerous subsequent publications. Radcliffe-Brown's own fieldwork was in the Andaman Islands and in Australia, and he noted in his paper (1952: 18) that virtually the same tale, of the destruction of the original society of all the animals, occurs in both places. In New South Wales, the story goes that in the beginning all animals lived together. Then the bat killed his two wives, which was the first occurrence of death. His brothers-in-law called a corroboree, caught the bat, and threw him into the fire. This started a war of all against all, with fire as the weapon. The animals now all bear the scars of fire and no longer live together in a single society. In the Andamans, the story is very similar (and, I might add, so too are /Xam and other San versions). Radcliffe-Brown (1952: 16-

18) also remarks on the pairing of Eaglehawk and Crow, found in the myths of different parts of Aboriginal Australia and on the Northwest Coast of North America. Eaglehawk and Crow are opponents in conflict, and the birds encode both kinship obligations and moral codes. For example, in Western Australia, Eaglehawk is Crow's mother's brother, and therefore his potential father-in-law and one to whom he should provide food. But in myth, Crow kills a wallaby and keeps the meat for himself, and that violation in noted. (This also explains why crows do not hunt, but steal carrion instead.)

Wilhelm Bleek and his family (including Lloyd) are often said to have been interested in /Xam because they believed it was close to the *Ursprache* of all humankind. Of course, I do not believe that it is, and have used /Xam as my example here simply because it is an example that I know. However, I do believe that the mythologies of world are based on universal structural principles. I also believe that they *might* preserve elements of a very deep mythological system dating to the time of *Homo sapiens* migration. Certainly, there are enough similarities in the mythologies of the world to suggest that, along with language, myths travelled across the continents. The possibilities for language change were far greater than those for myth change. Myths changed by combining and re-combining elements, or *mythèmes* as Lévi-Strauss calls them, to create new mythological systems, but almost always within larger systems of systems recognizable from continent to continent (see, e.g. Lévi-Strauss 1978). It is no accident that Wilhelm Bleek's (1864) collection of Khoekhoe texts was called *Reynard the fox in South Africa*.

6. Conclusion

I do not deny the importance of practical communication, or of neurological or other anatomical factors, or of music, ritual, exchange, or the complexification of kinship in the origins and evolution of language. I argue here simply that mythology, and its probable antecedents story-telling and legend, should be added to the list. Mythology does not perhaps explain the origin of language, but it does explain in part why language needs to be as complex as it is.

I referred at the beginning to examples of linguistic complexity, and perhaps I should add here that /Xam has its fair share, for example, at least 24 verbal particles which go before the verb to indicate mood and tense, and some 6 verbal suffixes to indicate duration or repetition of action, emphasis, or passive voice (D. F. Bleek 1929/30: 161-167). With nouns, there are at least 14 different ways to form a plural: by reduplicating the simple form, reduplicating the emphatic form, joining the simple and emphatic forms, and so on (D. F. Bleek 1928/29:

88-93). We have seen some of the former in the mythic sentence presented in this paper. Without such constructions, there can at best be only conversation. Narrative, and with it myth, upon which both the social and the symbolic worlds depend, requires much more linguistic baggage to make it work.

References

Barnard, A. (1985). *A Nharo wordlist with notes on grammar*. Durban: Department of African Studies, University of Natal.

Barnard, A. (2003). !Ke e: /xarra //ke – Multiple origins and multiple meanings of the motto. *African Studies*, 62, 243-250.

Bleek, D. F. (1928). *The Naron: A Bushman tribe of the central Kalahari*. Cambridge: Cambridge University Press.

Bleek, D. F. (1928/29). Bushman grammar: A grammatical sketch of the language of the /xam-ka-!k'e. *Zeitschrift für Eingeborenen-Sprachen*, 19, 81-98.

Bleek, D. F. (1929/30). Bushman grammar: A grammatical sketch of the language of the /xam-ka-!k'e (continuation). *Zeitschrift für Eingeborenen-Sprachen*, 20, 161-174.

Bleek, D. F. (1956). *A Bushman dictionary* (American Oriental Series, vol. 41). New Haven: American Oriental Society.

Bleek, W. H. I. (1864) *Reynard the fox in South Africa: Hottentot fables and tales*. London: Trübner.

Bleek, W. H. I. & Lloyd, L. C. (1911). *Specimens of Bushman folklore*. London: George Allen & Company.

Hewitt, R. L. (1986). *Structure, meaning and ritual in the narratives of the Southern San* (Quellen zur Khoisan-Forschung, Band 2). Hamburg: Helmut Buske Verlag.

Hollmann, J. C. (Ed.) (2004). *Customs and beliefs of the /Xam Bushmen*. Johannesburg: Witwatersrand University Press.

Lévi-Strauss, C. (1955). The structural study of myth. *Journal of American Folklore*, 78, 428-444.

Lévi-Strauss, C. (1978). *Myth and meaning*. Toronto: University of Toronto Press.

Lewis-Williams, J. D. (1981). *Believing and seeing: Symbolic meanings in southern San rock paintings*. London: Academic Press.

Radcliffe-Brown, A. R. (1952). The comparative method in social anthropology. *Journal of the Royal Anthropological Institute*, 81, 15-22.

Visser, H. (2001). *Naro dictionary: Naro-English, English-Naro* (fourth edition). Gantsi: Naro Language Project / SIL International.

Whorf, B. L. (1956). *Language, thought, and reality: Selected writings of Benjamin Lee Whorf* (J. B. Carroll, Ed.). Cambridge, MA: M.I.T. Press.

SYMMETRICAL ARTEFACTS, INTERNAL REWARD AND LANGUAGE PRECURSORS IN THE HEAD

BRIAN BAYLY

E&ES Department, Rensselaer Polytechnic Institute, 110 Eighth Street Troy NY, 12180, USA

Present-day people derive pleasure from rhymes, rhythms and repetitive visual patterns, that is, from instances of similarity. Similarity is the basis for grouping items into categories and so setting up abstract general concepts such as *ripeness* or *weight*. In present times, such grouping by similarity is a source of pleasure; the current plethora of concepts and words denoting them derives partly from pleasure in forming them. Then the question arises: how far back in prehistory has this pleasure been a motivation? Both beads and handaxes suggest by their symmetry that hominins may have derived this pleasure-in-the-head or internal reward as far back as Acheulian time: at this time, the motivation to construct abstract general concepts and thus expand language may have already been present. The timing is open to question but the pattern of inference connecting symmetry to language is particularly direct.

1. Introduction

In exploring the evolution of language, part of the art is to find indicators in the archaeological record of stages in the development of hominins' mental life. In an oversimplified view, two stages can be distinguished. In the first, communication between hominins concerns objects, moods or events that are present to the communicators or are remembered by them; topics of communication are limited to things that already exist. In the second stage, abstract general concepts such as *weight* are referred to in communication. Speaker and hearer both rely on experience with actual objects but the abstract property *weight* is a concept created by them, and creation of concepts has no limits. It is reaching the second stage that sets language free, that enables the amazing expansion into the language of today; but two intermediate steps are essential before the second stage is entered. First, a few abstract general concepts have to be formed privately in some hominins' minds and second, the concepts have to be labeled in private before public labels can be agreed upon (Steels, 1996; Tallerman, 2009:197). Soon a stage is reached in which a concept can be taught --- introduced into a learner's mind from out of a mind where the concept is already alive, but there must be a stage in which a few individuals separately conceive and possess some particular abstract concept and discover that a companion has something parallel in mind.

At such a moment, communication about an abstract concept can begin. Once abstract concepts become a topic for communication, the power of language is unleashed, its use becomes adaptive, and growth is assured. But when an abstract concept first arises privately in the head of an individual its adaptive value is slight and questions of motivation arise: why would a hominin form an abstract concept in the first place? The theme of the present contribution is that forming an abstract concept from a group of instances is intrinsically a pleasure: getting pleasure from forming general concepts is a crucial motivation. Without that motivation, language stagnates; with it, language frees itself from referring only to the here-and-now and expands without limit. Now, the pleasure of forming an abstract concept from instances can be related to the symmetry of artefacts (handaxes and beads), and thus the artefacts serve as indicators of the presence of an essential prelinguistic attribute of mind.

For brevity, the train of thought is presented through positive statements, alternatives and debatable points being deferred. Throughout, the example provided by Tallerman (2009) is followed, of considering the critical moments when essential early concepts were first formed privately in the minds of certain hominins, as prelude to the invention of words to denote them. Amidst progress in modeling the relevant processes, the need for attention to motivation is noted by Laskowski (2008).

A completely different line of argument (d'Errico et al., 2005; Botha, 2008) links beads and other ornamentation to self-awareness. This argument concerns a later stage in the evolution of language and does not attach special significance to symmetry.

2. Symmetrical artefacts: beads and handaxes

The beads in question from several African locations (d'Errico et al., 2005; Bednarik, 2005:539, 2008) are discs of ostrich egg shell about 7 mm in diameter with a central hole. Their outlines are nearly perfectly circular. Eggshell fragments have no natural circular character; thus one has to suppose that the shape was intentionally produced. Once produced, such beads might have had utility as gifts or for barter or display but any such use is secondary, deriving from the beads' primary quality of attractiveness. One concludes that the maker of the beads or some associate in the community was sensitive to symmetry and valued it for its aesthetic/hedonic effect.

The symmetry of handaxes has evoked comment since the early discoveries, but here the influence of utility is more uncertain. Some degree of symmetry contributes to the utility of the tool, but it has been claimed (e.g. Kohn & Mithen, 1999) that in some examples the degree of symmetry goes beyond what utility could require. The transition point is discussed in Section 6, Dating; here it is assumed simply that at some point the utility-limit is passed and that the record does include some instances of symmetry produced for aesthetic/hedonic effect, as with the beads.

3. Pleasure from symmetry --- present-day humans

A symmetrical object is one in which two or more parts are alike, and in the present-day human mind alikeness is a source of pleasure (Humphrey, 1973; Fost, 1999). People enjoy rhymes, rhythms, repeated visual patterns, a photograph and a matching memory, anything recognized as familiar, two similar eddies in a stream, or an eddy seen today and an eddy in memory from yesterday. The hedonic effect is usually small, so much so that its presence has attracted little attention, but it is widely recognized as present. And a physiological conclusion can be drawn: the present-day human brain contains a system that has as input two items that are alike and has as output a usually-tiny spasm of pleasure. The system is multi-modal or supra-modal, operating across sounds, sights and odors at a "high" cortical level (Plailly *et al.*, 2007). It operates equally on mental representations constructed from perception or from retrievals from memory.

4. Alikeness and categories

As mentioned briefly in the Introduction, the basis for most abstract general concepts such as *weight* is a group of instances. It is possible that a few concepts of this type are generated by single dramatic events but the great majority of concepts are generated by classifying or categorizing. The role of prototypes is debatable but for present purposes the role of prototypes does not need to be resolved; the point in view here is that *pleasure* is involved:

"... (other animals) do not extract characters for the mere fun of the thing, as men do." – William James (1892).

"... men ... take pleasure in classificatory activity ..." – Nicholas Humphrey (1973).

Classifying, categorizing and *forming an abstract general concept* are closely allied; to classify is to assign items to categories, and the features that the objects in a class have in common constitute a concept based on that class (with allowance for exceptions and fuzziness). A hominin who sees an eddy in a stream today will recall an eddy seen the day before and associate them merely for the pleasure involved --- no question of utility applies. And by repetition and accumulation, the common features shown by many eddies get reinforced in mind while the accidental features of separate instances get forgotten. By such means, a general concept is born with no motivation except pleasure.

5.   A continuum of pleasures

The overall purpose is to link the shaping of symmetrical artefacts to the forming of abstract general concepts, and for this purpose a series is presented: a bead's circular symmetry, a handaxe's bilateral symmetry, a neat Y-shaped twig, the right and left sides of a leaf, two similar leaves, two similar eddies in a stream, one eddy observed and one remembered, or a group of eddies one can recall from memory. In a present-day person, all of these yield pleasure and it is the same pleasure --- from alikeness --- all down the list. The conclusion is that a hominin with an aptitude for enjoying symmetry in physical objects has also the aptitude for enjoying the construction of private general concepts in the head.

[Contrary to the continuity just suggested, it might be pointed out that at one end of the putative continuum we are in the material world, whereas at the other end we are engaged wholly with non-material mental effects (or material only to the extent that any mental process has a neural correlate), and these seem like incommensurable realms. But this suggestion fails upon review of the vision process. The parts of the vision system close to perceived objects detect edges, extents, motions and colors; these raw or low-level effects set in motion a series of transformations of the signal into higher-level forms. The high-level process in the cortex of "seeing a leaf" is almost as far removed from any physical leaf as the process of remembering a leaf. Both lead to mental representations, and there is no need to suppose that the hedonic system activated by two representations' alikeness is at all affected by the remote regions where the representations had their source.]

6.   Dating

The uncertainties presented by dating are different for the two types of artefact: with the earliest-claimed beads there is possible allochthony whereas with handaxes there is possible utility.

A large number of occurrences of ostrich eggshell beads are reviewed by d'Errico *et al.*, (2005). They constitute evidence of a tradition dating back to at least 40 ka BP but not significantly earlier than that. By contrast, certain beads from southern Libya that are similar in material and geometry (Bednarik, 2005, 2008) are described by Ziegert (1998) as associated with Acheulean material. Such an isolated occurrence is suspect unless confirmed; the beads themselves have not been dated and the association might be due to some post-Acheulean disturbance of material. But an Acheulean date for symmetry in beads is not inconsistent with evidence from handaxes if handaxe symmetry can be accepted as aesthetic/hedonic.

Utility in handaxes is of two forms: handaxes have primary utility as tools and secondary utility for display, barter or as gifts. But the latter is termed secondary because it derives from a primary quality in the object: the object must be attractive or admirable to serve these functions. Handaxes are thus created to be either attractive or merely serviceable. Experiments such as those of Machin *et al.* (2007) tend to show that only a low degree of symmetry is needed for effectiveness as a tool, and thus suggest that if a high degree of symmetry is seen an aesthetic effect was intended; and Acheulean handaxes have constantly earned comment on their symmetry. These considerations reduce the extent to which the Libyan beads constitute an anomaly, though the beads' age remains precarious and in need of further study.

7. Discussion

The evolution of language is like a braided river, both long and broad with many interweaving channels. Within this big picture the pleasure-effect described above is strictly limited in occurrence but possibly critical nonetheless, as follows.

The scenario envisaged is alive with hominins already using language --- possibly song-like, possibly holophrastic. They direct one another's attention, express moods, issue commands etc. Their speech has utility both practical and social: it helps to get things done and fosters social wellbeing. Its use brings rewards --- successful cooperations (including mating), enhanced status etc. --- but these are external rewards, in contrast to the internal reward induced in humans by alikeness. (Certain non-humans, e.g. bower-birds, appear alert to alikeness but here again the reward may be external.) With such a scenario in view, of flourishing speech about the here-and-now, one may ask what might prompt excursions into the abstract.

First example: a hominin is likely at some time to see a fire's smoke and a patch of mist or cloud at the same time. He or she may then get pleasure from noting that both are diffuse, and thus begin to construct concepts such as *diffuse* and perhaps *ephemeral*. These have no immediate use but help language to escape from the bounds of utility.

Second example: suppose a hominin Alpha helps Beta on two occasions. The occasions may differ in every respect except that on both occasions Alpha was helpful. The episodes may influence Beta's future actions directly, but in addition Beta may contemplate the feature that the occasions had in common, purely for the pleasure of it. Eventually, perhaps in an effort at coalition-building, Beta wishes to indicate Alpha's character to a third member. Thus, after being formed, the concept *helpful* turns out to have utility --- but it is pleasure, not utility, that engenders the concept in the first place.

[A good memory for instances of helpfulness etc. is adaptive and over many generations could permeate a population regardless of pleasure. But pleasure and consequent categorizing greatly accelerate the process (Johnston, 1999, 2003)].

Third example: evolution of syntax depends on conserving the structure of utterances across content. Even in communication about concrete particulars, ambiguity is diminished by word-order conventions, by having the structure of one sentence match the structure of another. Again Johnston's (1999) point carries weight: the spread of a behavior such as making sentence-structures match is greatly accelerated if emotional valence, an internal reward, is attached.

Contrary to the above examples and reverting to the big picture, great quantities of categorizing are done *not* in the Steels-Tallerman manner (Harnad, 2005). But the examples illustrate moments when the Steels-Tallerman process runs, with pleasure-from-alikeness as the motivation, and such moments may have been pivotal in liberating language into the realm of the imaginative.

8. Conclusion

The symmetry of some beads and handaxes suggests that the makers or associates in their communities valued symmetry on aesthetic/hedonic grounds. In present-day people, stimuli yielding this type of hedonic response form a continuum that runs from tangible symmetrical objects to intangible pairings or matchings of abstract representations in the head --- for example, memories of two eddies in a stream seen on separate previous days. From this behavior in the present it is concluded that the bead and axe makers were apt to enjoy composing groups of items that had features in common, purely for the internal reward. And such groups are the basis for abstract concepts such as *ripeness*, as opposed to particular items such as *this apple*. Forming such abstract general concepts is an essential step forward from a language tied to particulars to a language with the unlimited potential seen today; and the artefacts suggest (subject to confirmation) that this step may have been taken, at least privately in the minds of some individuals, as early as Acheulean time. The timing remains uncertain, but the inference from utility-free symmetry (whenever established) to the enlargement of language is particularly direct.

Acknowledgments

Encouragement and support from W.D. Means and valuable comments from A. S. Black are gladly acknowledged.

References

Bednarik, R. G. (2005). Middle Pleistocene beads and symbolism. *Anthropos,* 100, 537-552.

Bednarik, R. G. (2008). Beads. In H. Selin (Ed.) *Encyclopaedia of the history of science, technology and medicine in non-western cultures* (pp. 395-399). New York: Springer.

Botha, R. (2008). Prehistoric shell beads as a window on language evolution. *Language and Communication,* 28, 197-202.

d'Errico, F., Henshilwood, C., Vanhaeren, M. and van Niekirk, K. (2005). *Nassarius krausianus* shell beads from Blombos Cave: evidence for symbolic behavior in the Middle Stone Age. *Journal of Human Evolution,* 48, 3-24.

Fost, J. W. (1999). Neural rhythmicity, feature binding, and serotonin: a hypothesis. *The Neuroscientist,* 5, 79-85.

Harnad, S. (2005). Language and the game of life. *Behavioral and Brain Sciences,* 28, 497-498.

Humphrey, N. (1973). The illusion of beauty. *Perception,* 2, 429-439.

James, W. (1892). *Psychology.* New York: Henry Holt and Co.

Johnston, V. S. (1999). *Why we feel: the science of human emotions.* Reading, MA: Perseus.

Johnston, V. S. (2003). The origin and function of pleasure. *Cognition and Emotion,* 17, 167-179.

Kohn, M. and Mithen, S. (1999). Handaxes: products of sexual selection? *Antiquity,* 73, 518-526.

Laskowski, C. (2008). The emergence of a lexicon by prototype-categorizing agents in an infinite world. In A. D. M. Smith, K. Smith and R. Ferrer i Cancho (Eds.), *The evolution of language (EVOLANG 7)* (pp. 195-202). New York: World Scientific Publications.

Machin, A. J., Hosfield, R. T. and Mithen, S. J. (2007). Why are some handaxes symmetrical? Testing the influence of handaxe morphology on butchery effectiveness. *Journal of Archaeological Science,* 34, 883-893.

Plailly, J., Tillmann, B. and Royet, J.-P. (2007). The feeling of familiarity of music and odors: the same neural signature? *Cerebral Cortex,* 17, 2650-2658.

Steels, L. (1996). Perceptually grounded meaning creation. In M. Tokoro (Ed.), *Proceedings of the international conference on multiagent systems (ICMAS-96)* (pp. 338-344). Menlo Park: AAAI Press.

Tallerman, M. (2009). The origin of the lexicon: how a word-store evolved. In R. Botha and C. Knight (Eds.), *The prehistory of language* (pp. 181-200). New York: Oxford University Press.

Ziegert, H. (1998). Acheulean settlements at Lake Fezzan, Libya *Libya Antiqua, Annual of the Department of Antiqities, Libya,* NS 4, 254-259.

LINGUISTIC ADAPTATION AT WORK?
THE CHANGE OF WORD ORDER AND CASE SYSTEM
FROM LATIN TO THE ROMANCE LANGUAGES

CHRISTIAN BENTZ

Department of Linguistics, University of Heidelberg, Hauptstraße 207-209, 69117 Heidelberg, Germany

MORTEN H. CHRISTIANSEN

Department of Psychology, Cornell University, Ithaca, NY 14853, USA

Understanding language evolution in terms of cultural transmission across generations of language users raises the possibility that some of the processes that have shaped language evolution can also be observed in historical language change. In this paper, we explore how constraints on production may affect the cultural evolution of language by analyzing the emergence of the Romance languages from Latin. Specifically, we focus on the change from Latin's flexible but OV (Object-Verb) dominant word order with complex case marking to fixed SVO (Subject-Verb-Object) word order with little or no noun inflections in Romance Languages. We suggest that constraints on second language learners' ability to produce sentences may help explain this historical change. We conclude that historical data on linguistic change can provide a useful source of information relevant to investigating the cognitive constraints that affect the cultural evolution of language.

1. Introduction

If language has evolved primarily through cultural transmission (e.g., Christiansen & Chater, 2008), then language evolution and language change may not be clearly distinct in a theoretical sense. Rather, it may be expected that the processes proposed to underlie patterns of historical language change (e.g., grammaticalization) also have been at play across the longer timescale of language evolution (e.g., Heine & Kuteva, 2009). Thus, diachronic change may be construed as a microcosm of language evolution and potentially provide a rich source of data to illuminate potential constraints on linguistic adaptation.

In this paper we ask: Are there diachronic data on language change that indicate that constraints on human cognition have shaped language on a historical time scale? To answer this question, we consider as a case study the

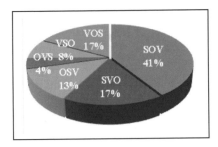

Figure 1. The frequencies of different word orders in Latin (based on Pinkster, 1991:72).

change from Latin to the Romance Languages, focusing on how limitations on production may affect linguistic adaptation. We sketch an account that highlights production as one of the multiple cognitive constraints influencing historical language change. This account highlights the sequencing problems a second language (L2) learner faces when producing a sentence. Finally, we broaden our discussion of the mutual relationship between L2 acquisition and language evolution beyond Latin and the Roman languages to English and Chinese. Together, these observations corroborate our suggestion that historical language change may be construed as *linguistic adaptation* to cognitive and social constraints.

2. The Diachronic Change from Latin to the Romance Languages

Taking the development of Latin towards modern Romance languages as an example of linguistic adaptation, we concentrate on simple transitive sentences because they can be considered the neutral prototype of other more complicated constructions (Slobin & Bever, 1982). There are two interesting changes to this sentence type occurring in the time span between Latin (~500 BC – AD 500) and recent Romance languages:

    i.   While Latin had a seven case system, all subsequent Romance languages use fewer cases.

    ii.   The word order in simple transitive sentences has changed from OV (foremost realized in SOV and OSV) to SVO.

Consider for example the following aphorism by Vergil:

(1)   *Fata   viam   invenient*
       fate-NOM-PL way-ACC-SG   find-3P-PL-PRE-ACT

(2) *I fati trovano una via* (direct Italian translation)

Latin makes use of the accusative marker to indicate who finds whom: *fata via-m*, but in Italian the marker has vanished and the problem of assigning thematic roles is solved by using a strict SVO word order. The nature of the change in word order has been the subject of some debate among specialists of Romance languages (e.g., Pinkster, 1991; Lee, 2002; Salvi, 2004). We therefore tabulated the number of sentences with different {S,O,V} ordering in simple declarative sentences. Using the two complete sets of counts from the classical period (Caesar and Petronius) and the later *Peregrinatio* (AD 400) from Pinkster (1991), we obtained the distribution shown in Figure 1. As Pinkster notes, S preferably takes initial position and O precedes V more often than the other way around. This displays the OV pattern as predominant, albeit in a flexible system. In contrast, modern Romance languages are widely assumed to have a clear predominance of SVO word order (Harris 1988; Lee, 2000; Salvi, 2004). For example, Slobin and Bever (1982) report word order frequency data for Italian indicating a clear predominance of SVO sentences (adults: 82% SVO, 2% SOV, 0 % OSV; children: 72% SVO, 1% SOV, 1 % OSV). Thus, usage of the OV patterns has declined to a minimum in Romance languages, such as Italian.

3. Production Constraints as a Source of Language Change

Past work investigating how cognitive constraints may shape language change has primarily focused either on limitations on learning (e.g., Polinksy & Van Everbroeck, 2003) or parsing (e.g., Hawkins, 2004). Because comprehension can typically be accomplished by integrating partial information, whereas production requires specifying the complete utterance, we suggest that the latter may cause more problems for L2 learners and therefore become a factor in the shaping of languages with many non-native speakers.. Consider the diagram in Figure 2, illustrating the complex dependency relationships within the previous Latin sentence in (1). Subject agreement information has to 'bypass' the direct object to get to the verb. This is likely to complicate processing further in sentences with embedded structures due to memory limitations (Hawkins, 2004). Moreover, the information required to inflect the direct object correctly, namely the thematic role assigned by the verb, is not given until the end of the sentence. Thus, thematic role assignment has to be 'back-projected' from the verb to the subject and object, complicating the left-to-right sequencing of words in language production. The more complex the sentence, the more complex the role assignment becomes. In the example of a ditransitive sentence in (3), the speaker already has to assign three roles and therefore inflect two nouns:

(3) *Magister*   *puell-ae*   *libr-um*   *dat*
    teacher-NOM-SG   girl-DAT-SG   book-ACC-SG   give-3P-PRE

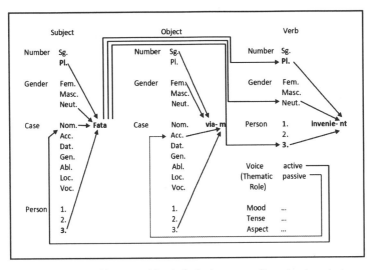

Figure 2. SOV with case marking in the Latin sentence *Fata viam invenient*.

This complexity contrasts with the much simpler set of dependency relationships shown in Figure 3 for the Italian transitive sentence in (2). Crucially, all arrows proceed from left to right, except the one assigning the thematic role of agent to the subject (mapped onto the voice character of the verb). But as the subject does not inflect according to the thematic role in Italian (at least for proper nouns) this is not a problem. Thus, Italian SVO word order

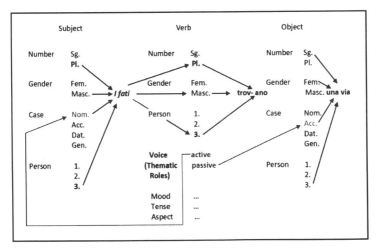

Figure 3. SVO without case marking in the Italian sentence *I fati trovano una via*.

fits well with a simple left-to-right sequence production mechanism. Obviously there is a tradeoff between two constraints within such simple transitive sentences. On the one hand, the verb should follow the subject because then the information regarding agreement of person and number is available when the verb has to be inflected. On the other hand, the verb should precede both subject and object to facilitate case marking. Given these constraints, the change from Latin OV and case marking of proper nouns to Italian SVO and no case marking makes sense for a left-to-right sequencing production system.

4. Meeting the Needs of Adult L2 Learners of Latin

Native speakers of Latin would, of course, have been able to learn, process, and produce constructions such as (1) and (3) despite their complex dependency relationships, just as children are able to understand *who did what to whom* in Turkish, another heavily case-marked language with flexible but OV-biased word order (Slobin & Bever, 1982). Therefore we suggest that an important pressure toward the simpler dependency relationships found in the Romance languages came primarily from adult L2 learners, and only to a smaller extent from L1 acquisition. As the Roman Empire grew, (Vulgar) Latin became its *lingua franca* and thus 'recruited' large numbers of non-native speakers. This may be seen as a large-scale historical parallel to the change from *esoteric* to *exoteric* communication, described by Wray and Grace (2007): Whereas the former is shaped by children's learning abilities, allowing the existence of idiosyncratic regularities that are hard for adult learners to master, the latter is tailored to the need for cross-group interactions, oftentimes by adult L2 learners. Thus, the problems facing adult L2 learners of Latin SOV (respectively OSV) word order and case marking when producing a sentence as sequential *output* may have provided an important pressure towards the Romance SVO without case marking.

But is there evidence that the 'recruitment' of non-native speakers might have impacted the structure of Latin? Herman and Wright (2000) describe the Latin speech community between 100 BC and 500 AD, suggesting that speakers of other languages (e.g., slaves, merchants, inhabitants of the Romanized provinces) were continuously integrated into the wider Latin speech community on a large scale. This led to the atypical situation in which non-native L2 learners in many geographical areas outnumbered native speakers of Latin. Based on a detailed analysis of changes to Latin's formerly rich case system, Herman and Wright argue that the large amount of L2 speakers is likely to have shaped Vulgar Latin both in terms of morphology and syntax. The overall result would have been an increasing number of confusions between cases that previously had been distinctive: Ablative constructions were replaced by nouns with accusative markers and dative was used with prepositions to indicate possession instead of the classical genitive. Importantly, for our purposes, Herman and Wright note that (2000: 54), "The accusative was originally used for the direct object of a transitive verb, and transitivity itself increased. Many verbs in Classical Latin were followed by a noun in the genetive, dative, or ablative case, but in Vulgar texts these verbs tend to take an accusative." Because the word order in the period of Vulgar Latin still displayed mainly OV patterns, the tendency to over-generalize accusative case may be seen as a consequence of the difficulty of 'back projecting' thematic roles outlined in Figure 2. As a consequence of this ambiguous use of the case markers, the full system could no longer be maintained, and it shrank to a minimum. Therefore another strategy for solving *who did what to whom* dependencies was needed and emerged in later centuries in the form of a fixed SVO word order.

5. Possible Effects of L2 Acquisition beyond the Romance Languages

The claim that fixed SVO word order without case marking should be easier to use by L2 learners than flexible OV word order with case marking may appear problematic when compared to the typological frequencies of the world's languages. Standard typological analyses in terms of number of languages indicate that SOV word order is predominant: SOV 497; SVO 435; VSO 85; VOS 26; OVS 9; OSV 4 (Haspelmath et al., 2005: 330). However, if we look at the number of speakers that each language has, then a different picture emerges. Figure 4 shows the number of speakers for the twenty most frequently spoken languages in the world (*SIL Ethnologue online version*) and their respective word order according to the online version of WALS (Haspelmath et al., 2005). Adding up the numbers of speakers of these languages, a different pattern emerges: roughly 2,390 million speakers of SVO languages against 894 million of SOV languages. Even when taking statistical error into account (+/- 25%) SVO still outnumbers SOV by far in terms of number of speakers.

Strikingly, this predominance of SVO patterns is mainly due to the fact that the three most widespread languages: Chinese, English and Spanish are SVO languages. Perhaps English and Chinese have also been subject to pressures from L2 learners? Although there is much debate over why and when exactly the word order changed from SOV or OSV (with tendency to be flexible) in Old English to SVO in modern English (see Pintzuk, 1999, for discussion), it is nevertheless widely agreed that it changed in this way. In the case of Modern

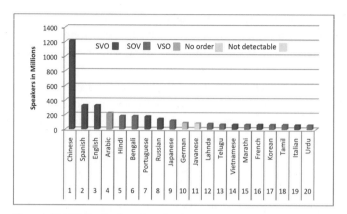

Figure 4. WALS distribution of word order patterns mapped onto SIL counts.

and Old Chinese, Xu (2006) argues that in earlier periods, Mandarin was a typologically "mixed language" because it oscillated between verb-object (VO) and object-verb (OV) word orders. However, in a text-count study of written and spoken Modern Mandarin, Sun (1996) found that 90% of the syntactic objects followed the verb (VO), whereas OV with grammaticalized verb-constructions marking agent/patient dependencies only occur in 10% of the sentences, pointing to SVO as the dominant word order. When these observations are combined with our analysis of Latin, we may speculate that production pressures from L2 learners can push OV languages with complex systems of solving *who did what to whom* ambiguities toward a fixed SVO word order with little or no additional marking.

6. Conclusion

Because there seems to be a tradeoff between strict SVO word order without case marking and flexible OV word order with additional morphological markers (Greenberg, 1966: Universal 41), it is an interesting fact that all Romance languages 'chose' the first strategy to solve ambiguities relating to *who did what to whom* in simple transitive sentences. In this paper, we have suggested that this change may be an example of how language adapts to the human brain. In particular, the difficulties in determining the relevant dependency relationships and generating the appropriate sequence of case-marked words would make L2 Latin learners prone to errors. L2 production pressures may furthermore have played a role in the similar shift from a relatively flexible word order to fixed SVO in English and Chinese, both of which have historically recruited a large number of L2 speakers. More generally, our analyses suggest that historical language change can be used as a source of data for understanding the kind of constraints that may have shaped linguistic adaptation over evolutionary time.

Acknowledgements

C.B. would like to thank the German Academic Exchange Service (DAAD) for funding via the program *Kurzfristige Aufenthalte zur Anfertigung von Abschlussarbeiten*, his thesis adviser in Germany, Prof. Dr. Klaus-Peter Konerding for providing new vistas for him in Cognitive Linguistics, and last but not least Daniela Schwarzmaier de Recacoechea for her helpful comments.

References

Christiansen, M.H., & Chater, N. (2008). Language as shaped by the brain. *Behavioral and Brain Sciences, 31*, 489–509.

Greenberg, J. H. (2005). *Language Universals: with special reference to feature hierarchies.* Berlin: Mouton de Gruyter.

Herman, J. & Wright, R. (2000). *Vulgar Latin.* University Park, PA: The Pennsylvania State University Press.

Harris, M. (1988). *The Romance languages.* London: Routledge.

Haspelmath, M.; Dryer, M. S.; Gil, D. & Comrie, B. (Eds.) (2005). *The world atlas of language structures.* Oxford: Oxford University Press.

Hawkins, J.A. (2004). *Efficiency and complexity in grammars.* OUP.

Heine, B. & Kuteva, T. (2009). *The genesis of grammar. A reconstruction.* Oxford: Oxford University Press.

Lee, C. (2000). *Linguistica romanza.* Rome: Carocci.

Pinkster, H. (1991). Evidence for SVO in Latin? In Wright, R. (Ed.), *Latin and the Romance languages in the early Middle Ages* (pp. 69-82). London: Routledge.

Pintzuk, S. (1999). *Phrase structures in competition: Variation and change in Old English word order.* New York: Garland.

Polinksy, M & Van Everbroeck, E. (2003). Development of gender classifications: Modeling the historical change from Latin to French. *Language, 79*, 356-390.

Slobin, D.I. & Bever, T.G. (1982). Children use canonical sentence schemas. A crosslinguistic study of word order and inflections. *Cognition, 12*, 229-265.

Sun, C. (1996). *Word-order change and grammaticalization in the history of Chinese.* Stanford, CA: Stanford University Press.

Wray, A. & Grace, G.W. (2007). The consequences of talking to strangers. Evolutionary corollaries of socio-cultural influences on linguistic form. *Lingua, 117*, 543-578.

Xu, D. (2006). *Typological change in Chinese syntax.* Oxford: Oxford University Press.

INVARIANTS AND VARIATION IN BIOLOGY AND LANGUAGE EVOLUTION: EXTENDED ABSTRACT

ROBERT C. BERWICK

Department of EECS & Brain and Cognitive Sciences, MIT,
Cambridge, MA 02139, USA
berwick@csail.mit.edu

Among the many puzzling questions about language, two are salient: First, why are there *any* languages at all, evidently unique to the human lineage. Second, why are there *so many* languages? These are in fact the basic questions of origin and variation that so occupied Darwin and other evolutionary thinkers and comprise modern biologys explanatory core: why do we observe this particular array of living forms in the world and not others – the key problem of reconciling the underlying unity of organisms with their apparent diversity, invariance and variation. Here we examine these two questions from the viewpoint of modern linguistics, biology, and dynamical system theory.[a]

Turning to the first question, why should there be any languages at all, apparently an autapomorphy? Apparently, until very recently in evolutionary time, the question would not have arisen: there were no languages. There were, of course, plenty of animal communication systems. But they are all radically different from human language in structure and function. Human language does not even fit within the standard typologies of animal communication systems – Marc Hauser's, for example, in his comprehensive review of the evolution of communication. It has been conventional to regard language as a system whose function is communication. This is indeed the widespread view invoked in most selectionist accounts of language, which almost invariably start from this interpretation. However, to the extent that the characterization has any meaning, this appears to be incorrect, for a variety of reasons which we will outline in this talk. Language can of course be used for communication, as can any aspect of what we do: style of dress, gesture, and so on. And it can be and commonly is used for much else. Statistically speaking, for whatever that is worth, the overwhelming use of language is internal — for thought.

To answer the origins question we must thus consider the special properties of language. The most elementary property of our shared language capacity is that it

---

[a]This represents joint work with N. Chomsky and P. Niyogi.

enables us to construct and interpret a discrete infinity of hierarchically structured expressions: discrete because there are 5 word sentences and 6 word sentences, but no 5 and 1/2 word sentences; infinite because there is no longest sentence. Language is therefore based on a recursive generative procedure that takes elementary word-like elements from some dictionary store, call it the lexicon, and applies repeatedly to yield structured expressions, without bound. To account for the emergence of the language faculty – hence for the existence of at least one language – we have to face two basic tasks. One task is to account for the "atoms of computation," the lexical items — commonly in the range of 30–50,000. The second is to discover the computational properties of the language faculty. This latter task in turn has several facets: we must seek to discover the generative procedure that constructs infinitely many expressions in the mind, and the methods by which these internal mental objects are related to two interfaces with language-external (but organism-internal) systems: the system of thought, on the one hand, and also to the sensorimotor system, thus externalizing internal computations and thought. This is one way of reformulating the traditional conception, at least back to Aristotle, that language is sound with a meaning.

Various kinds of generative procedures have been explored in the past 50 years. One approach familiar to linguists and computer scientists is phrase structure grammar, developed in the 1950s and since extensively employed. The approach made sense at the time. It fit very naturally into one of the several equivalent formulations of the mathematical theory of recursive procedures — Emil Post's rewriting systems — and it captured at least some basic properties of language, such as hierarchic structure and embedding. Nevertheless, it was quickly recognized that phrase structure grammar is not only inadequate for language but is also quite a complex procedure with many arbitrary stipulations, not the kind of system we would hope to find, and unlikely to have emerged suddenly.

Over the years, research has found ways to reduce the complexities of these systems, and finally to eliminate them entirely in favor of the simplest possible mode of recursive generation: an operation that takes two objects already constructed, call them X and Y, and forms from them a new object that consists of the two unchanged, hence simply the set with X and Y as members. Provided with conceptual atoms of the lexicon, this operation, iterated without bound, yields an infinity of hierarchically constructed expressions. If these can be interpreted by conceptual systems, the operation provides an internal "language of thought."

Insofar as it is correct, the evolution of language will reduce to the emergence of this operation, the evolution of conceptual atoms of the lexicon, the linkage to conceptual systems, and the mode of externalization. Any residue of principles of language not reducible to this operation and optimal computation will have to be accounted for by some other evolutionary process — one that we are unlikely to learn much about, at least by presently understood methods, as Lewontin 1998 notes.

Notice that there is no room in this picture for any precursors to language — say a language-like system with only short sentences. There is no rationale for postulation of such a system: to go from seven-word sentences to the discrete infinity of human language requires emergence of the same recursive procedure as to go from zero to infinity, and there is of course no direct evidence for such "protolanguages." Similar observations hold for language acquisition, despite appearances, a matter that we put to the side here.

Crucially, this operation yields the familiar displacement property of language: the fact that we pronounce phrases in one position, but interpret them somewhere else as well. Thus in the sentence "guess what John is eating," we understand "what" to be the object of "eat," as in "John is eating an apple," even though it is pronounced somewhere else. This property has always seemed paradoxical, a kind of "imperfection" of language. It is by no means necessary in order to capture semantic facts, but it is ubiquitous. It surpasses the capacity of phrase structure grammars, requiring that they be still further complicated with additional devices. But it falls within the notion of a single operator building hierarchical objects, automatically.

To see how, suppose that the operation has constructed the mental expression corresponding to "John is eating what." A larger expression can be constructed by the hierarchical combinator in two ways: one can add something from *within* the expression, so as to form "what John is eating what"; and one can add something new, yielding "guess what John is eating what." That carries us part of the way towards displacement. In "what John is eating what," the phrase "what" appears in two positions, and in fact those two positions are required for semantic interpretation: the original position provides the information that "what" is understood to be the direct object of "eat," and the new position, at the edge, is interpreted as a quantifier ranging over a variable, so that the expression means something like "for which thing x, John is eating the thing x."

These observations generalize over a wide range of constructions. The results are just what is needed for semantic interpretation, but they do not yield the objects that are pronounced in English. We do not say "guess what John is eating what," but rather "guess what John is eating," with the original position suppressed. That is a universal property of displacement, with minor (and interesting) qualifications that we can ignore here. The property follows from elementary principles of computational efficiency. In fact, it has often been noted that serial motor activity is computationally costly, a matter attested by the sheer quantity of motor cortex devoted to both motor control of the hands and for oro-facial articulatory gestures.

To externalize the internally generated expression "what John is eating what," it would be necessary to pronounce "what" twice, and that turns out to place a very considerable burden on computation, when we consider expressions of normal complexity and the actual nature of displacement. With all but one of the occurrences of "what" suppressed, the computational burden is greatly eased. The one occurrence that must be pronounced is the most prominent one, the last one created: otherwise there will be no indication that the operation has applied to yield the correct interpretation. It appears, then, that the language faculty recruits a general principle of computational efficiency for the process of externalization.

The suppression of all but one of the occurrences of the displaced element is computationally efficient, but imposes a significant burden on interpretation, that is parsing, hence on communication. The person hearing the sentence has to discover the position of the gap where the displaced element is to be interpreted. That is a highly non-trivial problem in general, familiar from parsing programs. There is, then, a conflict between computational efficiency and interpretive-communicative efficiency. Universally, languages resolve the conflict in favor of computational efficiency. These facts at once suggest that language evolved as an instrument of internal thought, with externalization a secondary process. There is a great deal of evidence from language design that yields similar conclusions; so called "island properties," for example, that block the displacement of elements that are "too far" from their original source, assisting parsing by forcing computation to be local; e.g., in "what did the man who bought read", "what" has been displaced from within the phrase "the man who bought what", and this is blocked.

There are independent reasons for the conclusion that externalization is a secondary process. One is that externalization appears to be modality-independent, as has been learned from studies of sign language in recent years. The structural properties of sign and spoken language are remarkably similar. Additionally, acquisition follows the same course in both, and neural localization seems to be similar as well. That tends to reinforce the conclusion that language is optimized for the system of thought, with mode of externalization secondary.

Note further that the constraints on externalization holding for the auditory modality also appear to hold in the case of the visual modality in signed languages. Even though there is no physical constraint barring one from 'saying' with one hand that "John likes ice-cream" and "Mary likes beer" with the other hand, nevertheless it appears that one hand is dominant throughout and delivers sentences (via gestures) in a left-to-right order in time, linearized as in vocal-tract externalization, while the non-dominant hand adds markings for emphasis, morphology, and the like. Indeed, it seems possible to make a far stronger statement: all recent relevant biological and evolutionary research leads to the conclusion that the process of externalization is secondary. This includes the recent and highly publicized discoveries of genetic elements putatively involved in language, specifically, the FOXP2 regulatory (transcription factor) gene. FOXP2 is implicated in a highly heritable language defect, so-called 'verbal dyspraxia.' Since this discovery it has been intensely analyzed from an evolutionary and comparative standpoint, with small amino acid differences between the human variant and other primates and non-human mammals posited as the target of recent positive natural selection, perhaps concomitant with language emergence (Fisher et al., 1998; Enard et al., 20021 and with similarities between those same two amino acids in humans and Neandertals also suggested as possibly significant with respect to language (Krause et al., 2007.)

However, we might ask whether this gene is centrally involved in language or, as now seems more plausible, is part of the secondary externalization process (or, in . Recent discoveries in birds and mice over the past few years point to an "emerging consensus" that this transcription factor gene is not so much part of a blueprint for internal syntax, the narrow faculty of language, and most certainly not some hypothetical 'language gene' (just as there no single genes for eye color or autism) but rather part of regulatory machinery related to externalization (Vargha-Khadem 2005; Groszer, et al. 2008; Geschwind et al, 2009, the latter an attempt to find the downstream targets regulated by FOXP2.). Taken together, it seems that FOXP2 aids in the development of serial fine motor control or its planning, oro-facial or otherwise: the ability to literally put one 'sound' or 'gesture' down in place, one point after another in time. In this respect it is worth noting that members of the KE family in which this genetic defect was originally isolated exhibit a quite general motor dyspraxia, not localized to simply their orofacial movements.

If this view is on the right track, then FOXP2 is more akin to the blueprint that aids in the construction of a properly functioning input-output system for a computer, like its printer, rather than the construction of the computer's central processor itself. From this point of view, what has gone wrong in the affected KE family members is thus something awry with the externalization system, the "printer," not the central language faculty itself. If this is so, then the evolutionary analyses suggesting that this transcription factor was under positive selection approximately 100,000 years ago (in itself arguable) could in fact be quite inconclusive about the evolution of the core components of the faculty of language, syntax and the mapping to the "semantic' (conceptual-intensional) interface. It is challenging to determine the causal sequence: the link between FOXP2 and high-grade serial motor coordination could be regarded as either an opportunistic pre-requisite substrate for externalization, no matter what the modality, as is common in evolutionary scenarios, or the result of selection pressure for efficient externalization 'solutions' after the hierarchical combinator arose. In either case, FOXP2 becomes part of a system extrinsic to core syntax/semantics.

It may well be of course that the externalization link is more indirect and subtle: that FOXP2 helps to build part of the input-output system for vocal learning where one must externalize and then re-internalize song/language — sing or talk to oneself. This would remain a way to 'pipe' items in and out of the internal system, and serialize them, possibly a critical component to be sure, in the same sense that one might require a way to print output from a computer. There is suggestive evidence that this is the case. We will examine one case from that of birdsong and its metrical or rhythmic structure, relating this to the basic combinatorial operation. A second line of evidence follows from the work done by Carol Chomsky several decades ago on the Tadoma method used by deaf-blind individuals to acquire language from simply feeling the external vibrations of the cheek and vocal cords (eg, Helen Keller). Evidently, adult-like language mastery is possible even under such deprived conditions as long as there has been *some* exposure to actual language input before age 1–1.5. (The precipitating cause of their medical condition is generally childhood encephalitis.) If there is no prior language exposure whatsoever — they become deaf/blind before age 1 — then such individuals are never able to acquire language.

An individual with this new combinatorial capacity would have had many advantages: capacities for complex thought, planning, interpretation, and so on. The capacity would be partially transmitted to offspring, and because of the selective advantages it confers, it might come to dominate a small breeding group, though as with all such novel mutations, there is an issue about how an initially small number of copies of such an allele might survive, despite a large selective advantage. In any case, when the beneficial mutation has spread through the group, there would be an advantage to externalization, so the capacity would be linked as a secondary process to the sensorimotor system for externalization and interaction, including communication as a special case. It is not easy to imagine an account of human evolution that does not assume at least this much, in one or another form. Any additional assumption requires both evidence and rationale, not easy to come by.

Most alternatives do in fact posit additional assumptions, grounded on the language as communication viewpoint, presumably related to externalization as we have seen. In a recent survey Számadó and Szathmáry (2006) list what they consider to be the major alternative theories explaining the emergence of human language: these include: (1) language as gossip; (2) language as social grooming; (3) language as outgrowth of hunting cooperation; (4) language as outcome of 'motherese'; (5) sexual selection; (6) language as requirement of exchanging status information; (7) language as song; (8) language as requirement for tool making or the outcome of toolmaking; (9) language as an outgrowth of gestural systems; (10) language as Machiavellian device for deception; and finally, (11) language as 'internal mental tool.'

Note that it is only this last theory, language as internal mental tool, that does not assume, explicitly or implicitly, that the primary function of language is for external communication. But this leads to a kind of adaptive paradox, since animal signaling ought to then suffice. Számadó and Szathmáry note: "Most of the theories do not consider the kind of selective forces that could encourage the use of conventional communication in a given context instead of the use of 'traditional' animal signals... thus, there is no theory that convincingly demonstrates a situation that would require a complex means of symbolic communication rather than the existing simpler communication systems" (2006:559). They further note that the language-as-mental-tool theory does not suffer from this defect. However, they, like most researchers in this area, do not seem to draw the obvious inference but instead maintain a focus on externalization and communication.

Proposals as to the primacy of internal language — similar to Harry Jerison's observation (1973) about language as an "inner tool" — have also been made by eminent biologists. At an international conference on biolinguistics in 1974, Nobel laureate Salvador Luria was the most forceful advocate of the view that communicative needs would not have provided "any great selective pressure to produce a system such as language," with its crucial relation to "development of abstract or productive thinking." The same idea was taken up by Francois Jacob, who suggested that "the role of language as a communication system between individuals would have come about only secondarily ... The quality of language that makes it unique does not seem to be so much its role in communicating directives for action" or other common features of animal communication, but rather "its role in symbolizing, in evoking cognitive images," in molding our notion of reality and yielding our capacity for thought and planning, through its unique property of allowing "infinite combinations of symbols" and therefore "mental creation of possible worlds."

Investigation of language design can yield evidence on the relation of language to the sensorimotor system and thought systems. As noted, there is mounting evidence to support the natural conclusion that the relation is asymmetrical in the manner illustrated in the critical case of displacement. Externalization is not a simple task. It has to relate two quite distinct systems: one is a sensorimotor system that appears to have been basically intact for hundreds of thousands of years; the second is a newly emerged computational system for thought. We would expect, then, that morphology and phonology — the linguistic processes that convert internal syntactic objects to the entities accessible to the sensorimotor system — might turn out to be quite intricate, varied, and subject to accidental historical events. Parameterization and diversity, then, would be mostly — possibly entirely — restricted to externalization resulting from complex and highly varied modes of externalization, which, furthermore, are readily susceptible to historical change.

This leads directly to our second salient question, why are there seemingly *so many* languages — why is there a Tower of Babel, with languages clumped into types? Instead we find that sometimes language groups can stably co-exist; at other times they may change, often quite rapidly. The solution to this variation problem turns out to be precisely the same as in modern evolutionary biology: the interaction of a particulate system of inheritance from generation to generation, sometimes imperfect, within a system that internally admits a limited range of possibilities. As with biological organisms, language variation does not admit infinitesimally fine gradations: we saw one example earlier, that of the 'head-first', 'head-final' property of languages that distinguishes, e.g., English from Japanese or German, so that we say 'eat apple' as opposed to 'apple eat'. Internally – however language is engaged as a mental tool – there is no need to distinguish among these different linear orders, which is a property forced by the externalization system of speech or gesture. Evidently one of the 'solutions' to the externalization problem is to choose one order or another.

In research covering the past 15 years, Partha Niyogi and I have shown that this provides the basic ingredients for setting up a dynamical system model for language evolution and change in a population framework, exactly as in evolutionary biology. The idea is to move away from the conventional view that language is to be thought of as externalization in an "idealized, homogeneous speaker-hearer community." This change in point of view should be emphasized. At least from the seminal work of Gold (1967), there has been a tradition of inquiry into computational models of language acquisition, where a learner acquiring a target grammar from its linguistic experience interacts with speakers of this grammar, generally positing that this experience is consistent with a *single* target grammar. Such models assume an idealized, homogeneous speaker-hearer population. We have now revised this: First, learning occurs in a population setting with potential variation in the attained grammars or languages of its members. Second, language acquisition is the mechanism by which language is transmitted from the speakers of one generation to the next. We call this newer formulation the *population view* of language acquisition and change, and the resulting models "Social Learning" or SL models. Here each learner is exposed to data from multiple individuals in a community. When individuals learn from a single source, the evolutionary dynamics that results is necessarily linear, leading to a single stable equilibrium from all initial conditions, and it can be shown that this is insufficient to model either the dynamics of stable language systems or the dynamics of language change. In contrast, in SL models the dynamics is potentially nonlinear. Bifurcations — like the freezing of water into ice — arise only in SL models. These are linguistically interpretable and as described below provide a new kind of explanatory construct for the patterns of rapid change often observed in historical linguistic change. The fixed points of these systems correspond to externally observable possible patterns of language change, e.g., historical changes in English, with the fixed points being the "end points" of possible language systems.

Returning to the two initial salient questions, we now have at least some suggestions — reasonable ones we think — about how it came about that there is even one language, and at the same time why languages can appear to vary so widely and still clump into stable groups — the latter a reflection of the fixed points possible in a system grounded on the transmission of language from one generation to the next as described above. The outcomes appear to be highly diverse, but they have an essential unity, reflecting the fact that humans are in fundamental respects identical, just as they are all part of the same biological tree of life, a conclusion that might well have found favor with Darwin himself.

FROM NEURONS TO SIGNS

DENIS BOUCHARD

Département de linguistique, Université du Québec à Montréal
Montréal, H3C 3P8, Canada

Human language is the result of a cascade of consequences from an initial mutation which provided a new "representational" capacity to some mirror neurons. This initial mutation has high evolvability. The mutation coincidentally allowed representations of the two substances of signs to meet in human brains, thus accounting directly for signs. Recursivity is a result of the self-organization triggered by the choatic system that emerged from this system of signs.

1. Introduction

Inquiry into the origin of language must explain why it took the form that it did. There are numerous structural properties which are attributed to language. It would be a formidable task to look at hundreds of properties in the light of the origin of language. I investigate two properties for which there is a very broad consensus among scholars: saussurean signs and type-recursion (the embedding of a phrase of type X into a phrase of type X). If we can explain why language evolved with these two basic properties, we are heading in the right direction.

2. Language as a neurological side-effect

Language seems to have evolved to fit some kind of communication or thought process, because that is how we often use language today. So the fit corresponds to what we do with language, an unsurprising panglossian conclusion. However, the human brain did not evolve for these functions. The emergence of language is a side-effect of a new kind of neuron.

There is a crucial distinction between humans and other primates which has recently been discovered and which informs us on what evolution did to make the human brain language ready. The difference is not in the brain plan (Deacon 2003): it is in the way some human mirror neurons function. Recent comparative studies on mirror neurons show that these "elementary particles" differ in an important way in the brain of humans and in the brain of other primates.

Some human mirror neurons get activated in absentia: humans do not have to see or hear an action for these neurons to react. Thus, Meltzoff et Moore (1997) observed that infants spontaneously correct their erroneous imitations of facial expressions. Moreover, infants imitate absent actions, that is, actions previously, but not currently, observed. Monkeys, on the other hand, merely replicate what is immediately perceptible. Also, Gallese (2003) argues that the simulation processes occurring during motor imagery in humans are different: they are triggered by an internal event. This indicates that the "resonance" mechanism has gained sophistication in humans compared to monkeys. Brain imaging reveals that the human brain has intra-representational systems (IRS) of neurons which can "represent" internal events, i.e., brain activations which are triggered by representations of events instead of events themselves, and which produce representations of events with no brain-external realization (Iacoboni et al. 2004; Jacob & Jeannerod 2004). This intra-representation is fundamental to Hurley's simulationist view that the same neuronal system one uses in one's own actions is also used off line to understand similar observed actions. She shows "how layered mechanisms of control, mirroring, and simulation can enable distinctively human cognitive capacities for imitation, deliberation, and mindreading" (Hurley 2008: 1). Crucially, these IRSs which encode non-realized goals are unique to humans (Rizzolatti 2005, Hurley 2008). This sets the stage for language, more precisely, for the core elements of language: signs.

3. A sign is born

IRSs are structures and mechanisms for active perception (Hurley 2008). This is a typical instance where a small mutation brought about complex phenotypic changes. I hypothesize that these neurological systems are what makes language possible: they provide the mechanisms for the saussurean sign to emerge.

In order to have signs, there has to be a way for elements of the conceptual and perceptual substances to meet in the brain. IRSs provided our ancestors with stable and productive mental representations that enable this linking. A linguistic sign is a relation between a representation of a perceptual element (the signifiant) and a representation of a conceptual element (the signifié). The key to the emergence of signs is therefore to have a way for this relation to take place in the brain. The central question is in which way exclusive to humans the vocal phenomenon enters into the brain. The answer is provided by the recently uncovered biological properties of the human brain pertaining to the IRSs.

IRSs explain how a vocal element could take on the function of signifiant. A vocal element activates an IRS. This IRS creates a representation of that vocal element in the brain. Perceptive and motoric elements are already brain-internal, but as categorial systems linked with brain-external elements. IRSs crucially provide the additional possibility to process these perceptual and motoric elements off-line in the brain, detached from the external world. Once a vocal element is "mentalized" in this way, it can be subjected to meta-representational processes. In particular, the vocal element can be linked to a meaning because IRSs give these dissimilar elements a similar nature which makes the linking possible. I claim that it is this particular property of human brains that makes signs possible, and predict that tests will reveal that the storage, production and understanding of signs depend on the activation of particular IRSs.

IRSs provide a plausible and testable explanation for the emergence of the linguistic sign. The human specificity of these IRSs explains why we have signs and other animals don't. We do not have a brain that "has" language (in the sense of innate principles and parameters of a Universal Grammar) but instead a language-ready brain with neurons unique to our species (IRS) that provide us with a qualitatively different memory. This system took on this other function of linking percepts and concepts after it was in place, as a side-effect.

Signs have very low evolvability. As Bickerton (2009) indicates, it is very unlikely that they evolved from an animal communication system, because the system would have to go through three concurrent transitions: it would have to be decoupled from situations, from current occurrence, and from the limbic system. Since syntax and semantics depend on words, and morphology and phonology "build" words, they may all be not evolvable. We face a paradox. On the one hand, the faculty of language seems to be an implausible trait for a living organism if we apply evolvability conditions directly to language as a complex system or as having certain functions for communication or organizing thought. On the other hand, language exists with all these components.

The solution to the paradox is to look for evolvability not at the functional level, but at the subpersonal level of the neurological substance. Only at that level can we determine the specifications that a biological organism has to meet to have a system with the properties that we observe in human language. IRSs have high evolvability because they are in continuity with the mirror neuron systems which are found in the brain of other primates: IRSs are off-line activations of such systems in essentially the same parts of the brain.

Arbib (2004) proposes the following evolutionary progression towards intra-representational neuronal systems. First, precursor systems for grasping evolved to provide the subtle visual feedback needed for the control of dexterous hand movements, allowing the organism to evaluate its progress towards some goal and correct its movement accordingly. The second stage was a mirror system resting on the organism's ability to map its body on (or from) that of another, and recognize which action that organism is conducting. Finally came a capacity for imitation, i.e., to go from recognizing a novel action by another to adding the action to its repertoire by means of a representation of it: the organism can achieve the observed goal by some coordinated control program abstracted from the observed pattern of movement. Each of these steps has high evolvability. Moreover, as Deacon (2008) observes, the size and the concomitant increase in regional differentiation of cerebral cortex are evolvability features of human brains which result in more afferent axons projecting to a greater number of regions in the cortex. This allows more intra-brain interactions, and so enhances the evolvability of IRSs which are triggered by other "brain events" instead of external events.

This continuity at the subpersonal level contrasts with the discontinuity which IRSs produce at the functional level: their new representational capacity had the side-effect that percepts and concepts could meet through their representations, and this got language started by allowing the formation of signs/words. The innovation of language greatly increased functional complexity, but (contra Deacon 2008) the transition to words did not necessitate a relaxation of selection in order to decouple ACSs from situations, current occurrence, and the limbic hard-wiring. Words are not the result of a decoupling but of an override. Vocalizations did not get decoupled from the limbic system so that they could be used symbolically. Instead, some vocalizations tied to the limbic system (and others if there were any) became represented in the IRS and it is these representations that took on the role of signifiant, leaving the limbic system generally intact.

4. The epigenetic factor: self-organization due to building materials

Once signs emerge, they quickly proliferate and self-organization kicks in, deriving the apparent complexity of language. As in the case of other biological systems, IRSs are complemented by epigenetic self-organizing constraints which emerge from interactions of properties of building materials which limit adaptive scope and channel evolutionary patterns (Jacob 1982). Since the representation of any percept can potentially be linked to the representation of any concept, there are innumerable possibilities. Therefore, IRSs introduce a new chaotic system in the brain. As in other chaotic situations, chance meetings are progressively amplified by material properties and result in clusterings, in order out of chaos. For instance, out of the chaotic passages of termites, concentration points are created by chance droppings: these points become more important as they attract more passages, and the outcome is termite mounds with complex structures (Prigogine & Stengers 1984).

In language, the potential chaotic dispersions of arbitrary signs are constrained by material constraints which restrict the linguistic sign system in a way that maximizes contrastive dispersion.

4.1. *Contrastive dispersion of percepts and combinatorial phonology*

Vocal percepts cluster in a few particular "hot spots" among the innumerable, chaotic possibilities we can produce and perceive. As in other chaotic systems, the clusterings depend on frequency and accumulation, which result from ease of production and distinctness of perception. Thus certain vocalizations are easier to pronounce and require less energy: this is likely to favor their use and increase their frequency (Lindblom 1992). Also, the human perceptual systems set upper bounds on the distinctions which we can perceive or produce as signifiants. Nowak et al. (1999) found that the demands of discriminability (as well as memory and time to learn) constrain the system to a fairly small set of signals. Oudeyer (2005) shows in simulations that canalisation by the vocal tract and general acoustic theory define eight discrete regions of a tube like the vocal tract which afford greatest acoustic contrast for least articulatory effort, and these correspond to places of articulation in natural languages.

The small number of clusters "automatically brings it about that targets are systematically re-used to build the complex sounds that agents produce: their vocalizations are now compositional" (Oudeyer 2005: 444). How could that be? Where does the compositional percept come from? The answer is again in the material properties of the elements. Vocalizations occur in time. So our perceptual system captures the linear properties of vocalizations when they are produced, in particular the linear relationship between two vocal clusters, the most salient one being linear adjacency. The linear adjacency of two vocal percepts is therefore a percept, and it can be represented by an IRS, just like any percept. The relational percept of juxtaposition is already in the stock of our perceptual system, hence it is available for IRSs that link concepts and percepts. Another material property of vocalizations is intonation: therefore, another perceptual element represented by IRSs is the tone superimposed on a phoneme, of which there are only a few distinctive values due to contrastive dispersion.

Crucially, in an arbitrary system, the percept represented by an IRS and linked to a concept can be any element among those recognized by the perceptual system: a phoneme, a juxtaposition, or an intonation. Under arbitrariness, it makes no difference whether the represented element is simple or complex. The accoustic image can be a single phoneme, or the relational percept of juxtaposition applying any number of times to phonemes, as well as any of the available intonations on these elements. These complex elements remain within the limits of what humans can distinctively perceive or produce because their parts have the appropriate qualities. Phonological compositionality therefore comes from two properties of vocalizations: they are temporally linearized, which provides the percept of juxtaposition as a signifiant; additionally, the material property of intonation provides tone as a signifiant.

As a result of all these constraints, a limited number of discrete phonemes and their combinations emerged from self-organization in the chaotic system of the speech sounds represented by IRSs: they constitute the potential signfiants.

4.2. *Contrastive dispersion of meanings*

Material properties and self-organization also affect the conceptual interface of the linguistic system. Here too order arises out of chaos and clusters are formed in the mass of the conceptual substance as a result of frequency and accumulation. The more a situation has some importance and/or is encountered frequently by the organism, the more likely concepts associated with it will be activated. The accumulations self-organize on the concepts most used by the organism. It is this "usefulness" which makes the signifiés tend to correspond to fairly broad and/or usual categories of things, actions, qualities, etc. (Locke 1690:15), basic-level concepts (Rosch et al. 1976, Murphy & Lassaline 1997) whose names are among the first common nouns learned by children (Brown 1958: 20). Discrete meanings are formed in the mass of the conceptual substance (Saussure 1916) as a result of maximizing contrastive dispersion across the space for signifiés. These clusters have to be relatively few in number due to storage limitations of the brain, hence they tend to have fairly broad meanings. This does not adversely affect the communicative or thinking functions of language because linguistic signs reside in organisms that independently have an inferential system that supplies the required complementary information.

4.3. *Self-organization and syntax*

I hypothesize that combinatorial syntax also emerged out of chaos due to self-organization. The element of the conceptual system which IRSs represent the most frequently is the relation of predication, since it is common to all the attributions of properties. Predication is the broad meaning *par excellence*, it is the meaning which creates the strongest concentration point in the chaos of IRS representations of meanings. Moreover, on the perceptual side, the most frequent elements are temporal sequencing and intonation. These happen to be relational percepts. So the hottest accumulation point in the mass of the conceptual substance is the relation of *predication*, and the hottest accumulation points in the mass of the perceptual substance are the two relational percepts *juxtaposition* and *intonation*. These accumulation points in their respective domains are so overwhelmingly dominant that the probability of links between *predication* and *juxtaposition/intonation* reaches a point where these links inevitably accumulate and crystallize. Therefore, given these prior properties, I predict that computational simulations will show that human languages inescapably develop combinatorial signs involving predication as a signifié, and juxtaposition and intonation as signifiants. Thus compositional syntax is also a consequence of self-organization arising out of the chaos created by IRSs.

Combining signs by means of a combinatorial sign produces a complex sign, i.e. a phrase with a compositional meaning and a compositional signifiant. Assuming that uni-signs fall into one of the lexical categories/types like noun, verb, adjective, preposition, and also that the category of a complex sign is the category of one of its immediate constituents (this endocentricity following from the parsimonious assumption that the only primitives are lexical and combinatorial signs), type-recursion occurs when a restraining sign or one of its elements happens to be of the same type as the restrained sign whose category projects and determines the category of the complex sign. Therefore, I predict that, given these additional prior properties, computational simulations will also show that type-recursivity is a side-effect of the combinatorial capacity of "syntactic" signs. In short, the presence of IRSs in human brains explains both saussurean signs and type-recursion. They no longer pose insoluble challenges for natural selection.

References

Arbib, Michael. 2004. The Mirror System Hypothesis. Linking Language to Theory of Mind. *Interdisciplines*.

Bickerton, Derek. 2009. *Adam's Tongue*. New York: Hill and Wang.

Brown, Roger. 1958. *Words and things*. New York: Free Press.

Deacon, Terrence W. 2003. The Co-evolution of Language and the Brain, Interview conducted at the studios of KCSM, September 5, 2003. San Mateo: PBS.

Deacon, Terrence W. 2008. Relaxed selection and the role of epigenesis in the evolution of language. In *Biological Foundations and Origin of Syntax*, eds. Derek Bickerton and Eors Szathmáry. Cambridge, MA: MIT Press.

Gallese, V. 2003. A neuroscientific grasp of concepts: From control to representation. *Philosophical Transactions of the Royal Society* 358:1231-1240.

Hurley, Susan. 2008. The shared circuits model (SCM): How control, mirroring, and simulation can enable imitation, deliberation, and mindreading. *Behavioral and Brain Sciences* 31:1-58.

Iacoboni, M., Molnar-Szakacs, I., Gallese, V., Buccino, G., Mazziotta, J., and Rizzolatti, Giacomo. 2004. Grasping intentions with mirror neurons. *Society for Neuroscience Abstracts* 254.

Jacob, François. 1982. *The possible and the actual*. New York: Pantheon.

Jacob, Pierre, and Jeannerod, Marc. 2004. The Motor Theory of Social Cognition. A Critique. *Interdisciplines*.

Lindblom, Björn. 1992. Phonological units as adaptive emergents of lexical development. In *Phonological Development: Models, Research, Implications*, eds. C. Ferguson, L. Menn and C. Stoel-Gammon, 565-604. Timmonium, MD: York Press.

Locke, John. 1690/1964. *An essay concerning human understanding*. Cleveland: Meridian Books.

Meltzoff, A.N., and Moore, M.K. 1997. Explaining facial imitation. A theoretical model. *Early Development and Parenting* 6:179-192.

Murphy, G.L., and Lassaline, M.E. 1997. Hierarchical structure in concepts and the basic level of categorization. In *Knowledge, concepts and categories*, eds. K. Lamberts and D.R. Shanks, 93-132. Cambridge, MA: MIT Press.

Nowak, Martin, Krakauer, David, and Dress, Andreas. 1999. An Error Limit for the Evolution of Language. *Proceedings of the Royal Society of London* 266:2131-2136.

Oudeyer, Pierre-Yves. 2005. The self-organization of speech sounds. *Journal of Theoretical Biology* 233:435-449.

Prigogine, Ilya, and Stengers, Isabelle. 1984. *Order out of Chaos*. New York: Bantam Books.

Rizzolatti, Giacomo. 2005. The mirror neuron system and imitation. In *Perspectives on Imitation*, eds. Susan Hurley and Nick Chater. Cambridge, MA: MIT Press.

Rosch, E., Mervis, C.B., Gray, W.D., Johnson, D.M., & Boyes-Braem, P. 1976. Basic objects in natural categories. *Cognitive Psychology* 8:382-439.

Saussure, Ferdinand de. 1916. *Cours de Linguistique Générale. Critical edition prepared by Tullio de Mauro*. Paris: Payot.

CULTURAL RATCHETING RESULTS PRIMARILY FROM SEMANTIC COMPRESSION

JOANNA J. BRYSON

Artificial Models of Natural Intelligence, University of Bath
Bath, BA2 7AY, United Kingdom
jjb@cs.bath.ac.uk

Humans acquire far more of their behaviour from conspecifics via culture than any other species. Our culture is larger because it accumulates, where other species' seem to stay approximately the same size (Tomasello, 1999). This chapter attempts to clarify the problem of cultural accumulation by distinguishing between the *size* of a culture that can be transmitted from one generation, and the *extent* of culture transmitted. A culture's size is determined largely by ecological constraints, and certainly homonins (and some other species) show adaptations to facilitate this. But the exponential accumulation hypothesised by (Tomasello, 1999) I claim cannot be accounted for this way, but rather is a consequence of increasing information value in semantic components. This process can be achieved through memetics — semantics will be selected for which transmits the most information. Thus cultural evolution achieves compression of information, generating increased extent in culture even when maintaining a fixed size. I support my argument with evidence from simulations explaining the size of culture (Čače and Bryson, 2007), and simulations demonstrating selection for increased extent Kirby (1999).

1. Introduction

Although language is undoubtedly a cultural artifact of unique utility, the evolution of language may best be viewed as one aspect of a general exceptional human capacity to evolve culture. By *culture* here I mean behaviour acquired from conspecifics by means other than genetic transmission (Richerson and Boyd, 2005; Bryson, 2008). For the last decade we have known that other species share with us the fact that some part of their behaviour repertoire is cultural (Whiten et al., 1999; van Schaik et al., 2003; Perry et al., 2003); more recently we have realized some of it is even taught (Franks and Richardson, 2006; Thornton and McAuliffe, 2006). Thus humanity's uniqueness is a question of extents: both the quantity of culture per individual, and the persistence of recognisable elements of culture across generations.

Many people have attempted to explain why human culture is uniquely large and complex. However, many of the hypothesised mechanisms might themselves be consequences of our accumulation of culture. For example, Beppu and Griffiths (2009) claim that cultural ratcheting requires the communication of beliefs about hypotheses. Clearly, cultural accumulation is accelerated by such a process. But if the bald statement that there can be *no* accumulation without it were true, then there could be no explanation of how we acquired the ability to communicate beliefs about hypotheses in the first place.

Ironically, Beppu and Griffiths (2009) base their work on a simulation which demonstrates exactly the sort of mechanism that leads to accumulation without beliefs or intentions. Their methodology is based on the iterated-learning paradigm invented by Kirby (1999), yet they (and their reviewers) overlook the result that made the paradigm famous. In Kirby's simulation, *the culture itself evolves to be more replicable*, without any change in the agents that transmit it. It does this through a process of regularisation: in later cultures, semantics is represented more efficiently. The process is not magic — it is the simple consequence of selection. Here the selective pressure is just the fixed number and length of transmissions an agent will hear in its lifetime. Where variation generates alternative mechanisms for expression, the most likely mechanisms to be transmitted to the next generation are the most general. Irregular forms may never be heard, and therefore drop out of the culture, unless they refer to very frequently-referenced notions. For such frequent references, selection from limited transmission favours brevity over generality. Thus even in a simple simulation, a fixed size for a culture is sufficient selective pressure to generate cultural accumulation.

I begin this chapter by explaining my thesis in better detail. I then analyse the results of Beppu and Griffiths (2009), showing an error in the mathematical model they present, and accounting for their experimental results. I use the concepts introduced in this analysis to examine what factors do account for ratcheting. I finish by re-addressing the question of human exceptionalism.

2. Thesis and Key Definitions

The fundamental claim of this article is that cultural ratcheting doesn't just mean transmitting more information, or at least not more bits of data. For real animals as for Kirby's simulated agents, the amount of communication from one generation to the next is largely determined by biological constraints such as lifespan or the carrying capacity of an environment. Lifespan determines how long the agents have to learn; carrying capacity determines how many agents can live near enough to each other to routinely transmit information. Our lifespan has not changed much compared to other apes. We can certainly support a more dense population, and we have learned to transmit behaviour faster, through teaching. But the majority of this increased rate of communication isn't about the number of signals, but about their quality. Essentially, the elements of culture that get selected *through* as well as *for* transmission between generation are those with the most meaning per transmission.

To clarify this, think about transmitting arithmetic. Imagine two societies that transmit how to add every possible pair of numbers between 1 and 999. One culture does this by rote, the other teaches only 0–9 by rote, and then a few rules that enable adding numbers of up to 3 digits length. For the purpose of clarity in this paper, I will define *size* such that the size of the rote culture is significantly larger than that of the rule-based culture. But I will say that the *extent* of the two cultures is the same. *Size* is roughly the number of bits physically transmitted between individuals. *Extent* is the range of behaviours the culture enables.

Thus the fundamental claim of my article is that the size of the culture is set largely by biological constraints. Of course, the qualification *largely* matters here. Practices such as systematic teaching do increase the amount of information that can be reliably transmitted from one individual to the next. Other practices like agriculture fall somewhere between my two categories, since the effect of communicating culture relevant to food production (rather than some other kind of culture) is to increase the population density, thus addressing some biological constraints. This is a sort of increased cultural richness, though not the semantic one I am emphasising. My claim is that the main contributing factor to cultural ratcheting is the accumulation of increasingly powerful concepts. Or, using the terms just introduced, my thesis is that human-like exponential cultural ratcheting requires cultural extent increasing without cultural size.

3. Cultural Accumulation Cannot Require Accumulated Culture

Recently, Beppu and Griffiths (2009) reported that observing the behaviour of others is not sufficient to produce cumulative cultural evolution. They base this claim on two sources of evidence. First, they argue mathematically that transmission must necessarily result in a loss of information, making reference to the children's game of telephone [US] or Chinese whispers [UK]. In this game, one person whispers a message to someone who has not heard it. After some number of such transmissions the final and original message are compared for amusement.

This signal-degradation observation has been both made and addressed before. Dawkins (2000) uses exactly the same metaphor to describe biological and memetic evolution. He then goes on to explain how errors introduced by noise are in the vast majority of cases corrected in true Darwinian selection by processes that apply rules for signal correction. In the Bayesian terms Beppu and Griffiths utilise, the point is that the receiver has priors as well as the sender, and in perceiving the message is able to correct for most noise. Sperber and Hirschfeld (2006) make largely the same observation in the specific context of modern human culture. In a reaction against the prior over-emphasis on imitation which Beppu and Griffiths (2009) are also responding to, Sperber and Hirschfeld credit their massive-modularity hypothesis with providing the additional information necessary for interpreting observed events. Information accumulated from some combination of genetics, individual experience and previously-acquired culture allows informed perception which effectively boosts a transmitted signal back to its original strength.

This is precisely why the game telephone requires whispering: not only to remove the chance of overhearing, but also to remove a great deal of linguistic information. This increases the probability of transmission error. Note that even so the message will still be perceived as language — no game of Chinese whispers ever ends with someone making white noise. Real cultural transmission is not so much like this game as like real telephone communication, where repeaters in the network amplify the signal in order to retain the signal over distance.

Of course there are some errors in transmission. More importantly, some individuals will die without ever transmitting some of the knowledge they have acquired culturally. In a sustainable cultural system, losses due to either death or corruption must be compensated for by individual discovery. For a culture to maintain its size, innovation merely needs to compensate, for growth, innovation must exceed loss. Errors of transmission may in themselves result in useful innovation, particularly if the 'error' is due to an intelligent perceiver making a 'correction' to a signal that is more sensible than the original transmission. This process can operate either with or without the awareness of a sentient receiver. Where transmission is perfect and entirely reliable, there would be no evolution and indeed no change.

Returning to Beppu and Griffiths (2009), the authors seek to verify their results with a second information source: live experiments. Taken in even a cultural-evolutionary context, the experiments are rather short, and they detect no significant accumulation from simple imitation. However, when the experimenters radically increase the amount of information transmitted by allowing the demonstrators to describe their hypotheses, accumulation becomes detectable. I suspect that the power of the initial form of the experiment is not sufficient that the apparent insignificance of its results are meaningful. That the level of accumulation is far lower with less information is unsurprising.

4. Determinants of Culture's Size and Extent

In previous work Čače and Bryson (2007) have presented a simulation model showing the spread and fixation of a tendency for the altruistic communication of food-processing strategies. By analysing this model, we can identify the factors determining the size of a culture. Basically, the size of a culture is determined by the probability of any particular piece of information being transmitted. Factors determining this probability include: the rate of information transmission, the maximum lifespan of an individual, and how many other agents an individual observes in the average time interval.

In the Čače and Bryson (2007) version of our simulation, individual bouts of communication transmit perfectly. Knowledge only leaves the simulation when an agent dies without transmitting it. It enters the system through a process of individual discovery. These discoveries occur at a low, fixed rate — for example, five percent of the population may discover one thing in their lives, and the rest discover nothing. What they discover is random and may already be known in the local population. At the beginning of he simulation, knowledge is present at the rate of discovery — the population knows about 0.05 things. Over time this builds to an equilibrium value, where that equilibrium is determined primarily by the transmission probability.

The extent of culture is determined by the size of culture multiplied by the average behavioural utility of its content. In the our simulation, the extent of the the culture is fixed by its size, because all knowledge is equally valuable and takes equally long to transmit. This is the exact opposite of the case for the Kirby (1999) simulation described earlier. There, the size of the culture is fixed, but the expressivity of what is transmitted increases as that which is expressed becomes regularised. Frequently used terms become shorter even at the costs of regularity, while infrequently used terms must either be regular or be likely to be lost before transmission to the next generation.

For another example of increasing 'quality' of transmitted culture, Bechlivanidis (2006) has extended the Čače and Bryson (2007) simulation to include foods of varying quality, including 'bad' foods that it was detrimental to eat. As before, agents were equally likely to discover on their own any of the available foods, and further they were not able to individually judge a food's quality or long-term effects, but continued eating it out of habit or social influence. However, simple biology results in the culture favouring good foods. Healthier individuals are more likely to live long, and thus have more opportunity to socially influence those around them.

Bechlivanidis' work demonstrates that the Čače and Bryson results are robust to false beliefs being held and communicated. It also allows us to explore additional circumstances that can lead to enhanced cultural evolution. For example, if the agents attended preferentially to the most prestigious individual available, the culture grows faster because all agents tended to have better knowledge and therefore to be able to support a denser population. Prestige could rely on even simple indicators like apparent age. Note that contrary to a small detail of Richerson and Boyd (2005), prestige-led imitation proves adaptive even though the prestigious individuals receive nothing in return for the attention of their neighbours.

In general then, higher-quality information will be selected for if available. In line with the experimental outcomes of Beppu and Griffiths (2009), the extent of culture can grow more rapidly if abstract rules rather than raw data can be transmitted. Obviously, once cultural artifacts like language and religion evolved they massively facilitated cultural accumulation. Similarly, new concepts such as *self*, *desires* and *other* must massively increase the amount the range of plans available to cognition, by compressing a wide range of phenomena into relatively simple accounts (c.f. Donald, 1991).

5. Why Humans are Special

Why doesn't cultural ratcheting happen for all species? It's possible, of course, that it *is* happening for some species, but that they are still in a phase hominids were in only half a million years ago, with very little visible change in technology. However, the biological constraints on culture size reflect a set of tradeoffs well away from the niche of most species — for example, long lives and high cognitive plasticity for retention of information. Certainly large brains are expensive; probably the hominid ones co-evolved with our culture (Aiello, 1997; Silk, 2007). Notably, the recent period (50,000 years) of rapid cultural evolution has actually accompanied a significant *reduction* in hominid brain size. This could reflect the onset of modern language making transmission so easy that an adaptive advantage was still conferred even with reduced memory capacity.

It is nevertheless striking that wild chimpanzee culture seems to be of relatively fixed size. Further, chimpanzee culture seems to be recoverable within two generations after an artificial troop of orphaned chimpanzees is reintroduced into a naturalistic setting (Whiten, personal communication). One possible reason for this is that there are also *ecological* limits on the adaptive size and stability of cultures. If all chimpanzees persistently fed on particular optimal species for too long, those food sources would go extinct. It may be ecologically advantageous that chimpanzees continue to discover and move between new food sources from time to time.

Why then are humans such an exception? For some time I have been promoting the idea that the key difference between humans and other primates is simply that we are the only primates capable of temporally-precise imitation (Bryson, 2001, 2004, 2008, 2009). That is, humans are the only primate demonstrating the ability to precisely replicate not just snap-shot final postures, but entire temporal trajectories of variable values over many degrees of freedom (e.g. pitch, volume, formants). This allows the encoding of substantially more information, such as might allow arbitrary patterns to be encoded redundantly and thus robustly. I have previously argued that the difference between hominids and other vocal imitators such as song birds may be that our capacity for second-order referential reasoning, derived from the primates' complex social structures. This in turn allows for compositionality, which in turn facilitates the sort of holophrasis evolution originally hypothesised by Wray (1998), and to some extent modelled by Kirby (1999), whose simulations assume recursion. This theory may be unnecessarily elaborate, however. Our common ape ancestor was already larger (though notably not longer-lived) than other vocal imitators, and may have more easily been able to support large brains and therefore large memories for a large lexicon.

6. Conclusion

To return to my primary point, I have argued that ratcheting is not just about innovation or increasing the number of things transmitted in a culture, but rather primarily due to increasing the behavioural productivity of the average piece of culturally-transmitted information. I motivated this by arguing against the claim that simplistic transmission necessarily leads to degradation and loss. First, this loss is ameliorated by the expectations of the receiver, and second, to the extent it exists it can be compensated for by some rate of individual innovation. This point is critical to understanding the origins of language and sophisticated meta-cognition (beliefs about our beliefs.) Any scientific explanation of these phenomena must rest on culture accrued without them.

I have illustrated my arguments with several published simulations. These demonstrate that processes exist such as my argument describes. We cannot prove that these are the processes that lead to cultural evolution in humans, but a scientific theory is never proven certainly. Theories are judged by their likelihood given currently available data. The demonstrated existence of appropriate processes certainly increases the likelihood they might have played a role in our cultural history.

References

Aiello, L. C. (1997). Brains and guts in human evolution: The Expensive Tissue Hypothesis. *Brazilian Journal of Genetics*, 20(1).

Bechlivanidis, C. (2006). An examination of the role of prestige in cultural evolution with the aid of agent-based modelling. Technical Report CSBU–2006–21, Department of Computer Science, University of Bath, UK.

Beppu, A. and Griffiths, T. L. (2009). Iterated learning and the cultural ratchet. In *The 31st Annual Meeting of the Cognitive Science Society (CogSci 2009)*, pages 2089–2094, Amsterdam. Lawrence Erlbaum Associates.

Bryson, J. J. (2001). Embodiment vs. memetics: Does language need a physical plant? In Pfeifer, R. and Westermann, G., editors, *Developmental Embodied Cognition (DECO-2001)*, Edinburgh.

Bryson, J. J. (2004). Language needs second-order representations and a rich memetic substrate. In *Evolution of Language 5*, Leipzig, Germany. talk.

Bryson, J. J. (2008). Embodiment versus memetics. *Mind & Society*, 7(1):77–94.

Bryson, J. J. (2009). Representations underlying social learning and cultural evolution. *Interaction Studies*, 10(1):77–100.

Čače, I. and Bryson, J. J. (2007). Agent based modelling of communication costs: Why information can be free. In Lyon, C., Nehaniv, C. L., and Cangelosi, A., editors, *Emergence and Evolution of Linguistic Communication*, pages 305–322. Springer, London.

Dawkins, R. (2000). Foreword to Susan Blackmore's *Meme Machine*, pages *vii–xvii*. Oxford University Press, second edition.

Donald, M. (1991). *Origins of the modern mind: Three stages in the evolution of culture and cognition*. Harvard University Press, Cambridge, MA.

Franks, N. R. and Richardson, T. (2006). Teaching in tandem-running ants. *Nature*, 439(7073):153.

Kirby, S. (1999). *Function, Selection and Innateness: the Emergence of Language Universals*. Oxford University Press.

Perry, S., Baker, M., Fedigan, L., Gros-Louis, J., Jack, K., MacKinnon, K., Manson, J., Panger, M., Pyle, K., and Rose, L. (2003). Social conventions in wild white-faced capuchin monkeys: Evidence for traditions in a neotropical primate. *Current Anthropology*, 44(2):241–268.

Richerson, P. J. and Boyd, R. (2005). *Not By Genes Alone: How Culture Transformed Human Evolution*. University Of Chicago Press.

van Schaik, C. P., Ancrenaz, M., Borgen, G., Galdikas, B., Knott, C. D., Singleton, I., Suzuki, A., Utami, S. S., and Merrill, M. (2003). Orangutan cultures and the evolution of material culture. *Science*, 299(5603):102–105.

Silk, J. B. (2007). Social components of fitness in primate groups. *Science*, 317(5843):1347.

Sperber, D. and Hirschfeld, L. (2006). Culture and modularity. In Carruthers, P., Laurence, S., and Stich, S., editors, *The Innate Mind: Culture and Cognition*, volume 2, pages 149–164. Oxford University Press.

Thornton, A. and McAuliffe, K. (2006). Teaching in wild meerkats. *Science*, 313(5784):227–229.

Tomasello, M. (1999). *The Cultural Origins of Human Cognition*. Harvard University Press, Cambridge, MA.

Whiten, A., Goodall, J., McGew, W. C., Nishida, T., Reynolds, V., Sugiyama, Y., Tutin, C. E. G., Wrangham, R. W., and Boesch, C. (1999). Cultures in chimpanzees. *Nature*, 399:682–685.

Wray, A. (1998). Protolanguage as a holistic system for social interaction. *Language and Communication*, 18(1):47–67.

ITERATED LEARNING OF MULTIPLE LANGUAGES FROM MULTIPLE TEACHERS

DAVID BURKETT

Computer Science Division, University of California, Berkeley
Berkeley, CA, 94720, USA
`dburkett@cs.berkeley.edu`

THOMAS L. GRIFFITHS

Psychology Department, University of California, Berkeley
Berkeley, CA, 94720, USA
`tom_griffiths@berkeley.edu`

Language learning is an iterative process, with each learner learning from other learners. Analysis of this process of iterated learning with chains of Bayesian agents, each of whom learns from one agent and teaches the next, shows that it converges to a distribution over languages that reflects the inductive biases of the learners. However, if agents are taught by multiple members of the previous generation, who potentially speak different languages, then a single language quickly dominates the population. In this work, we consider a setting where agents learn from multiple teachers, but are allowed to learn multiple languages. We show that if agents have a sufficiently strong expectation that multiple languages are being spoken, we reproduce the effects of inductive biases on the outcome of iterated learning seen with chains of agents.

1. Introduction

Natural languages change as they are passed from person to person and from generation to generation. Although many explanations have been proposed for these changes, one way to analyze the process is to focus on the iterative nature of language learning: people learning a language are being taught by other people who themselves previously learned that language. Formal analysis of this "iterated learning" process has yielded some important insights into how learners' biases affect the languages likely to be used by a population (Kirby, 2001). In particular, it has been shown that if we assume the learners are Bayesian agents who compute posterior distributions over languages based on their prior beliefs and evidence from the previous generation of learners, then the iterated learning procedure will converge on a population whose preferences reflect the learners' prior beliefs (Kirby, Dowman, & Griffiths, 2007; Griffiths & Kalish, 2007). This relationship between the prior beliefs of a population and the stationary distribution over linguistic characteristics is important for understanding the evolution of human language use. For example, it suggests that we should more closely examine universal properties of natural languages, since they are likely to reflect the biases underlying human language learning.

Most analyses of iterated learning with Bayesian agents have assumed that each learner receives linguistic data from exactly one member of the previous generation. This has led to the criticism that such learning dynamics are unrealistic and do not adequately model the full range of linguistic evolutionary processes (Niyogi & Berwick, 2009). However, a recent study begins to address this critique, showing that if learners consider evidence from the entire previous generation of speakers, then the results of iterated learning with Bayesian agents do not depend entirely on the learners' prior beliefs (Smith, 2009). Instead, the population comes to almost entirely speak one language, and the initial composition of the linguistic community is important. In particular, learners can consistently overcome their prior beliefs if they are learning from a multi-speaker population whose distribution of languages conflicts strongly enough with this prior.

Although the results of iterated learning with multiple teachers seems to conflict with earlier findings, there is a sense in which this model has an unusual dynamics. Each learner is attempting to decide on a single language despite the fact that the population that the learner is using as a source of evidence is, in the aggregate, multilingual. The learners are violating the principle of Bayesian rational analysis (Ferdinand & Zuidena, 2009) by making an unjustified assumption that only one language is being spoken. An alternative is that the learner not only assumes that the evidence is coming from multiple speakers, but also assumes that different speakers may be speaking different languages (see Figure 1).

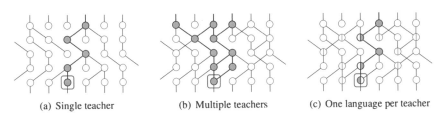

| (a) Single teacher | (b) Multiple teachers | (c) One language per teacher |

Figure 1. (a) If each learner learns from a single teacher in the previous generation, then the learning dynamics for infinitely sized discrete generations are equivalent to those for chains of individual learners, as each learner's ancestry is still a single chain. (b) If learners still learn a single language, but get data from multiple teachers, then we see different learning dynamics. (c) However, as learners consider multilingual hypotheses, in the limiting case where each teacher is assumed to speak a different language, we recover the learning dynamics from a single chain of learners.

One way to allow hypotheses consistent with data received from multiple speakers is to directly estimate the probabilities of words. We show that if learners adopt this approach, the iterated learning procedure will converge to reflect their prior beliefs, as in the simpler single teacher formulation. However, this learning model makes the most sense in a context where it is reasonable to interpolate between the languages spoken by one's predecessors: say, when learning from teachers who speak different dialects of the same basic language. In order for learners to deal appropriately with truly divergent inputs, we need a more complex learning process that explicitly models the possibility that they need to learn multiple complete linguistic systems. Intuitively, we expect that if learners are able to appropriately separate their input into distinct languages, then the learning dynamics will resemble those from the single teacher setting, as shown in Figure 1 (c). We test this intuition by modeling learners of this sort, and showing that in simulations, iterated learning with learners who believe that they are receiving data from multiple languages once more converges on the learners' prior beliefs.

2. Iterated Learning with Bayesian Agents

For Bayesian agents, learning is modeled as a statistical inference about the hypothesis h that generated data d. The agent computes the posterior distribution:

$$p(h|d) \propto p(d|h)p(h) \tag{1}$$

where $p(h)$ is the agent's prior distribution over hypotheses, and $p(d|h)$ is a likelihood expressing the probability of data d being generated for hypothesis h.

In iterated learning, the data that each agent learns from is generated from the previous generation of learners. If we let $p_t(h)$ represent the proportion of agents speaking language h at time t and assume that each learner receives data generated by one teacher, the probability of an agent receiving data d at time t, $p_t(d)$, is:

$$p_t(d) = \sum_h p_t(h)p(d|h) \tag{2}$$

Similarly, if each learner samples a hypothesis from $p(h|d)$, the next generation's distribution over hypotheses is: $p_{t+1}(h) = \sum_d p_t(d)p(h|d)$, with $p(h|d)$ as given in Equation 1. This is the model considered in previous analyses of iterated learning by Bayesian agents, and results in convergence of $p_t(h)$ to the prior $p(h)$ as $t \to \infty$ (Griffiths & Kalish, 2007).

This model can be extended to allow multiple teachers. Assume that the data d consists of a collection of independently produced words, w, with $p(d|h) = \prod_{w \in d} p(w|h)$. The case where all the words are generated by a single teacher is given by expanding Equation 2 as $p_t(d) = \sum_h p_t(h) \left(\prod_{w \in d} p(w|h) \right)$. If we allow each word to be potentially generated by a different teacher, as in the alternate model used in Smith (2009), we have to select a new hypothesis for each word, resulting in the modified distribution:

$$p_t(d) = \prod_{w \in d} \left(\sum_h p_t(h)p(w|h) \right) \tag{3}$$

Smith (2009) showed that when this model was used with a hypothesis space consisting of two hypotheses, each having one highly diagnostic word, $p_t(h)$ converged to a distribution that was dominated by one hypothesis, with the specific hypothesis resulting from an interaction between the prior and the initial proportion of the population who used that hypothesis.

The Bayesian inference described in Equation 1 is intended to identify which single hypothesis generated a collection of words, d. Therefore, the learners are making an estimate that is consistent with data generated according to Equation 2, but *not* with data generated according to Equation 3. Therefore, to properly model a Bayesian learner who receives data according to Equation 3, we need to consider a different hypothesis space: one that takes into account the fact that the learner is receiving data from multiple underlying distributions. This will be the focus of the remainder of this paper.

3. Learning Distributions over Words

One way to allow hypotheses consistent with data received from multiple speakers is to directly estimate the probabilities of words from the vocabulary. This results in a continuous hypothesis space: for a vocabulary of size V, a hypothesis h is a member of the V-dimensional simplex. For the simple two-word vocabulary used by Smith (2009), h can be summarized by a single parameter $\theta \in [0, 1]$, and the production probabilities can be written as $p(w|\theta) = \theta^{\delta(w,w_0)}(1-\theta)^{\delta(w,w_1)}$, where δ is the Kroenecker's delta function. Note that with this production probability, we can rewrite Equation 3 as:

$$p_t(d) = \prod_{w \in d} \left(\int_\theta p_t(\theta)p(w|\theta)d\theta \right) = E_t(\theta)^{n_0} \left(1 - E_t(\theta)\right)^{n_1}$$

where $E_t(\theta)$ is the mean of the current generation's distribution over hypotheses $p_t(\theta)$, and $n_i = \sum_{w \in d} \delta(w, w_i)$ for $i \in \{0, 1\}$. Because our hypothesis space is equivalent to the set of Bernoulli distributions, the conjugate prior is the beta distribution.[a] Therefore, we define $p(\theta)$ to be a beta prior, with hyperparameters α and β, which results in an iterated Bayesian learning process equivalent to the Wright-Fisher model of genetic drift (Reali & Griffiths, in press).

Given the equivalence to the Wright-Fisher model, we expect that the iterated learning procedure will converge to a distribution over θ that is closely related to the prior (Reali & Griffiths, in press). To verify this, we ran a simple computational simulation. Recall that under our transmission model, the behavior of an entire generation of learners can be summarized by a single value: $E_t(\theta)$. We assume learners select a hypothesis by sampling from their posterior distribution over hypotheses, so linearity of expectation makes this straightforward to compute

---

[a]More generally, for a vocabulary of size V, the conjugate prior is the V-dimensional Dirichlet.

from $E(\theta|d)$, the posterior mean. $E_{t+1}(\theta) = \sum_d p_t(d)E(\theta|d)$. Fortunately, due to the conjugacy of the beta prior, $E(\theta|d)$ has a simple form: $\frac{\alpha+n_0}{\alpha+\beta+n_0+n_1}$.

Following Smith (2009), we ran simulations for various proportions of w_0 spoken in the initial population, assuming an infinite population of learners. We fixed $|d| = 3$. Varying this parameter resulted in slower convergence as $|d|$ increased, but did not affect the qualitative results. We also experimented with different values of α, but fixed $\beta = \frac{2}{3}\alpha$ so that the expected value of θ under the prior was always 0.6, slightly favoring w_0. The results of our simulations are in Figure 2. The main finding is that under all the settings under consideration, the proportion of w_0 spoken in the population converged to 0.6. In other words, this model exhibited the expected convergence to a proportion favored by the prior.

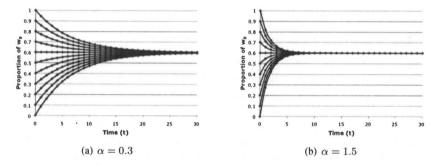

(a) $\alpha = 0.3$ (b) $\alpha = 1.5$

Figure 2.   Simulation results for the two hypothesis model. Here, the number of words seen by each learner $|d| = 3$, and the prior is parameterized with $\beta = \frac{2}{3}\alpha$, favoring proportions of w_0 close to 0.6.

4. Learning Distributions over Languages

A more general way to deal appropriately with multiple linguistically divergent teachers is for learners to explicitly consider arbitrary sets of languages, but to shift the hypothesis space from individual languages to *distributions* over languages. Thus, a learner is simultaneously inducing from data *which* languages are being spoken by the previous generation and their relative frequencies. We use h to refer to a full hypothesis: a distribution over languages, l, where each language l is a distribution over words w. For example, in the two-word setting, there might be two languages: l_0, where w_0 is spoken with probability 0.95 and w_1 with probability 0.05, and l_1, where those probabilities are reversed. A bilingual agent with a slight preference for l_0 can be represented as having hypothesis $h_{0.6}$, where $p(l_0|h_{0.6}) = 0.6$ and $p(l_1|h_{0.6}) = 0.4$.

The Dirichlet process (DP) (Ferguson, 1973) provides a suitable family of priors for this hypothesis space. A DP prior has two parameters: α, which affects the learner's prior belief in the number of languages being spoken (a learner with a higher value of α will tend to predict a larger number of distinct languages), and a base distribution G_0, which is a distribution over languages, specifying which languages are preferred.

4.1. *Inference*

Exact inference in the space of distributions over languages under a DP prior is intractable. However, we can approximate the dynamics of the Markov chain by running Monte Carlo simulations with collections of artificial agents separated into discrete generations. Procedurally, these simulations are straightforward. We start out with an initial collection of agents, A_0. Each of these agents receives some data according to the starting conditions of that simulation (see Section 4.2 for details). Then, based on that data, the agent picks a specific hypothesis. We then create a new generation of agents, A_1. Each agent in A_1 receives data generated by the agents in A_0, and chooses its own hypothesis accordingly. This procedure is iterated for some fixed number of generations, with each agent in A_t receiving data collectively from the agents in A_{t-1}.

There are thus two steps that we have to perform repeatedly. First, given some data d, we need to be able to draw a sample from the posterior distribution $p(h|d)$. Though we omit the mathematical details here, a sample can be obtained efficiently by using a Gibbs sampler based on the Chinese Restaurant Process (Aldous, 1985). The second step is to sample some data, d, from a collection of agents, A. We sample each word independently according to a multistep procedure. First, an agent a is selected uniformly from A. Then, a language is sampled according to that agent's hypothesis. Finally, the word is sampled from the selected language. This procedure is repeated for each word in the data. The number of words in the data, $|d|$, is fixed as before. This amounts to drawing each word according to: $p(w) = \sum_{a \in A} \frac{1}{|A|} \sum_l p(l|h_a) \sum_w p(w|l)$.

4.2. *Simulations*

We ran simulations of this learning procedure using the 260-language compositional vs. holistic setting from Griffiths and Kalish (2007). In this setting, each word, w, represents a form-meaning pair, (x, y), where x and y each have a two-bit representation. Each language corresponds to a mapping between forms and meanings on which its production probabilities depend. The holistic languages range over all $4^4 = 256$ possible mappings between the 4 forms and 4 meanings, whereas the compositional languages map each bit individually, and thus range over only $2^2 = 4$ possible mappings. The actual production probabilities are:

$$p(x,y|l) = p(y)p(x|y,l) = \begin{cases} \frac{1}{4}(1 - \epsilon) & y \text{ maps to } x \text{ in } l \\ \frac{1}{4}\frac{\epsilon}{3} & \text{otherwise} \end{cases}$$

with ϵ a free parameter. The base distribution, G_0, is parameterized by p_0, determining the probability of a compositional language. The distribution selects uniformly given the class of language:

$$G_0(l) = \begin{cases} \frac{p_0}{4} & l \text{ is compositional} \\ \frac{1-p_0}{256} & l \text{ is holistic} \end{cases}$$

For these simulations, we fixed the number of agents in each generation: $|A| = 100$, and each agent learned from a data set of fixed size: $|d| = 20$. We set $\epsilon = 0.05$ and ran the simulations for 50 generations each. There are three different types of starting conditions: in "holistic," 90% of the starting data was generated by a particular holistic hypothesis (one with minimal overlap with the compositional hypotheses) and the remaining 10% was drawn uniformly from the set of possible words. In "compositional," 90% of the starting data was generated by a particular compositional hypothesis. In "uniform," all the starting data was generated uniformly. We report values for various settings of α and p_0. Here, the values reported are the total final probabilities of compositional hypotheses, averaged over 50 runs.[b] The results are in Figure 3.

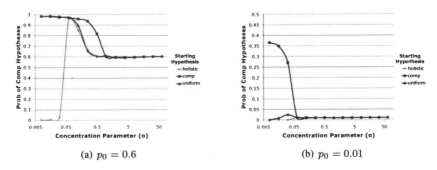

(a) $p_0 = 0.6$ (b) $p_0 = 0.01$

Figure 3. Simulation results with a richer pool of languages and multilingual learners. As the concentration parameter α increases, so does the extent to which the learner expects teachers to speak different languages. p_0 controls the strength of the prior in favor of compositional hypotheses.

The general trend of these results is that for low values of α, the population of learners tends to converge to the hypothesis most favored by the initial conditions, whereas for high values of α, we see convergence to the prior. This is consistent with previous work, which can be viewed as limiting conditions of this framework: as $\alpha \to 0$, we obtain a prior assumption by the learner that only one language is being spoken in the general population, as in Smith (2009), while as $\alpha \to \infty$, we obtain an assumption that each individual word is generated from a separate

---

[b]For smaller values of α, the individual hypotheses most consistent with the starting data were favored, whereas for larger values of α, the probabilities of individual hypotheses were generally uniform over each hypothesis class.

hypothesis, which is equivalent to the learning dynamics from Griffiths and Kalish (2007) (see Figure 1). Thus, the concentration parameter of the DP prior provides a natural way to interpolate between these two patterns of results.

5. Conclusion

The simulations we have presented show that when an agent's hypothesis space explicitly takes into account the possibility of receiving input from multiple teachers with possibly divergent hypotheses, then iterated Bayesian learning generally converges to reflect learners' inductive biases, as when agents learn from only a single teacher. However, if we explicitly encode a bias in the agent towards believing that the teachers all share a single hypothesis, then we may observe results that more closely align with initial data conditions. These results provide a way to understand how learners might learn from multiple teachers, but nonetheless show significant effects of inductive biases in the languages that they come to speak.

References

Aldous, D. (1985). Exchangeability and related topics. In *Lecture notes in mathematics* (Vol. 1117, p. 1-198). Springer, Berlin.

Ferdinand, V., & Zuidena, W. (2009). Thomas' theorem meets Bayes' rule: a model of the iterated learning of language. In *Proceedings of the 31st Annual Conference of the Cognitive Science Society*.

Ferguson, T. S. (1973). A Bayesian analysis of some nonparametric problems. *Annals of Statistics*, *1*, 209-230.

Griffiths, T. L., & Kalish, M. (2007). Language evolution by iterated learning with Bayesian agents. *Cognitive Science*, *31*, 441-480.

Kirby, S. (2001). Spontaneous evolution of linguistic structure: an iterated learning model of the emergence of regularity and irregularity. *IEEE Transactions on Evolutionary Computation*, *5*, 102-110.

Kirby, S., Dowman, M., & Griffiths, T. L. (2007). Innateness and culture in the evolution of language. *Proceedings of the National Academy of Sciences*, *104*, 5241-5245.

Niyogi, P., & Berwick, R. C. (2009). The proper treatment of language acquisition and change in a population setting. *Proceedings of the National Academy of Sciences*, *106*, 10124-10129.

Reali, F., & Griffiths, T. L. (in press). Words as alleles: Connecting language evolution with Bayesian learners to models of genetic drift. *Proceedings of the Royal Society, Series B*.

Smith, K. (2009). Iterated learning in populations of Bayesian agents. In *Proceedings of the 31st Annual Conference of the Cognitive Science Society*.

ON PROTOLINGUISTIC "FOSSILS": SUBJECT-VERB VS. VERB-SUBJECT STRUCTURES[1]

EUGENIA CASIELLES

Classical and Modern Languages, Literatures and Cultures, Wayne State University,
487 Manoogian Hall, 906 W. Warren
Detroit, MI 48202, USA

LJILJANA PROGOVAC

Department of English, Wayne State University, 5057 Woodward
Detroit, MI 48202, USA

This paper questions the assumption that subject-verb (SV) structures are basic and primary and shows instead that these apparently simple structures are quite complex informationally, intonationally, semantically, and syntactically. In contrast, we point out that verb-subject (VS) structures, particularly those involving unaccusative verbs and sentence focus, are simpler and better candidates for primary structures from an evolutionary point of view. From this perspective, Agent-first (SV) structures, which have been mentioned as examples of protolinguistic "fossils" (e.g. Jackendoff 2002), are not as basic as previously thought.

1. Linguistic "fossils"

Recently, linguists interested in the origin and evolution of human language have looked at modern languages in search of traces of previous evolutionary stages. Jackendoff (1999, 2002) suggests that not only are previous stages present in the brain, but also that 'their "fossils" are present in the grammar of modern language itself' (2002:236). Based on evidence from child language, second language acquisition, aphasia, pidgin languages and ape research, Jackendoff (2002) has proposed that the formation of compound nouns such as *snowman* and rules found in Klein and Purdue's (1997) *Basic Variety* such as 'Agent First' and 'Focus Last' could be considered protolinguistic 'fossils.'

Progovac (2008a, 2008b, 2009) has extended the fossil analysis to what she calls Root Small Clauses of modern languages (e.g. *Problem solved. Me first!*),

---

[1] For good comments on various aspects of this paper, we are grateful to four anonymous reviewers, as well as to audiences at the 2009 Michigan Linguistics Society Meeting at the University of Michigan-Ann Arbor and at the Ways to Protolanguage Conference in Toruń, Poland.

arguing that these are "half clauses," that is, clauses that lack at least one functional layer, that of Tense Phrase (TP), and show no evidence of tense, agreement, or structural case on the subject. Our paper considers Subject-Verb vs. Verb-Subject structures against this evolutionary framework.[2]

2. A closer look at Subject-Verb structures

Subject-Verb (SV) structures such as *John ran* look simple enough and are usually assumed to be the next stage after noun-noun combinations in the evolution of language. It is often taken for granted that the simplest syntactic structure involving a noun and a verb would be an Agent followed by an Action. A closer look at SV structures in present-day languages, however, points to certain complexities.

From the point of view of information packaging, unless they exhibit a special intonation (*JOHN ran*) or a special syntactic structure (*John was run over by a truck*; *It was John who ran*, etc.), SV structures are interpreted as involving an informational dichotomy, a division between what the sentence is about, the point of departure, usually referred to as the *topic* or *theme*, and what is predicated of that topic, the *focus*, *comment* or *rheme*.[3]

As for the nature of the event encoded, SV structures at least in SVO languages are typically *categorical* statements, also referred to as *double judgments* (Kuroda 1972, Lambrecht 1994, Sasse 1987, 2006). Categorical statements are constituted of two successive acts: choosing an entity and making a statement about it. They thus involve a subject (or predication base) and a separate predicate, forming a dichotomy, in contrast to *thetic* statements discussed below.

Current syntactic analyses of such SV structures also reflect a relative complexity. For example, in Generative Grammar these apparently simple structures involve generation of the subject inside the Verb Phrase and movement of the subject to a preverbal position: [$_{TP}$ John [$_{vP}$ John ran.]] (see e.g. Chomsky 1995, Koopman & Sportiche 1991).

The intonation of SV structures parallels their information and syntactic structure and results in two intonation units. Thus, as Chafe (1974) and Sasse (1987, 2006) have pointed out, an SV sentence such as *Mary is singing* would have two accents, one on the subject and one on the predicate: *MAry is SINGing*.

---

[2] For some additional recent works relevant to the evolution of syntax, see Botha & Knight (2009), Heine & Kuteva (2007), Hurford (2007), Locke (2009), and the references therein.

[3] It should be noted that there are two different types of information dichotomies involving the combination of focal and non-focal elements: Topic-Comment and Focus-Background. The difference between these two dichotomies is not relevant for the arguments in this paper. For a detailed discussion, see e.g. Casielles (2004), Erteschik-Shir (2007), Lambrecht (1994), and the references therein.

Semantically, the subject in SV structures can exhibit a variety of thematic roles, including Agent, Theme, or Experiencer (e.g. Fillmore 1968): *John opened the door* (Agent); *The door opened* (Theme); *John likes baseball* (Experiencer).

Given all these considerations, SV structures are not so simple after all: they involve different thematic roles, two intonational units, syntactic movement, a separation between a predication base and a predicate, and a division between a topic and a comment or focus. Interestingly, there is some evidence from the language acquisition literature pointing to difficulties with 'simple' SV structures. Thus, non-target null-subject structures are pervasive in child English (see Bloom 1990, Hyams & Wexler 1993, and Rizzi 1994, among many others). That is, children produce isolated predicates like *ran* instead of complete SV structures like *John ran*. In addition, children learning languages with fixed SVO word order, such as English or French, produce structures like *Go truck; Come car; Tomber papa* ('fall papa'), where the subject has not been moved to the sentence-initial position (Pierce 1992).

Thus, SV structures, many of which involve Agent First rules, might not be as simple as we previously thought. If so, are there any structures involving a verb and a noun, which could be more complex than noun-noun compounds but less complex than SV structures?

3. Verb-Subject structures

Although in modern English the order Verb-Subject (VS) is not productive any more, it does show up in sentences such as *In went Robin Hood; There appeared a ship on the horizon; Next to the fireplace stood a large old sofa; Sitting on the bed was his long lost brother.* In many other languages, which include Italian, Spanish, Russian, Serbo-Croatian, Bulgarian, Hungarian, Modern Greek, Albanian, Swahili, Tolai, Wikchamni, Modern Arabic dialects, and Chinese (Sasse 1987), this order is quite productive. For example in Spanish the unmarked order with verbs of appearance such as *arrive* is precisely VS *Llegó Juan* (arrived John). This is also the case in languages like Serbian: *Stigao (je) Jovan* (arrived (AUX) John).

Now, let us see if these VS structures are any simpler than the SV structures we considered in the previous section. From the point of view of information packaging, VS structures illustrated above do not involve a dichotomy of focal and non-focal elements. Instead, they are simple wide focus units (Lambrecht's 1994 Sentence Focus). More specifically, in a sentence such as *Llegó Juan* (arrived John)*; Aquí viene María* (here comes María), there is no topic, and the whole sentence (the predicate together with the subject) is considered to be the focus, with one informational unit encompassing the whole structure.

As for the organization of the event, these VS structures do not involve categorical statements, but thetic statements, also referred to as *simple judgments*

(Kuroda 1972, Sasse 1987, 2006). These statements do not separate the entity from the event, but merely express a state of affairs, where a new situation is presented as a whole. In thetic statements the entity involved in the event is viewed as part of the event and forms a unit with it. Thus, while a categorical statement says something about an entity, a thetic statement poses the existence of a certain state of affairs. From this perspective, a sentence such as *Llegó Juan* does not predicate something of John, in the traditional sense of predication, but merely asserts the arrival of John (Sasse 1987, 2006).[4]

Syntactically, these structures do not involve movement of the subject from a VP-internal position to a VP-external position. In fact, in most current analyses there is no movement involved whatsoever. That is, the subject remains in its VP-internal position: [$_{TP}$ [$_{vP}$ *Llegó Juan.*]]; [$_{TP}$ *There* [$_{vP}$*appeared a ship.*]] Verbs of (dis)appearance such as *arrive, come, go, appear, vanish*, etc. are known in the syntactic literature as unaccusative verbs and contrast with so-called unergative verbs (Levin and Rapapport 1995, Perlmutter 1978). What is interesting about these verbs is that they do not take an agent, but rather a theme (see below).[5] The two syntactic positions (postverbal vs. preverbal) are so different that in some languages like Spanish or Italian Bare Nouns (nouns without determiners) are allowed postverbally (*Juegan niños* (play children)), but not preverbally (**Niños juegan* (children play)). [6] In these languages, when the event and subject form a unit characteristic of thetic expressions, the subject does not need a determiner. However, it has to be preceded by a determiner in categorical, double judgment statements, such as *Los niños juegan* (the children are playing). Similarly, VS structures in Arabic show only partial agreement between the subject and the verb, suggesting again a relative simplicity of VS structures.

The intonation of these VS structures is also simpler. Thus, as Navarro Tomás (1974) points out for Spanish, while a sentence with SV order such as *La*

---

[4] A reviewer asks if thetic statements are non-compositional. Although it is possible that precursors of this structure were holistic, thetic statements in modern languages are considered to be compositional. The difference between categorical SV structures with agents, on the one hand, and thetic structures with themes, on the other, is that the former involve an external argument, whereas the latter involve an internal argument. It is widely assumed in the syntactic literature, including Minimalism (e.g. Chomsky 1995), that themes are internal arguments, generated in the projection of the lexical verb, VP, while agents are external arguments, generated outside of the VP.

[5] Notice that the underlying order for subjects of unaccusative verbs (*Llegó Juan; There appeared a ship.*) differs from that of unergative verbs (*John ran*). In the former case the underlying subject follows the verb [$_{TP}$ [$_{vP}$ *Llegó Juan.*]], while in the latter case, it precedes the verb: [$_{TP}$ John [$_{vP}$ ~~John~~ ran.]]. This postulated difference explains, among other things, why unaccusative subjects can find themselves following the verb, even in the final (surface) derivation of essentially SVO languages.

[6] See Casielles (1996, 2004), Contreras 1986, Longobardi (1994) and Torrego (1989), among others.

puerta se ha cerrado 'The door has closed' involves two intonational units (*La puerta* | *se ha cerrado*), the VS structure *Se ha cerrado la puerta* (has closed the door) only involves one. This is also the case with comparable VS structures in other languages, such as Serbian: *Pala vlada* (fallen government; 'The government has collapsed.') vs. *Vlada je* | *pala*. Notice that in English, where the VS order is not productive, the difference can be marked by a single accent on the subject. As pointed out by Sasse (1987, 2006), the English equivalent of *Llegó Juan* (arrived John) involves a single accent on the subject and no accent on the predicate, *JOHN arrived*, in contrast to the double accent in a categorical sentence such as *MAry is SINGing*.

From a semantic point of view, the thematic role of these postverbal subjects does not vary nearly as much as is the case with SV categorical statements, discussed in the previous section. The actions involved in these structures typically take a theme rather than an agent. Consequently, the subjects in these structures have a tighter connection with the verb, being internal, rather than external, arguments. In addition, many of the verbs involved in these VS constructions are semantically predictable and merely serve to introduce the focus of the assertion as in *Cae la nieve* (falls the snow; 'It is snowing').

In sum, the discussed VS structures involve a unique thematic role (theme), one intonational unit, a simple event+entity unit, no syntactic movement, and no informational dichotomy, but a single focus encompassing the whole structure. In other words, these VS structures are one unit semantically, intonationally, syntactically, and informationally, in contrast to SV structures, which form various dichotomies. We would like to propose that the VS structures under consideration are evolutionarily more primary than SV structures. If this is on the right track and thetic, especially unaccusative, statements are primary, the expression of an argument's involvement in an event as a theme, i.e. themehood, may have preceded the expression of agenthood in language evolution.[7]

Although in modern languages thetic statements may exhibit some sophisticated grammatical features (tense, agreement, etc.), they must have been quite basic in earlier stages. In fact, some languages like Serbian can be shown to exhibit constructions that correspond very closely to what can be considered the earlier versions of these VS structures. In addition to regular VS structures, Serbian also has short VS structures with limited agreement and no Tense. The examples like *Pala vlada* or *Stigao Jovan* illustrated above are missing an auxiliary and have been analyzed in Progovac (2008a,b) as incomplete utterances, lacking Tense and the Tense Phrase. Even more radically, in

---

[7] As one reviewer rightly points out, in addition to establishing what came first in language evolution, it is also necessary to hypothesize about how one stage led to another, and in this particular case, how these primary VS structures gave way to the eventual predominance of S(O)V(O) order across languages. It may be that the introduction of agency and agenthood, superimposed upon a VS unaccusative structure, led to the transition to SV(O), starting with transitive structures and then generalizing also to intransitive structures in many languages.

examples such as *Nestalo struje* (disappeared electricity; 'Electricity is out.') not only does the verb fail to agree with the subject noun (the verb is Neuter, and the noun Feminine), but the subject also surfaces in the genitive case, rather than the expected nominative case.[8]

As mentioned above, VS structures occur in child language even in cases where the target language does not allow for them (cases like *Come car; Go truck*). As Baker and Greenfield (1988) have noted, there might be a cognitive reason why thetic structures, at least the ones involving verbs of appearance, are primary. They note: "The very first acts of perceptual activity in the neonatal period grow out of a pattern of fixation to a novel stimulus (or as one might call it new information)" (1988:4).[9] Interestingly, this cognitive property may also be shared by other primates (Donald 1991 and Hurford 2007).

4. Some conclusions

In this paper we have questioned the assumption that SV structures are simple and primary and we have shown that these apparently basic structures are quite complex informationally, intonationally, semantically, and syntactically. In contrast, we have pointed out that VS structures, particularly those involving (unaccusative) verbs of appearance and movement are simpler and better candidates for primary structures in the evolution of human language. From this perspective, Agent-first (SV) structures, which have been mentioned as examples of protolinguistic 'fossils' (Jackendoff 2002), might not be as primary as previously thought. Although more evidence needs to be gathered, if this is on the right track, we expect thetic statements to be crosslinguistically simpler, acquired earlier, and easier to process.

---

[8] A reviewer points out that Jackendoff might have been referring to simpler Agent-First structures and not those found in modern languages. Although it is possible that there might have been simpler Agent-First SV structures (and simpler unaccusative VS structures), in this paper we look at modern languages and compare the intonation, semantics, syntax, and information packaging of comparably simple SV and VS structures (*John sang* vs. *JOHN arrived*). Our prediction is that, other things being equal, unaccusative+theme structures will be simpler than agent–first structures.

[9] Greenfield (1973) used different techniques to teach her daughter Lauren, age 11 months, the word *dada*. Pointing to her father and saying *dada* in his static presence didn't work. However, as Baker & Greenfield (1988: 4) point out: "...Lauren learned to attach meaning to the double syllable when her father appeared in the room. Lauren noticed his appearance and the appearance was labeled 'dada' by the mother. In other words Lauren learned the meaning of her first word, 'dada,' when the father was a novel or changing stimulus, eliciting perceptual orientation."

References

Baker, N. and Greenfield, P. (1988). The development of new and old information in young children's early language. *Language Sciences*, 10.1, 3-34.

Bloom, P. (1990). Subjectless Sentences in Child Language. *Linguistic Inquiry*, 21, 491-504.

Botha, R. and Knight, C. (eds.). (2009). *The Cradle of Language*. Oxford: Oxford University Press.

Casielles, E. (1996). On the misbehavior of bare nouns in Spanish. In C. Parodi et al. (eds.) *Aspects of Romance Linguistics: Selected Papers from the XXIV Linguistic Symposium on Romance Languages*. Washington D.C.: Georgetown University Press, 135-148.

Casielles, E. (2004). *The Syntax-Information Structure Interface: Evidence from Spanish and English*. New York: Routledge.

Chomsky, N. (1995). *The Minimalist Program*. Cambridge, MA: MIT Press.

Chafe, W. L. (1974). Language and consciousness. *Language* 50, 111-113.

Contreras, H. (1986). Spanish bare NPs and the ECP. In I. Bordelois, H. Contreras and K. Zagona (eds.) *Generative studies in Spanish syntax*. Dordrecht: Foris.

Donald, M. (1991). *Origins of the Modern Mind: Three Stages in the Evolution of Culture and Cognition*. Cambridge, MA: Harvard University Press.

Erteschik-Shir, N. (2007). *Information Structure. The syntax-Discourse Interface*. Oxford: Oxford University Press.

Fillmore, C. (1968). The Case for Case. In E. Bach and Harms (eds.) *Universals in Linguistic Theory*. New York: Holt, Rinehart, and Winston, 1-88.

Givón, T. (2009). *The Genesis of Syntactic Complexity: Diachrony, Ontogeny, Neuro-cognition, Evolution*. Amsterdam/Philadelphia: John Benjamins.

Greenfield, P. (1973). Who is Dada?: Some aspects of the semantic and phonological development of a child's first words. *Language and Speech*, 16, 34-43.

Heine, B. and Kuteva, T. (2007). *The Genesis of Grammar. A Reconstruction*. Oxford: Oxford University Press.

Hurford, J. R. (2007). *The Origins of Meaning: Language in the Light of Evolution*. Oxford: Oxford University Press.

Hyams, N. and Wexler, K. (1993). On the grammatical basis of null subjects in child language. *Linguistic Inquiry*, 24, 421-460.

Jackendoff, R. (1999). Possible stages in the evolution of the language capacity. *Trends in Cognitive Sciences*, 3.7, 272-279.

Jackendoff, R. (2002). *Foundations of Language*. Oxford: Oxford University Press.

Klein, W. and Purdue, C. (1997). The Basic Variety or Couldn't language be much simpler? *Second Language Research*, 13, 301-347.

Koopman, H. and Sportiche, D. (1991). The position of subjects. *Lingua*, 85: 211-258.

Kuroda, S.-Y. (1972). The categorical and the thetic judgment. Evidence from Japanese syntax. *Foundations of Language*, 9, 153-185.

Lambrecht, K. (1994). *Information Structure and Sentence Form*. Cambridge: Cambridge University Press.

Levin, B. and Rappaport Hovav, M. (1995). *Unaccusativity at the Syntax-Lexical Semantics Interface*. Linguistic Inquiry Monographs 26. Cambridge: MIT Press.

Locke, J. L. (2009). Evolutionary developmental linguistics: Naturalization of the faculty of language. *Language Sciences*, 31, 33-59.

Longobardi, G. (1994). Reference and Proper Names: A Theory of N-Movement in Syntax and Logical Form. *Linguistic Inquiry*, 25.4, 609-665.

Navarro Tomás, T. (1974). *Manual de Entonación Española*. 4th edition. Madrid: Guadarrama.

Pierce, A. (1992). *Language Acquisition and Linguistic Theory. A Comparative Analysis of French and English Child Grammars. Dordrecht: Kluwer.*

Perlmutter, D. (1978). Impersonal passive and the Unaccusative Hypothesis. *Berkeley Linguistics Society*, 4, 159-189. University of California, Berkeley.

Progovac, L. (2008)a. What use is half a clause? In A. D. M. Smith, K. Smith and R. Ferrer i Cancho (eds.) *Evolution of Language: Proceedings of the 7th International EVOLANG Conference, Barcelona, Spain, 12-15 March 2008.* New Jersey: World Scientific, 259-266.

Progovac, L. (2008)b. Root Small Clauses with unaccusative verbs. In A. Antonenko, J. F. Bailyn and C. Y. Bethin (eds.) *Proceedings of FASL (Formal Approaches to Slavic Linguistics)* 16. Ann Arbor: Michigan Slavic Publications, 359-373.

Progovac, L. (2009). Layering of grammar: Vestiges of evolutionary development of syntax in present-day languages. In G. Sampson, D. Gil & P. Trudgill (eds.) *Language Complexity as an Evolving Variable*. Oxford: Oxford University Press, 203-212.

Rizzi, L. (1994). Early Null Subjects and Root Null Subjects. In T. Hoekstra and B.D. Schwartz (eds.) *Language Acquisition Studies in Generative Grammar*. Amsterdam: John Benjamins, 151-176.

Sasse, H.-J. (1987). The thetic/categorical distinction revisited. *Linguistics*, 25, 511-580.

Sasse, H.-J. (2006). Theticity. In G. Bernini and M. L. Schwartz, *Pragmatic Organization of Discourse in the Languages of Europe*. Berlin and New York: Mouton de Gruyter, 255-308.

Torrego, E. (1989). Unergative-unaccusative alternations in Spanish. *MIT Working Papers in Linguistics*, 10, 253-272.

NUMEROSITY, ABSTRACTION, AND THE EMERGENCE OF METAPHOR IN LANGUAGE

FREDERICK L. COOLIDGE AND THOMAS WYNN

University of Colorado at Colorado Springs

For the last two decades, a major question for paleoanthropologists has been the origins of modernity and modern thinking. Explanations such as symbolic culture, fully syntactic language, or abstract reasoning are all too often proffered without clear or adequate operationalizations. It is purpose of the present paper to suggest both an evolutionary cognitive basis for one aspect of modern thinking and modern language, metaphors, and to offer a potential neurological substrate.

In our attempt to trace the evolution of a more circumscribed component of modern cognition, we think the candidate trait should be shared, at least in part, by our closer nonhuman primates. The trait should also be evident early (ontogeny) in humans, and there should be some specifiable and demonstrable neurological substrate. Finally, there should be evidence that the trait unambiguously sets a foundation for modern thinking. We think this trait is numerosity, i.e., the ability to think about and reason with numbers.

1. Numerosity

The first noticeable fact about arithmetic is that it applies to everything, to tastes and to sounds, to apples and to angels, to the ideas of the mind and to the bones of the body. The nature of the things is perfectly indifferent, of all things it is true that two and two make four. Thus ... the leading characteristic of mathematics [is] that it deals with properties and ideas which are applicable to things just because they are things, and apart from any particular feelings, or emotions, or sensations, in any way connected with them. This is what is meant by calling mathematics an abstract science. (Whitehead, 1948, p. 3)

Numbers (and the computational operations they permit) are the central principle of organization. Both temporal and spatial structure, the most conspicuous domains necessary for sustaining existence and experience (as well as further dimensions exposed through mathematical analysis), is subservient (at least to a substantial yet circumscribed extent) to quantitative modeling and explanation. Because quantification strips phenomena of all qualities, the capacity to cognize and conceptualize numerical relations may be considered one of the basic orders of abstraction and minimally requires a capacity to cognize magnitudes and/or distinct numerical differences in small number values (e.g., subitization). Because numerosity and its symbolization in mathematical representation points to an essentially abstract cognitive capacity, it may be an important feral cognitive process in other, higher levels of abstractive thinking, or in other manifestations of modern thinking, such as metaphor use.

1.1 Numerosity in Non-Human Primates and Human Infants

Cantlon and her colleagues (e.g., Cantlon & Brannon, 2006; Cantlon, Platt, & Brannon, 2008) have aptly demonstrated that non-human primates (particularly monkeys) and humans share a nonverbal ability for numbers. As Ansari (2008) has recently speculated, such a system might have been evolutionarily adaptive because the evaluation of the magnitude of food, other resources, and predators probably served critically important survival functions. Food, resources, predation, and competition (including confrontation) are among the common situations in which numerical information is highly relevant and directly bears on reproductive success. As Feigenson, Dehaene and Spelke noted, "[human] infants opt to maximize the total quantity of food rather than the number of pieces of food" (2004, p. 309). Likewise, being able to recognize that one is outnumbered (magnitude and/or numerosity) is absolutely fundamental to survival. However, also being able to appreciate that 3 is better than 1, when the subject is apples, but 3 is worse than 1 when it comes to predators, is an essential reasoning component that is highly dependent upon numerosity.

1.2 Two Core Systems of Numerosity

Feigenson, Dehaene, and Spelke (2004) have proposed that there are two core systems underlying numerosity. One system has the ability to represent large but approximate numerical magnitudes and can be demonstrated in human children as young as six-months old. They also concluded this first core system was "noisy" (not exact) but clearly captured interrelationships among different large groups of numbers and that it was robust across various sense modalities. Their second core system was a precise and distinct appreciation for small numbers of individual objects (labeled *subitization*). In human infants, their research suggested a limit of 3 or 4 objects.

1.3 Neurological Substrate for Numerosity

It also has been aptly demonstrated that the primary neurological substrate for core systems of numerosity lies in both a superior region of the parietal lobes, the intraparietal sulcus (IPS; Ansari, 2008; Hubbard et al., 2008; Miller, Nieder, Freedman, & Wallis, 2003) and the prefrontal cortex (PFC), a region critical to goal-directed activity and inhibition. As noted earlier, human infants, many non-human primates, and other animal species share a basic non-symbolic numerosity capability. One implication of this finding is that the ability to judge basic numerical values is then obviously independent of language abilities yet probably an important evolutionary precursor to adult symbolic numerosity. Ansari (2005) found elevated PFC activity in preschool children who were yet naïve with regard to Arabic number symbols when dealing with number cardinalities (e.g., how many objects in a number symbol). Diester and Nieder (2008) found that neurons in the PFC and the IPS in monkeys showed selective activity when judging quantities of items and to visual shapes associated with varying quantities. These studies may suggest that the PFC may help to establish semantic associations between signs and abstract numerical categories. Cantlon, Brannon, Carter, and Pelphrey (2006) have noted that there are disparate theories about exactly how children map the meaning of number words onto their nonverbal representations of numbers. However, their work with fMRI imaging in 4 year-olds appears to demonstrate that there is non-symbolic number activation in the neurons of the IPS, and by 4 years of age, the IPS begins to respond more strongly to numerical judgments than shape changes. When adults are tested for symbolic numerosity, the IPS is also specifically activated but additional number-specific neurons are recruited in adjacent areas. For example, multiplication tables and other mathematical operations appear to rely on the left angular gyrus and the supramarginal gyrus (Dehaene, Spelke, Pinel, Stanescu, & Tsivkin, 1999). In developing the argument for our proposed link for numerosity as a feral cognitive process for higher level abstractions, Geschwind (1979) proposed that the angular gyrus transforms written words into inner speech. Ramachandram (2004), in studies of brain-damaged patients, has implicated the angular gyrus as critical to metaphor production and appreciation. Chiappe and Chiappe (2007) have found that better metaphor facility requires greater working memory capacity (e.g., Baddeley, 2007; Coolidge & Wynn, 2005). Furthermore, they found that measures of inhibitory control also predicted greater metaphor aptness. They speculated that the relevance of a metaphor requires the inhibition of highly salient but distracting and inappropriate features associated with a vehicle, and the appreciation and selection of those features that are both salient and relevant. In summary, there are numerous lines of evidence suggesting the IPS is the core part of a cerebral network that is critically important to non-symbolic and symbolic number processing. Furthermore, associated areas to the IPC like regions of the PFC, angular and supramarginal gyri additionally appear to facilitate not only advanced mathematical operations but also metaphor production and appreciation.

1.4 Numerosity and Metaphors

Metaphors have been considered a cognitive ability that facilitates thinking across different conceptual domains (e.g., Chiappe & Chiappe, 2007). It is also claimed that metaphors not only communicate human knowledge but allow for its creation and expansion (e.g., Lakoff & Johnson, 1999). In a metaphor such as "Love is a rose", the metaphoric vehicle "rose" transfers its attributions to the topic of "love." In this communication, a topic like "love" provides relevant dimensions for attributions. The vehicle "rose" provides various properties for these attributions. In metaphor theory, the relevant properties associated with this vehicle form a superordinate category. The category in this case is the class of "beautiful, ephemeral things." The category is superordinate in the sense that the literal meaning of "rose" is simply a type of flower, so it transcends its literal meaning. If a person hears "love is a rose," they understand 'rose' as referring to the superordinate category that includes "love" as a member. It is important to note that the literal category "rose" (a type of flower) is not relevant to the actual metaphor, except that it helps form the superordinate category. It is also important to note that particular attributions of the vehicle are not only irrelevant but inappropriate to the topic. For example, the nitrogen-fixing bacteria in the roots of the vehicle roses are not relevant to the topic love, and furthermore, that aspect must be inhibited. Thus, inhibition is an important feature of metaphor production and comprehension. In addition, the relevant attributions must be attended to while other attributions must be repressed.

It may also be no mere coincidence that the angular gyrus, in the inferior parietal lobes, plays a crucial role in both the mental representation of numbers as actual quantities and their manipulation (Dehaene, 1997) and in the process of metaphorizing (Ramachandran, 2004). As already noted, metaphors give rise to superordinate categorization, and thus, the creation and expansion of knowledge. If we consider the dual core systems of numbers, especially subitizing, as inherently abstractive processes, then metaphor production allows the apprehension of abstract number concepts in more concrete yet symbolic terms. Lakoff and Núñez (2000) have argued that every language has a system of spatial relationships. They also propose that conceptual metaphors are a central cognitive mechanism of the extension from basic arithmetic to higher levels of mathematics, and they also propose the understanding of sophisticated applications of numbers requires non-numerical source domains. We would argue that they may have stated their case too conservatively. Indeed, it is an interesting phenomenon that infants can subitize and judge the relative size of larger sets well before they have any coherent linguistic abilities. In some respects, this suggests they have mathematical abilities independent not only of language but also of meaning. Nonetheless, we would hypothesize that inherent in these dual systems of numerosity is a feral cognitive basis for set theory, that is, conceptual schemas for images become intuitive and pre-attentive well before facility with language. Our reasoning is thusly: a set of numbers creates an image schema for a container schema, where there is an exterior (outside the set of numbers), a boundary (delineating the set of numbers from other sets of numbers or anything else), and an interior (the target set of numbers). Certainly, spatial relations are ubiquitous to all cultures, and they must have a basis in some cognitive process so why not numerosity? Lakoff and Núñez note that the concept of containment is absolutely central to mathematics and that mathematics makes use of many other embodied concepts used in everyday life. So, unlike Lakoff and Núñez who thought that mathematics exapted upon preexisting nonnumerical cognitive abilities, we would propose that our mathematical capabilities were built upon the feral cognitive processes of basic numerosity. Moreover, even the development of conceptual primitives such as image schemas (container schemas) and set theory is based upon the cognitive processes of numerosity. If we assume that preexisting neurological processes have long been in place such as the simultaneous activation of two distinct areas of the brain, which results in *conflation,* the cognitive embodiment of two different aspects of experience, then a single complex experience may be created. As Lakoff and Núñez have argued, it is by way of such conflations that cross-domain neural links are generated, and they in turn give rise to conceptual metaphors. Again, we find it no mere coincidence that the parietal lobes have long been known to be the site of cross-modal sensorimotor integration and the home to numerosity.

2. Parietal Lobe Expansion

The human fossil record now indicates, at least morphometrically (and verified statistically), that it is not the frontal lobes that best distinguish the brains of archaic members of the genus *Homo* and *Homo sapiens* but the parietal lobes. Recent work by Emiliano Bruner (2004, 2010) documents not only a more general parietal lobe hypertrophy but a particular expansion in the superior region of the parietal lobe, the IPS. Bruner also hypothesized that parietal lobe expansion was accompanied by a discrete cognitive shift. His best guess for the nature of this shift comes from the traditional understanding of parietal lobe functions: visual-spatial integration, sensory integration, multimodal processing, and social communication. The cognitive repercussions of IPS expansion itself are far from being understood, but it is a region that has been linked to the generation of concepts and numerosity. In addition, inferior displacement of the supramarginal and angular gyri, both structures of the inferior parietal lobe that are known to be linked to inner speech and metaphor production, would be an indirect consequence of superior parietal expansion. The significance of this development for the evolution of language cannot be understated, as we have noted the well-established function that has linked the IPS to numerosity.

3. Conclusions

We have proposed that the core systems of numerosity may have instantiated the human cognitive ability for basic and higher level abstraction. We have reviewed the evidence that these core systems of numerosity are inherently abstractive processes, and provocatively, appear to be independent of language functions initially, as they are exhibited in human infants and nonhuman primates. Thus, we would first propose that the human ability for abstractive thought may have had its prototypic basis in the abstraction involved in numerosity. It has also been well established that the IPS is primarily responsible for these core systems of numerosity. We also reviewed the evidence that the apprehension of the number of apples or the number of predators, as processed in the IPS, is shared with prefrontal cortices, as well as subcortical structures and the temporal-parietal-occipital juncture, for additional processing and decision-making. We are also proposing that the cognitive nature of these perceptions produces image schemas, in the language of Lakoff and Núñez (2000), particularly container schemas (exterior, boundary, interior). The concept of containment is essential to much of mathematics and such schemas are the link between spatial perceptions and language, which help to make human thought intuitively grounded in set theory and relationships between sets. Furthermore, set theory and image schemas (like container schemas) provide a concrete basis for conjunctive and disjunction reasoning. The former reasoning process creates a basis for establishing commonalities (a superordinate category) between two different sets. The latter reasoning process establishes a basis for determining unshared elements between two sets. Lakoff and Núñez also noted that there exists special cases of examining complex physical objects (like people) and determining there is a special internal structural organization. This process *conflation*, which implies the simultaneous activation of two distinct areas of the brain, further results in the cognitive embodiment of two different aspects of experience. Conflation ultimately yields a single complex experience (superordinate category). We would propose that these conflations give rise to conceptual metaphors. And thus, we come to the crux of our arguments: the 32,000 year old Hohlenstein-Stadel figurine (half-human, half-lion) may be the best, earliest evidence for fully modern thinking because it probably represents the symbolization of a conceptual metaphor, i.e., people are like lionesses or lionesses are like people. The figurine was not only the creation of superordinate category (lion-people) but also, in all likelihood, the external referent and physical embodiment of a conceptual metaphor. Certainly, metaphorical reasoning had some prototypic cognitive basis or bases as it is very unlikely to have arisen "whole-cloth." We would propose that metaphoric reasoning was adaptively selected because of its ability to create new knowledge and readily transmit that knowledge and that its prototypic roots appear to have begun in the feral cognitive processes involved in basic numerosity. We have also proposed noted that other cognitive functions are used in conjunction with metaphoric reasoning, such as inhibitory processes of the PFC, because the latter help to refine the quality of a conceptual metaphor by mentally de-emphasizing irrelevant or inappropriate properties. At the minimum, we are suggesting that the neural and cognitive bases for numerosity provide a model for the understanding of the evolution of modern abstractive thinking.

References

Ansari, D. (2008). Effects of development and enculturation on number representation in the brain. *Nature Reviews, 9*, 278-291.

Ansari, D., Garcia, N., Lucas, E., Hamon, K., & Dhital, B. (2005). Neural correlates of symbolic number processing in children and adults. *Neuroreport, 16*, 1769–1773.

Baddeley, A. (2007). *Working memory, thought, and action*. Oxford, UK: Oxford University Press.

Bruner, E. (2004). Geometric morphometrics and paleoneurology: Brain shape evolution in the genus *Homo. Journal of Human Evolution, 47*, 279-303.

Bruner, E. (2010, October). *Morphological differences in the parietal lobes within the human genes: A neurofunctional perspective.* A paper presented at the workshop - A multidisciplinary approach to the evolution of the parietal lobes, Burgos, Spain.

Cantlon, J. & Brannon, E. (2006). Shared system for ordering small and large numbers in monkeys and humans. *Psychological Science, 17*, 401-406.

Cantlon, J. F., Brannon, E. M., Carter, E. J., & Pelphrey, K. A. (2006). Functional imaging of numerical processing in adults and four-year-old children. *PLoS Biology, 4*, 844-854.

Cantlon, J., Platt, M., & Brannon, E. (2008). Beyond the number domain. *Trends in Cognitive Sciences, 30*, 1-9.

Chiappe, D. L., & Chiappe, P. (2007). The role of working memory in metaphor production and comprehension. *Journal of Memory and Language, 56*, 172-188.

Coolidge, F. L., & Wynn, T. (2005). Working memory, its executive functions, and the emergence of modern thinking. *Cambridge Archaeological Journal, 15*, 5-26.

Dehaene, S. (1997). *The number sense.* Oxford: Oxford University Press.

Dehaene, S., Spelke, E., Pinel, P., Stanescu, R., & Tsivkin, S. (1999). Sources of mathematical thinking: Behavioral and brain-imaging evidence. *Science, 284*, 970-974.

Diester, I., & Nieder, A. (2008). Complementary contributions of prefrontal neuron classes in abstract numerical categorization. *The Journal of Neuroscience*, *28*, 7737–7747.

Feigenson, L., Dehaene, S., & Spelke, E. (2004). Core systems of number. *Trends in Cognitive Sciences, 8*, 307-314.

Geschwind, N. (1979). Specializations of the human brain. *Scientific American, 241*, 180-199.

Hubbard, E. M., Piazza, M., Pinel, P., & Dehaene, S. (2009). Numerical and spatial intuitions: a role for posterior parietal cortex? In L. Tommasi, L. Nadel, & M. A. Peterson (Eds.), *Cognitive biology: Evolutionary and developmental perspectives on mind, brain and behavior* (pp. 221–246). Cambridge, MA: MIT Press.

Lakoff, G., & Johnson, M. (1999). *Philosophy in the flesh: The embodied mind and its challenge to Western philosophy.* New York: Basic Books.

Lakoff, G., & Núñez, R. E. (2000). *Where mathematics comes from: How the embodied mind brings mathematics into being.* New York: Basic Books.

Miller, E. K., Nieder, A., Freedman, D. J., & Wallis, J. D. (2003). Neural correlates of categories and concepts. *Current Opinion in Neurobiology, 13*, 198-203.

Ramachandran, V. S. (2004). *A brief tour of human consciousness: From impostor poodles to purple numbers.* New York: Pi Press.

Whitehead, A. N. (1948). *An introduction to mathematics.* Oxford: Oxford University Press.

SELF-ORGANIZATION AND EMERGENCE IN LANGUAGE
A CASE STUDY FOR COLOR

JOACHIM DE BEULE AND JORIS BLEYS

Artificial Intelligence Lab, Vrije Universiteit Brussel, Belgium

{joachim,jorisb}@arti.vub.ac.be

A computational language game model is presented that shows how a population of language users can evolve from a brightness-based to a brightness+hue-based color term system. The shift is triggered by a change in the communication challenges posed by the environment, comparable to what happened in English during the Middle English period in response to the rise of dyeing and textile manufacturing *c*. 1150–1500. In a previous model that is able to explain such a shift, these two color categorization strategies were explicitly represented. This is not needed in our model. Instead, whether a population evolves a brightness- or a hue-based system is an emergent phenomenon that depends only on environmental factors. In this way, the model provides an explanation of how such a shift may come about without introducing additional mechanisms that would require further explanation.

1. Introduction

There are thousands of languages in the world, differing not only in the words and grammatical elements of form they employ, but also in the conceptual distinctions they make explicit. Moreover, these languages are not static: in all of them a co-evolution of meaning and form continues to take place (see e.g. Fernandez-Ordonez (1999)). Still, there are (near-)universals of language and language evolution that require an explanation (Heine & Kuteva, 2002).

For many years, language universals were mainly ascribed to genetic predispositions (Chomsky, 1980; Pinker & Bloom, 1990; Hauser, Chomsky, & Fitch, 2002). Today, most are thought to be the result of environmental and cultural rather than genetic factors (Steels, 2000; Croft, 2007; De Beule, 2008). Nevertheless, there are still only very few demonstrations, in the form of a computational model for instance, that explain the appearance of complex regularities in the evolution of natural languages without ultimately relying on built in mechanisms. Iterated learning for example explains the emergence of compositionality by relying on a strongly developed capacity and 'desire' of language learners to generalize from examples, and on the assumption that language transmission is limited by a learning bottleneck (Kirby & Hurford, 2002; Smith, Kirby, & Brighton, 2003).

This paper presents a model that demonstrates the kind of conceptual refocusing that occurred in English between the Old English period *c*. 600–1150 and the

Middle English period *c*. 1150–1500, when the English color term system moved from being predominantly based on brightness to predominantly based on a combination of brightness and hue(Casson, 1997). Similar shifts also occured in other languages (MacLaury, 1992).

A previous model (Bleys & Steels, 2009) explained such shifts by introducing an additional level of competition and selection between two explicitly represented and predefined language strategies (Steels, 2009): one for a brightness- and one for a brightness+hue-based color term system. The current model shows that this extra level is not required. Rather, these language strategies emerge for free. The current model thus reproduces a non-trivial phenomenon without relying on additional mechanisms that in turn would require further explanation.

In the next section, the model is described in detail. It is essentially a prototype-based flexible extension to multiple dimensions of the model presented in (Puglisi, Baronchelli, & Loreto, 2008). It also bears similarities with the model described in (Wellens, Loetzsch, & Steels, 2008). The results section shows that the model can exhibit a shift from a brightness- to a hue-based color system when triggered by environmental and communicative challenges, similar to those experienced by speakers of Old English as a result of the development of dyeing and textile manufacturing. The discussion and conclusion section ends the paper.

2. The Model

The model is a language game model in which participants (or agents), each equipped with simple communication abilities, engage in repeated communicative interactions that eventually lead them to align their linguistic inventories. At each time step, two agents are randomly chosen from a population to play a game. They are presented with two distinguishable color samples, one of which is identified to the speaker agent as the topic of the game. The speaker agent then has one chance to describe the topic color, based on his current inventory of color terms and following a procedure described below; if the hearer agent correctly identifies the intended topic color, the game succeeds; otherwise the correct topic is revealed and the game fails.

Agents perceive the colors in the game as points in their private perceptual color space. The linguistic inventory of an agent simply consists of stored exemplar colors in its perceptual space, each linked to one or more color terms. All exemplars linked to the same term are said to form a *linguistic category* (Puglisi et al., 2008). If an exemplar is part of several linguistic categories (in other words, if it is linked to several color terms) then its main linguistic category is the one corresponding to the most recently added color term. To describe the topic color (i.e., find or create a color term to associate with the topic color), a speaker agent first determines which stored exemplar colors most closely match each of the new perceived colors. Standard Euclidian distance in color space is used for this. It then faces one of three conditions:

(a) If both perceived colors match the *same color exemplar* (and hence map to the same color term), the speaker agent stores the new color that is further away from the shared color exemplar as a new exemplar. This new exemplar is then associated with all the color terms of the original exemplar, as well as with a newly created term. Furthermore, the new term is also associated with all previously stored exemplar colors in the main linguistic category of the original exemplar that are closer to the new exemplar than to the other perceived color. As such a new linguistic category is formed for the new term.

(b) If the perceived colors map to *different color exemplars but with identical main linguistic categories*, then a new term is associated with the exemplar closest to the topic color only if the agent's current self-estimated success rate is below 70%.[a] This ensures (relative) stability while retaining flexibility in case of a drop in success.

c If the two perceived colors map to *different color exemplars with different main linguistic categories*, then both colors may still be stored as new exemplars for their respective color terms if they are far away from other color exemplars (as determined by a constant parameter representing the smallest distinction in perceptual color space that agents are still able to perceive).

In each of these cases, the speaker then utters the color term now associated with the main linguistic category of the topic color.

The hearer agent's task is to choose the perceived color that is the best match for the term uttered by the speaker. It does so by first looking up which of its own color exemplars are closest to the two perceived colors and then checking whether either is associated with the uttered term. It then chooses the perceived color corresponding to whichever exemplar is linked to the speaker's term (and making a random choice if both or none of the exemplars are). The game succeeds if the hearer correctly identifies the topic color. The hearer agent may also add exemplars to its private perceptual color space using a procedure similar to that used by the speaker agent (steps (a)–(c) above), but taking into account that the topic color belongs to the linguistic category of the term used by the speaker).

Finally, if the game was a success, then the exemplar colors closest to the topic color in both agents are marked as belonging *only* to the linguistic category associated with the color term used in the game. This extra alignment mechanism helps to ensure that *shared* linguistic categories emerge as conventional collections of color exemplars all linked to the same color term in a meaningful and useful way. It extends the approach introduced in (Puglisi et al., 2008) to the case of multiple dimensions and applies it to regions in perceptual space determined by points rather than by explicit boundaries.

---

[a] Agents keep track of their personal success in games as a running average.

We conclude our description of the model with two remarks. First, note that although the model makes no explicit reference to the notion of *globally shared* linguistic categories, they still emerge as a result of agents' local attempts to improve their language game performance. This forms a first example of how the model explains a feature of language as an emergent phenomenon (Puglisi et al., 2008).

Secondly, the model also makes no reference to specific linguistic strategies. It works for any number of dimensions and has no prior preferences among them. Still, as will be shown in the next section, it is capable of supporting a shift from an initially stable brightness-based language system to a new, hue-based language system. Each of these systems is the result of the same "universal" strategy responding to changing conditions, where this universal strategy is simply that of self-organization.

3. Results

For convenience of presenting results, simulations were performed in two dimensions, called the *brightness* and *hue* dimensions, each ranging from 0 to 1. The minimal distance between colors in perceptual space still noticeable to agents was set to 0.05. We ran repeated simulations of the model consisting of two stages.

In Stage 1, the topic and other colors in each game were always set to be well apart in the brightness dimension (at least one-fifth of its range, or 0.20). No bias was employed in the hue dimension. Thus, this stage corresponds to Old English usage, in which people only communicated color distinctions when the brightness channel was salient. In the following section, it will be shown that this case predominantly leads to brightness-based color term systems.

In Stage 2, the bias is removed from the brightness dimension, and samples are distributed randomly across both brightness and hue dimensions. This corresponds to an increased need to communicate color distinctions even when differences in brightness are not salient. Such a change reflects the increased communication challenge that is hypothesized to have occurred due to the rise of dyeing and textile manufacturing. Consequently, a shift occurs from a now insufficient brightness-based system to a better adapted brightness+hue-based system.

3.1. *Stage 1*

Figure 1 on the left shows the the average success rate over time across all agents, along with the average number of color terms in the population. After first going through a phase of exploration in which new terms are proposed, the agents manage to reach a reasonable success rate ($\simeq 85\%$) with on average a rather small number of color terms ($\simeq 3.5$–recall that unused color terms may disappear during a successful game).

The left of Figure 2 shows the perceptual space of a typical agent after Stage 1, together with the exemplar colors amassed by the agent. Exemplar colors in the

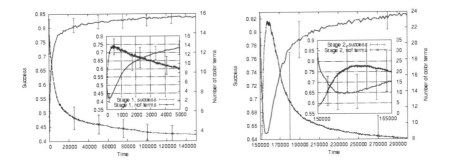

Figure 1. Average success rate and number of color terms in Stage 1 (left) and Stage 2 (right).

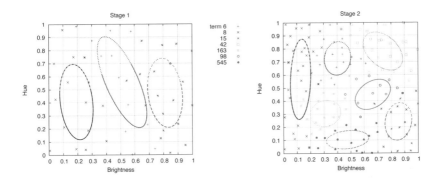

Figure 2. Example of color exemplars and (approximated) linguistic categories in the perceptual color space of an agent after Stage 1 (left) and Stage 2 (right), showing a shift from a brightness-based to a brightness+hue-based color system.

same linguistic category are shown using the same color. This agent's system can be considered brightness-based: its color categories are insensitive to hue (i.e., they all span the entire range of hue values) while they effectively partition the brightness dimension.

To provide a more precise quantitative basis for this measure, we performed a principal component analysis of the exemplar colors in each category. A linear approximation of the category was then obtained as an ellipse with major and minor axes along the principle components and with major and minor radii proportional to the standard deviations of the exemplars along them. These ellipses are also shown in Figure 2. A color category can now be defined to be brightness-based if its approximating ellipse is oriented along the brightness dimension and has a large eccentricity (in other words, if its shape is stretched out along the brightness dimension).

To obtain an "average category" that can be used to compare these values across the different stages (i.e., for different kinds of environmental bias arising from the distribution of color samples), we can now also average over all color categories from different agents and different runs, or rather over their elliptic directions and eccentricities. Figure 3 shows three average categories each based on 100 simulations involving five agents. In each of the three runs, a different environmental bias was employed. The large ellipse corresponds to the end of Stage 1

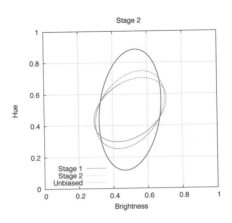

Figure 3. Average (linear approximations of) linguistic categories resulting from different environmental biases. The large red ellipse corresponds to a brightness-based system induced when the presented pairs of colors are required to differ by at least 0.2 in brightness (Stage 1). The middle ellipse shows how the average category shifts toward being based on both brightness and hue in response to a removal of the bias (Stage 2.) Finally, the inner ellipse corresponds to skipping Stage 1 (i.e., to having no environmental bias from the beginning) and is included for reference.

and is clearly brightness-based: it extends over the entire hue dimension, and thus can distinguish only between color percepts based on brightness. Its major axis lies along the direction (Brightness $= 0.96$, Hue $= 0.10$) and its eccentricity is 0.89. It can be compared with the smallest ellipse, which represents the average category arising in a completely unbiased environment, effectively skipping Stage 1. Its major direction is $(0.49, 0.45)$, meaning that it does not distinguish color percepts based specifically on either brightness or hue.

From these results, we can conclude that after Stage 1, agents have evolved an efficient color term system, on average containing around three to four mainly brightness-based color terms.

3.2. Stage 2

Figure 1 on the right shows how the success rate and the number of color terms change after the switch to an unbiased environment. As new challenges are encountered, the success rate starts to fall, and new terms are tried out. Then alignment dynamics take over until a successful color system is established again, but with on average around twice as many terms ($\simeq 8$).

Figure 2 shows how the color system from Stage 1 (left) has changed in Stage 2 (right). The intermediate ellipse in Figure 3 shows the average linguistic category after Stage 2. Clearly, a shift has occurred from a brightness-based color term system to a more neutral system based on the full color space: the linguistic categories from Stage 1 have become sensitive also to hue (i.e., they no longer span the entire range of hue values) and new, additional categories have emerged to fill the resulting gaps.

4. Discussion and conclusion

We have presented a computational language game model that is capable of showing effects similar to those observed in natural languages.

Many of the assumptions made in the model are vast oversimplifications of reality, and in particular may not properly model the details of perceptual color space.[b] Despite these simplifications and the relatively small number of assumptions it makes, it can still explain how color systems based on brightness or hue can emerge in a biased environment, without any built-in biases toward either kind of system or strategy. Instead, environmental changes in the kinds of color distinctions necessary to succeed at the language game are sufficient to push the model toward more useful strategies. These results are qualitatively the same as what happened in English during the Old English to Middle English color system shift.

The model does assume (models of) language users that are willing to play a game, which captures aspects of daily life communications between human interlocutors. It therefore takes seriously the fact that language serves a function and is best studied within the context of its use, in particular as it is subjected to the alignment dynamics induced by local, communicative usage interactions. Such interactions may be sufficient to account for the emergence of useful language strategies (such as the brightness- and hue-based color systems demonstrated here) as well as other universals of language, even in the absence of strong genetic biases.

Acknowledgments

The authors thank Nancy Chang for her incredibly detailed and invaluable comments that made it possible to considerably improve the paper. Joachim De Beule is funded by the ComplexDis European sixth framework project (FP6-2005-NEST-PATH). Joris Bleys is funded through a fellowship of the Institute of

---

[b]For example, D'Andrade and Egan (1974) show that brightness is cognitively more salient than hue, a result that could interfere with results presented in this paper. Note, however that our model could easily be adapted to investigate the impact of such differences in salience.

the Promotion of Innovation through Science and Technology in Flanders (IWT-Vlaanderen).

References

Bleys, J., & Steels, L. (2009). Linguistic selection of language strategies, a case study for color. In *Proceedings of the 10th european conference on artificial life (lncs)*. Springer-Verlag.

Casson, R. (1997). Color shift: evolution of english color terms from brightness to hue. In C. Hardin & L. Maffi (Eds.), *Color categories in thought and language* (p. 224239). Cambridge: University Press, Cambridge.

Chomsky, N. (1980). *Rules and representations*. Oxford, UK: Blackwell.

Croft, W. (2007). Language structure in its human context: new directions for the language sciences in the twenty-first century. In P. Hogan (Ed.), *Cambridge encyclopedia of the language sciences*. Cambridge: Cambridge University Press.

D'Andrade, R., & Egan, M. (1974). The color of emotion. *American Ethologist, 1*, 49-63.

De Beule, J. (2008). The emergence of compositionality, hierarchy and recursion in peer-to-peer interactions. In A. D. M. Smith, K. Smith, & R. F. i Cancho (Eds.), *Proceedings of the 7th international conference on the evolution of language* (p. 75-82). World Scientific.

Fernandez-Ordonez, I. (1999). Le'ısmo, laísmo, loísmo: estado de la cuestion. In I. Bosque & V. Demonte (Eds.), *Gramatica descriptiva de la lengua espanola* (Vol. 1, p. 13191390). Espasa Calpe, Madrid: Real Academia Éspanola.

Hauser, M. D., Chomsky, N., & Fitch, W. T. (2002). The faculty of language: What is it, who has it, and how did it evolve? *Science, 298*, 1569-1579.

Heine, B., & Kuteva, T. (2002). *World lexicon of grammaticalization*. Cambridge University Press, Cambridge, MA.

Kirby, S., & Hurford, J. (2002). The emergence of linguistic structure: An overview of the iterated learning model. In A. Cangelosi & D. Parisi (Eds.), *Simulating the evolution of language* (p. 121-148). London: Springer Verlag.

MacLaury, R. E. (1992). From brightness to hue: An explanatory model of color-category evolution. *Current Anthropology, 33*(2), 137-186.

Pinker, S., & Bloom, P. (1990). Natural languages and natural selection. *Behavioral and Brain Sciences, 13*, 707-784.

Puglisi, A., Baronchelli, A., & Loreto, V. (2008). Cultural route to the emergence of linguistic categories. *PNAS, 105*(23), 7936-7940.

Smith, K., Kirby, S., & Brighton, H. (2003). Iterated learning: a framework for the emergence of language. *Artificial Life, 9*(4), 3710386.

Steels, L. (2000). Language as a complex adaptive system. In M. Schoenauer, K. Deb, G. Rudolph, X. Yao, E. Lutton, J. J. Merelo, & H.-P. Schwefel (Eds.), *Proceedings of parallel problem solving from nature vi*. Berlin, Germany: Springer.

Steels, L. (2009). Can evolutionary linguistics become a science? *Journal of Evolutionary Linguistics, 1*(1).

Wellens, P., Loetzsch, M., & Steels, L. (2008). Flexible word meaning in embodied agents. *Connection Science, 20*(2), 173-19.

PROSODIC FEATURES IN NORTHERN MURIQUIS VOCALIZATIONS

DIDIER DEMOLIN
Université libre de Bruxelles, Belgium

CÉSAR ADES
Universidade de São Paulo, Brazil

FRANCISCO D. C. MENDES
Pontifícia Universidade Católica de Goiás, Brazil

This paper presents a preliminary description and analysis of prosodic features (amplitude, duration and rhythm) observed in Northern muriquis vocalizations. The northern muriqui (*Brachyteles hypoxanthus*) is an endangered primate species which lives in Atlantic forests of Minas Gerais and Espirito Santo, Brazil.

1. Introduction

The northern muriqui (*Brachyteles hypoxanthus*) is an endangered species of primates from Brazil (Strier 1999) that lives in multi-male fission-fusion societies in the Atlantic Forest (Strier et al, 1993). This paper presents a preliminary analysis of some characteristics of northern muriquis vocalizations. The originality of these vocalizations was shown in several recent publications (Mendes 1995, Ades & Mendes 1997, Strier 1999, Mendes & Ades 2004, Demolin, et al. 2008) that emphasize the structure and possible functions of sequential exchanges, defined as the vocalization of an individual and the response(s) of different group members, one at a time with a single call each and with little or no overlap between adjacent calls. Vocalizations within sequential exchanges are composed of a variety of acoustic forms that can be qualitatively distinguished from other vocalizations of the species' repertoire (Mendes & Ades 2004). The acoustic repertoire present in sequential exchanges includes vocalizations classified as short and long neighs (Strier,1999), and whinnies and screams (Nishimura et al., 1988). A more common distinction is that between staccatos (calls composed of short elements of less than 100ms) and neighs (at least one element longer than 100ms; Mendes, 1995, 1997; Ades & Mendes, 1997; Mendes & Ades, 2004; Arnedo et al., 2009).

2. Prosody and muriquis vocalizations

2.1 Prosody

In human languages the basic acoustic properties of a sound (pitch, loudness, duration) and the distinctive use of speed and rhythm are known as prosodic features. The linguistic use of pitch or melody defines the intonation system of a language, and different levels of pitch (the perceptual correlate of fundamental frequency -f0-) are used to express meanings. Loudness (the perceptual correlate of intensity), another important prosodic feature, is often mentioned as the correlate of stress. Syllables loudness refers to stressed or unstressed syllables. The increase or decrease of volume conveys various emotional states and some other more subtle differences in meaning. In human languages, the individual segments (the consonants or the vowels) in a syllable may also vary in length. The tempo, the high or low rate of speech production, and the rhythm of a sentence, depending of where the stress falls and the differences in syllable structure, are other prosodic features of human languages. All prosodic features occur within sentences.

One important feature of prosody in human speech is the possibility to produce modulations of f0 that are independent of intensity (Ohala 1970, Demolin 2007). Up to now this feature has not been observed in non-human primate vocalizations and may constitute an important difference with humans. Indeed most frequency modulations in non-human primate vocalizations seem to accompany amplitude modulations. The sensation of pitch that is heard from non-human primates is, likely, not directly derived from f0 but inferred from the frequency spacing of the harmonics of f0. In addition, the source of most non-human vocalization is quite unstable, a condition which triggers non-linear phenomena such as biphonation, subharmonics, frequency breaks and deterministic chaos (Riede et al. 2004, Demolin et al. 2008).

This paper presents a preliminary description and analysis of prosodic features (amplitude, duration and rhythm) observed in Northern muriquis sequential exchange vocalizations, and a brief discussion on the relevance of muriquis to the comparative study of prosody in non-human and human vocalizations.

3. Study site, data and method

3.1 Study site

Data were collected at the Reserva Particular do Patrimônio Natural– Feliciano Miguel Abdala (19° 50' S, 41° 50' W), a private reserve of Atlantic forest in the state of Minas Gerais, Brazil (Strier 1999). The study group (Matão group) varied in size from 39 to 42 individuals during data collection, including 8 adult males, 2 sub-adult males, 12 adult females, and 5 sub-adult females, besides juveniles and infants. The group was also frequently visited by 6 itinerant males, particularly when Matão females were in estrus (Strier et al, 1993). This same group had been extensively studied since 1982, so its degree of habituation to human observers and their individual patterns of facial dispigmentation allowed for both close range recordings (i.e. less than 15 meters) and identification of callers.

3.2 Data

Spontaneous vocalizations were recorded with a Marantz PMD430 cassette recorder and a Sennheiser ME-88 directional microphone between September of 1990 and February of 1991, during a broader study of the species overall vocal repertoire and the patterns of social interactions involving vocalizations (Mendes 1995, Mendes & Ades 2004). Our sample consisted of 318 vocalizations characteristic of sequential exchanges that had good signal to noise ratio. Vocalizations in our sample were emitted by several members of the Matão group: 12 adult males (n= 88: 34 neighs and 54staccatos), 1 subadult male (n=7: 4 neighs and 3 staccatos), 16 adult females (n= 216: 78 neighs and 138 staccatos) and 2 subadult females (n= 11: 1 neigh and 10 staccatos). Subadult individuals were underrepresented since only adult individuals had been recorded both during focal and ad libitum sampling (Altmann, 1974), while subadult muriquis were only recorded ad libitum (i.e. when they were close to adult focal animals). The smaller number of adult males' recordings, when compared to those of females, reflect the larger number of resident females in the group, and possibly a gender difference in rate of vocalizations (Arnedo et al., 2009). Both ad libitum and focal samplings were obtained during different months of the two seasons (i.e. wet and dry) and at different times of days. Sequential exchanges were actually the most frequent types of vocal interaction during Mendes (1995, 1997) study, and occurred throughout the day at variable behavioral (e.g. feeding, traveling, resting), social (e.g. whole group, small or large feeding parties, temporary fissions of different composition) and spatial contexts (e.g. cohesively, individuals evenly spread, group spread in parties).

3.3 Method

Vocalizations were digitized and archived at a sampling rate of 44.1 kHz and 16-bit accuracy through a Signal/RTS system. The system consisted of a Gateway 2000 486 - DX2 66 computer, a DSP board, and an A/D converter, as well as two softwares (Signal and RTS) and an interface supplied by Engineering Design (Beeman, 1989). Before 16 bits digitizing, original recordings were submitted to a low pass (10,000 Hz) high pass (200 Hz) anti-alias filter. For the acoustic analyses we used the Software Signal Explorer 7.2 and WinpitchPro that allow making various types of analyses (spectrograms, fo and amplitude curves, FFT and LPC spectra).

4. Muriquis prosodic features

4.1 Utterances and prosodic contour

The unit in which prosodic features are found in muriquis vocalizations is defined as an utterance. This is made of the combination of a number of basic elements that we call syllables. Mendes (1995) has identified 14 elements or syllables (4 short and 10 long) that can be combined to make these utterances. The paper focuses only on the prosodic features involved in these utterances; therefore the rules combining syllables to generate utterances will not be discussed here. The prosodic contour of an utterance is made, in the vast majority of the cases, by a rising and falling pattern. In our sample, the majority of staccatos (n= 133. 66.19%) and neighs (n=71, 60.68%) started with a low amplitude syllable, repeated or followed by a number of other syllables rising in amplitude and/or duration until a peak of intensity at the second half of the utterance, followed by a sharp fall or by one or several syllables of decreasing amplitude and reduced duration until the final element. All individuals in our sample produced at least one vocalization with this "slow up and fast down" contour (type 1, see Figure 1). The "reverse" pattern of prosodic contour (type 2), beginning with a sudden attack or a rapid crescendo at the first half of the utterance, followed by a slow decrease in intensity, was the only type of contour more common in neighs (n=30) than in staccatos (n=8), and was produced by 5 males and 10 females. "Monotonous" utterances (type 3), with very little intersyllabic modulations in amplitude/frequency and in duration, were reported in 27 staccatos and 2 neighs of 5 males and 9 females. Finally, we bundled a variable set of calls (n=47: 14 staccatos and 33 neighs) that were recorded for 4 males and 16 females into a fourth type of prosodic contour that we called "multiple shifts". These were vocalizations with relatively low amplitude, and with more than one visible cycle of modulation of either intensity/frequency or duration, often sounding like two or more different utterances were being produced by the same individual. With the exception of one male and one female, who consistently produced vocalizations of type 1 prosodic contour, all 19 individuals with more than 3 vocalizations in our sample produced vocalizations with either 2 (3 females), 3 (2 males and 5 females) or all 4 (3 males and 6 females) types of prosodic contours.

4.2 Amplitude/frequency

Figure 1 is an illustration of amplitude and frequency modulations that are very frequent and characteristic of muriquis vocalizations. These modulations of amplitude and frequency are produced in an utterance made of the repetition of short syllables. From the second repetition on there is a progressive rise in the amplitude and frequency of the first harmonic's frequency in the spectrum. This is accompanied by a gradual increase in the duration of each syllable. The reason for the equal space between the harmonics is that the sound is more than likely produced in a close/open acoustic tube with a uniform section (Demolin et al. 2008). Figure 2 is an utterance showing the repetition of different short syllables in strings and their combination with a long syllable. Strings are made of the combination of short syllables in which only the second syllable is repeated a number of times. The long syllable has a much greater amplitude and duration than the short one and is the peak syllable of the utterance.

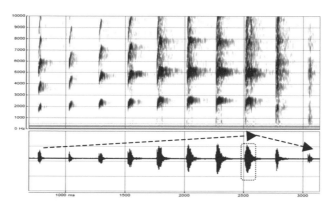

Figure 1. Utterance showing the repetition of a single short syllable modulated in amplitude/frequency and duration. Arrows show the rising falling pattern of the utterance. The peak syllable is surrounded.

Long syllables, when they are repeated, are often produced without interruption and present modulations similar to that of a vibrato. This is illustrated at Figure 3 showing four repetitions of the same long syllable

4.3 Rhythm

Rhythm is produced by the repetition and the combination of syllables within utterances. Figure 2 shows strings combining two short syllables in which only the second syllable is repeated 2 and 3 times after the first syllable. The number of repetitions is however not limited and is quite variable. This is a very frequent pattern observed in staccatos and neighs of all individuals with more than 5 vocalizations of our sample.

Other rhythmic effects are produced by the repetition of a single syllable with concomitant amplitude and duration modulations (Figures 1 and 2).

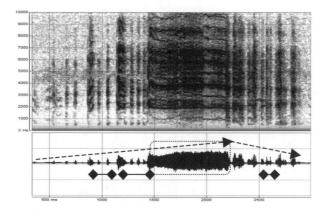

Figure 2. Utterance showing the combination of short syllables modulated in amplitude/frequency and duration with a long syllable. Arrows show the rising falling pattern of the utterance. The peak syllable is surrounded. Strings made of the combination of two short elements are indicated below the audio waveform.

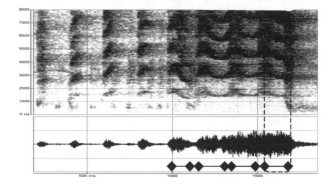

Figure 3. Utterance showing the combination of short and long syllables. The peak syllable is surrounded. The four repetitions of an identical long syllable are indicated below the audio waveform.

5. Discussion

Data from this paper present a preliminary description and analysis of prosodic features in muriquis vocalizations. For the moment it is difficult to define any function for the features mentioned in this paper. Prosodic features of non-human primate calls such as rising and falling frequency/amplitude and modulation of duration may not only inform about characteristics of the caller (e.g. affective state – Koda, 2008) but also stimulate a similar affective state in listeners (Bachorowski & Owren, 2003; Snowdon & Teie, 2009). Alternatively, a conspicuous stressed syllable within the prosodic contour might call the attention of listeners to specific parts of the utterance, such as its onset or upcoming end, or a particular syllable. For instance, the common "slow up fast down" type of prosody, with a conspicuous stressed syllable towards the end of the vocalization, might facilitate the turn-taking of group members during exchanges. There is still a lot of research to do to associate prosodic features to any function (emotive or other) in muriqui vocalizations. As far as prosody in non-human primates may inform about the origins and evolution of different aspects of language (e.g. motherese- Koda, 2008; non-verbal cues of affect– Scherer, 2003) and of other combinatorial forms of human communication (i.e. music – Snowdon & Teie, 2009), muriquis are likely candidates for future comparative studies. These monkeys provide a rare example of vocalizations with complex prosody used in variable social contexts. The same prosodic contour type may be used for staccatos and neighs. These are composed of different combinations of syllable types. In addition, intensity peaks (i.e. stressed syllables) may fall on short or long syllables (Mendes, 1995). The effects of prosodic features such as contour and rhythm on call variability are indeed quite striking. Vocalizations emitted by different individuals during the same exchange may vary both in composition and prosodic features, giving the impression that different messages might be exchanged among group members, much like a conversation (c.f. Snowdon & Cleveland, 1984; Mendes, 1997). Finally, we wish to emphasize the importance of prosodic features in muriquis vocalizations from an evolutionary point of view. Up to now, no clear evidence of prosody has been shown in non-human primate vocalizations. The prosodic features found in muriquis (i.e. amplitude/frequency, duration, rhythm) do not include melody (f0 contours) but they pattern in clear utterances. These are different from what is found in human language only by the lack of f0 modulations independent from amplitude. This shows two very important points. First, it suggests that the origin and evolution of a crucial character of language, such as prosody, can be described by the gradual modification of some of its features. Second, this raises the fundamental question of the potential meaning of these utterances. Future research should address these issues.

References

Ades, C. and Mendes, F.D.C. (1997). Uma aproximação etológica às vocalizações do muriqui. *Temas em Psicologia*, 3, 135-149.

Arnedo, L.F.; Mendes, F.D.C. & Strier, K.B. (2009). Sex differences in vocal patterns in the northern muriquis (*Brachyteles hypoxanthus*). *American Journal of Primatology*. DOI: 10.1002/ajp.2076.

Bachorowski, J. & Owren, M.J. (2003). Sounds of emotion: production and perception of affect-related vocal acoustics. *Annals of the NewYork Academy of Science*, 1000, 244-265.

Beeman, K. (1989). *Signal User's Guide*. Belmont: Engineering Design.

Candisani, L.(2004). *Muriquis*. São Paulo: DBA, Artes Gráficas.

Demolin, D. (2007). Phonological universals and the control and regulation of speech production. In Solé, M-J., Ohala, M. & Beddor, P. (Eds.) *Experimental approaches to phonology.* Oxford: Oxford University Press, 75-92.

Demolin, D. Ades, C. & Mendes, F.D.C. (2008). Some observations on the acoustics and articulatory capacities of northern muriquis (*Brachyteles hypoxanthus*). *Primate Tiding,* 16, 7-17.

Koda, H. (2008). Short term acoustic modifications during dynamic vocal interactions in nonhuman primates: implications for origins of motherese. In: Masataka, N. (Ed.) *The origins of Language: unraveling evolutionary forces.* Tokyo: Springer, 59-73.

Mendes, F. D. C. (1995). *Interações vocais do muriqui.* PhD Dissertation, Universidade de São Paulo, Brazil.

Mendes, F.D.C. (1997). Padrões de interação vocal do muriqui. In: Ferrari, S.F. (Ed.) *A Primatologia no Brasil V.* Belém: Editora da UFPA, 94-118.

Mendes, F.D.C. and Ades, C. (2004). Vocal sequential exchanges and intragroup spacing in the Nothern Muriqui *Brachyteles arachnoides hypoxanthus. Anais da Academia Brasileira de Ciências,* 76, 399-404.

Nishimura, A., Fonseca, G.A.B., Young, A.L., Strier, K.B., Mittermeier, R.A. & Valle, C.M.C. (1988). The muriqui, genus *Brachyteles.* In Mittermeier, R.A., Rylands, A.B., Coimbra-Filho, A. & Fonseca, G.A.B. (Eds.) *Ecology and behavior of neotropical primates vol. 2.* Belo Horizonte: Sociedade Brasileira de Primatologia.

Ohala, J.J. (1970). Aspects of the control and production of speech. *Working Papers in Phonetics,* 15. Berkeley, UCLA.

Riede, T., M.J. Owren and A.C. Arcadi (2004). Nonlinear acoustics in pant hoots of common chimapnzees (*Pan Troglodytes*): frequency jumps, subharmonics, biphonation, and deterministic chaos. *American Journal of Primatology,* 64, 277-291.

Scherer, K.R. (2003).Vocal communication of emotion: a review of research paradigms. *Speech Communication,* 40, 227-256.

Snowdon C.T.& Teie, D. (2009). Affective responses in tamarins elicited by species-specific music. *Biology Letters,* DOI: 10.1098/rsbl.2009.0593.

Snowdon, C.T.& Cleveland, J. (1984). "Conversations" among pygmy marmosets. *American Journal of Primatology,* 7, 15-20.

Strier, K.B. (1999). *Faces in the forest: the endangered Muriqui monkeys of Brazil,* 2nd edition. Boston MA: Harvard University Press.

Strier, K.B., Mendes, F.D.C., Rimoli, J. & Rimoli, A.O. (1993). Demography and social structure of one group of muriquis (*Brachyteles arachnoides*). *International Journal of Primatology,* 14, 513-526.

HAVE YOU ANYTHING UNEXPECTED TO SAY? THE HUMAN PROPENSITY TO COMMUNICATE SURPRISE AND ITS ROLE IN THE EMERGENCE OF LANGUAGE

JEAN-LOUIS DESSALLES

Telecom PARISTECH, 46 rue Barrault, Paris, France
&
ILCAA, Tokyo University of Foreign Studies, Tokyo, Japan

Individuals devote one third of their language time to mentioning unexpected events. We try to make sense of this universal behaviour within the Costly Signalling framework. By systematically using language to point to the unexpected, individuals send a *signal* that advertises their ability to anticipate danger. This shift in display behaviour, as compared with typical displays in primate species, may result from the use by hominins of artefacts to kill.

1. Theoretical Context

Human language has several remarkable features. It is a massive phenomenon (M): human individuals are involved more than six hours a day in spontaneous language activities (Mehl & Pennebaker, 2003) and speak some 15 000 words on average during that time (Mehl *et al.*, 2007). Information is available in abundance, due to the existence of talkative individuals (T). Many conversations deal with futile matters that are unlikely to affect the participants' survival (F). Speakers do not (or loosely) discriminate who will hear what they say (D), and most interactions in a group are *not* one-to-one (Dunbar *et al.*, 1995). Many conversational topics are narratives, *i.e.* they report on some current or past unexpected event (U) (Tannen 1984; Eggins & Slade 1997; Norrick, 2000); This behaviour: drawing attention to unexpected situations, is a human distinctive feature (Tomasello, 2006) that shows up early in childhood (Carpenter *et al.* 1998). Human beings learn and understand huge lexicons made of tens of thousands of words and set phrases (L). Most individuals willingly engage in conversational behaviour (W) with no noticeable difference between sexes (S) (Mehl *et al.*, 2007). And sharing conversational time strongly correlates with establishing and maintaining social bonds (B) (Dunbar, 1996).

Usual accounts of altruistic behaviour are at odds with these facts. Kin selection (Fitch, 2004) has problems with M, F, D, L, B. Reciprocal cooperation (Nowak, 2006) conflicts with T, F, D and indirect reciprocity (Nowak & Sigmund, 2005) conflicts, in addition, with W. Group selection (Sober & Wilson, 1998) conflicts with M, T, W, and in its warrior version (Bowles, 2006) also with S. Though each of these theoretical difficulties should be discussed in more detail, we must observe that these traditional models of altruism cannot be straightforwardly applied to the case of human language. Moreover, none of them positively predicts any of the first seven facts in the above list.

Other accounts of costly behaviour include sexual selection (Miller, 2000) and Costly Signalling Theory (CST) (Gintis et al., 2001). Sexual selection, when applied to language, is however incompatible with facts M, S and B. The case of CST will be examined in the next section.

We will first consider how CST can be applied to language. It requires that the quality advertised by speakers be specified. We then describe a study showing how the human mind detects and interprets unexpected events. We interpret the systematic communication of unexpected situations in our species (fact U above) as a way for individuals to advertise their ability to spot unexpectedness. This advertising behaviour makes sense within the CST framework if language emerged in the new context created by the use of artefacts to kill.

2. Can Costly Signalling Theory Account for Human Language?

CST (Zahavi & Zahavi, 1997; Gintis *et al.*, 2001) appears to be the most promising model to explain the above list of facts concerning spontaneous language, despite some initial beliefs about the contrary (Zahavi & Zahavi, 1997:222). In CST, individuals send signals, even if this involves a significant cost, to advertise a definite quality Q. They benefit from being perceived as possessing Q. In the social version of CST (Dessalles, 1999; Gintis et al., 2001), individuals establish social bonds based on Q. Social bonds are systematically beneficial to chosen signallers. They benefit followers as well, but only if the chosen partner really had Q, in other words if the signal was honest in the first place. CST shows that, under certain conditions, honest signals emerge and remain stable.

It is tempting to invoke CST to account for the existence of language, as it would correctly predict facts labelled T, D, W, B in our list. There are, however, several problems. One of them is that CST is apparently incompatible with M: the fact that everyone speaks, and speaks a lot. Within CST, signalling is competitive. This generates a threshold, below which it is not worthwhile signalling. The honesty of signals relies precisely on this fact: only high-quality individuals benefit from signalling, while the others have better time saving the cost, as they have little hope of return. We addressed this issue elsewhere (Dessalles 2006), by showing that when the competition is decentralized, even low-quality individuals benefit from signalling their true quality. The fact that social bonds imply spending time together (Dunbar, 1996) is crucial in this respect: individuals must recruit their friends among individuals who have available time left. This constraint creates a situation in which friends turn out to be matched by quality. In such situation, everyone benefits from signalling.

The major remaining problem concerning CST is that it leaves the advertised quality Q unspecified. The constraints are the following:

- Joining an individual with higher Q should bring more benefit to followers;
- Cheating on Q should be difficult for signallers.

Importantly, cost is not a necessary ingredient of CST! Cost might be borne by cheaters rather than signallers (Lachman et al. 2001), and in some cases cheating might simply be impossible, *e.g.* if recipients can check the validity of the signal. In the next sections, we explore the possibility that one prime quality advertised through language is the ability to notice unexpected states of affairs.

3. Unexpectedness in Language

Some 25% to 40% of language time is devoted to mentioning immediate or past events (Eggins & Slade, 1997; Dessalles, 2008), especially through conversational narratives (Norrick, 2000). To appear interesting to listeners, these events must appear unexpected, *i.e.* they must contrast with the listener's expectations about the world (see below for a more technical definition). We will show how this unique property of human communication can make sense within CST.

Unexpectedness can be given a formal definition. In their attempts to define randomness, mathematicians developed a concept known as Complexity (in the Kolmogorov sense). The complexity C of a situation is the minimal information needed to reconstruct it unambiguously. Though objective (*i.e.* observer-independent) complexity cannot be computed, observer-dependant C can be easily calculated in most concrete cases, as shown in table 1 (see www.unexpectedness.eu, or (Dessalles, 2008) for more details).

Table 1: Complexity computations

Parameter	C	Remark
Distance d to the event	$\log_2(\pi d^2/a)$	a is the typical surface of the event.
Time distance t to the event	$\log_2(t/a)$	a is the typical duration of event.
Social relatedness	$\log_2 r$	r is the rank of the acquaintance in the observer's address or cell phone shortlist.
Celebrity	$\log_2 r$	r is the rank of the person in an ordered list (see note).
Feature f	$\log_2 r$	r is the rank of the notion in an ordered list (see note).

Note: ranked lists can be obtained through Web search engines, or through temporal ordering (events being ranked by elapsed time), or by experimenting with individuals' reaction times in recognition tasks. r is ideally the minimal rank obtained through such means.

Unexpectedness is defined as a complexity drop:

$$U = C_w - C \tag{1}$$

C_w stands for the expected complexity, *i.e.* the minimal information needed for the known world to produce the situation. Table 2 shows the contribution of various parameters to unexpectedness (see www.unexpectedness.eu, or (Dessalles, 2008) for more details).

The claim is not that the human brain performs these computations formally. However, individuals seem to have clear intuitions about how these various parameters affect unexpectedness. For instance, they intuitively know that a fire breaking out next block is more unexpected, and thus more interesting to tell, than the same fire occurring five kilometres away. They intuitively know that coincidences are all the more unexpected, and thus interesting, as the two coincident facts share common features (making $C(s_2|s_1)$ smaller). And they know that it is highly unexpected to bump into one's neighbour P in a remote place L (*e.g.* a village in India), much more unexpected indeed than a mere encounter with some forgotten former colleague in the train station nearby (what the difference $C(P) - C(L)$ captures). The study presented in the next section puts these intuitions to the test.

Table 2: Unexpectedness computations

Parameter	U	Observation
Distance	$2 \log_2(D/d)$	D is the typical distance to similar events (estimated by the distance to the last remembered instance).
Time	$\log_2(T/t)$	T is the typical distance in the past to similar events (estimated by the time distance to the last remembered instance).
Rarity	$\log_2(1/F) - C(f)$	F is the occurrence frequency of feature f.
Atypicality	$0.7\, k^2 - C(f)$	The situation lies at k standard deviations along feature f from its prototype.
Coincidence	$C(s_1) - C(s_2\|s_1)$	Conditional complexity $C(s_2\|s_1)$ measures the minimal information needed to reconstruct s_2 from s_1.
Encounter	$C(L) - C(P)$	The observer bumps into P at location L.

4. Unexpectedness and Conversational Interest

A corpus of 18 short narratives was presented to 101 French participants (see (Dimulescu & Dessalles, 2009) for a detailed description of the experiment). For each story, participants had to choose among two options (randomly selected out of three possible values) the one that makes the story more interesting. The following stories (originally in French) illustrate, in turn, the influence of time distance, the role of atypicality, the importance of common features in coincidences, and the influence of social proximity (* signals when results are statistically significant $p < .05$).

➢ For a year, I had been thinking of changing my mobile phone at SFR (mobile operator). I finally decided to do so even if I had to pay a part because I did not have enough Red Square Points. I bought the new phone at 13:00. [---] I got a message from SFR: "Change your mobile, SFR offers you 15 000 Red Square Points."

Options: (a) At 13:10; (b) At 14:00; (c) Two weeks later.

Results: (a)/(b): 29/4* – (b)/(c): 28/6* – (a)/(c): 31/3*

➢ Wednesday, the city of Amiens police seized [---] kg of heroin at number 13 rue Fafet.

Options: (a) 10 – (b) 5 – (c) 2.

Results: (a)/(b): 28/13* – (b)/(c): 20/11 – (a)/(c): 21/8*

➢ I'd just bought a small Peugeot 106 ColorLine for 2000 euros. I had tried it the day before and it was very good. I turned the key, I started, I left the property of the former owner of the car when, coming from the left without looking, another [---] crashed into me.

Options: (a) Peugeot 106 ColorLine – (b) Peugeot 106 – (c) Peugeot.

Results: (a)/(b) 24/8* – (b)/(c) 32/4* – (a)/(c) 28/5*

➢ Two weeks after my car had been stolen, the police informed me that a car that might be mine was for sale on the Internet. They showed me the ad. The phone number had been identified. It was the mobile phone number of [---].

Options: (a) my office colleague – (b) a colleague of my brother's – (c) someone of my neighbourhood.

Results: (a)/(b) 25/6* – (b)/(c) 24/10* – (a)/(c) 26/7*

Participants altogether never preferred the least unexpected option (c). For 17 stories out of 18, the most unexpectedness option (a) was significantly ranked best. This is in perfect accordance with the major role played by unexpectedness in conversational interest. We now show that this role may owe its origin to our phylogeny.

5. Discussion

The human universal propensity to signalling unexpected events and the corresponding demand by listeners matches the CST prerequisite that it is used to display a social quality. What kind of quality? Candidates do not abound. There is one hypothesis, however, that seems to offer a consistent account.

It is a fact that at some point in our phylogeny, individuals started to use stones, sticks or weapons to kill at no risk (what chimpanzees do not do). This new behaviour dramatically transformed hominin politics (Woodburn 1982; Boehm 2000:177; Bingham, 2001). If anyone can kill anyone at no risk, e.g. during sleep, to be on one's guard is not enough. Individuals must rely on friends' alertness. In this context, ideal friends are those who are best able to anticipate danger. Language would have emerged as a way to advertise this ability.

In most species, danger is easy to anticipate. The gazelle knows that lions are dangerous, and it knows what the safe distance is. Chimpanzee males know that wandering close to territorial limits puts their life at risk. The problem is significantly harder for hominins: danger may come from group mates who may strike anywhere anytime by surprise. How can the unexpected be anticipated?

The present account of the evolutionary emergence of language instantiates CST in the following way: individuals, through their conversational utterances, advertise their ability to surprise others. By preferring to join and remain close to the most talented individuals in this game, listeners increase their viability as they diminish the probability of being taken by surprise. In a context of easy killing, information replaces muscular strength as main asset for success. Male chimpanzees display their muscles, whereas human beings advertise their informational abilities through language. Note that, as required by CST, it is difficult to cheat on unexpectedness, as the unexpected character of reported events can be easily checked by listeners.

This model accounts for all the facts listed at the beginning of this paper. In particular, noticing futile facts (*F*), such as the current date (09/09/09), can make a successful communicative act (in this example, the date is interesting, not because it is consequential, but merely because it is 'too' simple and thus unexpected). The model predicts that various levels of talkativeness will coexist (*T*); it predicts no discrimination of listeners (*D*), no sex difference (*S*), and of course a strong correlation between conversation and social closeness (*B*). It is, in addition, one of the few models that account for the existence of plethoric lexicons (*L*): the set of unexpected situations is by definition unbounded, and one must be potentially able to describe all of them, especially the rarest ones, with enough precision for their unexpected character to be correctly appraised.

In the hominin world in which riskless killing becomes possible, individuals secure their safety by choosing the right friends, those who are most able of keeping them informed of any unusual situation going on. This is the only way to prevent the danger of being taken by surprise. The initial emergence of language may be the consequence of this situation: individuals strive to display their ability to notice anything unexpected, as it is the best way, as predicted within the CST framework, to build efficient social networks.

References

Carpenter, M., Nagell, K. & Tomasello, M. (1998). Social cognition, joint attention, and communicative competence from 9 to 15 months of age. *Monographs of the Society for Research in Child Devel.*, 255(63), 1-143.

Bingham, P. M. (2001). Human evolution and human history: A complete theory. *Evolutionary anthropology*, 9 (6), 248-257.

Boehm, C. H. (2000). *Hierarchy in the forest: the evolution of egalitarian behavior*. Harvard, MA: Harvard University Press.

Bowles, S. (2006). Group competition, reproductive leveling, and the evolution of human altruism. *Science*, 314, 1569-1572.

Carpenter, M., Nagell, K. & Tomasello, M. (1998). Social cognition, joint attention, and communicative competence from 9 to 15 months of age. *Monographs of the Society for Research in Child Dev.*, 255 (63), 1-143.

Dessalles, J-L. (1999). Coalition factor in the evolution of non-kin altruism. *Advances in Complex Systems*, 2 (2), 143-172. http://www.dessalles.fr/papiers/pap.evol/Dessalles_99091402.pdf

Dessalles, J-L. (2006). Generalised signalling: a possible solution to the paradox of language. In A. Cangelosi, A. D. M. Smith & K. Smith (Eds.), *The evolution of language*, 75-82. Singapore: World Scientific. http://www.dessalles.fr/papiers/pap.evol/Dessalles_05112301.pdf

Dessalles, J-L. (2008). *La pertinence et ses origines cognitives - Nouvelles théories*. Paris: Hermes-Science Publications. http://pertinence.dessalles.fr

Dimulescu, A. & Dessalles, J-L. (2009). Understanding narrative interest: Some evidence on the role of unexpectedness. In N. A. Taatgen & H. van Rijn (Eds.), *Proceedings of the 31st Annual Conference of the Cognitive Science Society*, 1734-1739. Amsterdam, NL: Cognitive Science Society. http://141.14.165.6/CogSci09/papers/367/paper367.pdf

Dunbar, R. I. M. (1996). *Grooming, gossip, and the evolution of language.* Cambridge: Harvard University Press.

Dunbar, R. I. M., Duncan, N. & Nettle, D. (1995). Size and structure of freely forming conversational groups. *Human nature, 6* (1), 67-78.

Eggins, S. & Slade, D. (1997). *Analysing casual conversation.* London: Equinox.

Fitch, W. T. (2004). Evolving honest communication systems: Kin selection and 'mother tongues'. In D. K. Oller & U. Griebel (Eds.), *The evolution of communication systems: a comparative approach*, 275-296. Cambridge, MA: MIT Press.

Gintis, H., Smith, E. A. & Bowles, S. (2001). Costly Signaling and Cooperation. *Journal of Theoretical Biology, 213*, 103-119.

Lachmann, M., Számadó, S. & Bergstrom, C. T. (2001). Cost and conflict in animal signals and human language. *Proc. Natl. Acad. Sci., USA, 98* (23), 13189-13194.

Mehl, M. R. & Pennebaker, J. W. (2003). The sounds of social life: A psychometric analysis of students' daily social environments and natural conversations. *Journal of Personality and Social Psychology, 84* (4), 857-870.

Mehl, M. R., Vazire, S., Ramírez-Esparza, N., Slatcher, R. B. & Pennebaker, J. W. (2007). Are women really more talkative than men?. *Science, 317*, 82.

Miller, G. F. (2000). *The mating mind.* New York: Doubleday.

Norrick, N. R. (2000). *Conversational narrative: storytelling in everyday talk.* Amsterdam: John Benjamins Publishing Company.

Nowak, M. A. (2006). Five rules for the evolution of cooperation. *Science, 314*, 1560-1563.

Nowak, M. A. & Sigmund, K. (2005). Evolution of indirect reciprocity. *Nature, 437* (27), 1291-1298.

Sober, E. & Wilson, D. S. (1998). *Unto Others. The Evolution and Psychology of Unselfish Behavior.* Cambridge, MA: Harvard University Press.

Tannen, D. (1984). *Conversational style - Analyzing talk among friends.* Norwood: Ablex Publishing Corporation.

Tomasello, M. (2006). Why don't apes point?. In N. J. Enfield & S. C. Levinson (Eds.), *Roots of human sociality: Culture, cognition and interaction*, 506-524. Oxford: Berg Publishers.

Woodburn, J. (1982). Egalitarian societies. *Man, 17*, 431-451.

Zahavi, A. & Zahavi, A. (1997). *The handicap principle.* New York: Oxford University Press.

THE INNATENESS OF LANGUAGE: A VIEW FROM GENETICS

KARL C. DILLER AND REBECCA L. CANN

Department of Cell and Molecular Biology (Genetics), John A. Burns School of Medicine, University of Hawaii at Manoa, 1960 East-West Road, Honolulu, Hawaii 96822 USA

Language is a defining characteristic of the biological species *Homo sapiens*. But Chomskian Universal Grammar is not what is innate about language; Universal Grammar requires magical thinking about genes and genetics. Constraints of universal grammar are better explained in an evolutionary context by processes inherent in symbols, and by such processes as syntactic carpentry, metaphor, and grammaticalization. We present an evolutionary timeline for language, with biological evidence for the long-term evolution of the human capacity for language, and for the co-evolution of language and the brain.

1. Introduction

1.1. *Darwin and Broca*

We keep hearing that in 1866 the Linguistic Circle of Paris stopped accepting papers on the origin of language because those papers were speculatively silly. But why 1866? And why Paris? In 1866 intellectuals in Paris were talking about Pierre Paul Broca and Charles Darwin. Broca, a neurologist, had just discovered an area of the brain essential for speech, and Clémence Royer's controversial French translation of Darwin's *Origin of Species* had recently come out. By 1866 it was clear that one could no longer talk about the origin of language without considering the biological substrates of language and biological evolution. In reaction, the Linguistic Circle was founded in 1866 as a conservative Catholic-monarchist organization specifically to counter positivist and evolutionary thought in linguistics. But for the Anthropological Society, founded by Broca, who was also a champion of Darwin, any speculation about the origin of language outside the framework of biological evolution would be regarded as magical thinking.

1.2. *Magical thinking about genetic mutations for language*

From a biological point of view, one sees a surprising amount of magical thinking among linguists and paleoanthropologists, even 150 years after Darwin and Broca -- only now the magical thinking is couched in the vocabulary of genes and genetics. For example, Berwick and Chomsky (forthcoming) envision a scenario in which "in the very recent past, maybe about 75,000 years ago," [i.e. well after fossil human brains had reached their modern size and proportion], "an individual...underwent a minor mutation that provided the operation Merge," which allowed for recursive structured thought. "At some later stage," they say, "the internal language of thought was connected to the sensorimotor system," that is, to the "external" modalities of speech and hearing and sign language, "quite possibly a task that involves no evolution at all."

Likewise the paleoanthropologist Richard Klein has argued that there must have been a recent mutation for language about 50,000 years ago to explain an increase in cultural artifacts appearing at that time (Klein 1997). The implication is that if you don't have sophisticated preserved cultural artifacts as evidence, you don't have language.

Although single mutations can have devastating results for disease or disability, it is magical thinking to believe that a single recent mutation could cause something as complex as the origin of the biological capacity for language or for recursive thought.

We will present a long timeline for the coevolution of language and the brain in the genus *Homo*. But first, to clear the way for a biological perspective on the evolution of language, the Chomskian approach to Universal Grammar must be rejected. Universal Grammar is not what is innate for language.

2. Chomskian Universal Grammar is not what is innate for language

2.1. *Chomskian Universal Grammar and natural selection*

In critiquing behaviorism, Chomsky did us a great favor by emphasizing the biological species-specific nature of language. But then the first conceptual shift of generative grammar was to turn away from considering species behavior to focusing on the internal individual language of an ideal speaker -- 'I-language.' Almost by definition I-language is primarily for thought, not communication. External languages ('E-language'), e.g. English and Dutch, were regarded as secondary or derived epiphenomena. For purposes of the theory, the ideal speaker-hearer was placed in a pure ideal speech community with no variation. To solve the logical problem of language acquisition, language acquisition was regarded to be instantaneous. In that fixed and static context, the theory demanded universal grammar to be innate so that children could universally learn language in impoverished language environments without teaching. It is no wonder that Chomsky was skeptical whether evolution by natural selection could account for the Universal Grammar derived from this model.

In their classic paper, Natural Language and Natural Selection (1990), Pinker and Bloom tried to reconcile the generative linguistics of twenty years ago with the theory of evolution by natural selection. Both Chomsky and the paleontologist Stephen J. Gould had been questioning whether language could be explained by natural selection. Pinker and Bloom say, "Since we are impressed both by the synthetic theory of evolution and by the theory of generative grammar, we hope that we will not have to choose between the two." To reconcile the two, however, they had to recast the theory of generative grammar. Their argument is based on two "facts," one of which was that "language shows signs of complex design for the communication of propositional structures" (p.47). Communication is basic to their view of language, as it is to most people, but Berwick and Chomsky are still arguing that communication is a secondary phenomenon which came after the minor mutation for Merge that allowed structured thought. Even allowing for a genetic mutation, Berwick and Chomsky are reluctant to put it in the context of natural selection, preferring to recast evolution in terms of physical constraints and other processes with much of the language faculty evolving as a spandrel, as accidents or for purposes other than language.

We *do* have to choose between generative linguistics and the theory of natural selection for language, but if we reject generative linguistics, we still have to account for the phenomena explained by universal grammar.

2.2. *There is no need for a minor mutation for Merge or recursion*

A mutation for Merge or for linguistic recursion is not necessary if we recognize that recursion is common in the natural world and implicit in symbolic systems.

Recursion in the natural world. Chomsky and his collaborators have argued that while the human faculty of language, broadly speaking (FLB), may have homologs or analogs with other animals, the only thing which makes human language unique (the Faculty of Language Narrow Sense, FLN) is recursion. Hauser, Chomsky, and Fitch (2002) proposed that the "FLN comprises only the core computational mechanisms of recursion as they appear in narrow syntax and the mappings to the interfaces."

It is not at all clear, however, that recursion is so unique in the natural world. In living systems biochemical processes are used over and over again in hierarchical structures. For example, FOXP2 is a transcription factor that regulates several hundred genes in hierarchical structures at different places and different times in the life cycle.

Recursion and universal grammar for free. Terence Deacon (2003) argues that recursion is implicit as a semiotic universal in symbolic reference. Symbols, as predicates, are free and variable in reference and require an indexical argument to refer the predicate to a specific context. "Table" can refer to many things and we need modifiers and the like to let us know which table we are referring to. In English, the verb "carry" inherently requires subject and object arguments: we want to know *who* carried *what.* Deacon argues that "the kinds of thing that can be substituted for argument variables can themselves be predicates (with their own argument variables), exemplifying the possibility for recursion implicit in symbols (p. 133)." This, he maintains, is a semiotic universal not tied to human language or neural systems. In sum, he argues that "major universals of grammar may come for free, so to speak, required by the nature of symbolic communication itself (p.138).

William O'Grady (2005) goes a step further by working out how the effects associated with universal grammar can come for free in the process of building sentences. Universal grammar requires an interface with a mostly unspecified processing system. O'Grady shows how a processing system with the right characteristics can compute and build sentences of the appropriate sort without the need for universal grammar. Adopting the metaphor of a carpenter building without architectural blueprints, he shows that the properties of a broad range of phenomena associated with universal grammar (agreement, control, binding, *that* trace effects, and others) follow from the manner in which sentences are built by a processor whose primary concern is simply to minimize the burden on working memory.

3. A biological perspective on the evolution of language

3.1. *Language is a defining characteristic of Homo sapiens.*

Biologists would agree that language is a defining characteristic of *Homo sapiens.* In that sense, as Lenneberg used to argue, it is more like bipedal gait, which has no history in the species, than like writing, which has a clear history and is not universal among humans. Language would have been fully present at least as far back as 200,000 years ago, with "Mitochondrial Eve" (Cann et al. 1987) and with the first anatomically modern *Homo sapiens* fossil skulls.

Species-specific behavior does not necessarily mean species exclusive. Bipedal gait is a defining characteristic of *Homo sapiens*, but also of *Homo erectus, Homo habilis,* the australopithecines, and even, in a more primitive way, the 4.4 million year old Ardipithecus ramidus. The presumption of evolutionary biology is that the capacity for language and language itself also have a long history, and were co-evolving in the genus *Homo* with the tripling in brain size beginning 2 million years ago.

3.2. *The importance of speech in the evolution of language*

In experiments trying to teach human languages to chimpanzees, the most salient deficit among chimpanzees is their almost total inability to speak or even mimic English words. Even when raised as a child in diapers in a human home, and even after extensive behaviorist training, ability to mimic speech is almost nonexistent. Yet chimpanzees are able to understand spoken English words and communicate using basic signs of American Sign Language and special ideographs on computer keyboards. Except for speech, the cognitive abilities of the great apes would provide a good starting place for the evolution of language.

A question arose, did manual sign language serve as a transitional system leading to spoken language? The reverse is more likely, that modern sign languages are enabled by cognitive mechanisms evolved for spoken language. If American Sign Language is just as good a language as spoken languages are, then it is unlikely that humans would have undergone the difficult evolutionary task of developing neuromuscular control of the vocal tract. Except among deaf people, speech is a universal feature of human language.

Although the lips, tongue, vocal cords, breathing mechanisms, etc., are homologous between humans and apes, gaining voluntary neuromuscular control to coordinate these organs for speech was a major evolutionary task, not to mention the subtle changes in shape of some of these organs to accommodate efficient speech. When one looks at the extensive areas of the human brain dedicated to control of the vocal tract and to the processing of speech, one sees evidence of natural selection for speech function.

3.3. *Coevolution of language and the brain*

Human brain size tripled in the last 2 million years from the 350cc of Australopithecines to the 600cc of *Homo Habilis*, the 900cc of *Homo erectus* and the 1350cc of modern *Homo sapiens.* Some of this increase is required by increased body size, but the increase in brain power is still impressive.

Berwick and Chomsky (2008) quote a suggestion by Striedter that human language may have emerged automatically from increased brain size. This suggestion does not work. Microcephalics, human beings with chimpanzee-sized brains, can learn language to the kindergarten level by the time they are twelve, so it is clear that it is not the absolute size of the brain that matters but the structure and connectedness of the brain.

A true evolutionary novelty, like language, presumably involves mutation in gene regulation. With the whole genomes of chimpanzees and humans available we can search for regulatory gene shifts, especially those involved in neuronal architecture. Many human-specific regulatory RNA's have been discovered. For example, two genes that are highly expressed in the brain, CCDC55 and SEMA46, are regulated by small RNAs that are the target of recent positive natural selection in humans (Zhang, Lu, and Cui 2008). These newly regulated genes yield neurons with altered metal, ion, and nucleotide binding activities, along with changes in protein transport and cell cycle control.

Not all parts of the brain increased at the same rate: Broca's area and other language processing areas are among the areas that increased proportionately more than average. In biology we expect form and function to evolve together. When we see fossil dinosaur skeletons we confidently say which ones could fly. Likewise when we see increases in motor cortex controlling the vocal tract and increases in motor association cortex serving the vocal tract (Broca's area), we can be confident that we are seeing the evolution of the ability to speak. Our assumption here is that the first symbols of language were spoken words.

4. FOXP2 and other genes and mutations relating to language

Despite immense complexities that have come with more study, FOXP2 has held up as a gene of interest for the evolution of language. It is not a simple "grammar gene" as the popular talk was in 1990. It is a transcription factor that turns genes on or off -- several hundred of them (Vernes et al. 2007). The action of FOXP2 is so essential in so many parts of the body that there were no changes in FOXP2 protein from chimpanzee back to the common ancestor with mouse. But there were two amino acid changes in the human line since the common ancestor with chimpanzee. Were these related to the origin of speech and language? Circumstantial evidence suggest that maybe this is so, beginning with the KE family whose hereditary speech and language disability led to the discovery of FOXP2. FOXP2 is implicated in bird song, ultrasonic vocalization of mice, and echolocation of bats (see references in Diller and Cann 2010). This evidence points to a role in vocalization, or a possible role for speech.

Using genomic evidence, we have dated the human mutations in FOXP2 to 1.8 or 1.9 million years ago (see Diller and Cann, 2009). This date would coincide with the starting point of the dramatic expansion of the human brain areas involved in speech and language processing.

The complexities of the action of FOXP2 are seen in the example of CNTNAP, which is downregulated or inhibited by FOXP2. CNTNAP is involved in cortical development and axonal function. High levels are found in language related areas. Yet in the developing human cortex, lamina with the most FOXP2 have the lowest levels of CNTNAP. So we have the complexity that although both FOXP2 and CNTNAP seem to be positively correlated with speech, they are also negatively correlated with each other.

Not all genes which cause language difficulties when mutated are relevant to the evolution of language. For example, the fragile X syndrome, caused by a mutation in the FMR-1 gene, shows language development problems in humans, but the mouse model also shows the accompanying mental retardation, tremors and seizures, along with characteristically large ears and testicles and long faces. This gene works at a very basic level for proper development of neural connections in the developing brain and does not specifically target language.

Changes in generalized brain-size genes also say little for language evolution. A human mutation in the CMAH gene about 2.7 million years ago stopped production of an enzyme that inhibits brain cell growth (Chou et al. 2002). Release of this brake on growth may have been a prerequisite for reorganizing the brain for speech and language, but it does not explain the reorganization. Likewise for genes that when disabled cause microcephaly, e.g. microcephalin and ASPM. Since microcephalic brains are language capable, these genes did not likely have any effect on language evolution.

Linguists who focus too much on design are likely to be disappointed in biological evolution, which is more like tinkering than like design. Single mutations often cause disease, disability, and dramatic disruption of systems. It usually takes many adjustments for a system to adapt positively.

5. An Evolutionary timeline for language

On the basis of evidence from neuroanatomy and genetics, we argue that the first spoken words were used at least by the time of the emergence of genus *Homo* more than 2 million years ago. The first speakers were probably not very articulate at first, and literal pointing with the index finger probably provided the first indexical arguments to provide reference for these spoken symbolic words.

Homo erectus developed a brain double the size of chimpanzee brains, and, we argue, was on the way to building up a decent language through processes of syntactic carpentry, metaphor, and grammaticalization. Those processes do not require a major break between a "protolanguage" and full language. At the beginning, *Homo erectus* was probably not very good at language, but brain evolution would enable improvement.

Tool use was also not that sophisticated at first. Hand axes flaked only on one side were adequate until after *Homo erectus* had colonized Asia and Europe.

Homo erectus also controlled fire and Wrangham (2009) argues that the improved nutrition enabled by cooking was important for neurodevelopment as well as for the major changes in the digestive tract seen in modern humans (and reflected in the rib structure of *Homo erectus).* At first, however, *Homo erectus* was probably awkward at controlling fire. The first organized hearths appear in China 800,000 years ago.

After a million and a half years of coevolution of language and the brain, by the time of Mitochondrial Eve and the first fully modern *Homo sapiens* skulls 200,000 years ago, the biological evidence indicates that we had full language capabilities, fully modern languages, and a brain capable of higher cognition.

References

Berwick, R. and Chomsky, N. (forthcoming). The Biolinguistic Program: The Current State of its Evolution and Development In A-M. Di Sciullo and C. Agüero (Eds.), *Biolinguistic Investigations.* Cambridge MA: MIT Press.

Cann, R. L. et al. (1987). Mitochondrial DNA and human evolution. *Nature* 325: 31-36.

Chou, H. H. et al. (2002). Inactivation of CMP-N-acetylneuraminic acid hydroxylase occurred prior to brain expansion during human evolution. *PNAS,* 99 (18), 11736-41.

Deacon, T. W. (2003). Universal Grammar and Semiotic Constraints. In M. H. Christiansen and S. Kirby (Eds.), *Language Evolution* (pp. 111-139). Oxford: Oxford University Press.

Diller, K. C. and Cann, R. L. (2010 forthcoming). Genetic influences on language evolution: an evaluation of the evidence. In M. Tallerman and K. Gibson (Eds.), *Handbook on Language Evolution.* New York: Oxford University Press.

Diller, K. C. and Cann, R. L. (2009). Evidence against a genetic-based revolution in language 50,000 years ago. In R. Botha and C. Knight (Eds.), *The Cradle of Language.* Oxford: Oxford University Press.

Hauser, M. D, Chomsky, N., & Fitch, W. T. (2002). The Faculty of Language: What is it, Who has it, and How did it Evolve? *Science, 298.* 1569-1579.

Klein, R. G. (1997). Biological and behavioral origins of modern humans. Lecture, 11/8/97 *http://www.accessexcellence.org/bioforum/bf02/.*

O'Grady, W. (2005). *Syntactic Carpentry: an emergentist approach to syntax.* Mahwah, NJ: Lawrence Erlbaum Associates, Publishers.

Pinker, S. & Bloom, P. (1990). Natural language and natural selection, *Behavioral and Brain Sciences, 13*, 707-784.

Wrangham, R. (2009). *Catching Fire: how cooking made us human.* New York: Basic Books.

Zhang, Q, et al. (2008). Nature Precedings: hdl:10101/npre.2008.2127.1

A NEW THEORY OF LANGUAGE AND ITS IMPLICATIONS FOR THE QUESTION OF EVOLUTION

DANIEL DOR AND EVA JABLONKA

Tel Aviv University

1. Introduction

In a series of articles (Dor and Jablonka 2000, 2001, 2004, forthcoming), we have argued that the entire process of the evolution of language was driven, from the very beginning, by the cultural evolution of language as a socially-constructed communication technology. The new technology changed human societies in such fundamental ways, that individual survival eventually came to depend (more and more) on the individual's ability to participate in the activities of language – and individuals began to be selected (behaviorally, cognitively, emotionally and, eventually, genetically) for their linguistic capacities. Based on some of the most recent developments in Evolutionary Theory (West-Eberhard 2003, Jablonka and Lamb 2005), our model provided an explicit characterization of the biological-cognitive side of the process – beginning with a new understanding of the role of innovation (and particularly social innovation) in evolutionary processes, and ending with the developmental complexities involved in the partial genetic accommodation of the capacities required for the participation in innovative social activities, such as the activity of language. The model, however, was also based on a programmatic proto-theory of language as a communication technology (Dor 1999, 2000, 2005), and because of that, it remained at the programmatic level in terms of the social evolution of language itself. In Dor (2009), the program finally matured into a full-fledged theory, which allows for the construction of an explicit hypothetical narration of the social process that brought the technology of language from its moment of invention to its current state. In our talk, then, we will begin with an overview of the theory, and then present the hypothetical narration of the process that the theory entails.

2. Language and Experience: A Theory of Language as a Social Technology

The theory of language as a communication technology, developed in Dor (2009), is based on a particular understanding of the dialectic relationship between language and the world of *private experience*. The process of experiencing is the foundation of our lives as mental creatures: We live in experience. Experiencing includes not just everything that we call feeling, thinking, understanding, seeing, hearing, imagining, wishing, and so on - but also, importantly, everything that happens in our nervous system when we act, when we move, touch, react, try, succeed and fail. The most important thing to understand about experience, then, is that it is always private. We experience on our own, within ourselves, even when we experience together. Because of that, our private experiences are always different, even when we experience the same thing, and they are always, in many ways, inaccessible to others. We are forever separated from each other by *experiential gaps*.

All the active systems of communication used by biological species, apart from language (and possibly the dancing rituals of the bees), are systems of *experiential communication*. They allow for the experience of the communicator to be directly experienced by the interlocutor, in circumstances of direct experiential contact, where the interlocutors experience together, and the experiential gap between them is momentarily reduced. Because of that, these systems are locked within the here-and-now of the communication event. We, humans, share many of these systems with the other species. We have also taken experiential communication a major step forward, with the emergence of mimesis (Donald 1991).

It is only with language, however, that human speakers can communicate experiences that cannot be directly experienced by their listeners. The functional essence of language, what makes it unique, is the fact that it allows for communication *across* the experiential gaps between speakers and their listeners: Speakers do not try to make their experience perceptibly present to the listener. The experiential strategy is abandoned in principle. Instead, speakers provide their listeners with a code, a plan, a skeletal list of the basic co-ordinates of the experience – which the listeners are then expected to use as a scaffold for experiential imagination. Language is a technology of *instructive communication*: Speakers instruct their listeners' imaginations.

The technology consists of two components - the symbolic landscape and the communication protocol. The symbolic landscape is what we usually think of as the lexicon of the language, but it is much more than just a list of words and constructions. It is a huge semantic web, a radically-simplified *model* of the world of experience. The model is a socially-constructed compromise: It reflects the entire history of negotiation and struggle, within the linguistic community, over what should be properly thought of as a normative worldview. The communication protocol is a set of socially-negotiated procedures for the process of linguistic communication. Just like the signs of the symbolic landscape, the procedures emerge from the struggle over norms – this time, the norms of communication. The two components allow speakers to channel through the socially-constructed world of the symbolic landscape skeletal descriptions of their private experiences – which the listeners then imagine into experiential interpretations.

The key to this unique technology is the fact that it requires a huge amount of collective effort to make it work. The entire functional logic of the system depends on the foundational act of experiential *mutual-identification* - by speakers and listeners - prior to actual communication. Speakers have to go through a long process in which they mutually-identify elements of their experiences of the world which are similar enough for communication, and sign them in mutually-identified ways. And they have to mutually-identify elements of their communicative experiences and zoom-in, together, on procedures that would allow the listeners to imagine reasonably accurate interpretations to the speakers' utterances.

Mutual-identification is a collective activity of a very complex type. For two individuals, A and B, to mutually-identify an element of their experience, they have to go through the following process: One of them (A) has to direct the attention of the other (B) to the relevant experience (by pointing, for example); B should realize: 'A is directing me towards this particular experience'; A and B should mutually-acknowledge the identification of the experience (by eye contact, gesture or another experiential expression); and both should realize: 'We have identified the same experience'. To the extent that they also mark the mutually-identified experience with a mutually-identified sign, they may now talk about the experience when it is not available for direct experiencing, by using the agreed sign to invoke the memory of the experience in the mind of the other.

3. The Pre-History of Language: The Invention of Mutual - Identification

This conception of language positions the collective activity of mutual-identification at the center of the question of the origin of language. Even if the apes have some of the social and cognitive pre-conditions for the activity (such as a theory of mind), they definitely do not mutually-identify. Language could thus only be invented after groups of pre-linguistic hominids invented and stabilized the activity of mutual-identification as such. We suggest that mutual-identification could only have emerged as an innovative solution to a very specific type of problem – the problem *experiential dependency*: One individual experiences something that calls for action but he or she cannot act on the basis of the experience; another individual is in a position to act, but he or she does not experience the thing that actually calls for action; and the survival of both depends on the capacity of the first to direct the second to the relevant experience. Much of what we know today about the great revolutions of *Homo erectus* – both in terms of material culture (Ambrose 2001, Wrangham 2009), and social structure, including the emergence of alloparenting (Blaffer-Hrdy 2009) – suggests that *erectus* communities could not have stabilized their innovations without solving the problem of experiential dependency – which they did by upgrading their systems of experiential communication into systems of mimesis. Mimetic communication allowed, for the first time, for systematic mutual-identification. As mimetic communication stabilized, associations emerged (and came to be mutually-identified) between directive gestures and mimetic vocalizations – associations that, as such, may not have played an important role in the lives of the communities. They only assumed their full significance when innovative communicators began to experiment with their usage for communication about experiences that lay beyond the here-and-now of the communication event. This, we claim, in line with Tomasello (2008), could only have happened in special circumstances of enhanced social trust. The associations became the first words. The first prototype of the technology of language was invented.

4. The History of Language: Three Stages of Technological Innovation

Every technology develops through a long and complex line of gradual modifications, punctuated from time to time by a technological revolution. Language is no exception. As we see it, the technology of language has gone through three stages, with two revolutions between them:

The first functioning prototype of the technology, comprising of sets of mutually-identified signs, allowed for communication of the type that the acquisition literature calls holophrastic communication. It allowed speakers to refer their listeners to a limited (but growing) set of mutually-identified experiences – using a single sign per utterance. As the invention stabilized and developed, it began to produce new patterns of interaction between its speakers; a collective worldview began to emerge; and sets of linguistic sounds began to be mutually-identified and isolated from the experiential continuum of mimetic vocalization (this was the beginning of phonetics).

At a certain moment, when the set of mutually-identified experiences reached a certain level of complexity, a new technical possibility emerged: Some experiences came to be associated with more than a single sign, and speakers began to utter the relevant signs together - one after the other. This was the revolution of *compositionality*, and it brought language into the second stage of its evolution. The expressive power of language increased dramatically; patterns of semantic structure began to emerge on the symbolic landscape; and totally new habits of discourse began to be formed. As speakers gradually increased the number of signs they uttered together, and as they did it more quickly, patterns of linearization appeared, and together with them – the first patterns of phonology.

At this point, the increasing complexity of the entire system began to produce problems of interpretation of a totally new order, and communities began to develop sets of mutually-identified norms for linguistic communication. This was the third revolution: The birth of the communication protocol. As the protocol developed, increasingly complex clusters of norms (morphological, syntactic and others) came to regulate the on-line process of experience-to-speech translation.

Throughout the entire process, individuals were selected for their ability to work with the technology. When language was already deep in the second stage of its evolution, and for many different reasons, fast speech came to be an important individual challenge. From the speech revolution, taking place within the social-linguistic environment of late *erectus* - a human species not yet specifically adapted to language - emerged *Homo sapiens*, as a new human species physiologically adapted to fast speech. It is not the case that we have language because we are a species of speakers. We are a species of speakers because we have language.

References

Ambrose H. A. (2001). Paleolithic Technology and Human Evolution. *Science* 291: 1748 -1753.

Blaffer-Hrdy, S. (2009). *Mothers and Others: The Evolutionary Origins of Mutual Understanding*. The Belknap Press of Harvard University Press.

Donald, M. (1991), *Origins of the Modern Mind: Three Stages in the Evolution of Culture and Cognition*. Cambridge, MA: Harvard University Press.

Dor, D. (1999). From Symbolic Forms to Lexical Semantics: Where Modern Linguistics and Cassirer's Philosophy Start to Converge. *Science in Context* 12, 4, 493-511.

Dor, D. (2000), From the Autonomy of Syntax to the Autonomy of Linguistic Semantics: Notes on the Correspondence between the Transparency Problem and the Relationship Problem. *Pragmatics and Cognition* 8: 325–356.

Dor, D. (2005). Towards a Semantic Account of That-Deletion in English. *Linguistics*, 43, 2, 345-382

Dor, D. (2009). *Language and Experience: A General Theory of Language as a Communication Technology*. Tel Aviv Ms.

Dor, D. and Jablonka, E. (2000), From cultural selection to genetic selection: a framework for the evolution of language. *Selection* 1-3:33-55.

Dor, D. and Jablonka, E. (2001), How Language Changed the Genes: Towards an Explicit Account of the Evolution of Language. In: Trabant, J. (ed.) *Essays on the Origin of Language*. Berlin: Mouton, pp.149-175.

Dor, D. and Jablonka, E. (2004), Culture and Genes in the Evolution of Human Language. In: Goren-Inbar N. and J.D. Speth (eds.) *Human Paleoecology in the Levantine Corridor*. Oxbow Books, pp. 105-114.

Dor, D. and Jablonka, E. (forthcoming). Plasticity and Canalization in the Evolution of Linguistic Communication: An Evolutionary-Developmental Approach. In: Larson, Richard, Viviane Deprez and Hiroko Yamakido (eds.), *The Evolution of Human Language*. Cambridge University Press.

Jablonka, E. and Lamb, M.J. (2005). *Evolution in Four Dimensions: Genetic, Epigenetic, Behavioral and Symbolic Variation in the History of Life*. MIT Press.

Tomasello, M. (2008). *Origins of Human Communication*. MIT Press.

West-Eberhard, M. J. (2003). *Developmental Plasticity and Evolution*. Oxford: Oxford University Press.

Wrangham R. (2009), *Catching Fire: How Cooking Made Us Human*. Basic books

HORIZONTAL TRANSMISSION OF CALL FEATURES IN
KILLER WHALE DIALECTS

OLGA A. FILATOVA

Department of Vertebrate Zoology, Faculty of Biology, Moscow State University,
Vorobiovy gory, 1/12, Moscow 119992, Russia

ERICH HOYT

Whale and Dolphin Conservation Society, 29A Dirleton Avenue, North Berwick, Scotland
EH39 4BE, UK

ALEXANDR M. BURDIN

Alaska Sealife Center, P.O.Box 1329, 301 Railway Ave., Seward, AK 99664, USA

1. Introduction

In humans language passes from mother to offspring by the process of vocal learning. Vocal learning is common among birds (Kroodsma & Miller, 1996), but less studied and probably rare for non-human mammals. Among mammals vocal learning was shown only for cetaceans (Caldwell & Caldwell, 1972; Richards et al., 1984; Payne & Payne, 1985; Janik & Slater, 1997), true seals (Phocidae) (Ralls et al., 1985), some bats (Jones & Ransome, 1993; Boughman, 1998). Geographic variations in acoustic repertoires typical for many terrestrial mammals are usually a result of geographic isolation and pass from generation to generation genetically, rather than by vocal learning (Conner, 1982).

The specific vocal traditions of sympatric or neighbouring groups or sub-populations of mammals are called dialects (Conner, 1982). Ford (1991) showed that killer whale groups in the Northeast Pacific have unique vocal repertoires of discrete call types and documented various levels of sharing of discrete call types between groups: certain groups shared a number of discrete call types and others had entirely different call repertoires. The basic unit of the North Pacific resident killer whale's social organization is the "matriline", which consists of a living female and several generations of her offspring (Bigg et al., 1990). One or several matrilines comprise "pod" – a group of whales that share a unique repertoire of discrete calls. Set of pods which share a number of discrete call types is called "clan".

Killer whales acquire discrete call repertoires from their mothers through the process of vocal learning, like human children which learn the language from their parents. Some observations suggest that not only vertical (from mother to offspring) vocal learning can occur in killer whales, but also horizontal (between adult animals). Ford (1991) showed that killer whales in the wild sometimes mimic the discrete calls from the dialects of other pods, and Bain (1986) described that an Icelandic killer whale in captivity started to use calls from the dialect of its pool mate from British Columbia. Deecke et al. (2000) showed that a slight changes in N4 call structure over 12-year period occurred simultaneously in two matrilines of the same pod, which suggests the existence of intra-pod horizontal transmission of vocal features. However, inter-pod horizontal call type transmission is not studied to date. In human languages horizontal transmission is a common phenomena, constantly affecting the process of language development and change. The aim of this study was to examine if similarities and differences of calls in killer whale dialects can reveal the existence of inter-pod horizontal transmission of vocal traditions in killer whales.

2. Methods

We examined the patterns of call sharing in 11 pods of resident killer whales from Avacha Gulf, Kamchatka, Russian Far East. Discrete calls of resident killer whales fall into two main categories: monophonic calls, which are used mostly for intra-group communication, and biphonic calls, which are used mostly for inter-group communication (Filatova et al., 2009). We have compared the similarity of one monophonic and one biphonic call type between killer whale pods. Monophonic K1 type represents the low-frequency squeak-like sound which is shared by all 11 pods with substantial variations between pods (fig. 1). Biphonic K5 type is higher-frequency call which is shared by all but one pod with substantial variations between pods (fig. 2). The only pod which lacks K5 type produces K6 type which is highly similar to K5 type.

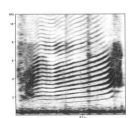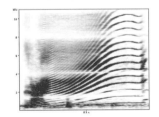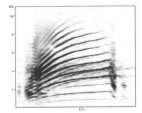

Figure 1. Examples of K1 calls from three different pods.

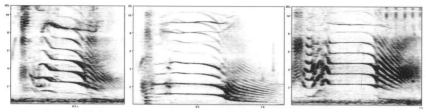

Figure 2. Examples of K5 calls from three different pods.

To examine call similarity between pods, we have measured time and frequency parameters in five K1 calls and ten K5 calls from each pod using AviSoft SASLab Pro software. In K5 calls we have measured time and sideband interval in the beginning, middle and the end of each syllable (fig. 3).

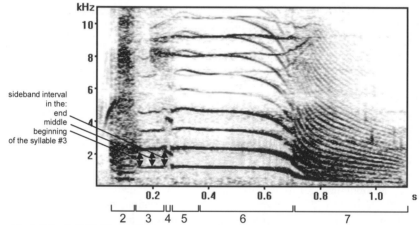

Fig. 3. K5 call divided into syllables (2-7) from which the measurements were done. Sideband interval measurements are shown for the syllable #3.

In K1 calls we have measured sideband interval in 6 regularly spaced points. We have used the absolute (sideband interval) and relative (frequency modulation between the measurements) frequency parameters as well as duration of syllables (for K5 calls only) to perform cluster analysis by the average values of K1 and K5 calls from each pods. To illustrate the patterns of call similarity, we have created dendrograms of similarity by K1 and K5 calls for all 11 pods using Euclidean distances measurement and weighted pair-group average linkage (fig. 4).

3. Results and discussion

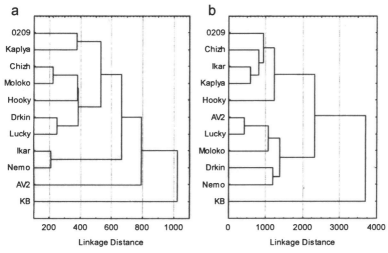

Figure 4. Dendrograms of K1 (**a**) and K5 (**b**) call type similarity for 11 pods.

The dendrograms (fig. 4) show that the call similarity between pods is not consistent for monophonic K1 and biphonic K5 types: pods that have similar K1 calls have different K5 calls and vice versa. For example, Ikar and Nemo pods have similar K1 calls but very different K5 calls, while Ikar and Kaplya pods have similar K5 calls and different K1 calls (fig. 5).

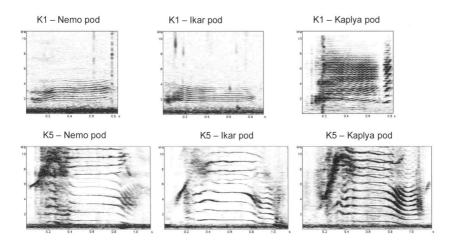

Figure 5. K1 and K5 types of Nemo, Ikar and Kaplya pods.

The classical model of killer whale dialect development suggests that pod fission and variation in discrete calls occurs gradually over several generations. According to this hypothesis, newly formed sister pods initially spend a significant amount of time together and share most of the calls of their ancestral pod. Over time, because of copying errors of calls between generations and fewer contacts between sister pods, calls change progressively and repertoires diverge. This hypothesis does not consider that killer whales can copy call features from other pods they contact with. Deecke et al. (2000) showed that changes in call structure occurred simultaneously in two matrilines of the same pod, which suggests that killer whales can copy call features from the related matrilines. In Kamchatka waters matrilines from different pods often travel together, and some matrilines associate more often with matrilines from other pods than with their own pod (Ivkovich at al. 2009). It is likely that killer whales can borrow some call features from other matrilines they usually travel with. However, to explain the different degree of divergence of K1 and K5 call types across pods, the speed of adopting call features should differ in these call types.

Alternatively, the observed call similarity can evolve if different call types change with various speed in different pods. For example, in Nemo, Ikar and Kaplya pods (fig. 5) the ancestral pod possibly had the dialect similar to Ikar pod, and after the pod division K5 call have changed in Nemo pod and K1 call – in Kaplya pod. However, it is unlikely because K1 and K5 calls appear to play the opposite roles in communication (Filatova et al., 2009), therefore the speed of change should be consistent within the call type. This scenario also contradicts the finding of Deecke et al. (2000) that that one call type was changing and another type was stable during 12 years in both studied matrilines, which suggests that the speed of call change is consistent in calls of the same type.

It is not known why different call types might change with different speed, but we can find the analogous process in human languages. Some words are easily replaced by the synonyms borrowed from other languages, but the other remain stable over the long periods (Swadesh, 1955). These "basic" words are usually the most concrete and important in everyday life. Killer whale discrete calls doesn't appear to have concrete meaning like human words (Ford, 1989), but we can suggest that the stable and changing call types should exist because of their role in killer whale communication. Killer whales mate more often between clans rather than within clans (Barrett-Lennard, 2000), which suggests that they probably estimate the relationships between pods by dialect similarity to prevent inbreeding. Copying call features between pods would reduce the effectiveness of inbreeding avoidance, so we can suggest that some call types should not be affected by horizontal transmission. Therefore, some call similarities between killer whale pods are the true markers of their relatedness, and others are the results of call copying between pods, which explains the controversial patterns of call similarity between pods. This situation is analogues to similarity of native and loan words between human languages. Further investigation of killer whale dialects can probably reveal more parallels with human languages, which will enable the comparative studies that can benefit research in both fields.

Acknowledgements

This research was supported by the Whale and Dolphin Conservation Society, Humane Society International, the Rufford Maurice Laing Foundation, and the Russian Fund for Fundamental Research, grant #08-04-00198-a.

References

Bain, D.E. (1986). Acoustic behavior of *Orcinus*: sequences, periodicity, behavioral correlates and an automated technique for call classification. In Behavioral Biology of Killer Whales (Ed. by B. C. Kirkevold and J. S. Lockard), pp. 335-371. New York: A. R. Liss.

Barrett-Lennard, L. G. (2000). Population structure and mating patterns of killer whales (*Orcinus orca*) as revealed by DNA analysis. PhD thesis. University of British Columbia, Vancouver.

Bigg, M. A., Olesiuk, P. F., Ellis, C. M., Ford, J. K. B. & Balcomb, K. C. (1990). Social organization and genealogy of resident killer whales (*Orcinus orca*) in the coastal waters of British Columbia and Washington State. Rep. Int. Whaling Comm., Spec. Issue No. 12, 383-405.

Boughman, J.W. (1998). Vocal learning by greater spear-nosed bats. Proc. R. Soc. Lond. B Biol. Sci., 265, 227-233.

Connor, D. A. (1982) Dialects versus geographic variation in mammalian vocalizations. Anim. Behav., 30, 297-298.

Caldwell, M. C. & Caldwell, D. K. (1972). Vocal mimicry in the whistle mode by an Atlantic bottlenosed dolphin. Cetology, 9, 1-8.

Deecke V.B., Ford J.K.B. & Spong P. (2000) Dialect change in resident killer whales: implications for vocal learning and cultural transmission. Anim Behav, 60, 629-638.

Filatova O.A., Fedutin I.D., Nagaylik M.M., Burdin A.M. & Hoyt E. (2009) Usage of monophonic and biphonic calls by free-ranging resident killer whales (*Orcinus orca*) in Kamchatka, Russian Far East. Acta ethol DOI 10.1007/s10211-009-0056-7

Ford, J.K.B. (1989). Acoustic behavior of resident killer whales *(Orcinus orca)* off Vancouver Island, British Columbia. Can. J. Zool., 67, 727-745.

Ford, J.K.B. (1991). Vocal traditions among resident killer whales (*Orcinus orca*) in coastal waters of British Columbia. Can. J. Zool., 69, 1454-1483.

Ivkovich, T.V., Filatova O.A., Burdin A.M., Sato H. & Hoyt E. (2009) The social organization of resident-type killer whales (*Orcinus orca*) in Avacha Gulf, Northwest Pacific, as revealed through association patterns and acoustic similarity. Mamm. Biol., doi:10.1016/j.mambio.2009.03.006

Janik, V.M. & Slater, P.J.B. (1997). Vocal learning in mammals. Advances in the Study of Behavior, 26, 59-99.

Jones, G. & Ransome, R. D. (1993). Echolocation calls of bats are influenced by maternal effects and change over a lifetime. Proc. R. Soc. Lond. B Biol. Sci., 252, 125-128.

Kroodsma, D.E. & Miller, E.H. (1996). Ecology and evolution of acoustic communication in birds. New-York: Cornell Univ. Press.

Payne, K. & Payne, R. (1985). Large scale changes over 19 years in songs of humpback whales in Bermuda. Z. Tierpsychol., 68, 89-114.

Ralls, K., Fiorelli, P. & Gish, S. (1985). Vocalizations and vocal mimicry in captive harbor seals, *Phoca vitulina*. Can. J. Zool., 63, 1050-1056.

Richards, D. G., Wolz, J. P. & Herman, L. M. (1984). Vocal mimicry of computer-generated sounds and vocal labeling of objects by a bottlenosed dolphin, *Tursiops truncatus*. J. Comp. Psychol., 98, 10-28.

Swadesh, M. (1955) Towards greater accuracy in lexico-statistic dating. International Journal of American linguistics, 18, 121–137.

INFORMATION AND INFLUENCE IN ANIMAL COMMUNICATION

JULIA FISCHER

Cognitive Ethology Laboratory, German Primate Center,
Kellnerweg 4, 37077 Göttingen, Germany

KURT HAMMERSCHMIDT

Cognitive Ethology Laboratory, German Primate Center,
Kellnerweg 4, 37077 Göttingen, Germany

There is currently considerable disagreement about the value of different theoretical accounts that have been employed to explain the evolution of communication. In this paper, we review some of the core tenets of the 'adaptationist' and the 'informational' account. We argue that the former has its strength mainly in explaining the evolution of signals and the maintenance of honest signaling, while the latter is indispensible for understanding the cognitive mechanisms underpinning signal usage, structure, and comprehension. Importantly, the informational account that incorporates linguistic concepts is necessary prerequisite to identify which design features of language are shared with nonhuman primates or other animals, and which ones constitute derived traits specific for the human lineage.

1. Background

1.1. *A conceptual conundrum*

Explaining the evolution of language is a challenge – not only because of the scarce data available for the early stages in the human lineage. Explaining the evolution of communication more generally also constitutes a major evolutionary puzzle, although certainly not because a lack of empirical evidence. Rather, we are faced with a conceptual conundrum as previous attempts to explain the evolution of communication have made use of different theoretical approaches that provide explanations at different levels. This has led to both confusion and sometimes unproductive friction, which also affects the research on animal communication that searches to explain the evolution of language from a comparative perspective. In this paper, we will present and discuss some recent contributions to the debate. In particular, we will examine evolutionary accounts that generally focus on explaining signal evolution and contrast them to informational accounts that have been adopted to explain the processing of signals. The informational account has recently come under attack, and it has been argued that the concept of information is useful as a by-product as best (Scott-Phillips, 2008), or not at all (Rendall, Owren, & Ryan, 2009). Instead, the argument goes, animal communication can be understood best in terms of the influence that signals putatively have on recipients. We will argue in favor of an integrative account that acknowledges the strengths but also shortcomings of both explanatory approaches.

2. Explaining communication

2.1. *The adaptationist account*

The 'adaptationist' account seeks to explain the evolution of signaling behavior and the maintenance of honest signaling. Game theoretical models that take into account the costs and benefits associated with signaling are employed to identify evolutionary stable strategies. Such models have shown that the distribution of interest is crucial for understanding the conditions under which honest signaling can arise. Specifically, when interests diverge, signaling must be costly to maintain honesty. When interests overlap, or when subjects interact repeatedly, cheap signaling may evolve (for an excellent introduction see Searcy & Nowicki, 2005).

Within this framework, there is a strong focus on distinguishing signals from other forms of behavior. One classic definition was provided by Maynard Smith and Harper who proposed that signals can be defined as "any act or structure which alters the behaviour of other organisms, which evolved because of that effect, and which is effective because the receiver's response has also evolved" (Maynard Smith & Harper, 2003, p. 3). Scott-Phillips (2008) provided an extension of that definition and described signals as "any act or structure that (i) affects the behaviour of other organisms; (ii) evolved because of those effects; and (iii) which is effective because the effect (the response) has evolved *to be affected by the act or structure*" (p. 388, italics ours). Within this framework, signals are distinguished from cues and coercion on the presence or absence of specific evolution on the signaler's and recipient's side, respectively (Table 1).

Table 1. Distinguishing between signals, cues and coercion within the adaptationist approach to explain the evolution of signaling behavior. Adapted from Scott-Phillips 2008.

	Signaller's behaviour evolved for purpose of affecting receiver?	Receiver's response evolved to be affected by signaller's behaviour?
Signals	+	+
Cue	–	+
Coercion	+	–

Notably, this account implicitly assumes that the interests of signaler and receiver overlap, otherwise there would be no reason to assume that the receiver's response evolved "to be affected"[1]. According to this view, the term 'signal' would be reserved for the narrow range of communicative interactions where interests overlap. Whenever interests diverge, signals would need to be defined as coercion. This becomes particularly curious when interests change over time, such as during parent-offspring conflict. In such cases, signaling of need will eventually turn into coercion, although the structure of the behavior (e.g. noisy screams) does not vary.

The advantage the above cited distinction between signals and coercion is that it stresses the importance of considering the distribution of interests when seeking to explain the evolution of communicative 'acts or structures' (Searcy & Nowicki, 2005). Otherwise, it seems more plausible to reserve the term 'coercion' for behaviors other than communicative acts or structures, which are used to manipulate another subject's behavior (e.g. push, pull, displace etc.). It also hampers the discourse about communication because each time, one needs to specify whether one talks about signals or coercion. In the following, we will therefore adopt a broader definition and use the term 'signal' for all acts or structures that have evolved for the purpose of communicating, i.e. altering the recipient's behavior – irrespective of whether or not the recipient's behavior has also evolved for that purpose.

Despite its strengths, there are also some major weaknesses with the adaptationist approach as advanced by Scott-Phillips. First and foremost, it does

---

[1] Scott-Phillips adapted the above scheme from Diggle and colleagues (Diggle, Gardner, West, & Griffin, 2007), but introduced some significant changes. In particular, Diggle et al. distinguished whether the act or structure "evolved owing to the effect *on the sender*" [italics mine], and whether it "benefits the receiver to respond".

not justice to the recipient's contribution to the equation. Tellingly, a wording such as "receiver's response evolved *to be affected* by signaller's behavior" [italics mine] carries the connotation that the receiver is a passive receptacle, unable to evolve its own strategies. It has long been known that this is not the case (Krebs, Dawkins, & Davies, 1984). Moreover, it does in fact very little to explain signal design.

2.2. The informational account

A large body of research in animal communication is implicitly or explicitly based on the assumption that communication can be characterized as the transfer of information from the signaler to the recipient. A caricature version of this conception, according to which the sender wraps information into little packages which are then sent to the recipient for further processing, has recently come under fierce attack (Rendall, et al., 2009). We believe that a serious informational account is indispensible when trying to understand the cognitive processes underlying signal production, usage, and responses to signals. That is, while an adaptationist account is particularly useful for explaining the function of signals and their evolution, the informational account is essential for describing the proximate mechanisms that subserve communicative behavior.

Information theory conceives information as a reduction of uncertainty (Shannon & Weaver, 1949). For those with an interest in animal cognition, this conception is useful because it connects communication to learning theory, which offers tools to analyze and predict how animals form associations between stimuli, stimuli and responses, as well as behaviors and outcomes of these behaviors (Rescorla, 1988). From a cognitive point of view, two questions are of particular interest: Firstly, how much 'executive control' animals have over the use and structure of their signals? Secondly, how do animals use signals (or cues, for that matter) to predict subsequent behaviors and upcoming events? In addition, it may be noted that all sensory research rests on the concept of information, when it seeks to explain how physical properties of the environment are coded, i.e. transduced by sensory structures into receptor and action potentials, respectively.

Information theory is agnostic with respect to 'meaning'. In animal communication, 'meaning' is generated when the recipient has learned that the occurrence of signal A reliably predicts event B. In colloquial terms, signal A has the potential to provide the information that B is imminent. Whether or not a signal reduces uncertainty information can only be determined from the recipient's perspective and depends on the context of occurrence, previous experience, preceding signals and so forth. Notably, from the recipient's perspective, any kind of behavior can be informative. In addition, insights from information theory stressed the importance of potential changes to the signal during transmission, and highlighted the selective pressure that different habitats may have on signal design. Moreover, it has been shown that animals respond adaptively to changes in acoustic signals that can be used to gauge signaler distance, such as effects due to reverberation (Naguib, 1995). In this sense, information theory also had a major impact on the way we relate signaling behavior to the environment in which it occurs.

3. Effects on receivers

3.1. *Physiological responses or cognitive creatures?*

It has been argued that studies of (nonhuman primate) acoustic communication should consider the influence that specific acoustic properties have on broadly conserved sensory and affective systems in listeners (Owren & Rendall, 2001; Rendall, et al., 2009). It is certainly true that sharp onsets may elicit startle responses. And likewise, it seems plausible that most nonhuman primates would respond aversively to loud and noisy screams. However, this view fails to capture many of the complexities of animal communication. Firstly, the diversity of alarm calls in different species, such as growls, barks, twitters and hoots, rejects a simplistic visceral explanation. Furthermore, nonhuman primates quickly learn to pay attention to the alarm calls of other species, such as the whistles and snorts of antelope, the calls of birds, or the growls of leopards. Even more strikingly, animals may respond to the absence of a signal, such as in the 'watchman's song' found in meerkats, where sentinels on guard regularly emit soft sounds. If they cede vocalizing, this signals the imminence of danger to their conspecifics (Manser, 1999). Clearly, such a behavior cannot be reduced to a simple physiological response. Secondly, calls with similar acoustic features can elicit different responses. For instance, baboon loud calls grade from more tonal into more noisy barks. While young infants generally fail to respond to either type, they proceed through a stage where they attend to both versions. From the age of 6 months on, they respond strongly to harsh barks while they have learned to ignore clear barks – unless the clear barks are uttered by their mother. Surely, physiological responses alone are not sufficient explain this differentiated development. Third, a number of studies have shown that monkeys may sort calls with different acoustic features into the same category. For instance, after hearing a Diana monkey's alarm call given in response to a leopard, they fail to respond to the playback of a leopard's growl (Zuberbühler, Cheney, & Seyfarth, 1999). In sum, we believe that an account that solely focuses on the influence of signals on largely hard wired physiological responses fails to explain much of communication, and certainly largely everything that is interesting from a cognitive point of view.

4. Nonhuman primate communication and the evolution of language

Although we strongly argue in favor of the informational account, this does not mean that we attribute linguistic capacities to the animals. Studies of the ontogeny of vocal production as well as the neurobiological foundations of vocal control in nonhuman primates suggest that the structure of primate vocalizations is largely innate. Unlike in most song-birds, exposure to species-specific calls is not a prerequisite for the proper development of the vocal repertoire. Nevertheless, developmental modifications occur. These can be mainly related to growth in body size, fluctuations in hormone levels, and arousal (reviewed in Hammerschmidt & Fischer, 2008). In terms of usage, current evidence suggests that, in nonhuman primates, the anterior cingulate cortex controls the initiation of vocalizations, facilitating voluntary control over call emission and onset. The periaqueductal grey (PAG) serves as a relay station (Jürgens, 2002). Because of the lack of voluntary control, nonhuman primates are unable to use their calls in a symbolic fashion. Although probabilistic combinations of calls do occur (Arnold & Zuberbühler, 2006), these do not appear to be driven by sets of rules applied by the sender. In contrast, learning plays an important role in the development of the comprehension of and the appropriate responses to calls. Listeners are able to attribute 'meaning' to single calls as well as to specific call combinations (J. Fischer, in press). In sum, nonhuman primate communication is characterized by a strong asymmetry in production and perception: whereas production is relatively fixed, perception is much more open-ended, and primates seem to be able to acquire an almost infinite number of sound-meaning associations. Yet, animals have no intention to transmit information, neither in terms of altering the mental state of others by the use of signals (Fischer, 2008; Seyfarth & Cheney, 2003). This notion fits with the view that nonhuman primates have no fully blown Theory of Mind (Premack & Woodruff, 1978).

Despite the fact that the structure of primate vocalizations appears fixed from birth, they nevertheless vary reliably with a number of signaler attributes such as size, age, sex, hormonal levels, and motivational state. Specific relations between motivational state and certain contextual situations allow listeners to use signals as predictors of upcoming events. Nonhuman primate communication functions efficiently with regard to social and ecological affordances, yet it is fundamentally distinct from human speech where members of a linguistic community agree on the referential content of utterances by convention, and where syntactical rules provide a means to generate infinite meaning.

5. Conclusion

To conclude, we believe that the adaptationist account is useful to understand the ultimate aspects of signaling behavior. It is important, however, to keep the recipients' interests in mind – these only rarely correspond to the signalers' goals. We argue that the informational account is indispensable to elucidate the cognitive underpinnings of communicative behavior. In conjunction with linguistic approaches, it provides a highly productive framework to study the evolution of language from a comparative perspective. Only conceptions that incorporate both accounts (Grafen, 1990) can address the complexities of the co-evolution of signaler and recipient.

Acknowledgements

We thank Robert Seyfarth for comments, and Dorothy Cheney, Klaus Zuberbühler, Bill Searcy, Tabitha Price, Urs Kalbitzer and Matthis Drolet for inspiration and discussion.

References

Arnold, K., & Zuberbühler, K. (2006). The alarm-calling system of adult male putty-nosed monkeys, Cercopithecus nictitans martini. *Animal Behaviour, 72*, 643-653.

Diggle, S. P., Gardner, A., West, S. A., & Griffin, A. S. (2007). Evolutionary theory of bacterial quorum sensing: when is a signal not a signal? *Philosophical Transactions of the Royal Society B-Biological Sciences, 362*(1483), 1241-1249.

Fischer, J. (2008). Transmission of acquired information in nonhuman primates. In J. H. Byrne (Ed.), *Learning and memory: A comprehensive reference* (pp. 299-313). Oxford: Elsevier.

Fischer, J. (in press). Nothing to talk about? On the linguistic abilities of nonhuman primates (and some other animal species). In U. Frey, C. Störmer & K. Willführ (Eds.), *Homo Novus - A Human Without Illusions*. New York: Springer.

Grafen, A. (1990). Biological signals as handicaps. *Journal of Theoretical Biology, 144*(4), 517-546.

Hammerschmidt, K., & Fischer, J. (2008). Constraints in primate vocal production. In U. Griebel & K. Oller (Eds.), *The evolution of communicative creativity: From fixed signals to contextual flexibility* (pp. 93-119). Cambridge. MA: The MIT Press.

Jürgens, U. (2002). Neural pathways underlying vocal control. *Neuroscience and Biobehavioral Reviews, 26*(2), 235-258.

Krebs, J. R., Dawkins, R., & Davies, N. B. (1984). Animal signals: Mind reading and manipulation *Behavioural ecology* (pp. 380-402). London: Blackwell.

Manser, M. B. (1999). Response of foraging group members to sentinel calls in suricates, Suricata suricatta. *Proceedings of the Royal Society of London Series B-Biological Sciences, 266*(1423), 1013-1019.

Maynard Smith, J., & Harper, D. (2003). *Animal Signals*: Oxford University Press.

Naguib, M. (1995). Auditory distance assessment of singing conspecifics in Carolina wrens: The role of reverberation and frequency-dependent attenuation. *Animal Behaviour, 50*, 1297-1307.

Owren, M. J., & Rendall, D. (2001). Sound on the rebound: Returning signal form and function to the forefront in understanding nonhuman primate vocal signaling. *Evolutionary Anthropology, 10*, 58-71.

Premack, D., & Woodruff, G. (1978). Does the chimpanzee have a Theory of Mind? *Behavioral and Brain Sciences, 1*(4), 515-526.

Rendall, D., Owren, M. J., & Ryan, M. J. (2009). What do animal signals mean? *Animal Behaviour, 78*(2), 233-240.

Rescorla, R. A. (1988). Behavioral studies of pavlovian conditioning. *Annual Review of Neuroscience, 11*, 329-352.

Scott-Phillips, T. C. (2008). Defining biological communication. *Journal of Evolutionary Biology, 21*(2), 387-395.

Searcy, W. A., & Nowicki, S. (2005). *The Evolution of Animal Communication*. Princeton: Princeton University Press.

Seyfarth, R. M., & Cheney, D. L. (2003). Signalers and receivers in animal communication. *Annual Review of Psychology, 54*, 145-173.

Shannon, C. E., & Weaver, W. (1949). *The Mathematical Theory of Communication*. Urbana, Illinois.

Zuberbühler, K., Cheney, D. L., & Seyfarth, R. M. (1999). Conceptual semantics in a nonhuman primate. *Journal of Comparative Psychology, 113*(1), 33-42.

A MOLECULAR GENETIC FRAMEWORK FOR TESTING HYPOTHESES ABOUT LANGUAGE EVOLUTION

W TECUMSEH FITCH

Department of Cognitive Biology, Faculty of Life Sciences, University of Vienna, Vienna Austria

MICHAEL A ARBIB

University of Southern California, Los Angeles, USA

MERLIN DONALD

Queen's University, Ontario, Canada

Because language doesn't fossilize, it is difficult to unambiguously time the evolutionary events leading to language in the human lineage using traditional paleontological data. Furthermore, techniques from historical linguistics are generally seen to have an insufficient time depth to tell us anything about the nature of pre-modern-human language. Thus hypotheses about early stages of language evolution have often been seen as untestable "fairy tales". However, the discovery of human-unique alleles, associated with different aspects of language, offers a way out of this impasse. If an allele has been subjected to powerful selection, reaching or nearing fixation, statistical techniques allow us to approximately date the timing of the selective sweep. This technique has been employed to date the selective sweep associated with FOXP2, our current best example of a gene associated with spoken language. Although the dates themselves are subject to considerable error, a series of different dates, for different language-associated genes, provides a powerful means of testing evolutionary models of language if they are explicit and span the complete time period between our separation from chimpanzees to the present. We illustrate the potential of this approach by deriving explicit timing predictions from four contrasting models of "protolanguage." For example, models of musical protolanguage suggest that vocal control came early, while gestural protolanguage sees speech as a late addition. Donald's mimetic protolanguage argues that these should appear at the same time, and further suggests that this was associated with *Homo erectus*. Although there are too few language-associated genes currently known to resolve the issue now, recent progress in the genetic basis for dyslexia and autism offers considerable hope that a suite of such genes will soon be available, and we offer this theoretical framework both in anticipation of this time, and to spur those developing hypotheses of language evolution to make them explicit enough to be integrated within such a hypothesis-testing framework.

1. Introduction

1.1. *Genes and Language*

Although the general idea that there is a human-specific genetic basis for language is an old one (Lenneberg, 1967), the ongoing genomic revolution offers exciting new prospects in understanding the genetic basis of human cognition generally, and language in particular (Ramus, 2006). In particular we are on the brink of discovering many genes that play important roles in various aspects of language, with many well-characterized candidate genes already identified. It is already clear that genes specifically "for" language alone are unlikely: we can rather expect a motley crew of rather general-purpose genes, such as transcription factors or genes involved in neuronal migration and circuit building, that have been shaped in the last six million years of human evolution to play roles in the various neural circuits that underlie language (Ramus and Fisher, 2009). We expect many, if not all, of the genes in language to be pleiotropic (playing a role in multiple aspects of organismic form and function); we further expect homologs of most "language" genes to be found in non-linguistic animals. We will henceforth use the shorthand LRG for such language-related genes, making no assumptions of a single function, or of a simple mapping between genes and adult cognition. But for those willing to embrace the inevitable complexity of the mapping between the language-related genotype and the human linguistic phenotype, the payoffs are likely to be considerable. Modern molecular biological tools promise to rival, or surpass those of contemporary neuroscience in their power to illuminate questions of human-specific cognition.

1.2. *FoxP2 as the first of many language-related genes*

The first clear example that we have of a language-related gene comes from the transcription factor FoxP2, which plays a role in speech-related oral-motor control (Vargha-Khadem *et al.*, 2005; Fisher and Marcus, 2006). The search for this gene started with KE, a large family in London, and involved both decades of hard work and a fair amount of luck (Vargha-Khadem *et al.*, 1995; Lai *et al.*, 2001). But most important for our argument is what happened, quite quickly, once this LRG was discovered and the full power of molecular biological techniques were brought to bear. As soon as the gene was identified, it was recognized as a new "forkhead box" gene, a large family of transcription factors of ancient provenance. A homolog of Foxp2 was found in mice and birds. The gene was then sequenced in multiple human populations and in nonhuman primates. All non-clinical humans were found to bear a single allele of FOXP2, which varies from that found in other apes, including chimpanzees (Enard *et al.*, 2002). This lack of variance in humans shows that the variant allele was subjected to a "selective sweep" in which alternative Foxp2 alleles were out-competed and lost, presumably due to some selective advantage conferred by the novel allele. Second, it has been possible to both knock-out the FoxP2 gene in mice, and to insert the human FoxP2 allele into a genetically-engineered mutant mouse (Shu *et al.*, 2005; Groszer *et al.*, 2008; Enard *et al.*, 2009). The latter studies show relatively subtle effects on innate mouse ultrasound vocalizations, and potentially more interesting effects on neuronal morphology that are expected to expect the cortico-striatal circuits involved in speech motor control. Third, and ultimately most significant for our understanding of language evolution, it was possible to use variance in the regions flanking this conserved allele to place a rough date on when this selective sweep occurred. Estimates from the original paper dated the sweep as happening 0-120,000 years ago (90% confidence intervals); to this date must be added the 10K-100K years that the human population has been expanding, to give an outer bound of about 220K years ago for the selective sweep (Enard *et al.*, 2002): which is to say very late in the six million years or so since our divergence from our last common ancestor (LCA) with chimpanzees. .

Several caveats are in order: FoxP2 is not solely a "language gene" or even solely neural: it is expressed in lungs and esophagus and is necessary for their proper development (Shu *et al.*, 2007). Furthermore, the KE family mutation is NOT a reversion to the ancestral state found in chimpanzees: it is novel variant which essentially knocks-out normal functioning. Finally, the new human variant of FoxP2, alone, is certainly not enough to give humans enhanced vocal control. Rather FoxP2 is part of a complex regulatory network, whose working are only beginning to be studied and understood, and comparative work on mammals and birds will play a key role in this research programme (Wada *et al.*, 2006) -- genes alone are not enough.

1.3. *Genetic Timing of Events in our Evolutionary Past*

Timing estimates of the FoxP2 selective sweep are only approximate. When the FoxP2 allele was recovered from Neanderthal bones (Krause *et al.*, 2007), it was found to share the same variant base pairs as modern *Homo sapiens*. Since Neanderthals and humans diverged some 300K-500K years ago, this came as a surprise, and its significance remains debated (cf. Coop *et al.*,

2008). Although either contamination of the Neanderthal bones by modern humans, or some limited hybridization between humans and Neanderthals, cannot be definitively ruled out at present, recent investigations suggest that the gene may in fact have been selected to two selective sweeps, and that the two amino acids that have been the focus of most discussion may not be the only focus of selection (Ptak *et al.*, 2009). Thus, estimated dates for selective sweeps will only be approximate at best, and single genes will not alone reveal our evolutionary history. Nonetheless, as more LRGs are identified, we can expect the *sequence* of selective sweeps to be quite informative, even if error bars remain quite broad. This offers considerable hope to begin testing hypotheses developed about human language evolution. In order for this potential to be fulfilled, an explicit theoretical framework for testing evolutionary hypotheses is required, one that allows us to identify and compare contrasting predictions made by multiple different models of language evolution.

2. Models of Language Evolution: Many Flavors of "Protolanguage"

Consideration of a substantial number of current hypotheses about the evolution of language reveals certain commonalities. Virtually all modern hypotheses involve some intermediate stage of hominin evolution, a system that provided a necessary evolutionary stepping-stone language but was not yet fully linguistic. Three well-known examples are:

1. **Gestural Protolanguage**: Early hominins communicated using a meaningful, syntactically-complex visual-manual gestural system before the evolution of speech (Condillac, 1747; Hewes, 1973).

2. **Musical Protolanguage**: Early hominins possessed a complex, learned vocally-based communication system, more similar to song than to language, and this system predated both propositional meaning and complex syntax (Darwin, 1871; Mithen, 2005)

3. **Lexical Protolanguage**: Early hominins used a simple, propositionally-meaningful spoken system, involving separate meaningful words but no complex syntax (Bickerton, 1990; Jackendoff, 1999)

Each of these models shares a hypothetical stage (or stages) of hominid evolution in which a system sharing some but not all traits characterizing modern human language existed, one or more hypothetical "protolanguages". Each of these models have their advantages and disadvantages (cf. Fitch, 2005; 2010), all share the core feature that they break down language into several components, and hypothesize that one of these components evolved before the others and was a core feature of protolanguage. A necessary component of any such model of protolanguage, then, is that it suggests an acquisition order, in phylogenetic time, of different components present in modern human language.

3. Explicit Predictions of Four Models of Protolanguage

Unfortunately, the models just sketched above are not complete: though each focuses on some aspect of the modern human language faculty, they do not attempt to cover all of the changes that have occurred since our LCA with chimpanzees (as reconstructed based on humans and living apes). We will now explore the predictions that follow from four models of human language evolution that paint a more complete picture.

Bickerton's lexical protolanguage (Bickerton, 1990) presents a rather simple and intuitive ordering of language components. He assumes that vocal control and meaningful words composed the first level of protolanguage, with some combinations of words occurring but no complex syntax (agreement, phrase structure, anaphora, etc). Thus, by this model, vocal control (speech) would have led the way, with basic propositional semantics and a propensity to share information close behind. Complex syntax was last on the scene.

Darwin's musical protolanguage hypothesis, which suggests a stage in which music-like song preceded propositional meaning, makes the clear prediction that laryngeal control, adequate for song, preceded semantics (Darwin, 1871). As elaborated by Fitch, this model splits syntax into a simpler phrasal component (with combinatoriality and hierarchy) which should have come quite early (as part of song) and both propositional meaning and "complex syntax," as described above, coming very late.

Donald's (1991) model of "mimetic protolanguage" is quite similar to Darwin's, except that the capacity for song would have been just one component of a broader, multi-modal "mimetic" capacity. Although the timing predictions of this model are similar to Darwin's, the capacities themselves should be different: the model suggests that imitation in all domains (vocal, movement, artistic) should be closely linked at the mechanistic and genetic levels.

Finally, **Arbib's** (2005) model of gestural protolanguage, more nuanced than the ones mentioned above, suggests a long period of interaction between gestural imitation and vocal imitation, but in general predicts gestural and semantic capacities preceding vocal imitative capacities. Syntax, deployed in gestural protolanguage, would already be well-developed before any complex vocal language came on the scene. These predictions are assembled in Table 1.

Table 1. Predicted order of acquisition of language-related traits.

	Vocal Learning	Propositional Semantics	Complex Syntax
Musical	first	last	late
Lexical	first	middle	last
Mimetic	early	late	late
Gestural	middle	first	late

4. Discussion: Future Candidate Genes

Many more LRGs need to be identified and understood for the approach we have outlined here to be viable. Fortunately, recent work on the genetic basis for **developmental dyslexia** (hereafter "dyslexia") and autism offer considerable grounds for optimism in this regard. We focus here on dyslexia, since the genetic bases for this relatively common cognitive disorder have been the focus of impressive progress recently (Galaburda *et al.*, 2006). Dyslexia is defined as significant impairment of reading ability in the face of overtly normal verbal and cognitive skills and educational opportunity. Nonetheless, considerable research shows that many dyslexics show subtle abnormalities in phonological processing, suggesting that genes in which a disruption of expression can lead to dyslexia may normally play a role in speech production and/or perception and phonology more generally. Thus these candidate genes provide a promising source of future LRGs. Four well-established candidate genes are listed in Table 2, following (Galaburda *et al.*, 2006; Paracchini *et al.*, 2007)

Table 2. Candidate Genes for Developmental Dyslexia.

Gene name	Function	Gene Family	Chromosal Location
ROBO1	Axon guidance across commisures	SLIT-protein receptor	3p
DCDC2	Neural/axonal migration	DCx	6p
KIAA0319	Cell-surface molecule	??	6p
DYX1C1	Neural migration	Nuclear protein, brain	15q

All of these genes were identified because variation in the non-coding portions of the gene were linked, in different studies, to a dyslexic phenotype. Ongoing research is focused on determining what roles these genes play *in vivo*, a research programme typically focused on rodent models in which reading is obviously impossible. Obviously, the shorthand term "dyslexia genes" would be very misleading here: all of these genes play a role in normal neural development, and the human variants probably affect gene expression patterns rather than protein identity. Nonetheless, when expression patterns of these genes are affected experimentally in rats, defects in neural structure results that are phenomenologically-similar to defects identified in some dyslexic human brains. It is already clear from this research that any simple-minded one-to-one relationship between such genes and a complex, culturally-embedded phenotype like dyslexia will be insufficient, and that a sophisticated, computationally-based model of the function of various neural circuits involved in phonology will be required to make sense of the role these genes play in brain development (Poeppel and Embick, 2005; Ramus, 2006). Fortunately, this research is progressing at a rapid pace.

A final set of candidate genes comes from recent breakthroughs in understanding genetic predisposing factors for autism. Recent work has uncovered several candidate genes associated with susceptibility to autism, but has also underscored the complexity and heterogeneity of this phenotype. This work suggests that, as for the candidate genes involved in dyslexia, patterns of gene expression (in this case mediated by gene copy-number variation) may be critical. Again, an embracing of a complex set of interacting neural networks will be required to make sense of this system. Autism is often thought of as a specifically "social" disorder, with the key deficit being an ability or proclivity to utilize "theory of mind" (Baron-Cohen, 1995). However, autism is also typically associated with language disorders (Abrahams and Geschwind, 2008). Since theory of mind is itself more highly developed in humans than in other primates, this is another human-specific trait, associated with language, that must have evolved since our separation with chimpanzees. By hypothesis, these candidate LRGs would play a role in social, communicative aspects of language, and thus be more tied to propositional semantics than to (say) phonology or vocal imitation. Thus novel alleles of such genes would be predicted as latecomers by the musical protolanguage hypothesis, but early on the scene by lexical protolanguage models. Again, such predictions will need to be refined as our understanding of the actual roles of these genes develops, but these candidates round out the considerable promise of this molecular approach.

References

Abrahams, B. S., and Geschwind, D. H. (2008). "Advances in autism genetics: on the threshold of a new neurobiology," Nature Reviews Genetics 9, 341-355.
Arbib, M. A. (2005). "From monkey-like action recognition to human language: An evolutionary framework for neurolinguistics," Behavioral and Brain Sciences 28, 105–167.
Baron-Cohen, S. (1995). Mindblindness (MIT Press, Cambridge, Mass.).

144

Bickerton, D. (1990). *Language and Species* (Chicago University Press, Chicago, IL).

Condillac, É. B. d. (1971 (1747)). *Essai sur l'origine des connaissances humaines* (Scholar's Facsimiles and Reprints, Gainesville, FL).

Coop, G., Bullaughey, K., Luca, F., and Przeworski, M. (2008). "The Timing of Selection at the Human FOXP2 Gene," Molecular Biology and Evolution 25, 1257-1259.

Darwin, C. (1871). *The Descent of Man and Selection in Relation to Sex* (John Murray, London).

Donald, M. (1991). *Origins of the Modern Mind* (Harvard University Press, Cambridge, Massachusetts).

Enard, W., Gehre, S., Hammerschmidt, K., et al (2009). "A humanized version of Foxp2 affects cortico-basal ganglia circuits in mice," Cell 137, 961-971.

Enard, W., Przeworski, M., et al. (2002). "Molecular evolution of FOXP2, a gene involved in speech and language," Nature 418, 869-872.

Fisher, S. E., and Marcus, G. (2006). "The eloquent ape: genes, brains and the evolution of language," Nature Reviews Genetics 7, 9-20.

Fitch, W. T. (2005). "The evolution of language: A comparative review," Biol Philos. 20, 193-230.

Fitch, W. T. (2010). *The Evolution of Language* (Cambridge University Press, Cambridge).

Galaburda, A. M., LoTurco, J., Ramus, F., Fitch, R. H., and Rosen, G. D. (2006). "From genes to behavior in developmental dyslexia," Nature Neuroscience 9, 1213-1217.

Groszer, M., Keays, D. A., et al (2008). "Impaired Synaptic Plasticity and Motor Learning in Mice with a Point Mutation Implicated in Human Speech Deficits " Curr. Biol. 18, 354-362.

Hewes, G. W. (1973). "Primate communication and the gestural origin of language," Current Anthropology 14, 5-24.

Jackendoff, R. (1999). "Possible stages in the evolution of the language capacity," Trends Cog. Sci. 3, 272-279.

Krause, J., Lalueza-Fox, C., et al. (2007). "The derived FOXP2 variant of modern humans was shared with Neandertals," Curr Biol 17, 1908-1912.

Lai, C. S. L., Fisher, S. E., Hurst, J. A., Vargha-Khadem, F., & Monaco, A. P. (2001). "A forkhead-domain gene is mutated in a severe speech and language disorder," Nature 413, 519-523.

Lenneberg, E. H. (1967). *Biological Foundations of Language* (Wiley, New York, NY).

Mithen, S. (2005). *The Singing Neanderthals: The Origins of Music, Language, Mind, and Body* (Weidenfeld & Nicolson, London).

Paracchini, S., Scerri, T., and Monaco, A. P. (2007). "The genetic lexicon of dyslexia," Annual Review of Genomics and Human Genetics 8, 57-79.

Poeppel, D., and Embick, D. (2005). "Defining the relation between linguistics and neuroscience," in *Twenty-First Century Psycholinguistics: Four Cornerstones*, edited by A. Cutler (Lawrence Erlbaum, London), pp. 103-120.

Ptak, S. E., Enard, W., Wiebe, V., Hellmann, I., Krause, J., Lachmann, M., and Pääbo, S. (2009). "Linkage Disequilibrium Extends Across Putative Selected Sites in FOXP2," Molecular Biology and Evolution 26, 2181-2184.

Ramus, F. (2006). "Genes, brain, & cognition: A roadmap for the cognitive scientist," Cognition 101, 247-269.

Ramus, F., and Fisher, S. E. (2009). "Genetics of language," in *The Cognitive Neurosciences IV*, edited by M. S. Gazzaniga (MIT Press, Cambridge, MA), pp.??-872.

Shu, W., Cho, J. Y., et al (2005). "Altered ultrasonic vocalization in mice with a disruption in the *Foxp2* gene," Proceedings of the National Academy of Sciences, USA 102, 9643-9648.

Shu, W., Lu, M. M.,et al. (2007). "Foxp2 and Foxp1 cooperatively regulate lung and esophagus development," Development 134, 1991--2000.

Vargha-Khadem, F., Gadian, D. G., Copp, A., and Mishkin, M. (2005). "FOXP2 and the neuroanatomy of speech and language," Nature Reviews Neuroscience 6, 131-138.

Vargha-Khadem, F., Watkins, K. E., Alcock, K., Fletcher, P., and Passingham, R. (1995). "Praxic and nonverbal cognitive deficits in a large family with a genetically-transmitted speech and language disorder," PNAS 92, 930-933.

Wada, K., Howard, J. T., et al (2006). "A molecular neuroethological approach for identifying and characterizing a cascade of behaviorally regulated genes," PNAS 103, 15212-15217.

EMERGENCE OF AKTIONSARTEN:
THE FIRST STEP TOWARDS ASPECT

KATERYNA GERASYMOVA

SONY Computer Science Laboratory Paris,
6, Rue Amyot, Paris, 75005, France
gera@csl.sony.fr

Slavic aspect has remained a mystery for centuries and continues to fascinate linguists. The genesis of this intricate grammar category is even a greater puzzle. This paper aims at computationally reconstructing the prerequisite for aspect – the emergence of a system of markers for Aktionsarten. We present an experiment where artificial language users develop a conventional system as the consequence of their distributed choices in locally situated communicative acts.

1. Introduction

Little is understood about the evolution of the infamously complex Slavic aspect. The literature on this subject is highly controversial. It is traditionally assumed that the aspectual system was already fully developed in the earliest Slavonic texts. Presumably already in Old Church Slavonic (established by Saints Cyril and Methodius in the 9th century AD) no verbs were exempted from the aspectual opposition which is identical with that in the modern Slavic languages (Dostal, 1954; Vaillant, 1966). Other scholars disagree with this view due to considerable discrepancies between verbal usage in Old Russian and modern Russian (Ruzicka, 1957). Additionally, some recent work (Bermel, 1997; Dickey, 2007) indicates that aspect as we know it in Russian today was sorted out much later, in the 16th-17th centuries. Not all scholars accept these recent results. However, even if one supports the more traditional view of a rather stable system it only reschedules but does not answer the question: How did this system come to existence?

In his exciting and comprehensive work, Forsyth (1972) proposes successive steps of how aspect could emerge and develop in complex tension with tense. He suggests that the perfectivity of a prefixed verb is basically nothing more than a by-product of the word-building process by means of which forms with new semantic nuances – new Aktionsarten – were derived. Further, he points to revealing statistics of modern as well as Old Russian concluding that aspectual opposition resides essentially in the contrast between simple verbs and their prefixal counterparts – those with new Aktionsarten – which nowadays account for ca 80 percent of the total verb occurrences. Another elaborate hypothesis about the origin of aspect is presented by Maslov (1961). Although it differs from that of Forsyth (1972) in later stages, the beginning of aspect remains the same – the existence of the general principle of prefixation to derive new Aktionsarten.

We propose to trace the genesis of aspect through computational simulations, since processes that took place long ago are notoriously difficult to verify otherwise. With this paper focusing on the prerequisite of Slavic aspect development, namely derivation of new Aktionsarten through prefixation, we demonstrate the emergence of prefixal forms in artificial populations.

This paper consists of two parts. The first part explains through a case study of Russian that aspect in Slavic languages is very distinct from a sporadic expression of aspect in other languages, and it addresses some historical facts. In the second part, we report on an experiment where a prefixal system becomes conventionalized in an artificial community, ending with discussion and future work.

2. Linguistic Background

2.1. *Dimensions of Aspect*

Russian aspect is notorious for its complexity. However, it is omnipresent in the grammar, and every verb in all forms and tenses expresses aspect. Moreover, it is the *primary* temporal distinction made by verbs in all modern Slavic languages and by far outranks tense. Russian aspect involves two dimensions: the *grammatical* category of aspect and the *semantic* category of Aktionsart. Grammatical aspect is manifested as a contrast between Perfective and Imperfective. Perfective aspect expresses the action as a *total event* summed up with reference to a single *juncture*, and Imperfective is characterized by the absence of that notion (Forsyth, 1972). The *juncture*, or position of the event's boundary, is fundamental for the Aktionsart of the verb, but the notion of perfectivity does not discriminate between the different possible positions (Bickel, 1997; Stoll, 1998). For example, the *ingressive* Aktionsart expresses the notion of beginning of an event, as in the verb заговорить (*zagovorit'*, 'start-talking.PFV'), whereas the Perfective sums up this beginning as a single undividable whole presenting it as a total event. Similarly, the *terminative* Aktionsart is characterized by focusing on the final boundary of the corresponding event, as in договорить (*dogovorit'*, 'finish-talking.PFV'), and the Perfective expresses this final phase of *talking* as a total.

2.2. *Morphology*

The morphology of Russian aspect mirrors the complexity of its semantics. In contrast to many other languages such as Turkish and English, it is the Perfective rather than Imperfective which is the marked member of the opposition, and there are numerous morphological markers expressing it. Russian verbs can be roughly divided into 'simple' verbs, consisting of a stem and a conjugated ending, e.g. читать (*čitat'*, 'read.IPFV'), щипать (*ŝipat'*, 'pinch.IPFV'), and 'complex' verbs, which are derived from the latter by the addition of aspectual markers, e.g. by pre-fixation перечитать (*perečitat'*, 're-read.PFV'), выщипать (*vyšipat'*, 'pinch out.PFV'). Simple verbs typically describe activities and are Imperfective. The addition of a prefix changes the aspect of simple verbs into Perfective. Russian has nineteen verbal prefixes that productively form Perfective (Krongauz, 1998).

In modern Russian, verbs can undergo more than one aspectual derivation. After a prefix is added to the simple verb, which made it Perfective, the so-called imperfectivizing suffixes can flip the verb's aspect to Imperfective again. But historically, the second imperfectivization developed only after the prefixal derivatives became 'perfective'. As already mentioned, awareness of the aspectual opposition is focused in the contrast between simple imperfective and prefixed perfective forms (and not between the latter and secondary imperfectives) which together account for ca 80 percent of the total verb occurrences (Forsyth, 1972).

2.3. *Historical development of aspect*

What is is known for sure is that Old Church Slavonic had a complex set of tenses, including a Present, two Past tense forms (Aorist and Imperfect), a Future, and four periphrastic tenses (Perfect, two Pluperfects, Future Perfect, see Andersen, 2006). In this proto-system aspect was nascent, but dominated by tense. In the modern Slavic languages we see a reversal of roles, and the dominant factor, aspect, displays typologically unusual behavior (Dahl, 1985).

In his attempts to trace the origin of aspect, Forsyth (1972) wonders: What is so special about the prefixation in Slavonic as compared to e.g. Latin, which did not develop a grammatical system of aspect? In the latter language, prefixes were used purely for derivation of new words, e.g. in Latin *fēci* 'made, did' → *confēci* 'accomplished', which is a new verb lexeme with more precise lexical meaning distinct from that of the simple verb, and which could be used in any syntactic function in the sentence. In Slavonic, however, prefixes had the dual role of providing not only lexical derivatives but also *Aktionsart* modifications of the basic verb (e.g. temporal modifications), and the disposition for the latter resulted in the spread of a generalized meaning of *totality* of the action, differing from, but overlapping with the Aktionsarten (as it is in modern Russian). Thus, the analogous process became linked with the grammatical meaning, not necessarily of actual completion of the action as an objective fact, but essentially with the syntactically restricted functions of expressing result, aim, sequence, condition, etc. Forsyth assumes that such meaning of totality developed first in one or another tense/mood form and only gradually spread until it embraced the whole paradigm.

Together with the fact that also in Old Russian the great majority of verb forms, at least in written texts, are simple verbs and primary prefixed 'perfectives' (Forsyth, 1972), the conclusion seems inescapable that the prefixed forms are at the heart of aspect. In sum, perfectivity of a prefixed verb is the consequence of the word-building process – Aktionsarten derivation. Thus, the derivation of new temporal modifications of verbs is the fundament of the origin of Slavic aspect.

3. Experiment

Derivation of Aktionsarten is the precondition for the development of Slavic aspect and is the subject of our modeling. We aim at demonstrating how such a system can be developed as the consequence of distributed processes whereby language users continuously shape and reshape their language in locally situated communicative interactions. Since our focus is not on lexicon formation (Steels, 1996), the interacting agents are assumed to operate a fully developed lexicon.

3.1. *Language Game for Aspect*

The setup of the experiment is inspired by psychological studies of Stoll (1998), who investigated how Russian children develop their understanding of aspect. Toddlers were interviewed after watching pairs of short movies, each illustrating what would be described by a different aspectual form of the same verb stem. Analogically to children, artificial agents in our experiment observe pairs of events differing in temporal semantics and afterwards engage in dialogs about these events. The experiment is framed as an incarnation of a *Language Game* (Steels, 2001) and consists of routinized communicative acts of identical form between members of an artificial community. A single interaction is best explained by looking at an example interaction between two agents – speaker and listener.

Example interaction Both agents perceive a shared context consisting of two events of the same kind but with different temporal semantics, e.g. *Michael read for a while* versus *Masha read the whole time*. The speaker chooses one event from the context as a *topic* she wants to communicate about, e.g. *Michael read for a while*. The communicative goal of the speaker is to ask a question about the protagonist of the topic. The question should unambiguously discriminate the protagonist, here this means that the event's temporal structure has to be incorporated into the question. For example, *Who read for a while?* discriminates Michael because only he was involved in the action for a short period of time (Masha was reading the whole time). Then, the speaker verbalizes the constructed question[a]. The hearer parses and interprets the meaning of the question by comparing it to the facts in the context. If the hearer is able to answer the question, i.e. identify the protagonist of the topic by comprehending the included temporal semantics, she verbalizes her answer by saying *Michael*. Otherwise, she gives up. The correct answer means communicative success, no answer is a failure. In the case of either incorrect or absent answer, the speaker reveals the desired answer. Based on the

---

[a]Language processing of agents is implemented in the Fluid Construction Grammar (FCG, see www.fcg-net.org); the details can be found in Gerasymova, Steels, and van Trijp (2009).

outcome, both agents consolidate their grammatical knowledge by increasing or decreasing the scores of constructions as well as creating or deleting them.

3.2. Cognitive Mechanisms

In order to be able to deal with communicative problems, agents are equipped with cognitive problem-solving tactics. These cognitive mechanisms consist of problem diagnostics and repair strategies and are crucial for the emergence process.

Inability to express meanings Imagine the speaker is confronted with the context as in the example interaction: there are two events *Michael read for a while* versus *Masha read the whole time*. Let us suppose that her chosen topic is the event where *Michael read for a while*, so she tries to verbalize the question *Who read for a while?*; especially the temporal semantics *for a while* of the corresponding reading has to be incorporated into the question, because this information is essential to make the question discriminative. She starts producing and, with the help of a given lexicon, produces the utterance: *Who read?* Rather than transmitting this utterance directly to the hearer, the speaker first *re-enters* – parses – it to predict the effect it might have on the hearer (Steels, 2003). Obviously, the parsed meaning does not correspond to the intended one and does not single out the topic-event as necessary. There are consequently two hypothesis for the answer. The failed production forces the speaker to examine what went wrong, and finally the inability to express the intended meaning *for a while* is detected.

To repair this problem, the speaker invents [b] a new marker, e.g. *hippi-* or *po-* as in Russian, to cover the needed meaning *for a while* and attaches it to the verb. There is empirical evidence of such language inventions, e.g. deaf children confronted with an atypical learning environment and without a tutor spontaneously invent a gesture system to communicate (Goldin-Meadow & Mylander, 1983). Thereafter, the speaker tries to produce again and this time succeeds.

Inability to parse strings Imagine the listener encounters the problem that she cannot entirely parse the question uttered by the speaker, e.g. *Who hippi-read?* from the above example. The linguistic parts that can be processed are *who* and *read*, but the newly invented prefix *hippi-* is left unprocessed. This leads to ambiguity in the interpretation of the topic (since both events are about *reading*) and consequently two hypotheses about the protagonist involved in the event. Because of this ambiguity, the interaction fails and the speaker reveals the right answer.

The listener tries to learn from this shortfall and stores the observed marker. Additionally, she can discover its semantics by searching the context for the meaning that could differentiate *Michael* from *Masha*, since questions are assumed to

---

[b]The agent could also reuse a device already existing in the language system, e.g. spatial preposition (*po* is preposition in Russian), but this possibility is not yet included into the presented model.

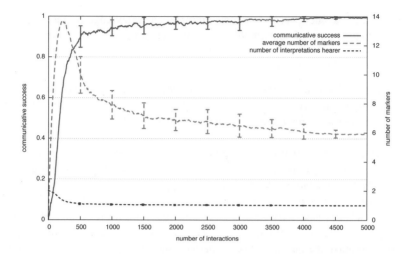

Figure 1. Communicative success (fraction of successful games in the last 100 interactions) and inventory of markers in a population of 10 agents playing 5000 aspect language games (avg. 10 runs).

be discriminative. The distinctive feature for *Michael* is the temporal structure of his *reading*, which is *for a while*, in contrast to the *ongoing reading* of *Masha*. Thus, the stored string of the marker is associated with this deduced information.

3.3. Results

Let us look at the development of a prefixal system in a community. In the world of agents, different events can take place and exhibit six temporal semantic features: *begin, finish, once, for a while, ongoing, complete*. Hence, grammatical markers for *ingressive, terminative, semelfactive, delimitative, durative, telic* Aktionsarten, respectively, should pop up in the population driven by the need to express these when communicating about events. Fig. 1 displays the communicative success and inventory of markers throughout the game, averaged over 10 runs. The beginning is characterized by the overshoot of the required number of markers and later phases display their convergence on the optimal number of six. The communicative success grows very quickly when the sufficient amount of markers starts floating in the population. There are however synonyms, which can be seen in Fig. 2 that zooms into one simulation and captures the development of markers.

By their invention, markers are assigned a score of 0.5 that is updated over time using a scoring mechanism (lateral inhibition) which rewards markers that were used often and successfully in communication and punishes competitors. Some

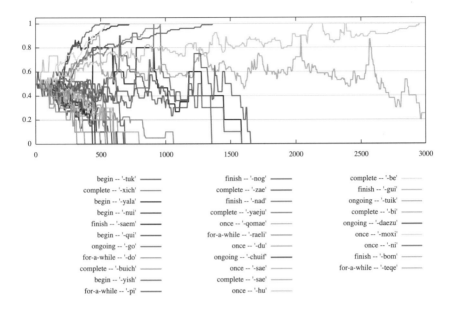

Figure 2.   Development of markers for Aktionsarten in a population of 10 agents (population avg.).

markers lose the competition, reach the minimal score of 0.0 and are eliminated from the inventory. Others reach the maximum score of 1.0 and win the battle.

Through repeated interactions of the aspect language game, the population of agents was able to develop a conventional system of markers for Aktionsarten.

4. Conclusion and Future Work

This paper presented the first step in reconstructing processes responsible for the evolution of Slavic aspect and their dynamics computationally. The prerequisite for aspect – the emergence of a conventional system of markers for Aktionsarten – was successfully tackled. For that, we pinpointed situations that necessitate the expression of new semantic nuances of events and their incorporation into a language system. We also identified cognitive mechanisms required by the members of a community, such as the ability to identify the cause of failures in communication and to be inventive enough to dare creative usage of already established morphemes or even brand new forms. Future work will be devoted to further steps tracing and modeling the evolution of aspect. Therewith, we target at core controversies in both Slavic and cognitive linguistics, controversies that are important for our understanding of language evolution and human cognition in general.

Acknowledgements

Reported research was funded by the EU project ALEAR. We thank the people working on Babel2 at the VUB AI lab and at Sony CSL Paris for their contributions in making such a superb environment for doing sophisticated language experiments. We are greatly in debt to Luc Steels for making this work possible.

References

Andersen, H. (2006). Grammation, regrammation, and degrammation: Tense loss in Russian. *Diachronica, 23*(2), 231–258.

Bermel, N. (1997). *Context and the Lexicon in the Development of Russian Aspect.* University of California Press.

Bickel, B. (1997). Aspectual scope and the difference between logical and semantic representation. *Lingua*(102), 115-131.

Dahl, Ö. (1985). *Tense and aspect systems.* Blackwell.

Dickey, S. (2007). A Prototype Account of the Development of Delimitative *po*-in Russian. *Cognitive Paths into the Slavic Domain*, 326–371.

Dostal, A. (1954). *Studie o vidovém systému v staroslověnštině.* Prague.

Forsyth, J. (1972). The nature and development of the aspectual opposition in the Russian verb. *The Slavonic and East European Review, 50*(121), 493-506.

Gerasymova, K., Steels, L., & van Trijp, R. (2009). Aspectual morphology of Russian verbs in Fluid Construction Grammar. *Proceedings of the 31th Annual Conference of the Cognitive Science Society*, 1370-1375.

Goldin-Meadow, S., & Mylander, C. (1983). Gestural communication in deaf children: noneffect of parental input on language development. *Science, 221*(4608), 372-374.

Krongauz, M. A. (1998). *Pristavki i glagoly v russkom jazyke: semantičeskaja grammatika.* Moscow: Jazyki russkoj kul'tury.

Maslov, Y. S. (1961). Rol' tak nazyvaemoj perfektivacii i imperfektivacii v processe vozniknovenija slavjanskogo glagol'nogo vida. *Issledovaniya po slavyanskomu yazykoznaniyu.*

Ruzicka, R. (1957). *Der Verbalaspect in der altrussischen Nestorchronic.* Berlin.

Steels, L. (1996). A self-organizing spatial vocabulary. *Artificial Life, 2*(3), 319-332.

Steels, L. (2001). Language games for autonomous robots. *IEEE Intelligent Systems*, 16-22.

Steels, L. (2003). Language re-entrance and the 'inner voice'. *Journal of Consciousness Studies, 10*(4-5), 173–185.

Stoll, S. (1998). The role of aktionsart in the acquisition of Russian aspect. *First Language, 18*(54), 351–376.

Vaillant, A. (1966). *Grammaire comparée des langues slaves: vol. 3–le verbe* (Vol. 3). Paris: C. Klincksieck.

TALKING ABOUT BIRDS, BEES, AND PRIMATES, TOO. IMPLICATIONS FOR LANGUAGE EVOLUTION

KATHLEEN R. GIBSON

*Departments of Neurobiology and Anatomy and Orthodontics,
University of Texas Health Science Center, Houston.
6516 M.D. Anderson Blvd, Suite 371
Houston, Texas, USA 77030*

This paper reviews findings on comparative primate and animal cognition. It suggests that although modern human linguistic, cognitive, and motor behaviors differ profoundly from those of great apes, primarily with respect to required mental constructional skills, an early hominin with ape-like capacities could have used non-innate, referential signals. To determine the most probable selective agents that may have motivated these first steps towards language evolution, it is necessary to look beyond the non-human primates to a wider range of animal species. When this is done, foraging adaptations emerge as the most probable selective agents for cooperative breeding and for the cognitive and behavioral suite that would eventually lead to language.

1.1. *Introduction*

A half century ago, in 1960, when I began my college career, Cartesian views of vast qualitative mental gaps between humans and other animals dominated introductory psychology and anthropology texts. It was alleged that only humans make tools, have culture and can symbolize and that, while laboratory rats can learn via conditioning and newly hatched geese via imprinting, only humans have rational thought and higher intellectual capacities. By my senior year, the tide had begun to change with as yet unpublished reports of tool-making chimpanzees in the Gombe Stream. Before the decade was out, Washoe's alleged linguistic accomplishments stunned the academic community. After Washoe, reports of remarkable ape accomplishments just kept coming and coming.

Despite the continued invocation of Morgan's Canon, by the time of the 1990 Wenner-Gren conference on Tools, Language and Cognition in Human Evolution, the tide had changed (Gibson & Ingold, 1993). Descartes was out. Darwin was in. For many, the differences between apes and humans were now considered to be differences of degree rather than of kind, and the great cognitive divide was now deemed to lie between great apes and other animals, rather than between apes and humans. The new evolutionary challenge was to prove that birds, cetaceans, maybe even dogs and spotted hyenas, are just as smart as (or even smarter than) chimps.

During this time frame, beginning in the late 1960's and early 1970's, anthropologists and others primarily interested in human evolution, but not especially knowledgeable about linguistics and little concerned with linguistic society bans or Chomsky's pronouncements, resurrected discussions of language evolution (See for example, de Grolier, 1983; Harnard, Steklis, & Lancaster, 1976). Indeed, the findings on animal behavior seemed to both give new legitimacy to and partially propel such studies. Certainly, for the most part, these early discussions focused on the initial emergence of language-like communicative systems, i.e. on those aspects of language evolution for which animal studies would appear most pertinent.

The linguistic community responded to initial claims of language competent apes as well as to language evolution scenarios based on them, by justifiably pointing to the vast differences between the ape "language" performances and fully developed language. To non-linguists, such as myself, linguists also seemed to be continually redefining language from symbolism, to syntax, to recursion. Similar redefinitions of humanity were also offered by other scholars eager to preserve the animal-human divide. However, each time others set new linguistic and cognitive bars, primatologists or other animal behaviorists challenged them with new findings. Thus, to some extent, studies of early language evolution and animal cognition developed synergistically, each helping to spur the other's development. One result of this half century of research findings and debate is that we now have a huge corpus of data on the cognitive, communicative, and social capacities of non-human primates and an ever emerging corpus of the capacities of other animals. Another is that language evolution has become a respected subfield of linguistics, one that even merits it own series with Oxford University Press.

Yet, in the nearly half century since Washoe and the discovery of tool-making chimps, we have yet to achieve consensus on a number of key issues pertinent to the animal-hominin cognitive and communicative transition. We still debate whether differences between humans and other animals are matters of degree or kind, what, if any language-relevant cognitive and neurological processes are uniquely human, and whether the original language-like communications were vocal or gestural. Indeed, we still debate which animals serve as the most relevant study subjects. Great apes, animals with the most elaborate vocal communication systems, savannah living monkeys and even insects (Bickerton, 2009) have all been suggested as the most appropriate models.

Many investigators do agree that social behaviors served as the prime selective agents for language evolution, but what social behaviors? Group bonding, gossip, sexual selection, Machiavellian manipulation, menstrual strikes, cooperative breeding, cooperative hunting, and motherese have all been suggested, but these are not all the same thing, and there is no reason to believe they evolved simultaneously or selected for the same communicative and cognitive skills. Moreover, the view that the first steps towards language-like communications arose as foraging adaptations has not yet died (Bickerton, 2009; Gibson & Jessee, 1999; Parker & Gibson, 1979), and some argue for still other selective scenarios such as predator defense.

This paper briefly reviews actual and potential future contributions of animal studies to our understandings of the evolution of human language and cognition from the perspectives of studies of both our closest phylogenetic kin and more distantly related animal species. It suggests that the initial impetus towards the use non-innate, referential communication occurred in extractive foraging contexts.

1.2. *What monkeys and apes can tell us.*

Studies of great apes and other primates have long been favored by most students of human evolution, because they are our closest phylogenetic relatives. It is generally recognized that if all descendents of a common ancestor possess a particular trait, the common ancestor most likely also possessed that trait. Consequently, studies of great apes and, to a lesser extent, of old world monkeys, provide the greatest potential for determining the sensorimotor, communicative, neurological, and cognitive capacities of the earliest hominins: hence, the potential start-point from which the earliest proto-language-like behaviors emerged. Such studies also have the strongest potential for determining the sensorimotor and cognitive advances required for the emergence of advanced forms of human language and cognition from more ape-like predecessors.

Such studies have already contributed a great deal. For one we now know that although members of all great ape species, if reared in captivity, can learn to use referential gestural or visual symbols and that many behaviors once thought to be uniquely human can be found in rudimentary form our primate brethren. Nonetheless, ape achievements in many behavioral domains fall far short of those of modern humans, and it now seems clear that enhanced mental combinatorial and hierarchical constructional skills underlie many aspects of these ape-human differences particularly in the realms of dance, athletics, speech, syntax, tool-making, music, and social computations. (See, for example, Gibson, 1990; Gibson and Jessee, 1999; Greenfield, 1991). These enhanced combinatorial and constructional capacities appear to be facilitated by enhancements of at least three basic processes involving diverse neurological components: (1) the minimalist process, merge, (2) working memory, and (3) the production of discrete, individuated movements and perceptions.

The cognitive, sensorimotor, and communicative capacities of the earliest hominins would surely have more closely resembled those of the common great-ape-human ancestor than those of modern humans. Based on the communicative achievements of bonobos, such as Kanzi, chimpanzees, such as Washoe, orangutans, such as Chantek, and other captive apes, however, it is likely that these capacities would have been sufficient to provide early hominins with the potential to communicate using non-innate, referential gestures or other visual signals. All that was needed was the motivation, something that appears to mostly lacking in wild ape populations today.

1.3. *Why we must study other animals as well*

Although questions of motivation and selective agents for the earliest emergence of language-like behaviors are sometimes treated as unknowable, clues can be gained by expanding our perspectives from great apes and other primates to a much wider range of animal species. Convergent evolution of similar traits in very distantly-related species, now known as homoplasy, often occurs in response to similar environments. Whales and dolphins, for example, have developed external body shapes quite similar to those of fish in response to aquatic environments. Other lesser known examples include the grasping hands and prehensile tails of some arboreal amphibians and reptiles.

Although no animal is known to have a fully developed language or the broad human-like cognitive suite which renders human languages both possible and useful, the complex vocalizations of many birds and cetaceans put rudimentary primate vocal skills to shame, and Alex, a recently deceased gray parrot, reportedly, had language-like capacities equivalent to Kanzi and other "language-trained" apes (Pepperberg, 2002). In addition, many non-primate animals exhibit behaviors similar to those thought to require advanced cognitive capacities when found in humans and apes. For example, Betty, a deceased New Caledonian Crow, could fashion tools that were seemingly more complex than any yet made by a chimpanzee (Weir, Chappell, & Kalcenik, 2002). Scrub jays not only cache food, but remember where they cached it and whether other jays were watching. (Dally, Emery & Clayton, 2006) Dogs, understand pointing gestures more readily than apes (Hare & Tomasello, 2005). The architectural constructs of bees, termites, and beavers are far more complex than primate nests. The ability to socially transmit information, once considered uniquely human, has been found in many animals including honey bees, ants, naked mole rats, rats, water buffalo, and carnivores (Bickerton, 2009; Box and Gibson, 1999). The list goes on. Given the diverse sensorimotor and neurological capacities which underpin these various animal behaviors, it is, in my opinion, premature to draw conclusions about the relative intelligence of various species based on these overt behaviors. What is clear, however, is that many behaviors once thought unique to humans or other primates can be found throughout the animal kingdom and, in many cases, these have known adaptive functions.

1.4 *All signs lead to foraging*

Although these varied animal achievements reflect a diversity of selective pressures, the most common ones relate to foraging. Group size, often touted as the major selective advantage for language, has long been known to largely reflect the interactions of adaptations for foraging and predator avoidance. Most animal social transmission of information relates to foraging information, specifically to the types and location of food resources (Box & Gibson, 1999). This is true for insects, bees, rats, pigeons, rabbits and naked mole rats. In contrast, although many animals do advertize their own presence via scent marking, singing and/or territorial calls, there are no known examples of animal "gossip" about the activity of con-specifics. Purported examples of animal "teaching" primarily occur in contexts of adult carnivores providing their young with opportunities for practice with prey. Reported examples of episodic memory and theory of mind in scrub jays occur in the contexts of food-caching.

Perhaps, most importantly, humans are now recognized as cooperative breeders (Hrdy, 2009). In many species, cooperative breeding is clearly a foraging adaptation associated with the provisioning of young (e.g. many birds and social carnivores) and/or with the collection and production of shared food resources that can be used by both adults and young (e.g. honey bees, naked mole rats, leaf-cutter ants). Humans, of course, also provision post-weanling young and share food resources among adults, and they do so cooperatively in the sense that mothers, fathers, grandparents, and older siblings all help provision young group members, and unrelated adults often share with each other.

The recognition that humans are cooperative breeders is a key advance for our understanding of language evolution for two reasons. (1) Much linguistic information consists of honest signals, and it has long been a puzzle why such should have developed in Machiavellian societies. Cooperative breeders, however, do benefit from shared information. (2) Like, human infants, the young of some cooperative breeding species babble or engage in other conspicuous behaviors that serve to attract the attention of older individuals.

A key question is when cooperative breeding first arose in the hominin line. In 1979, based on comparative studies of tool-using animals, Sue Parker and I proposed that, when faced with environmentally-induced shortages of easily obtained foods, early hominins would have engaged in obligatory, tool-assisted extractive foraging on a variety of high-energy embedded foods, such as nuts encased in hard shells, underground tubers, scavenged bone marrow and brains, meat scavenged from thick hides, burrowing animals, shellfish, and encased insects and insect products such as honey. We further suggested that the provisioning of post-weanling young would have arisen as soon as early hominins of all ages became dependent on extracted foods that could only be obtained by using tools that required strength or skills not present in the very young, and that, in such circumstances, young hominins would have been motivated to communicate their feeding needs and desires via pointing and other simple forms of referential communication. Hence, the provisioning of tool-assisted extractive foods may well have set the stage for the emergence of cooperative breeding and for the initial emergence of referential communication.

The extractive foraging hypothesis proved prophetic, in terms of subsequent findings of tool-using behaviors in other animals, including chimpanzees, cebus monkeys, and New Caledonian crows. Its emphasis on the relationship between the extraction of high energy foods and relative brain size was compatible with the subsequently proposed expensive tissue hypothesis. Moreover, nearly all current hypotheses about the earliest hominin foraging adaptations focus on some form of extractive foraging, such as scavenging of brains and bone marrow and the exploitation of tubers. Extractive foraging is also a highly probable predecessor for the hunting of large game, because, humans can only open the hides of large game by using tools. Tool-assisted omnivorous extractive foraging and cooperative breeding would not, in and of themselves, have selected for complex linguistic skills, but they could well have jump-started the language- evolution process.

References

Bickerton, D. (2009). *How humans made language: How language made humans.* New York: Macmillan, Hill and Wang.

Box, H. O. & Gibson, K. R. (Eds.) (1999). *Mammalian social learning: comparative and ecological perspectives.* Cambridge: Cambridge University Press.

Dally, J. M., Emery, N. J. & Clayton, N. (2006). Food caching Western Scrub-jays keep track of who was watching when. *Science, 312,* 1662-1665.

de Grolier, E. (ed.) (1983). *Glossogenetics: The origin and evolution of language.* London: Harwood Academic Publishers.

Gibson, K. R. (1990). New perspectives on instincts and intelligence: Brain size and the emergence of hierarchical mental constructional skills. In S. T. Parker and K. R. Gibson (Eds,) *Language and intelligence in monkeys and apes: Comparative developmental perspectives.* (pp. 97-128). Cambridge: Cambridge University Press.

Gibson, K. R. & Jessee, S. (1999). Language evolution and the expansion of multiple neurological processing areas. In B. King (Ed.), *The origins of language: What non-human primates can tell us.* (pp. 189-228). Santa Fe, NM, School of American Research Press.

Gibson, K. R. & Ingold, T. (eds.) (1993). *Tools, language and cognition in human evolution.* Cambridge: Cambridge University Press.

Greenfield, P. M. (1991). Language, tools, and the brain. The development and evolution of hierarchically organized sequential behavior. *Behavioral and Brain Sciences, 14,* 531-595.

Hare, B. & Tomasello, M. (2005). Human-like social skills in dogs? *Trends in Cognitive Science, 9,* 439-444.

Hrdy, S. B. (2009) *Mothers and others: The evolutionary origins of mutual understanding.* Cambridge, MA: Harvard University Press.

Harnard, S. R., Steklis, H.D., & Lancaster, J. (Eds.) (1976). *Origins and evolution of language and speech: Annals of the New York Academy of Science, 280*, 445-454.

Parker, S. T. & Gibson, K. R. (1979). A model of the evolution of language and intelligence in early hominids. *Behavioral and Brain Sciences, 2*, 367-407.

Pepperberg, I. (2002). The Alex studies: Cognitive and communicative abilities of grey parrots. Cambridge: Harvard University Press.

Weir, A.A.S., Chappell, J. & Kacelnik, A. (2002) Shaping of hooks in New Caledonian crows. *Science, 297*, 981.

THE EFFECT OF SOCIAL POPULARITIES ON LINGUISTIC CATEGORIZATION

TAO GONG

Department of Linguistics, Max Planck Institute for Evolutionary Anthropology, Deutscher Platz 6, Leipzig, 04103, Germany

This paper adopts the category game model that simulates the coevolution of categories and their word labels to explore the effect of social structure on linguistic categorization. Instead of detailed social connections, we adopt social popularities, the probabilities with which individuals participate into language games, to denote quantitatively the general characteristics of social structures. The simulation results show that a certain degree of social scaling could accelerate the categorization process, while a much high degree of social scaling will greatly delay this process.

1. Introduction

Social structures abound in human societies, primate communities, and colonies of some other species (e.g., ants), and social competences (e.g., coalition and competition) are also found in some non-human species. Some of these social factors, existing prior to human language, could have casted their influence on language evolution (Dunbar, 1996). Sociolinguists have already explored the influence of social factors on language change. For instance, Thomason and Kaufman (1988) have illustrated that the social facts of particular contact situations mainly determine the contact-induced language change, and Labov (2001) has shown that language-external factors such as social networks, identity, and gender could determine linguistic variations. In addition, modeling social systems as complex networks can offer new insights on social science research, and this approach has been recently adopted to study historical linguistic change (e.g., Bhattacharjee, 2003) and other sociological phenomena (e.g., Malsch & Schulz-Schaeffer, 2007). In this line of research, the earlier studies adopted simple networks to represent human communities, such as row (Livingstone, 2001), lattice (e.g., Nettle, 1999), and ring (e.g., Kirby, 2000). And later on, some complex networks revealed from sociological studies, such as small-world and scale-free networks, were considered (e.g., Ke, 2004), in which an individual is a node and a communication among individuals is an edge connecting nodes. Many simulations have shown that the longer the social distance among individuals, the weaker the influence these individuals could cast upon each other, and that the more social connections an individual has, the more influential this individual becomes to affect others.

This way of denoting social relations by particular connections among individuals is reasonable in large-scale communities. In small-scale societies, however, since any individual may directly interact with anyone else, it is unrealistic to define actual connections among individuals. One way to overcome this is to adopt a weighted, fully-connected network, but it is still difficult to specify the actual weights of edges based on the frequency information obtained from empirical evidence. Instead of local, particular connections, a global way to denote quantitatively the general characteristics of social structures is necessary. Considering this, in this paper, we define an individual's *social popularity* as the probability with which this individual participates into communications with others, and use the distribution of all individuals' social popularities to reflect the characteristics of the whole structure. Based on the category game model (Puglisi et al., 2008) that simulates the categorization process involving the evolution of both lexical items and semantic categories, we conduct a simulation study under different distributions of social popularities to explore the effect of social factors on linguistic categorization and discuss the role of social structures in language evolution.

The rest of the paper is organized as follows: Section 2 reviews the category game; Section 3 introduces the power-law distributions of social popularities; Section 4 discusses the simulation results; and finally, Section 5 evaluates our way of characterizing social structures.

2. The Category Game

Semantic categories are culture-dependent conventions shared by individuals for understanding the environment (Gardner, 1985). Their emergence may undergo a self-organization process via iterated interactions among individuals (Lakeoff, 1987). The category game model (Puglisi et al., 2008) theoretically simulates the emergence of common categories that share similar semantic boundaries and identical lexical labels.

This model involves a population of N artificial individuals. Starting from scratch, these individuals, through iterated games, dynamically generate a highly shared pattern of linguistic categories to distinguish stimuli from a perceptual channel. For the sake of simplicity and not losing generality, the perceptual channel is represented by the interval [0, 1), and each stimuli a real number in this continuous space. A categorization pattern is a partition of the interval [0, 1) into sub-intervals, or *perceptual categories*. Individuals have dynamical inventories of form-meaning associations that link categories with their word labels and evolve during iterated games. In each game, two players (a speaker and a listener) are selected from the population and a scene of M (≥ 2) stimuli chosen from the interal [0, 1) is presented, any two of the stimuli cannot appear at a distance smaller than *dmin*, and one stimulus in this scene is the speaker's topic in this game for the listener to perceive. Figure 1(a) illustrates the game procedure based on two games and Figure 1(b) illustrates the categorization process shown in this model.

As shown in Figure 1(b), all individuals initially have only a perceptual category [0, 1) with no associated words. In the first phase of the evolution, the pressure for discrimination makes the number of perceptual categories increase, and many different words are adopted by different individuals for categories having similar boundaries. Such synonymy reaches a peak and then dries out. When on average only one word is recognized by the whole population for each perceptual category, the second phase intervenes, during which words expand their dominion across adjacent perceptual categories, joining these categories into *linguistic categories*. The coarsening of these categories becomes slower and slower, with a dynamical arrest analogous to the physical process in which super-cooled liquids close to the glass transition (Mézard et al., 1987). In this long-lived, almost stable phase, usually after 10^4 games per individual, the categorization pattern has a degree of sharing between 90% and 100% and remains stable for 10^5 to 10^6 games per individual. If one waits for a much longer time, the number of linguistic categories is observed to drop down, caused by the slow diffusion of category boundaries that ultimately takes place due to small size effects. In this study, we focus on the shared pattern in the stable phase between 10^4 and 10^6 games per individual.

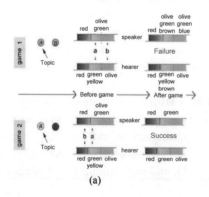

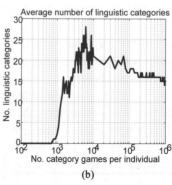

(a) (b)

Figure 1. (a) Two examples of the category game (adapted from Puglisi et al., 2008). The round objects are stimuli presented, among which the topics are pointed. The colorful banners represent individuals' perceptual channels, separated by bars into perceptual categories, whose inventories of words are listed above or below. In game 1, since the two stimuli fall into the same category, the speaker discriminates the topic ("a") by creating a new boundary in his/her rightmost perceptual category at the position (a+b)/2. Two new categories are created, both inheriting the word-inventory ("green" and "olive") of their parent category, and two new words are invented respectively for these new categories ("brown" and "blue"). Then, the speaker browses the list of words associated to the category that contains the topic. If a previous successful game using this category occurred, its winning word is sent to the listener; otherwise, the newly created word for this category ("brown") is sent. Since the listener does not have this word in his/her inventory, he/she cannot understand it, and the game *fails*. Then, the speaker points at the topic for the listener to discriminate, and the listener adds the speaker's word to the inventory of his/her corresponding category. In game 2, the topic "a" is already discriminated by the speaker in a perceptual category whose winning word is "green". Then, "green" is sent to the listener, who also knows this word and points at the topic contained in his/her corresponding category. This game is *successful*. Then, both individuals eliminate all competing words in their used perceptual categories whose boundaries might not match exactly, but leave the word "green" only. If ambiguity arises (the speaker's word is associated to more than one category that contains the topic), the listener takes a random choice. (b) The categorization process in a random category game simulation, N=50 and *dmin*=0.01, indicated by the average number of linguistic categories per individual over 50 runs under the same settings.

3. The Representative Distribution of Social Popularities

Sociological research has discovered that instead of uniformity, in many social and linguistic phenomena, such as sexual contact (Lijeros et al., 2003), rumor spread (Moreno et al., 2004), and size ranking of language families (Stauffer et al., 2006), the elements and interactions among them follow a power-law relation (Newman, 2003, 2005). Such a relation is also characteristics in many self-organizing systems, and factors such as preferential attachment (Barabási & Albert, 1999) can lead to this relation in those systems. A power-law relation of two quantities x and y is defined as $y = ax^{-\lambda}$, where a is a scaling parameter, x represents an element or interaction in a given system, y calculates the frequency of this element or interaction, and λ distinguishes different distributions. As summarized by Newman (2003), the λ values in many real-world power-law distributions lie in the interval [0.0 3.0]. For instance, it is 1.0 in the frequency ranking of words, 2.0 in the email exchange network, and 3.0 in the citation network.

In our study, we let social popularities follow power-law distributions: x is individual index (rank) from 1 to N, y calculates the popularity for an individual with index x to participate in communications, and a is set to make sure the sum of all probabilities is 1.0. We choose some sampling λ values: 0.0, 1.0, 1.5, 2.0, 2.5, and 3.0. When λ equals 0.0, all individuals have the same probability to communicate with others. This resembles the random case in which individuals are communicating randomly with each other. As λ increases, individuals having smaller indices become more popular than those having bigger indices, and they tend to communicate much frequently with each other but occasionally with those having bigger indices. Notice that there is a mathematical relation between the λ in the power-law, rank-frequency distribution used in this model and λ' in the power-law, cumulative distributions of node degrees: $\lambda' = 1 + 1/\lambda$.

4. The Simulation Results

In our simulation, $N=50$, *dmin*=0.01, individuals conduct 10^6 category games per individual, and their popularities follow the power-law distributions with the sampling λ values. We define two indices to evaluate the categorization process: a) *Overlap*, calculating the average degree of alignment of linguistic categories among individuals, a high value of which indicates that individuals tend to develop categories having similar boundaries; b) *Understanding Rate* (*UR*), calculating the percentage of successful category games in all pairs of individuals, a high value of which indicates that individuals tend to use identical labels to describe stimuli for categories with similar boundaries.

Figure 2 shows the simulation results. High *Overlap* of linguistic categories and *UR* are obtained after 10^6 category games per individual. Compared with the random case (λ=0.0, the solid line), social popularities cast an influence on the categorization process. With the increase in λ, under a fixed number of category games, *Overlap* of perceptual categories becomes smaller. When λ is bigger than 1.5, *Overlap* of linguistic categories starts to drop greatly. Meanwhile, when λ increases from 0.0 to 1.5, the increase in *UR* occurs earlier than that in the random case, which suggests that a certain degree of social scaling can accelerate the emergence of a common set of categories with similar boundaries and identical word labels; when λ exceeds 1.5, however, the increase in *UR* occurs much later, which indicates that a high degree of social scaling could actually delay the emergence of a common set of categories. The simulation results are similar when $N=100$ or $N=200$, and as shown in (Puglisi et al., 2008), a decrease in *dmin* cannot greatly change the categorization process.

These results illustrate a boundary λ value (around 1.0) in power-law distributed social popularities, below which categorization is accelerated, but beyond which this process is delayed. An increase in λ makes individuals with smaller indices have more opportunities to take part in category games, and update and spread their category patterns to others, thus helping to accelerate categorization in the whole population. However, a high λ value will cause individuals with bigger indices to lack opportunities to develop their category patterns and align their patterns towards those of the popular ones. This delays the increase in *Overlap* and *UR*, and more category games are needed for the whole population to achieve a common set of categories. Due to these two aspects of influence, a power-law distribution with an intermediate λ value becomes a compromise for maintaining both a certain degree of social scaling and a common set of linguistic categories. In addition, considering the relation between rank-frequency and cumulative node degree distributions, $\lambda' = 1 + 1/\lambda$, the boundary λ value (1.0) in the former type of power-law distributions roughly corresponds to the λ' value (2.0) in latter type of power-law distributions. Seen from Newman (2003), the power-law distributions of many language-related social activities have their λ' values around 2.0, such as the email exchange (2.0) and the telephone call (2.1) networks. This provides an empirical support for the boundary λ value shown in our study.

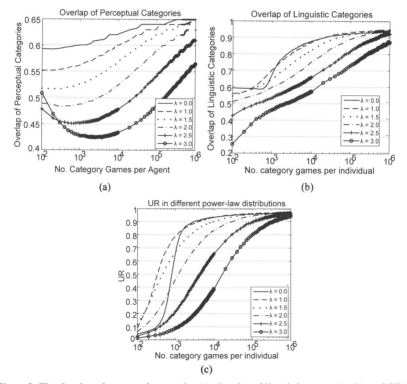

Figure 2. The *Overlap* of perceptual categories (a), *Overlap* of linguistic categories (b), and *UR* (c) in different power-law distributions. Each point is calculated using 20 runs under the same settings.

5. Discussions and Conclusions

Language evolves primarily via social contact among a finite number of individuals. Based on the category game model, we show that a certain degree of social scaling can efficiently develop a common set of semantic categories among individuals, while too much social scaling actually reduces this process. Instead of particular social connections, we adopt the concept of popularity, first used by Nettle (1999), and use the distributions of individual popularities to represent the characteristics of the whole structure. This approach helps summarize the general features shared in various kinds of social structures, requires only a few probability parameters whose values can be obtained from some empirical evidence, and allows statistical analyses to examine the results and provide quantitative understanding on human language, social factors, and their mutual interactions. As shown in Newman (2003), apart from power-law distributions, there are other topological features that are also important in characterizing social communities, and different types of network typology may share functional equivalence on linguistic tasks. The effects of other network typology on language evolution can be studied as well using the same approach. In addition, the category game model is restricted to lexical evolution. To better understand the social structure effect on language evolution, complex language models that concern both lexical and syntactic evolutions should be considered. A preliminary study, based on a lexicon-syntax coevolution model, has shown some similar results about the intermediate λ value in power-law distributions (Gong et al., 2008), which indicates that the power-law relations in a community of individuals is an *independent* factor to influence the average successful rate of language games among individuals.

Acknowledgements

The author acknowledges the support from the Alexander von Humboldt Foundation in Germany, and thanks Prof. Vittorio Loreto and Dr. Andrea Puglisi from Sapienza Universita' di Roma, and Dr. Andrea Baronchelli from Universitat Politecnica de Catalunya for their comments on this work.

References

Barabási, A-L. & Albert, R. (1999). Emergence of scaling in random networks, *Science*, 286, 509-512.

Bhattacharjee, Y. (2003). From heofonum to heavens. *Science*, 303, 1326-1328.

Dunbar, D. (1996). *Grooming, gossip, and the evolution of language.* Cambridge, MA: Harvard University Press.

Gardner, H. (1985). *The mind's new science: A history of the cognitive revolution*. New York: Basic Books.

Gong, T., Minett, J. W., & Wang, W. S-Y. (2008). Exploring social structure effect on language evolution based on a computational model. *Connection Science*, 20, 135-153.

Ke, J-Y. (2004). *Self-organization and language evolution: System, population and individual*. Doctoral Dissertation, City University of Hong Kong.

Kirby, S. (2000). Syntax without natural selection: How compositionality emerges from vocabulary in a population of learners. In C. Knight (Ed.), *The evolutionary emergence of language: Social function and the origins of linguistic form* (pp. 303-323). Cambridge: Cambridge University Press.

Labov, W. (2001). *Principles of linguistic change: Social factors*. Oxford, UK: Basil Blackwell.

Lakoff, G. (1987). *Women, fire, and dangerous things*. Chicago, IL: University of Chicago Press.

Lijeros, F., Edling, C. R., & Amaral, L. A. N. (2003). Sexual networks: Implications for the transmission of sexually transmitted infections. *Microbes and Infection*, 5, 189-196.

Livingstone, D. (2001). The evolution of dialect diversity. In A. Cangelosi and D. Parisi (Eds.), *Simulating the evolution of language* (pp. 99-117). London: Springer-Verlag.

Moreno, Y., Nekovee, M., & Pacheco, A. F. (2004). Dynamics of rumor spreading in complex networks. *Physical Review E*, 69, 1-7.

Stauffer, D., Schulze, C., Lima, F. W. S., Wichmann, S., & Solomon, S. (2006). Non-equilibrium and irreversible simulation of competition among languages. *Physica A*, 371, 719-724.

Malsch, T. & Schulz-Schaeffer, I. (2007). Socionics: Sociological concepts for social systems of artificial (and human) agents. *Journal of Artificial Societies and Social Simulation*, 10. http://jasss/soc/surrey.ac.uk/10/1/11.html.

Mézard, M., Parisi, G., & Virasoro, M. (1987). *Spin glass theory and beyond*. New York: World Scientific.

Nettle, D. (1999). Using social impact theory to simulate language change. *Lingua*, 108, 95-117.

Newman, M. E. J. (2003). The structure and function of complex networks, *SIAM Review*, 45, 167-256.

Newman, M. E. J. (2005). Power laws, distributions and Zipf's law. *Contemporary Physics*, 46, 323-351.

Puglisi, A., Baronchelli, A., & Loreto, V. (2008). Cultural route to the emergence of linguistic categories. *Proceedings of the National Academic of Sciences*, 105, 7936-7940.

Thomason, S. G. & Kaufman, T. (1988). *Language contact, creolization, and genetic linguistics*. Los Angeles, CA: University of California Press.

EXPLORING THE ROLES OF MAJOR FORMS OF CULTURAL TRANSMISSION IN LANGUAGE EVOLUTION

TAO GONG

Department of Linguistics, Max Planck Institute for Evolutionary Anthropology, Deutscher Platz 6, Leipzig, 04103, Germany

Cultural transmission is the primary medium of linguistic interactions. We propose an acquisition framework that involves the major forms of cultural transmissions, such as vertical, oblique and horizontal transmissions. By manipulating the ratios of these forms of transmission in the total number of transmission across generations of individuals, we analyze their roles in language evolution, based on a lexicon-syntax coevolution model. The simulation results indicate that all these forms of transmission collectively lead to the dynamic equilibrium of language evolution across generations.

1. Introduction

Human language is transmitted mainly via *cultural transmission* (the process of language adaptation in a community via various kinds of communication among individuals of the same or different generations, Christiansen & Kirby, 2003). Generally speaking, there are three forms of cultural transmission: a) *horizontal transmission (H)*, communications among individuals of the same generation; b) *vertical transmission (V)*, in which a member of one generation talks to a biologically-related member of a later generation; and c) *oblique transmission (O)*, in which any member of one generation talks to any non-biologically-related member of a later generation. Besides empirical studies, computational modeling that incorporates these forms of transmission has joined the endeavour to tackle problems of language evolution. This line of research has started from the Iterated Learning Model (ILM, Kirby, 2001), in which V transmission across single-individual generations is simulated and a limited exposure to the previous generation's linguistic instances is shown to trigger the origin of a compositional language in the future generation's language learner (*the bottleneck effect*). This effect is also shown in a laboratory experiment (Kirby et al., 2008) and proved in some Bayesian learning models (e.g., Kirby et al., 2007). Some later versions of ILM (e.g., Smith & Hurford, 2003) started to incorporate multi-agent generations and both V and O transmissions.

Meanwhile, some new models have been developed (e.g. Vogt, 2005), which uses two probability parameters to restrict the choices of speakers and listeners from adults or children during transmission. However, this probability approach implicitly involves the child-talking-to-adults transmission, which contaminates the effects of other forms on language evolution (Gong et al., in press).

In this paper, we modify this probability approach by proposing three parameters to control respectively the probabilities of H, V, and O transmissions. In this acquisition framework, children can talk to each other via H transmission, and adults talk to children via V or O transmission. These probability parameters are less dependent on the actual numbers of transmission and the particular language models. We use a ternary plot to vividly show that each form of transmission has its respective role in language evolution and all these forms have collectively led to a dynamic equilibrium of language evolution. The rest of the paper is organized as follows: Sec. 2 briefly reviews the language model; Sec. 3 describes the acquisition framework and simulation setup; Sec. 4 discusses the simulation results; and Sec. 5 gives the conclusions.

2. The Lexicon-Syntax Coevolution Model

This model was designed to study if a population of interacting *individuals* (artificial agents), based on some general learning mechanisms, can develop a compositional language out of a holistic signaling system (Gong, 2009). The evolved communal language is *systematic*, consisting of a set of lexical items and simple consistent word order(s). This model has two key features. First, it simulates the development of idiolects. Based on pattern extraction, individuals extract recurrent patterns in exchanged utterances into lexical items; based on semantic and sequential guidance of lexical items in exchanged utterances, individuals categorize lexical items with identical semantic roles and similarly ordered with respect to other lexical items in utterances; and based on categories and local orders among them, individuals form up global orders to regulate lexical items and encode simple predicate-argument meanings (Hurford, 2007) in utterances. The linguistic knowledge is represented by lexical rules, syntactic rules, and categories. Second, this model implements an *implicit meaning transfer* during dyadic transmission. Both the speaker and the listener refer to their own linguistic knowledge in production and comprehension. In production, the speaker can randomly create a holistic rule to map the chosen meaning, if its linguistic knowledge fails to encode that meaning; in comprehension, besides linguistic knowledge, some nonlinguistic, *unreliable* cue (which may or may not contain the speaker's intended meaning) may assist interpretation. Based on a standard, strength-based competition, individuals select their linguistic rules among the competing ones. Without direct meaning check, if the combined strength of the listener's used rules exceeds a *confidence threshold*, both individuals award their used rules (by increasing their strengths) and penalize (by decreasing their strengths) other competing ones; otherwise, both penalize their used rules in this transmission. In this way, the linguistic knowledge of these two individuals will become similar, which resembles the process of *conventionalization* (a social agreement for meaning–utterance associations). Both of these features make this model suitable to simulate language acquisition in children, and provide an appropriate level of complexity to discuss the role of cultural transmission in language evolution. Please refer to Gong (2009) for a detailed description of the major components, the transmission scenario, and the adopted learning mechanisms of this model, and a systematic discussion of the effects of various parameters that control those learning mechanisms.

3. The Language Acquisition Framework

Fig. 1 shows this framework. In each generation, a fixed number of randomly chosen adults each produce an offspring (child) that initially has no linguistic knowledge. Then, during a learning stage, each child develops his/her idiolect by learning from an adult via Parent-to-Child (V) or Adult-to-Child (O) transmission or from another child via Child-to-Child (H) transmission. The ratios of these forms are respectively manipulated by *PCrate*, *ACrate* and *CCrate*. During transmission, there is no global fitness guiding a child to learn from a specific adult or child. After the learning stage, children become adults and replace their parents, and a new generation begins.

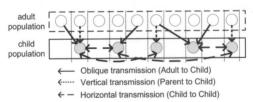

Figure 1. The acquisition framework that involves the three major forms of cultural transmission.

Strictly speaking, this is a pure cultural evolution setup without inheritance of biological features during reproduction. But it is still necessary to distinguish V and O transmissions. If there is more than one of V transmission, a child keeps sampling from its parent. If there is more than one of O transmission, however, a child can sample from more than one adult. Considering that this child may interact with the offspring of those adults in H transmission, O transmission may play a different role from V transmission on language evolution. In addition, it is necessary to distinguish adults and children. Considering *the critical period hypothesis* (Penfield and Roberts, 1959), we assume that only children update their linguistic knowledge in transmission, adults do not. Then, H transmission is distinct from V and O transmissions. Furthermore, PCrate, ACrate and CCrate control the percentages of different forms of transmission in the total number of transmission involving multiple individuals during the learning stage, instead of the number of transmission in which a particular new child is involved.

Table 1. The parameter settings. The left table lists the basic parameters for communications and acquisition framework. Please refer to Gong (2009) for the discussion of the effects of parameters for communications. The right table lists the 54 cases in each set of simulations. There are three extreme cases: the case of purely horizontal transmission (PCrate=ACrate=0.0, CCrate=1.0) is excluded, since it is obvious that in this case no language is transmitted across generations and children in each generation are creating their own communal language via horizontal transmission; the case of purely vertical transmission (PCrate=1.0, ACrate=CCrate=0.0) is discussed separately in Sec. 4, and so as the case of purely oblique transmission (PCrate=CCrate=0.0, ACrate=1.0).

	Parameters	Values	Cases	PCrate	ACrate	CCrate
For communications	Semantic space	64	1	0.0	0.1	0.9
	Individual memory size for lexical rules	60	2	0.0	0.2	0.8
	Individual memory size for categories	20	3	0.0	0.3	0.7
	Individual memory size for syntactic rules	20	⋮			
	Extraction rate of lexical/syntactic rules	0.25	9	0.0	0.9	0.1
	Creation rate of holistic rules	0.25	10	0.1	0.0	0.9
	Strength adjustment in competition	0.1	11	0.1	0.1	0.8
	Amount of strength adjustment in forgetting	0.01	⋮			
	Reliability of cue	0.6	18	0.1	0.8	0.1
	Confidence threshold	0.75	19	0.2	0.0	0.8
	No. of utterance exchange per transmission	20	⋮			
For the acquisition framework	Population size	10	51	0.7	0.2	0.1
	No. of adults each producing 1 offspring	5	52	0.8	0.0	0.2
	No. of transmissions in the learning stage	200	53	0.8	0.1	0.1
	No. of generations	100	54	0.9	0.0	0.1

The roles of different forms of transmission on language evolution are studied based on the understandability of the communal language. We define three indices: a) *understanding rate (UR) within a particular generation ($UR_{i,i}$)*, calculating the average percentage of integrated meanings understandable to each pair of individuals after the learning stage, based only on their linguistic knowledge; b) $UR_{i,i+1}$, calculated as UR between individuals from Generations i and $i+1$; and c) $UR_{1,i}$, calculated as UR between individuals from Generations 1 and i. High $UR_{i,i+1}$ indicates that a communal language is accurately understood by individuals across consecutive generations. High $UR_{1,i}$ indicates that an initial language is largely preserved in later generations. We conduct two sets of simulations, whose parameter settings are listed in Table 1. In the first set, the adults in Generation 1 only share a limited number of holistic rules to express few integrated meanings; in the second set, the adults in Generation 1 share a compositional language capable of expressing all integrated meanings. In each set, 54 cases are considered based on *PCrate*, *ACrate* and *CCrate* (see Table 1).

4. The Simulation Results

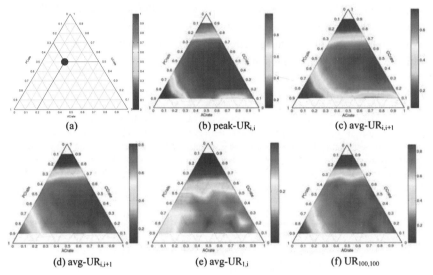

(a)   (b) peak-$UR_{i,i}$ (c) avg-$UR_{i,i+1}$

(d) avg-$UR_{i,i+1}$ (e) avg-$UR_{1,i}$ (f) $UR_{100,100}$

Figure 2. (a) The patch corresponds to the case PCrate=0.3, ACrate=0.2, CCrate=0.5, and its value is 1.0, based on the color map beside). (b)(c): the simulation results in the first set of simulations. (d)-(f): the simulation results in the second set of simulations. Each value is calculated based on 20 runs.

We adopt surface ternary plots to show the results. Figure 2 shows how to read in such plots and the results of the two sets. For the first set, we measure peak-$UR_{i,i}$ and avg-$UR_{i,i+1}$ in 100 generations; for the second set, we measure avg-$UR_{i,i+1}$ and avg-$UR_{1,i}$ in 100 generations. In the second set, peak-$UR_{i,i}$ appears in Generation 1, since all adults initially share a common compositional language. Therefore, we measure $UR_{100,100}$. The tendencies shown in these results are less dependent on the number of transmission during the learning stage and the number of individuals replaced in each generation, except that the absolute values of those indices in different settings could be different.

These results can be analyzed based on the UR values in different regions of the plots. Near the left angle, V transmission is dominant (PCrate is high, ACrate and CCrate are low), and the low UR values show that if the learning stage has mainly V transmission, both the origin of a common language with good understandability and the maintenance of an initial compositional language cannot be achieved. A further check based on the simulations with different numbers of purely V transmission (PCrate=1.0, ACrate=CCrate=0.0) confirms this finding (Gong et al., in press). It differs from the finding in ILM (e.g., Smith & Hurford, 2003), where purely V transmission can trigger a communal language with good understandability. This difference is due to the implicit meaning transfer in our language model. In the first set, while talking to children, adults in early generations, due to lacking linguistic knowledge, have to introduce new expressions. Since children have no linguistic knowledge, comprehension of these expressions relies on cues, and the occasional "wrong" cues having meanings different from adults' intended ones may cause children to develop some salient knowledge. Without V or O transmission, children develop independently their linguistic knowledge. After they replace adults and talk to new children, the idiolects among individuals will continue to diverge. In the second set, adults in Generation 1 have already shared some linguistic knowledge, but the unreliable cues still cast their influence, especially when adults talk to children not yet acquiring much linguistic knowledge. Without other forms of transmission, this influence could accumulate to such an extent that the communal language after a few generations becomes quite distinct from the initial one. Therefore, purely V transmission in a multi-individual population fails to trigger or maintain a communal language with good understandability.

Near the top angle, H transmission is dominant (PCrate and ACrate are low, CCrate is high), during which children can be either speakers or listeners, and both speakers and listeners update their linguistic knowledge. This two-way conventionalization is efficient to spread linguistic knowledge among individuals, thus helping their idiolects to converge. H transmission is good at maintaining high understandability within generations, and the two-way conventionalization may help diffuse some salient linguistic knowledge to the population, thus introducing changes in the communal language. However, H transmission occurs only among children, without sufficient other forms of transmission to get a broad sample of adults' language, what children develop in H transmission is a set of salient rules different from those of the adults. After being adults, without sufficient V or O transmission, they cannot provide enough instances of their idiolects to new children, who will keep randomly creating their own idiolects. Therefore, as shown by the low UR values, a communal language with good understandability cannot be preserved across generations via mainly H transmission.

Near the right angle, O transmission is dominant (PCrate and CCrate are low, but ACrate is high). This form of transmission has a similar role as V transmission by providing children with instances of the previous generation's language, but it allows one child to sample from multiple adults, thus making it more efficient than V transmission to spread linguistic knowledge of multiple individuals to new children. This results in the higher UR values in this angle than those in the left. In addition, only children update their linguistic knowledge in O transmission, adults do not. This one-way conventionalization of idiolects is less efficient than H transmission, which explains why the UR values in the first set are lower than those in the second set of simulations. A further check of simulations with purely O transmission shows that the UR value in this case is lower than those in the regions with many rounds of O transmission but a few of H transmission, which suggests the necessity of other forms of transmission, such as H transmission.

These three regions illustrate the relative roles of V, O, and H transmissions on language evolution. In all these plots, the highest UR values are obtained in the regions with some low values of PCrate but high values of either ACrate or CCrate. This shows that either V or O transmission is necessary for spreading language across generations and H transmission is also needed to maintain the understandability of the communal language within generations. In addition, during these forms of transmission, some salient knowledge may diffuse to the whole population, which introduce changes in the communal language, which causes the maximum values of $UR_{1,i}$ in these plots are not much high, compared with $UR_{i,i}$ and $UR_{i,i+1}$. All these results indicate that all these forms of transmission are necessary to trigger a communal language with good understandability and to largely preserve an initial communal language across generations. They also reveal a *dynamic equilibrium* of language evolution: in a cultural environment involving sufficient these three forms of transmission, individuals from consecutive generations can well understand each other ($UR_{i,i+1}$ is high), but language change is inevitable in the long run (UR_{ini} is not high). This equilibrium is collectively achieved by these three forms of transmission.

5. Conclusions

This paper proposes a multi-agent acquisition framework to discuss the roles of three major forms of cultural transmission in language evolution. Both V and O transmissions help maintain an initial language to a certain extent, and H transmission is necessary for maintaining the understandability of the communal language and diffusing linguistic variation. A reasonable combination of these forms of transmission can not only efficiently trigger a communal language but also largely maintain it across generations of language learners. These findings are insightful on research of other cognitive, political or economic activities that are also culturally transmitted. And the current framework can be modified to involve other forms of transmission (e.g., grandparent-grandchild transmission) or adopt continuous generation replacement or family structures. Both of these can help better understand the role of cultural factors on language evolution.

Acknowledgements

The author acknowledges the support from the Alexander von Humboldt Foundation in Germany, and thanks Prof. William S-Y. Wang and Dr. James W. Minett from the Chinese University of Hong Kong for their useful comments.

References

Christiansen, M. H. & Kirby, S. (2003). Language evolution: Consensus and controversies. *Trends in Cognitive Sciences*, 7, 300-307.

Gong, T. (2009). *Computational simulation in evolutionary linguistics: A study on language emergence.* Taipei: Institute of Linguistics, Academia Sinica.

Gong, T., Minett, J. W., & Wang, W. S-Y. (in press). A simulation study exploring the role of cultural transmission in language evolution. *Connection Science.*

Kirby, S. (2001). Spontaneous evolution of linguistic structures: an iterated learning model of the emergence of regularity and irregularity, *IEEE Trans. Evolutionary Computation*, 5, 102-110.

Kirby, S., Dowman, M., & Griffiths, T. (2007). Innateness and culture in the evolution of language. *Proceedings of the National Academy of Sciences*, 104, 5241-5245.

Kirby, S., Cornish, H., & Smith, K. (2008). Cumulative cultural evolution in the laboratory: An experimental approach to the origins of structure in human language. *Proceedings of the National Academy of Sciences*, 105, 10681-10686.

Penfield, W. & Roberts, L. (1959). *Speech and brain-mechanisms.* Princeton, NJ: Princeton University Press.

Smith, K. & Hurford, J. (2003). Language evolution in populations: Extending the Iterated Learning Model. In W. Banzharf, T. Christaller, P. Dittrich, J. T. Kim, and J. Ziegler (Eds.), *Proceedings of the 7th European conference on artificial life* (pp. 507-516). Berlin: Springer-Verlag.

Vogt, P. (2005). On the acquisition and evolution of compositional languages: sparse input and productive creativity of children. *Adaptive Behaviour*, 13, 325-346.

HOW TO IDENTIFY THE UNITS, LEVELS AND MECHANISMS OF LANGUAGE EVOLUTION

NATHALIE GONTIER

Marie Curie Outgoing Research Fellow, Division of Paleontology, American Museum of Natural History, New York City, New York & Centre for Logic and Philosophy of Science, Vrije Universiteit Brussel, Pleinlaan 2, 1050 Brussels, Belgium

When evolutionary biologists and epistemologists investigate the evolution of life, they deconstruct the problem into three research areas: they search for the units, levels and mechanisms of life's evolution. Here, it is investigated how a similar approach can be applied to evolutionary linguistics. A methodology is proposed that allows us to identify and further investigate the units, levels and mechanisms of language evolution.

1. Introduction

Evolutionary epistemologists and biologists agree that life is a highly complex, hierarchically-structured phenomenon. It is too complex to study as a whole, and scholars have therefore found it useful to decompose the study of life's evolution into the search for the units, levels and mechanisms of evolution (Campbell, 1960; Hull, 1980; Lewontin, 1970). Here, it will be argued that evolutionary linguists can benefit from applying a similar approach to the study of the evolution of language.

Many evolutionary linguists agree that language is a highly complex and heterogeneous phenomenon. It can come in both spoken and signed forms and each language is composed of syntax, morphology, semantics, etc. Furthermore, language is anatomically associated with specific morphological structures of the human body (e.g. the supralaryngeal vocal tract, the way we curl our fingers to sign) and brain (Wernicke's and Broca's area). The recognition of this heterogeneity of language as well as the multiplicity of morphological structures that allow us to have language implies that if we want to know how language evolved, we need to study the evolution of all these different elements. Put in evolutionary epistemological jargon, all these elements can be considered as *units* of language evolution.

Most evolutionary linguists will further acknowledge that language is partly a biological phenomenon and partly a cultural phenomenon. It is a biological phenomenon because of these morphological and neurological language-related structures. It is also a cultural phenomenon that "transcends" our biological make-up because newborn infants are unable to develop a full language by themselves. Rather, they learn the language that is spoken in their "language community" through frequent interactions with their parents and peers. In evolutionary epistemological jargon, these neurological, cognitive and socio-cultural aspects of language can be considered *levels* where language evolves.

Finally, many evolutionary linguists also investigate how specific evolutionary mechanisms can explain the evolution of (aspects of) language. Natural selection has been implicated as one of the major evolutionary mechanisms underlying language evolution (Pinker & Bloom, 1990). But also derivatives of, or alternatives to this mechanism have been associated with the evolution of language. Examples include the Baldwin effect, Ratchet effect, niche construction, etc. In evolutionary epistemological jargon, this implies that the aforementioned *evolutionary mechanisms* are not only applicable at an evolutionary biological level, but also at a cultural level. We therefore need to examine how the same mechanism can be implicated in both biological and extra-biological phenomena.

In other words, although neither the units and levels of selection debate, nor evolutionary epistemological jargon has been explicitly implemented in evolutionary linguistics, we can understand the research that is being done as exactly such an endeavour of identifying units, levels and mechanisms of language evolution. In fact, a quick dive into the literature allows us to make the following, tentative list of possible units, levels and mechanisms of language evolution (table 1).

Table 1 A tentative listing of different units, levels and mechanisms of language evolution

Units	Levels	Mechanisms
(Language-related) genes? brain regions? mirror neurons? The supralaryngeal vocal tract? home signs? Pointing? Idio- socio-dialects? ToM? Machiavellian Intelligence? Syntax? Lexicon? Semantics?	Genetic? Neuronal? Brain? Cognitive? The individual/ ontogenetic? Linguistic (language in itself)? The group? Socio-Cultural/ the language Community? The species?	Natural, sexual selection? Drift? Neural Darwinism? The Baldwin effect? The Ratchet effect? Niche construction? Co-evolution?

How then can we make the identification of units, levels and mechanisms in evolutionary linguistics more explicit? By introducing the following five clusters of evolutionary epistemological questions: (1) How many units of language evolution are there? (2) How many levels of language evolution are there? (3) Which of these units and levels are necessary and/or sufficient for language to evolve? (4) How do the different units interact, how do the different levels interact, and how do the units and levels in turn interact with each other? Can we order them hierarchically? (5) How many evolutionary mechanisms underlie the evolution of these different units? How do these evolutionary mechanisms work? In the following sections, it will be demonstrated how the implementation of these questions can be beneficial to the field of evolutionary linguistics, for it will be shown how they cast new light upon existing problems and help build more complete theories on how language evolved.

2. Three evolutionary epistemological heuristics of language evolution

How exactly is it that we can examine a certain trait, feature, event, ... from now on designated as x, as a unit, level or mechanism of language evolution? Three evolutionary epistemological heuristics are provided that answer these questions.

2.1. *The unit heuristic*

How do we know that x is a unit of language evolution? The heuristic outlined in table 2 suggests that we can identify x as a unit of language evolution if and only if we can identify a level where x evolves, and a mechanism according to which x evolves.

Table 2 Is x (a feature, trait, space, event, element, ... that is presumed relevant for language evolution) a unit in/of language evolution? read from left to right and top-down

?	Try to prove that it is a unit of language evolution (1 example suffices). Thus go to **yes**.		
Y E S	**Where?** At which **level** is x the subject of language evolution.	Not one level found? X is not a unit, go to **no**.	
		One/multiple level(s)? (Justifies that x is a unit.)	Via which **evolutionary mechanism(s)** does x evolve?
	Since **when**?	When did x first originate in time and when did it become a unit of language evolution?	
	How does this unit x **interact** with other units?	Can this unit be divided into one or several **subunits**? If so, are they also units in language evolution?	
		Can this unit be absorbed into one or several **super units**? If so, are they also units in language evolution?	
	Can this unit also be regarded as a **level** and/or **mechanism** of language evolution?	? & yes: try and treat the unit as a level and/or a mechanism, go to **level and/or mechanism**.	
	Relevance?	Is the unit x **sufficient** and/or **necessary** for language evolution?	
N O	Level and/or mechanism?	? or Yes: go to **level** and/or **mechanism**.	
		No. Window?	Yes: treat x accordingly.
			No: treat x as irrelevant.

In other words, a language unit is defined extensionally and even ostensively, by pointing out the level where, and the mechanism by which, it evolves. This approach differs from traditional approaches in evolutionary epistemology (EE) where units are defined by intrinsic properties such as replication (Dawkins, 1982: 162), interaction (Hull, 1981), or reproduction (Griesemer, 2000). Instead, this paper is written from a pragmatic point of view. It asks how we can identify units, not how we can define them. We can identify units by pointing out the level where they evolve, and the mechanism(s) by which they evolve.

If one is able to identify x as a unit of language evolution, the heuristic goes on to suggest that we locate the origin of x in time. Thus, we need to ask when x originated and when it became part of language evolution. The *FOXP2* gene for example (Vargha-Khadem, 2005) is a very old gene and cannot have been a unit of language evolution from its origin in fungi onwards. Nonetheless, at some point in time, it became associated with language.

The problem of hierarchies is tackled by asking if the unit can be subdivided into smaller subunits or embedded into larger superunits. If so, it is recommended that these sub- and superunits are also investigated as possible language evolution units. Because of the fact that no intrinsic definition is given to what a unit might be, we might find it useful to ask whether x, even if it is a unit, might also be a level or even a mechanism of language evolution. Pointing (Leavens, Hopkins, Bard, 2005; Tomasello, 2000), for example, might be a unit of language evolution, but it might also serve as a level where other units such as problem solving evolve.

Once we have considered all these questions, we are much better able to evaluate the importance of x, both in the evolution of language as well as in theorizing on the matter. We examine the importance of x by investigating if the unit is necessary and/or sufficient for language evolution; and necessary and/or sufficient in a theory on language evolution. In other words, the heuristic enables us to evaluate whether more research needs to be conducted or not.

If, on the other hand, we were not able to identify x as a unit of language evolution, we might ask if it is a level or a mechanism of language evolution. If neither, x might provide us with a *window* on language evolution. The concept of a window of language evolution was first introduced by Botha (2006). A window is not an actual unit of language evolution but a phenomenon that allows us to draw inferences on how language evolved. Examples given by Botha are current ape signing, Pidgin languages, Creoles and hominin tools.

2.2. *The level heuristic*

How do we know that x is a level of language evolution? By recursively identifying units that evolve at that level and mechanisms that are active on these units that evolve at this level (table 3). In other words, x is a level of language evolution if and only if one can point out at least one unit that evolves at this level according to one evolutionary mechanism.

Specific to this heuristic is that it asks for the ontological status of the level. Although the primary goal of this article is to pragmatically identify the different units, levels and mechanisms involved in language evolution, we cannot circumvent some metaphysical considerations, especially when we introduce levels of language evolution. If we argue, for example, that there exists a cultural realm, or a linguistic community, we need to investigate how real and material they are, or whether they are merely concepts invoked to facilitate theory formation. Anthropologists and linguists have been heavily criticized for assuming that culture or language can form a superorganic structure, especially when it is claimed that this superorganic structure can have an existence independent from this organic level (Sapir, 1917). Of course, neither language nor culture can exist without the presence of real human beings, but neither culture nor language can be reduced to living organisms or even groups. Language and culture can be "carried" by individuals, groups and material things. From an epistemological point of view, it can therefore be useful to postulate the existence of hierarchies, which enable one to analyse the existing data more analytically.

Table 3 Is x (a feature, trait, space, event, element, ... that is presumed relevant for language evolution) a level in/of language evolution? (read from left to right and top-down)

?	Try to prove that it is a level of language evolution (1 example suffices). Thus go to **yes**.		
Y E S	How many/which language **units** evolve at this level?	Not one language unit, x is not a level of language evolution, go to **no**.	
		One/multiple unit? (Justifies that x is a level.)	
	How many **evolutionary mechanisms** are active at (not on) this level?	Equals the question: how many evolutionary mechanisms are active upon the units that evolve at this level. (testing device)	
	What is the **ontological status** of the level?	The level is an **abstract notion** that facilitates theory formation/ an **exiting entity**.	
	Since **when**?	Locate the origin of x in time or when it becomes necessary to invoke x as an abstract notion in the theory	
	How does this level x **interact** with other levels?	Can this level be divided into **sublevels**? If so, are they also units in language evolution?	
		Can this level be absorbed into **superlevels**? If so, are they also units in language evolution?	
	Can this level also be regarded as a **unit** and/or **mechanism** of language evolution?	? & yes: try and treat the level as a unit and/or mechanism, go to **unit and/or mechanism**.	
	Relevance?	Is the level x **sufficient** and/or **necessary** for language evolution?	
N O	**Unit and/or mechanism**?	? or Yes: go to **unit** and/or **mechanism**.	
		No. Window?	Yes: treat accordingly.
			No: treat x as irrelevant

It is necessary to ask about the ontological status in order to be able to complete the next step prescribed by the heuristic. This step asks one to locate the origin of the level in time (when it is an existing entity), or to pinpoint when it becomes epistemologically necessary to invoke the level in the theory.

Afterwards, it can be asked if we can subdivide existing levels or embed them into higher levels, and as such one can try to establish ontological or at least epistemological hierarchies. This also allows us to identify new levels.

As was the case with units, it is useful to ask if levels might simultaneously be units or mechanisms of language evolution. Linguistic communities might serve as a level for the evolution of idiolects and sociolects, but they can themselves also be units of cultural evolution.

Finally, these research questions will again allow us to more firmly evaluate how necessary and/or sufficient the level is in the evolution of language and in theory formation on the subject.

If, on the contrary, we were not able to identify x as a level of language evolution, we can again recursively ask if x is either a unit or a mechanism of language evolution or whether it provides a window on language evolution.

2.3. *The mechanism heuristic*

How do we know that x is a mechanism involved in the evolution of language? X can be recognized as a mechanism of language evolution if and only if we are able to identify units of language evolution whereupon x is active, at a certain level of language evolution. If one or multiple such units are identified, x is indeed a mechanism involved in the evolution of language.

Specific to this heuristic is that it subsequently asks *how* the mechanism works. It is especially here that previous work done in the field of EE can be applied. When faced with questions about how natural selection can be equally applied to biological and extra-biological phenomena, evolutionary epistemologists have found it useful to abstract templates of natural selection. Campbell (1960) argued that natural selection works according to a blind variation and selective retention scheme. This means that each time we can identify something to vary blindly and to be selectively retained, it evolves by means of natural selection regardless of whether that something is a gene, phenotype, cognitive trait, or linguistic feature. Furthermore, the template has heuristic potential: it informs you on how the mechanism works and how we can identify it to be active. Lewontin (1970: 1) abstracted the following logical skeleton of natural selection: phenotypic variation, differential fitness and the heritability of that fitness. Hull (1981) has introduced a template of replicators, interactors and lineages. According to Hull, environmental interaction forms the basis for differential variation (different replicators) and this results in the evolution of different lineages. So far, only Hull's heuristic has been applied to linguistics. Croft (2000) introduced the notion of a lingueme, a linguistic meme (a replicator), that can be understood as a unit of selection. Linguemes are carried by individuals that belong to different speech communities. Their interactions induce variations in the linguemes, and natural selection can subsequently act upon this variation.

Evolutionary mechanisms can be active in many kinds of evolution (the evolution of the brain, the evolution of culture, life, etc.). It is therefore necessary to locate in time when a certain evolutionary mechanism became active, specifically in language evolution.

We can also ask ourselves if the evolutionary mechanism can be divided into submechanisms or embedded into larger supermechanisms. Some authors argue that the ratchet effect is a form of evolution by means of natural selection, others argue that it is a different mechanism. In the latter case, we have to demonstrate how it can work independently from natural selection, in the former we need to examine how it is embedded in natural selection.

Table 4 Is x (an evolutionary mechanism, feature, trait, space, event, element, … that is presumed relevant for language evolution) an evolutionary mechanism involved in/on language evolution? (read from left to right and top-down)

?	Try to prove that x is an evolutionary mechanism involved in language evolution. Thus go to **yes**.	
Y E S	On how many **units** is this evolutionary mechanism working?	Not one unit: x is not an evolutionary mechanism involved in language evolution, go to **no**.
		One/multiple unit(s). (Justifies that x is an evolutionary mechanism involved in language evolution.)
	At (not on) how many **levels** of language evolution is this evolutionary mechanism active?	Equals the question: the units that are subjected to this evolutionary mechanism, at how many levels are they subjected to it?
	How does the mechanism work? Which **conditions** need to be met in order for the evolutionary mechanism to occur? Answer requires (universal) **EE formulas** of the workings of the mechanism.	
	Since **when**?	Locate in time when these conditions are met regarding each unit and each level = when the evolutionary mechanism became a mechanism involved in language evolution at that unit and/or level.
	How does this mechanism x **interact** with other mechanisms involved in the evolution of language?	Can this mechanism be divided into **sub-mechanism(s)**? (Depends on the presence of subconditions.) If so, are they also mechanisms of language evolution?
		Can this mechanism be absorbed into a **super-mechanism(s)**? (Depends on the existence of a mechanism that allows to combine different mechanisms into one single mechanism.) If so, are they also mechanisms of language evolution?
	Is this mechanism also a **unit and/or level** of language evolution?	? & yes: try and treat the mechanism as a unit and/or level, go to **unit and/or level**.
	Relevance?	Is the mechanism x sufficient and/or necessary for language evolution?
N O	**Unit and/or level**?	? or Yes: go to **unit** and/or **level**.
		No. Window? — Yes: treat x accordingly.
		No: treat x as irrelevant

It is also useful to ask ourselves whether the mechanism itself is either a unit or a level of language evolution. Because no intrinsic definition is given with regards to what a mechanism is, such a possibility cannot be excluded a priori.

Finally, answering these questions again allows us to rigorously evaluate the importance of the mechanism in language evolution and theories thereof. If, on the other hand, no unit has been found upon which the mechanism is active at a certain level of language evolution, we might examine if x is a unit or a level of language evolution, or if it provides us with a window on language evolution. If it is neither, x can be treated as irrelevant for the evolution of language.

3. Conclusion

At present, scholars are studying a variety of phenomena that are implicated in language evolution. Unfortunately, the nature of these phenomena is not always clear, and neither is it obvious how the different elements under study relate to one another and fit in the puzzle of language evolution. The heuristics provided here allow for the identification, examination and evaluation of the different units, levels and mechanisms of language evolution. As such, they enable us to build unifying theories of language evolution.

References

Botha, R. (2006). On the Windows Approach to language evolution. *Language & Communication,* 26 (2), 129-143.

Campbell, D.T. (1960). Blind variation and selective retention in creative thought as in other knowledge processes. *Psychological Review,* 67(6): 380-400.

Croft, W. (2000). *Explaining language change: An evolutionary approach.* Essex: Pearson.

Dawkins, R. (1982). Replicators and vehicles. In N.R. Brandon and R.M. Burian (Eds.) (1984), *Genes, organisms, populations* (pp. 161-79). Cambridge, MA: MIT Press.

Griesemer J. (2000). Development, culture and the units of inheritance. *Philosophy of Science,* 67, S348-S368.

Hull, D.L. (1981). Units of evolution. In N.R. Brandon and R.M. Burian (Eds.) (1984), *Genes, organisms, populations* (pp. 142-159). Cambridge, MA: MIT Press.

Leavens, D.A., Hopkins, W.D. & Bard, K.A. (2005). Understanding the point of chimpanzee pointing: Epigenesis and ecological validity. *Current Directions in Psychological Science,* 14 (4), 185-9.

Lewontin, R. (1970). The levels of selection. *Annual Review of Ecological Systems,* 1, 1-18.

Pinker, S., & Bloom, P. (1990). Natural language and natural selection. *Behavioral and Brain Sciences, 13,* 707-784.

Sapir, E. 1917 Do we need a superorganic? *American Anthropologist,* 19, 441-7.

Tomasello, M. (2000). *The cultural origins of human cognition.* Cambridge, MA: Harvard University Press.

Vargha-Khadem, F. et al. (2005). *FOXP2* and the neuroanatomy of speech and language. Nature Reviews, *Neuroscience,* 6, 131-138.

LINGUISTIC ANALOGY FOR
CREATIVITY AND THE ORIGIN OF LANGUAGE

TAKASHI HASHIMOTO, MASAYA NAKATSUKA, TAKESHI KONNO

School of Knowledge Science
Japan Advanced Institute of Science and Technology (JAIST)
Nomi, Ishikawa, Japan, 923-1292, JAPAN
hash@jaist.ac.jp, m-naka@master.email.ne.jp, t-konno@jaist.ac.jp
`http://www.jaist.ac.jp/~hash/index-e.html`

Through a constructive study of grammaticalization as a potentially important process of language evolution, we have found two findings. One is that linguistic analogy, which applies linguistic rules extendedly, is a very critical for language acquisition and meaning change. The other is that inferences based on the recognition of similarity and contingency among particular meanings can realize unidirectional meaning change, a remarkable characteristic of grammaticalization. We discuss the significance of these findings in the context of the origin and the evolution of language, especially the role of linguistic analogy in creativity. Based on the discussion, a hypothetical scenario of the origin and the evolution of language is proposed.

1. Introduction

The purpose of the study of language origin is to clarify the biological evolutionary process of physical and cognitive characteristics making human language possible. That of language evolution is to reveal the cultural evolutionary process of complexification and structuralization of initial language into present languages. Grammaticalization is a kind of meaning change in which lexical items come to bear grammatical functions, and is a critical feature of human language. The remarkable characteristics of grammaticalization are its universality and unidirectionality. The former means that the same kind of changes are found in many languages in the world without language contact (Heine & Kuteva, 2002b). The latter means that changes from function to content words are extremely rare. Due to these characteristics, grammaticalization is thought of as playing an important role in the evolution of language (Hurford, 2003; Heine & Kuteva, 2002a, 2007). Further, these characteristics imply a universal mechanism in human cognition to cause characteristic meaning change like grammaticalization. Thus, inquiring cognitive mechanisms realizing grammaticalization will be useful in understanding language origin.

In this paper, from the viewpoint of creativity of language, we discuss cognitive mechanisms and biases studied in (Hashimoto & Nakatsuka, 2006, 2008), in which those causing unidirectional meaning changes have been studied using an evolutionary constructive approach (Hashimoto, Sato, Nakatsuka, & Fujimoto, 2008). The important cognitive mechanism providing this creativity is *linguistic analogy*, which is an ability to extend the application of linguistic rules. We finally show a hypothetical scenario of the origin and the evolution of language based on the constructive study.

2. Summary of Model and Findings from Simulation

As constructing a model of cognitive mechanism, we accept a hypothesis by Hopper and Traugott (2003) that reanalysis and analogy are indispensable for grammaticalization. We reconsider reanalysis and analogy as cognitive abilities of language users and define two abilities: the ability of "reanalysis" is to decide the way to segment sentences according to one's own knowledge, and that of "linguistic analogy" is to extend construction rules to forms to which the rules have not yet been applied. Note that linguistic analogy is not the same as usual analogy, which is to transfer information from source to target subjects based on similarity. For linguistic analogy, it is considered that similarity is not necessary, but actual exhibition of this ability is constrained by cognitive biases.

We adopt an agent model of iterated learning framework used in (Kirby, 2003), in which agents transmit linguistic knowledge over generations, with two extensions, one is to deal with functional meanings and the other is to introduce two cognitive biases. We summarize the basic model, and then explain the extensions. The detail of the basic model is in (Kirby, 2003).

Using a generalization learning algorithm, a language learner learns linguistic knowledge from a speaker. The speaker utters sentences (forms) corresponding to meanings given with its own linguistic knowledge. The learner becomes a speaker in the next generation after learning a series of meaning-utterance pairs. Linguistic knowledge is represented by a context-free grammar, which is a set of rewriting rules making connections between meanings and forms. The learning algorithm consists of three operations: chunk, merge, and replace[a]. Chunk and replace operations were found to correspond to reanalysis and linguistic analogy, respectively (Hashimoto & Nakatsuka, 2006).

Because functional meaning is missing in (Kirby, 2003), we introduced three tense meanings, past, present and future into the model in order to observe meaning change from content to functional, like from "go" to "be going to", a typical example of grammaticalization in English. Meaning given to agents has a propositional form, "[tense]verb(noun, noun)", where there are 3 tenses, 5 verbs, 5 nouns, and the two nouns used must not be the same, thus the number of possible mean-

---

[a]The replace operation is only explained but not named in (Kirby, 2003), so we named it in (Hashimoto & Nakatsuka, 2006). Note that "merge" in (Kirby, 2003) is a kind of category integration, and is different from "Merge" in minimalist program.

186

ings are 300.

We introduced two cognitive biases: co-occurrence and pragmatic extension, since it was found that unidirectional meaning change was not realized merely introducing functional meanings. Co-occurrence is the recognition of contingency as a basis of metonymic inferencing. In this model, we set co-occurrence between the meanings "go" and "future", namely, the probability of appearing meaning "[future]go(noun, noun)" is double than the other meanings. Pragmatic extension is the recognition of similarity as a basis of metaphoric inferencing. We set pragmatic extensions between the meanings "go" and "walk" and between "go" and "run". The agent can divert rules consisting of "walk" or "run" in order to express the meanings of "go". These two settings modify the learning and the use of linguistic knowledge in a particular way, thus they are considered to work as cognitive biases for language users.

It is found that linguistic analogy is very important for development of expressivity of linguistic knowledge (Fig. 1(Left)). Namely, linguistic analogy plays a critical role in generalization in language acquisition. Linguistic analogy is also virtually indispensable for meaning change (Fig. 1(Right))(Hashimoto & Nakatsuka, 2006).

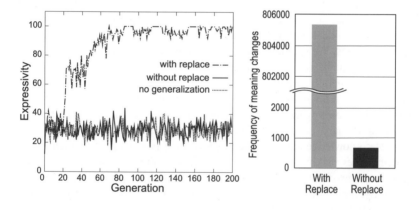

Figure 1. The effect of cognitive mechanisms: (Left) The development of expressivity with generations for three settings about cognitive mechanisms: all three operations (labeled by "with replace"); chunk and merge ("without replace"); and no operation, i.e., just memorizing ("no generalization") are shown (result of a typical run). 70 randomly selected meanings are given at each generation. Two biases are not introduced. The expressivity is the ratio of meanings describable with linguistic knowledge to all possible meanings. Only agents with all three learning operations can develop expressivity, while agents missing the replace operation stay at the same level as those without generalization learning mechanism. (Right) The differences in the frequencies of meaning changes between with and without the "replace" operation (accumulation of 100 runs).

The effects of two cognitive biases are summarized as follows: the recognition of similarity increases the frequency of meaning changes (Fig. 2(Left)), and the recognition of contingency provides unidirectional meaning changes (Fig. 2(Right)). Thus stable unidirectional meaning change is realized by the combination of metaphoric and metonymic inferencing (Hashimoto & Nakatsuka, 2008).

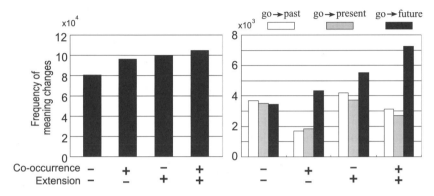

Figure 2. The effect of cognitive biases (accumulation of 100 runs) (Hashimoto & Nakatsuka, 2008): There are four settings in introducing the two biases. The symbols $+$ and $-$ indicate whether each bias is introduced or not, respectively. (Left) The frequencies of meaning changes for the four settings. The differences in frequencies between $(--)$ and $(-+)$ and between $(--)$ and $(++)$ are statistically significant, while that between $(--)$ and $(+-)$ is not. Thus, introducing pragmatic extension promotes the frequency of meaning changes. (Right) The frequencies of meaning changes from the meaning of "go" to three tense meanings. Introducing co-occurrence doubles the meaning changes, compared to the situations without co-occurrence. The other meaning changes from "go" are at the same level as those to "past" and to "present".

3. Creativity through Linguistic Analogy

We discuss linguistic analogy from the viewpoint of creativity. At first, we explain "replace" operation which corresponds to linguistic analogy: If both a meaning and a form of a word rule are included in a sentence rule, the corresponding parts in the sentence rule are replaced by a variable with the same category label as the word rule. For example, suppose that a learner acquires linguistic knowledge,

$$N/\text{girl} \quad \rightarrow \quad /\text{GIRL}/ \, , \tag{1}$$

$$S/[\text{present}]\text{read}(\text{girl}, \text{book}) \quad \rightarrow \quad /\text{GIRL READ BOOK}/ \, , \tag{2}$$

where S is a category label for sentences. In these rules, both the meaning "girl" and the form /GIRL/ in the word rule (1) are included in the sentence rule (2), respectively. In this case, the sentence rule (2) is replaced by

$$S/[\text{present}]\text{read}(N/x, \text{book}) \rightarrow /x \text{ READ BOOK}/ \, . \tag{3}$$

The "replace" operation provides the basis of extended application of rules. If this agent has other word rules in the category N, the new rule can be applied to such word rules. For example, if the learner has a word rule, N/stone $\rightarrow$ /STONE/, then he/she can produce an utterance /STONE READ BOOK/. But, he/she has never seen or heard such a situation that "[present]read(stone, book)", since the utterance is not learned through experience but created through extended inference. The ability of linguistic analogy provides an important feature, that language users can refer to entities away from "here, now, and I", which is called *displacement* and is thought of as particular and unique to human language.

Linguistic analogy enables language users to create novel expressions. Such expressions, however, are not always valid and meaningful. In order to be used for communication with others or for thought about reality, such expressions have to make sense[b]. Two ways, at least, can be supposed for the sense-making, one is to change both the interpretation of the expression and the conceptualization of the reality, and the other is to change the reality. The former way is to reinterpret the expression to be true or to be meaningful by changing an entity referred to by the words in the expression. At the same time, the entity referred to must be re-conceptualized. For example, the word /STONE/ is reinterpreted as an indication to an obstinate person who is reading a book, rather than a kind of material. Here, the interpretation of the word is changed and the interpretation of the reality, an obstinate person, is also re-conceptualized as an entity like stone. This leads to novel metaphors and artistic/poetic representations. The latter way is to change the world itself for the novel expression to become reasonable and meaningful. For the above example, if the speaker creates a stone statue of a reading person, or more interestingly, a reading machine with stone, the novel expression can be reasonable. Thus, this leads us to contrivances and (technical) innovations. Both ways are manifestations of creativity through producing novel expressions by linguistic analogy and making sense of novel expressions. We suppose that linguistic analogy can exert creative power after the acquisition of basic ontology about the world, which is plausible both ontogenetically and phylogenetically.

We can consider extensions of the number system as an instance of creativity through such a process. Suppose that a learner experiences situations such as "there are two cows" and "there are three baskets with two apples each", and abstracts such experiences to mathematical expressions of multiplication with natural numbers like "$1 \times 2 = 2$" and "$2 \times 3 = 6$", respectively. If the learner acquires the rule of multiplication, he/she will be able to answer expressions with unknowns such as "$5 \times 2 = x$", "$x \times 3 = 9$" and "$x \times x = 9$". In the last expression, the right-hand side must be a number that is limited to the square of an integer. Namely, it is considered that the application range S of a construction rule,

---

[b]We suppose that some of novel expressions may be ignored and some may be taken seriously. The latter expressions should make sense.

"$x \times x = S$", is the set of squared numbers. If the learner exhibits the ability of linguistic analogy, he/she can produce an expression like "$x \times x = 7$" by expanding the application range of the rule to any natural number. This is a meaningless expression, since there is no answer in the system of natural numbers, which is acquired through experience. If the learner creates a new number, $x = \sqrt{7}$, then the expression can be meaningful. This is an introduction of square root, that is, the extension of the number system to the system of irrational numbers[c].

The way to extend a concept is summarized as follows: at first to acquire a rule from experiences through abstraction and induction, then to produce a novel expression by extended application of the rule, and finally to make sense of the novel expression. This way can afford further extensions of concept. The extension to the system of complex numbers is realized by extended application of $\sqrt{P}$ with a positive number "P" to a negative number, and the introduction of an imaginary unit to justify a novel expression $\sqrt{-1}$. Note that the rule acquired at the first stage must have a slot or a variable part in order to be used in an extended way, such as "be going to V", where V is a slot for a verb of action. Fixed idioms like "rain cats and dogs" cannot be extended. Thus, rule acquisition at the first stage is not just finding a pattern in experiences, but extraction of a pattern with slots, which includes abstraction and inductive generalization.

4. A Hypothesis about Origin and Evolution of Language

We further discuss the creativity of linguistic analogy in the context of human evolution. Stone tools had been produced since the *Homo* genus appeared around 2 million years ago, but the diversity of tools was limited. *Homo sapiens* produced stone tools with great diversity in space and in functions 50,000 yeas ago. Arts also developed after 50,000 years ago. Archaeological evidence of wall paintings, imaginary statues such as human-like bodies with an animal heads, and stones with symbolic scratches have been found. Such major developments in arts and cultures are called the cultural explosion (Mithen, 1996).

The developments of arts and tools can be considered as manifestations of creativity through linguistic analogy. They correspond to novel metaphors and technical innovations, and also to the two ways of sense-making of novel expressions mentioned above: changing both the interpretation of the expression and the conceptualization of the reality, and changing the reality. After 50,000 years ago, humans also succeeded the exodus from Africa and expanded their habitats over most of the world, including the polar regions and islands in the oceans. For this achievement, the linguistic creativity could be used to solve severe environmental problems through making tools, clothes, houses and ships.

We consider that the adaptive function of language must be its creative power,

---

[c]We can extend mathematical theory in such a way, but in reality, it is thought that the square root was considered to be the length of a diagonal line through an equilateral rectangle (square).

rather than the communicative function, which is thought of as an exaptation as some scholars insist. The creative power of language causes the autonomous development of its diversity and complexity through linguistic analogy beyond the direct experiences of language users. The diversity and complexity of language can affect the diversification and the complexification of concepts and world though sense-making. There may be coevolutionary processes of diversification and complexification among language, concepts, thoughts and the world.

Was the transition of humans' capacity due to acquiring the ability of linguistic analogy gradual or sudden? We investigate how the expressivity changes, by controlling the probability of applying the "replace" operation, P_r, in our model. In this simulation, learners use the "replace" operation according to the probability P_r, when they have chance to use the operation in the process of generalization learning. As shown in Fig.3, the expressivity drastically drops at a very low level of P_r. This suggests that the transition is a sudden change. When language learners obtain the ability of linguistic analogy, namely, extended application of acquired rules, no matter how little of this ability, they can acquire full language.

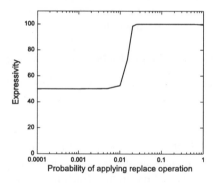

Figure 3. The change of expressivity in terms of the probability of applying "replace" operation: The expressivity reaches 100% for $P_r > 0.01$, and drastically decreases at $P_r = 0.01$.

As a summary of this paper, we propose a hypothetical scenario about the origin and the evolution of language based on the above findings and considerations. Humans, not only modern but also ancestral, were capable of communication using memory-based symbol systems, called proto-languages[d]. Around 50,000 years ago, *Homo sapiens* acquired the ability of linguistic analogy and

[d]Brain size developed greatly since the *Homo* genus appeared. The evolved brains might have been devoted to memorizing fruitful lexical items, constructions, and short sentences through experience. The fact that *Homo sapiens* has a smaller brain than *Homo neanderthalensis* can be supporting evidence for the difference between proto-(memory-based) language and modern (rule-based and productive) language.

suddenly became able to autonomically develop linguistic knowledge. Only modern humans attained displacement and linguistic creativity. Thanks to this ability their creativity realized the cultural explosion and the exodus from Africa. Thus, the origin of modern language should be thought of as before or around 50,000 years ago in *Homo sapiens*. Then, grammaticalization occurred through cognitive biases of the metaphoric and metonymic inferencing. Grammaticalization with linguistic analogy brought the evolution of language through coevolutionary processes of diversification and complexification among language, concepts, thoughts, and the world. Those processes enabled languages to develop into the present (full-fledged) languages in complexity and structure.

References

Hashimoto, T., & Nakatsuka, M. (2006). Reconsidering Kirby's compositionality model: Towards modelling grammaticalization. In A. Cangelosi, A. D. M. Smith, & K. Smith (Eds.), *The evolution of language, proceedings of the 6th international conference (evolang6)* (pp. 415–416). Singapore: World Scientific.

Hashimoto, T., & Nakatsuka, M. (2008). Unidirectional meaning change with metaphoric and metonymic inferencing. In A. D. M. Smith, K. Smith, & R. F. Cancho (Eds.), *The evolution of language, proceedings of the 7th international conference (evolang7)* (pp. 433–434). Singapore: World Scientific.

Hashimoto, T., Sato, T., Nakatsuka, M., & Fujimoto, M. (2008). Evolutionary constructive approach for dynamic systems. In G. Petrone & G. Cammarata (Eds.), *Recent advances in modelling and simulation* (pp. 111–136). Vienna: I-Tech Books.

Heine, B., & Kuteva, T. (2002a). On the evolution of grammatical forms. In A. Wray (Ed.), *The transition to language* (pp. 376–397). Oxford: Oxford University Press.

Heine, B., & Kuteva, T. (2002b). *World lexicon of grammaticalization*. Cambridge: Cambridge University Press.

Heine, B., & Kuteva, T. (2007). *The genesis of grammar: A reconstruction*. Oxford: Oxford University Press.

Hopper, P. J., & Traugott, E. C. (2003). *Grammaticalization*. Cambridge: Cambridge University Press.

Hurford, J. R. (2003). The language mosaic and its evolution. In M. H. Christiansen & S. Kirby (Eds.), *Language evolution* (pp. 38–57). Oxford: Oxford University Press.

Kirby, S. (2003). Learning, bottlenecks and the evolution of recursive syntax. In T. Briscoe (Ed.), *Linguistic evolution through language acquisition* (pp. 173–203). Cambridge: Cambridge University Press.

Mithen, S. (1996). *The prehistory of the mind: a search for the origins of art, religion, and science*. London: Thames and Hudson.

APPLICATIONS OF THE PRICE EQUATION TO LANGUAGE EVOLUTION

GERHARD JÄGER

Seminar für Sprachwissenschaft, University of Tübingen, Wilhelmstr. 19-23
72074 Tübingen, Germany
gerhard.jaeger@uni-tuebingen.de

In the early seventies, the bio-mathematician George Price developed a simple and concise mathematical description of evolutionary processes that abstracts away from the specific properties of biological evolution. In the talk I will argue argued that Price's framework is well-suited to model various aspects of the cultural evolution of language. The first part of the talk describes Price's approach in some detail. In the second part, case studies about its application to language evolution are presented.

1. Introduction

Ever since the development of the evolutionary model in biology in the mid-nineteenth century, people have noted a certain affinity of the evolutionary logic and the development of natural languages. The following well-known citation from Darwin's *The descent of man* perfectly captures this intuition:

> "The formation of different languages and of distinct species, and the proofs that both have been developed through a gradual process, are curiously parallel. ... Max Müller has well remarked: 'A struggle for life is constantly going on amongst the words and grammatical forms in each language. The better, the shorter, the easier forms are constantly gaining the upper hand, and they owe their success to their inherent virtue.' To these important causes of the survival of certain words, mere novelty and fashion may be added; for there is in the mind of man a strong love for slight changes in all things. The survival or preservation of certain favoured words in the struggle for existence is natural selection." ((Darwin, 1871):465f.)

In the last one or two decades, this analogy has been re-discoverd by many researchers that are interested in natural language. The success of the EVOLANG conference series is proof of that.

Still, there is no agreement yet how exactly the analogy between biological and linguistic evolution should be spelled out in detail. So while there is a strong interest now in evolutionary approaches to linguistic issues, there is little consensus so far about how exactly language evolution should be conceptualized. The main topic of debate, as far as I can see, is the issue what are the *replicators* in language evolution. The term "replicator" (in the sense of a unit of evolution) was coined by Richard Dawkins in his 1976 book *The Selfish Gene*. According to Dawkins' view, the basic unit of evolution in biology is the gene, the physical carrier of heritable information. Dawkins also argues that any evolutionary process must be based on a population of replicators, i.e. counterparts of genes. He actually invents a new term, "meme", as a unit of replication in cultural evolution.

If this logic is valid, the first step in developing a theory of language evolution is to identify the linguistic units of replication. This proves to be a surprisingly difficult task. There are essentially three modes of replication that play a role in the acquisition and usage of natural language:

1. the biological inheritance of the human language faculty,

2. first language acquisition, which amounts to a vertical replication of language competence from parents (or, more generally, teachers) to infants, and

3. imitation of certain aspects of language performance in language usage (like the repetition of words and constructions, imitation of phonetic idiosyncrasies, priming effects etc.)

It is fairly clear what replicators are for the biological evolution of the language faculty. Since this is just one aspect of biological evolution in general, the carriers of heritable information are of course the genes. For the other two aspects of language evolution, the question is not so easy to answer. What are replicators in iterated language acquisition—entire I-languages? Single Rules? Parameters? Lexical items? The same difficulties arise with respect to replication via language usage. Candidates for the replicator status are phonemes, morphemes, words, constructions etc., or single instances of them (i.e. features of utterances), or mental representations of such instances (so-called "exemplars") etc. A considerable amount of the recent literature on language evolution is actually devoted to foundational questions like this one.

The main point I want to make in the talk is that this issue is actually of little relevance in my view. For one thing, I tend to be sceptical about the usefulness of methodological discussions anyway. The proof of the pudding is in the eating—a certain approach is useful if (and only if) it leads to insightful analyses of linguistic facts. If this is missing, even the most sophisticated discussion of foundational issues will not make up for the lack of it. But quite apart from this general issue, I will try to argue that the programme for analysing cultural evolution that can be extracted from the work of George Price is perhaps better suited to conceptualize

language evolution than Dawkins' memetics or related approaches that assume a
very detailed analogy between the cultural and the biological sphere.

2. The Price equation

George Price was (among many other things) a bio-mathematician who made several breakthrough discoveries about the mathematics of natural selection around
1970. (He also was a very remarkable, if extravagant person, and I will devote
some time of my talk about his life—in the meantime, the interested reader is
referred to the short biography (Schwartz, 2000).) Around 1971, Price wrote a
manuscript titled "The Nature of Selection". It was only published posthumously
in 1995 ((Price, 1995)). There he sketched a programme for a general theory of
evolution (or "selection", as he calls it) which includes biological evolution in the
neo-Darwinian sense but encompasses various other kinds of natural and cultural
evolution as well. The abstract of the paper starts with:

> "A model that unifies all types of selection (chemical, sociologi-
> cal, genetical, and every other kind of selection) may open the way to
> develop a general 'Mathematical Theory of Selection' analogous to
> communication theory." (Price 1995:389)

The first paragraph of the paper deserves to be quoted in its entirety:

> "Selection has been studied mainly in genetics, but of course there
> is much more to selection than just genetical selection. In psychol-
> ogy, for example, trial-and-error learning is simply learning by se-
> lection. In chemistry, selection operates in a recrystallisation under
> equilibrium conditions, with impure and irregular crystals dissolving
> and pure, well-formed crystals growing. In palaeontology and ar-
> chaeology, selection especially favours stones, pottery, and teeth, and
> greatly increases the frequency of mandibles among the bones of the
> hominid skeleton. *In linguistics, selection unceasingly shapes and
> reshapes phonetics, grammar, and vocabulary.* In history we see po-
> litical selection in the rise of Macedonia, Rome, and Muscovy. Simi-
> larly, economic selection in private enterprise systems causes the rise
> and fall of firms and products. And science itself is shaped in part by
> selection, with experimental tests and other criteria selecting among
> rival hypotheses." (Price 1995:389, emphasis added)

Even though Price did not develop a theory of selection in the sense he probably envisioned it, the paper gives good arguments why the Price equation should
be the cornerstone of such a theory.

The centerpiece of his theory is the **Price equation**, a difference/differential
equation (or a system thereof) that quantitatively describes selection processes. In

the next paragraphs I will give a very brief description of the underlying conceptualization; the interested reader is referred to (Price, 1995), which is very readable and not overly technical.

The minimum requirement to apply the Price equation are two populations, P and P'. It is implicitly assumed that P' is later in time than P, and that P' is somehow derived from P. The prototypical interpretation would be two generations of the same population, where the elements of P' are the offspring of the individuals in P. Furthermore, there must be a correspondence function from P' to P, i.e. each element of the later population is assigned to exactly one individual of the former population. Again, in the prototypical interpretation this would be biological replication. However, the populations and the functional relation between them could be anything—the sets of utterances in a language community at two points in time and an imitation relation, the sets of mental grammars of people in a group at two points in time, two sets of FOXP2 molecules ...—you name it.

The Price equation describes how a certain quantitative character X changes from P to P'. Again, this character can be anything you like—the proportion of head-final structures in a corpus, the number of rules in a context-free grammar, the average length of final consonants in function words etc. The rate of change of x follows the following law:

$$f\Delta x = Cov(f, x) + E(f\Delta x). \tag{1}$$

Here f is the fitness, i.e. the average number of objects from P' that are related to some object from P.

The right hand side of the Price equation consists of two parts. The first term, $Cov(f, x)$, captures the effect of natural selection. If the character x has a positive covariance with fitness, individuals that have a high value of x tend to have a high fitness and thus many offspring. Therefore there are many descendants of indivudals with a high x-value in P'. If replication is faithuf, i.e. if parent and offspring share the value of x, the average value of x in P' will increase.

However, replication may be unfaithful. This is modeled by the second term, $E(f\Delta x)$. This expresses the average change in value of x between parent and offspring.

If this one-step selection process is iterated and the sequence of generations can be approximated by a continuous time, the Price equation becomes an ordinary differential equation, which is even more perspicuous

$$\dot{E}(x) = Cov(f, x) + E(\dot{x}) \tag{2}$$

3. Conclusion

The main purpose of the talk is to bring the conceptual framework that underlies the Price equation to the attention of linguists that are interested in evolutionary modelling. Price's framework has several attractive features that are briefly recapitulated here:

- Price's framework is very general. It does not over-emphasize certain features of biological evolution that are specific to biology rather than to the notion of evolution via selection—like assuming discrete units of heritable information or the dual ontology of genotype and phenotype. Rather, it focuses on population dynamics as such.

- There are no specific requirements about what the nature of the populations involved or the correspondence relation betwen them is. It is thus clear that evolution and selection are a perspective under which empirical phenomena can be studied, rather than being objective properties of these phenomena. Identifying a certain set as an evolving population and a certain relation between stages of this set as replication (i.e. correspondence) is a matter of practicality and usefulness, not of truth or falsity.

- In particular, Price's framework does not require anything like copying fidelity of replicators to be applicable. If a certain process does in fact involve faithfully replicating entities, this simplifies the analysis because the second term of the Price equation can be dropped in this case. However, this is a matter of convenience, not of principle.

- While Price's framework admits considerable methodological freedom, it enforces an absolutely rigorous analysis, once the basic modelling decisions are made.

In the talk I will present several applications of the Price equations to problems in language evolution, ranging from a re-formulation of Martin Nowak's model of the evolution of Universal Grammar to various versions of exemplar dynamics. My point is not so much to present novel models and hypotheses but to illustrate how using the Price equation helps to clarify the conceptual foundations of a particular model. As Jelle Zuidema (p.c.) once fittingly put it: *"The Price equation helps to clear your mind."*

The original sources for the Price equation are (Price, 1970, 1972). In the biological literature, Price's approach has been applied mainly in the context of group and kin selection; see for instance (Sober & Wilson, 1998) and (Okasha, 2006). So far Price's framework has attracted little attention in the language evolution literature. Notable exceptions are (Zuidema, 2005) and (Clark, 2009).

References

Clark, B. Z. (2009). *Evolutionary frameworks for language change: The Price equation approach.* (manuscript, Northwestern University)

Darwin, C. (1871). *The descent of man, and selection in relation to sex.* London: John Murray.

Dawkins, R. (1976). *The selfish gene.* Oxford: Oxford University Press.

Okasha, S. (2006). *Evolution and the levels of selection.* Oxford: Clarendon Press.

Price, G. R. (1970). Selection and covariance. *Nature, 227*(5257), 520–521.

Price, G. R. (1972). Extension of covariance selection mathematics. *Annals of Human Genetics, 35*(4), 485-490.

Price, G. R. (1995). The nature of selection. *Journal of Theoretical Biology, 175*(3), 373-388.

Schwartz, J. (2000). Death of an altruist. *Lingua Franca: The Review of Academic Life, 10,* 51–61.

Sober, E., & Wilson, D. S. (1998). *Unto others.* Harvard University Press.

Zuidema, W. (2005). *The major transitions in the evolution of language.* Unpublished doctoral dissertation, University of Edinburgh.

INTERPLAY BETWEEN LANGUAGE, NAVIGATION AND KIN SELECTION

DIMITAR KAZAKOV

Computer Science Department, University of York, Heslington
York, YO10 3EP, UK

It has been suggested that human language emerged as either a new, critical faculty to handle recursion, which linked two other existing systems in the brain, or as an exaptation of an existing mechanism, which had been used for a different purpose to that point. Of these two theories, the latter appears more parsimonious, but, somewhat surprisingly, has attracted less attention among researchers in the field. Navigation is a prime candidate for a task that may benefit from being able to handle recursion, and we give an account of the possible transition from navigation to language. In the described context, it appears plausible that the transition adding the crucial component of human language was promoted by kin selection. We show that once language is present among its speakers, it reinforces the mechanisms of kin selection, boosting such behaviour that benefit one's kin, and any such behaviour in turn boosts the use of language. The article also describes a mechanism through which language is used *in lieu* of kin markers to promote altruistic behaviour between potentially large communities of unrelated individuals.

1. Introduction

In 2002, we proposed an evolutionary model for the emergence of language that voiced a number of ideas (Kazakov & Bartlett 2002). In hindsight, the article appears to have caught the zeitgeist of linguistic research, and anticipated trends that were to become a topic of discussion among much of the relevant research community thanks to the now notorious 'HCF' paper on the faculty of language, which appeared in Science only a month later (Hauser, Chomsky & Fitch 2002). In this article, we revisit some of our original ideas, and focus on two aspects of language that would have assisted its spread, namely, its ability to assist kin selection among its speakers, and its potential to serve, through its variations and dialects, as a substitute for a kin marker that could transfer the benefits of kin-directed altruism to larger and open communities, which are not restricted to groups of relatives.

2. Language and Navigation

The first of our ideas was that there is a great similarity, indeed, an isomorphism, between the processes and representations needed for language syntax and navigation. More specifically, we postulated a link between planning a route as a sequence of landmarks, and generating/parsing a sentence as a sequence of words, and described a language use scenario in which

> *"Information about resource location is shared in the form of paths, consisting of sequences of landmarks that are to be seen along the way to the target destination."* (Kazakov & Bartlett 2002).

The article also pointed out that the same (regular) grammar rules could be used for both internal path planning and to generate sentences (to give directions). An example of such rule would be

River   MyCave, pine_tree, birch_tree, meadow   (1)

where MyCave and River are the starting, resp. end point of a particular path, and the other three symbols are the landmarks to follow along the way. MyCave and River can also be seen as non-terminals of a regular grammar, if there are other rules describing paths taking one to or away from these locations, and a rule, such as MyCave ← BigOakTree, landmark1, landmark2 can be combined with the above rule to describe a path from the big oak tree to the river. The transition from navigation to giving directions would only require the ability to designate the landmarks along the generated path, an action that could be delegated to either gesture or speech.

When HCF suggested looking for parallels between the formal computations involved in communication and other domains, including navigation, we anticipated a number of research projects in this area to follow soon, and felt that our own research agenda was receiving a boost after seeing Hauser's comment in a post-HCF interview:

> *"Constructing a sentence, and going from A to Z through a series of landmarks, could involve similar series of neural computations"* (Wade 2003).

The HCF paper discussed two alternatives for the uniquely human faculty to apply recursion to communication - that it either evolved in humans specifically as a link between the sensory-motor and conceptual-intentional systems, or it was already there, possibly shared with other animals, to serve another purpose. To study the possible origins of syntax in navigation, and whether the underlying mechanism is uniquely human, one would have to study the type of computation involved in various navigational tasks, and whether different animal species are able to perform them. Navigation using landmarks can be of varying complexity, from simply recalling a previously observed path to combining two or more paths to create a novel journey (Bartlett 2006). The generic task of going from A to B though can always be seen as equivalent to traversing a finite state automaton, since it involves derivations of rules of a regular grammar. Of course, such a grammar may contain recursion, *e.g.*, in the form of a pair of mutually recursive rules that make one go in circles. The HCF paper did not specify whether such iterative behaviour was to be deemed human-specific, and the corresponding faculty – part of the FLN, but research by Fitch and Hauser (2004) (already mentioned in HCF), in which they tested the ability of cotton-top tamarins to recognise regular and context-free ("phrase structure") grammars in spoken language, showed their intention to test this possible dividing line between us and other species. Their experiment followed in part the design of a well-known earlier experiment with infants (Marcus *et al.* 1999), but with some important differences, *e.g.*, it did not use disjoint sets of terminals for training and testing; other criticisms have also been voiced (Liberman 2004). Regardless of any potential flaws, the experiment tested the monkeys' ability to parse *spoken* context-free languages, rather than look for a non-linguistic behaviour involving recursion shared by several species. So, from this it would seem that instead of looking for an apparatus to handle recursion that is not uniquely human, the experiment tested the less parsimonious hypothesis that humans evolved a new faculty, and verified that it was not present in one particular species, which, presumably, was chosen to be close enough to us to make such difference significant.

We argue that the isomorphism between navigation and language (Kazakov & Bartlett 2002) is a proof that a vast number of species, including non-mammals, and probably insects (Collet 1992), are capable of performing computations, which could be seen as equivalent to parsing regular languages. A link between language and navigation in the context of the underlying neural circuitry was already discussed in O'Keefe and Nadel's treatise on the hippocampus (1978), and Hermer-Vasquez *et al.* (1999) make a closely related point, that there is a common structure underlying language and orientation. O'Keefe's more recent work on cognitive maps and spatial aspects of language (O'Keefe 1999) also links the two cognitive abilities in question.

We have proposed navigation tasks that are equivalent to parsing context free languages, and outlined the design for experiments with animals, which in many ways would be analogous to Marcus *et al.*'s experiments with infants (Kazakov & Bartlett 2005). If, for instance, one was able to demonstrate that rats, or another genetically distant species, were able to learn to perform a navigational task that required abstract computation equivalent to parsing a context-free language, this could provide the required evidence that other species possess the apparatus needed to handle recursion, and give strong support to the exaptation hypothesis on the origins of recursion. Similarly, it would be interesting to compare experiments with human subjects on navigation as carried out by Maguire *et al.* (2003) with experiments involving language, and look for common patterns of neural activation for the pairs of path-planning and sentence-parsing tasks. In doing this, one could also discriminate between tasks involving different classes of abstract computation, *e.g.*, going from A to B (resp. parsing regular languages) compared to going from A to B and back following the same route. The latter task spells out a palindrome of landmark names, say, ACDBDCA, and requires the use of memory in a way identical to the one needed by the parser of a context-free grammar.

Bartlett (2006) (see Chapter 7) describes multi-agent simulations which compare the relative benefits to the population of using various forms of landmark based navigation and sharing (communicating) the equivalent instructions between agents. Several classes of navigation/communication are considered: (1) wondering at random, (2) heading/searching for a landmark near a resource, (3) following a known path of landmarks, and, ultimately, (4) planning and following new paths to resources based on the knowledge of a network of previously explored paths. Giving directions based on these navigational abilities would correspond to (a) no communication (no information to be shared),

(b) one-word utterances, (c) repeating memorised sentences (made of landmark names), and (d) producing sentences from a regular grammar. The simulations look at populations of agents with different combinations of navigational and communicative faculties, where the only constraint is that the class of language employed by an agent does not surpass the complexity of its navigation. So, for instance, there would be agents of type (1-a) − no route planning, no communication or (3-b) − navigating known paths and sharing directions by naming a beacon (single landmark); (2-a), (2-b), (3-a), (3-c) and (4-a) − (4-d) are also considered. The simulations are run repeatedly and the survival rates of adjacent types of agent, *e.g.*, (3-b) *vs* (3-c) or (1-a) *vs* (2-a) compared through a t-test. All statistically significant differences are in favour of the next more complex navigational behaviour, everything else being equal. Not so with language – increasing the complexity of communication may be beneficial or harmful, depending on the environment. For instance, sharing the exact path to the most recently visited resources outperforms the benefits of sharing potentially novel paths to resources in some experimental settings, depending on the amount of resource (food) in the environment and the speed with which it decays, as paths to previously visited locations of quickly perishable resources are not likely to be very useful. One can derive from these experiments that the selective pressure for more complex navigation is universal, whereas selective pressure for more complex language depends on environmental factors, such as the availability and durability of resources available. In all cases, naming a beacon and pointing another agent in that direction has proven beneficial (or at least not harmful) when compared to non-cooperation. One should however bear in mind our previous results that sharing information may be outperformed by sharing in kind in certain environmental circumstances (Bartlett & Kazakov 2005). The above suggests, *inter alias*, a positive pressure for a protolanguage used to name a beacon, as soon as this type of navigation becomes plausible and offers advantages over some of the alternatives (scent trailing, footstep tracking…), for instance, after a change to a dryer climate, which means more open landscapes where longer distance landmark-based navigation would seem appropriate and beneficial.

3. Language and Kin Selection

We have proposed that language could have emerged as a form of kin selection (Kazakov & Bartlett 2002; 2003) – a theme since also taken up by other researchers (Fitch 2004). Here the above mentioned link between navigation and language is only relevant as it makes giving directions a likely topic of early human conversations, although it is worth mentioning that this assumption is given more weight by our further studies – showing that sharing directions to food resources is particularly valuable where such resources are encountered in relatively large quantities, but perishable (Bartlett & Kazakov 2005). This, of course, is the case with large kills or carcasses, where the hunter/scavenger can only consume and carry away a relatively small part of the food available. Therefore, the potential benefits of human communication for this particular use would have grown considerably with the substantial increase of meat in the human ancestors' diet. A 'long shot' that may be worth mentioning in this context is the fact that FOXP2, a gene linked with the ability to handle syntax, is also involved in the development of the gut, thus providing another potential link between food, its location, and human communication.

Focusing on the link between language and kin selection – naturally, sharing directions to food resources with relatives could be seen as fitting the kin selection mechanism. A closer look shows that Hamilton's rule $B.r > C$ (Hamilton 1964), linking the benefit B of an action to its recipient, the cost C to the donor, and their degree of relatedness r, is satisfied under certain conditions which we have studied in simulations (Turner & Kazakov 2003; Bartlett & Kazakov 2005). Although sharing information about resources with one's kin does appear a plausible scenario for the birth of language, it is clear that language did not remain limited to discussing one specific topic, neither did it stay directed only to relatives. However, whatever the initial step towards language, once it appeared in some form, it can be shown that it would have reinforced the processes of kin selection. First of all, food calls or other forms of sharing information about resources would result in raising the likelihood that the speaker and hearer would be in close proximity (Kazakov & Bartlett 2003) – as they both would tend to visit the locations of those resources. As a result, this would increase the chance of their having offspring together, which in time would replace the potentially unrelated parents with siblings, which still share a language, but are also related, giving a better ground in this way to the processes of kin selection.

It is worth noting that the example of the Australian Aboriginal Songlines (Kazakov & Bartlett 2003) provides a modern day example of a very ancient social phenomenon, which combines explicit sharing of navigational information among kin with variations of the practice that can be seen as reciprocal altruism between unrelated speakers, thus answering some of the criticism (Tallerman 2008) directed to later proponents of the link between language and kin selection, such as Fitch (2004).

Another important mechanism through which language could extend the benefits of kin-directed communication to groups of unrelated individuals is by serving as a substitute for a kin marker. We simulated small talk between agents (Kazakov & Brennan), whose only purpose was to indentify the degree of `linguistic relatedness'` as proportional to the degree of mutual understanding, in an environment where the vocabulary of each agent evolved over time following the well-known 'naming games' model (Steels 1996). The results confirmed that although not as common as in the case of genuine kin selection, altruistic behaviour based on this definition of kin selection could also emerge and remain relatively stable in this setting, promoting the sharing of information. Identifying one self with a group of speakers of a given vernacular could have been a crucial transition, allowing all forms of cooperation, including non-verbal, to take place among much larger and open groups of individuals, even if language itself did not bring any other direct benefits. Ignoring the exact origins of the linguistic 'Big Bang', this theory does not contradict any other hypothesis on this subject, e.g., Dunbar's (1993), but simply describes a mechanism akin to kin selection which guarantees the robust character of linguistic behaviour, once it emerged.

4. Conclusions

It appears important to redress the balance in current research and put more effort into studying the possibility of language, and recursion in particular, being an exaptation, rather than a new trait evolved solely by humans. The much smaller mutation such exaptation would require, together with the boost that language would receive, once present, through the mechanisms of kin selection, whether based on genuine relatedness or linguistic similarity, would seem to offer a more plausible explanation for the apparent sudden birth and subsequent rapid spread of language, when compared to the hypothesis that an important, and complex part of the faculty of language appeared suddenly in humans, and has only ever been used for this purpose alone.

References

Bartlett, M. (2006). *Language as an Exaptation: Simulating the Origin of Syntax*. PhD Thesis, Department of Computer Science, University of York.

Bartlett, M. and D. Kazakov (2005). The Origins of Syntax: from Navigation to Language. *Connection Science* 17(3-4).

Collett, T.S., E. Dillmann, A. Giger and R. Wehner (1992) Visual landmarks and route following in desert ants. *J Comp Physiol A* 170:435-442.

Dunbar, R.I.M. (1993), *Coevolution of neocortical size, group size and language in humans*, Behavioral and Brain Sciences 16 (4): 681-735.

Fitch, W. T. (2004) Kin Selection and "Mother Tongues": A Neglected Component in Language Evolution. In D. Kimbrough Oller and Ulrike Griebel, editors, Evolution of Communication Systems: A Comparative Approach, pages 275-296. Cambridge, MA: MIT Press.

Fitch, W. T. and M. D. Hauser (2004). Computational Constraints on Syntactic Processing in a Nonhuman Primate. *Science,*303:377 -- 380.

Hamilton, W. D. (1964). The Genetical Evolution of Social Behaviour I, II. *Journal of Theoretical Biology*, 7.

Hauser, M. D., Chomsky, N., and Fitch, W. T. (2002) The Faculty of Language: What Is it, Who Has It, and How Did It Evolve?, *Science*, 298:1569--1579.

Hermer-Vasquez, L., E. S. Spelke, and A. S. Katsnelson (1999). Sources of flexibility in human cognition: Dual-task studies of space and language. *Cogn. Psychology*, 39:3–36.

Kazakov, D. and M. Bartlett (2002). A Multi-Agent Simulation of the Evolution of Language. In Marko Grobelnik, Marko Bohanec, Dunja Mladenic and Matjaz Gams (eds): The *Proc. of Information Society Conference IS'2002*, p.39-41, Ljubljana, Slovenia, Josef Stefan Institute, October 2002.

Kazakov, D. and M. Bartlett (2003). *Social Learning through Evolution of Language*. In the Proceedings of the 6th International Conference on Artificial Evolution (EA'03), Université de Provence, France, 27-30 October 2003.

Kazakov, D. and M. Bartlett (2004). Co-operative Navigation and the Faculty of Language. *Applied Artificial Intelligence*, **18**.

Kazakov, D. and M. Bartlett (2005). *Could Navigation Be the Key to Language?* In the Proc. of EELC'05, pp. 50-55.

Kazakov, D. and O. Brennan. Investigating Cooperation Dynamics in a Population of Communicating Agents. *In manuscript.*

Liberman, M. (2004). *Hi Lo Hi Lo, it's off to formal language theory we go.* Language Log, http://itre.cis.upenn.edu/~myl/languagelog/archives/000355.html.

Maguire E., H. Spiers, C. Good, T. Hartley, R. Frackowiak and N. Burgess (2003). Navigation expertise and the human hippocampus: a structural brain imaging analysis. *Hippocampus* 13:208–217.

Marcus, G. F., Vijayan, S., Bandi Rao, S., and Vishton, P. M. (1999). Rule-learning in seven-month-old infants. Science, 283, 77-80.

O'Keefe, J. (1996). The spatial prepositions in English, vector grammar, and the cognitive map theory. In *Language and Space*, P. Bloom, M.A. Peterson, L. Nadel, and M.F. Garrett, eds., Cambridge, MA: MIT Press, pp. 277-316.

O'Keefe, J. and L. Nadel (1978). *The Hippocampus as a Cognitive Map*. Oxford University Press, Oxford.

Steels, L. (1996). The Spontaneous Self-organisation of an Adaptive Language. In S. Muggleton, Machine Intelligence 15, Oxford University Press.

Tallerman, M. (2008). Kin selection and linguistic complexity. *In:* A. D. Smith, K. Smith & R, Ferrer i Cancho, ed. *The evolution of language: proceedings of the 7th international conference.* New Jersey: World Scientific, pp. 307-314.

Turner, H. and D. Kazakov (2003). Stochastic Simulation of Inherited Kinship-Driven Altruism. In *Adaptive Agents and Multi-Agent Systems*, LNAI, vol. 2636, Springer.

Wade, N. (2003) Early Voices: The Leap to Language. *New York Times*, 15 July 2003.

CHILDREN LEARN SOUND SYMBOLIC WORDS BETTER: EVOLUTIONARY VESTIGE OF SOUND SYMBOLIC PROTOLANGUAGE

SOTARO KITA, KATERINA KANTARTZIS

School of Psychology, University of Birmingham
Birmingham B15 2TT, UK

MUTSUMI IMAI

Faculty of Environmental Information, Keio University
Fujisawa, 252-8520, Japan

Recent studies showed that three-year old children learned novel words better when the form and meaning of the words were sound symbolically related. This was the case for both children learning a language with a rich sound symbolic lexicon (Japanese) and that without (English). From this robust nature of sound symbolic facilitation, it was inferred that children's ability to use sound symbolism in word learning is the vestige of protolanguage consisting largely of sound symbolic words. We argued that sound symbolic protolanguage was able to refer to a wide range of information (not just auditory events). It had the added advantage that it was relatively easy to develop a shared open-class lexicon and it provided a stepping stone from a holophrastic protolanguage to a combinatoric protolanguage.

1. *Introduction*

One of the most celebrated characterizations of language is the arbitrary link between form and meaning (de Saussure, 1916/1983). However, it has also been recognized that the sound and meaning of a word can have a motivated "natural" link. This is called sound symbolism. The most familiar type of sound symbolism can be seen onomatopoeias (e.g., "bowwow" for barking of dogs) in which speech sound imitates an auditory event. However, sound symbolism goes far beyond sound-to-sound mappings. For example, novel words with /i/ (e.g., "mil") and those with /a/ (e.g., "mal") are judged to be more appropriate label for small objects and large objects, respectively (Sapir, 1929).

Many (but not all) languages of the world have a large grammatical class of sound symbolic words. Such word classes are called "ideophones" (African languages), "mimetics" (Japanese), and "expressives" (Southeast Asian languages). A large sound symbolic lexicon is found in most languages spoken in sub-Saharan Africa, Southeast Asia and East Asia (including Japanese) as well as in some indigenous languages in South America and Australia (Kita, 1997, 2001; Nuckolls, 1999; Voeltz & Kilian-Hatz, 2001). Indo-European languages do not have a large grammatically class of sound symbolic words. This is interesting in light of the fact that some of the non-Indo-European languages in Europe such as Basque and Finnish have a large sound symbolic lexicon (Ibarretxe-Antuñano, 2006; Mikone, 2001). The fact that a wide range of languages have an extensive sound-symbolic lexicon indicates that this is a resilient feature of human language faculty.

The variation across languages as to the size of their sound symbolic lexicons provides with us an opportunity to investigate whether children's ability to use sound symbolism in word learning is robust against this variation. We investigated sound symbolic facilitation of word learning in three-year old children learning Japanese (with a large sound symbolic lexicon) and those learning English (without a large sound symbolic lexicon). We will discuss how sound symbolic facilitation of word learning in both groups of children sheds light on theories of language evolution.

2. *Word learning Experiments with Children: Sound Symbolic Advantage*

Sound symbolism can help children overcome one of the challenges of word learning. Namely, a word can logically have an infinite number of possible referents when they learn the word in an ostensive situation (i.e., "Look! Rabbit!" as an adult points at a rabbit hopping across the field) (Quine, 1960). Three-year old children suffer from this problem when learning a new word referring to action (Imai, Haryu, & Okada, 2005). Imai and colleagues taught children a novel verb while showing a video clip of a person performing an action with an object. Subsequently, they asked the children to choose the referent of the verb from two video clips: one with the same action performed on a different object (the correct choice), one with a different action performed on the same actor (the incorrect choice). Three-year old children failed to pick the correct choice in this task. In other words, three year olds did not zero-in on its referent action in the video clip as the referent of the verb. They instead considered the object to be an equally relevant aspect of the scene. We adapted this experimental paradigm in new studies to investigate whether sound symbolism helps children make the link between a novel action word to the action. Furthermore, we carried out experiments with children learning Japanese (Imai, Kita, Nagumo, & Okada, 2008) and those learning English (Kantartzis,

Kita, & Imai, 2009) to see if children benefit from sound symbolism regardless of whether the language they are learning has a large sound symbolic lexicon.

In the new studies, the experiment consisted of the training phase and test phase (as in Imai, et al., 2005). In the training phase, we taught a novel action word (e.g., "Look! He is doing nosunosu!") to a child while showing a video clip with an actor walking in a particular manner (See Figure 1). The word taught either sound symbolically matched the action (the sound symbolic match condition) or not (the sound symbolic mismatch condition). The words were novel in both Japanese and English. The degree of sound symbolic match between the word and the action had been established by pre-testing the materials with Japanese and English speaking adults.

'nosunosu'

Figure 1. An example of manner of walking used in the word learning experiment with three year olds. This "heavy and slow" manner was judged to be a good sound symbolic match with the novel word "nosunosu" by English and Japanese-speaking adults in the pretest of the materials.

The training phase is followed by the test phase, in which we presented two video clips and asked the child to point to the correct referent of the novel action word (e.g., "Which one is doing nosunosu?"). One of the video clips showed the same action by a different actor (the correct choice) and the other video clip showed a different action by the same actor (the incorrect choice). The sound symbolic words and video clips used in the experiments with English speaking children were taken from the experiment with the Japanese speaking children[1].

---

[1] A couple of items (i.e., sound symbolic words and video clips) in the Japanese experiment were not used in the English experiment because English adults in a pretest did not rate these items as good a sound symbolic match as other four items. The remaining four items in the English experiment were judged to have a good sound symbolic match by both Japanese and English speaking adults.

The results were the same for Japanese-speaking and English-speaking three-year olds (Imai, et al., 2008; Kantartzis, et al., 2009). That is, they both performed significantly better in the sound symbolic condition than in the non-sound symbolic conditions[2]. In the sound symbolic condition, the children were able to pick the correct choice significantly above chance in the sound symbolic conditions, whereas they were at chance in the non-sound symbolic conditions. In other words, when the word sound symbolically matched the referent action, children were able to generalize the verb to a new situation on the basis of the identity of the action.

The above indicates that sound symbolism helped children to zero-in on the manner of walking as the referent, overcoming Quine's problem. This was the case regardless of whether the language they were learning had a rich sound symbolic lexicon (Japanese) or not (English).

3. Sound Symbolic Facilitation as the Vestige of Sound Symbolic Protolanguage

Interestingly, children benefited from sound symbolism in word learning even if they were learning English. As English does not have a large sound symbolic lexicon, there is no obvious practical advantage for such a facilitatory effect. This opens up the possibility that all children are biologically endowed to develop an ability to use sound symbolism in word learning because of our evolutionary history. We propose that our ancestors once used a protolanguage largely consisting of sound symbolic words (Kita, 2008; Ramachandran & Hubbard, 2001), and children's ability to use sound symbolism in word learning is the vestige of sound symbolic protolanguage.

The idea for sound symbolic protolanguage has not been taken seriously in the literature partly because previous research considered only onomatopoeias (e.g., "bowwow") and concluded that the type of encodable information is extremely limited. For example, Müller (1866) rejected the idea of sound symbolic

---

[2] There were two types of non-sound symbolic conditions. In the first type, we used non-sound symbolic non-words that have the typical shape of other non-sound symbolic words in the languages (e.g., "nekeru" in Japanese, "blicking" in English). In the second type, we used the same set of non-words as in the sound symbolic condition (e.g., "nosunosu" in both Japanese and English), but combined them with actions that did not sound symbolically match the words. Children's poor performance in the latter condition indicates that any features of sound symbolic words such as reduplication and polysyllabic structure were not the cause of children's success in the sound symbolic condition. If that were the case, children should have performed equally well in the sound symbolic match condition and in the second non-sound symbolic condition. On the contrary, children performed significantly better in the sound symbolic condition than in the non-sound symbolic conditions.

protolanguage on such grounds, "no process of natural selection will ever distill significant words out of the notes of birds or the cries of beasts" (p.354) (Müller, 1866, as quoted by Limber 1982). However, sound symbolic words in modern language can refer to a wide range of information. For example, Japanese sound symbolic words can refer to many domains of information (Kita, 1997, 2008): visual properties ("pikapika", flashing), tactile properties ("nurunuru", slimy in a unpleasant way), olfactory properties ("puun", smelly), gustatory properties ("piripiri", spicy hot as in chili pepper), emotional state ("sowasowa", nervous), pain ("chikuchiku", stinging pain), manner of motion ("goro", a heavy object rolling), etc.[3]. Thus, sound symbolic protolanguage may have also been able to refer to a wide enough range of information to be useful as means of communication.

4. Advantages of Sound Symbolic Protolanguage Hypothesis

The idea of sound symbolic protolanguage has the following two theoretical advantages. We here summarize the arguments from (Kita, 2008). First, it may explain how our ancestors could develop a shared open-class lexicon (Ramachandran & Hubbard, 2001). As soon as cross-modal mapping between various types of information and sound or articulation evolved, then our ancestors had a tool to develop a shared lexicon relatively quickly. Second, it may explain how protolanguage developed from a holistic phase (Wray, 2000), in which a single word encoded complex information, to a combinatoric phase, where complex information is encoded by a linear combination of words with simpler meaning. In sound symbolic words, words that share meaning, by definition, have common sound features. For example, consider Japanese sound symbolic words, "goro" (a heavy object rolling), "guru" (a heavy object rotating), "koro" (a light object rolling) and "kuru" (a light object rotating). For these words, it is transparent that voicing of the first consonant encodes the weight of the object, the combination of velar stops and /r/ encodes circular movements, and the vowels encodes finer properties of the manners of movement. In other words, it is easy to extract a subpart of words that have consistent meaning, leading to morphological decomposition. This could be the first step towards the combinatoric property, robustly seen in modern language (Senghas, Kita, & Özyürek, 2004).

---

[3] However, there are some interesting restrictions on the type of information sound symbolic words encode (Kita, 2008). The following types of information are not sound symbolically coded: properties of the agent of action, localization of events in time (e.g., tense) and space (e.g., at one's house).

6. *Uneven distribution of sound symbolic words across modern languages*

If there was a sound symbolic protolanguage, from which all modern languages have stemmed from, why do not all modern languages have a sound symbolic lexicon to the same degree? For example, why do Indo-European languages have a much smaller sound symbolic lexicon than some of African and Asian languages? The latter often has a large distinct word class for sound symbolic words. There are a couple of possibilities that are not mutually exclusive. First, genetic variability relating to the ability to use sound symbolism may have lead to the uneven distribution of rich sound symbolic lexicons across languages. The analogy can be drawn to the finding that speakers of tone languages share a certain genetic make-up that speakers of non-tone languages do not (Dediu & Ladd, 2007). It is possible that a certain genetic make-up promotes the use of sound symbolism, and speakers of languages like Indo-European languages do not have this make-up. Second, cultural differences in the values attached to sound symbolic words may have lead to the uneven distribution of rich sound symbolic lexicons (Nuckolls, 2004). For example, Zulu (South Africa) has traditionally had a large sound-symbolic lexicon, but younger speakers of Zulu know increasingly fewer sound symbolic words due to a negative image of such words (Childs, 1996). Namely, sound symbolic words are associated with rural Zulu identity, which rapidly urbanizing young Zulu speakers tend to disown (Childs, 1996). Similarly to the young Zulu speakers, the ancestors of the current speakers of Indo-European languages may have held cultural values that were not compatible with frequent use of sound symbolic words. This may have been the reason why current Indo-European languages do not have a large sound symbolic lexicon or a distinct word class for sound symbolic words.

Despite the uneven spread of a large sound symbolic lexicon across languages, speakers of Indo-European languages can detect cross-linguistically valid sound symbolism (Davis, 1961; Imai, et al., 2008; Iwasaki, Vinson, & Vigliocco, 2007; Kantartzis, et al., 2009; Maurer, Pathman, & Mondloch, 2006; Westbury, 2004). Thus, the ability to use universal sound symbolism is a robust feature of modern humans.

7. *Conclusion*

Sound symbolism helps children learn new words even if the language they are learning (e.g., English) does not have a large sound symbolic lexicon. We argued that children have this ability, even though it is not always useful, due to evolutionary history. More specifically, we proposed that our ancestors used protolanguage largely consisting of sound symbolic words, and children's ability to use sound symbolism in word learning is the vestige of this stage of language evolution. We argued that sound symbolic protolanguage would have been able to refer to a wide range of information. Emergence and development of a shared open-class lexicon might have been relatively easy in such protolanguage. Sound symbolic protolanguage may have also provided a stepping stone from a holophrastic protolanguage to a combinatoric protolanguage, which is closer to modern language.

Acknowledgements

This research was supported by Ministry of Education Grant-in-Aid for Scientific Research (#15300088) to Imai, by Daiwa Anglo-Japanese Foundation (5944/6131) to Kita and Imai, and by a Schilizzi Foundation fellowship to Kantartzis.

References

Childs, G. T. (1996). Where have all the ideophones gone? *Tronto Working Papers in Linguistics, 15*(2), 81-104.

Davis, R. (1961). The fitness of names to drawings: A cross-cultural study in Tanganyika. *British Journal of Psychology, 52*, 259-268.

de Saussure, F. (1916/1983). *Course in general linguistics (R. Harris, Trans.).* La Salle, IL: Open Court.

Dediu, D., & Ladd, D. R. (2007). Linguistic tone is related to the population frequency of the adaptive haplogroups of two brain size genes, ASPM and Microcephalin. *Proceedings of National Academy of Sciences of the United States of America, 104*, 10944-10949.

Ibarretxe-Antuñano, I. (2006). *Sound symbolism and motion in Basque.* München: Lincom.

Imai, M., Haryu, E., & Okada, H. (2005). Mapping novel nouns and verbs onto dynamic action events: Are verb meanings easier to learn than noun meanings for Japanese children? *Child Development, 76*(2), 340-355.

Imai, M., Kita, S., Nagumo, M., & Okada, H. (2008). Sound symbolism facilitates early verb learning. *Cognition, 109*, 54-65.

Iwasaki, N., Vinson, D. P., & Vigliocco, G. (2007). How does it hurt, "kiri-kiri" or "siku-siku"? Japanese mimetic words of pain perceived by Japanese speakers and English speakers. In M. Minami (Ed.), *Applying theory and research to learning Japanese as a foreign language* (pp. 2-19). New Castle upon Tyne: Cambridge Scholars Publishing.

Kantartzis, K., Kita, S., & Imai, M. (2009). Japanese sound symbolism facilitates word learning in English speaking children *Proceedings of the thirty first annual conference of the Cognitive Science Society* (pp. 591-595): Cognitive Science Society.

Kita, S. (1997). Two-dimensional semantic analysis of Japanese mimetics. *Linguistics, 35*, 379-415.

Kita, S. (2001). Semantic schism and interpretive integration in Japanese sentences with a mimetic: A reply to Tsujimura. *Linguistics, 39*, 419-436.

Kita, S. (2008). World-view of protolanguage speakers as inferred from semantics of sound symbolic words: A case of Japanese mimetics. In N. Masataka (Ed.), *Origins of language* (pp. 25-38). Tokyo: Springer.

Limber, J. (1982). What can chimps tell us about the origin of language? In S. Kuczaj (Ed.), *Language development, Vol. 2* (pp. 429-469). Hillsdale, NJ: Lawrence Erlbaum.

Maurer, D., Pathman, T., & Mondloch, C. J. (2006). The shape of boubas: sound-shape correspondences in toddlers and adults. *Developmental Science, 9*(3), 316-322.

Mikone, E. (2001). Ideophones in the Balto-Finnic languages. In F. K. E. Voeltz & C. Kilian-Hatz (Eds.), *Ideophones* (pp. 223-233). Amsterdam: John Benjamins.

Müller, F. M. (1866). *Lectures on the science of language.* New York: Scribner.

Nuckolls, J. B. (1999). The case for sound symbolism. *Annual Review of Anthropology, 28*, 225-252.

Quine, W. V. O. (1960). *Word and object.* Cambridge, MA: The MIT Press.

Ramachandran, V. S., & Hubbard, E. M. (2001). Synaesthesia - A window into perception, thought, and language. *Journal of Consciousness Studies, 8*(12), 3-34.

Sapir, E. (1929). A study in phonetic symbolism. *Journal of Experimental Psychology, 12*, 225-239.

Senghas, A., Kita, S., & Özyürek, A. (2004). Children creating core properties of language: Evidence from an emerging sign language in Nicaragua. *Science, 305*, 1779-1782.

Voeltz, F. K. E., & Kilian-Hatz, C. (Eds.). (2001). *Ideophones.* Amsterdam: John Benjamins.

Westbury, C. (2004). Implicit sound symbolism in lexical access: Evidence from an interference task. *Brain and Language, 93*, 10-19.

Wray, A. (2000). Holistic utterances in protolanguage: The link from primates to humans. In C. Knight, M. Studdert-Kennedy & J. Hurford (Eds.), *Evolutionary Emergence of Language : Social Function and the Origins of Linguistic Form* (pp. 285-302). West Nyack, NY: Cambridge University Press.

A SENSORIMOTOR CHARACTERISATION OF SYNTAX, AND ITS IMPLICATIONS FOR MODELS OF LANGUAGE EVOLUTION

ALISTAIR KNOTT

Dept of Computer Science, University of Otago, Dunedin, New Zealand
alik@cs.otago.ac.nz

In this paper I consider the possibility that language is more strongly grounded in sensorimotor cognition than is normally assumed—a scenario which would be providential for language evolution theorists. I argue that the syntactic theory most compatible with this scenario, perhaps surprisingly, is generative grammar. I suggest that there may be a way of interpreting the syntactic structures posited in one theory of generative grammar (Minimalism) as descriptions of sensorimotor processing, and discuss the implications of this for models of language evolution.

1. An optimistic idea about how to study language evolution

One way of studying language evolution is to investigate the interface between language and sensorimotor representations in modern humans. We know that there is an interface, of course, because we can talk about what we see and do in the world. But opinions vary about how much work is involved in converting sensorimotor signals into an utterance. If language is a Fodorian module, then a lot of work is involved, because there is no overlap between the sensorimotor mechanisms which create an episode representation and the syntactic mechanisms which express it as an utterance. But many cognitive scientists now argue that syntactic mechanisms supervene to some extent on sensorimotor ones (see e.g. Rizzolatti and Arbib, 1998; Barsalou, 1999; Hurford, 2003). The more overlap there is, the less specifically linguistic machinery we need to postulate, and the simpler a story we can tell about language evolution.

In this paper, I want to be optimistic, and entertain the scenario that syntactic mechanisms overlap extensively with sensorimotor ones. While this need not be the case, it would certainly be providential for language evolution theorists. For one thing, it would make it very likely that biological specialisations for language evolved as adaptations of sensorimotor mechanisms, as has already been proposed by several theorists (see e.g. Arbib, 2005; Fadiga *et al.*, 2006). Furthermore, given that our sensorimotor capabilities are relatively similar to those of other primates (see e.g. Tootell *et al.*, 1996; Iacoboni, 2006), we are probably within our rights to use the modern primate sensorimotor system as an approximation of the preadaptive platform from which language evolved. Models of the sensorimotor system would then provide a concrete starting point for relatively detailed hypotheses about how language evolved. In short, the possibility that syntactic mechanisms overlap extensively with sensorimotor mechanisms is one which language evolution theorists should think seriously about.

What would syntactic theory look like if language were indeed strongly grounded in sensorimotor mechanisms? Given that all humans have the same sensorimotor apparatus, one thing we expect is that there should be minimal differences between the grammars of different languages around the world. This seems like a setback, because languages around the world appear to differ quite a lot. In fact, the only way of maintaining our optimistic scenario is to assume that these differences are relatively superficial, and that at some deeper level of syntactic representation, the mechanisms for generating sentences are basically the same from one language to another.

Perhaps paradoxically, if we want to explore the best possible scenario a language evolution theorist could hope for, the syntactic framework we are drawn towards is Chomskyan generative grammar. This framework assumes that language is largely the product of an innate mechanism, which operates in the same way in every language. Accordingly, the syntax of a sentence is specified at an 'underlying' level, which reflects the operation of this innate mechanism and is relatively invariant across languages, and then at a more superficial level, which expresses how the underlying representation is rendered in different languages. Chomskyan generative grammar is a hunt for underlying syntactic representations (often abstract and arcane) which permit generalisations to be expressed about the syntax of different languages. If syntax supervenes heavily on sensorimotor mechanisms, such generalisations are to be expected.

Of course Chomskyan grammarians are normally also Fodorians, holding that the mechanisms responsible for language are *specific* to language. This possibility makes an account of language evolution especially difficult, as already noted, because there is a lot of language-specific machinery to evolve. On the alternative possibility that I am considering, the commonalities between languages are due to the fact that language supervenes heavily on sensorimotor mechanisms. If this is the case, then we expect to find the kind of underlying syntactic representations posited by Chomskyan linguists—but we also predict that they can be understood as descriptions of sensorimotor processing. This is quite a long shot, since the representations are developed by linguists without any reference to sensorimotor cognition at all. But the prediction can certainly be tested. We can proceed as follows. Take a simple concrete episode, which an observer can apprehend using sensorimotor mechanisms, and formulate a model of these mechanisms. Then take a sentence which reports this episode, and determine its underlying syntactic structure, within your favourite model of generative grammar. Is there any way of interpreting the syntactic structure as a description of mechanisms in the sensorimotor model? If there is, the prediction is borne out for this sentence/episode pair. If the interpretation also extends to other sentence/episode pairs, then it becomes possible to think of the language universals proposed within generative grammar as having a sensorimotor origin. A convincing sensorimotor interpretation of underlying syntactic representations would have many implications in linguistics. Most obviously it would open up new ways of studying these representations within the domain of sensorimotor neuroscience. But it would also be good news for language evolution theorists, for the reasons already given.

In the remainder of the paper I will report on my own investigation into the relationship between sensorimotor cognition and underlying syntactic representations. The investigation is described in detail in a book I am preparing (Knott, 2010); what I give here is a summary of the main ideas. The book focusses on a single concrete episode—a man grabbing a cup. In Section 2, I give a model of the sensorimotor processes involved in experiencing this episode. In Section 3, I give a model of the underlying syntactic structure of the the associated transitive sentence *The man grabbed a cup*, expressed within the Minimalist framework of Chomsky (1995). In Section 4 I argue that there is a natural sensorimotor interpretation of this syntactic structure, and I discuss what implications this interpretation might have for an account of language evolution, if it proves to be well-founded.

2. Outline of a sensorimotor model of a reach-to-grasp action

Research in sensorimotor cognition tends to focus on processes much smaller than the perception of a complete episode. There is a great deal of work on how individual objects are attended to and categorised, on how individual actions are executed and perceived, and on how attentional and motor processes are coupled during action execution and perception. I will begin by summarising what is known about these processes, and then outline my suggestion about how they combine during the experience of a complete episode.

Perceiving an object involves attending to it and classifying it. It is known that these processes happen in different neural pathways (Milner and Goodale, 1995), and in most models an object must be attended to before it can be categorised (see classically Treisman and Gelade 1980, and more recently Reynolds and Desimone, 1999). As regards action perception: it is fairly orthodox since the discovery of mirror neurons to assume that recognising a particular reach-to-grasp action activates the same premotor representations that are involved in executing this action. As regards the coupling of attentional and motor processes: it is well established that an agent typically attends to a target object before reaching for it (see e.g. Johansson and Westling, 2001). More recently, it has been found that observers watching a reach-to-grasp action saccade to the target object well before the agent's hand reaches it (Flanagan and Johansson, 2003). This is in line with computational models of hand action classification, which assume that the observer monitors the trajectory of the agent's hand in relation to the intended target (see e.g. Oztop and Arbib, 2002). In summary, recognition and execution of a reach-to-grasp action have much in common: in each case, the experiencer first attends to and classifies the intended target object, and then evokes a premotor action representation encoding the action being performed.

The way in which an experiencer identifies the agent of a reach-to-grasp action depends on whether he is observing the action or performing it. In the former case, the agent must be attended to as an external object. It has recently been found that observers of a reach-to-grasp action typically fixate the agent before saccading to the target (Webb *et al.*, in press). The initial saccade to the agent allows the agent to be classified or recognised, but also provides information about the agent's intentions, which is what allows the observer to make an anticipatory saccade to the target. In the latter case, where the experiencer of the action is also the agent, the mechanism which allows him to attribute the action to himself is quite different, involving recognition of a particular configuration of the motor system, in which high-level motor plans cause physical movements (see e.g. Farrer and Frith, 2002). The first operation in any action must be one which configures the motor system for action execution rather than action observation. This operation can be studied in an ERP paradigm. The earliest cortical indication of a forthcoming voluntary action is a bilateral signal called the Bereitschaftspotential (BP; Shibasaki and Hallett, 2006). Since the BP precedes lateralised activity in premotor areas reflecting a specific action being planned, it appears to encode a relatively pure 'decision to act', rather than a particular motor plan. I suggest that this operation is the means by which an experiencer establishes himself as the agent of his own actions; and therefore that the very first sensorimotor operation in both action perception and action execution is an action of 'attention to the agent'.

The picture which emerges from the above data is that experience of a reach-to-grasp action involves a canonical sequence of sensorimotor operations—and moreover that the sequence of operations is the same for action execution and action observation. The experiencer first attends to (and classifies) the agent, then attends to (and classifies) the target, and finally monitors the action to completion. In fact, during this latter process, there is evidence that the experiencer *reattends* first to the agent and then to the target. While the action is ongoing, the temporally extended pattern of signals in the sensorimotor system is characteristic of the agent as well as of the particular action being performed. When monitoring these signals, the experiencer evokes a representation of the agent as an animate entity, which is integrated with representations of the agent as a static object (Giese, 2000). When the action is complete, the agent is grasping the target object. A grasp action is a substantive motor action, but it is also an attentional action in the haptic modality, providing the agent with a new means of characterising the location and shape of the target object. Thus the target is attended to once when the action is being prepared, and again, in a different modality, when it is completed. Note that the actions of reattention to the agent and the target during action monitoring both allow the development of cross-modal object representations. The agent is attended to first as an object and then as an animate entity; the target is attended to first as an object and then as a motor state (i.e. a Gibsonian affordance).

The sequence of sensorimotor operations involved in experiencing a reach-to-grasp action according to the above account is summarised in Figure 1. Given

Initial context	Deictic operation	Reafferent sensory state	New context
$C1$	Attend to the agent	Attending to the agent	$C2$
$C2$	Attend to the target	Attending to the target	$C3$
$C3$	Activate 'grasp' action	Re-attending to the agent	$C4$
$C4$		Re-attending to the target	

Figure 1.   Sequence of sensorimotor operations involved in experience of a reach-to-grasp action

that the sequencing of operations is important, it is useful to model the process of experiencing a reach-to-grasp episode as a 'deictic routine' (Ballard *et al.*, 1997). A deictic routine is a sequence of attentional and motor operations, in which each operation brings about the sensorimotor context necessary to perform the next operation. Each item in the sequence has the same basic form: a **deictic operation** causes a transition from an **initial context** to a **new context**, generating as a side-effect a **reafferent sensory state**. Note that on this model, a reach-to-grasp episode can be stored in working memory as a planned sequence of sensorimotor operations. It thus lends itself particularly well to a 'simulationist' account of meaning (see e.g. Feldman and Narayanan, 2004; Gallese, 2005): the process of evoking a semantic episode representation can be understood as the process of internally replaying a stored sensorimotor sequence from working memory.

3. Outline of a syntactic model of transitive sentences

The syntactic framework I have adopted is that of Minimalism (Chomsky, 1995). In this framework, a sentence is represented at two syntactic levels: an underlying level of 'logical form' (LF), which is relatively invariant across languages, and a surface level of 'phonetic form' (PF). The LF of our example sentence *The man grabbed a cup* is shown in Figure 2. It is formed from applications of an abstract

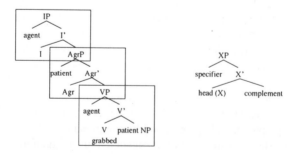

Figure 2.   Left: LF structure of *The man grabbed a cup*. Right: XP schema from which it is formed.

structure called an X-bar ('XP') schema, which is shown on the right of the figure. The LF of a clause is basically a right-branching structure of XP schemas.

An XP schema contains three positions: a **head** (which in the simplest case is occupied by a word), and a **specifier** and **complement** (which are occupied by other XPs which depend on the head). For instance, the verb *grabbed* sits at the head of VP; the specifier of VP holds an NP denoting the agent of the grab action, and its complement holds an NP denoting its patient. (The internal structure of NPs is omitted in the figure.) XP schemas are also contributed by grammatical elements; in our example sentence, IP and AgrP are associated with inflections on the verb agreeing with the subject and object NP respectively.

Note that the LF structure contains two positions each for the agent and the patient. In the Minimalist account, the agent and patient are generated at the lower positions, within VP, but they must raise to the higher positions in order to be assigned a syntactic feature called 'Case' — which at a first approximation is what distinguishes between nominative and accusative pronouns. The verb must also raise, by a different mechanism called 'head movement', to the head positions associated with its inflections: first to Agr, then to I. The surface (PF) form of the sentence is 'read out' at some point during these movement operations. How this happens is relatively unconstrained; different languages have different conventions about whether the subject, object and verb are read out 'high' or 'low', which result in different basic word orders (SVO, SOV etc).

Why is the Minimalist account of a simple transitive sentence so complicated? One reason is that Minimalism has wide coverage: the mechanisms which generate *this* sentence also generate a good proportion of the other sentences in English. Any wide-coverage grammar will give a complex syntactic analysis of any given sentence. But what makes Minimalism more complex than most syntactic theories is that it attempts to define a grammar of all languages, not just of a single language. By altering the conventions about how LF structures are read out at PF, the Minimalist account should be able to model a whole space of natural languages. It is surely laudable to look for a universal mechanism underlying the languages of the world. But even so, cognitive scientists tend not to like the Minimalist notion of LF. For one thing, Minimalism has problems as a linguistic theory. Recent work in linguistics has emphasised the importance of surface patterns in language (see e.g. Goldberg, 1995; Tomasello, 2003). As Jackendoff (2002) has incisively argued, the fact that PF supervenes entirely on LF makes it hard to account for these patterns. But perhaps more importantly, Minimalists make no attempt to relate the process of constructing an LF representation to any actual cognitive process. Notoriously, it is not a 'processing model'. But then what is it??

4. A sensorimotor interpretation of LF structure

My project is to look for a way of interpreting the LF of *The man grabbed a cup* as a description of the sensorimotor processes involved in experiencing an episode in which a man grabs a cup. There is in fact an interesting isomorphism between the LF representation just described and the sensorimotor model given in Section 2. The LF representation involves a right-branching structure of four XP schemas, associated respectively with the agent, the patient, the grab action, and again the patient. The sensorimotor model envisages a deictic routine with four phases: attention to the agent, attention to the target, activation of the 'grasp' motor programme, and reattention to the target (see Figure 1). Each XP schema has the same internal structure, and each phase in the deictic routine involves the same basic operations. In fact, I suggest we may be able to give a very general sensorimotor interpretation of an XP schema at LF, as illustrated on the left of Figure 3. Note that according to this interpretation, a right-branching sequence

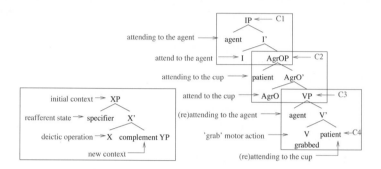

Figure 3. Left: sensorimotor interpretation of a single XP schema. Right: sensorimotor interpretation of the LF of *The man grabbed a cup*.

of XP schemas describes a sequence of deictic operations—i.e. a deictic routine. And the deictic routine which I argued for in Section 2 fits perfectly onto the LF structure of the associated sentence, as illustrated on the right of Figure 3.

This interpretation casts the Minimalist conception of LF in a completely new light. If it is legitimate, then maybe the abstract universal principles which Minimalists have derived from linguistic argumentation are not reflections of a modular language faculty, but of the fact that language is deeply grounded in sensorimotor cognition. For language evolution theorists, this is the providential scenario I began by considering. Of course, there is much work to be done to corroborate this idea. In the book I am preparing (Knott, 2010) I expand on the above analysis, arguing that there is a very natural sensorimotor interpretation of the movement of NPs from lower to higher positions in LF, and also of the raising of the verb head to higher head positions. I also argue that the sensorimotor interpretation of LF extends to several other syntactic structures: in particular, to the internal syntax of noun phrases, to the syntax of predication, and to intransitive and ditransitive sentences. I also argue that the sensorimotor interpretation of LF makes it possible to think of the Minimalist 'generative mechanism' as a model of a concrete cognitive process—one, moreover, which is involved in the generation and interpretation of sentences. Altogether this is a very radical reinterpretation of Minimalist syntax. But my hope is that it is still recognisable by Minimalists, while at the same time having a wider relevance for researchers interested in sensorimotor processing, language processing and language evolution.

References

Arbib, M. (2005). From monkey-like action recognition to human language: an evolutionary framework for neurolinguistics. *Behavioral and Brain Sciences, 28*(2), 105–167.

Ballard, D., Hayhoe, M., Pook, P., & Rao, R. (1997). Deictic codes for the embodiment of cognition. *Behavioral and Brain Sciences, 20*(4), 723–767.

Barsalou, L. (1999). Perceptual symbol systems. *Behavioral and Brain Sciences, 22*, 577–660.

Chomsky, N. (1995). *The Minimalist program*. Cambridge, MA: MIT Press.

Fadiga, L., Roy, A., Fazio, P., & Craighero, L. (2006). From hand actions to speech: evidence and speculations. In P. Haggard, Y. Rossetti, & M. Kawato (Eds.), *Sensorimotor foundations of higher cognition. attention and performance XXII* (pp. 409–434).

Farrer, C., & Frith, C. (2002). Experiencing oneself vs another person as being the cause of an action: The neural correlates of the experience of agency. *NeuroImage, 15*, 596–603.

Feldman, J., & Narayanan, S. (2004). Embodiment in a neural theory of language. *Brain and Language, 89*(2), 385–392.

Flanagan, J., & Johansson, R. (2003). Action plans used in action observation. *Nature, 424*, 769–771.

Gallese, V., & Lakoff, G. (2005). The brain's concepts: The role of the sensory-motor system in conceptual knowledge. *Cognitive Neuropsychology, 22*(3/4), 455-479.

Giese, M. (2000). Neural model for the recognition of biological motion. In G. Baratoff & H. Neumann (Eds.), *Dynamische perzeption* (pp. 105–110). Berlin: Infix Verlag.

Goldberg, A. (Ed.). (1995). *Constructions. a construction grammar approach to argument structure*. Chicago: University of Chicago Press.

Hurford, J. (2003). The neural basis of predicate-argument structure. *Behavioral and Brain Sciences, 26*(3), 261–283.

Iacoboni, M. (2006). Visuo-motor integration and control in the human posterior parietal cortex: Evidence from TMS and fMRI. *Neuropsychologia, 44*, 2691–2699.

Jackendoff, R. (2002). *Foundations of language: Brain, meaning, grammar, evolution*. Oxford: Oxford University Press.

Johansson, R., Westling, G., Backstrom, A., & Flanagan, J. (2001). Eye-hand coordination in object manipulation. *Journal of Neuroscience, 21*(17), 6917–6932.

Knott, A. (2010). *Sensorimotor cognition and natural language syntax*. Manuscript, Dept of Computer Science, University of Otago. (http://www.cs.otago.ac.nz/staffpriv/alik/publications.html)

Milner, R., & Goodale, M. (1995). *The visual brain in action*. Oxford: Oxford University Press.

Oztop, E., & Arbib, M. (2002). Schema design and implementation of the grasp-related mirror neuron system. *Biological Cybernetics, 87*, 116–140.

Reynolds, J., & Desimone, R. (1999). The role of neural mechanisms of attention in solving the binding problem. *Neuron, 24*, 19–29.

Rizzolatti, G., & Arbib, M. (1998). Language within our grasp. *Trends in Neurosciences, 21*, 188–194.

Shibata, H., & Hallett, M. (2006). What is the Bereitschaftspotential? *Clinical Neurophysiology, 117*, 2341–2356.

Tomasello, M. (2003). *Constructing a language: A usage-based theory of language acquisition*. Harvard University Press.

Tootell, R., Dale, A., Sereno, M., & Malach, R. (1996). New images from human visual cortex. *Trends in Neurosciences, 19*(11), 481–489.

Treisman, A., & Gelade, G. (1980). A feature integration theory of attention. *Cognitive Psychology, 12*, 97–136.

Webb, A., Knott, A., & MacAskill, M. (in press). Eye movements during transitive action observation have sequential structure. *Acta Psychologica*.

WHY ROBOTS?

MARTIN LOETZSCH

AI-Lab, Vrije Universiteit Brussel, Pleinlaan 2, 1050 Brussels, Belgium
Martin.Loetzsch@vub.ac.be

MICHAEL SPRANGER

SONY Computer Science Laboratory Paris, 6, Rue Amyot, Paris, 75005, France

In this paper we offer arguments for why modeling in the field of artificial language evolution can benefit from the use of real robots. We will propose that robotic experimental setups lead to more realistic and robust models, that real-word perception can provide the basis for richer semantics and that embodiment itself can be a driving force in language evolution. We will discuss these proposals by reviewing a variety of robotic experiments that have been carried out in our group and try to argue for the relevance of the approach.

1. Introduction

Computational modeling has become an invaluable tool for studying the origins and evolution of human languages. Mathematical investigations and computer simulations help us to test whether assumptions of a particular theory are explicit, detailed and consistent enough so that the operationalization of that theory can generate phenomena found in reality. Furthermore, computational models allow researchers to manipulate both external conditions as well as details of the assumed mechanisms in a controlled way that is not possible with human subjects. Standards for scientific experimentation using computer models are starting to be established within the evolution of language community (e.g. Cangelosi & Parisi, 2002; Steels, 2006) and work that follows these methodologies gets more and more accepted.

From the very beginning on, robots have been used to carry out experiments on the origins and evolution of language. And a question that is often asked by reviewers of such work is: *What is the added value of using robots for that particular study?* This is a very valid question and in fact a lot of the computational work on the evolution of language has been done successfully without robots. A common strategy is to scaffold all aspects related to perception (and often also conceptualization) by presenting agents with stimuli generated by world simulators of varying detail. Such generated stimuli can range from simple "meaning vectors" or readily pre-conceptualized semantic structures to more complex de-

Figure 1.   Robotic setup. Two robots are placed in an office environment consisting of colored objects, carton boxes and markers on the walls. Both robots engage in communicative interactions about objects in their environment.

scriptions of perceptual input that require further conceptualization. The advantage of this methodology is that researchers can focus on the "core" cognitive functions and representations that are involved in the processing and learning of language without having to deal with seemingly "remote" problems.

Why one would want to remove this scaffold can be easily answered when the topic of research is directly related to symbol grounding or human-robot interaction: such work simply requires to use robots. But for research on how and why a particular feature of language evolved, the value of using robots is much less obvious. And whereas other disciplines, such as the relatively new field of biorobotics, have already well-established criteria for judging whether a robotic implementation is a good model for a (biological) phenomenon (e.g. Webb, 2001), such a consensus does not exist for the field of language evolution. Nevertheless, as we will argue in this paper, there are clear and undoubtable advantages to using robots. In fact, we will claim that in order to start an investigation into language from the right point of view and to avoid getting trapped in solutions and theories of particular phenomena that are misleading or, even worse, false, robotic experiments are indispensable.

We will propose some answers to the question of "why robots?" by discussing a variety of language game experiments with Sony humanoid robots (Fujita et al., 2003, see Figure 1) that have been carried out in our group over the past few years. Compared to similar experiments based solely on computer simulations, setting up such experiments immediately becomes much more complex and difficult. In addition to finding the appropriate cognitive functions and representations for using and learning language, the robots have to be endowed with mechanisms for visual perception, joint attention and social interaction (pointing, non-linguistic feedback, etc.). In the next section, we will try to demonstrate that this additional effort is justified.

2. Why robots?

We will make four arguments for why the use of robots can lead to better models of language evolution: it increases the *realism* of models, it leads to more *robust* models, it provides *richer semantics* and, finally, real embodiment can serve as a *driving force* for language evolution.

2.1. Increased realism

One of the best-studied models on the origins of language is the naming game (Steels, 1995). In such a scenario, simulated agents of a population engage in local communicative interactions and over the course of many such interactions create and align a shared lexicon of proper names for individual objects. It is the simplest lexicon formation model that can be imagined and therefore proved to be an "E. coli paradigm" for investigating alignment strategies, mathematical proofs of convergence, impact of network structure and so on. Since it is such a simple model, it has also led to views that proper names are semantically simpler than words for kinds of objects (e.g. "red" or "block") and that they might be precursors of compositional communication systems (e.g. in Steels, 2005).

However, when this model is brought to real robots, as done by Steels, Loetzsch, and Spranger (2010), then it turns out that the dynamics of the grounded naming game differ drastically from the non-grounded version and that the underlying semantics of proper names are much more complex. Whereas in the non-grounded version word meanings refer directly to pre-given shared symbolic representations of individuals, in the grounded variant these representations need to be constructed from the continuous flow of visual perceptions. Since each individual physical object can be viewed from different angles and thus may look very different each time it is encountered by a robot, the agents can not know a priori whether a perception of an object belongs to the same individual or not. Additional heuristics, such as temporal-spatial continuity need to be employed to successively construct mental representations of individual objects. Consequently, tackling the emergence of proper names by using real robots introduces an additional level of realism because it forces researchers to incorporate processes for object individuation in their model instead of assuming them.

2.2. Robust models

Robots provide a tough testing ground for computational models in terms of their robustness. Agents can view a scene from different angles, lighting conditions may vary and thus the perceptions that two different robots have of the same physical object will never be the same. Even a single robot will perceive an object differently over the course of time due to camera noise, robot motion and general uncertainty in computer vision systems. Nevertheless, human concepts, such as, for example, the color red, are robust to such influences – we will recognize an object as red under very different lighting conditions and even subjects with color deficiencies are often able to communicate about colors.

One challenge stemming from real-world perception is *perceptual deviation*, i.e. that specific continuous features (e.g. position, shape, width and height, color information, etc.) computed by the vision system for an object differ drastically between the perception of speaker and hearer. For example one robot might perceive the height of an object as being 0.72 and the other one as 0.56. This will inevitably cause each agent to have a different notion of a word such as "high". Additionally, perceptual deviation makes the task of guessing what a novel word refers to (whether it is about an object as a whole, one particular sensory channel or a combination of features) harder than when simulated shared contexts are used.

The problem of inferring the meaning of an unknown word has been extensively studied in the field of artificial language evolution (e.g. Smith et al., 2006). However, many of these models work only when tested in shared simulated contexts and could not be successfully transferred to robotic scenarios. Trying to overcome this lack of robustness, Wellens, Loetzsch, and Steels (2008) proposed a lexicon formation model that challenged the way previous approaches represented word meanings and tackled the task of word learning. Perceptual uncertainty was put at the core of word meaning representations and thus the agents learned to rely less on sensory channels with higher perceptual deviation. As a result, the model was not only able to cope well with perceptual deviation but also turned out to scale better with increasing population size and larger meaning spaces in simulated environments (Wellens, 2008). Hence, using robots and not relying on simple world simulations can lead to qualitatively new models that exhibit properties closer to human language.

Furthermore, real-world perception can provide more structured stimuli than randomly created artificial contexts. For the domain of color, Bleys et al. (2009) systematically analyzed the impact of using robotic vision compared to artificial contexts (as used in anthropologic color research) on the performance of color naming games. They found their model to be robust with respect to perceptual deviation because perceived colors of objects are usually around prototypical centers of color categories.

2.3. *Rich semantics*

Rich conceptual structures are a requirement for the emergence of grammar. When one follows a functional perspective on language, then grammatical structure arises in large part due to the multiplicity and ambiguity of conceptualizing the world. More precisely, grammar gets shaped and adapted to solve problems emerging from ambiguity in interpretation or explosion of search in parsing and production (Steels & Wellens, 2006).

Prime examples for such phenomena can be found in the domain of space, where different ways of conceptualizing the same spatial scene compete. For example, the English utterance "in front of the TV" is ambiguous, because English allows speakers to conceptualize the world using *relative* or *intrinsic* frames of references (Levinson, 2003). The phrase can mean before the screen of the TV (intrinsic frame of reference, using the front of the TV) or before the screen from the viewpoint of the speaker. In many contexts there might be no difference between these two interpretations as they might happen to discriminate the same referent. But in certain cases English also requires speakers to disambiguate the meaning, by marking the particular conceptualization strategy used.

In order to have conceptual structures that leave room for ambiguities, the perceptual space underlying conceptualization needs to be complex enough so that the reality can be construed in different ways. Robotic models are a way to appreciate this: there are numerous ways of how interlocutors can be positioned relative to each other and hence how they view a scene, there is non-linear perceptual noise in position estimation and there are numerous ways to choose objects as reference points. Thus, rich perceptions of spatial setups have proven to be crucial for investigating the emergence of spatial perspective reversal (Steels & Loetzsch, 2009) and the alignment frames of reference choice (Spranger et al., 2009).

2.4. *A driving force for language evolution*

Many theoretical proposals of how language conveys meaning have focussed on the grounding of language in the body (Johnson, 1987), on how specific systems of language interact with sensorimotor processes and how semantic and syntactic structures become recruited from one domain to another, for example, from the bodily domain to the domain of space (MacLaury, 1989) or from space to time (Kuteva, 1999). Linguists, especially those in the cognitive linguistics tradition, have hypothesized that the adaptation and exaptation processes that guide such conceptual transfer are deeply rooted in the concrete embodiment of humans and our particular interaction with the environment.

For instance, Lemmens (2002) demonstrated how posture verbs such as *sit, stand, lie* become metaphorically extended to the domain of space in Germanic languages. Clear examples can be found in the Dutch language, where posture verbs have been extended from their original bodily meaning (their anthropocentric prototypical semantic structure denoting human postures) to animals, things and even abstract spaces and entities. In Dutch butter *lies* in the fridge and one even *sits* in an economical crisis.

To model such transfer processes, embodiment needs to be taken seriously because the interaction with the environment plays a crucial role both in constructing conceptual structures and linking them across different perceptual domains. For example Spranger and Loetzsch (2009) and Steels and Spranger (2009) used humanoid robots to show how the semantics of posture verbs can emerge from sensorimotor interaction, how these conceptual structures can be linked to language and, finally, how bodily representations can be metaphorically extended. It is hard to imagine how such processes could have been studied without using real robots because 1) the meaning of posture verbs is directly grounded in behavior and 2) perceptual capabilities and representations are at the heart of the exaptation process.

2.5. *Discussion*

It could be argued that all of the work cited above can be done in (sometimes complex) simulations, which would make setting up the experiments less difficult and time consuming, without decreasing the realism of models. This article in no way refutes the idea of simulating phenomena as an invaluable source of knowledge, inspiration and scientific progress. In fact, we ourselves have used simulations of different types ranging from full-blown world simulators including a simulated physical environment with agents, to simulators that reproduce the output of particular cognitive systems such as perception or conceptualization. In the process of building artificial systems to study certain aspects of language evolution one often anyway finds oneself building simulators for the purpose of testing and studying subsystems.

Setting up simulators seems easier on first sight, but in fact it is not. First, developing realistic simulations of complex interactions with a virtual world often turns out to be as difficult (if not even more) than dealing with actual robots. And second (more importantly), it entails a lot of decisions and assumptions that actually require justification.

When building a simulation one inevitably needs to make certain choices as to how the particular simulated entity behaves, what properties it has, for instance which noise and timing properties are assumed, but also which representations are the interface between the simulation and the system studied. These choices are governed by a set of explicit or implicit assumptions that restrain the test space of the system in question. This is true for physical simulations, where the choice amounts to which physical properties one includes in the simulation and how they are interacting with the studied system, as well as for more abstract simulations that for instance simulate the output of certain cognitive systems. These assumptions can of course be discussed and ideally researchers make an effort to find all hidden and implicit assumptions in their simulated models, but it seems hard to prove the realism of a particular model without showing its operation in the real world. After all "... physical robots cannot violate the laws of physics, even if those laws are unspecified by the investigator. The performance of a physical robot is immediately informative about what works and what does not" (Long, 2007, p.1193, see also Webb, 2000, p.552, for a discussion of simulated robots vs. real robots).

One point of computational modeling in this field is to operationalize and therefore test theories of language evolution in concrete experiments. And since language is a way of interaction of real agents in the real world, showing the adequacy of the proposed solution cannot be avoided by resorting to the success of a system in simulation. Hence, building a fully autonomous system interacting with the real world entails making certain choices on all levels of cognitive systems including perception and action, but building a simulation involves important choices and specific assumptions about how certain subsystems or the physical world works that need to be justified. While these choices are always explicit in a real world computational systems, they might be hidden and unnoticed in simulation based approaches.

3. Conclusions

This paper discussed how exploiting the rich sensorimotor interaction of real robots with a physical world is a valuable methodology for investigating the evolution of language. Computational models using real robots benefit from higher realism, increased robustness and richer semantics. Thus, this paper compiled evidence as to why the study of language evolution should encompass real robots, in turn, arguing for a "whole systems" approach that aims to integrate processes of embodiment, sensorimotor intelligence, cognition, and social interaction.

Acknowledgements

Reported research was partly funded by the EU project ALEAR and carried out at the Sony CSL in Paris and at the AI lab of the University of Brussels. We are extremely grateful to Masahiro Fujita, Hideki Shimomura and their team at the Sony Intelligent Systems Research Lab in Tokyo for giving the opportunity and support to work with the Sony humanoid robot.

References

Bleys, J., Loetzsch, M., Spranger, M., & Steels, L. (2009). *The grounded colour naming game.* To appear in Proceedings Roman-09.

Cangelosi, A., & Parisi, D. (2002). Computer simulation: a new scientific approach to the study of language evolution. In *Simulating the evolution of language* (pp. 3–28). New York, NY, USA: Springer-Verlag New York, Inc.

Fujita, M., Kuroki, Y., Ishida, T., & Doi, T. T. (2003). Autonomous behavior control architecture of entertainment humanoid robot SDR-4X. In *Proceedings of the IEEE/RSJ IROS '03* (pp. 960–967, vol. 1). Las Vegas, Nevada.

Johnson, M. (1987). *The body in the mind: The bodily basis of meaning, imagination, and reason.* University of Chicago Press Chicago.

Kuteva, T. (1999). On'sit'/'stand'/'lie'auxiliation. *Linguistics, 37*(2), 191–213.

Lemmens, M. (2002). The semantic network of dutch posture verbs. In J. Newman (Ed.), *The linguistics of sitting, standing and lying.* Amsterdam/Philadelphia: John Benjamins.

Levinson, S. (2003). *Space in language and cognition: Explorations in cognitive diversity.* Cambridge University Press.

Long, J. H. (2007). Biomimetic robotics: self-propelled physical models test hypotheses about the mechanics and evolution of swimming vertebrates. *Proceedings of the Institution of Mechanical Engineers, Part C: Journal of Mechanical Engineering Science, 221*(10).

MacLaury, R. (1989). Zapotec body-part locatives: Prototypes and metaphoric extensions. *International Journal of American Linguistics,* 119–154.

Smith, K., Smith, A. D. M., Blythe, R. A., & Vogt, P. (2006). Cross-situational learning: A mathematical approach. In *Symbol grounding and beyond: Proceedings of EELC 2006* (Vol. 4211, pp. 31–44). Springer Verlag.

Spranger, M., & Loetzsch, M. (2009). The semantics of SIT, STAND, and LIE embodied in robots. In *Proceedings of Cogsci'09.* Cognitive Science Soc.

Spranger, M., Pauw, S., & Loetzsch, M. (2009). *Open-ended semantics co-evolving with spatial language.* Submitted to Evolang 8.

Steels, L. (1995). A self-organizing spatial vocabulary. *Artificial Life, 2*(3).

Steels, L. (2005). The emergence and evolution of linguistic structure: from lexical to grammatical communication systems. *Connection Science, 17*(3/4).

Steels, L. (2006). How to do experiments in artificial language evolution and why. In *Proc. of Evolang 6.* World Scientific Publishing.

Steels, L., & Loetzsch, M. (2009). Perspective alignment in spatial language. In *Spatial language and dialogue* (pp. 70–89). Oxford University Press.

Steels, L., Loetzsch, M., & Spranger, M. (2010). A boy named sue. the semiotic dynamics of naming and identity. *submitted.*

Steels, L., & Spranger, M. (2009). How experience of the body shapes language about space. In *Proceedings of IJCAI 09.* Pasadena (CA).

Steels, L., & Wellens, P. (2006). How grammar emerges to dampen combinatorial search in parsing. In *Symbol grounding and beyond* (Vol. 4211, pp. 76–88). Rome, Italy: Springer Verlag.

Webb, B. (2000). What does robotics offer animal behaviour? *Animal Behaviour, 60*(5), 545–558.

Webb, B. (2001). Can robots make good models of biological behaviour? *Behavioral and Brain Sciences, 24*(6), 1033–1050.

Wellens, P. (2008). Coping with combinatorial uncertainty in word learning: a flexible usage-based model. In *Proceedings of Evolang 7.* World Scientific.

Wellens, P., Loetzsch, M., & Steels, L. (2008). Flexible word meaning in embodied agents. *Connection Science, 20*(2 & 3), 173–191.

LINGUISTIC ARGUMENTS PROBABLY ANTEDATE LINGUISTIC PREDICATES

ERKKI LUUK

Institute of Computer Science, University of Tartu, Postimaja pk 149, Tartu, 50002, Estonia

The received view is that the first distinct word types were noun and verb (Heine & Kuteva, 2002; Hurford, 2003a). Heine and Kuteva (2007) have suggested that the first words were noun-like entities. The present paper submits ten new arguments that support this claim. The arguments are novel implications of the reviewed evidence which is made to bear on the evolution of the linguistic predicate/argument (e.g. noun/verb) structure. The paper concludes that the evidence for noun-like entities antedating other word types is overwhelming.

1. Introduction[1]

It is generally agreed that argument and predicate are the syntactic (or propositional) functions of N and V, respectively (Anward, 2001; Helmbrecht, 2001). As pointed out by Hurford (2003b), the N/V structure does not align with the predicate/argument structure of FOPL (and SOPL). The conflict between the two above sentences implies a discrepancy between the predicate/argument structures of NL and FOPL/SOPL. In Luuk (2009a,b), I have characterized the predicate/argument system of NL as distinct from that of FOPL and SOPL (and possibly also of higher-order logics) in a number of respects. A property of this system is that nouns are linguistic arguments and verbs are linguistic predicates but the set of linguistic arguments and predicates is not restricted to nouns and verbs.

As suggested by Heine and Kuteva (2007, see also 2002), the first word type in language evolution was most likely a noun-like entity. The noun-like entities were not nouns in the modern sense, complete with grammatical marking and syntactic function (the latter is already precluded by the

---

[1] **Abbreviations:** ADJ adjective, ADP adposition, AUX auxiliary verb, DET determiner, FOPL first order predicate logic, LA linguistic argument, LP linguistic predicate, LP/A linguistic predicate/argument, N noun, N/V noun/verb, NL natural language, NP noun phrase, POSS possessive, SOPL second order predicate logic, TAM tense-aspect-mood, V verb

circumstance that the first words belonged to protolanguage which lacks syntax by definition – Bickerton, 1990; Jackendoff, 1999), but words which stood for time-stable, referential units expressing primarily thing-like concepts. As Heine and Kuteva (2007) define the first word type semantically (or denotationally), they can bypass the interdependence condition, characteristic of arguments and predicates in modern language. As syntactic functions, argument and predicate are interdependent, but their semantic motivation exhibits not interdependence but complementarity, opening the possibility that argumental entities appeared before predicative ones. Below is a meta-analysis contributing ten new arguments to the case for the evolutionary primacy of LA over LP. Heine and Kuteva's (2007) original arguments were the possibility of verbless pidgin sentences (in Russenorsk), evidence from spontaneous adult second language acquisition, and ample evidence from grammaticalization.

2. Ten arguments for the evolutionary primacy of linguistic arguments over linguistic predicates

1. LPs presuppose LAs they act upon. A predicate applies to a variable, whose value is provided beforehand (Hurford, 2003b). This is the reason why a language without LAs is almost inconceivable, whereas a language without LPs seems accessible enough. One can utter *ship Amsterdam tomorrow* and be understood that "a ship will arrive in or depart to Amsterdam tomorrow" but a nounless English construction expressing the same, though possible, is not likely to be univocally understood. J. L. Borges has explored the possibility of a nounless language in one of his short stories (Borges, 1964). The sample text he produces relies heavily on imagination and adjectives, whereas a verbless language can do with nouns alone. Asymmetry is inherent to P/A (and hence, to the LP/A – Luuk) structure (Hurford, 2003c). Budd (2006) has suggested that in complex systems with asymmetrical dependencies, the functionally necessary core component must have evolved first in relation to the 'unnecessary' ones. Among words, LAs are the prime candidates for the functionally necessary core component. The same holds in mathematical logic: a predicate presupposes a variable it applies to, while a variable can occur without a modifying predicate. See also point 6 below.

2. Children's early productive vocabularies are dominated by nouns, and infant comprehension of object names appears earlier than comprehension of relational terms (Fisher, 2002; Gleitman, 1993). Although it has been argued that early noun dominance is not universal cross-linguistically, the evidence for this is still

weaker than the evidence against it (Gentner & Boroditsky, 2001; Gopnik, 2000).

3. A virtual experiment (Steels, Kaplan, McIntyre, & Looveren, 2002) has identified a condition favoring nouns (i.e. LAs) for the first words – the condition that agents must have parallel non-verbal ways to achieve goals of interactions (e.g. pointing). Actions/changes are difficult to point to – other than, perhaps, by imitating or carrying them out. Accordingly, as compared to the first LAs, the first LPs would have been more elaborate in gestural modality. This in itself does not rule out the possibility that LPs came first, as it has, for instance, been proposed that language began as a "mixture of isolated grunts and gestures" (Bickerton, 2003, p. 81). However, the fact that language opted for vocal not gestural modality still favors LAs over LPs for the first words.

4. LAs appeal to geometrical and LPs appeal to kinaesthetic properties of images. As Pylyshyn has argued, the intrinsic properties of images are geometrical rather than dynamic, both because the spatial intuitions are among the most entrenched, and because there is evidence that geometrical and optical-geometrical constraints are built into the early-vision system. While we can easily imagine the laws of physics being violated, it seems nearly impossible to imagine the axioms of geometry or geometrical optics being violated (Pylyshyn, 2002). Prototypically, nouns are associated more with geometrical and verbs with kinaesthetic properties. However, kinaesthetic properties presuppose geometrical properties. For example, it is impossible to imagine movement without or outside space-time. This asymmetric dependency – the kinaesthetic properties of images depending on the geometric ones but not vice versa – together with the tendency of nouns to evoke geometric properties and the tendency of verbs to evoke kinaesthetic as well as geometric properties, suggests that nouns are cognitively more fundamental than verbs and verbs are cognitively more complex than nouns. This, in turn, suggests that nouns (LAs) may evolutionarily predate verbs (LPs).

5. Selective impairment of verbs is more frequent than selective impairment of nouns (Arevalo et al., 2007). There are two mutually nonexclusive explanations for this: 1. Extensive damage to the left hemisphere language areas induces the emergence of right hemisphere lexical abilities that are limited to high frequency concrete nouns (Crepaldi et al., 2006). 2. Selective impairment of verbs is a function of argument structure complexity that is regularly associated with verbs. It has been shown that the impairment is greater with 3-place than 2-

place verbs, and 2-place than 1-place verbs (Kim & Thompson, 2000). Moreover, production of argumental nouns like the Italian *passegiata* 'a walk', *risata* 'laughter', *pugnalata* 'a stab', etc. is impared at an equal level with production of argumental verbs (Collina, Marangolo, & Tabossi, 2001). I point out that all these findings are consistent with two hypotheses. (1) The N/V double dissociation in aphasia is an effect of the conceptual P/A double dissociation in the brain (the circumstance that argumental nouns are impared at an equal level with argumental verbs refers to the conceptual P/A rather than the LP/A double dissociation). (2) The N/V double dissociation is an effect of argument structure complexity. It is difficult to disentangle (1) from (2), as they have many correlated features. I conclude that the fact that the processing of LPs is more specialized and/or resource demanding than the processing of LAs suggests that the latter may be evolutionarily more fundamental.

6. In all natural languages, LP is the cornerstone of syntax. Cf. Ross (1972, p. 325): "nouns are more inert, syntactically, than adjectives and adjectives than verbs". NL syntax is based on the principle that LPs take arguments that are differentiated by analytic (adpositions, word order) and/or synthetic (morphological) case markers. Thus, there seems to be an equivalence relation between NL syntax and LP (i.e., if a system has LPs, it has NL syntax; and if it has NL syntax, it has LPs). In addition, the utility of LAs without syntax is obvious but the utility of LPs without syntax is dubious (although imperatives can be syntactically independent, as they are optimized for producing and parsing speed). The hypothesis that LP is equivalent to syntax, together with the axiom that there was no syntax in the beginning (Jackendoff & Pinker, 2005), favors LA over LP for the first words. Bickerton remarks that symbol and syntactic structure can be dissociated – the latter without the former is useless, whereas the former is useful per se. He further argues that this logico-pragmatical dissociation has a historical counterpart: "a variety of factors /---/ suggest that, in the evolution of our species, symbolism may have preceded syntax by as much as two million years" (Bickerton, 2003, p. 81). It is a possibility, then, that the historical dissociation between symbol and syntax is distantly reflected in NL structure in the form of the LP/A distinction.

7. In analyzing the syntactic functions of major parts of speech, it has been frequently suggested that the function of nouns (including pronouns and proper names) is the most basic one. For a simplified language model, it has been found that noun is the only constituent class that all sentences have in common

at the highest level of constituent-structure (Lyons, 2004). Referring to Jespersen, Lésniewski and Ajdukiewicz, Lyons conveys that nouns are "categories of the first degree" and that "all other parts of speech are derived, complex categories. Categories of the second degree combine with categories of the first degree (according to the principles of well-formedness /---/) to form sentences /---/" (Lyons, 2004, pp. 219-220). In analyzing semantic classes (situation, event, place, time etc.) Anward writes that "while the semantic class of person/thing seems lexicalizable by nouns, other semantic classes can be lexicalized in several ways" (Anward, 2001, p. 730).

8. Nichols has formulated two important principles of historical morphology: 1. Headward migration: "If any adposition or piece of affixal morphology moves, it will go from dependent to the head of the constituent, not vice versa" (Nichols, 1986, p. 86). 2. Reduction: the original dependents get cliticized and eventually become morphological markers of their head. Principle 1 suggests that the initial marking is more likely to appear on dependent. Together, the principles suggest a morphological migration pattern from dependent to head (e.g., from N to V). The fact that, cross-linguistically, verbal morphology appears to be richer than nominal morphology, is consistent with this. Although the evidence for it circumstantial, it is not unreasonable to suspect that the morphology appeared on older elements first. As morphology obscures lexical items' form and meaning, the latter have to be sufficiently conventionalized before any morphology can attach to them. It is plausible that older elements are more conventionalized than younger ones. Second, statistically, the longer an element has been around, the more chances it has had to attract morphology. Thus, the default assumption would be that the element that became a dependent is older than the element that became its head. An analysis of constituent types and their head-dependent relations confirms this. Cf. the following table (based on Helmbrecht, 2001, p. 1425):

Table 1. Constituent types and head-dependent relations

Constituent	Head	Dependent
1. NP	N	ADJ
2.	ADP	N
3. Clause	V	N
4.	AUX	V

From Heine and Kuteva (2002, 2007) it follows that, in three pairs (2, 3, 4), the dependent element is older than the head element. In one pair (1), the situation is the other way around. Thus, the evidence for the dependent element being older than the head element is stronger than the evidence for the contrary. Combined with the considerations put forth by Heine and Kuteva (2002, 2007), this adds up to a modest evidence that, in pair 3, N is older than V.

9. There are more nouns than verbs, and more productive noun than verb derivation in the world's languages (Gentner, 1981; Gentner & Boroditsky, 2001). This also suggests that nouns may predate verbs. In a system with fixed asymmetric dependencies between categories, one would expect the members of the evolutionarily older category to be more fundamental and (at least statistically) more numerous and varied.

10. The grammatical marking associated primarily with nouns – DET and POSS – has a more substantial role in the lexicon than the marking associated primarily with verbs (TAM and voice). In the world's languages, there is at least one example of TAM on DET (in Chamicuro – Nordlinger & Sadler, 2004). I know of no examples of DET or POSS on TAM or voice. This asymmetry – DET and POSS being more independent than TAM and voice – begs an explanation. A plausible explanation is that DET and POSS antedate TAM and voice. The circumstance that lexical items' form and meaning have to be sufficiently conventionalized before they can be modified by markers (cf. point 8) lends some additional support to the hypothesis that LAs predate LPs.

3. Conclusion

In reconstructing early language, Heine and Kuteva (2007) propose that at stage 1 there was only one lexical category, namely "nouns" (time-stable, referential units expressing primarily thing-like concepts), and substantiate their claim with three arguments. The present paper presents ten new arguments, gathered from a variety of domains, that support this claim. By itself, none of the thirteen arguments is sufficient to establish the primacy of LA over LP, but taken together, the evidence is overwhelming.

References

Anward, J. (2001). Parts of speech. In M. Haspelmath, E. König, W. Oesterreicher & W. Raible (Eds.), *Language typology and language universals. An international handbook* (Vol. 1, pp. 726-735). Berlin; New York: Walter De Gruyter.

Arevalo, A., Perani, D., Cappa, S. F., Butler, A., Bates, E., & Dronkers, N. (2007). Action and object processing in aphasia: From nouns and verbs to the effect of manipulability. *Brain and Language, 100*(1), 79-94.

Bickerton, D. (1990). *Language and species*. Chicago: University of Chicago Press.

Bickerton, D. (2003). Symbol and structure: A comprehensive framework for language evolution. In M. H. Christiansen & S. Kirby (Eds.), *Language evolution: The states of the art* (pp. 77-93). Oxford: Oxford University Press.

Borges, J. L. (1964). *Labyrinths: Selected stories and other writings*. New York: New Directions Pub. Co.

Budd, G. E. (2006). On the origin and evolution of major morphological characters. *Biological Reviews of the Cambridge Philosophical Society, 81*(4), 609-628.

Collina, S., Marangolo, P., & Tabossi, P. (2001). The role of argument structure in the production of nouns and verbs. *Neuropsychologia, 39*(11), 1125-1137.

Crepaldi, D., Aggujaro, S., Arduino, L. S., Zonca, G., Ghirardi, G., Inzaghi, M. G., Colombo, M., Chierchia, G., & Luzzatti, C. (2006). Noun-verb dissociation in aphasia: The role of imageability and functional locus of the lesion. *Neuropsychologia, 44*(1), 73-89.

Fisher, C. (2002). The role of abstract syntactic knowledge in language acquisition: A reply to Tomasello (2000). *Cognition, 82*(3), 259-278.

Gentner, D. (1981). Some interesting differences between nouns and verbs. *Cognition and Brain Theory, 4*, 161-178.

Gentner, D., & Boroditsky, L. (2001). Individuation, relativity, and early word learning. In M. Bowerman & S. Levinson (Eds.), *Language acquisition and conceptual development* (pp. 215-256). New York: Cambridge University Press.

Gleitman, L. R. (1993). A human universal: The capacity to learn a language *Modern Philology, 90*(Supplement), S13-S33.

Gopnik, A. (2000). *Theories, language and culture: Whorf without wincing*. New York: Cambridge University Press.

Heine, B., & Kuteva, T. (2002). On the evolution of grammatical forms. In A. Wray (Ed.), *The transition to language* (pp. 376-397). Oxford: Oxford University Press.

Heine, B., & Kuteva, T. (2007). *The genesis of grammar: A reconstruction*. New York: Oxford University Press.

Helmbrecht, J. (2001). Head-marking vs. Dependent-marking languages. In M. Haspelmath, E. König, W. Oesterreicher & W. Raible (Eds.), *Language typology and language universals. An international handbook* (Vol. 2, pp. 1424-1432). Berlin; New York: Walter De Gruyter.

Hurford, J. R. (2003a). The language mosaic and its evolution. In M. H. Christiansen & S. Kirby (Eds.), *Language evolution: The states of the art* (pp. 38-57). Oxford: Oxford University Press.

Hurford, J. R. (2003b). The neural basis of predicate-argument structure. *Behavioral and Brain Sciences, 26*(3), 261-283; Discussion 283-316.

Hurford, J. R. (2003c). Ventral/dorsal, predicate/argument: The transformation from perception to meaning. *Behavioral and Brain Sciences, 26*(3), 301-311.

Jackendoff, R. (1999). Possible stages in the evolution of the language capacity. *Trends in Cognitive Sciences, 3*(7), 272-279.

Jackendoff, R., & Pinker, S. (2005). The nature of the language faculty and its implications for evolution of language (reply to Fitch, Hauser, and Chomsky). *Cognition, 97*(2), 211-225.

Kim, M., & Thompson, C. K. (2000). Patterns of comprehension and production of nouns and verbs in agrammatism: Implications for lexical organization. *Brain and Language, 74*(1), 1-25.

Luuk, E. (2009a). The noun/verb and predicate/argument structures. *Lingua, 119*(11), 1707-1727.

Luuk, E. (2009b). *The noun/verb and predicate/argument structures.* Dissertationes Linguisticae Universitatis Tartuensis (Vol. 12). Tartu: Tartu University Press.

Lyons, J. (2004). A notional approach to the parts of speech. In B. Aarts (Ed.), *Fuzzy grammar: A reader* (pp. 213-223). Oxford; New York: Oxford University Press.

Nichols, J. (1986). Head-marking and dependent-marking grammar. *Language, 62*(1), 56-119.

Nordlinger, R., & Sadler, L. (2004). Tense beyond the verb: Encoding clausal tense/aspect/mood on nominal dependents. *Natural Language & Linguistic Theory, 22*, 597-641.

Pylyshyn, Z. W. (2002). Mental imagery: In search of a theory. *Behavioral and Brain Sciences, 25*(2), 157-182; Discussion 182-237.

Ross, J. R. (1972). *The category squish: Endstation hauptwort.* Paper presented at the Eighth Regional Meeting, Chicago Linguistic Society, Chicago.

Steels, L., Kaplan, F., McIntyre, A., & Looveren, J. V. (2002). Crucial factors in the origins of word-meaning. In A. Wray (Ed.), *The transition to language.* Oxford: Oxford University Press.

TOWARDS A SIMULATION MODEL OF DIALOGICAL ALIGNMENT

ALEXANDER MEHLER, PETRA WEIß, PETER MENKE, ANDY LÜCKING

Text Technology, Bielefeld University, Universitätsstraße 25,
Bielefeld, D-33615, Germany
`Alexander.Mehler@uni-bielefeld.de`

This paper presents a model of lexical alignment in communication. The aim is to provide a reference model for simulating dialogs in naming game-related simulations of language evolution. We introduce a network model of alignment to shed light on the law-like dynamics of dialogs in contrast to their random counterpart. That way, the paper provides evidence on alignment to be used as reference data in building simulation models of dyadic conversations.

1. Introduction

Simulation models of language evolution mainly start from a simplified notion of dialog. In simulation rounds of such models, a sender is typically selected at random to generate a signal for the listener *without considering any turn taking among the agents*. We call this scenario a *single-turn scenario* and contrast it with *multi-turn scenarios* where turn taking takes place in simulation rounds. By turn taking we refer to the fact that interlocutors continue to change their roles as sender and listener (Sacks, Schegloff, & Jefferson, 1974). Simulation models mostly disregard this dynamics that non-randomly structures communication.

At first sight, turn taking has been modeled in several simulations. Padilha and Carletta (2002), e.g., simulate turn taking with respect to multimodality. However, these simulations focus on discourse-managing strategies. Current research on dialog systems also makes use of simulations to improve strategies of the artificial systems (Scheffler & Young, 2002). Further, there are simulations where interaction among agents is only possible in subsequent rounds, which renders modeling of round-internal turn taking impossible. Steels and Loetzsch (2009), e.g., describe an experiment with robots with the purpose of perspective alignment where agents align to the speaker's usage strategy for ambiguous spatial expressions.

So far, little is known about the impact of *dialogical* communication on the outcome of language evolution. To study this impact, a simulation model is needed that *embeds* a simulation model of multi-turn communication. A central aspect of the dynamics of dialogs is *alignment* (Pickering & Garrod, 2004), which is a largely automatic, resource-saving process of structural coupling among interlocutors on several linguistic, e.g., lexical (Clark & Wilkes-Gibbs, 1986), syntactic

(Branigan, Pickering, & Cleland, 2000) and semantic (Garrod & Anderson, 1987; Garrod et al., 2007) levels that simplifies communication. The basic mechanism underlying alignment is *priming*: linguistic representations are primed by utterances so that (features of) expressions get copied within an agent dyad. Priming operates *intra-* and *inter*personally, that is, on two channels: a horizontal, "monological" one within a speaker and a vertical, dialogical one between speakers. The latter is based on a reciprocal dyadic exchange, which involves role switching, that is, turn taking.

This paper presents a model of *lexical* alignment in the framework of naming games (Jäger, 2006). It approaches reference data for simulation models of a certain class of real dialogs to be embedded into simulation models of language evolution (Kirby & Hurford, 2002). We introduce a network model according to a multi-turn scenario to separate the law-like dynamics of dialog from its random counterpart: Section 2 describes the experiment that we performed to get empirical data; Section 3 and 4 use this data to build a model of dialog lexica that allows for automatically classifying dialogs according to their (non-)alignment.

2. The Naming Game in an Experimental Perspective

Language use in free dialogs is hardly controllable so that experimental paradigms have been developed to elicit semi-spontaneous dialog situations where some degree of control over the topic of conversation is possible: the *referential communication task*, the *maze game* and the *map task* (Krauss & Weinheimer, 1966; Garrod & Anderson, 1987; Anderson et al., 1991). Based thereon, we developed the *Jigsaw Map Game* (JMG; Weiß et al., 2008) that allows for naturalizing experimental dialogs by encouraging face-to-face interaction with participants who mutually perceive and communicate in a multimodal way. In the JMG, parameters like dialog organization are controlled by regulating the game's flow and balancing partner roles. The JMG goes as follows: two participants cooperatively position objects (e.g., cuboids or cones) on a common interaction table according to a predefined arrangement. The arrangement is designed in a way that some objects stand out because of size. They define so called critical objects with two possible names (e.g., *ball* or *bowl*). The cooperative character of the game emerges by the fact that each partner only gets partial information about the final arrangement. This is realized by instruction cards that contain the constellation of three objects at a time: two already positioned and one new object to be placed by the partner in the next step. Guided by these cards, partners communicate in turns which object the other should pick next from a personal object box (*object identification*) and where it has to be placed on the table (*object placement*) until the whole arrangement is completed. This way, it is possible to analyze the names the interlocutors use to identify the objects. In the following sections, we take all our empirical data from JMG-based experiments. More specifically, we recorded and annotated 19 dialogs manifesting this experimentally controlled naming game.

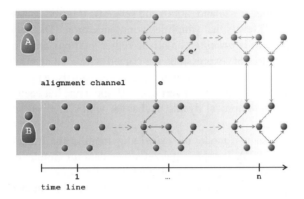

Figure 1.   Schematic representation of a bipartite time-aligned network series.

3. A Network Model of Alignment in Communication

Interpersonal alignment is brought forward by the turn taking of interlocutors. Simulation models mainly disregard this process, although it affects the build-up of dialog lexica and the transfer of linguistic representations. We introduce a graph model of such lexica that does not simply count items shared by interacting agents but captures (the strength of) lexical associations and the time course of alignment. This is done in terms of *bipartite Time-Aligned Network (TAN) series* as illustrated in Fig. 1. It presents the gradual build-up of a dialog lexicon by two interlocutors A and B: at the beginning (time point 1), both agents start with a set of unlinked lexical items. For an agent, this set presents the subset of items of his overall lexicon that are actually activated during his conversation. Thus, vertices in Fig. 1 denote lexical items. Henceforth, we represent dialog lexica as labeled graphs $L_t = (V, E_t, \mu_t, \mathcal{L})$ weighted by μ_t and indexed by points in time $t = 1..n$ at which they are built. We assume that vertices are labeled by the surjective function $\mathcal{L} : V \to L_V$ for the set of labels L_V (i.e. lemmata). Each time an interlocutor produces a linguistic output, the series proceeds to the next time point. We assume that L_t is divided into two subgraphs $L_{t_A} = (V_A, E_{t_A}, \mu_{t_A}, \mathcal{L}_A)$ and $L_{t_B} = (V_B, E_{t_B}, \mu_{t_B}, \mathcal{L}_B)$ according to the distribution of L_t over A and B at time t. In Fig. 1 this corresponds to a column of the TAN series. Note that $\mathcal{L}_X : V_X \to L_{V_X}, X \in \{A, B\}$, is the bijective restriction of $\mathcal{L}$ to V_X, while μ_{t_X} is the restriction of μ_t to E_{t_X}.

By continuing their communication, agents gradually span edges in the lexicon. This is done by *inter-* or *intra*personal links. To see that remember that in the JMG, a dialog is divided into rounds each of which corresponds to a focal object or topic (e.g., *ball* or *cone*). Thus, for each time point t of a JMG we can identify the focal topic $x = focus(t)$ at t. Now we induce links in the lexicon as follows:

- If at time t agent $X, X \in \{A, B\}$, uses the item l to express $focus(t)$ that

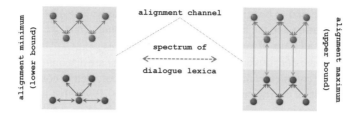

Figure 2. A graph-theoretical representation of turning points of lexical alignment.

has been expressed by $Y \neq X$ in the same round by l, we span an *interpersonal* link between $v_A \in V_A$ and $w_B \in V_B$ where $\mathcal{L}_A(v_A) = \mathcal{L}_B(w_B) = l$, e.g., edge e in Fig. 1. Links of this sort cross the *alignment channel* between A and B. If the link already exists, its weight $\mu_t(e)$ is increased by 1.

- If at time t agent $X \in \{A, B\}$ uses item l to express $focus(t)$, we generate an *intrapersonal* link between $v_X \in V_X$, $\mathcal{L}_X(v_X) = l$, and all other vertices labeled by items that X has used in the same round of the game, i.e., items that are equally used as l (see, e.g., edge e' in Fig. 1). Once more, if the links already exist, their weights (initially set to 1) are augmented by 1.

·*Note that without turn taking there would be no interpersonal links in this model.* The graphs $L_1, \ldots, L_n$ define a time series where each time point corresponds to a network. Since each of them is decomposable into subgraphs L_{t_A} and L_{t_B}, we speak of a bipartition. This model easily allows for representing turning points of alignment as shown in Fig. 2: on the left side, a dialog lexicon occurs without any link across the alignment channel. This happens, e.g., if the interlocutors never use the same item to speak about the same topic. That is, *the interlocutors use different words or the same words differently so that their dialog lexicon is nonaligned.* The right part of Fig. 2 shows the opposite case. Such a situation occurs if *both interlocutors use the same words the same way so that their dialog lexicon is completely aligned.* Obviously, lexica emerging from real dialogs enter into the middle of these extremal points. We assume that this happens law-like so that we can apply complex network theory (Barrat, Barthélemy, & Vespignani, 2008) to analyze the networking of dialog lexica as described in the next section.

3.1. *Quantifying Dialog Lexica*

Bipartite TAN series allow for analyzing intra- and interpersonal links of lexical items, that is, lexicon structure. This is done by means of the following indices:

- The average geodesic distance $\hat{L}(G) = 1/\binom{|V|}{2} \sum_{\{v,w\} \in [V]^2} \delta(v, w)$ where $[V]^2$ is the set of all subsets of 2 elements of V and $\delta(v, w)$ is the geodesic distance of v and w in G. Since at the beginning of lexicon formation vertices tend to be unlinked, this index gives unrealistically small values if $\hat{L}$ is restricted to the largest connected component. Thus, we normalize it to capture all pairs of vertices: $L(G) = 1 - ((\sum_{\{v,w\} \in [V]^2} \delta(v,w))/(n^2(n - 1))$, where $\delta(v,w) = n - 1$, $n = |V|$, if v and w are disconnected. L ranges from 0 (completely disconnected graph) to 1 (completely connected graph).

- The cluster coefficient C_{ws} (Watts & Strogatz, 1998) that together with L describes small worlds. Additionally, we compute its weighted extension C_w (Barrat et al., 2008) and its counterpart C_{br} (Bollobás & Riordan, 2003).

- The weighted cluster coefficients $\langle C_w(k) \rangle$ and $\langle C_w^{ns}(k) \rangle$ (Serrano, Boguñá, & Pastor-Satorras, 2006), which, as C_w, evaluate edge weights. Basically, we interpret the weights of links as indicators of the strength of association among the interlinked items: the higher the weight, the stronger their usage-based relation, the higher the association of the one if the other is primed.

- A measure of cohesion $coh(G) = \frac{\sum_{v \in V} d_G(v)}{|V|^2 - |V|}$ that scores the cohesion of G as the ratio of the number of its links in relation to the maximal number of possible links; $d_G(v)$ is the degree of v. We also compute the compactness index $cp(G)$ and $cp_{lcc}(G)$ of hypertext theory (Mehler, 2008).

- An index of modularity that for a given network measures the independence of its candidate modules. As we consider networks with two modules, we use the following variant of the index of Newman and Girvan (2004): $Q(G) = \sum_{i=1}^{2} (e_{ii} - a_i^2)$ where e_{ii} is the number of links within the ith part of the network and a_i^2 is the number of links across the alignment channel.

We hypothesize that aligned dialogs are distinguished from nonaligned ones by topological indices of the TAN series that represent them as tested below.

Our next step is to distinguish our model of the gradual build-up of dialog lexica from a random counterpart. This is done by algorithm that for a given TAN series computes a randomized series of equal order and size. It randomly rewires the last link of the series uniformly at random and then randomly deletes edges till the first link is reached. Then we compute a set of topological indices for each network state of each randomized series and, finally, average those indices over this set. In this way, we get for each topological index of Section 3.1 an expected value under the condition that the networking of the lexicon is at random.

4. Experimentation

In this section, we evaluate topological indices of dialog lexica regarding their relevance for alignment measuring. We start with two dialogs for which we know by human expert annotation that they manifest alignment and nonalignment, respectively. In Fig. 3 we present the value patterns of C_{ws} and $\langle C_w(k) \rangle$ based on three dialog lexicon graphs: the graph of the lexically nonaligned dialog $(-)$, the graph of its aligned counterpart $(+)$ and of its randomized counterpart averaged over 50 repetitions (rnd). As we focus on naming games, we account for nomi-

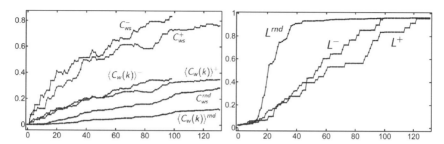

Figure 3. X-axis: time line. Y-axis: cluster values (left) and average geodesic distances (right) of a dialog manifesting nonalignment ($-$), alignment ($+$) and the random model (rnd).

nal units so that each time point in Fig. 3 corresponds to the utterance of a noun (according to the sequence of turns of the interlocutors) and the related update of the dialog lexicon graph. Fig. 3 is in line with our expectations: the randomized dialog lexica have relatively small cluster values. We also observe that the non-aligned dialog is distinguished from its aligned counterpart in terms of weighted and unweighted clustering. These relations are retained irrespective of the cluster coefficient in use. They are also retained if we evaluate the value pattern of Q: in case of nonalignment, modularity is more salient than in case of alignment, while the randomized dialog graphs show an unnaturally small modularity. Regarding geodesic distances L, the picture is somehow different (see Fig. 3): in line with network theory, a small L rapidly emerges in randomized dialog lexica. It also emerges more quickly in the nonaligned dialog compared to its aligned counterpart. In all three cases a small L of about two links characteristically emerges at the end of the dialog – that is, *dialog lexica are tiny small worlds*.

Supposed that topological indices of dialog lexica are really indicative of lexical alignment, they should allow for automatically classifying dialogs with a high F-score (i.e., harmonic mean of precision and recall). This is what we test now. We explore a corpus of 19 manually annotated JMG dialogs. 15 of them have been rated to manifest alignment, 4 have been judged to manifest nonalignment. The classifier should automatically reconstruct this human-based gold standard where a high F-score (up to 1) indicates a good classification, while a small F-score (down to 0) indicates a failure. For each of the lexicon graphs of the 19 dialogs (with an average duration of 11 minutes) we compute the set of indices described in Sec. 3.1. Thus, each dialog is represented by a vector of 10 indices (see Table 1). This allows for applying cluster analysis and to compute F-scores. The results are reported in Table 1. It shows that both baseline scenarios are outperformed: scenario I that assumes an equi-partition among the target classes and scenario II that knows their real sizes. We also see that 5 indices are enough to classify up to 95% of the dialogs correctly – *this shows that classifying dialogs by means of network analysis is feasible*. In Table 1, we also report feature combinations

Table 1. F-scores of dialog classification (above) and sensitivity analysis of the indices (below).

procedure	F-score	remark
QNA[Mahalanobis, hierarchical, complete linkage]	.945	5 out of 10 features
QNA[Mahalanobis, hierarchical, average linkage]	.746	all features
random baseline II	.703	known partition
random baseline I	.634	equi-partition

C_{br}	C_{ws}	L	cp	cp_{lcc}	coh	$\langle C_w(k)\rangle$	$\langle C_w^{ns}(k)\rangle$	C_w	Q	#
×	×	×			×				×	5
×	×	×	×	×	×					6
×			×			×	×	×	×	6
×	×	×			×	×	×	×	×	8
4	3	3	2	1	3	2	2	2	3	#

that provide the same F-score. They have been computed by means of a genetic algorithm for selecting feature subsets. Table 1 shows the features that are most reliably used throughout the different runs. Obviously, the cluster coefficient C_{br} performs best among all candidates considered here. We also see that weighted cluster coefficients are less indicative of alignment. Further, we get the information that the average geodesic distance L, the index of modularity Q, the cluster coefficient C_{ws} and the cohesion measure coh are reliable indicators of alignment vs. nonalignment. Thus, we conclude that the value patterns of these indices can serve as reference frames for building simulation models of the time course of dialogical alignment. By considering their value patterns a simulation model is informed about what naturally happens in dialogs of the sort of the naming game considered here.

5. Conclusion

We presented a network model of lexical alignment in a multi-turn scenario. It allows for distinguishing aligned from nonaligned dialogs. That way, our model provides reference data for simulation models of dialogical communication.

Acknowledgement

Financial support of the German Federal Ministry of Education through the project *Linguistic Networks*, of the German Research Foundation through the EC *Cognitive Interaction Technology* and the SFB *Alignment in Communication* is gratefully acknowledged.

References

Anderson, A.H., Bader, M., Gurman Bard, E., Boyle, E., Doherty, G., & Garrod, S. et al. (1991). The HCRC Map Task Corpus. *Language and Speech, 34,* 351-366.

Barrat, A., Barthélemy, M., & Vespignani, A. (2008). *Dynamical processes on complex networks.* Cambridge: Cambridge University Press.

Bollobás, B., & Riordan, O. M. (2003). Mathematical results on scale-free random graphs. In *Handbook of graphs and networks*. Weinheim: Wiley-VCH.

Branigan, H. P., Pickering, M. J., & Cleland, A. A. (2000). Syntactic coordination in dialogue. *Cognition, 25,* B13–B25.

Clark, H. H., & Wilkes-Gibbs, D. (1986). Referring as a collaborative process. *Cognition, 22,* 1–39.

Garrod, S., & Anderson, A. (1987). Saying what you mean in dialogue: a study in conceptual and semantic co-ordination. *Cognition, 27*(2), 181-218.

Garrod, S., Fay, N., Lee, J., Oberlander, J., & MacLeod, T. (2007). Foundations of representations: Where might graphical symbol systems come from? *Cognitive Science, 31,* 961–987.

Jäger, G. (2006). Convex meanings and evolutionary stability. In A. Cangelosi, A. D. M. Smith, & K. Smith (Eds.), *Proc. of EVOLANG6* (p. 139-144).

Kirby, S., & Hurford, J. R. (2002). The emergence of linguistic structure: An overview of the iterated learning model. In A. Cangelosi & D. Parisi (Eds.), *Simulating the evolution of language* (p. 121-148). London: Springer.

Krauss, R. M., & Weinheimer, S. (1966). Concurrent feedback, confirmation, and the encoding of referents in verbal communication. *Journal of Personality and Social Psychology, 4,* 343-346.

Mehler, A. (2008). Structural similarities of complex networks. *AAI, 22*(7&8), 619–683.

Newman, M. E. J., & Girvan, M. (2004). Finding and evaluating community structure in networks. *Physical Review E, 69*(2), 026113.

Padilha, E., & Carletta, J. (2002). A simulation of small group discussion. In *Proc. of EDILOG* (pp. 117–124).

Pickering, M. J., & Garrod, S. (2004). Toward a mechanistic psychology of dialogue. *Behavioral and Brain Sciences, 27,* 169-226.

Sacks, H., Schegloff, E. A., & Jefferson, G. (1974). A simplest systematics for the organization of turn taking for conversation. *Language, 50,* 696-735.

Scheffler, K., & Young, S. (2002). Automatic learning of dialogue strategy using dialogue simulation and reinforcement learning. In *Proc. of the 2nd int. conf. on Human Language Technology Research* (pp. 12–19).

Serrano, M. Á., Boguñá, M., & Pastor-Satorras, R. (2006). Correlations in weighted networks. *Physical Review E, 74,* 055101.

Steels, L., & Loetzsch, M. (2009). Perspective alignment in spatial language. In K. R. Coventry, T. Tenbrink, & J. Bateman (Eds.), *Spatial language in dialogue*. Oxford.

Watts, D. J., & Strogatz, S. H. (1998). Collective dynamics of 'small-world' networks. *Nature, 393,* 440-442.

Weiß, P., Pfeiffer, T., Schaffranietz, G., & Rickheit, G. (2008). Coordination in dialog: Alignment of object naming in the Jigsaw Map Game. In *Proc. of cognitive science 2007.*

EVOLUTION OF GRAMMATICAL FORMS

MIEKO OGURA

Linguistics Laboratory, Tsurumi University
Yokohama, 230-8501, Japan

WILLIAM S-Y. WANG

Department of Electronic Engineering, The Chinese University of Hong Kong
Shatin, Hong Kong, China

We examine the evolution of major grammatical forms and constructions as linguistic manifestations of human cognitive ability, based on historical data from English. We show that the complex linguistic system has arisen as more and more grammaticalized forms have accumulated. Word order and case go back to the earliest language. Tense, aspect, modality, gender, questions, negations, parataxis can be traced back to Proto-Indo-European, and they may go back further. Most crucial is the rise of embedding recursion and its product, the VO word order in Old English. This brought about the transition from the syntactic organization of the clause interwoven with discourse organization to the more strictly syntactic organization of the clause. With this transition, the periphrastic constructions of progressive, perfect and pluperfect, modal auxiliaries, periphrastic *do* and definite article arose due to speakers' desire to be more specific than was possible with the older forms. We also show the role of high-frequency words in the evolution of the grammatical forms.

1. Introduction

At the heart of grammaticalization theory is the idea that syntactic organization, and the overt markers associated with it, emerged from non-syntactic, principally lexical and discourse, organization. Modern complex linguistic systems could have arisen from simpler origins, as languages accumulated more and more grammaticalized forms (Hurford 2003). In this paper we would like to investigate the evolution of grammatical forms based on historical data from English as one example, because no comprehensive research has been done in any language from this perspective. We will examine how major grammatical forms and constructions arose and developed, and explain why they occurred at all. We will also show the role of word frequency in the actuation and implementation of grammatical forms.

We assume that the human language faculty, rather than being innately equipped with unique mental capacities for acquiring language, is a mosaic of many factors which have come together in a unique combination in humans. Many of these factors can be observed, often in a less powerful form, in other animals (Wang 1983, Hurford 2003). Thus we suppose that grammaticalization is the linguistic manifestation of human cognitive abilities.

2. Verbal Categories

2.1. *Tense and Aspect*

One cognitive domain that may have influenced, and perhaps even shaped, the evolution of language is mental time travel - the ability to mentally relive events in the past (episodic memory) or imagine events in the future. Language structure has evolved to express different points in time, including past, present and future, and to make other temporal distinctions, such as action completed versus action ongoing (Hurford 2007, Corballis 2008).

In Old English (OE) and Middle English (ME) there were two morphological tense markers: non-past and past. They go back to Proto-Indo-European (PIE) present and aorist. Non-past tense primarily refers to the present. It also indicates that an action is going on. Here it covers the function of the progressive in Present-Day English (PDE). It can also express the future. The past tense is primarily used to refer to past time. It is also used where we might expect the perfect, or past of past (pluperfect) in PDE.

To indicate that an action is ongoing, the BE-verbs *beon, wesan* and sometimes *weorþan* began to be used with V-*ende* construction in OE. To indicate the perfect and pluperfect, *habban* 'have' or BE-verbs began to be used with V-past participle in OE. *Willan* 'will' and *sculan* 'shall' were grammaticalized as auxiliaries to denote future time. These progressive, perfect, pluperfect and future constructions arose out of speakers' desire to be more specific than was possible with the older forms in the transitional period from the syntactic organization of the clause interwoven with discourse organization to the more strictly syntactic organization of the clause (see section 6).

2.2. *Modality*

The prelinguistic ancestors of humans had a whole range of different mental states such as believing, knowing, imagining and desiring (Hurford 2007). OE distinguished three modes - indicative, subjunctive and imperative morphologically. IE had four modes: indicative, subjunctive, optative and imperative. In general, the indicative is used to present a proposition as true. The subjunctive expresses expectation, hope, admonition, probability, the optative wish, unreal condition, statement contrary to fact, and the imperative command. However, there are many counter-examples. The indicative may be used where some doubt is expressed, and the subjunctive may be used where the proposition clearly expresses a fact.

Modal auxiliaries, *cunnan* 'can', *durran* 'dare', *magan* 'may', *motan* 'must', *sculan* 'shall', *willan* 'will', etc. developed from lexical verbs in OE. This may be due to speakers' desire to be more specific than was possible with the subjunctive form when the strictly syntactic organization of the clause appeared (see section 6). The collapse of the subjunctive mood in the course of late OE and ME due to simplification of the inflectional endings enhanced the grammaticalization of the modal verbs.

3. Nominal Categories

3.1. *Case*

We assume that case emerged originally to distinguish actor from patient in the SOV word order of the earliest languages (see section 4). The world's case-marking systems have evolved by the interplay between speaker's ease of learning and listener's ease of comprehension (Tallerman 2008). There were eight cases in PIE: nominative, accusative, genitive, ablative, dative, locative, instrumental, vocative, four cases in OE: nominative, accusative, genitive, dative, and only two cases in ME: common vs. genitive.

Adverbial constructions that could be coded by case-endings alone in OE already had alternants with prepositions (*sweord-um* and *mid sweord-um* 'with swords'), and this increased in ME. By the late fourteenth century, only possession was coded by morphological case (genitive); and even this had an alternant with a preposition (*England's Queen* vs. *the Queen of England*). There was no preposition in PIE, and prepositions have derived from adverbs.

3.2. *Gender*

Gender may be a covert noun category; overtly it is realized only in concord and anaphora, i.e. the main signal of gender in OE is the concordial relation between a noun and its modifiers and anaphors. This goes back to PIE. In a grammatical gender system, every noun belonged to masculine, feminine, neuter, which had no necessary semantic reference; on the grammatical level gender was a classifying device that predicted concord. In ME there was a shift towards a system in which sex (or the lack of it) was the primary or sole determinant. It was induced by the erosion of noun endings.

3.3. *Definite Article*

All languages have an inherent sense of definiteness. Some languages develop the overt expression of this, but others do not. All the West Germanic languages began to use their demonstrative around the sixth century where nowadays we would associate with the definite article. We assume that the overt expression of definiteness was motivated by speakers' desire to be clear and informative when clause combining became syntactically bonded (see section 6).

The OE deictic *se* (*seo*, *þæt*) fulfilled the function of both definite article and demonstrative adjective. In ME a clear-cut distinction developed between these two functions with the invariant form *the* taking the role of the former and the OE neuter form *þæt* > *that* beginning to function purely as a deictic.

4. Word Order

Newmeyer (2000) claims that the earliest human language had rigid SOV order. He considers that protolanguage had thematic structure, and the grammatical role – thematic role match, or the thematic role of syntactic positions is revealed more directly in SOV languages than SVO languages.

Goldin-Meadow et al. (2008) provide evidence for the proto-world SOV order. They asked speakers of four languages differing in their predominant word orders (English, Turkish, Spanish, and Chinese) to perform two nonverbal tasks: a communicative task (describing an event by using gesture without speech) and a noncommunicative task (reconstructing an event with pictures). They found that the speakers of four languages used the same order, actor-patient-act. This order may reflect a natural sequencing for representing events. Entities are cognitively more basic and less relational than actions, which might lead participants to highlight entities involved in an action before focusing on the action itself, thus situating Actor and Patient before Action. Moreover, there is a particularly close cognitive tie between objects and actions, which would link Patient to Action, resulting in an Actor-Patient-Act.

Goldin-Meadow et al. suggest that, initially, an emerging language co-opted the Actor-Patient-Action order used as a default pattern, thus displaying SOV order, which may have had the virtue of semantic clarity. But as the functions of language became more complex, additional pressures may have exerted their influence on language structure. We discuss the evolution of relative clause and the SVO order in section 6.

5. Questions and Negations

The trained animals can acquire the ability to perceive questions. They also know how to handle the notion of rejection and non-existence (Heine & Kuteva 2007). There were basic interrogative *Wh+-tero* 'which of two' and negative indicative *ne* and prohibitive in PIE. In OE and ME questions are either yes/no questions or wh-questions. Inversion of subject and finite verb is the rule in simple clauses of both types unless the wh-word is itself the subject in OE and ME.

ME also marks the beginning of the development of the auxiliary *do* in questions and negations. We assume that the periphrastic *do* was induced by the development of modal auxiliaries (for details, see Ogura 1993).

6. Complex Sentences

Complex sentences range in type from multiple nuclei that are juxtaposed under one intonation contour but have no overt morphological or syntactic indication of a grammatical relationship between them, to combinations of nucleus and margin in which this relationship is highly compressed. We can think of a cline of clause combining: parataxis > hypotaxis > subordination.

The emergence of linear adjacency of modifiers might well be the underpinning of hierarchical arrangement of words into phrase structures (Jackendoff 1999). We assume that the same mechanism operates in the clause combining. The juxtaposed paratactic clauses develop into higher-order hypotactic clauses and further subordinate clauses or, in its extreme form, embedding, by hierarchical arrangement. Recursion, or embedding recursion, is the product of a diachronic process of hierarchical arrangement of paratactic clauses.

Hauser, Chomsky & Fitch (2002) submit that a distinction should be made between the faculty of language in the broad sense (FLB) and in the narrow sense (FLN). They hypothesize that FLN only includes recursion and is the only uniquely human component of the faculty of language. But recursion appears in a wide range of human behaviors, and it is shared with other human cognitive domains and possibly other species.

The evolution of the relative clause is an evidence to support our claim. In OE there were independent sentences which assumed functions of relative clauses as shown in (1).[1] Here the shared NP is replaced with an anaphoric demonstrative pronoun, and the presence of a coordinating conjunction marks it not as a relative pronoun but as an anaphoric demonstrative pronoun.

(1) Eac þis land wæs swiþe afylled mid munecan.
    Also this land was exceedingly filled with monkes
    7[2] þa leofodan heora lif æfter scs Benedictus regule. (1086)
      they lived their lives after St Benedict's rule
'This land too was filled with monks living their lives after the rule of St Benedict.'

---

[1] The example is from A-manuscript in C. Plummer (ed.), *Two of the Saxon Chronicles Parallel*, 1892.

[2] 7 represents '&' (ampersand).

Then the anaphoric personal or demonstrative pronoun was placed at the beginning of the second clause as shown in (2).[3] This is the paratactic stage of adjunction in a relative clause.

(2) 7 <u>ealles</u> benæmde *þes he on Englalande hæfde* (1102/10-1)
     all   seized   that he in England   had
    'and seized all that he had in England.'

This paratactic adjunctive relative clause was embedded as a dependent clause immediately after its nominal head as shown in (3). Embedding took place by pulling the head noun to a position before the relative clause, because the moving the relative clause after the head noun inside the main sentence creates center-embedding. This also produced the word order change from OV to VO. The change started around the sixth century. Our discussions based on OE data can be extended to the evolution of the postnominal relative clause and the word order change from OV to VO in general (Ogura 2003).

(3) 7 sceawode <u>þet madmehus 7 þa gersuman</u> *þe his*
    inspected the jewell-house the treasures which his
    fæder ær gegaderode: (108[7]/167-8)
    father formerly gathered
'and inspected the treasury and the riches which his father had accumulated.'

The relative clause construction was originally not a grammatical entity but simply part of the way in which discourses are organized, coming to be grammaticalized as an embedded clause. Kemenade & Los (2006) discuss, based on the syntactic and discourse properties of the adverbs *þa* and *þonne* 'then', that OE discourse organization was closely interwoven with syntactic organization. The transition of Middle English is marked by the elimination of the multiple topics in OE, and results in a more strictly syntactic organization of the clause. We assume that the evolution of the relative clause and its product, the VO order, brought about the change in the organization of the clause. With this transition, the periphrastic constructions of progressive, perfect, pluperfect and modal auxiliaries, definite article and periphrastic *do* arose due to the speakers' desire to be more specific and informative than was possible with the older forms (see sections 2.1, 2.2, 3.4 and 5).

Hypotactic constructions developed from paratactic constructions include adverbial clauses ('when', 'because', 'conditional', and 'although'- clauses). PIE had coordinate conjunctions *and* and *or*, but no subordinate conjunctions.

---

[3] The examples in (2) and (3) are from C. Clark (ed.), *The Peterborough Chronicle 1070-1154*, 1957. The heads are underlined, and the relative clauses are italicized.

Subordinate conjunctions evolved for linking clauses into tighter amalgamations and had their sources in nouns, verbs, adverbs and pronouns.

7. Word Frequency and Grammaticalization

In OE we see a beginning of the development of progressive, perfect and pluperfect constructions, modal auxiliaries in the system of tense, aspect and modality. Verbs like *habban, beon, willan, sculan, cunnan, durran, magan, motan,* etc. already enjoyed the auxiliary status. We find that they are highly frequent verbs. When the words are frequently used, they become polysemous and the meanings become more general and abstract (Ogura & Wang 2008). We assume that grammaticalization proceeds when bleaching or generalization in meaning occurs through frequent use of lexical verbs in the contexts in which they are appropriately used. Furthermore, the change implemented itself from high-frequency verbs to low-frequency ones used with them.

The same process occurs in the rise of the definite article in OE. The definite article was derived from a demonstrative which occurred frequently, and the change proceeded from the high-frequency nouns to low-frequency ones used with it. But the situation is different in the development of periphrastic *do.* Periphrastic *do* was derived from high-frequency verb *do.* But the change occurred from the less frequent verbs. We assume that periphrastic *do* was not a direct manifestation of the cognitive ability, but it was induced by the development of modal auxiliaries. The old constructions in questions and negations persisted long in frequent verbs (Ogura 1993).

8. Conclusion

We have examined the evolution of major grammatical forms and constructions as linguistic manifestations of human cognitive ability, based on historical data from English. We have shown that the complex linguistic system has arisen as more and more grammaticalized forms have accumulated. Word order and case go back to the earliest language. Tense, aspect, modality, gender, questions, negations, parataxis can be traced back to PIE, and they may go back further. Most crucial is the emergence of embedding recursion and its product, the VO word order in OE. This brought about the transition from the syntactic organization of the clause interwoven with discourse organization to the more strictly syntactic organization of the clause. With this transition, the periphrastic constructions of progressive, perfect, pluperfect and modal auxiliaries, definite article and periphrastic *do* arose due to speakers' desire to express grammatical categories more specifically than was possible with the older forms. We have also shown the role of high-frequency words in the actuation and implementation of grammaticalization.

Acknowledgements

This work is supported by the grants from the Human Frontier Science Program and the Ministry of Education, Culture, Sports, Science and Technology of Japan to Mieko Ogura, and the Research Grants Council of the Hong Kong SAR to William S-Y. Wang.

References

Corballis, M. C. (2008). Time on Our Hands: How Gesture and the Understanding of the Past and Future Helped Shape Language. *Behavioral and Brain Sciences* 31:5, 517.

Goldin-Meadow, S. et al. (2008). The Natural Order of Events: How Speakers of Different Languages Represent Events Nonverbally. *PNAS* 105, 9163-9168.

Hauser, D. M.,N. Chomsky and W. T. Fitch (2002). The Faculty of Language: What Is It, Who Has It, and How Did It Evolve? *Science* 298, 1569-1579.

Heine, B. and T. Kuteva (2007). *The Genesis of Grammar: A Reconstruction.* Oxford University Press.

Hurford, J. R.(2003). The Language Mosaic and its Evolution. In M. H. Christiansen and S. Kirby (Eds.), *Language Evolution* (pp.38-57). Oxford: Oxford University Press.

Hurford, J.R. (2007). *The Origins of Meaning.* Oxford: Oxford University Press.

Jackendoff, R. (1999). Possible Stages in the Evolution of the Language Capacity. *Trends in Cognitive Science* 3/7, 272-279.

Kemenade, A. V. and B. Los (2006). Discourse Adverbs and Clausal Syntax in Old and Middle English. In A. V. Kemenade & B. Los (Eds.), *The Handbook of the History of English* (pp.224-248). Oxford: Blackwell.

Newmeyer, F. J. (2000). On the Reconstruction of 'Proto-World' Word Order. In C. Knight, M Studdert-Kennedy and J. R. Hurford (Eds.), *The Evolutionary Emergence of Language* (pp. 372-388). Cambridge: Cambridge University Press.

Ogura, M. (1993). The Development of Periphrastic *Do* in English: A Case of Lexical Diffusion in Syntax. *Diachronica* 12, 31-53.

Ogura, M. (2003). Evolution of Word Order. *Folia Linguistica Historica* XXV, 21-39.

Ogura, M. and W. S-Y. Wang (2008). Evolution of the Global Organization of the Lexicon. In A. D. M. Smith, K. Smith and R. Ferrer i Cancho (Eds.), *Evolution of Language* (pp.243-250). Singapore: World Scientific.

Tallerman, M. (2008). Case-marking Systems Evolve to Be Easy to Learn and Process. *Behavioral and Brain Sciences* 31:5, 534-535.

Wang, W. S-Y. (1983). *Exploration in Language Evolution.* Osmania University Press.

THE SILENCE OF THE STONES: ON THE ARCHAEOLOGICAL RECORD FOR (NEANDERTAL) LANGUAGE

WIL ROEBROEKS

Faculty of Archaeology, Leiden University, P.O. Box 9515, 2300RA Leiden, The Netherlands
w.roebroeks@arch.leidenuniv.nl

The last decade has been a very productive one for our knowledge of our closest extinct relative, *Homo neanderthalensis*. A wide variety of studies has focused on various aspects of the Neandertal skeletal record and how to read it (e.g. Hublin 2009; Weaver 2009), on the chemical composition of their bones and how that might inform us on their diet (e.g. Richards and Trinkaus 2009), on their geographical distribution and their archaeological record (e.g. Roebroeks 2008) and, very importantly, on their genetic characteristics (e.g. Green et al. 2008; Briggs et al. 2009). Genetic studies indicate that modern humans and Neandertals shared a common ancestor only 500,000 to 700,000 years ago, which is also the picture emerging from studies of their physical remains (Hublin 2009). Building on the same *Bauplan*, two different hominin lineages emerged, in Africa the ancestors of modern humans, and in western Eurasia the Neandertals, who vanished from the record around 35,000 radiocarbon years ago. Integration of genetic data with the other lines of evidence promises to yield major breakthroughs in our understanding of the differences and similarities between these two groups of hominins in the very near future.

With so many new data on this extinct relative, the EVOLANG 2010 conference is a good moment to take stock of what we think we know about the linguistic capacities of these hominins. Language is a system for expressing thoughts which can incorporate any one of several signalling systems, including speech, sign language and writing. But apart from the written form, none of these signalling systems fossilizes, and attempts to reconstruct the evolution of language from skeletal, genetic or archaeological "proxies" hence must build on a chain of (usually implicit) inferences and assumptions (Fitch 2009; Botha 2009). While little can be said in unambiguous terms here on the basis of the archaeological record (Roebroeks and Verpoorte 2009), much however might be learned by reviewing the archaeological data that some consider pertinent for this issue and by analyzing how various workers have dealt with these data in the context of the language evolution debate.

Table 1

Biological, behavioral, and cultural comparisons between the late Middle and Upper Paleolithic in Europe[a]

Late Middle Paleolithic (ca. 50 ka ^{14}C BP)	Upper Paleolithic (30 ka ^{14}C BP)
Neandertals	Modern humans
Robust, energetically costly bodies [1,2]	Gracile, energetically less costly bodies [1,3]
Efficient hunters, relatively narrow focus on large mammals [3,4,5]	Efficient hunters, with somewhat broader prey choice, including smaller game and fish[3,4,5]
Stable isotopes: top carnivores with heavy emphasis on larger mammals[6]	Stable isotopes: comparable to Neandertal signal, with some individuals consuming significant amounts of fish[6]
Distribution south of 55 degrees North[7]	Northward range expansion[7]
Lithic technology, including laminar reduction, discoidal and Levallois[7,8]	Variety of lithic reduction strategies, including bladelet production[7,9]
Thrusting spears, little investment in projectile technology[9]	Well-developed projectile technology in bone, antler, ivory, and stone[9,10]
Very limited investment in on-site structures[9]	Structured hearths common[9]
Burials, without grave goods[8]	Elaborate burials[8]
Use of pigments[11]	Figurative portable and parietal art, personal ornaments[10]

[a] References. 1 - Churchill, 2006; 2 - Sorensen and Leonard, 2001; 3 - MacDonald et al., in press; 4 - Hockett and Haws, 2005; 5 - Kuhn and Stiner, 2006; 6 - Richards, 2007; 7 - Roebroeks and Verpoorte, in press; 8 - Gamble and Roebroeks, 1999; 9 - Verpoorte, 2006; 10 - Mellars, 2004; 11 - Soressi and d'Errico, 2007.

Apart from the archaeological record there exists more data on Neandertals that may have a bearing on the issue, for instance skeletal and genetic evidence, but these datasets do not give an unambiguous signal as to how Neandertals may have expressed their thoughts either. As far as the Neandertal skeletal evidence goes, I refer to Fitch's (2009) excellent review of fossil cues to the evolution of speech. In this he concludes 1) that it is a simple but unfortunate fact that the key issues of the vocal tract do not fossilize, 2) any possible reconstructions are necessarily based on indirect lines of evidence, and 3) most attempts at vocal tract reconstruction fail to stand up to empirical scrutiny (Fitch 2009:132). In the genetic realm, the FOXP2 gene is generally thought to be important for the evolution of language, by helping to establish neuromuscular control of the organs of speech. There now is evidence (Krause et al. 2007) that Neandertals had the modern human mutations at FOXP2, which suggests that these mutations must have occurred some time before the above mentioned split between Neandertals and modern humans (Krause et al. 2007; Green et al. 2008). Diller and Cann have recently suggested that the selective sweep at FOXP2 occurred already around 1,8 to 1,9 million years ago, i.e. early in the history of the genus *Homo*, at or near the beginning of the process of dramatic brain growth.

It is on the basis of the archaeological record that many workers have come up with a chronology for the emergence of language. The wide field of EVOLANG-studies has in recent years produced a number of papers in which straightforward archaeological finds (e.g. engraved pieces of ochre, some *Nassarius* shells, or heated slabs of silcrete), after a treatment with a series of inferences, have become important building blocks for scenarios on the timing and location of the origin(s) of languages). Although such interpretations have been criticised (e.g. Botha 2008), their prominent presence in high-ranking journals and the sheer power of endless repetition might yield the impression that these archaeological contributions to the language origins debate are rock solid. In this paper I will suggest that this is not the case at all.

Whilst concentrating on the Neandertal record, I will briefly review the archaeological proxies that are currently used in the debate on language origins, and conclude that many of the most prominent claims regarding the evolution of language on the basis of the archaeological record are flawed. Language in any sense of the word does not leave any direct traces in the fossil record prior to the invention of writing - not in the way that for instance hunting behaviour or tool use does. As suggested elsewhere (Roebroeks and Verpoorte 2009) rather than the archaeological record indicating the presence of language, *we archaeologists have been using the concept of language to explain (changes in) the archaeological record.* This has very clearly been the case with the Neandertal record. The differences between the Neandertal record and the one of the Upper Palaeolithic modern humans in Europe are indeed striking (see Table 1, from Roebroeks 2008). They are usually interpreted as the result of Neandertals lacking "fully modern language", with the archaeological record clearly showing the presence of more complex language patterns by the time of the Upper Palaeolithic of Europe - and even tens of thousands of years earlier during the Middle Stone Age in southern Africa (e.g. Mellars 2005).

One problem with these cognitive explanations is that they often lead to tunnel vision, in which all of modern humans accomplishments in any domain are treated as far more complex and superior to anything the "archaics" ever accomplished. For instance, there exists solid and well-published data that European Neandertals from at least 200,000 years ago onward routinely used fire to synthesize from birch bark a glue for hafting stone tools to their handles. Chemically comparable pitches can easily be produced with modern technical methods, e.g. by using air-tight laboratory flasks and temperature control facilities. Such tars can only be produced within a small temperature interval, from between a minimum of 340°C to a maximum of 400°C, and in the absence of oxygen. How this was actually achieved by Neandertals (and later prehistoric modern humans) is not known yet. Brown *et al.* (2009) present detailed evidence for early modern humans at the site of Pinnacle Point in Southern Africa regularly employing heat treatment to increase the quality and efficiency of their stone tool manufacture process, 72,000 years ago. They infer that the technology required a novel association between fire, its heat and a structural change in stone with consequent flaking benefits that demanded "…an elevated cognitive ability". They also suggest that as these early modern humans moved into Eurasia, their ability to alter and improve available raw material and increase the quality and efficiency of stone tool manufacture may have been a behavioral advantage in their encounters with the Neanderthals. However, with this interpretation they completely ignore that by the current state of affairs, Neandertals used fire as an engineering tool to synthesize birch tar tens of thousands of years before some modern humans at Pinnacle Point decided to put their stone raw material in it.

An even more serious problem with these cognitive explanations is that they fail to address that "fully modern" humans created very diverse archaeological signatures, sometimes strongly resembling what Neandertals left behind in western Eurasian landscapes. The record of Tasmanian aboriginals for instance has many of the hallmarks of the Neandertal record (Holdaway and Cosgrove 1997). These and other case studies ((Speth 2004; Brumm and Moore 2005) serve to make the point that modern humans did repeatedly and over long periods produce archaeological records that in many or even all domains resembled the ones created by Neandertals (Roebroeks and Verpoorte 2009).

A focus on the ecology of Neandertal and modern human hunter-gatherers has yielded more productive straightforward alternatives for the cognitive explanations of the differences in the record. These explanations focus on the costs and benefits of various behavioural strategies and, in contrast to the cognition-based explanations, do account for the diversity within the record of modern human hunter-gatherers. By focusing on the different trade-offs hunter-gatherers had to deal with, they reduce the cherished "proxies" for language to the outcome of cost-benefit analyses, and hence remain silent as far as linguistic capacities of early humans are concerned.

In summary, our discipline's attempts to bridge the wide gap between the dirt of the archaeological record and the abstraction that is "language" have produced a series of very good "stories" but have scientifically been unsuccessful. They are often based on a chain of inferences and assumptions that are seldom made explicit and are only as sturdy as their weakest link. Botha's (2009) "conceptual anatomy" of the inferences drawn about language evolution in archaeology gives a lethal overview of the basic line of reasoning in this domain.

Despite of the negative outcome as far as language origins-studies are concerned, the field of human origins-studies as a whole has profited immensely from the language-centred debate: it has led to the production of an extensive and new database informing us on the variability within the Middle and Late Pleistocene archaeological record of "archaic" and modern humans and has opened avenues for explanation of this (and later) striking diversity. Study of the archaeological record has shown that simple categories (such as archaic versus fully modern human behaviour) that we archaeologists once used to productively work with (e.g. Binford 1989) are now beyond their use life. When originally launched, they served a good purpose as heuristic devices which forced us to look at the record in fresh and innovative ways, they functioned for some time by generating new research and new questions, but have by now become obsolete through the progress of our disciplines.

That is, finally, not to say that one has to doubt the communicative skills of Neandertals. For instance, given their accomplishments in hunting down large mammals with a very simple technology, it is probable that they invested heavily in the reduction of search costs - and hence in their knowledge of animal behaviour - as well as in communication and cooperation between individual hunters (Buckley and Steele (2002) have suggested that this indeed may have been the selective context for spoken language abilities). For modern hunter-gatherers obtaining the skills necessary to become a successful hunter takes a long time and goes on into adulthood (Kaplan et al. 2000). MacDonald (2007a; 2007b) has shown that a range of learning processes are involved in acquiring hunting skills; learning about animal behavior involves individual observation and imitation as well as limited instruction, and exposure to potentially useful information in linguistic forms or in hunting stories. While that is the case for extant hunter-gatherers, we have no information on Neandertals in this domain, but for their archaeologically visible success in hunting large and dangerous mammals. The archaeological record is simply silent on the linguistic capacities of hominins, prior to the advent of writing. We would do a lot better without "language" when developing falsifiable "stories" on the evolution of the human lineage.

References

Binford, L.R. (1989). Isolating the transition to cultural adaptations: An organizational approach. In: Trinkaus E (ed) *The Emergence of Modern Humans: Biocultural Adaptations in the Later Pleistocene.* Cambridge University Press, Cambridge, pp 18-41

Botha, R, (2008). Prehistoric shell beads as a window on language evolution. *Language & Communication* 28:197-212

Botha, R. (2009). Theoretical underpinnings of inferences about language evolution: the syntax used at Blombos Cave. In: Botha, R., Knight, C. (eds.) *The Cradle of Language.* Oxford University Press., New York, pp 93-111.

Briggs, A.W., Good, J.M., Green, R.E., Krause, J., Maricic, T., Stenzel, U., Lalueza-Fox, C., Rudan, P., Brajkovic, D., Kucan, Z., Gusic, I., Schmitz, R.W., Doronichev, V.B., Golovanova, L.V., de la Rasilla M., Fortea, J., Rosas, A., Pääbo, S. (2009). Targeted Retrieval and Analysis of Five Neandertal mtDNA Genomes. *Science* 325:318-321.

Brown, K.S., Marean, C.W., Herries, A.I.R., Jacobs, Z., Tribolo, C., Braun, D., Roberts, D.L., Meyer, M.C., Bernatchez, J. (2009a). Fire As an Engineering Tool of Early Modern Humans. *Science* 325:859-862.

Brown, K.S., Marean, C.W., Herries, A.I.R., Jacobs, Z., Tribolo, C., Braun, D., Roberts, D.L., Meyer, M.C., Bernatchetz, J. (2009b). Early modern humans used fire to improve the fracturing of silcrete in making tools in South Africa 72,000 years ago. *Science* 325(5942):859-862.

Brumm, A., Moore, M.W. (2005). Symbolic Revolutions and the Australian Archaeological Record. *Cambridge Archaeological Journal* 15(2):157-175.

Buckley, C., Steele, J. (2002). Evolutionary ecology of spoken language: co-evolutionary hypotheses are testable. *World Archaeology* 34(1):26-46.

Churchill, S.E. (2006). Bioenergetic Perspectives on Neanderthal Thermoregulatory and Activity Budgets. In: Harvati, K., Harrison, T. (eds.) *Neanderthals Revisited: New Approaches and Perspectives.* Springer, Dordrecht, pp 113-134.

Fitch, W.T. (2009). Fossil cues to the evolution of speech. In: Botha, R., Knight, C. (eds) *The Cradle of Language.* Oxford University Press., New York, pp 112-134.

Gamble; C., Roebroeks, W. (1999). The Middle Palaeolithic: a point of inflection. In: Roebroeks, W., Gamble, C. (eds.) *The Middle Palaeolithic Occupation of Europe.* University of Leiden, Leiden, pp 3-21.

Green, R.E., Malaspinas, A-S., Krause, J., Briggs, A.W., Johnson, P.L.F., Uhler, C., Meyer, M., Good, J.M., Maricic, T., Stenzel, U., Prüfer, K., Siebauer, M., Burbano, H.A., Ronan, M., Rothberg, J.M., Egholm, M,. Rudan, P., Brajkovic, D., Kucan, Z., Gusic, I., Wikström, M., Laakkonen, L., Kelso, J., Slatkin, M., Pääbo, S. (2008). A Complete Neandertal Mitochondrial Genome Sequence Determined by High-Throughput Sequencing. *Cell* 134:416-426.

Hockett, B., Haws, J.A. (2005). Nutritional ecology and the human demography of Neandertal extinction. *Quaternary International* 137:21-34.

Holdaway, S., Cosgrove, R. (1997). The archaeological attributes of behaviour: difference or variability? *Endeavour* 21(2):66-71

Hublin, J. (2009). The Origin of Neandertals. *Proceedings of the National Academy of Sciences* 106(38):16022-16027.

Kaplan, H., Hill, K., Lancaster, J., Hurtado, A.M. (2000). A Theory of Human Life History Evolution: Diet, Intelligence, and Longevity. *Evolutionary Anthropology* 9:156-185

Krause, J., Lalueza-Fox, C., Orlando, L., Enard, W., Green, R.E., Burbano, H.A., Hublin, J., Hänni, C., Fortea, J., de la Rasilla, M. (2007). The derived FOXP2 variant of modern humans was shared with Neandertals. *Current Biology* 17(21):1908-1912

Kuhn, S.L., Stiner, M.C. (2006). What's a Mother to Do? The Division of Labor among Neandertals and Modern Humans in Eurasia. *Current Anthropology* 47(6):953-980

MacDonald, K. (2007a) Cross-cultural Comparison of Learning in Human Hunting. Implications for Life History Evolution. *Human Nature* 18:386-402

MacDonald, K. (2007b). Ecological Hypotheses for Human Brain Evolution: Evidence for Skill and Learning Processes in the Ethnographic Literature on Hunting. In: Roebroeks, W. (ed) *Guts and Brains: An Integrative Approach to the Hominin Record.* Leiden University Press, Leiden, pp 107-132.

MacDonald, K., Roebroeks, W., Verpoorte, A. (2009). An Energetics Perspective on the Neandertal Record. In: Hublin, J-J., Richards, M.P. (eds.) *The Evolution of Hominin Diets: Integrating Approaches to the Study of Palaeolithic Subsistence.* Springer, Leipzig, pp 211-220.

Mellars, P.A. (2004). Neanderthals and the modern human colonization of Europe. *Nature* 432:461-465

Mellars, P.A. (2005). The Impossible Coincidence. A Single-Species Model for the Origins of Modern Human Behavior in Europe. *Evolutionary Anthropology* 14:12-27

Richards, M.P. (2007a). Diet Shift at the Middle/Upper Palaeolithic Transition in Europe? The Stable Isotope Evidence. In: Roebroeks, W. (ed.) *Guts and Brains: An Integrative Approach to the Hominin Record.* Leiden University Press, Leiden, pp 223-234

Richards, M.P. (2007b) Isotopic evidence for European Upper Palaeolithic human diets. In: Hublin, J.J. (ed.) *The Evolution of Hominid Diets: Integrating Approaches to the Study of Palaeollithic Subsistence.* Springer, Dordrecht, p XXX

Richards, M.P., Trinkaus, E. (2009) Isotopic evidence for the diets of European Neanderthals and early modern humans. *Proceedings of the National Academy of Sciences* 106 (38):16034-16039.

Roebroeks, W. (2008). Time for the Middle to Upper Paleolithic Transition in Europe. *Journal of Human Evolution* 55:918-926

Roebroeks, W., Verpoorte, A. (2009) A "language-free" explanation for differences between the European Middle and Upper Paleolithic Record. In: Botha, R., Knight, C. (eds) *The Cradle of Language.* Oxford University Press, New York, pp 150-166

Sorensen, M.V., Leonard, W.R. (2001) Neandertal energetics and foraging efficiency. *Journal of Human Evolution* 40:483-495.

Soressi, M., D'Errico, F. (2007) Pigments, gravures, parures: Les comportements symboliques controversés des Néandertaliens. In: Vandermeersch, B., Maureille, B. (eds.) *Les Néandertaliens: Biologie et cultures.* C.T.H.S., Documents préhistoriques 23, Paris, pp 297-309

Speth, J.D. (2004). Hunting pressure, subsistence intensification, and demographic change in the Levantine late Middle Palaeolithic. In:

Goren-Inbar, N., Speth, J.D. (eds.) *Human Paleoecology in the Levantine Corridor*. Oxbow Books, Oxford, pp 149-166

Verpoorte, A. (2006) *Neanderthal energetics and spatial behaviour. Before Farming 2006/3*:1-6

Weaver, T.D. (2009). The meaning of Neandertal skeletal morphology. *Proceedings of the National Academy of Sciences* 106(38):16028-16033

MINIMUM DESCRIPTION LENGTH AND GENERALIZATION IN THE EVOLUTION OF LANGUAGE

GIANCARLO SCHREMENTI, MICHAEL GASSER

School of Informatics and Computing, Indiana University
Bloomington, IN 47405, USA
gischrem@cs.indiana.edu

The purpose of language is to encode information, so that it can be communicated. Both the producer and the comprehender of a communication want the encoding to be simple. However, they have competing concerns as well. The producer desires conciseness and the comprehender desires fidelity. This paper argues that the Minimum Description Length Principle (MDL) captures these two pressures on language. A genetic algorithm is used to evolve languages, that take the form of finite-state transducers, using MDL as a fitness metric. The languages that emerge are shown to have the ability to generalize beyond their initial training scope, suggesting that when selecting to satisfy MDL one is implicitly selecting for compositional languages.

1. Introduction

One of the most basic cognitive activities is the discovery of patterns in one's environment. Patterns allow us to make sense of the world and provide a foundation for activities as varied as vision and reasoning. However, discovering patterns is often only useful if we can compress those patterns into something simple enough to store in memory or transmit to others. One of the prime examples of this activity is language, where we are taught as children to correlate experiences with their compressed encoding in language.

The compression in language occurs for two reasons, corresponding to the two actors involved in a communication. The first reason is that the comprehender of the communication doesn't want to be overwhelmed with a large communication that is difficult to process and learn. This first reason has been well recognized in language evolution research (Brighton, 2003), where it's argued that languages evolve to be more easily learned. What is often neglected is that the comprehender has a willing partner in this drive towards simplicity. The producer wants the communication to be short as well, to minimize energy expenditure. This second reason has been recognized at least as far back as Zipf (1949), but has seen only passing attention in the research of language evolution, usually in the form of the emergence of irregularity (Batali, 1998),(Kirby, 2001).

The producer and the comprehender are cooperating on this goal of simplicity, but they have competing interests as well. The producer, in trying to minimize energy expenditure, would love to compress everything to just one form. The comprehender, in trying to maximize interpretive accuracy, would prefer every meaning have a distinct form. So, both actors want a simple language but one favors compactness and the other fidelity. A measure of a successful evolved language needs to balance these two concerns.

One solution to this problem is the Minimum Description Length Principle (MDL) of Rissanen (1978), which is typically used to evaluate mathematical models of data by balancing two factors: the complexity of the model and the likelihood of the data to be generated if that model were true. These factors mirror the two concerns of the producer and the comprehender in communication. The complexity of the model can be measured by size of the encoding system and the size of the encoded data. The likelihood of the data can be measured as the likelihood of correctly decoding the data. Looking at encoding this way allows us to use the MDL principle as a guide in assessing the success or fitness of an encoding system.

Using description length as a fitness criterion means that we can evolve encoding systems that balance the needs of the producer with those of the comprehender. Then, the next question is: what kind of encoding systems succeed at this criterion? What sort of properties emerge over the course of the evolution? The question of emergent properties is at the heart of language evolution research and, like many authors, we are particularly interested in the property of compositionality.

Compositionality is the notion that language is made up of reusable components and rules for combining them. This powerful property gives human language the ability to generalize knowledge to both understand and produce an infinite variety of expressions. Thus the question of the nature of its emergence is of particular importance. One of the goals of this paper is to investigate whether compression systems evolved under the constraint of minimizing description length develop this property of generalization.

2. Methods

In order to model the evolution of the compression of patterns, the research here uses a genetic algorithm to search over possible finite-state transducers that encode a given set of patterns. The patterns are strings of characters from an input alphabet, that must be encoded into strings of characters from an output alphabet.

Finite-state transducers are simple machines that sequentially process input and for each input produce an output. These transducers make effective models of both encoding and decoding, because they can operate both forward and backward. Forward operation encodes patterns and backward operation, accomplished by reversing what is input and what is output for each transition, decodes them. An important caveat, is that a transducer with transitions that produce no output, may be non-deterministic when reversed. This is because there will be transitions that can be followed without processing any input, so there may be multiple paths that could be taken from a particular state.

The algorithm starts with a state-minimal finite state automaton that recognizes the entire set of input patterns. This automaton has a certain number of state transitions or edges, which in a transducer could output a character or an ϵ meaning no output. The genes in the genetic algorithm are the output characters on these edges. Each genome is a set of output characters, one for each edge in the initial automaton. These genomes can be combined with the structure of the automaton to form a transducer that encodes the set of input patterns. The search space for the genetic algorithm is then the range of possible outputs for each edge. It is important to note that the algorithm does not make use of communication between multiple agents. So, it does not model the evolution of language in the strict sense, but rather investigates what types of encodings emerge in the evolution that best satisfy the fitness criteria.

Before the fitness of the genomes can be assessed the transducer that they produce is compressed according to a compression criterion from Brighton (2005). The criterion is that any two states can be combined as long as the result doesn't change the encoding of any of the initial patterns and the two states to be combined don't have conflicting output edges, e.g. two edges reading the same character but outputting a different character. In order to prevent loops and so that the compression can be done iteratively, the two states to be combined also have to be at the same depth from the initial state.

Our model is not the only language evolution model to use finite-state transducers and minimum description length, an important inspiration for this work was Brighton (2005). The primary difference is that in Brighton's model the encodings the transducer produces are fixed. The MDL is used to guide the evolution of minimal transducers that produce those fixed encodings. In this model the encodings are not fixed, allowing for compression to evolve across a wide range of possible transducers simple and complex that produce a wide range of encodings.

2.1. *Formulas*

The transducer's fitness is calculated using a series of formulas that are grounded in the MDL principle. The fittest genomes are the ones that produce the most compact transducer and encodings while retaining accuracy in decoding back into the initial patterns. Equation (1) shows the fitness formula, $Norm$ is a normalization function that will be discussed later, DL is description length measured in bits and H is entropy measured in bits as well. Since a fitness metric should be maximized, the sum of the two normalized factors is subtracted from their maximal sum.

$$Fitness = 2.0 - (Norm(DL(Model)) + Norm(H(Data|Model))) \quad (1)$$

The producer's concerns are represented by Equation (2), which is composed of two parts, the description length of the transducer doing the encoding and the description length of the encodings of the input patterns. The producer would like to minimize both of these values. Equation (3) calculates the size of the transducer assuming each edge needs to be described, with N_{Edges} being the number of edges and N_{States} the number of states. The description length of the encodings is calculated according to Equation (4) which sums the length of the encodings and multiplies that sum by the cost of representing each output character. Each character in the output alphabet is assumed to occur with roughly equal frequency, so the cost of each character is the log_2 or lg of the size of the output alphabet.

$$DL(Model) = DL(Transducer) + DL(Encodings) \qquad (2)$$

$$DL(Transducer) = N_{Edges} * (2 * lg(N_{States})) \qquad (3)$$

$$DL(Encodings) = lg(AlphabetSize) * \sum_{pat} LengthOfEncoding_{pat} \qquad (4)$$

The comprehender desires accuracy in decoding, which in information-theoretic terms means that we don't want to be surprised by decoding patterns into something other than the originals. The amount of surprise given the encodings is calculated using the conditional entropy calculation in Equation (5). Remember, that the comprehender is using an encoding transducer that is reversed to do decoding, which means that there may be non-determinism in its processing. We want to know how many of the potential paths through the reversed transducer result in correctly decoding the compressed pattern back into the original. Taking the lg of this fraction gives us the amount of surprise in bits. There will always be at least one successful decoding path because the same transducer, in its original form, produced that encoding, so taking that same path in the reversed transducer will successfully decode it. The number of bits is then multiplied by the probability of encountering that encoding, which for the experiments in this paper is the same for every encoding.

$$H(Data|Model) = -\sum_{enc} p_{enc} * lg(\frac{SuccessfulDecodingPaths_{enc}}{TotalPaths_{enc}}) \qquad (5)$$

Now that we have some methods of calculating description length, we can return to the normalization function that was mentioned earlier. The two factors in the fitness calculation, that represent the concerns of the producer and the comprehender, don't necessarily have the same range of possible values. In order to keep them evenly balanced, they are both normalized by dividing by their maximum possible values. The values that would occur if no compression was done and accuracy was as poor as possible. The normalization results in each value ranging from zero to one, the closer to zero they both are the more fit the transducer is.

3. Results

In keeping with the linguistic theme of the investigation, the patterns in the input set are composed of components combined using a rule. This provides structure to the set that the transducer may encode. Each pattern is of the form NVN, where N is a string from a set called Nouns and V is a string from a set called Verbs. The rule for these experiments is that each of the nouns and the verb in the pattern must start with the same character.

3.1. *Experiment One*

In order to visually represent the transducers, the experiment here uses a small set with 4 Nouns and 2 Verbs, resulting in 8 strings that the transducer must encode. Additionally for simplicity, the input and output alphabets for the experiments are of size two, meaning they are bits represented by the characters a and b, with the addition of ϵ to represent null to the output alphabet. The input patterns for both experiments are shown in Table 1.

Table 1.   Input patterns

Experiment One		Experiment Two	
Nouns	Verbs	Nouns	Verbs
aba	aa	ababa	aaaa
bab	bb	babab	bbbb
abb		abbba	aabb
baa		baaab	bbaa
		aabaa	
		bbabb	

Using this pattern set, the first experiment ran a genetic algorithm with 20 genomes for 100 generations. Each generation went through a mutation in which 5% of the edges had their outputs randomly switched.

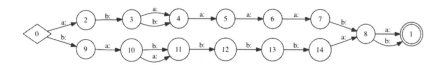

Figure 1.   Starting automaton

The fittest transducer from that run is described here. The initial automaton is shown in Figure 1 and the final compressed transducer is shown in Figure 2. This transducer when reversed has perfect accuracy in decoding, meaning for each

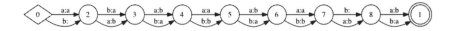

Figure 2.   Fittest transducer

pattern in the set there there is only one path that processes the encoding for that pattern and that path outputs the original input pattern correctly. As the transducer is clearly state and edge minimal for processing the pattern set, it is very fit as judged by description length. The only aspect that could be improved is shorter encodings for the pattern set. The left chart in Figure 3 shows the progression of fitness over the 100 generations of this experiment.

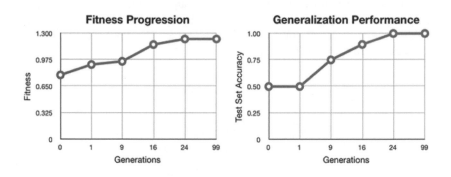

Figure 3.   Experiment One Results

In order to determine whether generalization has occurred as the encoding system has evolved, we need to look at a larger pattern set. This test set consists of every NVN combination totaling 32 different patterns, 4 times as many as were in the training set that was used to guide the evolution. The winning transducer, shown above, ended up having perfect accuracy in decoding its encodings of these 32 patterns. The right chart in Figure 3 shows the progression of this test set accuracy.

3.2. Experiment Two

In order to test whether this behavior continues for larger sets, a second experiment with a pattern training set of 36 patterns is investigated. This experiment has 6 Nouns and 4 Verbs, shown in Table 1, that are combined with the same rule as the first experiment. This experiment also had 20 genomes, but evolves them for 1000 generations as the genomes are much larger. The transducers for this experiment are too large to reproduce here.

The fitness progression of this experiment is shown in left chart of Figure 4. The test set for this experiment has 144 patterns and the plot of the generalization accuracy over the generations is shown in the right chart of Figure 4. This experiment doesn't end up with perfect accuracy like the previous one, but does evolve a structure with an encoding system that is able to generalize across the majority of the test set.

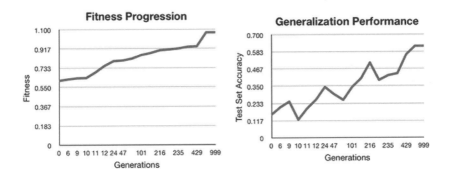

Figure 4.   Experiment Two Results

As can be seen from the dips in the generalization graph, this experiment frequently encounters local minima where fitness is higher but generalization is lower. This occurs because it generally requires fewer changes to the transducer to improve compression than it does to improve accuracy. The normalization functions are an attempt to remedy this situation by better balancing the two factors in the fitness function. In order to analyze the emergent properties of very fit transducers, the result shown here is one that successfully navigates these local minima to achieve a high level of fitness.

4. Conclusions

The work here shows finite-state transducers can be evolved to not only compress patterns, but to do it in a way that can be generalized to novel patterns. The MDL Principle is a powerful guide in evolving transducers that are both accurate and compact. This drive to compress while retaining accuracy is what encourages encodings to evolve that are compositional in nature. These compositional encodings allow the transducer to be reduced in size and still produce decodable output. In turn, this emergence of compositionality gives the transducer the ability to generalize its encoding rules to new input patterns.

The work builds on the idea from Brighton (2005) of using MDL as an evolutionary guide to compress transducers in order to promote generalization. This idea is developed to show MDL can be used to guide more than just transducer complexity but the evolution of the entire encoding system towards systems that display generalization behavior. Intriguingly, the results suggest description length may be able to be developed into a measurement of the presence of compostionality and/or generalization in an encoding system. Further work needs to be done to evaluate its relationship to the *assumption of optimal generalization*, used by Brighton (2003) and Kirby (2007), that measures how close a language is to a fully compositional one that distinctly represents each semantic feature.

Human language is a model of human experience and in the evolution of language there would be the same pressures facing it any other model would face. The MDL Principle formalizes these pressures and allows us to use them to simulate the emergence of properties we associate with language. Not only does it neatly capture these pressures but it provides an explanation for how compositionality emerged in language. It emerged because languages that are compositional better meet the pressures of conciseness and accuracy.

References

Batali, J. (1998). Computational simulations of the emergence of grammar. In J. Hurford, M. Studdert-Kennedy, & C. Knight (Eds.), *Approaches to the evolution of language: Social and cognitive bases* (pp. 405–426). Cambridge: Cambridge University Press.

Brighton, H. (2003). *Simplicity as a driving force in linguistic evolution.* Unpublished doctoral dissertation, Theoretical and Applied Linguistics, The University of Edinburgh.

Brighton, H. (2005). Linguistic evolution and induction by minimum description length. In M. Werning & E. Machery (Eds.), *The compostionality of concepts and meanings: Applications to linguistics, psychology and neuroscience* (pp. 405–426). Frankfurt: Ontos Verlag.

Kirby, S. (2001). Spontaneous evolution of linguistic structure: an iterated learning model of the emergence of regularity and irregularity. *IEEE Transactions on Evolutionary Computation, 5*(2), 102–110.

Kirby, S. (2007). The evolution of meaning-space structure through iterated learning. In C. Lyon, C. Nehaniv, & A. Cangelosi (Eds.), *Emergence of communication and language* (pp. 253–268). Springer Verlag.

Rissanen, J. (1978). Modeling by shortest data description. *Automatica, 14*, 465–471.

Zipf, G. (1949). *Human behavior and the principle of least-effort.* Addison-Wesley.

THOUGHTS ON EVOLUTION OF LANGUAGE FROM THE POINT OF VIEW OF BRAIN NEUROANATOMY AND DEVELOPMENT, AND OBJECT-ORIENTED PROGRAMMING

H. LEE SELDON

School of Computing and Design, Swinburne University of Technology Sarawak,
Jalan Simpang Tiga, Kuching, 93350, Malaysia

The evolution of language capabilities is closely linked to the evolution of human brain structures. Human brain auditory cortices are anatomically and functionally asymmetrical. Studies at the microscopic level have found a thinner cortex and more widely spaced neuronal columns in the left (dominant) hemisphere, which reasonably correlate with its greater ability to discriminate speech sounds. The nature of these differences is consistent with a "balloon model" of brain growth, which states that as the brain white matter grows, it stretches the overlying cortex. Thus, the amount and duration of brain growth is an important factor in acquiring the ability to perceive speech. Humans have a much longer brain maturation time than any other primates (or animals). This "extended maturation time" allows language capabilities to evolve in the brain over time, rather than requiring them to be present at birth. The extended maturation time also must have a genetic basis, but not one specific to language, and the HAR1, G72 and FOXP2 genes might well be examples of genes which affect cortical and white matter growth. Finally, if this neuronal system can learn language without depending on specific language genes, then what could be the origin of universal grammar? Natural human grammars, like object-oriented software programs, are constrained to describe our experiential universe – an idea mooted also by "the early Wittgenstein" and others. Insofar as humans mostly share the same experiential universe, our descriptions of it (our languages, some branches of mathematics) share many features; these common features can appear as a "universal grammar."

1. The relationship between language and the human auditory cortex

It is generally accepted that speech perception is lateralized in the human brain, being in the left hemisphere in most people. In the 1970's - 1980's I searched in the human auditory cortices of both hemispheres for a neuroanatomical correlate of lateralized speech perception. The spacing of cell columns is slightly wider on the left, and the dendrites there are oriented slightly "flatter" (Seldon, 1981a-b, 1982, 1985). The latter finding implies that tangential extent (width) of each neuronal cell column is slightly greater in the left hemisphere, thereby allowing a column to integrate more afferent input. The increased inter-column spacing on the left was even greater than could be accounted for by the flatter dendritic orientations and implied that neuronal columns on the left are more disjoint in their sampling of afferent inputs. Years later Harasty and I found that the left auditory cortex is also slightly thinner than the right (Harasty et al., 2003) - all these findings combined with those of Kaes (1907) to imply that white matter growth in and below the auditory cortices is asymmetrical (in the left versus right hemispheres). All this was summarized in a "balloon model" of cortical growth (Harasty et al., 2003; Seldon, 2005), which seemed to explain why the left hemisphere (in most people) could perceive speech signals better than the right hemisphere. The model states that during physical development, in addition to the well documented synaptic plasticity there is proliferation of myelin in and below the cortex, and that this white matter growth stretches the cortex like a balloon, causing it to become thinner and its elements (neuronal columns) to be pushed further apart. Functional columns could subdivide into more numerous and finer functional units with a greater capacity to discriminate afferent signals – this process extends further in the dominant hemisphere. Further measurements of human auditory cortices are consistent with this model (Seldon, 2006).

Other authors have also recently re-emphasized the importance of the white matter in understanding brain function. Fields (2008) has reviewed several studies which indicate the importance of environmental stimuli ("nurture") on white matter growth, and the consequent correlation between white matter volumes and levels of skill. He also described how the amount of activity in axons influences the growth of the myelin sheathes. (More activity -> more myelin -> better cognition.) Finally, he reviewed how defects in myelin formation are correlated with mental abnormalities (cf. also Seldon, 2007).

2. Hypothesis: Cortical and white matter growth and duration of growth are critical to language perception

Thus, neocortex and myelin growth and maturation seem to be important factors in the ability to perceive speech. So we have the hypothesis that the amount and duration of growth during exposure to speech are critical factors and that a longer duration allows the cortical neurons more time to learn to distinguish more speech sounds and combinations. Hemispheric asymmetry of growth might appear to be a factor, but such asymmetry is characteristic of many functions in mammals, birds and fish, and thus is not unique to either humans or language.

The size of the human brain regions associated with speech and language - the temporal and frontal lobes – distinguishes us from all of our living relatives. If the amount of white matter growth is important to linguistic abilities, then one should also consider the hypotheses of Gibson (1991) and Horrobin (2001). They proposed that the Homo sapiens speciation (about 130,000 years ago) was linked with a dramatic improvement in the metabolism of fatty acids, in particular of DHA and EPA, which led to a massive increase in the production of cell membranes in brain neurons and thus in the size and functional capacity of the brain. Disturbances in these metabolic pathways can lead to (less membrane production and) schizophrenia or "madness." This hypothesis does imply a link between brain size and functional capacity. However, total brain volume does not significantly differentiate Homo sapiens sapiens from other ancestors and relatives such as Homo erectus and Neanderthals, who have not left any record of significant grammatical language (Bickerton, 1996, p. 47). [If Neanderthals had mastered language, then it could not be considered uniquely human.] Therefore, size alone cannot account for grammatical abilities.

The new emphasis on development duration is supported by the observation that humans take much longer to mature than do other primates or animals (cf. review by Gopnik, 2009) or than did Neanderthals (cf. e.g. Ramirez Rozzi & Bermudez de Castro, 2004). However, accepting time, a continuous variable, as a determinant of linguistic capacities implies that the spectrum of such capacities could also be more continuous; human language might appear as a discrete step in capacity only because of the great differences in maturation times (together with the differences in cortical size etc.). Kenneally (2009) has reviewed recent studies which show that apes and other animals are capable of much more sophisticated communications than we have previously thought; the implication is that the gap in communicative ability is not so great as we have assumed. The chimpanzee Kanzi's unusual mastery of speech perception is a prime example supporting the development time hypothesis. His cortex, anatomically not different from other chimpanzees', was exposed to "language" during its entire growth period. Reports on so-called "wild children" suggest that without the long exposure period they do not master the whole complexity of language.

Other recent studies also emphasize the role of "extended immaturity" or "extended childhood" in the development of human features such as the ability to focus and to plan (Gopnik, 2009). She relates how altricial bird species such as crows have a longer immaturity and considerably greater learning capacity than precocial species such as chickens. She also explains how children can use their extended maturation period to "update ... their hypotheses about the world"

– this would include updating their language skills to match their experience. A related finding is that about 30,000 years ago Homo sapiens started living longer (Caspari & Lee, 2004); this might have been related to a longer maturation time. There is a corollary which says that the longer duration of growth can lead to more (distinct) individual final outcomes in keeping with probability theory (Seldon, 2007). (The more often you roll dice, the greater the number of different possible combinations of faces.) Final outcomes significantly different from the average may cause the affected individuals to have different "perceptions" than usual and/or to be labeled as mentally different, e.g. schizophrenic or genius (cf. also section 1). There is a high incidence of schizophrenia around the age of completion of cortical maturation.

3. Genetic basis of cortical and white matter maturation compared to genetic basis of language capabilities

The roles of size and maturation time suggest that in the search for a genetic basis of language, those genes which affect brain maturation or its end should also be considered, in addition to those implied by Horrobin (2001). It would also be interesting to study brain maturation and speech perception in cases of progeria or Werner's Syndrome. One very interesting genetic sequence, HAR1 (Human Accelerated Region 1), has been described by Pollard (2009). It affects cortical maturation and displays 18 base pair changes relative to the equivalent chimpanzee sequence. Another interesting gene has been described by Chumakov et al. (2002); G72 is implicated in cases of schizophrenia; it indirectly affects the NMDA receptor, which in turn has been implicated in myelin (white matter) metabolism. Fields (2008) mentions others which are known to affect myelin growth and behavioral performance.

FOXP2 is a much-studied regulatory gene which has been linked to language capabilities. The human and chimpanzee protein products differ in 2 amino acids. Konopka et al. (2009) have shown different regulatory effects of the two forms in cell lines, but the targets of the regulation are a large suite of genes implicated in basic cell processes (and thus in development and neuronal plasticity (Fisher and Scharff, 2009)). FOXP2 and several of its targets are especially apparent in the perisylvian (speech perception) cortex, but also in the cerebellum of fetal brains. However, it may have had the same form in Neanderthals as in Homo sapiens (Krause et al., 2007), which would contrast with the lack of other evidence of language among the Neanderthals.

4. Universal grammar could arise from specific human "language genes" or could be learned by less specific neocortical structures

This brings us to the question of whether there is a genetically based "innate grammar" and whether that defines the species Homo sapiens sapiens. Human language capabilities could be presumed due to the evolution of a "language organ" – of specific genes with an instantaneous effect - or to the evolution of a neuronal system with enhanced learning duration and capacity. Analogous to genetic evolution over a long period of time, a human neocortex with adequate maturation time can differentiate and refine its functional units to lead to specific, well adapted skills, including language. As described above, up to now there is little genetic evidence for a specific genetic "innate grammar," but there is mounting evidence for uniquely human genes affecting cortical and myelin development.

Assuming that the difference between humans and other primates is based on sequences such as HAR1 and FOXP2, then the multiple genetic changes must have accumulated over time. It is then more of an academic question whether one of the sequence of changes was "the defining speciation event."

5. Hypothesis: The source of universal grammar could be "compatibility with the experiential universe" instead of genes

The postulated genetic basis of language suggests an origin for language and grammar, whereas the brain size and maturation time described above suggests a mechanism for acquiring language and grammar. The "complexity of language" and "paucity of stimuli" arguments have been proposed to support the assumption of genetically determined grammar; the argument developed above leaves open the question of a source of universal grammar. This is where "object-oriented" programming (OOP) enters into the discussion. OOP is based on the description of "objects," their actions and relations – as are all natural human languages and even "animal communications." The objects (nouns), their descriptors (adjectives) and their relations (verbs, adverbs, prepositions) all derive from the experiential universe, i.e. the one we (and animals) perceive. The majority of afferent inputs to the brain speech or language perception areas come from our sensory organs and thus are ultimately derived from the universe we sense. Indeed, the purpose of communications in the animal world has been to describe the experiential universe.

This view has already been mooted by others, although perhaps not so explicitly. Wittgenstein's early views were that language was related to logic, and logic reflected "the a priori order of the world" (1953, §97); therefore, the structure of language derived from the worldly order. Although he later discounted the referential nature of language, viewing it only as a game with mutually agreed words and rules, *still* all of his examples could be mutually accepted only because they referred to mutual experiences. [Inner feelings cannot be mutually experienced.] Universal grammar would arise from "The tendency to look for something in common to all the entities which we commonly subsume under a general term" (Wittgenstein, 1958); it is the structural framework shared by all human grammars.

B.F. Skinner's behavioral model linked language with the perceived universe through stimuli and reinforcement, but his interpretation of these concepts was rather narrow. Although Chomsky (1959) originally rejected that model, his own more recent "minimalist program" emphasizes constraints imposed on language from external sources. "Economy of grammar ... investigates the possibility that human language design meets the Bare Output Conditions imposed on it from those systems with which it interfaces" (Cook & Newson, 2007, p. 249). Those conditions are restrictions imposed on "the language faculty" by systems such as our sense organs, which in turn derive their information from the experiential universe.

Deutscher (2005) wrote "from a very simple starting point and with modest raw materials, it is possible, in principle, to understand how the full complexity of language could have arisen. All that is needed are five main ingredients:

(i) A human brain (capable of learning a language, drawing analogies, thinking in terms of metaphor, and so on). (ii) Human beings who wish to communicate with each other for essentially the same purposes as those that motivate us today. (iii) Words for some simple physical objects and simple actions. (iv) A few natural principles of ordering, which stem from somewhere very deep in our cognition. (v) A bit of time." (Deutscher, 2005, p. 259)

Point (iii) refers to the "object orientation" of language; to point (iv), the ordering stems from our experiential universe; to point (v), Deutscher meant the time for generations of humans to develop a language, but it could also mean the maturation time within which our brains learn the words and the order.

Even the Amazonian Piraha language described by Everett (2008) is clearly linked to the experiential universe of its speakers.

About music, which is perceived by mostly the same brain regions as speech, Schwartz et al. (2003) wrote "Music, like the visual arts, is rooted in our experience of the natural world." They found that the acoustic frequencies in music parallel those in speech, i.e. those often found in our experiential world.

Thus, we are in a position to replace the strong nativist assumption of "an innate grammar" with a weaker and more general assumption that "all grammars which are consistent with the experiential universe are allowed." Because all grammars are constrained to be consistent with mostly the same universe, they all share many features which can be collectively called "a universal grammar." Until now all natural human grammars have been consistent with the experiential universe, as has Chomskyian universal grammar.

Thus, as the assumption of a biologically based innate grammar is unnecessary, so also it is unnecessary to make the strong assumption that there was one "first language" or "ur-language." It is allowable to assume that languages may have arisen in different places at different times. Due to the consistency constraints mentioned above, they would all of necessity still share many features.

In conclusion, the source of universal grammar has existed for a long time in the experiential universe. The mechanism for mastering the complexity of language has evolved in the neocortex via its synaptic plasticity and the proliferation of myelin, which over time help define ever more and finer functional neuronal units. The origin of this mechanism should be sought, among many places, in genes which affect neocortical growth and maturation time.

References

Bickerton, D. (1996) *Language and Human Behavior*. Seattle, USA: Univ of Washington Press.

Chomsky, N. (1959) Review of B.F. Skinner *Verbal Behavior. Language 35*, 26-58

Chumakov, I., Blumenfeld, M., Guerassimenko, O., Cavarec, L., Palicio, M., Abderrahim, H., et al. (2002) Genetic and physiological data implicating the new human gene G72 and the gene for D-amino acid oxidase in schizophrenia. *Proc Nat Acad Sci 99(21)*, 13675-13680

Cook, V.J. & Newson, M. (2007) *Chomsky's Universal Grammar. An Introduction*. Oxford, UK: Blackwell Publishing.

Deutscher, G. (2005) *The Unfolding of Language*. New York, USA: Henry Holt and Company

Everett, D. (2008) *Don't Sleep, There Are Snakes: Life and Language in the Amazonian Jungle*. New York, USA: Random House.

Fields, R.D. (2008) White matter matters. *Scientific American 3/2008*, 54-61

Fisher, S.E., Scharff, (2009) FOXP2 as a molecular window into speech and language. *Trends in Genetics 25(4)*, 166-177

Gibson, K.R. (1991) Myelination and behavioral development: A comparative perspective on questions of neoteny, altriciality and intelligence. In: Gibson K.R. & Petersen A.C. (Eds) *Brain Maturation and Cognitive Development*, New York, USA: Aldine de Gruyter, pp 29-63

Gopnik, A. (2009) When we were butterflies. *New Scientist 2719*, 44-45

278

Harasty, J., Seldon, H.L., Chan, P., Halliday, G., Harding, A. (2003) The left human speech-processing cortex is thinner but longer than the right. *Laterality 8(3)*, 247-260

Horrobin, D. (2001) *The Madness of Adam and Eve*. London, UK: Bantam Press.

Kaes, T. (1907) *Die Großhirnrinde des Menschen in ihren Maßen und in ihrem Fasergehalt*. Jena, Germany: Verlag Gustav Fischer.

Kenneally, C. (2009) So you think you're unique. *New Scientist 2657*, 29-34

Konopka, G., Bomar, J.M., Winden, K., Coppola, G., Jonsson, Z.O., Gao, F., Peng, S., Preuss, T.M., Wohlschlegel, J.A., Geschwind, D.H. (2009) Human-specific transcriptional regulation of CNS development genes by FOXP2. *Nature 462*, 213-217

Krause, J., Lalueza-Fox, C., Orlando, L., Enard, W., Green, R.E., Burbano, H.A., Hublin, J.J., Hänni, C., Fortea, J., de la Rasilla, M., Bertranpetit, J., Rosas, A., Pääbo, S. (2007) The derived FOXP2 variant of modern humans was shared with Neandertals. *Curr Biol. 17(21)*, 1908-12

Pollard, K.S. (2009) What make us human? *Scientific American 5/2009*, 32-37

Ramirez Rozzi, F.V., Bermudez de Castro, J.M. (2004) Surprisingly rapid growth in Neanderthals. *Nature 428*, 936-939

Schwartz, D.A., Howe, C.Q., Purves, D. (2003) The statistical structure of human speech sounds predicts musical universals. *J Neuroscience 23*, 7160-7168 (cited in Kenneally, C. (2008) *The First Word*. London, England: Penguin Books)

Seldon, H.L. (1981a) Structure of human auditory cortex. I. Cytoarchitectonics and dendritic distributions. *Brain Res 229*, 277-294

Seldon, H.L. (1981b) Structure of human auditory cortex. II. Axon distributions and morphological correlates of speech perception. *Brain Res 229*, 295-310

Seldon, H.L. (1982) Structure of human auditory cortex. III. Statistical analysis of dendritic trees. *Brain Res 249*, 211-221

Seldon, H.L. (1985) The anatomy of speech perception. Human auditory cortex. In A. Peters, E.G. Jones (Eds.) *Cerebral Cortex*, vol. 4 (pp. 273-327). New York, USA: Plenum Press.

Seldon, H.L. (2005) Does brain white matter growth expand the cortex like a balloon? Hypothesis and consequences. *Laterality 10(1)*, 81-95

Seldon, H.L. (2006) Cortical laminar thickness and column spacing in human temporal and inferior parietal lobes. Intra-individual anatomical relations. *Laterality 11(3)*, 226-250

Seldon, H.L. (2007) Extended neocortical maturation time encompasses speciation, fatty acid and lateralization theories of the evolution of schizophrenia and creativity. *Medical Hypotheses 69*, 1085-1089

Wittgenstein, L. (1953) *Philosophical Investigations*. Oxford, UK: Basil Blackwell.

Wittgenstein, L. (1958) *The Blue and Brown Books*. Oxford, UK: Basil Blackwell.

THE EVOLUTION OF SEGMENTATION AND SEQUENCING: EVIDENCE FROM HOMESIGN AND NICARAGUAN SIGN LANGUAGE

ANN SENGHAS

Department of Psychology, Barnard College of Columbia University
New York, NY, 10027, USA

ASLI ÖZYÜREK

Center for Language Studies, Radboud University Nijmegen,
& Max Planck Institute for Psycholinguistics, Nijmegen, 6525 XD, Netherlands

SUSAN GOLDIN-MEADOW

Departments of Psychology and Comparative Human Development,
University of Chicago, Chicago, IL, 60637, USA

Segmentation and combination is a fundamental and ubiquitous feature of modern human languages. Here we explore its development in newly emergent language systems. Previous work has shown that manner and path are segmented and sequenced in the early stages of Nicaraguan Sign Language (NSL) but, interestingly, not in the gestures produced by Spanish speakers in the same community; gesturers conflate manner and path into a single unit. To explore the missing step between gesturers' conflated expressions and signers' sequenced expressions, we examined the gestures of *homesigners*: deaf children not exposed to a sign language who develop their own gesture systems to communicate with hearing family members. Seven Turkish child homesigners were asked to describe animated motion events. Homesigners resembled Spanish-speaking gesturers in that they often produced conflated manner+path gestures. However, the homesigners produced these conflated gestures along with a segmented manner or path gesture and, in this sense, also resembled NSL signers. A reanalysis of the original Nicaraguan data uncovered this same transitional form, primarily in the earliest form of NSL. These findings point to an intermediate stage that may bridge the transition from conflated forms that have no segmentation to sequenced forms that are fully segmented.

1. Introduction

Information can, in principle, be organized in many ways, but certain patterns recur in language after language. One apparently universal organizing principle is the segmentation and sequencing of basic, categorical elements (Hockett,

279

1960, 1987). Where does this practice come from? Segmentation and sequencing is not the only way to bundle information – indeed, we use other ways of structuring information every day. For example, representations such as maps, paintings, and acted-out imitations of behaviors are structured highly iconically, that is, they derive their organization wholly from their referents. Patterns in such representations correspond, part-for-part, to patterns in the thing represented. Half of a city map represents half of the city, and the initial moment of acting out a behavior represents the initial moment of the behavior. In contrast, the sequenced patterns of language are not imitating the world it represents. There is no part of New York City that corresponds to the word "York."

In a series of studies, we have been tracing the steps that underlie the transformation from non-language to language. How does a system progress from unanalyzed, holistic representations to discrete, sequenced elements? The approach of much recent computational and experimental work has been to simulate the emergence of such features in a language (e.g., Christiansen & Kirby, 2003). This approach provides fruitful springboards for speculation about language evolution, but must be complemented by data from actual communities where new language systems have emerged *de novo*. Two types of such naturally emergent systems appear promising. These include *homesigns*, the gestural communication systems that develop in individual households that include a deaf member (Coppola & Newport, 2005; Goldin-Meadow, 2003) and *emergent sign languages*, which develop when such gestural systems are transmitted between individuals within a generation and across different generations (e.g., Nicaraguan Sign Language, Senghas et al, 2004; Al Sayyid Bedouin Sign Language, Sandler et al., 2005). These naturally developing systems provide unprecedented opportunities to track empirically the steps of human language emergence.

We begin by considering data from Nicaraguan Sign Language (NSL). In the late 1970s and early 1980s, rapidly expanding programs in special education brought together deaf children and adolescents in greater numbers than ever before (Kegl & Iwata, 1989; A. Senghas, 1995). Before that time, societal attitudes kept most deaf individuals at home, and the few schools and clinics available served small numbers of deaf youths for short periods, without continuing contact outside school hours (Polich, 1998; R.J. Senghas, 1997). Consequently, deaf Nicaraguan children had minimal contact with each other, and no contact with deaf individuals older than themselves. In this context, no sign language emerged, evidenced by the lack of language in today's adults over the age of 45.

Deaf enrollment in the new programs initially comprised approximately 50 students in 1977, growing to over 200 by 1981, and increasing throughout the 1980s (Polich, 2005). Although language instruction concentrated on teaching students to lip-read and to speak Spanish (with minimal success), the children spontaneously began to use gestures to communicate with each other. As they interacted socially on school buses, in the schoolyard, and later in their homes, students converged on a common vocabulary of signs and characteristic ways to express them – and a new language was born. The language has continued to develop and change as new waves of children enter the community each year and learn to sign from older peers. Today there are approximately 1000 signers of Nicaraguan Sign Language (NSL), ranging from 1 to 45 years of age.

This is not an unusual history for a sign language. Other languages have originated in a school context, and been passed from student to student ever since. What is special about the Nicaraguan case is that it has occurred recently enough that the originators of the language are still alive. Taken together with the generation that followed them, they provide a living historical record of a language as it develops through its earliest stages. For experimental purposes, it has been convenient to divide the community into age cohorts based on the year of arrival in the signing community. The first cohort includes those who arrived in the late-1970s and early-1980s; the second, those who arrived in the mid- to late-1980s; and the third, those who arrived since 1990. We can take advantage of this sequence of cohorts to explore the nature of the processes that shaped the language as it was passed from one cohort to the next.

2. Motion Event Expressions in an Emerging Sign Language

The description of motion events – such as the way a linguistic expression describes the event of an object rolling down an incline – offers a promising domain for detecting the segmentation and sequencing of basic elements. Perceptually, rolling is experienced as a holistic, unsegmented event that simultaneously includes rotation and linear displacement. However cross-linguistic work has shown that languages typically separate expressions of complex motion into elements that encode the manner and the path of motion, and combine these elements according to the rules of the particular language (Talmy, 1985). For example, English produces one word to express manner (*rolling*) and another to express path (*down*), and assembles them into the sequence *rolling down*. In an initial study (Senghas, Kita, & Özyürek, 2004), we examined whether NSL, over the course of its early development, represented motion in a holistic, iconic manner faithful to the physical motion, or with the discreteness and combinatorial structure typical of developed languages.

We asked ten signers from each of the three cohorts to describe a collection of motion events, such as a cat climbing up a drainpipe, or rolling down a hill. We also asked ten hearing Nicaraguans to describe the same events in Spanish, and observed their co-speech gestures. Each participant watched an animated video cartoon that included these events, and narrated its story to a peer. Deaf subjects signed their narratives. Hearing subjects spoke Spanish, and only their co-speech gestures were analyzed. The narratives were videotaped, and the expressions that described the motion events were analyzed with respect to how the different aspects of the motion were integrated. Specifically, we determined whether information about manner and path was (A) a conflated, simultaneous expression, with a single hand movement, or (B) a sequence of manner-only and path-only elements. Examples of these two types of expression are shown in Figure 1. Note that a single response could include both types.

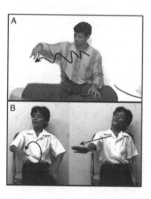

Figure 1. Examples of motion event expressions from participants' narratives. **(A)** Manner and path expressed simultaneously. In this example a Spanish-speaker describes a character rolling down a hill with a bowling ball in his belly; the gesture shown naturally accompanies his speech. Here manner (wiggling) and path (trajectory to the speaker's right) are expressed together in a single holistic movement. **(B)** Manner and path expressed sequentially. In this example a third-cohort signer describes the same rolling event in NSL. Here manner (circling) and path (trajectory to the signer's right) are expressed in two separate signs, assembled into a sequence (from Senghas, Kita, & Özyürek, 2004).

We found that Spanish-speakers always, and first-cohort signers often, produced manner and path together as a single holistic, conflated movement. In this way, their expressions matched the structure of events in the world. Second- and third-cohort signers preferred instead to separate events into sequences of pure, elemental manner-only and path-only signs (see Figure 2). These new expressions already include the segmentation and sequencing characteristic of language.

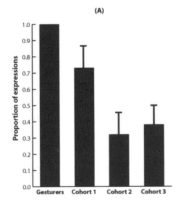 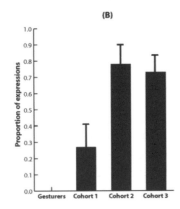

Figure 2. (**A**) The proportion of expressions with manner and path in which they are conflated within a single gesture or sign. Bars indicate mean proportions for individuals in each of the four groups; error bars indicate SE. All of the co-speech gestures and most of the first-cohort signers' expressions conflated manner and path. Second- and third-cohort signers produce relatively fewer expressions of this type. (**B**) The proportion of expressions with manner and path in which they are produced sequentially as manner-only and path-only elements. Such sequences are never observed in the co-speech gestures. First-cohort signers sometimes produce them; second- and third-cohort signers include them in most of their expressions (from Senghas, Kita, & Özyürek, 2004).

3. The Missing Step: Homesign

We have found what appears to be an abrupt transition from the holistic manner+path conflation produced by the Spanish speakers to the segmented manner–path sequence produced by the second- and third-cohort Nicaraguan signers. There is, however, a missing step. It is likely that prior to coming together for the first time in 1977, the Nicaraguan deaf children had been using gestures to communicate with the hearing people in their households – that is, that they were *homesigners*. Homesigners are deaf individuals whose hearing losses have prevented them from acquiring spoken language and who have not been exposed to sign language. Despite the absence of a model for language, homesigners use gesture to communicate and, importantly, their gestures display many of the properties found in natural language (Goldin-Meadow, 2003). Perhaps the homesigners who initially came together in Nicaragua had already begun the process of segmentation that has come to characterize NSL.

To explore this possibility, we studied seven homesigners in Turkey, ranging in age from 3;2 to 5;6 (years;months), who had learned neither a spoken nor a signed language. The homesigners were shown short animated video-clips of motion events highlighting manner and path (Özyürek et al. 2008) and were asked to describe what happened in each clip. During the narration, the children were given a picture of the initial scene of each event so that, if necessary, they could use pointing gestures to refer to the characters in the event. Children were videotaped at home every 1-3 months. The descriptions for this study came from six sessions for each child conducted over the course of a year. All of the children were congenitally deaf, with bilateral hearing losses (70-90 dB) and no other reported cognitive or physical abilities. The children's hearing parents had chosen to educate them using oral (i.e., non-signing) methods. At the time of our study, the children had received minimal or no speech therapy and, although they were able to produce an occasional Turkish word, did not combine words into sentences. In addition, none had been exposed to conventional sign language or had contact with another deaf child or adult.

We coded all of the gestures that the children used to convey motion information, and classified each gesture into one of three types: (i) manner gestures, e.g., the hand rotates in place; (ii) path gestures, e.g., the hand moves across space in a straight path; (iii) manner + path gestures, e.g., the hand rotates while moving across space in a straight path). (In many cases, the children enacted the manner or path of motion, or traced it on the picture that they were given; such responses were also coded as manner and/or path gestures.) Using criteria developed by Goldin-Meadow and Mylander (1984), we divided the gestures into sentence strings, and classified each sentence that contained information about both manner and path into one of three types: (i) Conflated only (containing only manner+path gestures); (ii) Sequenced only (containing both manner and path gestures and no conflated gestures; (iii) Mixed (containing a conflated gesture plus a manner and/or path gesture).

We found that almost half (49%, SD=18%) of the Turkish homesigners' expressions contained Conflated gestures alone, and relatively few (14%, SD=19%) contained Sequenced gestures alone. In this sense, the homesigners' pattern resembled the pattern found in the first cohort of Nicaraguan signers (cf. Figure 2). However, a sizeable percentage (34%, SD=15%) of the Turkish homesigners' gesture sentences were of the third type – a conflated gesture combined with one or more of its components. Thus, the homesigners appear to be in a transitional period with respect to segmentation – they were able to segment an action component out of the conflated motion, but they continued to produce the conflated form along with the segmented form (see Figure 3A).

Figure 3. Examples of Mixed gesture sentences. (A) A Turkish homesigner describes the jumping-up movement of a triangle figure. She first produces a gesture for the jumping manner, followed by a gesture conflating the jumping manner and the upward path; (B) A first-cohort NSL signer describes a character rolling down a hill with a bowling ball in his belly. He first produces a body gesture for the side-to-side waddling manner, followed by a gesture conflating both the waddling manner and the forward path.

If the gestures that the Turkish homesigners produce – their Mixed gesture expressions, in particular – reflect an early stage in the emergence of a language system, then we might expect to find Mixed expressions also in the first users of Nicaraguan Sign Language – that is, in first-cohort signers. To test this possibility, we reanalyzed the Nicaraguan data reported in Senghas et al. (2004), this time classifying the gesturers' and signers' expressions into the same three types – Conflated, Mixed, and Sequenced. The results are presented in Figure 4. The hearing Spanish-speakers relied predominantly on Conflated gestures to convey manner and path information. In contrast, the second- and third-cohort Nicaraguan signers relied predominantly on Sequenced gestures to convey manner and path information. The interesting group is the first cohort, who, as predicted, appears to be in a transitional state between the gesturers on one hand, and the more advanced signers on the other. The first cohort's preferred way of conveying manner and path information was to produce Mixed gesture expressions, that is, sentences containing a conflated manner + path gesture along with a segmented manner or path gesture (see Figure 3B).

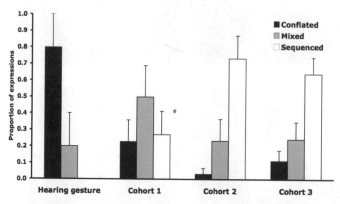

Figure 4. The proportion of expressions produced by the hearing Spanish speakers and the three cohorts of Nicaraguan signers, classified according to the segmentation of the manner and path components: Conflated (no segmentation), Mixed (partial segmentation), Sequenced (full segmentation). Error bars indicate SE.

4. Conclusion

By studying natural, present-day, emergent language systems, we have captured the earliest stages in the development of a fundamental property of human language: segmentation and sequencing. Learners presented with holistic, conflated gestures do not faithfully reproduce the gestures they see. Instead, they segment those holistic gestures into components and produce the components in a single gesture string. The roots of this process can be found even in a single-member communication system, that is, even in homesign. However, two types of transmission patterns are needed for the system to continue to develop and converge on a more mature, language-like form. The first is horizontal transmission across peers within a single generation. The effect of this process is evident in the differences seen between homesigners and first-generation NSL signers. Although the studies are not directly comparable, first-cohort signers seem to segment more than homesigners. The second type is vertical transmission from one generation to the next as new learners enter the community. The effect of this process is evident in the differences seen across the three cohorts of NSL signers. Here we see more and more segmentation in the later cohorts, with a sharp decrease in conflated forms.

It may be relevant that all of the learners in these studies were children, who, in the case of NSL, converged on a system with peers as children, and then passed the system on as adolescents and adults to new children. Evidently child learners have a natural inclination to analyze a linguistic signal as discrete and combinatorial, even if it is originally continuous and holistic. It is as if children see structure where there is none.

A segmented and sequenced format may not have evolved in the first language as quickly as it has in these modern emerging sign systems. We speculate that learners and languages have co-evolved to favor an analytical, combinatorial pattern. Once languages began to take on this form, children with a bias to analyze and segment would have a learning advantage, and these learning mechanisms would be favored over time. Once the bias was in place, any new languages to emerge would quickly take on a segmented, combinatorial structure, making it a universal linguistic feature. Today, when these learning mechanisms apply, segmented structures will dominate after a few short generations of transmission.

Acknowledgements

The research described in this paper was supported by grants from the National Institutes of Health (NIDCD) R01-DC05407 to A.S and R01-DC000491 to S.G.M. The content is the responsibility of the authors and does not necessarily reflect the views of the funding institutions. We would like to thank Burcu Sancer and Reyhan Furman for their help in collecting and coding the Turkish homesign data, Koc University, Istanbul, Turkey for logistic support, and the deaf children and families for their participation.

References

Christiansen, M & Kirby, S. (2003). Language evolution. Oxford University Press: Oxford

Coppola, M & Newport, E.L. (2005). Gramamtical subjects in homesign: Abstract linguistic structure in adult primary gesture systems without linguistic input , *Proceedings of the National Academy of Sciences*, 102 (52): 19249-19253

Goldin-Meadow, S. (2003). The resilience of language: What gesture creation in deaf children can tell us about how all children learn language. Psychology Press: NY

Goldin-Meadow, S., & Mylander, C. (1984). Gestural communication in deaf children: The effects and noneffects of parental input on early language development. *Monographs of the Society for Research in Child Development*, 49(3-4).

Hockett, C. F. (1960). The origin of speech. *Scientific American*, 203, 88-96.

Hockett, C. F. (1987). *Refurbishing our Foundations : Elementary Linguistics from an Advanced Point of View*. Philadelphia: J. Benjamins.

Kegl, J., & Iwata, G. (1989). Lenguaje de Signos Nicaragüense: A pidgin sheds light on the "creole?" ASL. In R. Carlson & S. DeLancey & S. Gilden & D. Payne & A. Saxena (Eds.), *Fourth Annual Meeting of the Pacific Linguistics Conference* (pp. 266-294). Eugene, OR.

Ozyurek, A., Kita, S., Allen, S., Brown, A., Furman, R., & Ishizuka, T. (2008). Development of cross-linguistic variation in speech and gesture: Motion events in English and Turkish. Developmental Psychology, 44 (4), 1040-1054.

Polich, L. (1998). *Social agency and deaf communities: A Nicaraguan case study*. Unpublished Ph.D. dissertation, University of Texas at Austin.

Polich, L. (2005). *The Emergence of the Deaf Community in Nicaragua: "With Sign Language You Can Learn So Much"*. Washington, DC: Gallaudet University Press.

Sandler, Wendy, Meir, Irit, Padden, Carol, and Aronoff, Mark. (2005). The Emergence of Grammar in a New Sign Language. *Proceedings of the National Academy of Sciences. Vol 102, No. 7*. 2661-2665.

Senghas, A. (1995). *Children's contribution to the birth of Nicaraguan Sign Language*. Unpublished Ph.D. dissertation, Massachusetts Institute of Technology, Cambridge, MA.

Senghas, A., Kita, S., & Özyürek, A. (2004). Children creating core properties of language: Evidence from an emerging Sign Language in Nicaragua. *Science*, 305(5691), 1779-1782.

Senghas, R. J. (1997). *An "unspeakable, unwriteable" language: Deaf identity, language & personhood among the first cohorts of Nicaraguan signers*. Unpublished Ph.D. dissertation, University of Rochester, Rochester, NY.

Talmy, L. (1985). Lexicalization patterns: Semantic structure in lexical forms. In T. Shopen (Ed.), *Grammatical Categories and the Lexicon,* Vol. III (pp. 57-149). Cambridge: Cambridge.

EXPLORING THE NATURE OF A SYSTEMATICITY BIAS: AN EXPERIMENTAL STUDY

ANDREW D. M. SMITH, BARBORA SKARABELA & MÓNICA TAMARIZ

Language Evolution and Computation Research Unit,
Linguistics and English Language,
The University of Edinburgh,
Dugald Stewart Building, 3 Charles Street, Edinburgh, EH8 9AD
{andrew;barbora;monica}@ling.ed.ac.uk

In this study, we tested the circumstances under which cultural evolution might lead to regularisation, even in the absence of an explicit learning bottleneck. We used an artificial language experiment to evaluate the degree of structure preservation and the extent of a bias for regularisation during learning, using languages which differed both in their initial levels of regularity and their frequency distributions. The differential reproduction of regular and irregular linguistic items, which may signal the existence of a systematicity bias, is apparent only in languages with skewed distributions: in uniformly distributed languages, reproduction fidelity is high in all cases. Regularisation does happen despite the lack of an explicit bottleneck, and is most significant in infrequent items from an otherwise highly regular language.

1. Introduction

One of the most striking features of language is its extensive use of conventionalised systematicity in representing and conveying meaning. Signal-meaning systematicity can be found at many levels of linguistic analysis, from simple morphological paradigms to complex syntactic and discourse constructions. The actual signal-meaning mappings in a particular language depend, as in any adaptive system, on the language's initial conditions (Gell-Mann, 1994), and the characteristics of its usage history, such as regularities which may have appeared by chance (Wray, 2002), the order in which items are learnt (Foss, 1968; Schyns & Rodet, 1997), or the way in which language use is negotiated (Galantucci, 2005). Researchers have proposed several different sources for linguistic systematicity, including cognitive biases (Pinker, 1999), the nature of the social and communicative context in which language is used (Wray & Grace, 2007), the frequency of the input (Bybee & Hopper, 2001), or a transmission bottleneck (Kirby, 2001).

A number of models, both computational (Brighton, Smith, & Kirby, 2005) and experimental (Kirby, Cornish, & Smith, 2008), have shown how a bottleneck on the transmission of linguistic items leads to the emergence of regularity and compositionality. It has, furthermore, been proposed as the mechanism which may have led to the emergence of compositional language from a holistic protolanguage (Kirby, 2002). It is not clear, however, that an explicit bottleneck is indeed a necessary and sufficient condition for regularity to arise, and so we present a study exploring the effects of frequency on the development of regularity in linguistic structure in the absence of an explicit transmission bottleneck.

We use an artificial language experiment with multiple languages which differ in the degree of regularity in their signal-meaning correspondences. Although artificial language systems have a long pedigree in psycholinguistic research, dating back to Esper (1925) and Wolfle (1933), it is only in recent years that they have begun to be used to investigate the adaptation and evolution of linguistic structure (Kirby et al., 2008; Beqa, Kirby, & Hurford, 2008; Tamariz & Smith, 2008). This study differs from existing artificial language experiments in that it studies the regularisation of internal linguistic structure, rather than the regularisation of inconsistent, unpredictable input (Hudson Kam & Newport, 2005; Wonnacott & Newport, 2005). We explicitly investigate the impact of the degree of regularity in the initial language (see also Tamariz & Smith, 2008) and the effects of different frequency distributions on language reproduction and regularisation, rather than using only languages with a uniform frequency distribution.

We focus on an exploration of how the *regularity of a language* and the *frequency distribution* of its items affect: (i) the fidelity with which the original form-meaning associations are reproduced; (ii) and the regularisation of irregular items. We predicted that languages would be reproduced better as their overall regularity increased; that within each language, regular items would be reproduced better than irregulars, and frequent items would be reproduced better than infrequents; and that if regularisation occurred, it would be most likely in infrequent items.

2. Method

Participants 44 monolingual English native speakers took part in the experiment, with four being excluded from the analysis (three due to software failure and one who failed to comply with the requirements of the study); each was paid £4.

Materials Participants were asked to learn pairings of pictures depicting familiar activities and nonsense words. Twelve different activities were chosen, using pictures designed to be culturally and linguistically neutral, and used by foreign language instructors; these pictures were then modified (by adding hair, clothing etc.) to produce two different versions: male and female[a]. Nonsense words were created according to English phonotactics, all containing three syllables (a bisyllabic root and a monosyllabic suffix); each language contained equal num-

---

[a]Original pictures are freely available at http://tell.fll.purdue.edu/JapanProj/ /FLClipart/; modified stimuli used in the experiment at http://www.ling.ed.ac.uk/ ~andrew/systematicity/gender_activity_stimuli.html.

bers of roots and suffixes with a variety of syllable structures (roots: VCV, VCCV, CVCV, CVCCV, CCVCV, CCVCCV; suffixes: CV; CVC). The experiment was developed using Psyscope X and run on laptops with Mac OS X.

Design Five types of experimental language were created, all sharing the same 24 meanings (12 activities x 2 genders), but having different words associated with these meanings. Two languages were created for each language type, differing in the forms of the roots and suffixes, but structurally identical. The language types differed in their level of regularity, or the degree to which there is a systematic correspondence between forms and their meanings. We measured regularity in signal-meaning correspondences along two dimensions: a root corresponding to the activity (e.g. swimming, drinking); and a suffix corresponding to the natural gender of the agent of the activity (male, female):

0% regular: The words for all twelve activities were compiled from 24 roots and 24 suffixes[b]. This language type is effectively fully holistic, with an independent phonological form for each meaning.

33% regular: Four activities had regular mappings (i.e. four roots and two suffixes for the eight meanings), while the other eight activities were compiled from 16 roots and 16 suffixes.

50% regular: Six activities had regular mappings, the other six were compiled from 12 roots and 12 suffixes.

67% regular: Eight activities had regular mappings, the other four were compiled from 8 roots and 8 suffixes.

100% regular: All twelve activities had regular mappings (i.e. twelve roots and two suffixes). This language type is fully compositional.

Each language was presented in two different distributions: with either a uniform distribution (all items were seen equally frequently) or a skewed distribution (half the items were seen nine times more frequently than the other half).

Procedure Participants were explicitly told that they would see pictures on the computer screen, with descriptions, and that they would subsequently be asked to remember which description went with which picture. Participants were seated in front of a computer screen in a quiet room on the university premises. Training consisted of exposure to the whole language via 240 exposures: at each exposure, the picture was presented first, followed 500ms later by a description below it (see

---

[b]Details of the forms in all the languages can be found at http://www.ling.ed.ac.uk/~andrew/systematicity/exptl_languages.html.

Fig. 1). In testing, individual pictures appeared on the screen, and participants were asked to type descriptions as they remembered. After testing, they completed a questionnaire and were debriefed on the aims of the experiment. Training and testing occurred over one self-paced session, which lasted on average 25 minutes.

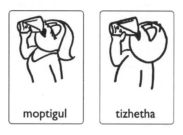

| moptigul | tizhetha |

Figure 1. Examples of two separate training exposures: each contains a picture of an activity paired with a nonsense word. Meanings are differentiated by the gender of the activity's agent. Words consist of a bisyllabic root (here: **mopti-, tizhe-**) and a monosyllabic suffix (here: **-gul, -tha**).

3. Results

3.1. *Reproduction Fidelity*

Figure 2 shows the reproduction fidelity of suffixes by initial language regularity. We ran a series of ANOVAs with regularity and frequency distribution of language as the independent variables, and found a significant effect of both variables on the reproduction fidelity of suffixes (frequency distribution: $F_{(1,38)} = 4.63, p = .04$; regularity: $F_{(4,35)} = 2.86, p = .04$), but a significant effect only of frequency distribution on the reproduction of roots (frequency distribution: $F_{(1,38)} = 10.29, p < .01$; regularity: $F_{(4,35)} = 0.50, p = .74$). Overall, suffixes are significantly better reproduced as the regularity of the language increases, and in uniformly distributed languages rather than in skewed languages. Roots are reproduced better in uniformly distributed languages, but equally well in languages with different levels of regularity. This latter finding is likely to be due to the nature of regularity in these artificial languages: if there is any regularity in the languages it tends to concern suffixes rather than roots, because a regular root occurs across only two lexical items, whereas a regular suffix can occur with up to 12 different roots.

Considering the frequency distributions separately, we found no significant effects on the reproduction fidelity of different forms in uniform languages: regular and irregular suffixes were reproduced equally well ($F_{(1,30)} = 1.13, p = .30$), as were regular and irregular roots ($F_{(1,30)} = 0.14, p = .71$). Regular forms

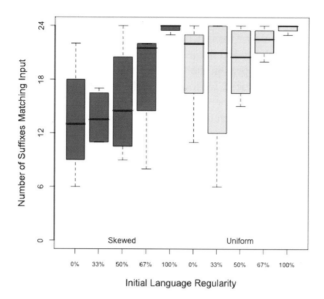

Figure 2.   Mean reproduction fidelity of suffixes, by frequency distribution and language regularity.

were reproduced equally well across the four language types[c] (suffixes: $F_{(3,12)} = 0.64, p = .61$; roots: $F_{(3,12)} = 1.05, p = .41$), as were irregular forms (suffixes: $F_{(3,12)} = 0.35, p = .79$; roots: $F_{(3,12)} = 0.33, p = .80$).

In skewed languages, however, regular suffixes were reproduced significantly better than irregular ones ($F_{(1,62)} = 10.12, p < .001$), and frequent suffixes were reproduced significantly better than infrequent ones ($F_{(1,62)} = 19.33, p < .001$). There is an additional interaction between item regularity and item frequency: the reproduction fidelity of infrequent irregulars is even lower than would be expected by combining the individual effects of regularity and frequency ($F_{(1,60)} = 4.53, p = .04$). The same is not true, however, for roots: although frequent roots are reproduced better than infrequent roots ($F_{(1,62)} = 35.86, p < .001$), regular and irregular roots are reproduced equally well ($F_{(1,62)} = 0.45, p = .51$).

3.2. Regularisation

In the cases in which reproduction is not faithful (such as the irregular infrequent items in the skewed languages), therefore, can we discern any trends towards reg-

---

[c]There are only four language types in these analyses because the 0% languages have no regular forms; likewise, 100% languages have no irregulars.

ularisation which might be regarded as a systematicity bias? Is there a tendency for participants to regularise forms which were originally irregular, and if so, what role do language regularity and frequency distributions play?

To examine what happens in the instances when originally irregular suffixes were not faithfully reproduced, we focused on the irregular items in the input languages. Regularisation was operationally defined as a change from an originally irregular suffix, which was therefore used on only one item in the input language, to a suffix which was used on multiple items in the output language to convey the *same* gender (i.e. either male or female). Zero suffixes were excluded, so deletion of the suffix across multiple items was not counted as regularisation in our analysis. The regularised suffix could therefore be either: (i) an originally regular suffix whose range has increased to encompass one or more irregular items; (ii) an originally irregular suffix whose range has increased to encompass one or more additional items; (iii) a novel suffix used on two or more items. According to these criteria, 8.75% of the originally irregular items were regularised (42 items in total: 9 originally regular suffixes; 20 originally irregular suffixes; 13 novel suffixes).

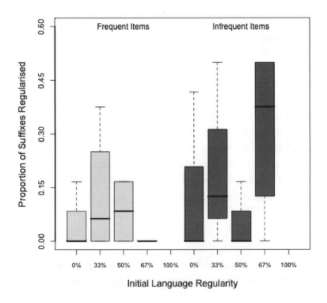

Figure 3. Regularisation of suffixes in languages with skewed frequency distributions, by item frequency and language regularity.

We ran a series of ANOVAs with language regularity and frequency distribution as the independent variables. While we predicted that regularisation would be more likely to take place in the skewed rather than the uniform languages, we did not find a significant difference between the two types of languages ($F_{(1,46)} = 0.91, p = .35$), nor did we find a significant trend towards regularisation with increasing language regularity ($F_{(3,44)} = 0.69, p = .56$). We further compared suffix regularisation in the languages with uniform frequency distributions, and found no significant difference between the process in languages with different degrees of regularity ($F_{(3,12)} = 1.14, p = .37$).

Figure 3 shows details of regularisation in the skewed languages. Although language regularity did not yield a significant effect overall ($F_{(3,28)} = 0.72, p = .55$), infrequent suffixes were marginally significantly more likely to undergo regularisation than frequent suffixes ($F_{(1,31)} = 2.91, p = .10$). Looking at this effect in more detail, we found that the difference in regularisation between frequent and infrequent irregulars is significant only in the language with the highest level of regularity[d] (67%, $F_{(1,6)} = 6.82, p = .04$). This is indicative of an interaction between language regularity and frequency, which may be obscured by the relatively low number of participants in this study.

4. Summary and Conclusion

The potential systematicity bias, which would be signalled by differences in reproduction fidelity between regular and irregular items, is more likely to be observed in languages with skewed frequency distributions rather than in languages where items occur with equal frequency, because uniform languages are better learnt. Regularisation is also affected by both frequency and the existing level of language regularity: although there is no difference between frequent and infrequent items from languages with relatively low levels of overall regularity, in languages with high regularity, infrequent irregulars are regularised while frequent regulars are reproduced more faithfully.

These results suggest that the skewed frequency distribution reveals the systematicity bias by acting as an *implicit* bottleneck, which makes it very difficult for language users to reproduce infrequent items accurately, and therefore leads to regularisation even in the absence of an explicit bottleneck. The meanings humans communicate about in social interactions are notably skewed in their frequency distribution — we talk about a few favourite things most of the time, and about many other things much less often. This study shows that such a distribution may have played a role in the evolution of language by promoting regularisation.

Acknowledgements

The authors acknowledge the support of ESRC Grant Award RES-062-23-1537.

---

[d]Note that regularisation cannot apply to fully regular (100%) languages.

References

Beqa, A., Kirby, S., & Hurford, J. R. (2008). Regular morphology as a cultural adaptation: Non-uniform frequency in an experimental iterated learning model. In A. D. M. Smith, K. Smith, & R. Ferrer i Cancho (Eds.), *The Evolution of Language (EVOLANG 7)* (pp. 401–402). World Scientific.

Brighton, H., Smith, K., & Kirby, S. (2005). Language as an evolutionary system. *Physics of Life Reviews, 2*(3), 177-226.

Bybee, J. L., & Hopper, P. J. (Eds.). (2001). *Frequency and the emergence of linguistic structure*. Amsterdam: John Benjamins.

Esper, E. A. (1925). *A technique for the experimental investigation of associative interference in artificial linguistic material*. Philadelphia: Linguistic Society of America.

Foss, D. J. (1968). Learning and discovery in acquisition of structured material – effects of number of items and their sequence. *Journal of Experimental Psychology, 77*(2), 341–344.

Galantucci, B. (2005). An experimental study of the emergence of human communication systems. *Cognitive Science, 29*, 737-767.

Gell-Mann, M. (1994). *The quark and the jaguar.* New York: Freeman.

Hudson Kam, C. L., & Newport, E. L. (2005). Regularizing unpredictable variation: the roles of adult and child learners in language formation and change. *Language Learning and Development, 1*(2), 151-195.

Kirby, S. (2001). Spontaneous evolution of linguistic structure: an iterated learning model of the emergence of regularity and irregularity. *IEEE Journal of Evolutionary Computation, 5(2)*, 102–110.

Kirby, S. (2002). Learning, bottlenecks and the evolution of recursive syntax. In E. Briscoe (Ed.), *Linguistic evolution through language acquisition: Formal and computational models* (pp. 173–203). Cambridge University Press.

Kirby, S., Cornish, H., & Smith, K. (2008). Cumulative cultural evolution in the lab: an experimental approach to the origins of structure in human language. *Proceedings of the National Academy of Sciences, 105*(31), 10681–10686.

Pinker, S. (1999). *Words and rules.* Weidenfeld & Nicolson.

Schyns, P. G., & Rodet, L. (1997). Categorization creates functional features. *Journal of Experimental Psychology: Learning, Memory and Cognition, 23*(3), 681–696.

Tamariz, M., & Smith, A. D. M. (2008). Regularity in mappings between signals and meanings. In A. D. M. Smith, K. Smith, & R. Ferrer i Cancho (Eds.), *The Evolution of Language (EVOLANG 7)* (pp. 315–322). World Scientific.

Wolfle, D. L. (1933). The relative stability of first and second syllables in an artificial language. *Language, 9*(4), 313-315.

Wonnacott, E., & Newport, E. L. (2005). Novelty and regularization: The effect of novel instances on rule formation. In A. Brugos, M. R. Clark-Cotton, & S. Ha (Eds.), *BUCLD29: Proceedings of the 29th Annual Boston Conference on Language Development*. Somerville, MA: Cascadilla Press.

Wray, A. (2002). *Formulaic language and the lexicon.* Cambridge: CUP.

Wray, A., & Grace, G. W. (2007). The consequences of talking to strangers: evolutionary corollaries of socio-cultural influences on linguistic form. *Lingua, 117*(3), 543-578.

OPEN-ENDED SEMANTICS CO-EVOLVING
WITH SPATIAL LANGUAGE

MICHAEL SPRANGER AND SIMON PAUW

Sony CSL Paris, 6 rue Amyot, 75005 Paris, France
spranger@csl.sony.fr

MARTIN LOETZSCH

VUB AI Lab, Vrije Universiteit Brussels, Pleinlaan 2, 1050 Brussels, Belgium

How can we explain the enormous amount of creativity and flexibility in spatial language use? In this paper we detail computational experiments that try to capture the essence of this puzzle. We hypothesize that flexible semantics which allow agents to conceptualize reality in many different ways are key to this issue. We will introduce our particular semantic modeling approach as well as the coupling of conceptual structures to the language system. We will justify the approach and show how these systems play together in the evolution of spatial language using humanoid robots.

1. Introduction

Linguists have long studied spatial language as an important foundation of communication in many languages of the world. Spatial utterances such as "the building left of the train station" are typically used to discriminate an object (sometimes referred to as *figure*) in a specific spatial scene. Such utterances can contain one or more *spatial terms* (e.g. *left*) (Carlson & Hill, 2009) as well as a marker or lexical item for a *reference object*, also called *trajector*, *landmark* or *ground* (in this case "train station")[a]. There are also other types of spatial utterances not involving an explicit reference object, for example "This ball here!". However, as already demonstrated by Steels and Loetzsch (2009) who made one of the first attempts on modeling spatial language with robots, talking about objects using spatial language inevitably involves some notion of perspective, hence the choice of a particular point of reference. As Levinson (2003) suggests, the study of spatial language is best framed using three distinctions: 1) *absolute* frames of reference that relate to fixed features of the environment, for instance, seaside/mountainside or gravity, 2) *intrinsic* frames of reference that are based on objects that have an

---

[a]There is quite some debate in linguistics as to how to define spatial language (Zlatev, 2007). Here we only consider utterances that involve spatial relational terms.

inherent orientation, e.g. humans have an inherent front, as in "the glass in front of you", and finally 3) *relative* frames of reference that allow to express spatial relations with respect to some object from the viewpoint of the observer, as in "left of the tree"[b]. Languages differ in which frames of reference they instantiate, e.g. the Mayan language Tzeltal features only an absolute frame of reference.

How language users choose a particular reference system to distinguish some object in the environment has been studied extensively in experimental psychology. It seems now clear that this choice depends not only on the saliency of the landmark (Carlson & Hill, 2009), but also on the prototypicality of the spatial position of the object, with respect to the category system and the particular frames of reference available to the speaker. Moreover, speakers align their choice of reference points during interactions (Pickering & Garrod, 2004).

The phenomena encountered in natural language make it clear that in order to study the evolution of spatial language, in particular the alignment of conceptualization and language strategies, we first need to answer the question how agents flexibly compose complex semantic structure, encode the semantic structure into syntactical structure and back, thus making themselves understood, and second we need learning operators that shape the particular way of how agents choose to express themselves in a given environment. Consequently, this paper first deals with our approach to representing semantic programs, called *Incremental Recruitment Language* (IRL), followed by an introduction to the system for producing and parsing utterances, called *Fluid Construction Grammar* (FCG). We then move on to present an experimental setup that tests the expressive power of the mechanisms for studying the evolution of spatial language. Lastly, we add learning operators to the system and explore how ambiguity arising in conceptualization can be resolved collaboratively by a community of agents, thereby highlighting how and why spatial language might have evolved.

This paper builds on extensive previous work. IRL has first been described in Steels (2000) and extended in Steels and Bleys (2005), Van Den Broeck (2008). FCG also has a long tradition of development in our lab (Steels & De Beule, 2006). Moreover this is not the first attempt to model spatial language. Steels and Loetzsch (2009) explained alignment of choice of perspective and Steels and Spranger (2009) highlighted exaptive mechanisms behind spatial language stemming from bodily meaning. However, the approach in this paper is unprecedented in terms of complexity of semantics, as well as integration of FCG, IRL and embodiment.

2. Flexible Representation of Conceptual Structure with IRL

What is the meaning of the utterance "the block to my left"? Presumably this utterance is an attempt to draw the attention of the hearer to some object in the

---

[b]Trees do not feature an inherent orientation, i.e. have no left side. It is thus the position of the observer in relation to the tree, that determines what is left of the tree.

Figure 1. IRL network representing the meaning of the utterance "the block to my left".

environment. In procedural semantics terms: the speaker wants the hearer to execute a program – a set of instructions that will lead him to identify the object in the environment that is the referent of the phrase. The steps that the hearer should follow are 1) search for objects in the environment that are blocks, i.e. filter the context of the interaction for things that belong to the class of blocks and than 2) filter for the blocks that are left of the speaker. This last operation can be split up even further into first put yourself in the position of the speaker and than filter for objects that are at the left side. In summary, the meaning of the utterance is in the particular combination of *cognitive operations* that are connected in a *network*.

Figure 1 shows a possible semantic structure for our example phrase. The network consists of nodes that represent cognitive operations, which are instantiations of cognitive mechanisms such as categorization, discrimination and so forth. This particular graph contains 1) the operation `filter-set-category` that filters a set using the category `block`, 2) the mechanism `geometric-transform` for changing perspective to the perspective of the `speaker` 3) the operation `filter-by-angular-category` that filters objects using the projective, angular category `left` and 4) `unique-element` as a check for uniqueness.

Each cognitive operation is characterized by a call pattern. For instance, `filter-set-category` has three slots (`filter-set-category ?target-set ?source-set ?category`) (marked by variables starting with ?) whic means that it can take three input/output arguments. Given a source set and a category, a target set will be computed, that contains items pertaining to the particular target category. Moreover, when a target set and a source set is passed, then `filter-set-category` tries to compute the category that can filter the source set and lead to the target set. Other combinations are also possible, if we only pass a source set, then all imaginable categories together with the target sets they produce from the source set are computed. How many such combinations are possible depends on the number of categories known to the agent. The categories, but also prototypes, as well as other semantic material that can be used in cognitive operations are called *semantic entities*.

We have already hinted at the linking of cognitive operations via variables. That is, the value computed by one cognitive operation can be input of another. Moreover, semantic entities can be explicitly represented in a network with *bind statements* that assign a value of a particular type to a variable. For exam-

ple, `(bind angular-spatial-category ?space-cat left)` introduces
the category left, so that it can be used by the `filter-by-angular-category-`
operation. When variables are explicitly bound, control flow in the network for
that particular variable is clear. But, it is extremely important to understand that in
all other cases it is not, mirroring the fact that natural language utterances in many
cases provide semantic material but leave the actual control flow unspecified or at
least under-specified. Whether the utterance "the block to my left' means 1) filter
by blocks, than 2) take the perspective of the speaker, and 3) search for left items,
or whether one should first search for items left of the speaker and for items in
that set, which are blocks, is ambiguous or at best irrelevant.

Next to the unspecified control flow, the system offers another dimension of
flexibility. Cognitive operations can be creatively combined into networks. When
speakers try to conceptualize a specific object in a specific scene they are trying to
construct networks that best discriminate the target object. Just as human speakers
try to conceptualize the world for spatial utterances by identifying good combinations of reference points, frames of reference and spatial categories, agents can
freely compose cognitive operations and search the space of possible networks for
good solutions, encodable by the particular conventionalized grammar. Trying to
interpret an utterance, agents are facing a search problem as well. An utterance
might only partially encode a network, which turns the process of understanding an utterance into a restoration of possibly intended meaning. For instance,
suppose you hear the phrase "left of the train station". In English this phrase is
ambiguous because it under-specifies how to precisely conceptualize the landmark
"train station", both intrinsic and relative frame of reference are possible. Which
interpretation of the two makes sense might be inferable from the context, nevertheless whichever choice one makes, one has filled in an operation that was not
explicitly coded in the utterance.

3. Encoding Conceptual Structure into Syntactic Structure using FCG

We now turn to FCG, the computational engine for verbalizing IRL networks.
FCG is specifically designed to support language evolution studies in a construction grammar approach. At the heart of the formalism are constructions, which are
bi-directional form-meaning mappings. Most importantly, FCG features mechanisms for tracking the usage patterns and the success of particular rules in the
inventory of agents. Constructions, as well as all other items known to agents,
be it its semantic entities, cognitive operations, or even IRL networks, are scored.
The score can be updated according to the success of particular items in communication and reflects how certain an agent is that the items lead to success.
Moreover, similarly to conceptualization, we understand the process of verbalizing conceptual structure as a a search process. Trying to produce an utterance
for an IRL network comprises searching for conventional lexical and grammatical
constructions that maximize communicative success.

Figure 2. Left: example scene consisting of yellow colored blocks, the target objects, as well as four possible frames of reference (two robots, one box and a marker on the wall). The box to the left is an allocentric reference point and can be used in relative and intrinsic frames of reference. The big barcode attached to the wall signifies a geocentric, absolute direction, similar to north on a compass. Right: world models extracted by each robot for this particular spatial setup (arrows – robots, blue rectangle – box, yellow circles – yellow objects, green line – major direction geocentric frame of reference).

FCG can produce phrases starting from IRL programs by adding words and syntactical structure on the form side. When producing, first lexical constructions are applied, mapping some of the conceptual substructure of an IRL network to words. Second, particular cognitive operators and variable links might be conveyed using grammatical markers, endings or word order. Successively syntactical structure is build, that partially encodes the structure of the IRL network. For instance, for the network in Figure 1, first lexical constructions map the categories `block` and `left` to words, followed by mapping the `get-speaker` operation onto the pronoun "me", followed by adding the marker indicating the role of "me" as landmark and so forth. In parsing the process is reversed. By successively applying constructions, conceptual structure is inferred from syntactical.

4. Experimental Setup

For our setup we equipped robots with mechanisms for composing semantic structure and for verbalizing, parsing and reconstructing such structure and released them into an office environment in which they roam around freely (see Figure 2). When they encounter each other, they play a *language game* (Steels, 2001) in which the task of one agent is to draw the attention of the interlocutor to an object in the environment. In order to understand the influence of the world onto the particular language system developed by agents in the course of consecutive interactions, we setup the world such that the scenes contain multiple target objects, which are indistinguishable in size, color and form. Consequently, the only difference between target objects is their spatial position. To understand speakers'

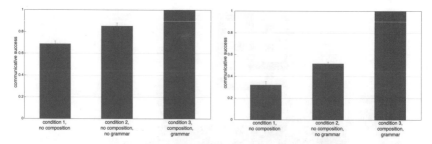

Figure 3. Experimental results I, three experimental conditions, two different sets of scenes. Left: scenes where robots are standing next to each other in all scenes, giving them a similar scene perception. Right: Difficult spatial setups with robots facing each other, looking at the scene from very different angles. Bars show the average communicative success over 20000 games. The benefit of allowing agents to compose complex meanings is evident. However, allowing for different frames of reference also leads to ambiguity, which can be resolved by introducing grammar.

choices for particular reference systems we spread wooden card boxes that are augmented by easily recognizable two dimensional barcodes in the environment. These objects function as reference objects besides the present robots. To run repeatable experiments, we recorded almost 400 scenes, differing in spatial layout. Some feature global reference systems, others only allocentric landmarks. Furthermore, the concrete spatial position of interlocutors is manipulated, such that in some scene agents face each other, whereas in others they have a very similar view on the scene.

5. Experimental Results I

We first investigated the general power of freely composing conceptual structure utilizing the reference systems, points and spatial categories. However, as in natural language, allowing for different ways of conceptualizing without clearly marking them leads to ambiguity. We thus also tested how language and, in particular, grammar can help disambiguate between the different ways of conceptualization by introducing a hand-crafted grammar, reminiscent of English distinctions between absolute, relative and intrinsic frames of reference. There are three experimental conditions: 1) agents are only given spatial categories like left together with cognitive operations to categorize the environment and ways to verbalize and parse categories; 2) agents are additionally given cognitive operations to conceptualize the context. Following the findings in human spatial language they are given different conceptualization strategies, i.e. absolute, intrinsic and relative frames of reference. Additionally agents are equipped with lexical items to denote the particular point of reference, but not the specific construal operation used. 3) agents are given a hand-crafted grammar, that marks complete conceptual semantic networks. Results (see Figure 3) show that indeed agents are better of using reference

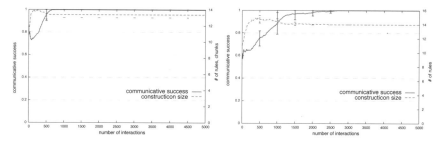

Figure 4. Experimental results II. These graphs show learning for population of 10 agents (10 runs avg) equipped with marker invention and alignment strategies. Left: simple spatial configurations. Right: difficult spatial setup (same as in Figure 3). Agents reach 100% communicative success in both cases (going from the middle bar in Figure 3 to the right bar). For simple spatial setups (left) convergence is much quicker, and the population invents two markers, since there are no global landmarks (one marker each for relative and intrinsic frames of reference). For the difficult spatial setups with global reference frames (right) convergence takes longer, mostly due to the interfering relative frames of reference and homonymy that is created when hearers reconstruct wrong networks.

points, but, even more so, should mark the particular conceptual operation used.

6. Experimental Results II

Given the promising results of scenario I, which suggest clear communicative advantages for grammar developments in spatial settings, we went on to explore how such a grammar can evolve. In this scenario, we equipped agents with grammar invention and adoption mechanisms, as well as alignment strategies. Moreover, agents were given lexical items to denote categories and reference points. However, in contrast to the third experimental condition of scenario I, they were not given a target grammar but only diagnostic and repair strategies, as well as an alignment mechanism called *lateral inhibition* (Steels, 1995).

Agents that are producing, diagnose ambiguity in their utterance when re-entering (Steels, 2003) – parsing utterance themselves before passing it to the hearer – that do not clearly distinguish between objects in the environment. In such cases agents can repair the shortfall by introducing marking constructions, which symbolize particular semantic structure, i.e. the cognitive conceptualization operation used (intrinsic, relative, absolute). In the process new markers are introduced in the population. Whenever an agent perceives a marker that he does not know, a diagnostic detecting missing items kicks in and triggers an adoption mechanism, that associates the marker with the meaning the hearer inferred. This can of course go wrong. As both agents at the end of the interaction have established the referent of the utterance the speaker produced, but they do not necessarily share the conceptual structure that discriminates it. The same problem occurs in human communication where the referent of the phrase "to the left of the train station" might accidentally coincide with conceptualizing the train station as a relative or intrinsic frame of reference. So agents face the problem of homonymy, which is resolved by laterally inhibiting competitors – punishing constructions that either express the same conceptual structure or use the same marker. However, agents align in spite of this problem (Figure 4), and incorrect mappings die out.

7. Conclusion

We have demonstrated how phenomena in human spatial language can be modeled using an open-ended, rich, conceptual system, that allows agents to flexibly combine cognitive operations into large conceptual structures and how such structures can be verbalized. Furthermore, we have presented a first attempt at in silico analysis of the subtle interplay of frames of reference choice and categorization strategy in spatial language. We, moreover, hypothesized learning mechanisms that can try to resolve naturally arising ambiguities in spatial language showing how and why agents evolve spatial language.

References

Carlson, L., & Hill, P. (2009). 7. Formulating Spatial Descriptions across Various Dialogue Contexts. *Spatial Language and Dialogue*, *1*(9), 89–104.

Levinson, S. (2003). *Space in language and cognition: Explorations in cognitive diversity*. Cambridge University Press.

Pickering, M., & Garrod, S. (2004). Toward a mechanistic psychology of dialogue. *Behavioral and Brain Sciences*, *27*(02), 169–190.

Steels, L. (1995). A self-organizing spatial vocabulary. *Artificial Life*, *2*(3).

Steels, L. (2000). The emergence of grammar in communicating autonomous robotic agents. In *Proceedings of ecai 2000* (pp. 764–769). IOS Publishing.

Steels, L. (2001). Language games for autonomous robots. *IEEE Intelligent Systems*, *16*(5), 16–22.

Steels, L. (2003). Language re-entrance and the Inner Voice. *Machine Consciousness*, 173.

Steels, L., & Bleys, J. (2005). Planning what to say: Second order semantics for fluid construction grammars. In *Proceedings caepia '05*.

Steels, L., & De Beule, J. (2006). Unify and merge in fluid construction grammar. In *Symbol grounding and beyond* (pp. 197–223). Berlin: Springer-Verlag.

Steels, L., & Loetzsch, M. (2009). Perspective alignment in spatial language. In *Spatial language and dialogue* (pp. 70–89). Oxford University Press.

Steels, L., & Spranger, M. (2009). How experience of the body shapes language about space. In *Proceedings of ijcai 2009*.

Van Den Broeck, W. (2008). Constraint-based compositional semantics. In *Proceedings of evolang 7* (pp. 338–345). Singapore: World Scientific Pub.

Zlatev, J. (2007). Spatial semantics. *The Oxford Handbook of Cognitive Linguistics*, 318.

LOST IN A LINGUISTIC JUNGLE: WHAT'S IN THE LANGUAGE FACULTY?

MAGGIE TALLERMAN

Linguistics Section, Newcastle University, Newcastle, NE1 7RU, UK

Evans & Levinson (2009) argue that language diversity is more robust than linguistic homogeneity, and also suggest that explanations for recurring patterns in language are not the product of an innate, evolved language faculty. I examine various kinds of evidence in favour of a specialized language faculty, and argue against the claim that typologically distinct languages must have distinct parsing systems.

1. Is linguistic diversity all that's out there?

In a provocative target article in *BBS*, Evans & Levinson (2009) set out the thesis that if we discount vital functional features required by all languages, such as negation, or the ability to form questions, then there are essentially no true language universals. They suggest that pervasive Chomskyan influence from within linguistics has given cognitive scientists the mistaken impression that there exists an uncontroversial set of language universals, and, furthermore, has resulted in an extreme nativist bias. By presenting examples of the massive superficial diversity of the world's languages, and by examining (and dismissing) some putative universals, they hope to demonstrate that:

> The fact is that it is a jungle out there: languages differ in fundamental ways – in their sound systems (even whether they have one), in their grammar, and in their semantics.

Thus, their views can be seen as an updated take on those of linguist/anthropologist Edward Sapir, a pioneering scholar of the indigenous languages of the Americas, who suggested in his 1921 book that language is "a human activity that varies without assignable limit", going on to argue that linguistic variation is essentially cultural, much like religion or art. More recently, another linguist with extensive experience of native American languages, Martin Joos, characterized (in fact, caricatured) the American structuralist position as believing that languages can "differ from each other without limit and in unpredictable ways" (1957: 96). Note, however, that these claims are not representative of the research agenda pursued by either linguist.

Evans & Levinson (E&L) acknowledge "biological underpinnings" for language (or at least, for certain restricted aspects of it), though they claim that "biology constrains and canalizes but does not dictate linguistic structures". Describing language as "a bio-cultural hybrid", E&L argue that linguistic diversity is the most remarkable biological property of language, NOT linguistic homogeneity. Their strongly-stated position is that there is no "fixed human language processing capacity", nothing corresponding to Universal Grammar (UG) – no "'language faculty' or innate specialization for language".

Certainly, there is far more linguistic diversity than was once suspected; in fact, this is what Sapir and Joos were both trying to put across: the more we study "exotic" languages, the more we learn about the extent of linguistic variation. This typological variation is indeed acknowledged in a recent paper by Chomsky (2005): "No one familiar with the field has any illusion today that the horizons of inquiry are even visible, let alone at hand, in any domain".

Thus, a simplistic nativist viewpoint is certainly not warranted, since it is a far from trivial matter to illustrate language universals at anything but a very abstract level. It is also surely true, as E&L argue, that grammatical relations such as "subject" cannot be defined such that we could pinpoint a set of properties common to any one grammatical relation in all languages – it may be convenient to use the same term to express the striking similarities across "subjects" in many unrelated languages, but there is no universally applicable definition (see, for instance, Dryer 1996).

However, E&L's claim that "it's a jungle out there" is certainly unjustified, since there exists other, compelling evidence for a language faculty, in the sense of specifically linguistic cognitive abilities. Here, I argue against two of E&L's major claims: first, the view that there is no innate specialization for language; and second, the view that languages with distinct typological characteristics cannot share a single, universal parsing system.

2. Is there a language faculty?

Despite the fact that E&L wish to take "explanations for the recurrent regularities in language out of the prewired mind", and also argue against the existence of "a fixed human language processing capacity", they do refer in positive terms to "our biological endowment for language". They also mention emergent signed languages, apparently in support of the latter notion – and surely, if anything argues for a language faculty it must be languages which arise *de novo* in deaf communities. However, E&L note that one such language, Al-Sayyid Bedouin Sign Language (ABSL), exhibits no duality of patterning, thus indicating, in E&L's view, that even this supposedly fundamental design feature of language is not universal. Aronoff et al. (2008) indeed report that ABSL, which first emerged about 70 years ago, lacks phonological contrasts. Crucially, and unlike in established signed languages, there are no minimal pairs in the ABSL lexicon (words like English *see* and *bee* which differ by just one meaningless contrastive element). However, Aronoff et al. also show that ABSL has all the remaining features we'd expect of a language: distinct word classes, morphology (in the form of compounding), a regular syntax with constituent structure, standardized word order, and embedding, including subordination. They argue that phonological contrasts only arise once a critical number of signs is reached; thus, in an emergent language, and in language evolution, duality of patterning might actually be the last property to appear. Far from supporting E&L's views about the linguistic jungle, emergent signed languages show just how a regular language can be built *ab initio*.

In fact, excellent evidence supoprts the idea of a language faculty, and also shows that natural languages don't vary without limit. Smith & Tsimpli (1995) outline work with the linguistic savant 'Christopher', who has autism, but also an usually developed facility with language learning. Christopher was well able to learn novel natural languages, but performed poorly on regular, but linguistically impossible aspects of an invented language, Epun. By contrast, cognitively 'normal' controls learned some of the impossible aspects easily. The authors had predicted that the controls would be able to compensate for the inability of their language faculty to cope with impossible grammar by using their 'general intelligence' and principles of inductive learning. Christopher's cognitive impairment, however, precluded the use of such 'central' strategies.

The really interesting differences between Christopher and the controls emerged over regular, structure-dependent but linguistically impossible constructions. First, negation in Epun involves a switch from SV to VS word order, but without the addition of any negative morpheme. Second, the past tense of transitive verbs requires the object to move to clause-initial position, giving OSV order in affirmative clauses and OVS order in negative clauses. All these patterns are consistent, but linguistically anomalous – natural languages just don't work this way. The control group mastered both constructions with ease, apparently resorting to non-linguistic cognitive strategies of induction at once. Christopher, however, had considerable and persistent difficulties with these impossible constructions, and never did learn them successfully, in stark contrast to his usual rapid acquisition of the complex grammatical rules of natural languages. So, though his general cognition is severely impaired, Christopher's linguistic faculty is intact, and 'recognizes' linguistic impossibility. These results emphatically challenge E&L's claim that "Language diversity is characterized not by sharp boundaries between possible and impossible languages".

Moreover, the fact that Christopher must rely on a purely linguistic faculty strongly supports the notion of a specialized linguistic module, some form of UG. E&L suggest that some kind of language faculty may account for systems that are clearly uniquely human (i.e. not shared by other primates), such as vocal learning, but that "Whether the higher, more abstract aspects of language reside in language-specific abilities, however, remains quite unclear". Given the contrast between Christopher and the controls in learning linguistically impossible constructions in Epun, such a stance is hard to maintain.

3. Is there a single parsing system?

One of E&L's main contentions concerns "the claimed universality of constituency". Discussing so-called non-configurational languages (NCLs) such as Latin, and many Australian languages, which allow free word order, E&L claim that "many languages do not have syntactic constituent structure". In fact, in such languages, "order and constituency are playing no signalling role for the hearer – they cannot therefore play a role in the parsing". E&L further claim that NCLs are parsed radically differently from, say, English: "the parsing system for English can't be remotely like the one for [NCLs]". But E&L present no experimental evidence in support of this astonishing claim.

Since the linguistic parsing system is surely under genetic control, it seems more likely that both non-configurational and configurational languages share a single parsing system. In both language types, the parsing system needs to discover contractual relationships between words and phrases, however this is expressed. In languages with rich verbal agreement or extensive case-marking, the elements of a noun phrase may (but need not) be discontinuous. The Australian language Wambaya, as Nordlinger (2006) notes, has "all the classic hallmarks of non-configurationality". In (1), the underscored items form a discontinuous subject, as indicated by the shared ergative case marking:

(1) <u>Nganki</u>   *ngiy-a*   lurrgbanyi   <u>wardangarringa-ni</u>   alaji
    this.ERG 3SF-PAST grab   moon-ERG   boy
    "The moon grabbed (her) child."   (1 – 3 are from Nordlinger 2006)

First, it is untrue that order and constituency play no role in such languages; in fact, ordering constraints of various kinds are common in NCLs; and the literature offers various tests for constituency. Both Wambaya and Warlpiri (another classic example of an NCL) display one strict ordering requirement (Nordlinger 2006, Hale 1973): the auxiliary must be in second position in its clause, i.e. either second word, as in (1) or second CONSTITUENT, as in (2) (auxiliaries italicized). (Note that a subordinate clause may precede the main clause, and it too counts as a constituent for auxiliary placement.)

(2) Naniyawulu   nagawulu   baraj-bulu   *wurlu-n*
     that.DUAL.NOM   female.DUAL.NOM   old.person-DUAL.(NOM)   3.DUAL-PROG
     duwa.
     get.up
     "Those two old women are getting up."   (Wambaya)

Crucially, the auxiliary cannot be, say, the third word in a four-word noun phrase; only a sequence of words which forms a CONSTITUENT can precede the auxiliary (see also Austin & Bresnan 1996: 218). Here, then, is concrete evidence for the reality of constituents in NCLs.

A further example from Wambaya is that a relative clause must be immediately preceded by the head noun, i.e. no discontinuity is allowed here. Nordlinger (2006) comments "Such ordering constraints provide strong evidence that the relative clause in these constructions forms a syntactic constituent with the head noun that it modifies". Moreover, in the most common type of relative clause in Wambaya, the auxiliary of the relative clause (in italics) must immediately follow the head noun (underlined):

(3) Ilinga gin-a   <u>galyurringi</u> *gi-n*   bardbi.
     hear   3SG.M.TRANS.SU-PAST water   3SG.INTRANS.SU-PROG run
     "He heard the water which was running."

Nordlinger points out that this shows the head noun to be a member of the subordinate clause (since an auxiliary is in second position in its clause), demonstrating that these elements "form a single syntactic constituent".

Tellingly, discontinuous noun phrases in NCLs are not necessarily identical in FUNCTION to continuous NPs, which means that constituency must be playing some role in the parsing. In Warlpiri, the following contrast occurs (Austin & Bresnan 1996: 235):

(4) <u>Kurdu-jarra-rlu</u> ka-pala   maliki   wajili-pinyi   <u>wita-jarra-rlu</u>.
child-DUAL-ERG PRES-3DU.SU dog.ABS chase-NONPAST small-DUAL-ERG
a) "Two small children are chasing the dog." OR
b) "Two children are chasing the dog and they are small."

(5) <u>Kurdu wita-jarra-rlu</u>   ka-pala   maliki   wajili-pinyi
child   small-DUAL-ERG PRES-3DU.SU dog.ABS   chase-NONPAST
"Two small children are chasing the dog."

Discontinuous NPs have either of the meanings shown in (4), whereas continuous NPs only display the 'merged' meaning shown in (5).

Finally, Austin & Bresnan (1996: 218) note that in Warlpiri, case markers may be omitted on all but the final word(s) of a continuous NP, as in (5), where *kurdu* 'child' is not case-marked, but case-markers cannot be omitted in discontinuous NPs, as in (4). They explicitly present this as a test for NP constituency. It seems evident, then, that both ordering constraints and clearly demarcated constituents occur in NCLs, contra E&L.

Second, there is clear evidence of both subcategorization/selectional restrictions and embedding in NCLs. It has often been assumed rather glibly that there is no clausal embedding in Australian languages, and E&L also argue against the universality of "recursion" (in the sense of embedding), citing the notorious case of Pirahv (Nevins et al. 2009 provide extensive reanalysis of data purported to show no embedding; Everett 2009 responds). Note, though, that Aronoff et al. (2008) report the presence of clausal subordination even in the first generation of ABSL speakers. For Wambaya, Nordlinger (2006) shows that on careful analysis, evidence for embedding does exist: an embedded clause commonly functions as the argument of a main clause verb of speech or perception, as with *ilinga* in (6) – a standard indication of subordination:

(6) Guyala ng-udi   *ilinga*   [injani g-a   yarru].
NEG   1SG.TRANS.SU-IRR.PRES remember where 3SG.INTRANS.SU-PAST go
"I can't remember where he went."

Incidentally, another ordering constraint emerges here too: the subordinate clause in this function must follow the main clause, whereas in other functions, the ordering is free.

Third, E&L would presumably predict that discontinuous constituents (clear hallmarks of non-configurationality) never occur in constituent structure languages – since their parsing systems should not be able to deal with these. But parsing in languages like English is perfectly able to cope with discontinuous constituents too, as in *A new discovery* was made *which changed the course of history,* or *Which country* do you think she comes *from* __ ?, where the dependency even occurs across a clause boundary. Recall, in fact, that relative clauses in Wambaya must immediately follow the head noun – a closer intregation than in the above example from English!

In sum, there is little justification for the claim that different parsing systems exist for different languages, a claim which, if true, would radically change the object of enquiry for evolutionary linguistics. If we believe that no species-specific language processor exists, it is hard to explain why only human primates can learn a natural language grammar. More probably, humans share a single parsing system, and perhaps languages themselves have evolved to fit the requirements of this system (Christiansen & Chater 2008).

4. A rapprochement? Bio-linguistic perspective vs. bio-cultural hybrid

Finally, it is worth noting that Chomsky's recent ideas on the evolution of the language faculty are in some ways strikingly similar to E&L's own position. For instance, Chomsky (2005: 6) suggests that three factors are at work in the ontogenetic development of language: the genetic endowment, experience, and "principles not specific to the faculty of language". These last include:

> (a) principles of data analysis that might be used in language acquisition and other domains; (b) principles of structural architecture and developmental constraints that enter into canalization, organic form, and action over a wide range, including principles of efficient computation, which would be expected to be of particular significance for computational systems such as language. It is the second of these subcategories that should be of particular significance in determining the nature of attainable languages.

Chomsky further notes that it is "quite reasonable to seek principled explanation in terms that may apply well beyond language, as well as related properties in other systems" and that moreover "we need no longer assume that the means of generating structured expressions are highly articulated and specific to language" (2005: 9). This seems to sit very well with E&L's position that the brain mechanisms needed for language are exaptations of earlier cognitive adaptations, and that language exploits "pre-existing brain machinery".

References

Aronoff M., Meir, I., Padden, C., & Sandler, W. (2008) The roots of linguistic organization in a new language. *Interaction Studies, 9*, 133–153.

Austin, P. & Bresnan, J. (1996) Non-configurationality in Australian Aboriginal languages. *Natural Language and Linguistic Theory, 14*, 215–268.

Chomsky, N. (2005). Three factors in language design. *Linguistic Inquiry, 36*, 1–22.

Christiansen, M. H. & Chater, N. (2008). Language as shaped by the brain. *Behavioral and Brain Sciences, 31*, 489–558.

Dryer, M. (1996). *Grammatical relations in Ktunaxa (Kutenai)*. Winnipeg, Manitoba: Voices of Rupert's Land.

Evans, N. & Levinson, S. (2009). The myth of language universals: Language diversity and its importance for cognitive science. *Behavioral and Brain Sciences, 32*(5).

Everett, D. (2009). Pirahv culture and grammar: A response to some criticisms. *Language, 85*, 405–442.

Hale, K. (1973). Person marking in Walbiri. In S. R. Anderson & P. Kiparsky (Eds.), *A Festschrift for Morris Halle* (pp. 308–344). New York: Holt, Rinehart, & Winston.

Joos, M. (Ed.) (1957). *Readings in linguistics. The development of descriptive linguistics in America since 1925*. New York: American Council of Learned Societies.

Nevins, A., Pesetsky, D., & Rodrigues, C. (2009). Pirahv exceptionality: A reassessment. *Language, 85*, 355–404.

Nordlinger, R. (2006). Spearing the emu drinking: Subordination and the adjoined relative clause in Wambaya. *Australian Journal of Linguistics, 26*, 5–29.

Sapir, E. (1921). *Language: An introduction to the study of speech*. New York: Harcourt, Brace.

Smith, N. V. & Tsimpli, I.-M. (1995). *The mind of a savant: Language learning and modularity*. Oxford: Basil Blackwell.

THE ROLE OF PRACTICE AND LITERACY IN THE EVOLUTION OF LINGUISTIC STRUCTURE

MÓNICA TAMARIZ, J. ERIN BROWN & KEELIN M. MURRAY

*Language Evolution and Computation, PPLS, The University of Edinburgh,
3 Charles Street, Edinburgh EH8 9AD, UK.
monica@ling.ed.ac.uk; erin@ling.ed.ac.uk; k.m.murray-3@sms.ed.ac.uk.*

Recent iterated language learning studies have shown that artificial languages evolve over the generations towards regularity. This trend has been explained as a reflection of the learners' biases. We test whether this learning bias for regularity is affected by culturally acquired knowledge, specifically by familiarity and literacy. The results of non-iterated learning experiments with miniature artificial musical and spoken languages suggest that familiarity helps us learn and reproduce the signals of a language, but literacy is required for regularities to be faithfully replicated. This in turn indicates that, by modifying human learning biases, literacy may play a role in the evolution of linguistic structure.

1. Introduction

Throughout the history of our species, language has been transmitted between generations by observation of the linguistic behaviour of conspecifics and subsequent practice of the skills learned during language use. Only structures that can be transmitted in this way (those that go through the "transmission bottleneck") exist in any language (Kirby & Hurford, 2002). Linguistic structure reflects the conditions where language is used and transmitted. Structure may thus emerge from individual processes such as our ability to establish relationships between symbolic units (Deacon 1997) or from pressures derived from social communication (Schoenemann, 1999) and the cultural transmission of language (Kirby & Hurford, 2002). One suggested source of linguistic structure related to both use and transmission is literacy, a powerful cultural institution that touches on all aspects of language. Literacy enhances phonological (Ehri, 1985) and morphological (Nunes et al. 2006) awareness and seems to be necessary for the segmentation of utterances into words (Olson, 1996; Ramachandra & Karanth, 2007), for grammaticality judgments related to syntax (de Villiers & de Villiers, 1972) as well as for the ability to analyze linguistic structure separately from semantic content (Karanth & Sutchira, 1983). This paper is concerned with the idea that cultural institutions like teaching and literacy may have modified the transmission bottleneck of

313

language, allowed different kinds of linguistic structures to exist and thus influenced the course of language evolution.

Recent experimental approaches to cultural evolution (e.g. Kirby, Cornish & Smith, 2008; Kalish, Griffiths & Lewandowsky, 2007) show how culturally learned and transmitted information comes to reflect the inductive biases of the learners. The biases at work in the above-mentioned studies include a preference for linear functions and a preference for regular mappings between signals and meanings in artificial miniature languages. In the case of the languages, the fact that the products of repeated transmission share some of the characteristics of language indicate that the evolving systems have successfully adapted to the learners' expectation of what a language looks like. This expectation may be influenced by innate and culturally acquired biases. The present study explores the role of culturally acquired knowledge on individual learning of language structure. Specifically, we look at the effect of literacy and of extensive experience of language on how the *structure* of artificial miniature language is learned and reproduced. We hypothesize that bias for regular mappings observed in recent studies (e.g. Tamariz & Smith, 2008; Kirby, Cornish & Smith, 2008) is enhanced by literacy as well as by familiarity with language forms and functions.

2. A musical artificial language experiment

In our investigation we turned to musical literacy as a proxy for orthographic literacy, since finding two groups of participants matched in all aspects except literacy proved impossible. Participants were shown artificial miniature musical (or spoken) systems consisting of mappings between tunes (or pseudo-words) and drawings and subsequently tested how well they had learned the systems. We manipulated two independent variables: participant literacy and level of regularity of the input languages.

2.1. Participants

85 undergraduate students were recruited through the university employment website. They fell into one of four categories: 1. Musician participants who had studied music at the University level beyond year one, could read musical notation and play an instrument proficiently and were currently practicing (the mean length of practice was 15.2 years). 2. Illiterate musicians who were required to play an instrument and practice regularly, but to have had no instruction in musical notation. This condition allows us to isolate the effects of literacy from those of extensive practice and familiarity with music. 3. Non-

musicians, who were required to have no musical background. 4. A fourth group of participants with no musical requirements was assigned to the Spoken language condition. Groups 1 and 4 were literate in their respective artificial languages, but, while spoken language usually has referential meaning, music usually has not. Comparing these two conditions may tell us something about the effect of habit of referentially linking the signals in the (musical or spoken) language with meaning

2.2. Materials

Three musical and three spoken languages each comprising 27 meaning-signal pairs were used in the experiment. The meanings used all languages 27 were visually presented figures (Tamariz & Smith, 2008) including all possible combinations of three shapes (square, circle, hexagon), three colours (red, blue, yellow) and inserts (star, dot, cross).
The musical signals were constructed by combining two-note intervals. The nine intervals used were perceptually distinct and positioned within the human voice range. All intervals had middle C (*C4*, 262 Hz) as the first note, followed by one of nine other notes (see Fig. 1).

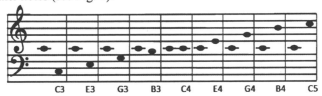

Figure 1. The nine signal units used to construct the signals for the musical languages. All two-note intervals begin with C4.

Each note in the interval was played as a pure tone for 330 ms and there were 150 ms of silence between them. Signals were constructed by concatenating three intervals, with 550 ms of silence between intervals. The spoken signals were the following nine consonant-vowel syllables: pe, mu, lo, tu, na, di, be, ga, ki.

Three languages (mappings of the above signals and meanings) were constructed. In the fully compositional language *L3*, color is regularly encoded in the first musical interval, shape in the second and insert in the third (e.g. figures of the same colour start with the same interval, and figures with the same insert have the same final interval). The partially compositional language *L2* generally follows the same pattern, but has some exceptions or irregularities in each meaning dimension. Random language *L1* contains no regular mappings. All materials were presented via a *Psyscope* script run on an Apple Macbook.

Participants were only exposed to one half of the signal-meaning items in the relevant language (L1, L2 or L3), as a 50% transmission bottleneck was in place. (They were, however, tested on all 27 meanings.)

2.3. Data analysis

We analyzed the fidelity of reproduction of the signals and the fidelity of reproduction of the compositional structure in the output languages. The *reproduction of the signals* was the number of times that a segment in the input language was reproduced exactly, in the same position for the same signal, in the output language. (Note that only signals in the items that were seen (those left after applying the bottleneck) were counted.) The *reproduction of the compositional structure* of the input language in the output language was quantified using *RegMap* (Tamariz, *in press*; Cornish, Tamariz & Kirby, *in press*), an information-theoretical tool designed to quantify the regularity of the mappings between two domains. The compositional patterns in the languages were quantified with partial *RegMap*. Partial *RegMap* is calculated for each meaning component-signal component pair (e.g. for colour and initial segment). The two conditional entropies $H(S|M)$ and $H(M|S)$ (Eqn. 1) of the cooccurrence frequency matrix between each meaning component variant M (e.g. red, blue, yellow) and signal component variant S (e.g. *be, ga, ki*) in a language are obtained. These are used in equations 2 and 3 to obtain *RegMap(S|M)* and *RegMap(M|S)*, which are combined in equation 4 to yield the corresponding partial *RegMap*. A partial *RegMap* value measures the confidence that a meaning component is reliably and unambiguously associated with a signal component, given a learner's experience of a language (reflected in the cooccurrence frequency matrix).

$$(1)\ H(X \mid Y) = -\sum_x \sum_y p(y)p(x \mid y)\log_2(p(x \mid y))$$

$$(2)\ RegMap(S \mid M) = 1 - \frac{H(S \mid M)}{\log(n_s)}$$

$$(3)\ RegMap(M \mid S) = 1 - \frac{H(M \mid S)}{\log(n_m)};$$

$$(4)\ RegMap(S,M) = \sqrt{RegMap(S \mid M) \times RegMap(M \mid S)}$$

Reproduction of the compositional structure of a language by a participant is the correlation (Pearson's r) between the partial *RegMap* values of the participant's input and output languages. This measure captures reproduction of the compositional structure independently of reproduction of the signal elements. For example, if the output of a participant exposed to language L3 maps colour to the first segment, shape to the second and insert to the third, the correlation will be high even if the actual segments he or she produces are different from those in the input language.

2.4. Procedure

Experiments were conducted individually and took approximately 30 to 45 minutes. 85 participants were run in total. They were told they would learn a language before they underwent three *training* phases and one testing phase, with breaks between phases. Each training exposure consisted of visual presentation of a meaning and, 50 msec later, auditory presentation of the corresponding musical or spoken signal. The signal was played through headphones three times, leaving silence (6 seconds for musical languages, 4.5 sec for spoken language) after each signal where participants were instructed to repeat it. During the *testing* phase, meanings were visually presented one at a time and the participants had to hum or say the corresponding signals. Participants' productions were recorded and later analyzed using Adobe Audition 1.5, which assigned the frequency of each note to the appropriate semitone. This analysis was checked by the experimenters.

2.5. Results and discussion

The levels of reproduction of the signals (Fig. 2a) reflect the degree to which participants learned and faithfully reproduced the signal segments and their positions during training; reproduction of the compositional structure (Fig. 2b) reflects the degree to which participants learned and faithfully reproduced the associations between signal segment positions and features of the meanings.

A two-way ANOVA of language (L1, L2, L3) and condition (non-musician, illiterate musician, musician, spoken) was carried out to assess the impact of condition and language on reproduction of signals and reproduction of structure. Results revealed significant effects of language ($p<0.001$ for signal reproduction; $p<0.01$ for structure reproduction), of condition ($p<0.001$ for both signal and structure reproduction) and a significant interaction for signal reproduction ($p<0.05$) but not for structure reproduction ($p=0.14$).

Further ANOVAs were then applied to pairs of conditions to obtain a more detailed picture. Comparing musicians with non-musicians reveals a strong effect of literacy and practice on the capacity to faithfully reproduce both the signals (effect of condition: $p=0.001$; effect of language: $p<0.01$; interaction $p<0.01$) and the compositional structure (effect of condition: $p<0.001$; non significant effect of language: $p=0.36$). This indicates that musicians were better able than non-musicians to remember and produce signals and structure; performance overall improved as the degree of structure of the input languages increased; and, when reproducing the signals, musicians' advantage increases in the more structured languages. On the other hand, the compositional structure of the three languages was reproduced to similar degrees of accuracy.

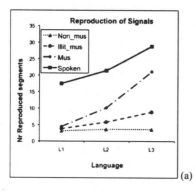 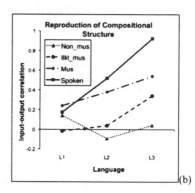

(a) (b)

Figure 2. Mean values of the reproduction of the signals and of the compositional structure of the input languages in the three languages and the four conditions. (a) Number of segments in participants' output languages that exactly matched the corresponding segment (in the same position) in their respective input languages. The theoretical maximum is 42, as we only take into account the 14 words participants were exposed to – remember a 50% bottleneck was in place during training. (b) Correlation (Pearson's r) of the nine partial *RegMaps* (which define the compositional structure of the language) in the input and output languages.

To separate the effects of practice from those of literacy, we compare the performance of illiterate musicians (who have practice but not literacy) with non-musicians (who have neither) and with musicians (who have both). Comparing illiterate musicians with musicians shows an effect of literacy both on reproduction of signals (effect of condition: $p<0.01$; effect of language: $p<0.01$; no significant interaction) and reproduction of compositional structure (effect of condition: $p<0.05$; effect of language: $p=0.05$; no significant interaction). Comparing illiterate musicians with non-musicians reveals an effect of practice on reproduction of signals (effect of condition: $p<0.05$; effect of language: $p=0.21$; no significant interaction) but not on reproduction of the compositional structure (effect of condition: $p=0.38$; effect of language: $p=0.18$). This indicates that practice and familiarity with music provides an advantage for reproducing the musical tunes, but not for noticing and reproducing the compositional structure of the system. For this task, literacy is required.

Comparing the results from the two language modalities (musical versus spoken) revealed an effect of modality of language on reproduction of signals (effect of modality p<0.05; effect of level of language structure: p<0.05; no significant interaction), indicating that the spoken signals were much better learned and reproduced than the musical tunes, even in the absence of structure (see results for Language 1 in Fig. 2). This may be due to a mismatch between the conditions: while musicians are proficient in reading and playing music, they do not produce musical vocal output as frequently as the students produce spoken vocal output. As for the ability to reproduce the compositional structure of the language, very interestingly, modality had no impact (p=0.20), but the level of language structure did (p<0.01). This suggests that musicians learned the musical languages' structure as competently as undergraduates learned the spoken language's structure, and they did so despite the fact that while spoken signals usually map to referential meaning, musical signals usually do not. This result strongly supports out hypothesis that literacy promotes learning and reproduction of compositional structure.

2.6. *Conclusion*

Adding to the literature on the effects of literacy on language processing, our results show how literacy impacts on learning and reproduction not only of the signals, but of the *compositional structure* of a miniature artificial language. While all the participants in our experiment were able to name the objects in their artificial languages, only the signals produced by (musically or orthographically) literate learners retained the compositional relationship with the meanings that was present in the languages they were exposed to. In other words, only literates were able to stably replicate the structure of their input languages.

Language structure evolves as it is transmitted over the generations, and is affected by individual learning biases. The present results suggest that literacy and training facilitate learning and reproduction of compositional structure, supporting the hypothesis that these factors biased the evolution of linguistic structure in the direction of increased compositionality.

Acknowledgments

Monica Tamariz was funded by a Leverhulme Trust Postdoctoral Fellowship, ESRC Grant RES-062-23-1537 and AHRC Grant AH/F017677/1; J. Erin Brown was funded by Scottish Funding Council and the University of Edinburgh's College of Humanities and Social Science and Keelin M. Murray was funded by ESRC Postgraduate Studentship ES/H012605/1.

References

Cornish, H. Tamariz, M. and Kirby, S. (in press). Complex adaptive systems and the origins of adaptive structure: what experiments can tell us. Special issue on Language as a complex Adaptive System. *Language Learning*: 59:4S1.

de Villiers, P.A. & de Villiers, J.G. (1972). Early judgment of syntactic and semantic acceptability by children. *Journal of Psycholinguistic Research*, 1(4), 294-310.

Deacon, T. (1997). They symbolic species. New York: Norton & Co.

Ehri, L.C. (1985). Effects of printed language acquisition on speech. In D.R. Olson, N. Torrance & A. Hildyard (eds.), *Literacy, language, and learning: The nature and consequences of reading and writing*, pp. 333–367. Cambridge: Cambridge University Press.

Kalish, M., Griffiths, T. & Lewandowsky, S. (2007). Iterated learning: Intergenerational knowledge transmission reveals inductive biases. *Psychonomic Bulletin and Review*, 14(2), 288-294.

Karanth, P. & Suchitra, M.G., (1993). Literacy acquisition and grammaticality judgments in children. In: Scholes, R.J. (ed.), *Literacy and language analysis*, Hillsdale, NJ: Erlbaum.

Kirby, S. and Hurford, J. (2002). The emergence of linguistic structure: An overview of the iterated learning model. In A. Cangelosi, and D. Parisi (Eds.) *Simulating the Evolution of Language*, pp. 121-148. Longon: Springer Verlag.

Kirby, S., Cornish, H., & Smith, K. (2008). Cumulative cultural evolution in the laboratory: an experimental approach to the origins of structure in human language. *Proceedings of the National Academy of Sciences*, 105(31), 10681-10686.

Nunes, T., Bryant, P. & Bindman, M. (2006). The effects of learning to spell in children's awareness of morphology. *Reading and Writing*, 19, 767-787.

Olson, D.R. (1996). Towards a psychology of literacy: on the relations between speech and writing. *Cognition*, 60, 83-104.

Ramachandra, V. & Karanth, P. (2007). The role of literacy in the conceptualization of words: Data from Kannada-speaking children and non-literate adults. *Reading and Writing*, 2(3), 173-199.

Schoeneman, P.T. (1999). Syntax as an emergent characteristic of the evolution of semantic complexity. *Minds and Machines*, 9, 309-346.

Tamariz, M. (in press). Could arbitrary imitation and pattern completion have bootstrapped human linguistic communication? *Interaction Studies*.

Tamariz, M. & Smith, A.D.M. (2008). Quantifying the regularity of the mappings between signals and meanings. In A. D. M. Smith, K. Smith & R. Ferrer i Cancho (eds.): *The Evolution of Language: Proceedings of the 7th International Conference on the Evolution of Language*, pp. 315-322.

ACQUISITION PREFERENCES FOR NEGATIVE CONCORD

JACQUELINE VAN KAMPEN

UiL OTS, Utrecht University, Janskerkhof 13
Utrecht, 3512 BL, The Netherlands

Negated sentences in Dutch child language are analyzed. It is argued that, rather than an innate UG structure, the child's acquisition procedure explains a temporary rise and fall of negative concord. It is further suggested that natural preferences of the acquisition procedure are a substantive source for grammatical universals. This evades the assumption that the evolution of the human brain as such has already produced an innate repertoire of grammatical universals.

1. A Trade off

One may have doubts whether little toddlers of less than 3 years old may acquire abstract principles of grammar when given no more than a set of elementary input sentences. If so, one may consider the conjecture that basic schemes of universal grammar (UG) are innate, wired into the human neural system a priori. The productive acquisition procedure could then be seen as filling in the schemes that were already there. The procedure implies that evolution in the prehistory of man must have somehow built in the features that allow the present verbal virtuosity of the species. This biological view implies a certain trade off between language acquisition steps and innate schemes. Everything in grammar that language acquisition is unlikely to deliver, suggests itself now as a welcome present from the evolution of the human brain. There is a certain ambiguity here. One may postulate that universal and typological features of grammar are those that are highly learnable for a general pattern recognizing intelligence. By contrast, one may as easily assume that universal and typological properties are so much hidden in the mass of the various data that they can only be recognized by an intelligence that is successfully predisposed to find them due to its innate scheme for grammar. This conceptual ambiguity between learnability versus grammar-specific a priories justifies that a conference on language evolution scrutinize specific cases of language acquisition in order to see what seems to be learnable anyway and what seems to be less so. In this light, I will consider the successive forms of single and doubly marked negation.

2. Negative Concord

There are three ways to mark a sentence as a negation, (i) a modal clitic on the finite verb, (ii) a modal clitic on the finite verb obligatorily supported by a negative adverb (negative concord), or (iii) a negative adverb alone. Negation in French shows the following historical development ('Jespersen's cycle': Jespersen 1917, Zeijlstra 2004).

(1) a. Je ne dis   (Old French)
    b. Je ne dis pas   (Modern French)
    c. Je ne dis   (colloquial French)

The order in the historic changes shows that we have here more than a simple choice between negation by a single element versus negation by two elements. The change is caused by different perceptions of the input, a difference in learning. When a cliticized element is no longer acquired as an essential marking, the single full-sized negation adverb suffices. But there is more to it.

Negative concord was present in 17th century Dutch, but Modern Dutch sentence negation is realized by means of a single adverb. In spite of the single adverb input, Dutch (and German) child language shows a well-defined period of negative concord (two negative markers for a single negative meaning). It appears spontaneously in periphrastic predicates (*wilnie eten niet* 'want not eat not') and disappears just after the acquisition of the V2 rule. The rise and fall of the second negative marking can be understood from successive reconstructions by the acquisition procedure. The acquisition procedure reconstructs a double negation in spite of the fact that the adult input has a single negative element only. One may see this as a very early default parameter setting for negative concord, but that is not needed. There is a more substantive and interesting explanation, as I will argue now.

3. Input Reduction

Child language does not consider all structures at the same time. The child cannot attend to all data at once and she does not even try to. She applies a massive data reduction instead, and she subsequently builds a grammar for the residue only. That residue determines what new facts can be accommodated. The reduction procedure needs no innate, biologically pre-wired, knowledge. It is based on ignorance.

The child's attention is first directed to binary word combinations in which each element allows an immediate interpretation in the speech situation (see also Jordens 2002). This implies that grammatical elements that are not pragmatically understood are left out of the initial utterances, although their frequency in the input is hundred or more times higher than the lexical items that are in fact reproduced. Two types of predicative structures dominate in early child language. The first type in (2) marks a kind of proto-illocution. It determines the sentence type (wish, statement, question).

(2) modal illocution operator (+ negation)
   a.   is (nie)   [assertion: *that is (not)*]
       is (clitic Neg)
   b.   hoefe (nie)   [wish: *I need (not)*]
       need (clitic Neg)
   c.   wil (nie)   [wish: *I want (not)*]
       want (clitic Neg)
   d.   hoort (nie)   [norm: *it belongs (not)*]
       belongs (clitic Neg)
   e.   kan (nie)   [possibility: *I can (not)*]
       can (clitic Neg)

The second type is a content element with characterizing function, a 'comment'.

(3) a.   ei (niet)
       egg (Neg)
   b.   bad (niet)
       bath (not)
   c.   pap-opeten (niet)
       porridge eat (Neg)
   d.   slapen (niet)
       sleep (Neg)

Both constructions can be followed by a negation element, as indicated in (2)-(3). The negative element in (2) is analyzed here as a clitic, as part of a fused modal illocution operator. It then gets a negative illocutive intention, something like 'negative name-giving' (2)a, 'negative wish' (2)b,c, 'negative norm' (2)d, 'impossibility' (2)e. An analysis of *kannie, hoefenie, magnie* as 'negative modal operator' is also present in Hoekstra & Jordens (1994) and Jordens (2002).

In a somewhat later development the recombination of reconstructed parts yields the forms in (4). See also Wijnen 2000 for the analysis of periphrastic predicates as a later development. The full supporting evidence is drawn from the negative sentences before, during and after the acquisition of the V2 rule in the Van Kampen corpus (two children) and Groningen corpus (four children). A comparison with the dense German Leo corpus (Behrens) is in preparation.

(4)   negative operator + comment (content *niet*)

     a. isse*nie* ~ ei [niet]   (Sarah 2;4.2)
         thatsnot egg not

     b. hoefe*nie* ~ bad [niet]   (Sarah 2;4.25)
         (I) neednot bath not

     c. (ik) hep*niet* ~ sjembad [niet]   (Sarah 2;4.27)
         (I) havenot swimming pool not

     d. hoort*niet*   ~ daar [niet]   (Sarah 2;5.22)
         (it) belongsnot there not

     e. kan*nie*   ~ vinden [niet]   (Tim 2;2)
         (I) cannot find not

     f. past*niet* ~ ijsbeer in [niet]   (Matthijs 2;4.24)
         ((there) fitsnot polar-bear in not

     g. hoefe*niet*   ~ pap opeten [niet]   (Thomas 2;4.14)
         neednot porridge eat not

     h. khoef*nie*~ s(l)apen [niet]   (Laura 2;4.21)
         (I) neednot sleep not

     i. zijn*nie*   ~ [niet] koud [niet]   (Laura 2;8.24)
         (they) arenot cold not

Since the two-part utterances in (4) were intended as a single negation, I analyze the negation element between brackets [*niet*] as a simultaneous and repetitive tag on the denotational element. A negation element *nie(t)* is the final element in both parts of the utterance.

(5)

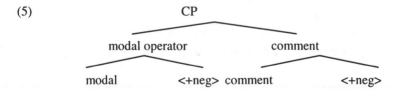

The doubling constructions appear just before the acquisition of V2nd, when complex sentences are still rare in the speech of the child. Therefore, the doubling constructions are not very frequent. They may easily be overlooked, but they are definitely there in the speech of the Dutch child, as has been shown by longitudinal graphs for the two girls.

The doubling of <+neg> need not arise from a deep intuition of the child about negative CPs. Their combination follows the general pattern of combining simplex or complex operator constructs with a context comment that will develop later in a grammatically-marked predicate. The result is a temporary doubling construction.

In this way, the doublings in (4) are not part of the input, but they will nevertheless arise from an acquisition procedure that combines pre-existing parts. The adult input is as in (6).

(6) Adult Dutch
   a.   ik hoef dat   niet t_V
       I need that   not   (I do not need it)
   b.   ik hoef het ei   niet t_V
       I need the egg   not   (I do not need the egg)
   c.   ik hoef niet t_V te eten
       I need not   to eat   (I do not need to eat)
   d.   ik hoef niet een ei t_V
       I need not   an egg   (I do not need an egg)

The adult Dutch sentences in (6) allow us to consider the child language forms in (2)-(4) as temporary reductions by the acquisition procedure. The negation element can become part of different remnants.

The acquisition of the V2 rule will reveal that the negative modals are to be analyzed as modals plus a cliticized negation marker. When all illocution operators in initial position are reinterpreted as a finite verb that takes part in <+finite>/<−finite> paradigm, all input patterns show that the negation markings follow the finite forms and precede the non-finite forms.

(7) a.   [hoenie]$_M$ => [hoef]$_M$ [niet .... t_M]
     b.   [hoenie] [ei eten] => [hoef]$_{<+finite, +M>}$ [niet$_{Neg}$ ei t_M (te) eten]$_{predicate}$

The negative modal clitic *nie* can now be recognized as placed at the beginning of the predicate (the characterizing comment) and not necessarily fused with the modal operator. The negative following the predicate disappears. As a matter of fact the double marked negative sentences disappear almost simultaneously with the acquisition of the verbal paradigm <+finite>/<–finite> and its characteristic positions, respectively sentence-initial/<+finite> versus predicate-final/<–finite>. This suggests an acquisition procedure that adds a binary opposition in category (<±finite>) and position (<sentence-initial operator> versus <predicate-final head>). Thereafter follows a uniform position for the negative element (<predicate initial>). Input reductions to elementary patterns, rather than a priori parameters, seem to determine the developmental steps.

Afrikaans has a similar double negation as in child Dutch. The modal verb and the negation *nie* appear also as a fused element see (8).

(8) Hy *kannie*   kom nie, want hy is siek.
     He cannot   come not, because he is ill

Afrikaans fits the present learnability analysis, but it succeeds to maintain the negative concord that was present in child Dutch before the V2 rule. See Biberauer (2008) for an analysis along the line of innate UG procedures.

Not all child languages show the Neg doubling constructions. It has not (or hardly) been attested in English. English has a restricted use of low negation. English uses mostly a dummy *don't* in front of the lexical verb. In Dutch 'object + verb' constructions, the negation element appears in predicate final position (*Ik wil dat ei niet eten*), a configuration no longer present in VO English at all (*I don't want to eat that egg*). The dummy *don't* is picked up by the English child as sentence negation (*no/don't want that egg*) from the start.

4. Perfect Language

This learnability perspective on universal and typological properties of grammar is not as far from present day theorizing as one may imagine, although it is definitely a different, non-nativist, point of view. Chomsky (2005) mentions three factors for the acquisition of grammar: (A) general cognitive abilities, (B) innate UG distinctions, and (C) input sentences. He considers, and prefers in principle, the possibility that the determinants in (B) can be minimalized to zero. In that case, a general combinatorial system (A) would suffice to derive a grammar from input (C) without support by (B)

Grammatical constructions themselves are seen as implementing a general scheme for categorical combination "Merge and Agree". This scheme is general enough to fall under (A). More specific grammatical properties could follow from (B), such as (i) the categorial system, (ii) the binarity of all combinations

(iii) the headedness of phrases, (iv) the hope that all restrictions on combinations follow from lexical properties (inclusiveness), (v) the recursivity of combinations, (iv) the locality of all grammatical restrictions.

My argument is that they may as well follow from natural preferences in the acquisition procedure. If the acquisition procedure is not pre-programmed for the properties just mentioned, it could nevertheless hang on to them assuming the following learning strategy (see also Van Kampen 2009).

Suppose *dog* is identified as <+N> in the sense of 'element that can be used as a topic-name' (Krifka 2007) and suppose further that the article *the* is identified as 'followed by <+N>'. A later appearing *[angry dog]* must then become <+N> given *the [angry dog]$_N$* . The element *angry* is <−N> (not a topic-name), and hence *[dog]$_N$* is the head of the phrase *the [[angry]$_{-N}$ dog]$_{+N}$*. The recursion in *the [angry [dark-haired dog]]* follows logically if the rule head on the left-hand side (N → A+N) is a repeatedly applied Merge. The binarity of the system was first a practical start and developed from there into a dominating property of the system. As such it is not necessarily an innate property of grammar, but rather a self-reinforcing tendency of the naïve acquisition procedure. A learner may have acquired the small phrase [β+γ]. When confronted with larger constructs, say [α+β+γ], there will be an immediate preference to hold on to the previous result [β+γ]. That favors the binary analysis [α+[β+γ]]. The pressure of such a learnability preference may in the long run impose on grammars the binarity principle. In general, let grammatical structures have the option to be (i) binary branching as well as multiple branching, (ii) headed as well as non-headed, (iii) conditioned by a local 'Agree' as well as non-locally (globally) conditioned. Then, in the long evolutionary run, the restricted system is likely to win the learnability competition on all these points.

Hence, the first principles of grammar may follow from the child's natural acquisition strategy, and need not constitute an innate scheme of grammar as such. Such a view does not explain why language should require a rather large brain in spite of the simplicity of the basic principles, why prehistoric man may have suffered from some kind of specific language impairment, or why first language acquisition is hardly possible after the age of 5 (whereas restarts are possible). Note though that the conjecture of an innate UG scheme does not answer such questions either. All such obvious questions require real models of the way the brain operates and that must be quite beyond the range of grammatical analysis as such. The suggestion that the initial limitations in child language might be due to a maturation of the young brain (Wexler 1999) runs in conflict with the findings about the acquisition of English in American adopted Chinese preschoolers (3000 children, aged 2½-6) (Snedeker et al. 2007). The children acquired English from child-directed speech without access to bilingual informants. They showed the same developmental patterns in language production as monolingual infants, i.e. input reduction and a gradual expansion of the grammar. Their brain must have been matured in China, nevertheless they follow the same reduction and reconstruction method as their native classmates had done two or three years earlier. I consider this natural mass experiment on language acquisition as supporting a non-nativist view on grammar.

References

Biberauer, Theresa (2008). Doubling and omission: insights from Afrikaans negation. In Sjef Barbiers, Olaf Koeneman & Marika Lekakou (Eds.), *Microvariation of syntactic doubling* (pp. 103-140). Bingley: Emerald.

Chomsky, Noam (2005). Three factors in language design. *Linguistic Inquiry, 36* (1), 1-22.

Haegeman, Liliane & Raffaella Zanuttini (1996). Negative concord in West Flemish. In Adriana Belletti & Luigi Rizzi (Eds.), *Parameters and functional heads: Essays in comparative syntax* (pp. 117-179). Oxford: Oxford University Press.

Hoekstra, Teun & Peter Jordens (1994). From adjunct to head. In Teun Hoekstra & Bonnie D. Schwartz (Eds.), *Language acquisition studies in generative grammar* (pp. 119-149). Amsterdam: John Benjamins.

Jespersen, Otto (1917). *Negation in English and other languages.* Copenhagen: Host.

Jordens, Peter (2002). Finiteness in early child Dutch. *Linguistics, 40,* 687-765.

Kampen, Jacqueline (2009). The non-biological evolution of grammar: Wh-question formation in Germanic. *Biolinguistics,* 3 (2-3), 154-185.

Krifka, Manfred. (2007). Functional similarities between bimanual coordination and topic/comment structure. In Shinishiro Ishihara, Michaela Schmitz & Anne Schwartz (Eds.), *Working papers interdisciplinary studies in information structure (ISIS)* 8 (pp. 39–59). Postdam: Universitätsverlag.

Snedeker, Jesse, Joy Geren & Carissa L. Shafto (2007). Starting over. International adoption as a natural experiment in language development. *Psychological Science, 18* (1), 79-87.

Wexler, Kenneth (1999). Maturation and growth of grammar. In William C. Ritchie & Tey K. Bhatia (Eds), *Handbook of language acquisition* (pp. 55-105). San Diego: Academic Press.

Wijnen, Frank (2000). Input, intake and the sequence of syntactic development. In Mieke Beers et al. (Eds.), *From sound to sentence* (pp. 163-186), Groningen: Centre for Language and Cognition.

Zeijlstra, Hedde (2004). *Sentential negation and Negative Concord.* Ph.D. dissertation University of Amsterdam. Utrecht: LOT.

THE PREDICABILITY TREE. HOW, AND WHY?

ROBERT VAN ROOIJ

Institute for Logic, Language and Computation, University of Amsterdam

The art of ranking things in genera and species is of no small importance and very much assists our judgment as well as our memory. You know how much it matters in botany, not to mention animals and other substances, or again moral and notional entities as some call them. Order largely depends on it, and many good authors write in such a way that their whole account could be divided and subdivided according to a procedure related to genera and species. This helps one not merely to retain things, but also to find them. And those who have laid out all sorts of notions under certain headings or categories have done something very useful.
Gottfried Wilhelm von Leibniz, New Essays on Human Understanding (Leibniz, 1704)

1. Introduction

According to the still dominant Chomskian tradition in linguistics, we are required to have *a priori* knowledge of some (universal) linguistics constraints, because otherwise it is impossible to learn a language (in such a short period of time). For this reason, a 'language faculty' evolved which 'contains' this type of knowledge. But even among grammatical sentences there is a distinction to be made between sensical and nonsensical ones. Also this distinction is based on some constraints. In this paper I will argue that one of these latter 'linguistic' constraints could better be thought of as ontological, or categorical knowledge: knowledge about fundamental ontological categories, or perhaps about the way we categorize our world. I will discuss whether this type of knowledge evolved as becoming part of our 'ontology faculty', or whether each child can learn it based on more general Bayesian principles.

The existence of ontological knowledge manifests itself through various phenomena: (i) anomalous sentences, (ii) natural co-predication, and (iii) natural classes. As for (i), we have a strong intuition that there is an important distinction between the non-true sentences (1-a) and (1-b):

(1)   a.   The cow was green.
        b.   The cow was an hour long.

Whereas (1-a) is an ok, but false sentence, (1-b) is not true, because it is 'unnatural', or 'anomalous': it involves a category mistake. Something very similar holds for (ii), it is easy to see that not all pairs of predicates can be combined naturally:

it is ok to say (2-a), but not to say (2-b):

(2)   a.   Either x is fat, or/and x is hungry.
        b.   Either x is fat, or/and x is an hour long.

Intuitively, whether it is contingent whether or not (2-a) is true, sentence (2-b) cannot even be true, because no entity can both be fat and an hour long.

As for (iii), finally, according to a long philosophical tradition (starting with Aristotle (1963), and recently defended by authors as diverse as Goodman (1965), Lewis (1983), and Gardenfors (2000)), not all classes are alike: some are 'natural' and others are not. The famous *paradox of confirmation* is one (among many) way(s) in which this distinction manifests itself: we state a law-like sentence as (3-a) rather than as (3-b):

(3)   a.   Ravens are black.
        b.   Non-black things are not ravens.

The reason seems to be that we prefer the subject of a law-like sentence to involve a natural class, or kind. (Aristotle observed that even for particular sentences there is a distinction between the natural 'Some logs are white' versus the less natural 'Some white things are logs'). Whereas the class, or concept of what it is to be a raven, seems to be 'stable', 'homogenuous', and 'projectable' (Goodman), this is not the case for the class of non-black things. Whether a term is more 'natural' than another, does not just depend on whether it is (logically) 'primitive' (like 'raven') or (logically) 'complex' (like non-black): the use of nominal, or substantive, terms as subjects of law-like sentences is much more natural than the use of adjectival terms.

These phenomena strongly suggest that the set of predicates, classes, or (if you want) ontological categories, are *structured*, and that not taking this structure into account gives rise to anomaly and 'paradoxes'. What is this structure, and why does it exist?

2. Ontological categories

Aristotle (1963) made a famous suggestion of how predicates, or 'ontological en-titties', are categorized. In the previous century, philosophers like Russell (1924) and Ryle (1938) made more concrete proposals, but only Sommers (1959) and Sommers (1963) developed an extremely simple (though not very well known) theory that could easily explain the above phenomena. The distinction between term/predicate- and sentence-negation is crucial for his account. Where a modern logician would say that 'x is non-even' is true for both 3 and John, because 'it is not the case that x is even' is true for both, Sommers more naturally claims that the former sentence is only true for 3, and neither true nor false for John. The class of things that is either 'even' or 'non-even' is called an ontological category. Something similar we do for every (primitive) predicate P, and we denote the category by $/P/$. Thus, $/P/$ is the set of objects to which the predicate P can sensibly be applied, whether truly or falsely. Predicate P is said to *span* the objects in $/P/$. The category $/Ape/$, for instance, spans all animals (including humans), just as the category $/Human/$. In Aristotelian terms, if X denotes a species, the category $/X/$ denotes the genus of X. The sets $/Socrates/$ and $/Quine/$ will (arguably) be identical (the set of all humans), and the sets $/Ape/$, $/Even/$, $/An\ hour\ long/$ will all be mutually exclusive. But not all non-identical categories are mutually exclusive. It seems reasonable to say that only human beings, and not apes, can be honest, or dishonest. But this means that $/Honest/$ is a proper subset of $/Human/$. Similarly, $/Human/$ can be seen as a subset of $/Animal/$, which can denote the set of all living things. Sommers' **Law of categorial inclusion** now says that categories (or predicates) can be hierarchically ordered in what is formally known as a (rooted) *tree* (which is a connected set with no cycles), also known as a 'predicability tree'. Stating it somewhat differently, it says that for any two categories $/X/$ and $/Y/$, either (i) $/X/ \cap /Y/ = \emptyset$, or (ii) $/X/ \subseteq /Y/$, or $/Y/ \subseteq /X/$. What Sommers' law excludes is there to be an individual x such that $x \in /X/ \cap /Y/$, although neither $/X/ \subseteq /Y/$ nor $/Y/ \subseteq /X/$. In later work, Sommers called this the M-rule or the principle of no downward convergence.

In terms of Sommers' theory we can explain the above phenomena. Let us say that $/X/$ and $/Y/$ are *compatible*, $U(/X/, /Y/)$, iff $/X/ \cap /Y/ \neq \emptyset$. First, (1-b) is anomalous, though (1-a) is not, because the categories used in the latter sentence are compatible, i.e., $U(/Cow/, /Green/)$, because $/Cow/ \subseteq /Green/$), but the categories used in the former sentence are not: $\neg U(/Cow/, /An\ hour\ long/)$. The same explanation can be given to the second phenomenon: (2-a) is ok, because $U(/Fat/, /Hungry/)$, but (2-b) is anomalous, because $\neg U(/Fat/, /An\ hour\ long/)$. To account for the third phenomenon, we have to say what it means to be the *natural subject*, in a subject-predicate sentence. The proposal is that (3-a) is ok because $/Raven/ \subseteq /Black/$, and that (3-b) is not, because $/Non - black/ \not\subseteq /Raven/$. Notice that the latter is true iff $/Black/ \not\subseteq /Raven/$, which means that although we have come close to accounting for the traditional distinction between substantial and accidental terms (incorporated in language by the distinction between nominals versus adjectives), it seems that we haven't yet accounted for the distinction between positive and negative terms.

There seem to be some obvious counterexamples to Sommers' theory, however. Men can be white, but not even, while mathematical numbers can be even, but not white. But this means that according to the theory, there can be no predicate X that is applicable to both man and to number. But, of course, both men and numbers can be rational. What Sommers' theory predicts is that this means that 'Rational' must be ambiguous. And this seems to be a correct predication. A similar correct prediction follows from another 'counterexample': The categories /Made of wood/ and /Was dead/ are incompatible. Still, neither 'The bat was made out of wood' nor 'The bat was dead' is anomalous. We have to (correctly) conclude that the two occurrences of 'The bat' denote something quite different. Perhaps a more interesting (though more disputable) example is the pair of sentences 'Holland is flat' and 'Holland is a democracy'. A table is in /Flat/ but not in /Democracy/. A political constitution is in /Democracy/ but not in /Flat/. But this means that according to the theory, the two occurrences of 'Holland' must denote different entities. And perhaps that is the way we have to think about it! (For the philosophers among us, consider examples given after Ryle: 'Descartes is 1.67 meter long' and 'Descartes thinks', and conclude that Descartes is made up of two categories/substances (or can be seen from two different angles): body and mind). Thus, the most obvious counterexamples can be explained away very naturally, and the theory even enables us to detect ambiguity.

Although Sommers' theory is not uncontroversial (for instance because it depends on a primitive notion of a sentence being anomalous, e.g Cogan (1971)), there is a lot of empirical evidence that suggests it is correct. Keil (1979) and Keil (1983) found empirical evidence that both adults and children follow Sommers' law to reason about the world. Moreover, children's trees are typically simpler than the ones of adults. That Sommers' law holds (if it does) or not is a logical possibility, but certainly not a logical necessity. It can be shown that the probability of generating a matrix that satisfies Sommers' law, or the M-constraint, is highly insignificant. Logically speaking, there is an indefinitely large number of different ways of conceptualizing the world. Why could all different categories not be mutually exclusive, or why couldn't they give rise to a full partial order? Why is the relation between ontological categories, or is our conceptualization of the world, constrained by Sommers' law? Why are these categories hierarchically ordered, giving rise to a tree?

3. Why hierarchical structure?

Giving that the *a priori* chance of a set of categories satisfies Sommers' law is so insignificant, why does our language still seem to obey it? The set of categories satisfies Sommers' law iff we organize our categories into a tree-structure. It is well-known (Johnson (1967) and Jardine and Sibson (1971)) that there exists a direct correspondence between any hierarchical system of clusters and a particular type of distance measure. Suppose that objects can be mapped to a metric space such that differences and similarities between these objects can be represented by a metric distance function, d, such that any objects x and y, $d(x,y) \geq 0, d(x,x) = 0$ and $d(x,y) = d(y,x)$. This metric gives rise to an (ultrametric) tree iff the following so-called uttrametric inequality holds: $\forall x, y, z : d(x,y) \leq d(x,z) = d(y,z)$. Thus, for any three objects x, y, and z for which the above inequality is true (and the inequality is strict), x and y are less distant from each other than either is from z.[a] This implies that x and y form a subtree (cluster) relative to z. But this correspondence between distance functions and trees (where each object can be seen as a set of features) only gives rise to the new question of why a metric should satisfy the ultrametric inequality.

One answer is that the distinctions between the objects in the world itself satisfy this constraint, i.e. the world is organized according to a strict non-convergent hierarchy. In evolutionary processes, this is not at all unnatural: all objects have an initial common structure and later develop additional distinctive feaures. An alternative (rather Kantian) answer is that Sommers' law is due to our internal psychological constraints on how we can 'see' the world. Such an answer is very similar to the answer Chomsky has given to the question how we can learn a language: without any *a priori* limitation this is impossible, because there are too many possibilities. But notice that our constraint will be very abstract: no innate concepts, but rather a structural limitation on how concepts can be related to one another, which is more in line with Gardenfors (2000)'s limitation on what a natural concept can be. If this is the answer, it seems we have to explain the way we actually seem to categorize in terms of a general advantage of hierarchical organization. The nobel prize winner Herbert Simon suggested in (Simon, 1969) that the existence of hierchical orders might be explained by reference to phylogenetic evolution. He argued that to represent information in a tree is one of the most stable ways to represent knowledge, and thus has evolutionary advantages: the relative stability of intermediate levels enables such systems to emerge more quickly through evolutionary processes.

Simon illustrated his idea with a parable of two watchmakers, Hora and Tempus. Each makes watches composed of 1000 parts each, but while those of Tempus have to be assembled in one whole, Hora's are made up of three levels of subassemblies of 10 elements each. So, Tempus has to make a complete assembly in one go, and it is assumed that if he is interrupted, the partially completed assembly will fall apart. Hence, for each interruption, he will lose more work, and he will take many more attempts to produce a complete assembly. Hora, on the other hand, has to complete 111 subassemblies for each complete watch, but she will lose less work for each interruption and will take far fewer attempts to make a complete assembly. If the probability of interruption is about 1 in 100, then Tempus will take around 4000 times as long as Hora to assemble a complete watch. Simon argued that the same principle of faster evolution of a complex structure consisting of relatively stable sub-structures will apply to any biological or social system and so such hierarchic systems are likely to be much more

---

[a]This assumption seems very strong, though. It demands not only that given two disjoint clusters, all intro-cluster distances are smaller than all inter-cluster distances, but also that all the inter-cluster distances are equal. Proposals to weaken the demands that still generate trees are given in Sattah and Tversky (1977), Corter and Tversky (1986), and Davis (1999).

334

common than non-hierarchic complex systems. Sampson (2005) has argued that Simon's argument is relevant for linguistics, but relates it to grammatical structure. Simon's argument seems not immediately relevant for motivating Sommers' constraint. But I think it still is: presenting knowledge of concepts/categories in a tree is very efficient (see also, among many others, Leibniz' quote above, and Bickerton, 1990). The oldest known tree diagram was drawn in the 3rd century AD by the Greek philosopher Porphyry in his commentary on Aristotle's categories. This tree diagram incorporates Aristotle's traditional method of defining new categories by genus and differentiae. The species 'Man', for instance, is defined by the genus 'Animal' and the differentia 'Rational'. This method is fundamental to artificial intelligence, object-oriented systems, the semantic web, and every dictionary from the earliest days to the present. Why? Because it allows us to define all terms without giving rise to cycles, but most of all because it greatly helps the child to figure out the fundamental categories of existence and what properties could be applied to what sorts of entities.

But it comes with a prize which I don't know whether we want to pay: we have to assume a set of primitive (positive) properties or attributes. Consider the predicates 'Tiger' and 'Non-Tiger'. The first denotes a kind (e.g. Kripke, Putnam), or natural class, but the latter does not. In terms of this distinction — or so say even extreme nominalists like Goodman (1965) and Quine (1960) — we can solve the problems of induction (and thus the possibility of doing natural science) and indeterminancy of translation, even if this distinction depends only on our (stable) interests. Even though $/Tiger/$ and $/Non - Tiger/$ denote the same category — the set of animals — there is a crucial difference between the predicates themselves: where the set of tigers can be determined by a *conjunctive* set of (primitive) positive attributes they all have in common, this cannot be done for the set of non-tigers. Of course, this depends very much on what we take to be a primitive attribute

Perhaps this means that Sommers' M-constraint is not innate — as suggested by Keil (1979) and Bickerton (1990) — but due to evolution. And indeed, Schmidt (2000) have shown that how Bayesian model selection can be used to learn the M-constraint given a hypothesis space including alternative models. Thus, our desire for efficiency has not resulted in an innate M constraint by evolution, but forces every individual to discover the M-constraint anew. For instance, it may be the result of people's tendency to classify objects into mutually exclusive categories. The prevalence of hierarchical classification can then be attributed to the added complexity involved in the introduction of cross classification with overlapping clusters.

References

Aristotle. (1963). *Categories*. London: Oxford University Press. (Translated with notes by J.L.Ackrill)

Bickerton, D. (1990). *Langauge and species.* The University of Chicago Press.

Cogan, R. (1971). A criticism of sommers' language tree. *Notre Dame Journal of Formal Logic, 17,* 208-310.

Corter, J., & Tversky, A. (1986). Extended similarity trees. *Psychometrika, 51,* 429-451.

Davis, E. (1999). Order of magnitude comparisons of distance. *Journal of Artificial Intelligence Research, 10,* 1-38.

Gardenfors, P. (2000). *Conceptual spaces. the geometry of thought.* MIT Press.

Goodman, N. (1965). *Fact, fiction, and forecast.* New York: Bobbs Merrill.

Jardine, N., & Sibson, R. (1971). *Mathematical taxonomy.* London: Wiley.

Johnson, S. (1967). Hierarchical clustering schemes. *Psychometrika, 32,* 241-254.

Keil, F. (1979). *Semantic and conceptual development. an ontological perspective.* Harvard University Press.

Keil, F. (1983). On the emergence of semantic and conceptual distinctions. *Journal of Experimental Psychology, 112,* 357-389.

Leibniz, G. (1704). *New essays on human understanding.* Cambridge: Cambrdigde University Press. (Translated by P. Remnant and J. Bennet)

Lewis, D. (1983). New work for a theory of universals. *The Australian Journal of Philosophy, 61,* 343-377.

Quine, W. V. O. (1960). *Word and object.* Cambridge: MIT Press.

Russell, B. (1924). Logical atomism. In J. Muirhead (Ed.), *Contemporary british philosophy: First statements, first series* (p. 359-383). London.

Ryle, G. (1938). Categories. *Proceedings of the Aristotelian Society, 38,* 189-206.

Sampson, G. (2005). *The 'language instict' debate.* London: Continuum.

Sattah, S., & Tversky, A. (1977). Additive similarity trees. *Psychometrika, 421.*

Schmidt, L. e. a. (2000). Nonsense and sensibility, inferring unseen possibilities. In *Proceedings of the 28th annual conference of the cognitive sciences society.* London.

Simon, H. (1969). *The sciences of the artificial.* Cambridge: MIT Press.

Sommers, F. (1959). The ordinary langauge tree. *Mind, 68,* 160-185.

Sommers, F. (1963). Types and ontology. *Phylosophical Review, 72,* 327-363.

STRATEGY COMPETITION IN THE EVOLUTION OF PRONOUNS: A CASE-STUDY OF SPANISH *LEÍSMO, LAÍSMO* AND *LOÍSMO*

REMI VAN TRIJP

Sony Computer Science Laboratory Paris
6 Rue Amyot
Paris, 75005, France
remi@csl.sony.fr

Pronouns form a particularly interesting part-of-speech for evolutionary linguistics because their development is often lagging behind with respect to other changes in their language. Many hypotheses on pronoun evolution exist – both for explaining their initial resilience to change as well as for why they eventually cave in to evolutionary pressures – but so far, no one has proposed a formal model yet that operationalizes these explanations in a unified theory. This paper therefore presents a computational model of pronoun evolution in a multi-agent population; and argues that pronoun evolution can best be understood as an interplay between the level of language strategies, which are the procedures for learning, expanding and aligning particular features of language, and the level of the specific language systems that instantiate these strategies in terms of concrete words, morphemes and grammatical structures. This claim is supported by a case study on Spanish pronouns, which are currently undergoing an evolution from a case- to a referential-based system, the latter of which there exist multiple variations (which are called *leísmo, laísmo* and *loísmo* depending on the type of change).

1. Introduction

Pronouns are commonly defined as substitutes for noun phrases that refer to persons or things in the discourse context. Interestingly enough, there is often a discrepancy between the morphosyntactic qualities of pronouns and the nominal system in the rest of the language (Comrie, 2005). In English, for example, full noun phrases are not marked for case, whereas pronouns distinguish between nominative and non-nominative (e.g. *he* vs. *him*). In most cases, the discrepancy means that pronouns still contain traces of an earlier grammatical stage of a language. This makes them interesting objects of study for evolutionary linguistics: not only because they hint at what the language once looked like, but also because they "cannot indefinitely uphold a grammatical category/property-based distinction alone [...]" (Howe, 1996, p. 63). In other words, pronoun evolution is strongly motivated by other, well-known developments in their language.

Many hypotheses have been proposed to explain why pronouns are initially resilient to change and why they eventually yield to evolutionary pressures. However, no one has offered a formal model yet that operationalizes these proposals and validates them in a computational model. This paper therefore presents a concrete multi-agent model that investigates the evolution of pronoun systems through a case study of Spanish, in which the pronouns are currently shifting from a case- to a referential-based system (Valenzuela et al., to appear). The model studies pronoun evolution at two different levels (Bleys & Steels, 2009; Steels, submitted):

1. The level of *language strategies*: Language strategies are sets of procedures for acquiring, expanding and aligning features of language. Language strategies allow speakers to become and remain proficient in their language, and also cause language change.

2. The level of *language systems*: Language systems are the concrete choices that instantiate particular language strategies in terms of an ontology, a lexicon and grammatical structures. Language systems allow language users to produce and parse conventional linguistic utterances.

As I will illustrate in the remainder of this paper, there is an interplay between both levels that strongly influence the ongoing evolution in Spanish.

2. A Case Study of Spanish Pronoun Evolution

The (Standard) Spanish personal pronouns still show traces of a previous case declension. This is most apparent in the third person, which differentiates among nominative, accusative and dative. The other pronouns, however, only distinguish between nominative and non-nominative. The third person pronoun also features a gender distinction between masculine and feminine in the nominative and accusative cases, but not in the dative case. This pronoun system (see Table 1) is known by scholars as the 'etymological system' (Valenzuela et al., to appear).

Table 1. Singular pronouns in Standard Spanish.

	Nominative	Accusative	Dative
1st Person	*yo*	*me*	*me*
2nd Person	*tú*	*te*	*te*
3d Person Masc.	*él*	*lo*	*le*
3d Person Fem.	*ella*	*la*	*le*

The etymological system is gradually changing into a 'referential system' in which the accusative and dative cases are collapsed. This does not mean that the system is simply impoverished: pronouns start to differentiate gender, number and noun class. Moreover, the pronouns have specialized into agreement markers as they can be used in a sentence along with the noun phrases they refer to:

(1) *Le   di   un regalo a mi madre.*
     him.3SG.DAT. give.1PAST   a gift   to my mother
     'I gave my mother a present.' (*lit.* 'to her I gave a present to my mother')

'Referential system' is in fact an umbrella term for covering multiple variations of the system that are not uniformly distributed in the regions of Spain, and that are still in competition with the etymological one (Fernández-Ordóñez, 1999). Depending on the particular flavour of the referential system, the variations are called *leísmo*, *laísmo* and *loísmo*.

Leísmo denotes the use of the pronoun *le* (etymologically a dative pronoun) instead of accusative *lo*. The most frequent occurrences are the use of *le* as a singular, masculine and personal pronoun (ex. (2)). The *Laísmo* variation concerns the use of the pronoun *la* (etymologically an accusative pronoun) instead of *le* with a feminine referent (ex. (3)). Finally, *loísmo* is the use of *lo* (etymologically an accusative pronoun) instead of *le* with masculine or neuter referents (ex. (4)).

(2)   *Le*   *vi*   *(a*   *Javier).*
       3P.SG.ACC   saw-1P.SG.PAST   (Person-Marker   Javier)
       'I saw him (Javier).'

(3)   *La*   *dio*   *un*   *regalo*   *(a   Maria).*
       her.DAT   gave-3P.SG.PAST   INDEF.ART.M   present   to   Maria
       'He gave a present to her (Maria).'

(4)   *Lo*   *dio*   *un*   *regalo*   *(a   Juan).*
       him.DAT   gave-3P.SG.PAST   INDEF.ART.M   present   to   John
       'He gave a present to him (John).'

3. Two Levels of Language Evolution

This paper assumes that the evolution described in the previous section is not happening by accident but that it is *motivated* given the other developments in the Spanish language, which has lost case marking in its noun phrases (in favour of word order and prepositional usage) and which has evolved explicit gender-marking (Valenzuela et al., to appear). Spanish pronoun evolution should thus be studied at two levels: the level of the *language system* and the level of the *language strategies*. Both levels are studied within the setting of a *language game*.

3.1. *Language System*

Studies of grammaticalization have abundantly shown that language users most of the time recycle existing forms into new functions. This is also true for the Spanish pronouns. Future innovations and changes in a language are therefore highly dependent on the already existing items in the linguistic inventory.

     The experiments therefore start with a population of agents that are equipped with the etymological pronoun system of Spanish, including an ontology, lexicon and grammar. The main challenge of this formalization is that speakers of Spanish are perfectly capable of recognizing and understanding when other speakers use

Etymological		Referential	

`lo`
`(syn-cat`
`(==1 (case ((NOM -)`
`(ACC +)`
`(DAT -)))`
`(gender M)))`
	`la`
	`(syn-cat`
	`(==1 (case ((NOM -)`
	`(ACC +)`
	`(DAT -)))`
	`(gender F)))`
		`loísmo`
		`(syn-cat`
		`(==1 (case ((NOM -)`
		`(ACC ?acc)`
		`(DAT ?dat)))`
		`(gender M)))`
			`laísmo`
			`(syn-cat`
			`(==1 (case ((NOM -)`
			`(ACC ?acc)`
			`(DAT ?dat)))`
			`(gender F)))`

`le`
`(syn-cat`
`(==1 (case ((NOM -)`
`(ACC -)`
`(DAT +)))`
`(gender ?gender)))`
		`le-feminine`
		`(syn-cat`
		`(==1 (case ((NOM -)`
		`(ACC -)`
		`(DAT +)))`
		`(gender F)))`
			`le-masculine`
			`(syn-cat`
			`(==1 (case ((NOM -)`
			`(ACC -)`
			`(DAT +)))`
			`(gender M)))`

Figure 1. *Left:* A simplified representation of the syntactic functions of *lo*, *la* and *le* in the etymological system. *Right:* The possible syntactic functions of the same pronouns in the referential system.

a particular variation such as *laísmo* or *loísmo*, so the agents have to be capable of dealing with variation as well and be aware of alternative uses. This has been achieved in Fluid Construction Grammar (De Beule & Steels, 2005; Steels & De Beule, 2006, also see www.fcg-net.org). An overview of the current implementation can be found in Valenzuela et al. (to appear).

Ontology. The experiments make use of a small ontology that consists of several objects and events. The objects differentiate between 'persons' (e.g. [JAVIER]) and 'non-persons' (e.g. [BOOK]). This distinction is not relevant for the experiments in this paper, but will be used for later stages of the case study (also see section 4). There are in total 28 objects that balance the gender distinction between masculine-feminine. Next, there are eight different events, of which five transitive (e.g. [TOUCH]) and three ditransitive events (e.g. [GIVE]).

Lexicon and Grammar. Each item in the ontology has a corresponding lexical entry (e.g. [CAT] – "gato"). The grammar consists of two argument-structure constructions for transitive and ditransitive events. These constructions take care of the correct word order and grammatical role assignment in production. In parsing, they help the hearer to retrieve 'who did what to whom'.

The pronouns *lo, la* and *le* are implemented as morphological rules that map a specific syntactic function to a particular form. The left of Fig. 1 illustrates the case and gender specification of the etymological system. The case-features of *lo* and *la* specify that they always play the accusative role (marked with a '+') and never the nominative or dative roles (marked with a '−'). The two pronouns only differ in the feature 'gender', which has the value 'M' (masculine) for *lo*, and 'F' (feminine) for *la*. *Le*, on the other hand, states that it always plays the dative role. However, it leaves its gender underspecified, which is marked by the variable '?gender' (indicated with a question mark). Indeed, the utterance *Le dio un regalo* will be ambiguous as to whether the speaker intended to say 'He gave **him** a present' or 'He gave **her** a present'.

3.2. *Language Strategies*

The language system will allow agents to produce and parse conventional utterances in Spanish that involve the etymological pronoun system. However, becoming and remaining proficient in a language also means that you know how to acquire innovations, how to expand the system if needed and how to adapt your linguistic inventory to changes in the speech community. These three components are operationalized in the form of *language strategies* (Steels, submitted).

Each language strategy is explicitly represented as a set of 'diagnostics' for detecting communicative problems, 'repair functions' for solving these problems and 'alignment functions' for adapting the linguistic inventory based on the communicative outcome of an interaction. Each language strategy also has a 'score' between 0 and 1 that reflects its strength or dominance in the language. The dominance of a strategy will decide on which communicative problems are considered more urgent by the language user, which repair functions have priority over the others, and which alignment functions have the biggest impact. Scores are updated using similar lateral inhibition dynamics as in previous language game experiments (Bleys & Steels, 2009).

A Strategy for Case. Given the loss of case marking in most of the Spanish language, I will assume here that the strategy for case is not productive anymore for Spanish speakers, and that it can at best be used for acquiring case distinctions and upholding this distinction because of frequency effects. The necessary learning mechanisms for a case strategy are described by van Trijp (2008).

A Strategy for Gender. It is a well-established fact that Spanish explicitly marks gender distinctions. The experiments therefore assume that the Spanish gender strategy has a high 'score' and that its associated diagnostics, repairs and alignment functions have priority over those of the case strategy. In total, the gender strategy has three diagnostics with three corresponding repair functions and one alignment function:

1. **A speaker** can *detect* whether the pronoun he used explicitly marked gender or not. If not, they can *repair* this problem by either recruiting another pronoun (typically *lo* or *la*) or by adapting *le* (see below). However, two conditions have to be met: (a) the score of the gender strategy must be higher than the score of the case strategy; and (b) the 'functional load' of the recruited pronoun must be covered by at least one other system in the language. The latter requirement means that there must be some formal way that hearers can notice that an innovation took place (see below).

2. **A speaker** can *detect* variation in the language when they know multiple possibilities for expressing the same meaning. This may cause an explosion of search effort during processing. The speaker can decide to *repair* this problem by introducing additional gender constraints on one of the pronouns (e.g. specify that *le* should only cover masculine referents).

3. **A hearer** can *detect* the novel use of a pronoun (e.g. *lo* or *la* in dative position) if the 'functional load' of case assignment is also carried by another system in the language. In this case, the word order specifications of the argument-structure constructions will effectively inform the hearer that there is a mismatch between the case specification of the pronoun and what was expected by the construction. The hearer can use this information for *repairing* the problem.

4. **Both speaker and hearer** will increase the confidence score of a pronoun if it was used in a successful interaction and punish pronouns that try to cover the same gender by decreasing their scores. In case of failure, only the score of the pronoun that was used is decreased.

Agents can autonomously test whether an innovation is incompatible with the old use of a pronoun. If so (typically when introducing new constraints), a new morphological rule is introduced that co-exists with the old one. If not, then the repair occurs directly in the recruited pronoun. The gender strategy can (but does not have to) lead to the four different morphological rules that are shown in the right of Fig. 1. Here we see that *lo* and *la* may evolve into non-nominative masculine and feminine pronouns, whereas *le* can remain a dative pronoun if it specializes in either masculine or feminine referents.

4. Experimental results and discussion

The above-mentioned language system and language strategies for case and gender were implemented in a population of ten agents that engage in a series of 'language games' (i.e. routinized communicative interactions). More specifically, agents play description games in which the speaker has to describe an event to the hearer. These events are randomly created by a scene generator based on the ontology of the agents. The speaker has to use a pronoun for one of the participants that play a role in the action. The game is a success if the hearer agrees with the description, and a failure if he disagrees. The agents will exploit this setting when adapting their language. For each language game, two agents are randomly picked to act as either the speaker or the hearer.

In all of the simulations, the population of agents succeeded in modifying their pronoun system such that it incorporates a novel gender distinction for indirect objects. The two graphs in Fig. 2 show examples of the global evolution between *lo*, *la* and *le* on the level of the language system. The Y-axis shows the percentage

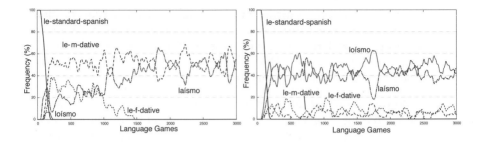

Figure 2.   Two times competition between different uses of *le, la* and *lo.*

of how often a pronoun was used during the last ten interactions that involved a ditransitive utterance, whereas the X-axis indicates the number of language games in the population.

The left graph shows a simulation where the agents went for the *laísmo* variation in which *la* emerges as a non-nominative feminine-marker. We see that the etymological use of *le* quickly disappears under influence of the new uses of *la* and also briefly of *lo*, but the form is nevertheless able to survive as a dative masculine pronoun. As the results show, whereas *le* used to take up 100% of the dative case, it now shares this function with *la* depending on the gender of the referent. The right graph shows another simulation where *le* has almost disappeared and been replaced by *lo* and *la*, which makes that the accusative-dative distinction has completely collapsed. This is the most frequent solution in the simulations, as *le* competes with both *la* and *lo*, but the latter two don't compete with each other.

It is striking that *leísmo* never occurs, whereas this is the most frequent variation in real life. This is due to the fact that there is already a gender differentiation in the accusative case, hence the gender strategy does not pressure the agents to make changes here. Indeed, most occurrences of *leísmo* in Spanish actually employ *le* as a pronoun for personal, animate and volitional referents (both masculine and feminine). This use of *le* probably follows a tendency in Spanish to differentiate person from non-person entities (Valenzuela et al., to appear). This hypothesis is supported by the form *a*, which emerged as a marker for person entities in direct object positions. The data therefore suggest that future experiments need to incorporate a third language strategy for marking the noun class or type.

5. Conclusions

This paper presented a multi-agent computational simulation in which a population of agents succeeded in evolving the etymological pronoun system of Spanish towards a more referential-oriented system, including the well-known *laísmo* and *loísmo* variations of this system. The simulations showed that this shift was made possible without loss of communicative success because of evolution on two levels: that of the language system and that of language strategies. The results also suggest that gender can only explain two types of variation in Spanish and that at least a third strategy is needed in future experiments to explain some of the observed phenomena in Spanish.

Acknowledgements

This research was partly funded by the EU FP7 ALEAR Project and the Sony Computer Science Laboratory Paris. I would like to thank Javier Valenzuela, Mar Garachana Camarero and Joe Hilferty for their thoughtful comments. Many thanks also go to Luc Steels, director of Sony CSL Paris and the VUB AI-Lab in Brussels, and my colleagues from both labs for the helpful feedback on this work.

References

Bleys, J., & Steels, L. (2009). Linguistic selection of language strategies. a case study for colour. In *Proceedings of the 10th european conference on artificial life*. Berlin: Springer.

Comrie, B. (2005). Alignment of case marking. In M. Haspelmath, M. S. Dryer, D. Gil, & B. Comrie (Eds.), *The world atlas of language structures*. Oxford: Oxford University Press.

De Beule, J., & Steels, L. (2005). Hierarchy in Fluid Construction Grammar. In U. Furbach (Ed.), *Ki 2005: Advances in artificial intelligence. proceedings of the 28th german conference on ai* (Vol. 3698, pp. 1–15). Berlin: Springer.

Fernández-Ordóñez, I. (1999). Leísmo, laísmo, loísmo: Estado de la cuestión. In I. Bosque & V. Demonte (Eds.), *Gramática descriptiva de la lengua española* (Vol. I, pp. 1319–1390). Madrid: RAE – Espasa Calpe.

Howe, S. (1996). *The personal pronouns in the germanic languages. a study of personal pronoun morphology and change in the germanic languages from the first records to the present day*. Berlin: de Gruyter.

Steels, L. (submitted). Can evolutionary linguistics become a science?

Steels, L., & De Beule, J. (2006). Unify and merge in Fluid Construction Grammar. In P. Vogt, Y. Sugita, E. Tuci, & C. Nehaniv (Eds.), *Symbol grounding and beyond.* (pp. 197–223). Berlin: Springer.

Valenzuela, J., van Trijp, R., Garachana, M., & Hilferty, J. (to appear). Variation in grammar and fluid construction grammar: A case study of the spanish clitic system.

van Trijp, R. (2008). The emergence of semantic roles in Fluid Construction Grammar. In A. D. Smith, K. Smith, & R. Ferrer i Cancho (Eds.), *The evolution of language. proceedings of the 7th international conference (evolang 7)* (pp. 346–353). Singapore: World Scientific Press.

PRIMING THROUGH CONSTRUCTIONAL DEPENDENCIES
A CASE STUDY IN FLUID CONSTRUCTION GRAMMAR

PIETER WELLENS, JOACHIM DEBEULE

AI-Lab,Vrije Universiteit Brussel, Pleinlaan 2,
Brussels, 1050, belgium
pieter@arti.vub.ac.be, joachim@arti.vub.ac.be

According to recent developments in (computational) Construction Grammar, language processing occurs through the incremental buildup of meaning and form according to constructional specifications. If the number of available constructions becomes large however, this results in a search process that quickly becomes cognitively unfeasible without the aid of additional guiding principles. One of the main mechanisms the brain recruits (in all sorts of tasks) to optimize processing efficiency is priming. Priming in turn requires a specific organisation of the constructions. Processing efficiency thus must have been one of the main evolutionary pressures driving the organisation of linguistic constructions. In this paper we show how constructions can be organized in a *constructional dependency network* in which constructions are linked through semantic and syntactic categories. Using Fluid Construction Grammar, we show how such a network can be learned incrementally in a usage-based fashion, and how it can be used to guide processing by priming the suitable constructions.

1. Introduction

According to Construction Grammar, linguistic knowledge is captured in a constructicon, which is an assembly of form-meaning pairings called constructions (Goldberg, 1995). Processing (i.e. producing or parsing) a sentence amounts to the successive application of constructions, gradually augmenting and transforming an initial meaning to a final form or vice versa.

In each step during processing out of tens of thousands of constructions only a few constructions can apply and of these even less will be correct thus pressuring both efficiency and accuracy. Acknowledging this, most flavors of Construction Grammar adopt a taxonomy of constructions capturing relations of schematicity, but other relations like polysemy, meronomy, inheritance have been proposed as well (see Croft and Cruse (2004) for an overview). Such relations are based on intrinsic properties that hold between the form or meaning of the connected constructions. But constructions can also be related by usage-based properties (i.e. properties that follow first and foremost from their actual use in processing). For example in (Saffran, 2001) it was shown that children are capable of tracking co-occurrence relations not only for word boundaries but also for syntactic patterns.

Such co-occurrence relations can also be captured in a network of constructions, linking them according to conventional usage patterns. Obviously learning these relations can be used to guide and optimize later processing. In addition, if these principles are operating continuously (i.e. at every usage event) this will have a major impact not only on the internal organisation of the constructicon but also on the way the language evolves and changes since it gives rise to self-enforcing loops entrenching patterns more quickly than they otherwise would.

In this paper we operationalize two usage-based construction networks, the second being an extension of the first. Operationalizing requires (1) a learning component that gradually builds and shapes the network on every use and (2) optimized language processing in terms of efficiency and accuracy by utilizing this network. First we introduce a network capturing the fact that certain constructions tend to precede others and show how this can be learned from a series of usage events given a pre-defined set of constructions in Fluid Construction Grammar. We also show how the acquired co-occurrence network combined with language processing capable of priming improves processing performance significantly. A second type of network, the *dependency network*, is based on more subtle and often intricate processing dependencies instead of simple co-occurrences. Such networks allow for an even greater improvement in performance by making the priming much more accurate. We thereby provide the basis for further investigating the influence of conventional constructional usage patterns on the further evolution of language in a computational fashion (e.g. in language game experiments).

2. Learning and using Causal Co-occurrences

In order to capture usage-based dependencies between constructions, we first need to specify in more detail how constructions are used during processing. We use Fluid Construction Grammar (FCG) (De Beule & Steels, 2005; Steels & De Beule, 2006), arguably one of the most advanced formalisms presently available for doing computational construction grammar. FCG has been developed primarily for investigating the emergence and evolution of artificial grammars among autonomous robots. Furthermore, FCG is not a theory of any particular language in that it remains neutral towards what kinds of semantic or syntactic features constitute constructions. As such, it provides the ideal skeletal substrate for implementing and testing a wide variety of empirical and theoretical findings in evolutionary linguistics.

In FCG language processing amounts to finding the correct chain of constructions so that applied in that sequence they will lead to a correct interpretation or production. Determining the appropriate sequence of constructions involves searching through a vast space of possible sequences. If however one construction is often observed to trigger another construction, it makes sense to record this information and use it in later processing. It is important to understand that we are

346

tracking these co-occurrences at the level of such application sequences and *not* for example at the surface form.

We kept track of causal co-occurrences between constructions as they were applied while processing a thousand randomly generated but valid sentences according to an FCG grammar based on the one documented in (Micelli, Trijp, & De Beule, 2009). The grammar contains 64 lexical constructions for 39 nouns, 18 adjectives, 4 verbs and 3 prepositions, and 16 grammatical constructions, in total amounting to a constructicon of 80 constructions suitable for parsing and producing sentences into and from their Frame Semantic meaning according to FrameNet (Fillmore, 1982; Baker, Fillmore, & Lowe, 1998).

After each sentence is processed, co-occurrences are recorded between the constructions involved, and a constructional causal co-occurrence network is gradually built up. A fragment of the resulting network is shown in Figure 1.

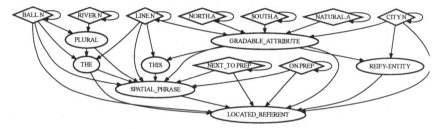

Figure 1.   A fragment of the learned causal co-occurrence network. Diamond shaped nodes represent constructions that appeared to be applicable without reliance on other constructions, i.e. only requiring initial meaning and form. Egg-shaped constructions on the other hand were observed to have a causal co-occurrence with other constructions, namely with those connected to them by incoming edges. For example, it was recorded that the plural construction causally co-occurs often with nouns like "ball" and "river", but not yet with other nouns like "line".

As the network is being improved after each new sentence, it is also used to reduce the number of constructions tried for processing the next sentence thus improving efficiency. Figure 2 shows the average number of grammatical constructions considered before an applicable one was found for each sentence.

As the first 300 sentences were processed, the network was being built up, and the number of constructions tried steadily decreased. After this, the average number of tried constructions stabilizes around seven, resulting in a vast improvement compared to the baseline case.

3. Constructional dependencies

Constructional dependencies are a more refined form of causal co-occurrence relationships and build on two related observations. First, in an application chain of constructions most of them can only apply when certain constraints are met. This

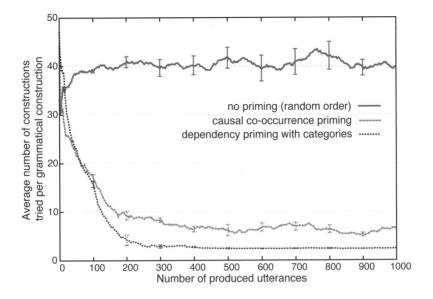

Figure 2. Evolution of the average number of grammatical constructions considered per construction applied while processing a new sentence. The top curve represents the baseline case corresponding to random search, amounting to on average about half of all constructions being tried each time. The middle curve shows how this can be improved by priming constructions according to a causal co-occurrence network. The bottom curve shows another improvement by using dependency based priming, amounting to an additional drop from around seven to around two constructions. This performance is also more stable and learned faster due to generalisation.

holds especially true for grammatical constructions in which these constraints can become quite abstract. For example, in English, the intransitive constructions will, during parsing, only be triggered if a Noun Phrase (NP) is observed directly preceding a Verb. During production, it expresses the fact that the subject NP in a 'Subject Verb' syntactic pattern fills the agentive participant role of the event evoked by the verb. The second and related observation is that these semantic and syntactic constraints are supplied by previously applied constructions. For example whether a constituent is a Noun Phrase or can play the agentive role in an event, and hence whether the intransitive construction will apply, depends on the constructions making up that constituent.

In more general terms, whether construction X should trigger doesn't just depend on what constructions applied before, but more specifically *on the semantic and syntactic categories supplied by these previously applied constructions*. In this view constructions are thus "communicating" with each other during processing through the categories that they require (from previous constructions) and supply (to later constructions). Categories thus become the main regulators of linguistic processing. This way, dependencies specify a *constructional dependency network* among the constructions in the constructicon.

In FCG the application of a construction involves a *match phase* in which its preconditions are verified and a *merge phase* in which the linguistic feature structure that is being built is modified. It is exactly the interplay of merges of earlier constructions and matches of later constructions that makes the tracking of dependencies possible. Indeed, when a construction matches with the linguistic feature structure only because of an earlier modification by another construction the matching construction is dependent on the earlier one. In pseudocode this is computed as follows:

```
————————————— Function LearnDependencies(applicationChain) —————————————
Loop
  ForEach laterConstruction in Reverse(applicationChain) do
  // We loop backwards over the applied constructions
    applicationChain ← Remove(laterConstruction, applicationChain);
    dependencyFound ← false;
    ForEach previousConstruction in Reverse(applicationChain) do
      matchedOnByLaterConstruction ← MatchedOn(laterConstruction);
      mergedByPreviousConstruction ← MergedBy(previoudConstruction);
      matchMergeIntersection ← Intersection(matchedOnByLaterConstruction,
                                             mergedByPreviousConstruction);
      If matchMergeIntersection
      then
        // laterConstruction is dependent on previousConstruction
        // either the intersection is already a category or we create it
        category ← FindOrCreateCategory(matchMergeIntersection,
                                        knownCategories);
        AddOrEntrenchDependencyLink(previousConstruction, category);
        AddOrEntrenchDependencyLink(category, laterConstruction);
        dependencyFound ← true;
    End ForEach;
    If dependencyFound == false
    then
      // laterConstruction is INdependent and gets marked as such
      AddOrEntrenchIndependencyLink(laterConstruction);
  End ForEach;
End Loop;
————————————————— End LearnDependencies —————————————————
```

The above code loops in reverse order over the applied constructions (i.e. the last one first) and checks for this construction what it matched on (i.e. its preconditions). Then it loops again over all constructions applied before this construction and checks how these construction applications modified the feature structure by their merge. If an intersection is found between this match and merge then a dependency is found. Essentially it means the later construction would not have been able to apply if it was not for the modifications of the earlier construction. When such a dependency is found either a new edge is added between the constructions or if there already is one it entrenches it more by incrementing its score. If no dependency is found then this is also recorded because it means the construction could be applied without any previous construction modifying the initial feature structure.

Capturing these sort of dependencies requires that not only the constructions are explicitly represented in the network but also the semantic and syntactic categories that constitute the dependencies. This is illustrated in Figure 3.

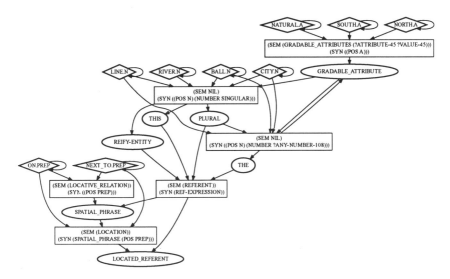

Figure 3. Fragment of the constructional dependency network learned from the exact same usage history as in Figure 1, but this time also capturing more subtle inter-dependencies between constructions besides causal co-occurrences. Square nodes hold semantic and syntactic categories as provided or required by constructions.

Explicitly representing the categories has the advantage that it makes priming of constructions much more accurate and at the same time more general. Consider for example the GRADABLE_ATTRIBUTES construction in Figures 1 and 3. It requires an adjective and a noun and assembles them in an Adjective-Noun phrase. In the simpler network of Figure 1, all nouns and adjectives that occurred together prime the construction, meaning that on the one hand it is primed too often (because it is primed *whenever* one of these nouns is observed, even if no adjective is observed yet), but on the other hand also that it is not primed often enough, because only previously encountered nouns and adjectives prime it. In the augmented network of Figure 3 however, the GRADABLE_ATTRIBUTES construction is primed only if *both* a noun and an adjective are observed, and even if they were not encountered before with this particular construction; as long as they are known in the network to be a noun and an adjective. The same effect is also observed in children when they cue in on syntactic information to produce novel utterances with nonce words (Tomasello, Akhtar, Dodson, & Rekau, 1997).

In the current model, the effect can also be illustrated by comparing the linkage of the LINE.N construction with the PLURAL construction in both networks. In the simple network, LINE.N and PLURAL are not yet connected, meaning that no sentence was ever encountered containing the plural form "lines". LINE.N is however linked to the THE construction, meaning that the phrase "the line" was observed. In the augmented network, observing "the line" connects LINE.N to THE through the intermediate noun-like category node. This node is in turn connected to PLURAL due to *another* observation *not* involving LINE.N. This way, the dependency between the LINE.N and the PLURAL constructions has also been captured without having observed it.

Dependency based priming allows an additional improvement of processing performance as can be seen in Figure 2. This time, on average only two out of eighty constructions need to be considered before a good one is found. This number is also more stable compared to a co-occurrence network.

4. Discussion and conclusion

There is a growing body of evidence supporting the hypothesis that acquiring a language involves the learning of usage-based dependency patterns among constructions (Tomasello, 1992; Saffran et al., 2008). There is also evidence that acquired patterns of constructional usages influence language processing, for example through the priming of frequently co-occurring constructions (Tomasello et al., 1997; Saffran, 2001).

In this paper we have shown how these two observations can be operationalized by performing a case study in Fluid Construction Grammar involving the learning of constructional dependency networks from randomly generated but valid sentences according to an FCG grammar documented in (Micelli et al., 2009). It was shown that such networks can be learned and allow to reduce the amount of processing required for parsing or producing a sentence. In addition, we have proposed to explicitly include semantic and syntactic categories in the network, providing the glue between constructions, and have shown how this leads to a powerful capacity to generalize from observations and an associated further reduction of processing load.

The processing efficiency and accuracy in humans is nothing short of amazing and the mechanisms regulating our capacity for language must have been under these evolutionary pressures at all times. If not it would have become to slow to use or could not expand to more than a limited lexicon. The model and results presented here show that language does indeed contain structure that allows one to build and shape a constructional dependency network which can be used to optimize both efficiency and accuracy. Moreover there is a non trivial connection between the dependencies we tracked in our networks and the hierarchical structure of language thus hinting that recruitment of these general cognitive capabilities might be a necessary requirement to learn and process hierarchical large scale language systems (Steels, 2007).

Moreover, if learning a language involves learning dependency patterns, and if using language involves employing the learned patterns, then language transmission, and hence language evolution, will also be influenced by dependency patterns. By operationalizing the learning and usage of dependency patterns, we have therefore provided a basis for investigating the role of dependency patterns in the evolution of language.

References

Baker, C. F., Fillmore, C. J., & Lowe, J. B. (1998). The Berkeley FrameNet Project. In *Proceedings of the 17th international conference on computational linguistics*. Morristown, NJ, USA: Association for Computational Linguistics.

Croft, W., & Cruse, A. (2004). *Cognitive linguistics*. Cambridge: Cambridge University Press.

De Beule, J., & Steels, L. (2005). Hierarchy in Fluid Construction Grammar. In U. Furbach (Ed.), *Ki 2005: Advances in artificial intelligence. proceedings of the 28th german conference on ai* (Vol. 3698, pp. 1–15). Berlin: Springer.

Fillmore, C. J. (1982). Frame semantics. In *Linguistics in the morning calm* (pp. 111–137). Seoul.

Goldberg, A. (1995). *Constructions: A construction grammar approach to argument structure*. Chicago: University of Chicago Press.

Micelli, V., Trijp, R. van, & De Beule, J. (2009). Framing fluid construction grammar. In N. Taatgen & H. van Rijn (Eds.), *the 31th annual conference of the cognitive science society* (p. 3023-3027). Cognitive Science Society.

Saffran, J. (2001). The use of predictive dependencies in language learning. *Journal of Memory and Language*, *44*, 493-515.

Saffran, J., Hauser, M., Seibel, R., Kapfhamer, J., Tsao, F., & Cushman, F. (2008). Grammatical pattern learning by human infants and cotton-top tamarin monkeys. *Cognition*, *107*, 479-500.

Steels, L. (2007). The recruitment theory of language origins. In C. Lyon, C. Nehaniv, & A. Cangelosi (Eds.), *Emergence of communication and language* (p. 129-151). Berlin: Springer Verlag.

Steels, L., & De Beule, J. (2006). Unify and merge in Fluid Construction Grammar. In P. Vogt, Y. Sugita, E. Tuci, & C. Nehaniv (Eds.), *Symbol grounding and beyond.* (pp. 197–223). Berlin: Springer.

Tomasello, M. (1992). *First verbs: A case study of early grammatical development*. Cambridge: Cambridge University Press.

Tomasello, M., Akhtar, N., Dodson, K., & Rekau, L. (1997). Differential productivity in young children's use of nouns and verbs. *Journal of Child Language*, *24*, 373-87.

THE MOVING TARGET ARGUMENT AND THE SPEED OF EVOLUTION

BODO WINTER

Department of Linguistics, University of Hawai'i at Manoa
Honolulu, 96822, USA

This paper discusses problems associated with the "moving target argument" (cf. Christiansen & Chater 2008, Chater et al. 2009, see also Deacon 1997: 329, Johansson 2005:190). According to this common argument, rapid language change renders biological adaptations to language unlikely. However, studies of rapid biological evolution, varying rates of language change and recent simulations pose problems for the underlying assumptions of the argument. A critique of these assumptions leads to a richer view of language-biology co-evolution.

1. Introduction

Are languages a "moving target" for biological evolution? According to Christiansen and Chater (2008) there could not have been any biological adaptations to language because languages change rapidly whereas biology needs stable targets to adapt to. This argument features prominently in the debate on the origins of language (e.g. Deacon 1997: 329, Johansson 2005: 190, Chater et al. 2009). The following three points highlight the structure of the argument:

(1) Premise 1   Biological evolution is slow.
     Premise 2   Language change is rapid.
     Premise 3   Slow biological adaptation needs stable targets.
     Conclusion   Biology could not have adapted to language.

2. The Uniformitarian Principle and some associated problems

The moving target argument covertly assumes that the rates of biological and cultural change we observe today are similar to the rates of change in the past. This inference has often been called the Uniformitarian Principle. The notion of "Uniformitarianism" goes back to Charles Lyell's *Principles of Geology* (1830) where he states that the processes which alter the shape of the earth remain unchanged through time. The principle has also been stated within the context of linguistics by Labov (1972: 275):

> "[T]he forces operating to produce linguistic change today are of the same kind and order of magnitude as those which operated in the past (...)"

The view that cultural (and likewise linguistic) change is a much faster process than biological evolution is common. For example, Dawkins (2006 [1976]: 190) states that "fashions in dress and diet, ceremonies and customs, art and architecture, engineering and technology, all evolve in historical time in a way that looks like highly speeded up genetic evolution" and with respect to language he says that languages seem to evolve "at a rate which is orders of magnitude faster than genetic evolution" (ibid. 189).

Dawkins' use of 'historical time' implicitly contrasts with 'geological time', which is thought to be the domain of evolution. This idea goes back to Darwin, who thought of evolution as something that cannot be observed by humans and that works on non-historical timescales:

> "We see nothing of these slow changes in progress, until the hand of time has marked the long lapse of ages, and then so imperfect is our view into long past geological ages, that we only see that the forms of life are now different from what they formerly were." (Darwin 1909–14., ch. 4)

However, during the past years more and more cases have been discussed in which biological evolution is observable "in real time" – the literature on this is extensive and constantly growing. A number of these cases will be reviewed here to show that rapid evolution is much more frequent than sometimes assumed:

- A very famous example of rapid evolution is the ongoing co-evolution of virulence in the myxoma virus and defense against the virus in Australian rabbits (Dwyer et al. 1990).
- An experiment was able to show that bacteria are able to develop resistance to certain temperatures after 200 generations (Bennet et al. 1990) – a timescale of just months.
- In a captive population of chinook salmons, the egg size decreased within 5 generations (Heath et al. 2003). Selection pressure on offspring survival selects for larger eggs whose offspring are more likely to survive. If this pressure disappears in captivity, egg size may change rapidly.
- Ritchie & Gleason (1995) describe song patterns of flies of the *Drosophila willistoni* sibling species group. They find differences in frequencies and interval pulses of song patterns which – given that the

involved species are closely related – are likely to be the result of rapid evolution due to sexual selection.

- Klerks & Levinton (1989) suggest that the evolution of metal resistance of an invertebrate to a metal-polluted site in Foundry Cove (New York) could have succeeded in 1 to 4 generations – 30 years after the onset of the pollution.
- O'Steen et al. (2002) were able to show how populations of guppies rapidly adapt to their environment: guppies in high-predation areas rapidly evolved better escape abilities than guppies in low-predation areas. This change happened in a period of between 15 and 20 years.

These are some of the many cases of rapid evolution mentioned in the literature. One could object that many of these changes are not due to natural conditions because they are in some ways connected to human intervention. There are, though, good examples of rapid evolution where humans play no role, most notably the Darwin's finches of the Galápagos Islands which rapidly changed their beak size after a climatic event occurred that devastated a major food resource (Grant & Grant 1993). One could also object that the examples do not pertain to human evolution. However, a number of human genetic traits show the signature of selection within the last few thousand years (Wang et al. 2006). Taken together, these examples highlight the fact that evolution does not always proceed slowly:

> "Our ideal world requires a constancy of evolutionary rate in all lineages. But rates are enormously variable." (Gould 1983: 363)

Since there is still considerable dispute as to what exactly determines the speed of evolution, it seems best to remain agnostic, with rapid evolution being seen as a possibility which should not be ignored.

3. The rate of cultural and linguistic change

These examples have shown that biological adaptation need not be slow. What about language change? Language change – and cultural change in general – seems to be almost entirely rapid. However, there are exceptions. For example, Diamond (1997) mentions the extremely slow cultural evolution (or sometimes the apparent lack of any evolution at all) in certain parts of the world due to detrimental geographical factors. A case in point is Tasmania, where there have not been any major technological advances for hundreds or even thousands of years. Also, there may be periods of time where the rate of evolution is different. For example, there is a huge gap between the Oldowan and the Acheulean stone producing techniques (cf. Johansson 2005), a transition which took approximately one million years.

Turning to language, linguists have discussed varying rates of change in the context of a critique of lexicostatistical methodology. A major criticism of lexicostatistics was the fact that it assumed constant rates of change (e.g. Teeter 1963). While Lees (1953) claimed that lexical retention rates cluster around a universal constant, Guy (1983) observed that Lee's sample is highly biased. In a classic paper, Bergsland & Vogt (1962) showed that some languages – in particular Icelandic, Armenian, Georgian and Greenlandic Eskimo (Inuit) – have higher retention rates than predicted by Lees' constant, while Blust (2000) shows that rates of change differ within the Austronesian language family. After splitting off from Proto-Malayo-Polynesian, some languages retained 58% of the Proto-Malayo-Polynesian vocabulary, whereas other languages retained only 5.2% after the same length of time.

Additional examples for varying rates of change come from the literature on phylogenetic modeling of languages: Although somewhat controversial, researchers have turned to estimate the 'half-life' of words (cf. Pagel 2007). Some of the words are estimated to have 'half-lifes' of approximately 70,000 years, which is similar to the rate of evolution of some genes (Burger et al. 2007). Other words are replaced faster. The varying rates of lexical displacement can be illustrated by looking at cognate sets: Where English speakers say "bird", Italians say "uccello", the French say "oiseau", the Spanish "pajaro", the Germans say "Vogel", the Greeks say "pouli" and Latin speakers said "avis". These forms do not form a cognate set as opposed, for instance, to "two" which has not been replaced in any of the Indo-European languages (Pagel 2009).

However, there are many examples of language change that seem rather rapid: vowels constantly shift; German is in the process of losing its genitive case marker; 'cool' and 'uber' change with almost every generation of kids. These examples constitute very interesting changes – but they do not constitute major changes. Most of the rapid changes of linguistic systems we can think of are changes in the inventory of categories: certain linguistic categories disappear, two categories might merge or one category might split into two.

There are, though, major changes that can be observed, e.g. the change of Nonthaburi Malay as an agglutinative language to a language of an isolating type, or the ongoing emergence of tonal contrasts in Korean. However, these shifts from one language type to another (agglutinative to isolating, non-tonal to tonal) usually need much more time and proceed in an incremental, step-by-step fashion over long periods. For example, Proto-Indo-European had a case system and while most European languages underwent specific changes (e.g. certain cases have been lost), all European languages retain a case system (with the notable exception of the marginal system in English).

When I speak of 'major' and 'minor' changes, I do not intend to imply that this is a qualitative distinction. I put forth the hypothesis that most of the fast changes we observe are among the more minor changes, while big changes need time – partly because they are constituted by a number of sequential small changes.

This hypothesis needs to be tested with large-scale typological databases, but crucially, it is a testable claim.

4. Biological adaptations for changing targets

To my knowledge no one has yet considered the implications of the work of Kashtan et al. (2007) for language evolution. Contrary to Christiansen and Chater's claim that biology could not have adapted to a moving target, Kasthan et al. (2007) find that "temporally varying goals can substantially speed evolution compared with evolution under a fixed goal" (ibid. 13711). As they point out, it might be expected that changing goals make evolution more difficult (ibid. 13711) but their model turns out to show that this is not necessarily the case.

They also find that "the more complex the problem at hand, the more dramatic the speedup afforded by temporal variations" (ibid. 13711). This is interesting with respect to language evolution because if anything can be thought of as a complex trait, it is language. If we believe Kashtan et al. (2007) that a moving target even increases the rate of evolution, the moving target argument can not only be criticized on the grounds of a critique of the Uniformitarian Principle (section 1 and 2) but also with respect to premise 3 which states that biological adaptation needs a fixed target.

5. A thought experiment on early language change

The following thought exercise is intended to show that it is not only possible but also quite likely that languages (or proto-languages) have changed more slowly in the past than they do today:

> Suppose, you are playing a game with a friend and you are given only one red die. The only thing you can do is throw the red die – once or maybe repeatedly. Only if you are given an additional die, let us say a green one, is there the possibility to change the order of the two dice. Now, more "complex" games are possible, e.g. throwing the red die three times, the green die three times etc. Given yet another colored die, the options of the game multiply. Crucially, the game can only be changed if there are enough elements in the game to be changed.

Something similar might have been the case in the early stages of language evolution – if one wants to avoid a saltational theory of language evolution it seems to be necessary to assume "simpler" stages of languages. This is something done by a large number of scholars who posit the existence of some form of intermediate proto-language before the advent of modern human languages.

With respect to these proto-languages we might ask questions such as: Can word order be changed if speakers only use single words? Can tone be changed in a meaningful way if the speakers of a proto-language have not yet started to employ tones to distinguish meanings? Can two categories be merged if there is only one category in the language? The answer to all these questions is obviously 'no'. Therefore, it is likely that language change was not only slow but severely limited. Because languages at a certain stage in the language-brain co-evolution were likely to have been less complex, they had fewer dimensions on which cultural change could have acted.

The crucial difference between this thought experiment and the rapid emergence of new languages we observe in creolization processes is that today 'the game' is not biologically constrained and therefore the inventory of categories and patterns can expand at astonishing rates in language genesis. However, the thought experiment pertains to biological constraints. Let us take working memory capacity as an example. If there were selective pressure on increasing working memory capacity in the early stages of language evolution, adaptations to this pressure would lead to longer sentences. These are more likely to exhibit more complexity and the ability to change this complexity in increasingly different ways.

6. Conclusions

In this paper, I have argued that the Uniformitarian Principle does not hold across the board and should be used with caution since rates of change differ. I have also put forth the possibility that linguistic change and biological evolution are on a similar and sometimes overlapping timescale. Other researchers have reached similar conclusions on different grounds, e.g. Nettle (2007: 10756) argues for a greater role of gene-culture co-evolution than previously suspected. In the comments to Christiansen & Chater's paper, over five commentators argue for a bigger role of co-evolution in the origins of language. Taken together, these considerations show that the extent of co-evolution as opposed to one-sided adaptation of language 'to fit the human brain' (Christiansen & Chater 2008: 489) has probably been underestimated. The picture that emerges is an evolution of language/culture and biology in tandem. In the initial stages, proto-languages did not change as much as modern languages but with some general biological adaptations to language (e.g. in the domain of working memory, cooperation etc.), there was more and more room for languages to change and at the same time, to increase the rate of change.

References

Bennett, A.F., Khoi, M.D., & Lenski, R.E. (1990). Rapid evolution in response to high-temperature selection. *Nature*, 346, pp. 79-81.

Bergsland, K., & Vogt, H. (1962). On the validity of glottochronology (with comments and reply). *Current Anthropology*, 3:2, pp. 115-53.

Blust, R. (2000). Why lexicostatistics doesn't work: the 'universal constant' hypothesis and the Austronesian languages. In: Renfrew, C., McMahon, A., & Trask, L. (2000). *Time Depth in Historical Linguistics*. (Papers in the prehistory of language, volume 1). Cambridge: McDOnald Institute for Archaeological Research.

Burger, J., Kirchner, M., Bramanti, B., Haak, W., & Thomas, M. G. (2007). Absence of the lactase-persistence-associated allele in early Neolithic Europeans. *Proceedings of the National Academy of Sciences of the USA*, 104, pp. 3736-3741.

Chater, N., Reali, F., & Christiansen, M. (2009). Restrictions on biological adaptation in language evolution. *Proceedings of the National Academy of Sciences of the USA*, 106, pp. 1015-1020.

Christiansen, M. H., & Chater, Nick (2008). Language as shaped by the brain. *Behavioral and Brain Sciences*, 31, pp. 489-558.

Darwin, C.R. (1859). *On the Origin of Species*. London: John Murray.

Dawkins, R. (2006 [1976]). *The Selfish Gene*. New York: Oxford University Press.

Deacon, T.W. (1997). *The Symbolic Species*. New York: Norton.

Diamond, J. (1997). *Guns, Germs and Steel: The Fate of Human Societies*. New York: W.W. Norton.

Dwyer, G., Levin, S.A., & Buttel, L. (1990). A simulation model of the population dynamics and evolution of myxomatosis. *Ecological Monographs*, 60, pp. 423–447.

Gould, S.J. (1983). *The Hen's Teeth and Horse's Toes*. New York: Norton.

Grant, R.B., & Grant, P.R. (1993). Evolution of Darwin's finches caused by a rare climatic event. *Proceedings: Biological Sciences*, 251, pp. 111-117.

Guy, J.B.M. (1983). On Lexicostatistics and Glottochronology. *Proceedings of the XVth Pacific Science Congress*, Dunedin, New Zealand. Manuscript, 36 pp.

Heath, D.D., Heath, J.W., Bryden, C.A., Johnson, R.M., & Fox, C.W. (2003). Rapid Evolution of Egg Size in Captive Salmon. *Science*, 299, pp. 1738-1740.

Huey, R. B., Gilchrist, G.W., Carlson, M.L., Berrigan, D., & Serra, L. (2000). Rapid Evolution of a Geographic Cline in Size in an Introduced Fly. *Science*, 287, pp. 308-309.

Johansson, S. (2005). *Origins of Language: Constraints on hypotheses*. Amsterdam: John Benjamins.

Kashtan, N., Noor, E., & Alon, U. (2007). Varying environment can speed up evolution. *Proceedings of the National Academy of Sciences of the USA*, 104, pp. 13711-13716.

Klerks, P.L., & Levinton, J.S. (1989). Rapid Evolution of Metal Resistance in a Benthic Oligochaete Inhabiting a Metal-polluted Site. *Biological Bulletin*, 176, pp. 135-141.

Labov, W. (1972). *Sociolinguistic Patterns*. Philadelphia: University of Pennsylvania Press.

Lees, R.B. (1953). The basis of clottochronology. *Language*, 29:2, pp. 113-127.

Lyell, C. (1830). Principles of Geology. Albemarle-Street: John Murray. URL: http://www.esp.org/books/lyell/principles/facsimile/

Nettle, D. (2007). Language and genes: A new perspective on the origins of human cultural diversity. *Proceedings of the National Academy of Sciences of the USA*, 104, pp. 10755-10756.

O'Steen, Shyril, Cullum, Alistair J., & Bennett, Albert F. (2002). Rapid evolution of espace ability in Trinidadian guppies (Poecilia reticulata). *Evolution*, 64:4, pp. 776-784.

Pagel, M., Atkinson, Q. D., & Meade, A. (2007). Frequency of word use predicts rates of lexical evolution throughout Indo-European history. *Nature*, 449, pp. 717–719.

Pagel, M. (2009). Human language as a culturally transmitted replicator. *Nature Genetics*, 10, pp. 405-415.

Ritchie, M.G., & Gleason, J.M. (1995). Rapid evolution of courtship song pattern in Drosophila willistoni sibling species. *Journal of Evolutionary Biology*, 8, pp. 463-479.

Teeter, K.V. (1963). Lexicostatistics and Genetic Relationship. *Language*, 39:4, pp. 638-648.

Wang, E.T., Kodama, G., Baidi P., & Moyzis, R.K. (2006). Global Landscape of Recent Inferred Darwinian Selection for Homo Sapiens. *Proceedings of the National Academy of Sciences of the USA*, 103, pp. 135-140.

Abstracts

WHAT IS SPECIAL ABOUT THE LANGUAGE FACULTY, AND HOW DID IT GET THAT WAY?

STEPHEN R. ANDERSON

Dept. of Linguistics, Yale University, PO Box 208366
New Haven, CT 06520-8366, USA
sra@yale.edu

A consideration of the communicative abilities of other animals makes it clear not only that no other species has a system with the essential properties of a human natural language, but also that there is no reason to believe that such systems are even accessible to animals lacking our specific cognitive capacities (Anderson, 2004). In every animal species that has been seriously investigated, it is clear that the specific properties of its communicative mechanisms are tightly grounded in specific properties of its biology. There must be some aspect of our biological nature, therefore, which has been distinctively shaped in the course of evolution to subserve our ability to acquire and use the languages we do (Pinker & Bloom, 1990). Let us call this aspect of human biology the "Language Faculty," without prejudice as to whether components of it might have other roles to play as well.

Some have argued that it is plausible to suggest that there is very little about the Language Faculty that is unique to humans and to its role in language: perhaps only the capacity for recursive elaboration of structure (Hauser, Chomsky, & Fitch, 2002). This claim has provoked heated debate between those who maintain a highly structured species-specific capacity devoted to the acquisition and use of language (Pinker & Jackendoff, 2005; Jackendoff & Pinker, 2005) and those who argue that most of what makes language possible in humans has substantive parallels in other domains and/or other species (Fitch, Hauser, & Chomsky, 2005; Samuels, 2009). I maintain that the participants in this discussion are largely talking past one another: while it is clear that analogs and even homologues of components of human biology relevant to language exist in other species, and in other cognitive domains, it is also clear that these components have been shaped distinctively in humans by their role in language.

Within Linguistics, there has similarly been argument over whether our ability to acquire and use language is the product of a distinctive faculty, or simply due to the confluence of capacities equally relevant to other domains. A component of that discussion has been controversy about whether the regularities we find across the whole range of human languages result from a distinctive and highly specific faculty, or are simply the inevitable outcome of external processes shaping language use and language change. This has made the process of discovering linguistic universals, and attributing them to the substantive character of the Language Faculty, particularly difficult: merely demonstrating that every language in the world conforms to a given generalization (even ignoring the problem of showing that this would also be true for all *possible* languages) does not support attributing that generalization to such a faculty if an alternative account in terms of external factors of usage and change is available.

Anderson (2008) suggests that this difficulty is more apparent than real. Supposing that external forces conspire to shape languages in particular ways, independent of the precise nature of the cognitive capacity underlying their acquisition and use, we should still expect that precisely these recurrent regularities would be incorporated into our biological nature by Baldwinian evolution, given the central role played by language in our ecological niche and the concomitant value of an ability to acquire the language of the surrounding community quickly and without excessive effort. Nativist and externalist accounts of linguistic regularities are therefore complementary, not contradictory. On this understanding, a highly specific Language Faculty is just what we predict if external forces of usage and change really can drive the emergence of recurrent cross-linguistic regularities.

References

Anderson, S. R. (2004). *Doctor Dolittle's delusion: Animals and the uniqueness of human language*. New Haven: Yale University Press.

Anderson, S. R. (2008). The logical structure of linguistic theory. *Language, 84,* 795–814.

Fitch, W. T., Hauser, M. D., & Chomsky, N. (2005). The evolution of the language faculty: Clarifications and implications. *Cognition, 97,* 179–210.

Hauser, M. D., Chomsky, N., & Fitch, W. T. (2002). The faculty of language: What is it, who has it, and how did it evolve? *Science, 298,* 1569–1579.

Jackendoff, R. S., & Pinker, S. (2005). The nature of the language faculty and its implications for evolution of language (reply to Fitch, Hauser, and Chomsky). *Cognition, 97,* 211-225.

Pinker, S., & Bloom, P. (1990). Natural language and natural selection. *Behavioral and Brain Sciences, 13,* 707–784.

Pinker, S., & Jackendoff, R. (2005). The faculty of language: What's special about it? *Cognition, 95,* 201–236.

Samuels, B. (2009). The third factor in phonology. *Biolinguistics,* 355–382.

ON THE ORIGIN OF UNIVERSAL CATEGORIZATION PATTERNS: AN *IN SILICA* EXPERIMENT

ANDREA BARONCHELLI

Departament de Fisica i Enginyeria Nuclear, Univ. Politecnica de Catalunya, C. Nord B4, 08034 Barcelona, Spain
andrea.baronchelli@upc.edu

TAO GONG

Dept. of Linguistics, Max Planck Institute for Ev. Anthropology, Deutscher Platz 6, 04103 Leipzig, Germany
tao_gong@eva.mpg.de

VITTORIO LORETO

Dip. di Fisica, Sapienza Universita' di Roma, P.le Aldo Moro 5, 00185 Roma, Italy
and Complex Networks Lagrange Laboratory, ISI, Torino, Italy
vittorio.loreto@roma1.infn.it

ANDREA PUGLISI

CNR-INFM-SMC and Dip. di Fisica, Sapienza Universita' di Roma, P.le Aldo Moro 5, 00185 Roma, Italy
andrea.puglisi@roma1.infn.it

The Category Game is a computational model designed to investigate how a population of individuals can develop a shared repertoire of linguistic categories, i.e. co-evolve their own system of symbols and meanings, by playing elementary language games (Puglisi, Baronchelli, & Loreto, 2008). Consensus is reached through the emergence of a hierarchical category structure made of two distinct levels: a basic layer, responsible for fine discrimination of the environment, and a shared linguistic layer that groups together perceptions to guarantee communicative success. The only parameter of the model is the Just Noticeable Difference (JND) of the agents defined as the smallest detectable difference between two stimuli. Remarkably, the number of linguistic categories turns out to be finite and small, as observed in natural languages, even in the limit of an infinitesimally small JND. As in pioneering work on the coevolution of language and meaning (Steels & Belpaeme, 2005), finally, the shared categorization is reached through pure cultural negotiation, but in the Category Game the individuals are addition-

365

ally able to categorize a continuum environment. The analogy with color categorization is therefore natural (Steels & Belpaeme, 2005; Puglisi et al., 2008), even though computational modeling implies a large number of (even drastic) simplifications.

Here we focus on the (much debated (Lakoff, 1987)) question of the origins of *universal* (i.e. shared) categorization patterns across cultures. In particular, we report on an *in silica* experiment pointing out that cultural and linguistic interactions can induce universal patterns in categorization provided that the human perceptual system is taken into account (Baronchelli, Gong, Puglisi, & Loreto, 2009). We simulate, through the Category Game model, a certain number of noninteracting populations each developing its own synthetic language. We find universal categorization patterns among populations whose individuals are endowed with the human JND function, describing the resolution power of the human eye to variations in the wavelength of the incident light (Long, Yang, & Purves, 2006). We furthermore show that, on the contrary, populations whose individuals' JND is uniform do not exhibit any signature of universality. In particular, we repeat the same statistical analysis performed in (Kay & Regier, 2003) and find that the difference between these two classes of simulated populations is in striking agreement with the difference between the experimental World Color Survey data and their randomized counterparts.

Remarkably, the model we present (i) incorporates a true feature of human perception (i.e. the human hue JND), and produces results (ii) testable against and (iii) in agreement with experimental data. Our work not only corroborates the findings of (Kay & Regier, 2003), but also validates the hypothesis that the universal properties of human visual system are probably involved in the regularities of color nomenclatures of the world's languages.

References

Baronchelli, A., Gong, T., Puglisi, A., & Loreto, V. (2009). Modeling the emergence of universal categorization. *Preprint arXiv:0908.0775, at http://arxiv.org/abs/0908.0775.*

Kay, P., & Regier, T. (2003). Resolving the question of color naming universals. *Proc. Natl. Acad. Sci. USA, 100*(15), 9085–9089.

Lakoff, G. (1987). *Women, fire, and dangerous things: What categories reveal about the mind.* Chicago: University of Chicago Press.

Long, F., Yang, Z., & Purves, D. (2006). Spectral statistics in natural scenes predict hue, saturation, and brightness. *Proc. Natl. Acad. Sci. USA, 103*(15), 6013–6018.

Puglisi, A., Baronchelli, A., & Loreto, V. (2008). Cultural route to the emergence of linguistic categories. *Proc. Natl. Acad. Sci. USA, 105*(23), 7936.

Steels, L., & Belpaeme, T. (2005). Coordinating perceptually grounded categories through language: A case study for colour. *Behav. Brain Sci., 28*(04), 469.

COORDINATION OF LANGUAGE STRATEGIES BASED ON COMMUNICATIVE FITNESS

JORIS BLEYS

Artificial Intelligence Laboratory, Vrije Universiteit Brussel
Brussels, 1000, Belgium
jorisb@arti.vub.ac.be

How one language strategy - a set of instructions to structure and express one particular subarea of meaning - allows a population of agents to self-organise their own language system that allows them to reach communicative goals in routinised interactions, is relatively well understood. How agents can align on which strategy to use when several strategies are available, has been explored far less (Steels, 2010). This paper investigates how linguistic selection based on communicative success, might be suitable for this purpose in a concrete case study.

The starting point of this case study is an observation in the history of English colours terms. In Old English the colour terms primarily had a brightness meaning sense but in the transition most colour terms shifted simultaneously to a hue sense. In the history of the term "yellow" for example, the OE term "geolo" meant "to shine" whereas ME "yelou" referred to the hue of specific objects, such as yolk, ripe corn or discoloured paper. Colour terms that have been introduced after this shift, never had a brightness sense (Casson, 1997).

We propose a language game model based on the colour naming game to model this observation. In this game, the communicative goal of the speaker is to describe one of the objects in a shared context to the hearer using only a single term that describes the colour of the object.

Each meaning sense is implemented as a different language strategy. Colour categories are represented by their prototype which represent the most prototypical colour of that category. Each prototype is a single point in a three dimensional perceptual colour space (CIE $L^*u^*v^*$), of which the L^* dimension corresponds to the brightness of a colour. In *brightness strategy* only the L^* dimension is taken into account during categorisation, whereas in the *hue strategy*, all dimensions are taken into account.

To model linguistic selection of language strategies, each agent keeps track of the communicative success of each strategy for each linguistic item in their inventory. This is the default strategy that is used in production or interpretation when an item is used. When the stored associations fail in a specific communicative challenge, the items will be re-interpreted using the other strategies that are available to the agent, starting from the strategy that is considered to be generally most fit by that agent. When the language system needs to be expanded, the agents will prefer the language strategy they consider to be generally most successful in previous interactions and that is suitable for the current communicative challenge.

The mechanisms proposed in this paper allow the agents to align on the strategies they use and give rise to some interesting dynamics. In some runs one strategy clearly becomes the most dominant one, whereas in others a shift occurs from one strategy into the other and both strategies continue to co-exist in the same language system (Fig. 1). The usage of the strategies reflects their fitness within the system.

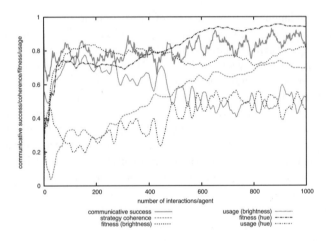

Figure 1. An experimental run in which initially the brightness strategy has a higher fitness than the hue strategy. After 400 interactions per agent, the fitness of the hue strategy overtakes the fitness of the brightness strategy, which is reflected in their usage.

References

Bleys, J., & Steels, L. (2009). Linguistic Selection of Language Strategies. A Case Study for Colour. In *Proceedings of the 10th European Conference on Artificial Life*. Berlin: Springer.

Casson, R. (1997). Color shift: evolution of English color terms from brightness to hue. In C. Hardin & L. Maffi (Eds.), *Color categories in thought and language* (pp. 224–239). Cambridge: Cambridge University Press.

Steels, L. (2010). Can evolutionary linguistics become a science? *Journal of Evolutionary Linguistics, 1*(1).

SAMPLERS, MAXIMISERS AND THE CULTURAL EVOLUTIONARY DYNAMICS OF LANGUAGE

RICHARD A BLYTHE

*SUPA, School of Physics and Astronomy, University of Edinburgh, Mayfield Road,
Edinburgh, EH9 3JZ, UK*
R.A.Blythe@ed.ac.uk

If language is an emergent product of both cognitive biases and human social interactions, then the structure of language and how it changes over time may provide valuable information about these biases, potentially bringing us closer to understanding their origins (Hruschka et al., 2009). Modelling and simulation is one way to discover the consequences of repeated interactions between agents, and how they may end up amplifying (or, indeed suppressing) these biases.

There has recently been a massive burst of activity within the statistical physics community, whereby the emergent properties of many repeated socially-inspired interactions between agents have been investigated (Castellano, Fortunato, & Loreto, 2009). Many researchers have studied whether one of two variant forms with the same function is ultimately adopted as a convention by a community, and if so, which one wins out. Despite the insights into complex interacting systems that physicists bring with them, a valid criticism of this work is that many models invoke ad-hoc rules that are simplistic in their treatment of cognition and lack empirical contact (Castellano et al., 2009).

A more systematic approach is possible, by thinking beyond specific rules and focussing on the type of bias that they imply. We consider three superficially distinct models, one in which speakers sample interlocutors' utterances randomly (Baxter, Blythe, Croft, & McKane, 2006), another in which agents negotiate referents for an object by eliminating other potential referents when a communicative act is deemed successful (Baronchelli, Felici, Caglioti, Loreto, & Steels, 2006), and another that investigates competition between two languages but permits the possibility of bilinguals (Castelló, Eguíluz, & San Miguel, 2006).

We have previously shown that these distinct models can be unified. An analysis of the relevant stochastic equations of motion allows one to identify three distinct biases operating within them (Blythe, 2009). One is a *maximising* bias, where agents seek to eliminate the minority variant. This quickly brings the community to consensus on the global majority variant. The second behaviour is pure *sampling*: both variants then fluctuate in frequency before one of them goes extinct. Both behavioural biases have been observed experimentally, e.g., in the work of Hudson Kam and Newport (2005); a formal cognitive basis for such behaviour has also been provided within a Bayesian learning framework (Reali & Griffiths, 2009). Finally, the model demonstrates the logical possibility of a third type of behaviour, where the two variants coexist indefinitely in equal numbers.

Here we further argue that these three emergent outcomes are generic in models that invoke maximising, linear sampling or "anti-maximising" behaviour, in various combinations and implementations. Whether individuals are variable or categorical users of a variant; whether the bias is in production, or perception, or both; whether they interact with many or few other members of the community; all are 'details' as regards the qualitatively distinct emergent outcomes that can be expected. Unfortunately, all are problematic from the point of view of observed language change. We will discuss consequences, e.g., for the systematisation of a holistic protolanguange (Kirby, Dowman, & Griffiths, 2007), and propose cultural evolutionary mechanisms that may plausibly describe actual instances of language change, speculating as to the kinds of cognitive processes that may underpin them.

References

Baronchelli, A., Felici, M., Caglioti, E., Loreto, V., & Steels, L. (2006). Sharp transition towards shared vocabularies in multi-agent systems. *Journal of Statistical Mechanics: Theory and Experiment*, , P06014.

Baxter, G. J., Blythe, R. A., Croft, W., & McKane, A. J. (2006). Utterance selection model of language change. *Physical Review E*, *73*, 046118.

Blythe, R. A. (2009). Generic modes of consensus in stochastic language dynamics. *Journal of Statistical Mechanics: Theory and Experiment*, , P02059.

Castellano, C., Fortunato, S., & Loreto, V. (2009). Statistical physics of social dynamics. *Reviews of Modern Physics*, *81*, 591–646.

Castelló, X., Eguíluz, V. M., & San Miguel, M. (2006). Ordering dynamics with two non-excluding options: Bilingualism in language competition. *New Journal of Physics*, *8*, 308.

Hruschka, D. J., Chrisiansen, M. H., Blythe, R. A., Croft, W., Heggarty, P., Mufwene, S. S., Pierrehumbert, J. B., & Poplack, S. (2009). Building social cognitive models of language change. *Trends in Cognitive Sciences*, *13*, 464–469.

Hudson Kam, C. L., & Newport, E. L. (2005). Regularizing unpredictable variation: The roles of adult and child learners in language formation and change. *Language Learning and Development*, *1*, 151–195.

Kirby, S., Dowman, M., & Griffiths, T. L. (2007). Innateness and culture in the evolution of language. *PNAS*, *104*, 5241–5245.

Reali, F., & Griffiths, T. L. (2009). The evoluation of frequency distributions: Relating regulatization to inductive biases through iterated learning. *Cognition*, *111*, 317–328.

ACOUSTIC VARIABILITY IN NONHUMAN PRIMATES: INDIVIDUALITY AND SOCIAL CONTEXT

HELENE BOUCHET, CATHERINE BLOIS-HEULIN, ALBAN LEMASSON

UMR6552 EthoS – Ethologie animale et humaine, University of Rennes 1 – CNRS, Station Biologique de Paimpont, France

A growing number of studies revealed that, to some extent, parallels can be found between nonhuman primates' vocal communication and human language (e.g. conversation-like vocal exchanges, referential communication and call combination). But at the same time, nonhuman primate calls are different from speech because of their very limited flexibility. This is intriguing for people interested in the evolution of communicative abilities and in the phylogenetic origin of language. It is now commonly admitted by the scientific community that social life played an essential role in this evolution. Interestingly, vocal plasticity in nonhuman primates is certainly limited but not inexistent and they are nice models to test the influence of social factors on acoustic variability. Several studies have shown that changing the group social composition triggered changes in individual vocal signatures. For example, replacing the harem male in a captive Campbell's monkeys group leads to a rearrangement of social networks and, in parallel, to fine acoustic modifications of the female contact calls conducting to vocal sharing between preferential partners. Here we propose two ways to test the potential influence of social factors on acoustic variability. Our questions were: 1) Does the social context of calling influence the level of intra/inter-individual variability? 2) Does the social system of the species play a role on the shaping of the vocal repertoire's variability?

We conducted call recordings in two primate species presenting interesting social differences. Red-capped mangabeys (*Cercocebus torquatus*) live in the wild in large multi-male and multi-female groups and their social organisation is, like most baboons and macaques, strongly based on frequent peaceful and agonistic interactions. Campbell's monkeys (*Cercopithecus campbelli campbelli*) live in the wild in small harem groups and their social organisation is, like most forest guenons, based on rare physical interactions and a discrete hierarchy. We investigated whether the level of intra/inter-individual variability depended on the call social function. We hypothesized that, as in several other animal species, the level of acoustic variability, notably the level of individual distinctiveness, would be higher in calls presenting a high social value (e.g. contact call types) than in calls presenting a low social value (e.g. alarm call types), the former being involved in affiliative dyadic interactions and the latter consisting in a communication at the group level. In humans, individual distinctiveness can also be accentuated or attenuated by speakers according to the macro context of communication depending on the size and the composition of the audience. We then hypothesized that the variability found in affiliative *versus* agonistic calls would depend on the species social system.

We studied in mangabeys and guenons respectively six and five call types for which we could associate a high, intermediary and low social value. Among highly social calls we compared in both species affiliative contact calls and agonistic threat calls. Intra- and inter-individual acoustic variability was assessed by measuring a set of temporal and frequential values in the same way for all call types. We measured respectively 1416 calls from 14 individuals in mangabeys and 1348 calls from 6 individuals in guenons. We found that the degree of the call social value predicted the level of variability. For instance, we found in both species a much higher potential for identity coding in affiliative calls used during dyadic exchanges than in less social calls like alarm calls (two to four times more variable). A strong difference between the two species was found in social calls associated to a negative value. While the level of variability of threat calls was almost as high as the one of affiliative calls in mangabeys, it was as low as the one of alarm calls in Campbell's monkeys, supporting the social system effect hypothesis.

This study highlights the determinant role played by social factors on the structuring of vocal repertoires and individual acoustic variability. It opens new perspectives of comparative research in animals for understanding how human language evolved and supports the general theory of a social-vocal co-evolution.

CONTEXTS OF LANGUAGE DIVERSITY

INGAR BRINCK

Department of Philosophy and Cognitive Science, Lund University, Sweden

Evans & Levinson (2009) claim that language is a "biocultural hybrid" of gene:culture co-evolution, and that a crucial fact for understanding the place of language in human cognition is its diversity or fundamental variation in form and content. A plausible case for language diversity must explain (1) how language systems can evolve and diversify as socio-cultural products under cognitive constraints on learning, and (2) how come children can learn and adults use any one of the alternative language systems. It is argued here that language is fundamentally pragmatic, and that this explains language diversity given a certain understanding of how behavior and environment specify each other (Brinck 2007; Clark 2008). From a system dynamics perspective it is considered how methods in, e.g., the theory of situated learning (Lane & Husemann 2008) might be used to explore the hypothesis.

(1) Evans' & Levinson's conception of evolution relates to a broader notion of context-dependence that places cultural and technological adaptation at centre-stage. Evolution involves continuous interaction between species and environment leading to new artifacts and behavior, potentially with a wide application such as language. Communication is a situated practice, controlled by local (causal) and global (socio-cultural) contextual features (Garfinkel & Sacks 1970). Internalized skills interact with the environment to produce action, whereas emerging behavior forms induce changes among existing conditions. In a constantly developing feedback loop (*spiral*), our ancestors' environment influenced the evolution of language, while the language shaped the environment. Given that every alternative language has evolved in a particular ecological niche, diversity is no surprise.

(2) Assuming cognitive constraints on learning, the multi-layered nature of language explains how verbal communication can be prolific and occur with such ease. Language relies for its proper functioning on a variety of cognitive, affective, and conative processes. Some occur in nonverbal communication

among nonhuman primates and human infants. Consider reference. Data from comparative, cognitive, and developmental psychology show that nonverbal reference can take many forms, some intentional, others automatic or reflexive (Brinck, 2008; Leavens et al., 2009; Senju & Csibra, 2008; Zlatev et al., 2008). Mechanisms for producing and responding to attention, imitation, gesture, and emotion occur on different processing levels in different formats, simultaneously working towards a common goal, thus enabling multi-layered communication. To optimize performance, behavior is tuned to local properties, explaining how come, in spite of diversity, language is accessible. To exemplify, referential skills are cue-driven and tuned to action contexts. Actions are encoded in detail, and apparently identical contexts may be handled differently by the same agent, because behavioral competence depends on local affordances and constraints.

References

Brinck, I. (2007) Situated cognition, dynamic systems, and art. *JanusHead*, 9(2), 407-431.

Brinck, I. (2008). The role of intersubjectivity for the development of intentional communication. In J. Zlatev, T. Racine. C. Sinha, & E. Itkonen (Eds.) *The Shared Mind: Perspectives on Intersubjectivity* (pp. 115-140). Amsterdam: John Benjamins Publ.

Clark, A. (2008). *Supersizing the Mind: Embodiment, Action, and Cognitive Extension.* Oxford: Oxford University Press.

Evans, N., & Levinson, S.C. (2009). The Myth of Language Universals. *Behavioral and Brain Sciences*, 32, 429-448.

Garfinkel, H., & Sacks, H. (1970). On Formal Structures of Practical Actions. In J.D. McKinney and E.A. Tiryakian (Eds.) *Theoretical Sociology* (pp. 337–66). New York: Appleton-Century Crofts.

Lane, D.C., & Husemann E. (2008). Steering without Circe: attending to reinforcing loops in social systems. *System Dynamics Review*, 24(1), 27-61.

Leavens, D.A., Russell, J., & Hopkins, W.D. (2009). Multimodal communication by captive chimpanzees (Pan troglodytes), *Animal Cognition* (published online 7 June).

Senju, A., & Csibra, G. (2008). Gaze following in human infants depends on communicative signals. *Current Biology*, 18, 668–671.

Zlatev, J., Brinck, I., & Andrén., M. (2008). Stages in the development of perceptual intersubjectivity. In F. Morganti, A. Carassa and G. Riva (Eds.) *Enacting Intersubjectivity: A Cognitive and Social Perspective to the Study of Interaction* (pp. 117-132). Amsterdam: ISO Press.

COORDINATED MULTI-MODAL EXPRESSION AND EMBODIED MEANING IN THE EMERGENCE OF SYMBOLIC COMMUNICATION

J. ERIN BROWN

Language Evolution and Computation, PPLS, The University of Edinburgh, 3 Charles Street, Edinburgh EH8, UK

The study of language evolution has a long tradition of connecting gestures to language origins (Condillac, 1746; Hewes, 1973). Modern theories point to gesture as the solution to a central problem: the emergence of symbolic communication. Prominent versions (Arbib, 2005; Corballis, 2002; Tomasello, 2008) share three critical features: i) early forms of communication consisted of pointing and pantomiming; ii) these gestures then became conventionalised and arbitrary, or symbolic; iii) at some point, the symbolic channel 'switched' and vocalisations became the dominant channel for symbolic communication. I agree that i) is a plausible stage in language evolution but contend that points ii) and iii) are less likely, as they do not follow the evolutionary principles of parsimony and continuity, nor do they provide a satisfactory explanation for the relationship between speech and gesture as it exists today (McNeill, 2005). In addition, arguments for this scenario rely on questionable assumptions regarding early hominid gestural and vocal abilities, the vocal channel's greater potential for creating arbitrary symbols and the role of speech in the instruction of manufacturing techniques.

Although these accounts recognise the powerful representational potential of gesture and consider the advantages of an additional, distinct modality of communication, they do not appear to fully appreciate the synergistic potential of both modalities together nor the limitations of a single modality on its own. If mimetic gestures became symbolic as postulated, the power of their 'natural' meaning would have been lost. Moreover, distributing meaning expression between symbolic and nonarbitrary forms provides cognitive and communicative benefits in language production and comprehension (Goldin-Meadow et al., 2001; Kelly et al., 1999), an advantage that would be sacrificed if gestures transitioned into arbitrary symbols. Though it is not claimed nonarbitrary gestures disappeared during this transition, this scenario does not allow for the same simultaneous nonarbitrary-and-arbitrary signaling distributed across modalities that would enable the cognitively demanding task of forming symbols.

Another problem for these theories is the 'switch' to vocalisations as the dominant vehicle for symbolic communication. If a symbolic gestural system arose, it would have been hugely advantageous and caused evolutionary forces to move toward manual signed language, thus making it very unlikely for speech to evolve (Emmorey, 2005). In addition, an evolutionary scenario in which signaling types shift between modalities entails multiple and significant evolutionary transitions.

A careful consideration of gesture research and the nonarbitrary nature of human communication can contribute substantially to our understanding of language origins. The representational power of gesture alone is not sufficient to explain how arbitrary forms came to carry meaning, as claimed in current gestural origins theories. It is the *coordinated multimodality* of human expression that provides the opportunity for bodily manifestations of meaning to be transferred to co-occurring vocal signals. If nonarbitrary gestures co-occurred with vocalisations early in hominid history, it presents an opportunity for sounds to become symbolic while preserving gesture's 'natural' meaning and retaining the cognitive and communicative benefits of gesturing. In this view, symbols arose in the modality in which they still occur today, thus obviating a 'switch' in symbolic channel in the course of human evolution.

References

Arbib, M., 2005. From monkey-like action recognition to human language: An evolutionary framework for neuroscience. *BBS, 28*, 105-124.

Condillac, E.B., 1746. Essai sur l'origine des connassances humaines, ouvrage ou l'on reduit a un seul principe tout ce concerne l'entendement. In *Oeuvres philosophiques de Condillac.* Paris: Georges LeRoy.

Corballis, M., 2002. *From hand to mouth: The origins of language.* Princeton University Press.

Emmorey, K., 2005. Sign languages are problematic for a gestural origins theory of language evolution. *BBS, 28*, 130-131.

Hewes, G.W., 1973. Primate communication and the gestural origin of language. *Current Anthropology, 12*, 5-24.

Kelly, S.D., Barr, D.J., Breckinridge Church, R. & Lynch, K., 1999. Offering a hand to pragmatic understanding: The role of speech and gesture in comprehension and Memory. *Journal of Memory and Language, 40*, 577-592.

McNeill, D., 2005. *Gesture and Thought.* Cambridge University Press.

Tomasello, M., 2008. *Origins of Human Communication.* MIT Press.

DO APE GESTURES HAVE SPECIFIC MEANINGS?: SHIFTING THE FOCUS FROM FLEXIBILITY TO SEMANTICITY

ERICA A. CARTMILL

Department of Psychology, University of Chicago, 5848 S. University Ave.
Chicago, 60637, USA

RICHARD W. BYRNE

School of Psychology, University of St Andrews, South Street
St Andrews, KY16 9JP, Scotland

Research has demonstrated that captive apes use gestures flexibly in different contexts and in accordance with some understanding of their recipients (e.g. Cartmill & Byrne, 2007; Pika, Liebal, Call, & Tomasello, 2005). This flexibility shows that ape gestures are intentional rather than automatic responses to external stimuli, but gives no indication that they can be used to communicate specific meanings. Discussions of meaning in ape gestures have largely focused on contextual flexibility or cataloguing the number of functions per gesture (e.g. Genty, Breuer, Hobaiter, & Byrne, 2009; Pika et al., 2005). The greater flexibility of gestural vs. vocal communication in great apes demonstrates that the system is less rigid and, in some ways, a seemingly better precursor to language (see Arbib, Liebal, & Pika, 2008; Pollick & de Waal, 2007). However, if gestures are used so flexibly that there is no predictable relationship between form and meaning, then they are not used to communicate *something*. By placing too much weight on the flexible use of gestures, researchers risk underestimating gesture meaning.

Researchers studying ape gesture should adopt a more probabilistic and systematic approach to meaning: one that incorporates our understanding of apes' flexibility in strategic communication but focuses on whether gestures are used predictably to elicit particular behaviors. Such an approach should identify cases where the final outcome of an interaction fulfills the apparent goals of some of the gestures in the exchange. Examples where the gesture's goal appears to be satisfied can be described as having *goal-outcome matches*. One can then attribute meaning to gestures that occur predictably with single matches and test these attributions of meaning using the rest of the dataset. Previous studies have assessed the "function" or "goal" of gestures by correlating form with context (e.g. Genty et al., 2009; Pika et al., 2005). The present approach extends this work significantly by using a subset of data to predict meanings and then testing those meanings using the whole dataset to determine what apes do when recipient responses do not match their gestures' attributed meanings.

I applied this methodology to 64 gestures produced by 28 captive orangutans (*Pongo pygmaeus* and *P. abelii*) to conspecifics housed in 3 European zoos. Out of a total of 1344 examples of "intentional" gesture, 698 had goal-outcome matches (most of the others received no reaction). Of the examples of gestures with goal-outcome matches, 29 gestures occurred more than 70% of the time with a single match, and an additional seven gestures occurred more than 50% of the time with a single match. Each gesture that met either of these meaning thresholds was found to have one of six meanings: *Affiliate/Play*, *Stop action*, *Look at/Take object*, *Share food/object*, *Co-locomote*, and *Move away*.

These attributions of meaning were tested by assuming that every example of a gesture (including those without goal-outcome matches) had the same meaning. I examined whether orangutans were more likely to persist following recipient reactions that did not match the meaning attributed to the initial gesture used. The type of recipient reaction (matching or not matching) significantly affected the gesturer's probability of persisting (χ^2=63.35, df=1, p<0.001). This supported the attributions of gesture meaning.

The results indicate that the gestural communication system of orangutans is composed of both ambiguous and meaningful gestures. Most meaningful gestures do not show a one-to-one correspondence between form and meaning, which allows them to be used with some degree of flexibility. Flexibility and semanticity therefore need not be mutually exclusive, and by redirecting the discussion of ape gesture from flexibility to meaning researchers can use attributions of meaning to make specific predictions about communication strategies and open up new comparisons to human language.

References

Arbib, M., Liebal, K., & Pika, S. (2008). Primate Vocalization, Gesture, and the Evolution of Human Language. *Current Anthropology, 49*(6), 1053-1076.

Cartmill, E., & Byrne, R. (2007). Orangutans modify their gestural signaling according to their audience's comprehension. *Current Biology, 17*, 1-4.

Genty, E., Breuer, T., Hobaiter, C., & Byrne, R. (2009). Gestural communication of the gorilla (*Gorilla gorilla*): repertoire, intentionality and possible origins. *Animal Cognition, 12*(3), 527-546.

Pika, S., Liebal, K., Call, J., & Tomasello, M. (2005). The gestural communication of apes. *Gesture, 5*(1/2), 41-56.

Pollick, A., & de Waal, F. B. M. (2007). Ape gestures and language evolution. *PNAS, 104*(19), 8184-8189.

BRAINS, GENES AND LANGUAGE EVOLUTION

MORTEN H. CHRISTIANSEN

Department of Psychology, Cornell University
Ithaca, NY 14853, USA
Santa Fe Institute
Santa Fe, NM 87501, USA

Why is language the way it is, and how did it come to be that way? Answering these questions requires postulating genetic constraints on language. A key challenge for language evolution research is therefore to explain whether such genetic constraints are specific to language or whether they might be more general in nature. In this talk, I argue that traditional notions of universal grammar as a biological endowment of abstract linguistic constraints can be ruled out on evolutionary grounds (Chater, Reali & Christiansen, 2009; Christiansen, Chater & Reali, 2009). Instead, the fit between the mechanisms employed for language and the way in which language is acquired and used can be explained by processes of cultural evolution shaped by the human brain. On this account, language evolved by 'piggy-backing' on pre-existing neural mechanisms, constrained by socio-pragmatic considerations, the nature of our thought processes, perceptuo-motor factors, and cognitive limitations on learning, memory and processing (Christiansen & Chater, 2008). Using behavioral, computational and molecular genetics methods, I then explore how one of these constraints—the ability to learn and process sequentially presented information—may have played an important role in shaping language through cultural evolution (Reali & Christiansen, 2009). I conclude by drawing out the implications of this viewpoint for understanding the problem of language acquisition, which is cast in a new, and much more tractable, form (Chater & Christiansen, in press).

References

Chater, N. & Christiansen, M.H. (in press). Language acquisition meets language evolution. *Cognitive Science*.

Chater, N., Reali, F. & Christiansen, M.H. (2009). Restrictions on biological adaptation in language evolution. *Proceedings of the National Academy of Sciences, 106*, 1015-1020.

Christiansen, M.H., Chater, N. & Reali, F (2009). The biological and cultural foundations of language. *Communicative & Integrative Biology, 2*, 221-222.

Christiansen, M.H. & Chater, N. (2008). Language as shaped by the brain. *Behavioral & Brain Sciences, 31*, 489-558.

Reali, F. & Christiansen, M.H. (2009). Sequential learning and the interaction between biological and linguistic adaptation in language evolution. *Interaction Studies, 10*, 5-30.

COULD EVO-DEVO SAVE CHOMSKY FROM THE EVOLUTIONARY PARADOX?

HANGJUN CHU

Institute of Linguistics, Beijing Foreign Studies University, No 2 Xisanhuan North RD Beijing, 100089, P. R. China

Chomsky's viewpoint on the evolution of language is quite controversial. (Pinker & Bloom, 1990; Newmeyer, 1998; Jenkins, 2000; Bickerton, 2005; Pinker & Jackendoff, 2005) On the one hand, many supporters believe that Chomsky, who benefits a lot from the new development of evolutionary theories, especially from the non-selectionist concepts such as "spandrel", "exaptation", and "known or unknown physical laws", provides a reasonable speculation on the origin and evolution of language (Jenkins, 2000), which probably can be termed as "neo-neo-Darwinism" (Piattelli-Oalmarini, 1989: 9); On the other hand, some critic argue that the "by-product" concept held by Chomsky is "utterly implausible" (Newmeyer, 1998: 313), and that the evolution of syntax attributed to a very lucky accident of "hopeful monster" mutation, is out of biology (Szabolcs Számadó, 2009: 18).

From Chomsky's own words, we can see that although "the specificity and richness of the language faculty" held in the early phases of generative grammar poses serious barriers to inquiry into how this faculty might have evolved, the Principles and Parameters (P&P) approach, which makes "a sharp distinction between process of acquisition and the format of the internal theory of a language", removes "a crucial conceptual barrier to the study of evolution of language". (Chomsky, 2007, p. 13-4) According to Chomsky, the idea of P&P approach mainly comes from both the intensive study of various languages and an analogy to the new development of biology, evo-devo theory. Chomsky (2005b) has recently written a paper to discuss the application of evo-devo to the study of language, in which the origin and evolution of language became a simple thesis of evo-devo. The impression given by Chomsky is that the exploration on the evolution of language faculty in the framework of P&P approach can greatly make use of the updated development of evolutionary theory---evo-devo. Then could evo-devo save Chomsky from the evolutionary paradox that subtly goes across natural selection and directly attributes the birth of the "merge" operation to a magic random mutation?

The form of every animal is the product of two processes---development from an egg and evolution from its ancestor. What evo-devo focuses on is the closely related relationship between these processes. The fundamental principles of evo-devo theory are that evolution has close relationship with development and the regulatory gene that controls the development of different organisms, is very conservative even across a long period. (Carroll, 2005) Chomsky (2005a, b, 2007) seems to have seized the soul of evo-devo correctly and makes two analogies in linguistics: from the relationship between development and evolution, Chomsky (2005a) finds three factors that can influence the development of language in an individual; and from the regulatory gene mechanism, he gets the idea that the interaction between invariant principles and alternative parameters can determinate the nature of language and language acquisition. Although those ideas, as Chomsky has said, truly get their origins from the parallel development in biology, they are just simple conceptual analogies without any direct relationship with evo-devo theory. We can not find any evolutionary mechanism for Chomsky's "hopeful monster" random mutation in the birth of "merge" operation in evo-devo. From the evo-devo perspective, more attentions should be paid to the epigenetic factors in language development and evolution, rather than just putting too much weight on language phenomenon on genetic instructions. (Deacon, 2003a, b, 2005) Meanwhile, the conservation of regulatory gene means that the reappropriation of old genes to new use is much more the normal case that organisms adopt than the creation of new genes, and instead of expecting too many new "language genes" produced just by magic mutation, the research of language evolution needs the mechanism, such as relaxed selection (Deacon, 2010), to reduce its heavy burden on genetic requirement.

From the analysis above, we can draw conclusions that (1) though evolutionary linguistics can greatly make use of evo-devo, Chomsky just makes a few analogies at the conceptual level and there is not a direct relation between his arguments on the magic mutation and the content of evo-devo theory; (2) Chomsky's viewpoint on language evolution can't get enough evidence from evo-devo, and in fact, some points of his arguments are contradictive to evo-devo; (3) what Chomsky says on the origin and evolution of language mainly comes from his language philosophy, not soundly based on biological phenomena.

Acknowledgements

Thanks to Prof. Terrence Deacon at UC, Berkeley for the helpful discussion, to Prof William S-Y Wang at the Chinese University of Hong Kong for his short comment, and to the anonymous referees for their insightful critique.

GESTURAL COMMUNICATION IN HUMAN CHILDREN: ONTOGENETIC PERSPECTIVE IN FAVOUR OF THE GESTURAL HYPOTHESIS OF LANGUAGE ORIGIN

HELENE COCHET & JACQUES VAUCLAIR

Center for Research in the Psychology of Cognition, Language & Emotion, Aix-Marseille University, Department of Psychology

The evolution of human language can be investigated from different points of view, including from an ontogenetic perspective. By presenting a number of arguments, including original data of our own, we aim to demonstrate the relevance of studying the development of communication in infancy to better understand the evolution of language.

Both neuroanatomical and behavioural studies have shown that gestures and speech entertain close relations during human ontogeny (e.g., Bates & Dick, 2002; Iverson & Thelen, 1999; Rowe & Goldin-Meadow, 2009), and given the cerebral lateralization of speech in humans, the investigation of manual laterality for communicative gestures can provide valuable clues regarding the nature of these speech-gestures links. Experimental and observational studies have reported that the production of communicative gestures, especially pointing gestures, is lateralized to the left cerebral hemisphere (e.g., Cochet & Vauclair, submitted). Interestingly, this right-sided bias for pointing gestures was reported to be stronger than for manipulative actions, whether it concerned hand use in simple reaching or in bimanual activities (Bates, O'Connel, Vaid, Sledge, & Oakes, 1986; Vauclair & Imbault, 2009). Hand preference for communicative gestures then appears to be independent of handedness for manipulative actions. This finding has led researchers to postulate the existence of a specific communication system in the left cerebral hemisphere, controlling both gestural and vocal communication, and which may differ from the system involved in purely motor activities.

Different patterns of laterality between communicative gestures and non communicative actions have also been observed in non human primates (in baboons: Meguerditchian & Vauclair, 2009; in chimpanzees: Hopkins, Russel, Freeman, Buehler, Reynolds, & Schapiro, 2005). Altogether, these results support the gestural theory of the origin of speech. The communication system in the left cerebral hemisphere, which is likely to be located in Broca's area (Gentilucci & Dalla Volta, 2007), might have served as a substrate for the evolution from a gestural communication system to a vocal one (Corballis, 2009).

In order to investigate in greater depth this hypothesis, we focused on the function of pointing gestures, in addition to their handedness. So far, three main functions have been described: children produce *imperative* pointing as a request for an object, *declarative expressive* pointing to share interest with the adult about a specific referent and *declarative informative* pointing in order to help someone by providing him/her needed information (Tomasello, Carpenter, & Liszkowski, 2007). Declarative pointing gestures, whose frequency increases when children grow old (Cochet & Vauclair, submitted), are thought to reflect more complex cognitive skills related to the understanding of others as attentional and intentional agents. We set up three experimental designs at day nurseries to elicit these three different pointing gestures in 48 toddlers between 15 and 30 months of age. A unimanual reaching task was also administered. Main results revealed that declarative gestures were more frequently accompanied by vocalizations than imperative gestures and that gaze alternation was more frequent in informative pointing compared to imperative and expressive situations. Furthermore, the difference in the degree of manual preference between manipulative actions and pointing gestures was the strongest for informative pointing.

As non human primates point imperatively to request food, but not declaratively (except a few language-trained apes), studying the emergence of declarative communication in human infants might point out some socio-cognitive prerequisites for the emergence of language. In this regard, investigating the development of declarative informative pointing is particularly relevant, as this gesture seems to benefit only the recipient of the signal, opening window into the development of cooperative abilities. Our results then suggest that such cooperative gestures may have played an important role in the evolution of human language and its cerebral lateralization.

This research was supported by a French National Research Agency (ANR) grant reference ANR-08-BLAN-0011_01.

THE PATH FROM POINT A TO POINT B: HOW GESTURES BECAME LANGUAGE IN NICARAGUAN SIGNING

MARIE COPPOLA

Departments of Psychology and Linguistics, University of Connecticut
Storrs Mansfield, CT 06269 USA

ANN SENGHAS

Department of Psychology, Barnard College, 3009 Broadway
New York, NY 10027 USA

How do new linguistic elements emerge? How are they changed from the pre-linguistic raw materials of their origin? To catch the very earliest stages of such a transformation, we turned to a young language – Nicaraguan Sign Language (NSL). Because NSL is only 30 years old, the pioneering generation that created it is around today, able to show us what the earliest Nicaraguan signing looked like. Members of different age cohorts today represent a living · "fossil record" of the language. Elements that served as likely linguistic precursors are also still observable, in present-day co-speech gestures and homesigns.

Here we take a humble gesture – the point – and follow its transformation into a linguistic element. This basic gesture often accompanies speech to indicate real-world locations and objects. As it transformed into a sign, we found an increase in its use to identify the participants in events rather than referring to locations or real-world objects. With this shift, points took on new linguistic functions, including indicating the subject of a verb, and serving as a pronoun.

Most deaf signers in Nicaragua learned to sign through social contact when they entered special education centers in Managua that were newly established and expanded rapidly starting in the late 1970s. Educators did not sign, but they did not prohibit their students from gesturing, and the children began to create a common communication system. What began as gesturing among fifty individuals became a full, rich sign language used by a community of over 1000.

To capture different periods in the language's emergence, we grouped participants into cohorts: Children who arrived in the late 1970s and early 1980s (now adults) form the first cohort, those who arrived in the mid- to late-1980s (now adolescents) form the second cohort, and those who arrived in the 1990s (now children) form the third cohort.

Going one level deeper in the fossil record, we compared these NSL signers to four deaf homesigners who never entered the programs in Managua. These homesigners have not acquired NSL; none has a regular communication partner who signs NSL, none uses NSL vocabulary or grammar. They represent the communication systems of deaf Nicaraguans before NSL developed.

We compared the same signed story (based on a cartoon) from four participants from each group along this continuum of language emergence: adult homesigners who never acquired a conventional sign language, and NSL signers who acquired the language at three successive periods during its emergence. How does the form and function of pointing change along this continuum?

We classified each instance of a point according to its endpoint (e.g., a nearby object, the signer's chest, or an empty space in front of the signer). We then determined the meaning and function of points and categorized them into *locatives*, which referred to locations (such as 'overhead' or 'to the left') and *nominals*, which referred to persons or objects (such as 'Tweety the bird' or 'the cage'). Note that both types entail a displacement of the referent from the real world and real objects. Such displacement is a fundamental symbolic characteristic of language that allows reference to entities and locations that are not in the here-and-now. As the points took on this symbolic function, we also examined whether and how they combined with other signs to form phrases.

Comparisons across our continuum revealed a shift in the use of the manual point, starting with mostly concrete, locative meanings, and later taking on more symbolic, abstract, and displaced nominal (and possibly pronominal) functions. While the frequency of locative points remained constant across participant groups, the frequency of nominal points increased significantly. The nominal forms also became integrated into the syntax of NSL. Thus, modern NSL points participate in constructions that give them a more categorical, less context-bound flavor than the co-speech forms that are their origin.

These uses of pointing differ strikingly from those of gestures accompanying speech. Indeed, the more the sign-like uses develop, the less they show the spatial and locative meaning associated with typical pointing gestures. In accord with findings from spoken language grammaticalization, a crucial step in the transformation of pointing gestures into abstract, recombinable linguistic elements seems to be the loss of locative semantic content. Thus, from the earliest to the most developed form of NSL, we find more points that refer not to locations but to entities, and that increasingly serve linguistic functions.

THE EMERGENCE OF STRUCTURE FROM SEQUENCE MEMORY CONSTRAINTS IN CULTURAL TRANSMISSION

HANNAH CORNISH & SIMON KIRBY

Language Evolution and Computation Research Unit, University of Edinburgh, Edinburgh, EH8 9AD, UK

MORTEN H. CHRISTIANSEN

Department of Psychology, Cornell University, Ithaca, NY 14853, USA

Iterated language learning has recently emerged as a method for experimentally exploring processes of cultural transmission in language evolution amongst humans. In this approach, miniature artificial languages are acquired by participants, and then transmitted to the next participant following a diffusion chain paradigm. This technique has revealed how an initially unstructured language can become structured and progressively easier to acquire over time (Kirby et al., 2008), adapting in a systematic way alongside the meanings being conveyed (Cornish et al., 2009). Importantly, participants are only seeking to reproduce the language given to them: there is no communication with other learners, and changes arise purely as a result of the cultural transmission process, not through deliberate invention by participants.

This previous work has focused exclusively on the cultural transmission of meanings and signals, and in particular, how the presence of structured meanings gives rise to compositional linguistic structures. The question remains, though, whether other types of cognitive constraints, in the *absence* of structured meanings, may affect cultural transmission via iterated learning, as suggested by Christiansen & Chater (2008). Accordingly, in this talk, we present the results from a novel iterated learning paradigm that seeks to investigate experimentally whether biases in sequence memory lead to the cultural evolution of structure, independent of any language-like task.

To isolate the effect of sequence memory constraints on cultural transmission, we ran an iterated version of a simple artificial grammar learning (AGL) task. Although AGL tasks have been primarily used to study implicit learning, the cognitive mechanisms employed in this task are likely the same as those used for artificial language learning (Perruchet & Pacton, 2006). Indeed, AGL tasks have been shown to activate the same part of Broca's area that is also involved in language (Petersson et al., 2004). Crucially, unlike previous iterated language learning tasks (e.g. Kirby et al., 2008), our iterated AGL task did not involve the transfer of meanings, only signals. Participants were exposed to a series of fifteen different consonant strings one by one, and asked to accurately reproduce them after a short delay (3000ms) following each presentation. Each string was seen six times in total, at which point the participants were asked to recall all fifteen strings in any order. The output from this final recall test was then recoded to eliminate potential typing biases and/or use of anagrams, and this became the input string-set for the next generation.

The initial string-sets used to begin each chain were carefully constructed to contain very little structure. Our predictions were two-fold: that by the end of the chains the string-sets would become 1) easier to acquire, and 2) more structured. These predictions were confirmed by standard information-theoretical measures of structure, such as entropy, and also by techniques drawn from the AGL literature (see Conway & Christiansen, 2005, and references within). In particular, measures of associative chunk strength (the amount of repetition of sub-sequences) and anchor strength (the specific sub-sequences at the beginning and end of strings) show that over time certain distributional patterns emerge in the string-sets, which facilitate learning. Strings within a set also evolve to become more similar to one another, again, facilitating better learning and recall. Thus, distributional structure relevant for language acquisition (Perruchet & Pacton, 2006) emerges across chains of learners.

The results from our new iterated AGL task thus demonstrate that constraints on sequence memory alone, amplified by processes of cultural transmission, may have been an important factor in shaping linguistic structure during the cultural evolution of language.

References

Christiansen, M.H. & Chater, N. (2008). Language as shaped by the brain. *Behavioral & Brain Sciences, 31*, 489-558.

Conway, C.M. & Christiansen, M.H. (2005). Modality constrained statistical learning of tactile, visual, and auditory sequences. *Journal of Experimental Psychology: Learning, Memory & Cognition, 31*, 24-39.

Cornish, H., Tamariz, M. & Kirby, S. (2009). Complex adaptive systems and the origins of adaptive structure: what experiments can tell us. *Language Learning, 59*, 191-209.

Kirby, S., Cornish, H. & Smith, K. (2008). Cumulative cultural evolution in the laboratory: An experimental approach to the origins of structure in human language. *PNAS, 105*(31), 10681-10686.

Perruchet, P. & Pacton, S. (2006). Implicit learning and statistical learning: Two approaches, one phenomenon. *Trends in Cognitive Sciences, 10*, 233-238.

Petersson, K.M, Forkstam, C. & Ingvar, M. (2004). Artificial syntactic violations activate Broca's region. *Cognitive Science, 28*, 383-407.

CROSS-MODALITY: REVIVING ICONICITY IN THE EVOLUTION OF LANGUAGE

CHRISTINE CUSKLEY, SIMON KIRBY, JULIA SIMNER

School of Philosophy Psychology and Language Sciences, University of Edinburgh,
3 Charles Street, Edinburgh, EH8 9AD, United Kingdom

Some of the earliest and most simplistic theories of the evolution of language have been coined "bow-wow" theories, positing that language sprung from utterances (forms) directly and iconically related to what they depict (meanings). In the relatively recent explosion of interest in language evolution, theories of this type have been largely forgotten or dismissed for two major reasons: (i) natural language is arbitrary, not iconic; and (ii) given that we use the auditory modality for communication, we are only able to iconically express meanings related to sound. I will argue that the former problem makes uninformed assumptions about language and language evolution, while the latter problem may find a solution in the study of cross-modality: connections between the senses. Moreover, an iconic protolanguage would offer a compelling solution to Harnad's (1990) symbol grounding problem: linguistic symbols are ultimately grounded in our perceptual system.

Objection (i), that natural language is arbitrary, makes two major errors. One, it assumes that because all languages make use of arbitrariness, that they are *exclusively* arbitrary. Non-arbitrariness and iconicity in language are historically understudied, but it is uncontroversial among those that do study it that almost all languages take advantage of some form of iconicity (Nuckolls, 1999; Tamariz, 2005). Directly iconic forms can be seen most obviously in onomatopoeia, but also occur in ideophones: words vividly depicting sensory events for native speakers (Dingemanse, 2009).

Two, this objection assumes language has always been as it is now. The concept of protolanguage allows for a smaller system preceding language. Simulations show that iconicity is favoured in small systems, but arbitrariness has greater advantages as the system expands (Gasser, 2004). Communication emergence experiments (Theisen, Oberlander & Kirby, in press) and documented change in sign languages (Pietrandrea, 2002) demonstrate a move from iconic to arbitrary in language growth and use.

This leaves the second objection to "bow-wow" theories: language occurs in the auditory modality, and utterances can only be iconic through the imitation of sound. However, this objection ignores the growing literature on the complimentary role gesture plays in language (Tomasello, 2008). Although the auditory modality is dominant, the gestural modality is also available for iconic expression.

Moreover, humans experience non-random cross-modal associations (e.g., Simner & Ludwig, 2009) allowing for all sensory experiences to be expressed through a single modality. These shared cross-modal biases allow both iconic expression and understanding: combined with the cognitive assets of shared intentionality and theory of mind (Tomasello, 2008), we are equipped and motivated to make inferences about the cross-modal nature of others' utterances.

In this paper, we will review the evidence for cross-modality relating to language, and present experimental evidence specifying the precise nature of the cross-modal biases involved. Ultimately, we will argue that these consistent biases provided a scaffold for an iconic spoken protolanguage.

References

Dingemanse, (2009) How To Do Things With Ideophones: Observations on the use of vivid sensory language in Siwu. *Presentation at the SOAS Research Seminar*, June 3, London.

Gasser, M. (2004) The origins of arbitrariness in language. *Annual Conference of the Cognitive Science Society*, 26.

Harnad, S. (1990) The symbol grounding problem. *Physica D*, 42, 335-336.

Nuckolls, J. (1999). The case for sound symbolism. *Annual Review of Anthropology*, 28, 225-252.

Pietrandrea, P. (2002). Iconicity and arbitrariness in Italian Sign Langauge. *Sign Langauge Studies*, 2:3, 296-321.

Simner, J. & Ludwig, V. (2009). What colour does that feel? Cross-modal correspondences from touch to colour. *Third International Conference of Synaesthesia and Art (Artecitta)*. Granada, Spain.

Tamariz, M. (2005). Configuring the Phonological Organization of the Mental Lexicon using Syntactic and Semantic Information. *Proceedings of the 27rd Annual Conference of the Cognitive Science Society*.

Theisen, C.A., Oberlander, J. & Kirby, S (in press) Systematicity and arbitrariness in novel communication systems. *Interaction Studies*.

Tomasello, M. (2008). *Origins of Human Communication*. Cambridge, Massachusetts: MIT Press

SQUIGGLE: LARGE-SCALE SOCIAL
EMERGENCE OF SIMPLE SYMBOLS

RICK DALE

GARY LUPYAN

Department of Psychology
The University of Memphis
Memphis, TN, USA

Department of Psychology
University of Pennsylvania
Philadelphia, PA, USA

Recently, several prominent studies have developed human experimental methods to explore the emergence and evolution of simple linguistic systems. In one line of research, often termed *iterated learning* (Kalish, Griffiths, & Lewandowsky, 2007; Kirby, Cornish, and Smith, 2008), human participants see word-picture pairings in an invented mini-language. The learner then reproduces these pairings, which become the training material for the next learner. Because learning is imperfect, subsequent generations produce gradually stable, systematic versions of the "language." Another line of work has explored how social coordination between participants produces simplified linguistic systems. Simon Garrod and Nicholas Fay and colleagues (Garrod, Fay, Oberlander, Lee, & MacLeod, 2007; Fay, Garrod, & Roberts, 2008) had participants function in pairs, creating line drawings to identify a referent picture among a list of candidates. After multiple rounds of interaction, participants create a simplified set of symbolic representations for images (see also Galantucci, 2005).

In the present work, we have loosely integrated both empirical approaches, and taken them in a new direction in a multiplayer communication game we call *Squiggle*. Players connect to the game engine via Internet, and create and interpret visual signs for real-world objects. Successful communication occurs when other players are able to match a previously created sign to its referent. As gameplay proceeds, we track the evolution of individual signs and study in real-time the transition from iconic to symbolic communication.

The Squiggle game consists of *speaking* trials in which a player is presented with a picture (common objects, faces, and place pictures) and has 4 seconds to draw a squiggle—a black and white line drawing created on a computer interface—such that another person would be able to match the squiggle with the picture. On a *listening* trial, a player is shown a previously created squiggle along with two pictures and has to select the picture they think the squiggle refers to. They are then provided with accuracy feedback. On speaking trials, a picture is randomly chosen to be "squiggled." On listening trials, an evolutionary algorithm, factoring in the novelty and previous comprehensibility of a squiggle in the database, determined whether a squiggle had an opportunity to be presented to the community of users for a randomly selected picture. The most successful squiggles remain in game play while less successful squiggles (those which are not reliably understood) gradually disappear. Initial data were collected from 60 players who produced about 1,400 squiggles and participated in 4,100 listening trials. Many players report the game to be very entertaining (even addictive) and several played for almost an hour or more.

Basic findings suggest that the same patterns observed in previous work occur in this large-scale online game. First, squiggles get simplified. The average size of a squiggle shrinks over gameplay. Second, the evolutionary algorithm produced stability for most images, despite opportunities for novel squiggles to replace them during listen trials. Third, while squiggles are drawn highly iconically at first, participants gradually use simplified squiggles that distinguish pictures from others in the same domain. Finally, we describe a referent set in which compositionality may be emerging (akin to Kirby et al., 2008).

Currently, we are extending this game-based approach to a massively multiplayer environment for the iPhone in the hope of getting thousands to play. This will permit explorations of language evolution hitherto inaccessible to human experimentation, including questions regarding social network connectivity, small-world network structure, and the emergence and interaction between human dialects. The approach therefore holds promise by allowing us to study the emergence of linguistic communities in real-time at a very large scale.

References

Fay, N., Garrod, S., & Roberts, L. (2008). The fitness and functionality of culturally evolved communication systems. *Philosophical Transactions of the Royal Society B: Biological Sciences, 363*(1509), 3553-3561.

Galantucci, B. (2005). An experimental study of the emergence of human communication systems. *Cognitive Science, 29*(5), 737–767.

Garrod, S., Fay, N., Lee, J., Oberlander, J., & MacLeod, T. (2007). Foundations of representation: Where might graphical symbol systems come from? *Cognitive Science, 31*, 961–987.

Kalish, M. L., Griffiths, T. L., & Lewandowsky, S. (2007). Iterated learning: intergenerational knowledge transmission reveals inductive biases. *Psychonomic Bulletin & Review, 14*(2), 288-294.

Kirby, S., Cornish, H., & Smith, K. (2008). Cumulative cultural evolution in the laboratory: An experimental approach to the origins of structure in human language. *Proc. of the National Academy of Sciences, 105*, 10681–10686.

USING SOFTWARE AGENTS TO INVESTIGATE THE INTERACTIVE ORIGINS OF COMMUNICATION SYSTEMS

PIETER DE BIE*, THOMAS SCOTT-PHILLIPS†, SIMON KIRBY†, BART VERHEIJ*

* Artificial Intelligence, University of Groningen
† Language Evolution and Computation Research Unit, University of Edinburgh
pdebie@ai.rug.nl

In contemporary research on the origins of human communication, games are used as a methodological tool (Galantucci, 2005; De Ruiter, Noordzij, Newman-Norlund, Hagoort, & Toni, 2007; Scott-Phillips, Kirby, & Ritchie, 2009). It has turned out that the ample degree of freedom allowed by the proposed games can be an impediment for the fruitful drawing of conclusions from the empirical findings: the creativity and flexibility of experimental participants leads to behavior that is hard to predict up front, allowing only post-hoc analysis (cf. Galantucci (2005)).

In the research reported here, an attempt is made to improve this situation by designing a game that can be played by a human player against a software agent. We hypothesize that this will provide an experimental setting that is sufficiently constrained for the design of experiments on the emergence of a communication system in which the test person's behavior is quantitatively measurable.

To test our hypothesis, a game has been defined that is sufficiently complex to allow for interesting communicative interaction to arise, but that is at the same time sufficiently simple to allow the design of software agents playing different strategies in the game. By the use of software agents, there is control over one of the players in the game, effectively reducing the range of expected behaviour of the second (human) player. The Embodied Communication Game (ECG) by Scott-Phillips et al. (2009) served as starting point for the design of our game. Current results are the design, analysis and implementation of a game and software agents with different strategies. The implemented strategies were derived from theoretical considerations and from the observation of human players playing the game.

In our game, there are a Sender and a Receiver (cf. De Ruiter et al. (2007)). The Sender controls a stick man situated in a box with four squares of one of four colours (red, yellow, blue, green). A colour might occur several times, or not at all. The stick man can travel from square to square. The Sender's goal is to communicate to the Receiver the colour of the square at the end of his turn. The Receiver watches a replay of the moves of the Sender, with all timing information removed, and with the squares grayed out. After watching the replay the Receiver has to decide on which of the four colours the Sender ended his turn. If the Receiver chooses the correct colour, both players gain a point. The goal for the players is to score the highest amount of points in succession.

Preliminary experiments have been performed to test whether the game indeed provides an experimental platform allowing the effective measuring of the behaviour of human players. We performed a 24 person experiment and tested two hypotheses. First, a less efficient signal is expected to be easier to recognize as a meaningful signal. Second, a highly repetitive signal is expected to be easier to detect than a signal without repetitions. We predicted higher scores for players paired with an inefficient, highly repetitive agent than for players paired with a highly efficient, not repetitive agent.

Inefficiency was measured as the number of moves used to travel from to the ending square minus the minimal number of moves required. Repetitiveness was measured by creating an algorithm that can detect oscillations, loops, corner oscillations and U-shapes in the moves of the Sender. The hypotheses were tested by creating four agents which all took on the signalling role. The agents used strategies differing in inefficiency and repetitiveness by using different signalling methods. One agent moved as efficient as possible, the others used combinations of oscillations and circles. Contrary to expectations, we found no significant differences in the scores between different agents. It seems that the agents' strategies were too difficult to understand; only one participant was able to score higher than what would be expected by chance.

We expected that replacing one participant with an agent and using a predefined signalling system would make the task easier. In fact, comparison with results from the ECG indicates that this made the task harder. This suggests that interaction is critical in constructing a shared signalling system. One possible reason is that the embodied behaviours of the signaller only make sense once the receiver has actually played that embodied role themselves. If so, researchers looking at these games may need to explore the space of designs more widely to find out what aspects of their games are crucial and what are not. Future work may need smarter agents that play both signalling and receiving roles.

References

De Ruiter, J., Noordzij, M., Newman-Norlund, S., Hagoort, P., & Toni, I. (2007). On the origin of intentions. In P. Haggard, Y. Rossetty, & M. Kawato (Eds.), (p. 593-610). Oxford University Press.

Galantucci, B. (2005). An experimental study of the emergence of human communication systems. *Cognitive Science: A Multidisciplinary Journal, 29*(5), 737 - 767.

Scott-Phillips, T. C., Kirby, S., & Ritchie, G. R. S. (2009). Signalling signalhood and the emergence of communication. *Cognition, 113*, 226-233.

THE PERCEPTUAL EFFECT OF AIR SACS

BART DE BOER

Amsterdam Center for Language and Communication, Universiteit van Amsterdam,
Spuistraat 210, 1012VT, Amsterdam, the Netherlands

1. Introduction

This paper presents work on air sacs that extends the work presented by de Boer, (2008a). In that paper, and before (Fitch, 2000) air sacs were identified as a likely feature of our evolutionary ancestors that may have been lost because of the evolution of speech. In the mean time, a more accurate understanding of air sac acoustics has been achieved (de Boer, 2008b; Riede *et al.*, 2008). Ape-like air sacs modify the acoustics of a vocal tract in three ways: they add a low-frequency resonance (near the resonance frequency of the air sac itself), they shift up the resonances of the vocal tract without the air sac, and they shift these resonances closer together. The question that is addressed in the present paper is how these changes influence perception of the difference between vocalizations.

2. The experiment

Two sets of three stimuli were generated with a simple two-tube model (Chiba & Kajiyama, 1942) that modeled [a], [ə] and [y] with and without air sacs. Subjects (22 undergraduate students with normal hearing) were asked in two tasks to identify whether stimuli with noise were either [a] or [ə] and [a] or [y] using an unforced-choice adaptive threshold method (Kaernbach, 2001). This method

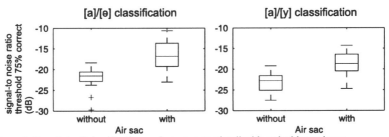

Figure 1. Box plots of classification performance on stimuli with and without air sac.

establishes the signal-to-noise ratio at which subjects perform halfway between chance and perfect classification (for two stimuli this is at 75% correct).

Figure 1 illustrates that subjects performed significantly better at classifying the stimuli without an air sac than at classifying those with an air sac (p < 0.001 with the Wilcoxon rank sum test). The difference in median threshold was 4.7 dB for classifying [a] and [ə] and 4.1 dB for [a] and [y].

3. Discussion

The higher signal-to-noise ratio required to classify stimuli with air sacs indicates that the perceptual distance between these stimuli is lower and that air sacs therefore reduce the acoustic difference that exists between articulations. This means that more articulatory effort is needed to make distinctive speech sounds when an air sac is present, lending support to the theory that humans have lost air sacs because of the evolution of speech. On the other hand, the difference is not very big. Therefore, other factors may be important as well. The extra resonance that air sacs provide has low frequency and this helps to exaggerate size. This might be less important for modern humans, and as air sacs do have important disadvantages (they can become infected, Lawson *et al.*, 2006), this might therefore also be a contributing factor to their disappearance.

References

Chiba, T., & Kajiyama, M. (1942). *The vowel: Its nature and structure*. Tokyo: Tokyo-Kaiseikan.

de Boer, B. (2008a). The joy of sacs. In A. D. M. Smith, K. Smith & r. Ferrer i Cancho (Eds.), *The evolution of language* (pp. 415–416). New Jersey: World Scientific.

de Boer, B. (2008b). *Modeling the acoustics of air sacs*. Paper presented at the Acoustic Communication by Animals, Corvallis, OR.

Fitch, W. T. (2000). The evolution of speech: A comparative review. *Trends in cognitive sciences, 4*(7), 258–267.

Kaernbach, C. (2001). Adaptive threshold estimation with unforced choice tasks. *Perception & Psychophysics, 63*(8), 1377–1388.

Lawson, B., Garriga, R., & Galdikas, B. M. F. (2006). Airsacculitis in fourteen juvenile southern bornean orangutans (*Pongo pygmaeus wurmbii*). *Journal of Medical Primatology, 35*(3), 149-154.

Riede, T., Tokuda, I. T., Munger, J. B., & Thomson, S. L. (2008). Mammalian laryngseal air sacs add variability to the vocal tract impedance: Physical and computational modeling. *Journal of the Acoustical Society of America, 124*(1), 634–647.

THE INFLUENCE OF LANGUAGE ON CONCEPT FORMATION IN ARTIFICIAL AGENTS

JOACHIM DE GREEFF, FRÉDÉRIC DELAUNAY AND TONY BELPAEME

School of Computing and Mathematics, University of Plymouth,
Plymouth PL4 8AA - United Kingdom
Joachim.deGreeff@plymouth.ac.uk

For any cognitive system to behave properly within a dynamic, ever changing natural environment, the ability to work with concepts is quite important. Humans display an ability to talk·about, reason over, infer and generate new concepts with remarkable ease, but for artificial agents this is far from trivial. In the case of human concept learning, it has been acknowledged by several authors that the formation of new concepts is heavily influenced by language. As such, the words used to describe a stimulus govern the way in which this data will be integrated into existing conceptual structures.

Several studies have shown that young children, in addition to learning directly from sensory exploration, rely on linguistic labels to acquire new concepts. Xu (Xu, 2002), for example, demonstrated how linguistic labels help 9-month old infants to establish a representation for different objects. Learning without linguistic labels, or with the presence of tones, sounds or emotional expressions is not as effective. Plunkett (Plunkett, Hu, & Cohen, 2008) came to the same conclusion in a controlled experiment in which they demonstrated how category formation in 10-month old infants is influenced by linguistic labels. Linguistic labels also have an effect on category learning in adults; adults who learn a new category did so significantly faster and showed more robust category recall when the learning experience was accompanied by novel linguistic labels (Lupyan, Rakison, & McClelland, 2007). This shows that linguistic labels facilitate category acquisition, both in pre-linguistic infants and adults. These insights tie in with linguistic relativism, which gained renewed attention as a series of experiments demonstrated how perception of stimuli and use of categories is influenced by language (Gilbert, Regier, Kay, & Ivry, 2006) (Majid, Bowerman, Kita, Haun, & Levinson, 2004).

In order to capture these insights, we developed a computational model in which a learning agent is able to learn new concepts through linguistic interaction with a teacher. To do so, we adapted interaction based on Language Games (Steels & Belpaeme, 2005) to a teacher-learner scenario. This allows for the usage of language as a steering mechanism in the acquisition of conceptual knowledge and associated meaning. A learning agent engages into a series of Language Games with a teacher, and thus gradually builds a repertoire of word-meaning mappings. To represent conceptual knowledge, we use a Conceptual Space (Gärdenfors, 2000), which consists of a geometrical representation within a number of quality dimensions with a metric, allowing for similarity measurement. Within a Conceptual Space, concepts can be stored as prototypes and associated with a lexicon of word labels. Newly perceived stimuli can be matched to existing conceptual prototypes and an appropriate linguistic expression can be found.

We propose that the model exhibits properties comparable to how young children learn new concepts; namely *language driven acquisition*, *fast mapping* and *overgeneralization*. The model is based on previous work as reported in (Greeff, Delaunay, & Belpaeme, 2009), in which we studied the effect of adding interactive features to the learning process. We then augmented the model with a Spreading Activation layer (Rumelhart, McClelland, & PDP Research Group, 1986) which allows for association between conceps, even when they are not perceptually similar. Typically the colour domain is used as a test case, but the model characteristics are general enough to be applied in any domain. We argue that our model is a feasible way of acquiring conceptual knowledge in a linguistic relativism spirit.

References

Gärdenfors, P. (2000). *Conceptual spaces: The geometry of thought.* Cambridge, MA: the MIT Press.

Gilbert, A., Regier, T., Kay, P., & Ivry, R. (2006). Whorf hypothesis is supported in the right visual field but not the left. In *Proceedings of the national academy of sciences* (p. 489-494).

Greeff, J. de, Delaunay, F., & Belpaeme, T. (2009). Human-robot interaction in concept acquisition: a computational model. *ICDL, 0*, 1-6.

Lupyan, G., Rakison, D. H., & McClelland, J. L. (2007). Language is not just for talking - redundant labels facilitate learning of novel categories. *Psychological Science, 18*(12), 1077-1083.

Majid, A., Bowerman, M., Kita, S., Haun, D. B. M., & Levinson, S. C. (2004). Can language restructure cognition? the case for space. *Trends in Cognitive Sciences, 8*(3), 108 - 114.

Plunkett, K., Hu, J., & Cohen, L. B. (2008). Labels can override perceptual categories in early infancy. *Cognition, 106*(2), 665–681.

Rumelhart, D. E., McClelland, J. L., & PDP Research Group the. (1986). *Parallel distributed processing, volumes 1 and 2.* Cambridge: MIT Press.

Steels, L., & Belpaeme, T. (2005). Coordinating perceptually grounded categories through language: A case study for colour. *Behavioral and Brain Sciences, 28*(4), 469-89. (Target Paper, discussion 489-529)

Xu, F. (2002). The role of language in acquiring object kind concepts in infancy. *Cognition, 85*(3), 223 - 250.

RECREATING DUALITY OF PATTERNING IN THE LABORATORY: A NEW EXPERIMENTAL PARADIGM FOR STUDYING EMERGENCE OF SUBLEXICAL STRUCTURE

ALEX DEL GIUDICE

Linguistics Department and Center for Research in Language, University of California – San Diego, 9500 Gilman Dr., La Jolla, CA 92093-0108

SIMON KIRBY

Linguistics and English Language, University of Edinburgh, 3 Charles Street, Edinburgh, EH8 9AD

CAROL PADDEN

Department of Communication and Center for Research in Language, University of California – San Diego, 9500 Gilman Dr., La Jolla, CA 92093-0503

1. Abstract

Duality of patterning (DoP) refers to the reuse and recombination of a small set of meaningless units to create a near-limitless set of meaningful morphemes. We develop an experimental paradigm to explore the development of DoP. In this paradigm, human participants (each representing one generation) learn a lexicon of *random visual symbols,* such that influence from their own language is minimized. Using a communication system similar to that of Galantucci (2005), participants use a digital stylus to draw symbols on a computer display but, critically, the mapping from the stylus to the screen is restricted in order to prevent the use of orthographic characters or pictographs. Participants recreate the set of symbols, and these are transmitted to the next participant in a diffusion chain through a process of iterated learning. This paradigm allows us to observe evolution of a cultural behavior such that no single participant is the driver of innovation and selection; instead the behavior is cumulatively developed across individuals.

A sample of the results is presented in Figure 1 (multiple diffusion chains were created, each consisting of 5 or more generations). Here we note few items remain unaltered by the fifth generation. Most symbols undergo small changes that accumulate over time (i.e. item #7). Lost symbols are generally replaced with novel symbols composed of segments present in other items in the lexicon. As items are modified and replaced in this way, a small set of subunits begins to pervade the entire lexicon. After several generations, items become more similar and these similarities lead to, and result from, the reuse and recombination of smaller units.

Figure 0: A sample of the lexicon. Row 1 represents the random initial lexicon, rows 2 and 3 represent the lexicon at later generations (3 and 5, respectively).

In subsequent experiments, we study how the pairing of meaning with each symbol influences the development of subunits based on semantic categories (such as abstract shapes and animate creatures) similarly to studies by Thiesen et al (to appear). Results of this paradigm suggest that an interaction of two or more factors may be partly responsible for the emergence of DoP: articulation and memory constraints. As each generation alters the symbols responding to tension between the production and perception systems, symbols become more similar and more difficult to recall. To overcome this, each "generation" modifies the set via small, often unintended, innovations in order to form distinctions within the set. In Figure 1 above, we see that by Gen 5 several symbol pairs differ only in a single feature. For example: Items #2 and #3 are mirror images of one another along the y-dimension. Items #9 and #3 differ by the direction line segments beneath the symbol.

Recently, Sandler et al. (to appear) argue that DoP is still emerging in a spontaneously created new sign language, Al-Sayyid Bedouin Sign Language (ABSL), whereas established older sign languages have contrastive phonological systems. This may be because sign languages have large articulatory spaces and can exploit iconicity, or a transparent form-meaning mapping. This paradigm may allow us to test articulatory constraints (by modifying the pad and stylus' ability to recreate symbols) and memory constraints (by varying the number of symbols in a set) in order to evaluate effects on subjects' output forms across generations.

Galantucci, B. (2005). An experimental study of the emergence of human communication system. *Cognitive Science*, 29, 737-767.

Sandler, W., Aronoff, M., Meir, I., Padden, C. (to appear). The gradual emergence of phonological form in a new language. *Natural Language and Linguistic Theory*.

Theisen, C.A., Oberlander, J., & Kirby.S, (to appear). Systematicity and arbitrariness in novel communication systems. *Interaction Studies*.

FROM HAND TO MOUTH: AN EXPERIMENTAL SIMULATION OF LANGAUGE ORIGIN

NICOLAS FAY & STEPHANIE LIM

School of Psychology, University of Western Australia, 35 Stirling Highway
Perth, WA6009, Australia

Though the language of gestures and that of voice be equally natural,
nevertheless the former is easier and less dependent on convention, for
more objects strike our eyes than our ears and shapes are more varied
than sounds. Rousseau (1781, p. 71)

Consideration of the origin of language was deemed futile by the Société de Linguistique de Paris in 1866, and all discussion on this topic was banned. This ruling reflects the fact that spoken language leaves no trace, prohibiting a study of language origin. Recently there has been a resurgence of interest in the science of language evolution (Fitch, 2007). Discussion of the origin of language has also been revived, although it has been largely speculative.

Three theoretical accounts of the origin of language have been proposed: vocalization, manual gesture and vocalization plus gesture. A vocalization account proposes that spoken language evolved from non-human primate alarm calls (MacNeilage, 1998). On this account spoken language emerged via the repeated association between sounds and their referents. In contrast, and in light of primates' greater manual (as opposed to vocal) dexterity, it has been argued that spoken language arose out of manual gestures (Corballis, 2003). On this account spoken language systems emerged from pantomime, where gestures were used to iconically communicate their referents. Unlike a situation where spoken language arose out of a full-blown gestural language, a combined account argues that gesture and vocalization supported each other's development until a fully-fledged spoken language was established (Arbib, 2005).

How are we to test the veracity of each account given that we have no fossil record? One way of overcoming the lack of linguistic fossils is by recreating a simplified historical record under laboratory conditions. That is, by having modern humans communicate a set of recurring concepts to a partner using vocalization, gesture, or vocalization plus gesture. Prohibiting participants from using their existing language system allows us to examine how different communication modalities lend themselves to the establishment of effective and efficient communication systems.

Forty-eight undergraduate students participated in exchange for payment or partial course credit. Participants completed the task in pairs. In each condition (*vocalization only, gesture only, vocalization plus gesture*) one participant (the director) tried to communicate a list of concepts (18 targets plus 6 distracters) to their partner (the matcher), such that their partner could identify each item from their (unordered) list. The experimental items fell into one of three categories: *Object* (rock, fruit predator, water, tree, hole, mud, rain), *Action* (fleeing, sleeping, fighting, throwing, chasing, washing, eating, hitting) and *Emotion* (tired, pain, angry, hungry, disgust, danger, happy, ill). Participants played six games, using the same item set on each game (presented in a different random order). Participants were not permitted to use spoken language. All communication was recorded audio visually.

Communication accuracy (% correct) increased across games 1-6 in each condition. However, accuracy was higher in the gesture (81.3% at game 1 and 94.4% at game 6) and vocalization plus gesture conditions (88.2% at game 1 and 95.8% at game 6) when compared to the vocalization only condition (37.5% at game 1 and 52.1% at game 6). Communication success was mediated by item type in the vocalization only condition (emotion > action > object), but not in the gesture and vocalization plus gesture conditions where all items were communicated equally well. Communication efficiency (time to successfully communicate each item) improved (i.e., decreased) across games 1-6 in each condition. There was no difference between conditions.

In conclusion, our results indicate that gesture is a more effective means of establishing a communication system where none exists. Our findings, albeit compromised by using modern humans, lend support to the theoretical position that spoken language arose out of manual gestures.

References

Arbib, M. (2005). From monkey-like action recognition to a human language: An evolutionary framework for neurolinguistics. *Behavioral and Brain Sciences, 28*(2), 105-167.

Corballis, M. C. (2003). From mouth to hand: Gesture, speech, and the evolution of right-handedness. *Behavioral and Brain Sciences, 26*(2), 199-260.

Fitch, W. T. (2007). Linguistics: An invisible hand. *Nature, 449*(7163), 665-667.

MacNeilage, P. F. (1998). The frame/content theory of evolution of speech production. *Behavioral and Brain Sciences, 21*(4), 499-546.

Rousseau, J. J. (1781). *Essay on the origin of language (Essai sur l'origine des langues).*

DOES INPUT MATTER? GESTURE AND HOMESIGN IN NICARAGUA, CHINA, TURKEY, AND THE USA

MOLLY FLAHERTY AND SUSAN GOLDIN-MEADOW

The University of Chicago, 5848 South University Ave
Chicago, IL 60637 USA

Science does not often have the opportunity to observe the genesis of a natural language. However, in the case of deaf individuals born into hearing families, language genesis can be observed as it happens. Deaf children born into non-signing hearing families often spend their early years unable to access their world's ambient language. In the most extreme case, deaf children who are unable to hear the spoken language surrounding them and who are not exposed to a conventional sign language develop their own gesture systems: homesigns. These homesign systems bear many of the hallmarks of mature languages, including stable word order, arbitrariness, and displaced talk (Goldin-Meadow, 2003, 2005) and grammatical categories (Coppola and Newport, 2005). When circumstances cause homesigners to come together for extended periods of time, the situation is ripe for the creation of a new full-blown language.

The new sign language in Nicaragua is the product of just this sort of situation. Deaf children brought their individual homesign systems with them to new schools founded in the 1970's (Polich, 2005). As they began to gesture and communicate with one another, they converged on a common system: Nicaraguan Sign Language was born. The language is now thriving, with nearly one thousand native users (Senghas & Coppola, 2001). But why did this new language grow so quickly? Though children create homesign systems in the absence of a conventional language, these systems do not arise in a vacuum. The raw materials for a homesign are the child's brain and the only accessible linguistic input in their environment: the gestures of the hearing people around them. Children around the world are born with equivalent mental resources, but the gestural input homesigners have to work with might differ.

In western cultures, hearing parents who have chosen to educate their deaf children orally are advised to use their voices whenever they communicate with their children; as a result, they rarely produce gestures without also producing speech. In contrast, hearing parents not committed to training their deaf children orally might be more open to producing gestures in the absence of speech. And gestures produced without speech have been found to display the

404

linguistic properties of segmentation and hierarchical combination, properties *not* found in gestures produced along with speech (Goldin-Meadow, McNeill & Singleton, 1996). Homesigners with this more language-like gestural input might create different, perhaps more linguistically complex, gesture systems than children exposed only to gestures that co-occur with speech. Our study takes the first step in exploring this possibility by examining gestural input to homesigners in four different cultures: Nicaragua, Turkey, the USA and China.

Four deaf homesigning children from each culture were observed at play in their homes with members of their family. Sessions were videotaped and coded. All vocal and gestural utterances directed toward the child by a family member were recorded. Utterances were classified based on whether they contained gesture without speech, gesture with speech, or speech alone. All children received utterances of all types, but the proportion varied by culture. The majority of the utterances that the Nicaraguan homesigners received contained gesture without speech (black bars). In contrast, almost all of the gestures that the children in the other three cultures received were produced along with speech (white bars). The American and Turkish children also received a sizeable number of utterances containing only speech (grey bars).

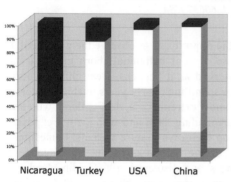

Figure 1. Input modality by culture.

Because the gestures they see are produced without speech, the Nicaraguan homesigners may be getting substantially richer input than the homesigners in other cultures. These gesture-alone utterances may be complex enough to serve as the raw linguistic materials for language creation, allowing the Nicaraguan homesigners to then create more complex homesign systems than those seen in other cultures. If so, the Nicaraguan environment may have been a particularly fertile environment for the birth of a new language, which could help to explain the rapid emergence and development that has been documented in the language over the past few decades.

Acknowledgements

This work was supported by NIH Grant RO1-DC000491 to S.G.M. and an NSF Graduate Research Fellowship to M.F.

DECEPTION, TELLS, AND THE EVOLUTION OF COMBINATORIAL COMMUNICATION

JACOB G. FOSTER

Complexity Science Group, Department of Physics and Astronomy, University of Calgary,
Calgary, T2N 1N4, Canada
jgfoster@ucalgary.ca

MATTHEW SLAYTON

Duke University
Durham, NC 27708, USA
matthew.slayton@duke.edu

Human language is characterized by an arbitrary association between signal and meaning and by the combinatorial assembly of larger units of meaning from smaller referential units (Lachmann, Számadó, & Bergstrom, 2001). The stabilization of honest signaling in such systems on evolutionary time scales remains an important theoretical challenge. Lachmann et al. (2001) propose that arbitrariness can be preserved by social enforcement of honest signaling, while combinatoriality requires that the punishment of deception be associated with whole messages rather than their components. Scott-Phillips (2008) suggests that social exclusion, fueled by gossip, provides a cheap mechanism for punishing deceptive signalers. But gossip about reputation can be deceptive, as all teenagers know, and hence it seems unlikely in the absence of modeling evidence that language can guarantee its own reliability and ensure honest signaling.

We propose that the reliability of signals in human language can be preserved by a group of largely involuntary, non-linguistic signals, which we call *tells*; as in poker, a tell is (often) a sign of deception. The sensitivity of humans to kinesic and paralinguistic channels and the use of these channels in mediating mammalian social relationships is well-known (Bateson, 2000). More recent work demonstrates that by measuring these largely involuntary channels one can predict the outcome of many social interactions in modern humans (Pentland, 2008). The effect of such involuntary channels on the evolution and stability of honest signaling in another channel has not been studied; we take a first step by analyzing the effect of tells on three game theoretic models of signaling, two standard and one combinatorial.

In the first game, two players decide whether to escalate a conflict (Gintis, 2009); the tell reveals whether the first player has signaled its relative strength honestly. The first player is under evolutionary pressure to minimize the probability p of giving a tell, and the second to become sensitive to smaller tells. The second game begins in an honest signaling equilibrium: the signaler provides information about the world via an arbitrary signal. We then change the payoffs to incentivize signaler deception. The tell alone cannot change the outcome; punishment following tells, however, preserves the signaling equilibrium for values of $p > p_{min}$, depending on the incentive and punishment for deception.

The third game is a model of combinatorial signaling. Lachmann and Bergstrom (2004) show that combinatorial signaling has a unique vulnerability to deception: individual signals can have a negative value of information (the receiver is worse off for having received that signal). This results from the fixed mechanism for combining signal components into signal meanings. Lachmann and Bergstrom (2004) suggest that this vulnerability explains why combinatorial communication has evolved so rarely. We find that honest combinatorial signaling can be stabilized when the probability of the signaler giving a tell exceeds a threshold set by the receiver's response strategy.

These games suggest that the combination of multiple signaling channels has rich strategic implications, worthy of further investigation; tells, in particular, provide a mechanism for stabilizing combinatorial communication against deception, and probably do so in concert with social enforcement. As primates, human ancestors possessed highly developed mechanisms for extracting information about social relationships from non-vocal and perhaps largely involuntary behaviors. The ability to read these behaviors could be recruited to stabilize combinatorial signaling in the primary channel, freeing our ancestors to gossip with confidence – and to talk about much more.

Acknowledgements

JGF is supported by iCORE and MS by an Angier B. Duke Scholarship. We thank E.A. Cartmill and M. Paczuski for insightful discussions.

References

Bateson, G. (2000). *Steps to an ecology of mind.* Chicago, IL: University of Chicago.

Gintis, H. (2009). *Game theory evolving.* Princeton, NJ: Princeton UP.

Lachmann, M., & Bergstrom, C. T. (2004). The disadvantage of combinatorial communication. *Proc. R. Soc. Lond. B, 271*, 2337–2343.

Lachmann, M., Számadó, S., & Bergstrom, C. T. (2001). Cost and conflict in animal signals and human language. *PNAS, 98*, 13189–13194.

Pentland, A. (2008). *Honest signals.* Cambridge, MA: MIT Press.

Scott-Phillips, T. C. (2008). On the correct application of animal signalling theory to human communication. In A. Smith, K. Smith, & R. F. i Cancho (Eds.), *The evolution of language* (pp. 275–282). London: World Scientific.

THE EVOLUTION OF SEMANTICS: A MEETING OF MINDS

PETER GÄRDENFORS

Cognitive Science, Lund University, Box 188
Lund, S-22100, Sweden

1. Semantics and the goal of communication

I will present a model of the evolution of semantics where meanings emerge as meetings of minds. What is new is that the focus will be on the *domains* of communication. I shall argue that the evolution of semantics can be interpreted as an increasing complexity of domains that communication builds on. An evolutionary benefit of this increase is that expanding communication allows for new forms of cooperation.

The basic function of communication is to coordinate actions. A communicative act is an invitation to cooperate (albeit sometimes an instance of deception). Normally, the goal is to make the minds of the communicators meet so that successful joint action can arise. When the communication concerns objects or events in the present environment, this can be achieved via joint attention. In more advanced forms of communication about non-present entities, this means coordinating minds (Warglien & Gärdenfors 2009, Gärdenfors & Warglien, to appear).

2. Domains of communication

The most basic domain for communication seems to be *emotional space*. In animal communication, expressions of emotional states are dominating. Not only different forms of vocal signals, but also facial expressions, body posture, etc, convey the emotional state of the signaller.

The second domain to consider is *visual space*. Animals (and humans) communicate nonverbally, in most cases unintentionally, by body position or gaze direction about objects or events in the environment. Following the direction of somebody's attention is a good way to vicariously learn about valuable features of the environment.

In particular, different forms of *pointing* employ the visual domain (Gärdenfors & Warglien, to appear). In imperative pointing the pointer expresses a goal with respect to the objects pointed at, typically to get hold of the object. Declarative pointing consists of one individual pointing to an object or spatial location and at the same time checking that the attendant focuses his or her attention on the same object or place (Bates 1976). In emotive declarative pointing (Brinck 2004, Tomasello et al. 2007), the pointer wants the attendant to share emotions concerning the object. This form of communication thus combines the emotional domain with the visual (mathematically this can be described as the communication taking place in the product space). In contrast, in goal-directed declarative pointing, the joint attention to the object is instrumental to the attainment of a goal. Goal-directed declarative pointing therefore also involves the *goal space*. In general, the actions of others communicate their goals.

Most animal communication is unintentional in the sense that the communicator has no intention to alter the state of the mind of the observer. However, some forms of gestures have been observed in non-human animals (Tanner & Byrne 1996, Pika & Mitani 2006). Declarative pointing is also intentional. More generally, *miming* can be an efficient way for the communicator to convey his or her goals and planned actions. Generally, this form of communication involves the *goal space*.

In order for communication to be able to refer to objects and events that are not present on the scene, the communicators must rely on their *mental* representations of objects and events. This is where *category space* becomes relevant. Words (or signs) "point" to categories that can be described as regions in conceptual spaces (Gärdenfors 2000). The conceptual spaces belong to the mental representations of the communicators. In order that cooperation be successful, these spaces must be coordinated (Warglien & Gärdenfors 2009). The development of a symbolic communication ability can therefore be seen as a transition from pointing in physical space to pointing in mental spaces.

3. Parallels with intersubjectivity

In earlier writings (Gärdenfors 2003), I have proposed that intersubjectivity ("theory of mind") should be split into four components: representing the emotions (empathy), attention, intentions and beliefs of others. The following table indicates that there is a tight connection between the components of intersubjectivity and the communicative domains presented above.

Table 1. Correspondences between components of intersubjectivity and communicative domains.

Intersubjectivity	Communicative domain
Representing emotions	Emotional space
Representing attention	Visual space
Representing intentions	Goal space
Representing beliefs	Category space

4. Parallels between communication and cooperation

Each of the four components can be turned into a form of joint intersubjectivity: joint emotion, joint attention, joint intention, and mutual belief. Each of these joint forms makes possible certain forms of cooperation. Joint emotions lead to "attunement" (Stern 1985). This requires communication in the emotional domain. Joint attention makes possible coordinated actions toward the attended object, for a example in a hunting situation. This requires communication in the visual domain. Tomasello et al. (2005) emphasize joint intention as the hallmark of humanity. Joint intentions make it possible to cooperate about non-present entities. This requires communication in the goal domain. Finally, joint beliefs are required for conventions and contracts. This requires communication in the category domain.

Acknowledgements

I gratefully acknowledge support from the Swedish Research Council for my own research and for the Linnaeus project *Thinking in Time: Cognition, Communication and Learning*.

References

Bates, E. (1976). *Language and Context: The Acquisition of Pragmatics*. New York: Academic Press.

Brinck, I. (2004). The pragmatics of imperative and declarative pointing. *Cognitive Science Quarterly*, *3(4)*, 429-446.

Gärdenfors, P. (2000). *Conceptual Spaces: The Geometry of Thought*. Cambridge, MA: MIT Press.

Gärdenfors, P. (2003). *How Homo Became Sapiens*. Oxford: Oxford University Press.

Gärdenfors, P., & Warglien, M. (to appear). The development of semantic space for pointing and verbal communication. To appear in J. Hudson, U. Magnusson & C. Paradis (eds.) *Conceptual Spaces and the Construal of Spatial Meaning. Empirical Evidence from Human Communication.* Cambridge: Cambridge University Press.

Pika, S. & Mitani, J. C. (2006). Referential gestural communication in wild chimpanzees (*Pan troglodytes*). *Current Biology*, *16(6)*, 191-192.

Stern, D. (1985). *The Interpersonal World of the Infant*. New York: Basic Books.

Tanner, J. E. & Byrne, R. W. (1996). Representation of action through iconic gesture in a captive lowland gorilla. *Current Anthropology*, *37*, 162-73.

Tomasello, M., Carpenter, M., Call, J., Behne, T. & Moll, H. (2005). Understanding and sharing intentions: The origins of cultural cognition. *Behavioral and Brain Sciences*, *28*, 675-691.

Tomasello, M., Carpenter, M., & Liszkowski, U. (2007). A new look at infant pointing. *Child Development*, *78*, 705 – 722.

Warglien, M., & Gärdenfors, P. (2009). Semantics, conceptual spaces and the meeting of minds. Manuscript.

DOES DEIXIS PRECEDE VOCABULARY DEVELOPMENT IN LANGUAGE-TRAINED APES?

KRISTEN GILLESPE-LYNCH[a,] YUNPING FENG[a,] PATRICIA M. GREENFIELD[a,]
SUE SAVAGE-RUMBAUGH[b]
HEIDI LYN[c]
CHRISTINA KHOU[a]

a. *Department of Psychology and FPR-UCLA Center for Culture, Brain, and
Development, University of California, Los Angeles CA 90095*

b. *Great Ape Trust of Iowa, Des Moines, IA 50320*

c. *Department of Psychology, Agnes Scott College, 141 E. College Ave,
Decatur, GA, 30030 USA*

Given the contextual flexibility of gestural communication by apes relative to their more context-bound vocalizations (Tomasello et al., 1994), many theorists have inferred that language was initially gestural (e.g. Hewes, 1973). If language emerged from gestures, the potential to use gestures to acquire words should be present not only in young humans, but also in juvenile chimpanzees and bonobos (when they are raised in language-enriched environments). This study examines whether deictic gestures supported the vocabulary development of a chimpanzee (Panpanzee) and a bonobo (Panbanisha) as well as analyzing their developing ability to pair gestures with signals of communicative intent.

Both deaf and hearing children's gestures are initially context bound (deictic) before becoming progressively more decontextualized (Caselli, 1983). Toddlers are significantly more likely to first indicate an object through deictic gesture and only later to name it than to first name and later gesture towards an object (Iverson & Goldin-Meadow, 2005). Do juvenile apes also progress from indicating objects through gesture to decontextualized reference through lexigrams (arbitrary visual symbols signifying words)? Qualitative analysis suggests that human children and apes combine a deictic gesture and a word before combining two words (Greenfield et al., 2008). Using a sampling method developed with human children (Iverson & Goldin-Meadow, 2005), the present study aims to determine if gesture plays a role in the emergence of language across the clade. We predict that like human toddlers, apes will first rely on gesture and only later use words to name objects.

Sampling from video footage of the daily interactions of Panpanzee and Panbanisha from 10 to 24 months of age, we are coding all gestures and lexigrams that are demonstrated during 2 hours a month for each ape. As in observational studies of human linguistic development, this sampling method provides an index of when gestures emerge relative to words. Once we have coded 30 hours of video for each ape, we will use chi-square analyses to determine if the number of items that were first observed to be referenced by deictic gestures exceeds the number that were first evidenced as lexigrams. Preliminary analyses based on 5 hours of video coding for each ape suggest that deixis may indeed precede lexigram use by language-trained apes. Panpanzee first referred to 7 items with deictic gesture and 2 items with lexigrams while Panbanisha referred to 5 items first with deictic gesture and 3 with lexigrams.

Because deixis may be a mechanism that helps members of the clade learn to use words, understanding the ways that deixis is marked as communicative across phylogeny and ontogeny is also important. Intentional communication is often defined by the presence of one of the following behaviors: attention getting behaviors, gaze alternation, or persistence. Because human deixis only gradually takes on communicative elements across ontogeny (Masur, 1983), we are also analyzing how often deictic gestures and lexigrams emitted by Panpanzee and Panbanisha co-occur with communicative signals during the sampled time frames.

Acknowledgements

The authors wish to acknowledge the assistance of the staff and administration of the Language Research Center, The Yerkes National Primate Research Center, The Great Ape Trust of Iowa, and the Jacksonville Zoo and Gardens where these data were collected. Funding for this study was provided by NIH grants HD-56232 and HD-38105.

References

Caselli, M. C. (1983). Communication to language: Deaf children's and hearing children's development compared. *Sign Language Studies, 39*, 113-143.

Greenfield, P. M., Lyn, H., Savage-Rumbaugh, S. E. (2008). Protolanguage in ontogeny and phylogeny: Combining deixis and representation. *Interaction Studies, 9*(1), 34-50.

Hewes, G. W. (1973). Primate communication and the gestural origins of language. *Current Anthropology, 14*, 5–24.

Iverson, J. and S. Goldin-Meadow (2005). Gesture paves the way for language development. *Psychological Science, 16*(5), 367-71.

Masur, E. F. (1983). Gestural development, dual-directional signaling, and the transition to words. *Journal of Psycholinguistic Research, 12*(2), 93-109.

Tomasello, M., Call, J., Nagell, K., Olguin, K., & Carpenter, M. (1994). The learning and use of gestural signals by young chimpanzees: A trans-generational study. *Primates, 35*, 137-154

WHY APE-HUMAN SIMILARITIES AND LEARNING MECHANISMS ARE IMPORTANT: A DEVELOPMENTAL AND CLADISTIC APPROACH TO THE EVOLUTION OF LANGUAGE.

PATRICIA M. GREENFIELD

*FPR-UCLA Center for Culture, Brain, and Development, Department of Psychology,
University of California, Los Angeles 90095, USA*

For the last thirty years species comparative approaches to the study of the evolution of language have shown a strong bias toward uncovering differences between apes and humans in their symbolic and communicative capacities. Flying in the face of the well established fact that chimpanzees and humans share 99% of their genes, researchers and scholars seem motivated to emphasize the uniqueness of human language at the expense of understanding its origins and foundations in primate communication. Another tendency in the field is to assume that only spontaneously manifest symbolic capacities are of interest and to ignore learning mechanisms that rely on social or nonlinguistic stimuli. In order to counter these trends, I will be presenting an alternative theoretical and methodological framework.

Its first tenet is that cladistic analysis (comparative study of species descended from a common ancestor) is an important tool for understanding the primate foundation of human language and communication.. This is because similarity of a characteristic across a clade (a phyologenetically related group of species with a common ancestor) indicates that it is likely to be an ancestral trait that is part of the genetic heritage of all members of the clade. Therefore, comparing behaviors across a clade is a research strategy that can uncover ancestral behavioral capabilities that served as the foundation for modern capabilities – in this case for language and communication. This theoretically based methodological point is particularly important because language, like other behavioral capabilities, does not leave fossils.

The second tenet is that earlier stages of development are more similar among members of a clade than are later stages of development. Therefore, comparing behaviors in very young members of each species across the clade is most likely to uncover evolutionary foundations for a particular system, in this case, language and communication.

Third, later capabilities build on earlier ones in both ontogeny and phylogeny. Therefore, the analysis of developmental transitions from one stage to another is useful in understanding both ontogeny and phylogeny. We therefore will examine behavioral development – in this case the development of language and communication – over time in each species,. But our analysis does not focus on time or age per se; instead it emphasizes the transitional learning mechanisms that drive symbolic and communicative development from one level to the next.

Fourth, earlier stages of development are more universal within a species than are later stages of development. This is because both ontogeny and phylogeny build on what is already there rather than erasing it, so both speciation and individual differences in development tend to be found in later rather than earlier stages of development, Therefore, sample selection and large sample size within each species is less important than when studying older members of a species: cross-species similarities early in life are likely to be robust across a wide range of species members.

Fifth, language evolved for communication. Therefore, the social stimuli provided by conversation should provide important developmental learning mechanisms.

Sixth, language evolved out of nonlinguistic behaviors and capacities. Therefore, nonlinguistic communication, specifically gesture, is a good candidate for a developmental learning mechanism.

These principles have animated a series of cross-species comparative studies that demonstrate common transitional mechanisms in the early development of symbolic communication and representation across the clade consisting of bonobo, chimpanzee, and human. According to the principle of cladistic analysis, these transitional mechanisms then become good candidates for mechanisms that lie at the very foundation of language evolution. While we rely heavily on a small number of members of each species – mainly because highly rare symbol-enculturated apes are at the heart of the research designs – the focus on *early* development means that our findings may not only constitute an existence proof, but also index species-typical capabilities held in common by all three species in the clade. We will provide evidence that three kinds of transitional mechanisms - gesture, dialogue, and social scaffolding - are utilized across the clade in the ontogeny of symbolic and communicative capacities. More specifically, we will show how, in bonobo, chimpanzee, and child, each of the three mechanisms leads to a similar developmental progression in symbolic representation or communication. We see these commonalities as a foundation from which human language, communication, and representation evolved after the phylogenetic split of the three species five million years ago. Rather than trying to figure out where human language went in its evolution, we are trying to figure out where it started. Learning where it started can give us critical information about the evolution of its most basic and robust characteristics. Learning where it started is also essential for understanding where human language has gone in the last five million years. Thus, it is not an either-or situation. Instead, the study of cross-species similarities complements and provides a context for the study of cross-species differences in language evolution.

EVOLVING LINGUISTIC COMPETENCE IN THE ABSENCE OF PERFORMANCE

MARC D. HAUSER

33 Kirkland St., Harvard Dept. of Psychology, Cambridge, MA 02138

There are many fascinating routes to studying the evolution of language, including explorations of the fossil record, game theoretic modeling, historical analyses, and comparative experiments on nonhuman animals. All have contributed in various ways to our understanding of the origins and subsequent evolution of language. And yet, there is a nagging feeling that much of the evidence is circumstantial, and that we will never deeply understand how our capacity for language started, and what selective pressures, if any, led to subsequent transformations in both structure and function.

In this talk I explore the evolution of our linguistic competence, and in particular, the kinds of capacities that animals may have in the absence of a comparable capacity to use these abilities in communication. I then use these results, and others from the field, to argue that though we have rich theoretical frameworks for exploring problems of language evolution, our methods are woefully deficient. As such, we need to carefully consider whether we will ever have the empirical goods to address the theoretical perspectives sketched.

I begin in Part 1 of the talk by laying out a theoretical framework that I find useful for thinking about questions of evolutionary origins and change. In Part 2 I turn to a set of comparative results that I believe are relevant to this framework. In particular, I discuss recent studies of nonhuman primates focusing on spontaneously available (i.e., untrained) competences for understanding symbols and simple rules, capacities that did not evolve *for* language, but were subsequently used by the language faculty. In Part 3, I turn to a new set of findings on humans, showing the interface between semantics and syntax, and in particular, revealing the constraints that evolutionarily ancient, domain-general computations have on domain-specific knowledge, and in particular, language-specific computations. In Part 4, I end by critically evaluating the kinds of contributions that comparative studies — including especially, my own — have provided to our understanding of language evolution. I end with a rather pessimistic conclusion: due to methodological limitations, comparative studies can not presently answer most of the fundamental questions concerning the syntactic and semantic structures that are ubiquitous in language, and consequently, we may forever be stuck in mystery and speculation concerning the origin and subsequent evolution of language.

Part 1. The theoretical framework I develop is based on the original paper I wrote with Chomsky and Fitch, but with subsequent clarifications and extensions. In particular, I argue that from an evolutionary comparative perspective, it make sense to ask which aspects of our language faculty are shared with other animals and which are unique, and of those capacities that are unique to our species, which are unique to language. This framework, when properly articulated, is not committed to any particular view of language, including theories targeting representational structure (e.g., minimalism) and evolutionary processes (e.g., adaptation and functional design).

Part 2. I begin by discussing new experiments on rhesus monkeys that explore how our capacity to comprehend and use symbols may have emerged, and in particular, how our capacity to understand the *duality of pictures* as both physical objects and representations of something else evolved in evolution and develops in human ontogeny. Based on a highly simplified task, results show that rhesus discriminate pictures of food from real food, discriminate pictures of food from pictures of non-food, this discrimination is based on visual inspection alone (i.e., no contact with the pictures), and in the absence of prior experience with pictures, as well as no training or reward. Thus, important aspects of our competence to recognize the symbolic duality of pictures evolved before our uniquely human capacity to create symbols. I then turn to a series of experiments that explore the capacity of primates to extract rule-like regularities from a structured input, with the aim of targeting some of the core syntactic properties of language. In one experiment with captive tamarins, I show that they have the capacity to acquire a simple affixation rule, distinguishing structures that contain specific prefixes with those that contain specific suffixes. In a second experiment, I show that captive chimpanzees share with human adults the capacity to spontaneously extract both category information and ordering information from a structured input. More specifically, both species primarily encoded positional information from the sequence (i.e., items that occurred in the sequence-edges), but generally failed to encode co-occurrence statistics. This suggests that a mechanism to encode positional information from sequences is present in both chimpanzees and humans, and may represent the default in the absence of training and with brief exposure. As many grammatical regularities exhibit properties of this mechanism, it may be recruited by language, and constrain the form certain grammatical regularities take.

Part 3. When children acquire language, they acquire not only the syntactic categories (e.g., nouns, verbs, determiners), but the rules by which such categories are ordered and arranged. Here I present the results of an experiment with human adults looking at the capacity to acquire a simple duplication rule (e.g., AAB or ABB), where the categories are syntactic (i.e., nouns and verbs). Although subjects readily processed the categories and learned repetition-patterns over non-syntactic categories (e.g., animal-animal-clothes), they failed to learn the repetition-pattern over syntactic categories (e.g., Noun-Noun-Verb, as in "apple-car-eat"), even when explicitly instructed to look for it. Further experiments revealed that subjects successfully learned the repetition-patterns only when they were consistent with syntactically possible structures, irrespective of whether these structures were attested in English or in other languages unknown to the participants. When the repetition-patterns did not match such syntactically possible structures, subjects failed to learn them. Results suggest that when human adults hear a string of nouns and verbs, their syntactic system obligatorily attempts an interpretation (e.g., in terms of subjects, objects and predicates). As a result, subjects fail to perceive the simpler pattern of repetitions --- a form of syntax-induced pattern deafness that is reminiscent of how other perceptual systems force specific interpretations upon sensory input.

Part 4. I conclude by summarizing the results presented, and critically evaluating my own comparative studies. In brief, though I think it is probably accurate to say that animals have evolved domain-general competences that are shared with humans, and these competences are relevant to the faculty of language in the broad sense, current methods for extracting the specific mechanisms in play are weak, and thus, not up to the job of testing between competing hypotheses. This puts us in a difficult position because comparative studies may simply be unable to generate the kind of data that are necessary to explore the evolution of language, and in particular, those aspects that are part of the broad language faculty and those which are part of the narrow faculty.

SIMULATING CREOLE AND DIALECT FORMATION

ZENA M. HIRA

Department of Life Sciences, Imperial College London,
South Kensington Campus, London, SW7 2AZ, UK

MARK BARTLETT

Department of Computer Science, University of York,
Heslington, York, YO10 5DD, UK

Human languages are in a constant state of change. New words are constantly being invented and old ones lost. Words change their meanings and pronunciations over time. In the extreme case, whole new languages are created, either through the merging of unrelated languages or the splitting of one language into many variants. These processes are known are creolisation and dialect formation respectively. The former is perhaps best known from those creoles which originated in the period of European colonization and slave trade and which still exist today in the Caribbean. In contrast, the latter process can be observed in a great many number of dialects and languages worldwide, such as the descent of the Romance Languages from Latin.

The use of computer modelling to study aspects of the evolution of language has become established over the past couple of decades. In particular, the naming games introduced by Steels (1995) have been very influential. Using this model, Steels showed how a shared vocabulary can emerge in a group of agents through a series of conversations involving two agents. The more times a word is used for an object, the stronger the association between the object and the word will become. New words can be added and words that do not have communicative success are removed.

Subsequently, Steels (1997) performed a limited evaluation of the element of distance in his game. In that paper, the agents are divided in clusters and eventually develop a stable vocabulary within the cluster and at the same time they become familiar with the words used in the other clusters. In effect they become bilingual. Our work extends this model to study what happens when clusters merge or divide, simulating the conditions in which creoles or dialects form respectively.

In order to introduce multiple populations into the model of Steels, we place agents in a two dimensional environment in which agents are more likely to talk to agents closer to them. Additionally, we allow for this environment to be split in half and ban all communication between the halves, creating two subpopulations which are linguistically isolated from each other.

Simulations of language contact were performed by beginning in a split environment and then, after allowing each group to interact for a specific amount of time, the entire population was left to interact together. For small populations, such simulations did indeed lead to the formation of "creole" languages, with words in the final combined language being taken from both the languages spoken by the initial subpopulations. However, as the groups of agents become larger the agents have trouble in converging to a single language. No name is dominant over the other but in the conversations about an object the agents end up using one of the two names developed in the groups but they can never decide which one they prefer. This may be seen as more analogous to the creation of bilingualism in the agents.

By reversing the earlier process, first allowing the whole population to interact before splitting it into two subpopulations, the divergence of a common language can be studied. The results observed are that the similarity of the resulting languages in the groups is strongly related to the amount of time the agents have spent together in a single group at the beginning. The longer the time they have spent the higher probability they have to end up using the same language.

References

Steels, L. (1995). A self-organizing spatial vocabulary. Artificial Life, 2(3), 319-332.

Steels, L. (1997) Language learning and language contact. In Daelemans, W.,Van den Bosch, A. and Weijters, A., (Eds), *Proceedings of the workshop on Empirical Approaches to Language Acquisition*, (pp. 11-24). Prague.

ECOLOGICAL AND SEXUAL EXPLANATIONS
FOR LARYNX LOWERING

JEAN-MARIE HOMBERT[1]

Dynamique du Langage, CNRS and University of Lyon
14, Ave Berthelot, 69363 Lyon Cedex 07, France

It has been shown that larynx lowering is probably not the key factor leading to the emergence of speech in Humans. Rather, it has been argued that larynx lowering is a process which allows males to produce lower frequency sounds and thus giving females the impression of a bigger (more powerful?) potential sexual partner (Fitch 2000, 2002, 2005; Ohala, 2000). Although the process of larynx lowering is found in a number of mammal species (deer, lions) with apparently a similar function, that of providing males with "impressive" vocalizations exaggerating their size (Fitch and Reby, 2001), it is not found in our closely related non-human primates. Why did our non-human primate cousins not develop a lowered larynx? One possible explanation is that these species possessed air sacs which fulfilled the same function. These laryngeal air sacs have the capacity to produce **lower** frequency sounds (de Boer, 2008; Gautier, 1971) but they are also able to produce **louder** sounds.

Our hypothesis is that the male common ancestor of non-human and human primates had laryngeal air sacs which were replaced by a lowered larynx in the line which led to Homo sapiens. Why did air sacs disappear? We propose an ecologically induced explanation. In a forest environment, it is very important to produce loud sounds for two reasons. First, forest environments often render difficult the visual identification of conspecifics. Second, sound propagation is dampened in forest environments. In such an ecological context air sacs were quite appropriate to produce both lower frequency and louder sounds. When our ancestors left a forested environment, the need for loud sounds was no longer necessary. In a savannah type of environment sounds propagate much more efficiently than in a forest environment and, in addition, it is easy to visually

---

[1] I wish to thank Guy Dubreuil, Jean-Pierre Gautier, Alban Lemasson, John Ohala and Regine Vercauteren Drubbel for useful comments and suggestions.

perceive other individuals of your group. However, in order to preserve the "exaggerated male size" the disappearance of air sacs had to be replaced by another mechanism. The ancestors of Homo sapiens selected a process used by a number of mammal species: the lowering of the larynx. Hyoid bone fossil data seem to indicate that Australopithecus afarensis had air sacs (Alemseged et al. 2006) but Homo heidelbergensis (Martinez et al. 2008) and Neandertals did not.

We will provide supporting evidence for our hypothesis through an examination of the relationship between the presence versus absence of vocal sacs among related species in contrasting ecological environments. Air sacs are present in species inhabiting forest environments, while they have disappeared in closely related species inhabiting savannah environments. The role of sexual dimorphism will also be discussed.

References

Alemseged, Z., Spoor, F., Kimbel, W. H., Bobe, R., Geraads, D., Reed, D., & Wynn, J.G. (2006). A juvenile early hominin skeleton from Dikika, Ethiopia. *Nature, 443*(7109), 296–301.

de Boer, B. (2008). The joy of sacs. In A. D. M. Smith, K. Smith and R. Ferrer i Cancho (Eds), *The Evolution of Language: Proceedings of 7th International Conference.* World scientific Publishing, 415-6.

Fitch, W. T. (2000). The evolution of speech, A comparative review. *Trends in Cognitive Sciences.* 4(7), 258-267.

Fitch, W.T. (2002). Comparative vocal production and the evolution of speech: reinterpreting the descent of the larynx. In: Wray A. (ed*.), The Transition to Language.* Oxford University Press, Oxford, 21-45.

Fitch, W. T. (2005) The evolution of language: a comparative review. *Biology and Philosophy,* 20, 193-230.

Fitch, W.T. and D. Reby. (2001). The descended larynx is not uniquely human. *Proc. R. Soc. Biol. Sci.* 268: 1669-1675.

Gautier, J. P. (1971). Etude morphologique et fonctionnelle des annexes extra-laryngées des cercopithecinae; liaison avec les cris d'espacement, *Biologica Gabonica,* VII (2), 229-267.

Hewitt, G. P., MacLarnon, A., & Jones, K. E. (2002). The functions of laryngeal air sacs in primates: A new hypothesis. *Folia Primatologica, 73,* 70–94.

Martínez, I., Arsuaga, J.-L., Quam, R., Carretero, J.-M., Gracia, A., & Rodríguez, L. (2008). Human hyoid bones from the middle Pleistocene site of the Sima de los Huesos (Sierra de Atapuerca, Spain). *Journal of Human Evolution, 54,* 118–124.

Ohala, J. J. (2000). The irrelevance of the lowered larynx in modern man for the development of speech, *Proceedings of the International Conference on the Evolution of Language,* Paris, 171-2.

DUALITY OF PATTERNING AS AN EMERGENT PROPERTY: EVIDENCE FROM A NEW SIGN LANGUAGE

ASSAF ISRAEL

Sign Language Research Lab, University of Haifa, Haifa, 31905, Israel

WENDY SANDLER

Department of English Language and Literature and Sign Language Research Lab, University of Haifa, Haifa, 31905, Israel

Duality of patterning – the existence of a meaningless phonological level as well as a meaningful level of morphemes and words -- is a fundamental design feature of human language (Hockett 1960). It seems reasonable to speculate that a combinatorial system of meaningless elements emerged from holistic forms, facilitating the creation of a sizable vocabulary of perceptually distinct words.

Empirical data about the origins of duality are hard to find, as all spoken languages have been around for millennia, or are descended from languages that have. Such data can be found in sign languages, however, since a sign language can arise at any time. Data from a new sign language suggest that duality of patterning – a phonological level of structure alongside meaningful words – does not arise at the outset, and that its emergence is gradual (Sandler et al in press).

The first deaf signers of Al-Sayyid Bedouin Sign Language (ABSL) were born about 75 years ago, and the language is now used by a community of about 150 deaf people and many of the 4,000 hearing people in the village. This language has regular word order (Sandler et al 2005) and prosodically marked phrasal constituents (Sandler et al 2008). However, we have not yet encountered minimal pairs, and we observe glaring variation in sign production across signers, of a kind that would blur phonological category boundaries of more established sign languages. It appears that signers aim for holistic iconic prototypes, and do not rely on discrete, meaningless combinatorial units to form signs.

The present study supports these observations by carefully measuring variation across signers in ABSL, and comparing it with sign productions in two other, more established sign languages, American Sign Language (ASL), and Israeli Sign Language (ISL), both of which have been shown to have phonological organization (Stokoe 1960; Meir and Sandler 2008). 47 features of the three major categories of sign formation – hand shape, location on or near the body, and type of hand movement – are coded for 15 signs as signed by 10 signers in each language. The results show more variation in nearly every subcategory in ABSL than in the other two languages (Israel 2009). Taken together with other criteria for phonological organization, the results support the claim that this new language does not yet have a level of structure consisting of discrete, meaningless, combinatorial units.

The cline of variation is consistently ABSL > ISL > ASL. ASL is the oldest of the three languages with the largest community, while ISL is about the same age as ABSL but developed through creolization in a larger and more diverse community. Our results indicate that the emergence of duality of patterning is gradual, and depends in part on social factors such as age, size, and diversity of the language community. If its emergence is gradual in a modern human community, it is reasonable to infer that the same was true in evolution.

References

Hockett, Charles. 1960. The origin of speech. *Scientific American.* 203, 89-96

Israel, Assaf. 2009. Sublexical variation in three sign languages. MA thesis. University of Haifa.

Meir, Irit and Wendy Sandler. 2008. *A Language in Space: The Story of Israeli Sign Language.* New York: Taylor Francis.

Sandler, Wendy, Aronoff, Mark, Meir, Irit, and Padden, Carol. in press. The gradual emergence of phonological form in a new language. In press. *Natural Language and Linguistic Theory.*

Sandler, Wendy, Irit Meir, Carol Padden and Mark Aronoff. 2005. The emergence of grammar in a new sign language. *Proceedings of the National Academy of Sciences* 102: 2661-2665.

Sandler, Wendy, Meir, Irit, Dachkovsky, Svetlana, Padden, Carol, and Aronoff, Mark. 2008. Prosody and linguistic complexity in an emerging sign language. In A. Smith, K. Smith, & R. Ferrer I Cancho (eds.) *The Evolution of Language: Proceedings of the 7th International Conference Evolang 7.* 489-490.

Stokoe, William. 1960. Sign language structure: An outline of the visual communications systems. *Studies in Linguistics, Occasional Papers 8.* Buffalo, NY: University of Buffalo.

RELAXATION OF SELECTION CAN LEAD TO SIGNAL VARIATION: AN EXAMPLE IN BIRDSONG

HIROKO KAGAWA[1,2], HIROKO YAMADA[1], RUEY-SINGH LIN[3],
TOSHIKAZU HASEGAWA[2], KAZUO OKANOYA[1]

[1]*Biolinguistics Laboratory, Brain Science Institute, RIKEN, 2-1 Hirosawa, Wako,
Saitama 351-0198, JAPAN;* [2]*Hasegawa Lab., University of Tokyo and JSPS;* [3]*Endemic
Species Research Institute, TAIWAN; Okanoya@brain.riken.jp*

Deacon (2003) proposed a novel mechanism by which a biological property gains complexity. In his theory, the term "masking" is used to refer to an environmental change that masks a particular selection pressure. Similarly, the term "unmasking" is used to indicate a process by which a selection pressure becomes effective. Birdsong conveys two messages: species identification and individual vigor. To ensure the former, the signal should satisfy one or more species-specific features. To ensure the latter, the signal should reflect individual characteristics related to vigor. The Bengalese finch is a domesticated strain of the white-rumped munia, an endemic finch of East Asia. The process of domestication occurred about 250 years ago, comprising approximately 500 generations. Bengalese finches sing syntactically and phonologically complex songs, whereas white-rumped munias sing simpler songs in both domains (Okanoya, 2004). Female Bengalese finches engage in more breeding behaviors when stimulated by complex songs, suggesting that song complexity in Bengalese finches evolved by sexual selection (Okanoya, 2004). However, the model of Ritchie and Kirby (2005) demonstrated the possibility that domestication alone could account for the evolution of song complexity by relaxing selection pressures. In their study, domestication was used as a condition to disable selection pressure for species identification. If a system arises in which the need for species identification exhibits natural variation, that system can be used to directly test Deacon's theory.

When several species of birds with similar plumage share the same environment (sympatric environment), birdsong should faithfully convey the species identification signal to avoid infertile hybridization. In Taiwan, white-rumped munias form mixed colonies with a closely related species, the spotted munia. We hypothesized that the rate of sympatry would affect song complexity. We conducted a field study at three locations in Taiwan: Huben (H), Mataian (M), and Taipei (T), where natural populations of white-rumped munias occur. During the summers of 2006-2008, we captured white-rumped munias using mist nets and recorded male songs. Totals of 30 (H), 23 (M), and 17 (T) male white-rumped munias were captured. The number of spotted munias at each location was also counted. Song linearity, an index of song simplicity, was calculated as (the number of song notes)/(the number of song note transition types). The value of this index equals one when the song sequence is completely linear and decreases when the song is less deterministic. The index is 1/N, where N is the number of song notes, when the song is completely random. The rate of sympatry was calculated as (the number of mixed flocks)/(the number of total flocks), where mixed flocks were those containing both white-rumped and spotted munias. We found that the rate of sympatry was lowest at Huben and higher at Taipei and Mataian (H < T, M; Fig. 1a). Song linearity was lowest (more complex) at Huben and greater at Taipei and Mataian (H < T, M; Fig. 1b). Therefore, the rate of sympatry corresponded with song linearity. These results were consistent with the prediction that lower pressure for species identification leads to higher complexity in birdsong.

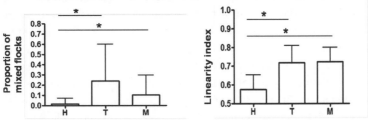

Although other factors including sexual selection (Okanoya, 2004) are undoubtedly involved, the process of masking, as demonstrated here, may account for some proportion of signal evolution in Bengalese finches, as suggested by Deacon (2003). Similar mechanisms should be considered when examining the evolution of human language.

References

Deacon, T. (2003). Multilevel selection in a complex adaptive system: the problem of language origins. In B. H. Weber and D. J. Depew (Eds.), *Evolution and learning: Baldwin effect reconsidered.* Cambridge, MA: MIT Press.

Okanoya, K. (2004). Song syntax in Bengalese finches: proximate and ultimate analyses. *Advances in the Study of Behaviour, 34,* 297–346.

Ritchie, G., & Kirby, S. (2005). Selection, domestication, and the emergence of learned communication system. *Proceedings of the Second International Symposium on the Evolutionary Emergence of Language and Communication.*

THE CO-INVOLVEMENT OF HANDS AND MOUTH IN UTTERANCE CONSTRUCTION: IMPLICATIONS FOR LANGUAGE ORIGINS THEORIES

ADAM KENDON

43 West Walnut Lane,
Philadelphia, Pennsylvania 19144, USA

The idea that language first emerged as a form of visible bodily action, - the "gesture first" view - has attracted supporters since the eighteenth century. Since the modern revival of this idea by Gordon Hewes in 1973, it has gained many adherents with Michael Corballis and Michael Tomasello (2008), among the most recent. It is attractive, perhaps, because we can observe, through such processes as the conventionalisation of pantomime, the emergence of language-like systems, as may be seen when primary sign languages come into being. However, the problem a "gesture first" theory always confronts is that modern languages are spoken and humans are highly specialised for speech. This means that "gesture first" advocates have to account for a switch from gesture to speech. None of the modern "gesture first" theorists offer a satisfactory account of this, while opponents of this position have argued that a "gesture stage" is unnecessary. Advocates of a "speech first" position, on the other hand, overlook or downplay the fact that when speakers engage in utterance, always to some extent, and often to a considerable extent, they produce an *ensemble* of speech *and* gesture. Studies of the way in which gesture is involved in utterance construction show that gestures function like partners with speech in the creation of coherently meaningful utterances. Furthermore, gestures enter into the fashioning of utterances in many different ways. They express emphasis and emotion, but they also express concepts, often by means similar to those found in sign languages. They also express meta-discursive and pragmatic aspects of the utterance (Kendon 2004). Neither "gesture first" advocates nor "speech only" advocates have considered seriously this co-involvement of speech and visible bodily action in utterance construction.

428

In this paper, this partnership of speech and gesture in utterance will be our starting point. Looking at the various forms of gestural expression, we note that referential gestures, whether deictic or representational, and gestures with pragmatic functions can often be seen as derived from manipulatory actions, as if the speaker is acting on, or in relation to, objects in a virtual physical environment, including other animate beings as objects. Appealing to MacNeilage's (2008) suggestion that the actions of speech are exaptions of the mouth actions of chewing and other eating actions, and considering the evidence from many different studies that suggest hand-mouth synergies of great phylogenetic antiquity (Gentilucci and Corballis 2006), we propose that the action systems used in speaking and gesturing are descended by modification from the hand-mouth action ensembles employed as the animal manipulates, modifies or appropriates and ingests parts of its environment, as it seeks for and grasps and processes food, or manages, manipulates and modifies its environment. These systems were recruited to symbolic functions when practical actions acted out in a "vicarious way" (as when an animal must decide between more than one course of action) were recognised by conspecifics as "as if" actions. It was this that made symbolic dialogues possible (Kendon 1991). On this view, important aspects of language are only secondarily communicative in origin and the co-invovlement of hands and mouth in utterance production is accounted for because of the development of shared control networks which originated in strategies that developed in relation to food getting and environmental manipulation. Language emerged, thus, from an *ensemble of oral and manual actions*, an ensemble still observed in utterance production in modern humans.

References

Gentilucci, Maurizio, and Michael C. Corballis. "From Manual Gesture to Speech: A Gradual Transition." *Neuroscience and Biobehavioral Reviews* 30 (2006): 949-60..

Kendon, Adam "Some Considerations for a Theory of Language Origins." *Man (N.S.)* 26 (1991): 602-19.

Kendon, Adam (2004). *Gesture: Visible Action as Utterance*. Cambridge: Cambridge U.P.

MacNeilage, Peter F. (2008). *The Origins of Speech*. Oxford: Oxford University Press.

Tomasello, Michael (2008). *The Origins of Human Communication*. Cambridge, MA: MIT Press.

EARLY LINKS BETWEEN ICONIC GESTURES AND SOUND SYMBOLIC WORDS: EVIDENCE FOR MULTIMODAL PROTOLANGUAGE

SOTARO KITA

School of Psychology, University of Birmingham,
Birmingham, B15 2TT, UK

ASLI ÖZYÜREK

Centre for Language Studies, Radboud University Nijmegen & Max-Planck Institute for Psycholinguistics
Nijmegen, The Netherlands

SHANLEY ALLEN

Dept. of Literacy and Language, Counseling and Development, Boston University,
Boston, MA 02215, USA

TOMOKO ISHIZUKA

Dept. of Linguistics, University of California Los Angeles,
Los Angeles, CA 9009-1543, USA

1. Iconic Gestures and Sound Symbolic Words: Motivated Link between Form and Meaning

When we speak, we spontaneously produce hand gestures that are co-expressive with speech. Many such gestures are "iconic gestures", which depict shape, motion and action based on similarity between gestural hand movement and the referent (e.g., flat hand moving downwards repeatedly to depict a water fall). This study addresses the question of how humans evolved to produce iconic gestures with speech, i.e., the origins of speech-gesture link.

In iconic gesture, form and meaning are related in a motivated (non-arbitrary) way. This is in sharp contrast with typical words with an arbitrary link between form and meaning. However, sound symbolic words also have form and meaning that are "naturally" related with each other, similar to iconic gestures. Many languages of the world, including Japanese, have a large class of sound symbolic words (Kita, 2008; Nuckolls, 1999). These words can refer to not only sounds (i.e., onomatopoeia) but also a wide range of non-auditory experiences including manner of movement (Kita, 1997, 2008).

2. Ontogenetic and Phylogenetic Linkage between Iconic Gestures and Sound Symbolic Words

We examined how the link between speech and iconic gestures develop in children. We presented animated cartoons to Japanese-speaking 3- and 5-year old children and adults (n = 20 in each group). They narrated the cartoons to another person, in which they spontaneously produced iconic gestures depicting the protagonists' movements. We analyzed linguistic and gestural expression of manner of motion (e.g. jumping, rolling). The statistical analysis revealed the following results. (1) Children had a stronger preference to use sound symbolic manner words to express manner of motion (e.g., "pyonpyon" for jumping and "korokoro" for rolling) than adults, as opposed to non-sound symbolic manner verbs (e.g., "tobu" for jumping and "kaitensuru" for rolling/rotating). (2) Sound symbolic manner words were more likely to be accompanied by co-expressive iconic gestures than non-sound symbolic manner verbs, and this tendency was especially strong in children. In other words, the speech-gesture link started out with sound symbolic words in ontogeny.

Based on the above results, we infer that the link between speech and iconic gesture started in sound symbolic words and spread to "ordinary" non-sound symbolic words with arbitrary form-meaning mapping. We propose that our ancestors once used a protolanguage that combined iconic gestures and sound symbolic words. In other words sound symbolic words may be the "missing link" in the explanation for why speech and iconic gesture are tightly coupled in modern humans. Our data is also compatible with the idea that sound-symbolic words and iconic gestures emerged simultaneously when our ancestors developed an ability to cross-modally represent information in an iconic way.

References

Kita, S. (1997). Two-dimensional semantic analysis of Japanese mimetics. *Linguistics, 35*, 379-415.

Kita, S. (2008). World-view of protolanguage speakers as inferred from semantics of sound symbolic words: A case of Japanese mimetics. In N. Masataka (Ed.), *Origins of language* (pp. 25-38). Tokyo: Springer.

Nuckolls, J. B. (1999). The case for sound symbolism. Annual Review of Anthropology, 28, 225-252.

COOPERATIVE BREEDING MODELS: IMPLICATIONS FOR THE EVOLUTION OF LANGUAGE

CHRIS KNIGHT

Comenius University, Fakulta sociálnych vied, Odbojárov 10/A, 820 05 Bratislava, Slovakia

CAMILLA POWER

Anthropology Programme, School of Humanities and Social Sciences, University of East London, E16 2RD, United Kingdom

The 'cooperative breeding' hypothesis (Hrdy, 2009) and the 'grandmother' hypothesis (O'Connell, Hawkes and Blurton Jones, 1999) have combined to establish a new orthodoxy that *Homo erectus* social structures were fundamentally female kin-bonded (and see Knight, 2008; Opie and Power, 2008). What are the implications for the evolution of language?

Hrdy accounts for the evolution of special hypersocial tendencies in genus *Homo* by arguing that strategies of cooperative breeding give rise to intersubjectivity – a willingness to share what I am thinking with you, and seek to know what you are thinking of my thoughts (Tomasello et al., 2005). Other great apes, especially machiavellian chimpanzees, are capable of mind-reading, but lack any intention of cooperating in allowing their own minds to be read. Precisely when an evolving hominin mother lets others take her baby off her hands, says Hrdy, selection pressures for two-way mind-reading are set up. The mother must be socially adept to elicit support and judge motivations of the alloparent towards her offspring; the baby, once handed over, must be monitoring carefully 'where's mum gone?', at the same time as probing for signs about the intentions of the new carer; while the alloparent, necessarily a relative in the original scenario, adopts a quasi-maternal role. A whole array of behaviours sprang up to help this variegated triad of mum, baby and allocarer to keep in contact: mutual gazing, babbling, kissfeeding. Hyperpossessive great ape mothers never needed such elaborate bonding mechanisms. The only other primates which have been heard babbling are tiny South American marmosets and tamarins, whose breeding systems are fully cooperative, involving shared care and provisioning of infants by allocarers. The ancestors of the first language-users, says Hrdy 'were already far more interested in others' intentions and needs than chimpanzees are.' (2009: 38)

While the cooperative breeding/grandmothering model offers a plausible explanation for language-ready brains, these conditions may be necessary but not sufficient for the historical evolution of actual languages. In proposing 'emotional modernity' among *H. erectus*, Hrdy makes clear that she is discussing the prequel to language and symbolic culture, refraining from speculation about the transition to full cognitive and linguistic modernity. What are the problems that are not solved by this scenario? Shared infant care will not increase fitness unless the offspring's psychological development prepares it for gaining reproductive success in adult life. Hrdy draws on analogy of cooperative breeding systems among callitrichids, examining male caring behaviours, but offers little discussion of how males among early *Homo* would have integrated into this framework of mutual understanding. How did problems of male dominance, violence and competition for mates get resolved? A cooperative childcare system implies quasi-sibling solidarity among children. Unless that principle of solidarity can be extended into adulthood, encompassing sexual relationships, selection for intersubjectivity will be limited and language will not evolve.

References

Hrdy, S. B. (2009). *Mothers and Others: the evolutionary origins of mutual understanding*. Cambridge, MA: Belknap Press of Harvard University Press.

Knight, C. (2008). Early human kinship was matrilineal. In N. J. Allen, H. Callan, R. Dunbar and W. James (eds) *Early Human Kinship. From sex to social reproduction*. Oxford: Blackwell Publishing, pp. 61-82.

O'Connell, J. F., K. Hawkes and N. G. Blurton Jones (1999). Grandmothering and the evolution of *Homo erectus. Journal of Human Evolution* 36: 461-485.

Opie, K. and C. Power (2008). Grandmothering and female coalitions. A basis for matrilineal priority. In N. J. Allen, H. Callan, R. Dunbar and W. James (eds) *Early Human Kinship. From sex to social reproduction*. Oxford: Blackwell Publishing, pp. 168-186.

Tomasello, M., M. Carpenter, J. Call, T. Beyne and H. Moll (2005). Understanding and sharing intentions: The origins of cultural cognition. *Behavioral and Brain Sciences* 28: 675-691.

CONTRIBUTIONS OF APHASIOLOGY TO LANGUAGE EVOLUTION RESEARCH

ANDREAS KYRIACOU

Department of Neuropsychology, Zürich University, Switzerland

SVERKER JOHANSSON

School of Education and Communication, Jönköping University, Sweden

Brain imaging techniques have greatly improved our understanding of cerebral language processing. Nevertheless, finding the neural correlates of linguistic operations seems to be no less a quest than in the field of consciousness, for which the mapping between psychological experiences and neural activation has been labelled *the* hard problem (Chalmers, 1995).

Poeppel and Embick (2005) argued that psycholinguistics and the neurosciences face a granularity mismatch and an ontological incommensurability problem. This lacking of a common basis concerns both the granularity levels at which the two disciplines investigate processes and the fundamental elements used and, consequently, prevents the formulation of theoretically motivated, biologically grounded and computationally explicit descriptions of language processes in the brain. To better align the two areas Poeppel and Embick suggest to use computational models, whose operations must be plausibly executable by neural assemblies and represent subroutines of linguistic computation.

We appreciate Poeppel and Embick's analysis and support their proposal to identify computationally explicit processes. Resorting to computer linguistics is however no guarantee that biologically plausible implementations are identified. Artificial neural networks can be built in a way that mimic human behaviour without basing on biology-inspired architecture, as exemplified by the Rumelhart & McClelland (1986) model of English past tense acquisition.

In order to aid the identification of the relevant atomic processes involved in language perception and production we evaluate a model of language evolution with findings from agrammatism research. Johansson (2005) suggested to work backwards from current grammars through a sequence of possible proto-grammars by removing pivotal structural features. Johansson's model consists of a four-step hierarchy, which supposedly reflects the appearance of fundamental properties in human language, for the existence of which there is wide agreement across different grammar theories: the emergence of structural constraints, most notably with respect to word order; the emergence of hierarchies, i.e. the occurrence of structured units within larger-scale structures; the emergence of flexibility in the transformational sense, allowing structures to be moved around; and lastly, the occurrence of recursion, proposed to be the only domain-specific computational capacity involved in language processing (Hauser, Chomsky & Fitch, 2002, but see also e.g. Kinsella, 2009).

We hypothesise that the biologically oldest capacities recruited for language processing are least likely to suffer selective impairments from brain injuries as they presumably evolved pre-linguistically. More recent abilities, notably the proposed capacity for recursion, are more likely to have been selected specifically for linguistic purposes. In contrast to their biologically older counterparts, such capacities may be more vulnerable to break-down and affect specific aspects of language production or perception in isolation.

We use findings from studies investigating the patterns of grammar deficits in aphasia patients to assess the proposed hypothesis and to demonstrate how far aphasiology can contribute to the quest of defining linguistic capacities that are evolutionarily layered and real in both linguistic-computational and neurological terms.

References

Chalmers, D.J. (2005) Facing Up to the Problem of Consciousness, *Journal of Consciousness Studies*, 2, 200-19.

Hauser, M., Chomsky, N. & Fitch, T. (2002) The Faculty of Language: What Is It, Who Has It, and How Did It Evolve?, *Science*, 298, 1569-79.

Johansson, S. (2005) *Origins of Language: Constraints on Hypotheses*. John Benjamins.

Kinsella, A. R. (2009) *Language evolution and syntactic theory* Cambridge: Cambridge University Press

Poeppel, D. & Embick, D. (2005). The relation between linguistics and neuroscience. In A. Cutler (Ed.), *Twenty-First Century Psycholinguistics: Four Cornerstones*. Lawrence Erlbaum.

Rumelhart, D. E. & McClelland, J. L. (1986). *Parallel Distributed Processing*, MIT Press.

Wickelgren, W.A. (1969) Context-sensitive coding, associative memory, and serial order in (speech) behavior. *Psychological Review*, 86, 44–60.

HOW IMPORTANT ARE WORDS FOR CONCEPTUAL COORDINATION?

CYPRIAN LASKOWSKI, MARTIN PICKERING

Language Evolution and Computation Research Unit, University of Edinburgh,
3 Charles Street, Edinburgh, EH8 9AD, United Kingdom
cyp@ling.ed.ac.uk

In attempting to explain how words first emerged in language evolution, it is often assumed that words map passively onto a pre-existing static conceptual system (e.g., Hurford, 2007). However, human thought is very flexible: we can conceptualise the same referent in many different ways, depending on the context and our goal. For instance, we may conceptualise a lion as a dangerous beast, a thrilling sight, an unusual dinner, etc. Moreover, concepts may have different scope for different people. As a result, one of the main functions of words may be to provide an efficient way to share and coordinate conceptualisations with others. Indeed, to the extent that people do conceptualise things differently, it is not easy to imagine how such gaps could be bridged without the help of words and language, and previous work has shown that verbal labels can enhance category learning (Lupyan, Rakison, & McClelland, 2007). Either way, looking into this issue could contribute to our understanding of how much the advent of public symbols transformed human cognition (Deacon, 1997). The question under empirical investigation here is thus the importance of words to conceptual coordination.

Before this issue can be addressed experimentally, there is an immediate methodological challenge. In particular, in order to assess the role of words in conceptual coordination, we need a way of getting at experimental participants' concepts without relying on words. The solution that will be adopted here is the use of free classification tasks (Malt, Sloman, Gennari, Shi, & Wang, 1999): participants partition a set of items into groups, and these groups are assumed to be referential snapshots of their concepts.

I present here an experiment within the free classification framework which pits the importance of words against that of referential information. Pairs of native English speakers conducted a sequence of thirty free classification tasks involving a fluid domain of triangle-like stimuli. In each task, participants had to individually sort a set of eleven stimuli into two categories, and to label their categories. Their goal was to partition the stimuli into the same (or as similar as possible) two groups as their partner (irrespective of the labels used). Participants could not interact or communicate freely during the experiment, but they did receive feed-back at the end of each task. All participants were shown their partnership's joint task score, and, depending on the condition that they were assigned to, either their partner's category groupings, category labels, both or neither (thus the experiment had a 2x2 between-pairs design).

The results revealed several patterns. First, although label agreement within pairs correlated with higher task scores, there were plenty of exceptions, where the participants used the same labels but differed in their category groupings, or achieved identical groupings despite using different labels. Second, averaging across the tasks, grouping feedback resulted in significantly higher scores, and these were higher still if accompanied by label feedback as well. On the other hand, label feedback on its own did not result in higher scores. Third, although there was a lot of fluctuation in scores even within pairs, they tended to go up over time, except in the groupings-only condition, where they stayed about the same. Due to these last two patterns, by the end of the experiment, the scores in the *both* condition were significantly higher than in the other three conditions. Thus it was only in the condition with both kinds of feedback that pairs started off with relatively high scores **and** improved over time.

Together, these results suggest that rich referential information is more useful than words for conceptual coordination, but that high levels of coordination can only be achieved when both types are available. Of course, it would be absurd to suggest that early hominins huddled together and explicitly sorted things into categories to coordinate their concepts. However, the current results shed light on the extent to which language may have revolutionised human cognition. Language does not seem to be crucial for conceptual coordination, but it does enhance it.

References

Deacon, T. (1997). *The symbolic species: the coevolution of language and the brain*. New York: Norton.

Hurford, J. R. (2007). *The origins of meaning: language in the light of evolution.* Oxford University Press.

Lupyan, G., Rakison, D. H., & McClelland, J. L. (2007). Language is not just for talking: labels facilitate learning of novel categories. *Psychological Science, 18*, 1077–1083.

Malt, B. C., Sloman, S., Gennari, S., Shi, M., & Wang, Y. (1999). Knowing versus naming: similarity and the linguistic categorization of artifacts. *Journal of Memory and Language, 40*, 230–262.

VOCAL ABILITIES IN A GROUP OF NONHUMAN PRIMATES

ALBAN LEMASSON

Ethologie animale et humaine UMR 6552, Université de Rennes 1, Station Biologique, Paimpont, 35380, France

KLAUS ZUBERBÜHLER

School of Psychology, University of St Andrews, St. Andrews, KY16 9JP, Scotland

Human language is too complex to have emerged in the absence of any evolutionary precursors, which suggests that primitive forms of pre-linguistic communication can be found in animals. Whether this was based on acoustic or gestural communication is an ongoing debate. An argument against a vocal origin is the absence of vocal flexibility and complexity in non-human primates. However, human language is primarily a vocal behaviour, and vocal flexibility – as assessed by vocal plasticity, semanticity, compositionality, and intentional signalling - is not a uniquely human trait. Our research focuses on the precursors of the various types of vocal flexibility in forest guenons (*Cercopithecus* spp). The vocal tract of nonhuman primates is in principle capable of producing speech-like sounds (Riede et al 2005) and one puzzle is why nonhuman primates do not make greater use of this feature. Instead, primates produce a finite range of calls that develop under strong genetic control. Within some call types, however, some flexibility can be seen at the level of call morphology, as for example demonstrated by socially-determined vocal plasticity and vocal sharing in Campbell's monkey contact calls used in conversation-like socially controlled vocal exchanges (Lemasson & Hausberger 2004; Lemasson et al 2010). Second, many primates produce acoustically distinct calls to specific external events, including Diana and Campbell's monkeys. In both species, the adult males and females produce acoustically different alarm calls to the same predator (Ouattara et al 2009a), but calls are meaningful to others, both within and between species. Alarm calls are not only predator-specific but also vary depending on the modality by which the predator is discovered, i.e. the visual or acoustic domain. In Campbell's monkeys females produced a complex alarm call repertoire, although differences were found between captive and wild individuals. Captive ones did not produce predator-specific calls but had a unique call to humans (Ouattara et al 2009a). For males, we found a repertoire of six call types, which could be classified into different morphs, according to the frequency contour and whether calls were trailed by an acoustically invariable suffix. Suffixed calls carried a broader meaning than unsuffixed ones (Ouattara et al 2009b). The six calls were concatenated into context-specific call sequences, following basic combinatorial principles (Ouattara et al 2009c). In sum, the vocal abilities in guenons go significantly beyond the currently assumed default case for nonhuman primates. Flexibility can be seen at all relevant levels, including limited control over call morphology, conversational rules, ability to produce context-specific calls, and some basic combinatorial properties. The data are at odds with a gestural origins of language theory. Gestural signals do not appear to play a key role in these species, while vocal flexibility is seen in all key components despite the fact that they have split from the human line about 30 million years ago. Field playback experiments will be needed to confirm whether receivers utilise these rich patterns to guide their behavioural decisions. But even in the absence of such evidence data suggest that a strong dichotomy between human language and nonhuman primate communication may no longer be tenable in the vocal domain. The visually dense forest habitat may have played a key role in the evolution of advanced vocalisation skills.

References

Lemasson, A., & Hausberger, M. (2004). Patterns of vocal sharing and social dynamics in a captive group of Campbell's monkeys. *Journal of Comparative Psychology, 118,* 347-359.

Lemasson, A., Gandon, E., & Hausberger, M. (2010). Attention to elders' voice in nonhuman primates. *Biology letters*: in press;

Ouattara, K., Zuberbühler, K., N'goran, K.E., Gombert, J-E., & Lemasson, A. (2009a). The alarm call system of female Campbell's monkeys. *Animal Behaviour, 78,* 35-44;

Ouattara, K., Lemasson, A. & Zuberbühler, K. (2009b). Campbell's monkeys use affixation to alter call meaning. *PloS ONE, 4,* e7808;

Ouattara, K., Lemasson, A., Zuberbühler, K. (2009c). Generating meaning with finite means in Campbell's monkeys. *P.N.A.S., 106,* 48;

Riede, T., Bronson, E., Hatzikirou, H. & Zuberbuhler, K. (2005). Vocal production mechanisms in a non-human primate: morphological data and a model. *Journal of Human Evolution, 48,* 85-96.

VOCAL DECEPTION FROM A HUNTER-GATHERER PERSPECTIVE

JEROME LEWIS

Department of Anthropology, University College London, London WC1E 6BT, UK

CHRIS KNIGHT

Comenius University, Fakulta sociálnych vied, Odbojárov 10/A, 820 05 Bratislava, Slovakia

It is well-known that primates – as opposed to, say, songbirds (Marler, 1970; Nottebohm, 1999) or cetaceans (Sayigh et al., 1990; Miller et al., 2004) – are poor vocal imitators, lacking volitional control over their vocal signals. It is equally evident that in this particular respect, humans are a puzzling aberration: evolution seems to have aligned us much closer to ravens or parrots than monkeys or apes! To explain this, it is not satisfactory to work backwards from speech. Speech in its modern form is a massively complex expression of the ability to control vocal signals. During earlier stages in the evolution of language, we would expect less developed capacities, more closely related to the situation among our primate cousins. We would also expect communicative reliance on manual and other visible gestures. This is simply because *all* primates (for obvious functional reasons) must be neurally equipped to cognitively sequence and control movements of their limbs, fingers and hands.

As and when enhanced capacities for vocal imitation and control in the human lineage evolved, we would expect selection pressures not initially for speech. Instead, on the model of songbirds and cetaceans, we might expect innovations serving purposes associated with vocal chorusing, song transmission, mimicry, deception and play. The evolutionary emergence of speech *depends* on the antecedent evolution of such vocal capacities; it cannot be invoked retrospectively to explain them.

There are good Darwinian reasons why non-human primates find it difficult to subject vocal communication to volitional control. Much more than facial or manual gestures, which are primarily useful in face-to-face interactions, the more complex sound signals of primates must carry over distances. This means that receivers are less in a position to immediately check veracity, hence more under pressure to insist on signal reliability. A vocal signal which can be manipulated at will is one which can easily be faked; if primate vocalizations are overwhelmingly 'hard-to-fake' it is because receivers over evolutionary time have listened to nothing else. Vocal signals whose acoustic properties suggested that they might possibly be fakes were ignored.

So what changed during the evolution of humans? One context in which hominins might routinely have deployed vocal manipulations could have been hunting, entailing deception of other species. Among Central African Forest hunters, sound signatures of the forest are systematically faked to lure prey. In this paper, we outline a model in which successful deception of non-humans, unable to develop resistance, is redeployed within human groups as the basis for mimetic storytelling, ritual and vocal play. In this perspective, 'language' is interpreted broadly, going beyond narrowly defined speech to consider all the ways that sounds can be strung together to effectively convey meanings.

References

Marler, P. (1970). A comparative approach to vocal learning: Song development in white-crowned sparrows *Journal of Comparative and Physiological Psychology*, **71**, 1-25.

Miller, P. J. O., Shapiro, A. D., Tyack, P. L. & Solow, A. R. (2004). Call-type matching in vocal exchanges of free-ranging resident killer whales, *Orcinus orca*. *Animal Behaviour*, **67**, 1099-1107.

Nottebohm, F. (1999). The anatomy and timing of vocal learning in birds. In: *The design of animal communication* (Ed. by Hauser, M. D. & Konishi, M.), pp. 63-110. Cambridge: MIT Press.

Sayigh, L. S., Tyack, P. L., Wells, R. S. & Scott, M. D. (1990). Signature whistles of free-ranging bottlenose dolphins, *Tursiops truncatus*: Stability and mother-offspring comparisons. *Behavioral Ecology and Sociobiology*, **26**, 247-260.

THE EMERGENCE OF SELF-ORGANIZATION IN LANGUAGE: EVIDENCE FROM ENGLISH WORD FORMATION

MARK LINDSAY

Department of Linguistics, Stony Brook University
Stony Brook, NY 11794, USA

MARK ARONOFF

Department of Linguistics, Stony Brook University
Stony Brook, NY 11794, USA

Certain subsystems of human languages can be profitably studied as self-organizing or emergent systems. In this presentation we will show that the birth of productive affixes from borrowed vocabulary can be treated as an emergent system, using modern databases and the Internet. We present two types of evidence. The first addresses the question of how a language borrows affixes at all. We examine the history of two suffixes in English, *-ment* and *–ity*, both of which came into English from French, using the OED on CD-Rom as a database. Both suffixes had their origins in words borrowed individually from French. Before 1600, the great majority of new words in *–ity* were borrowed; beginning around 1600, the percentage of coinages increased rapidly, soon reaching 80% and plateauing at 95% by 1800. Since 1900, only two words ending in *–ity* have been borrowed, while close to 500 have been coined. We thus have evidence that *-ity* became a productive suffix once there were enough exemplars for a tipping point to be reached, which is typical for self-organizing systems. The history of *–ment* shows that the story is not so simple. Here, although newly coined words outnumbered borrowed words two-to-one by 1600, paralleling *–ity*, the pattern never became a truly productive suffix. Since 1900, only 30 words ending in *–ment* have been coined, as opposed to almost 500 in *–ity*, showing that the number of exemplars is not the only factor in determining whether a system self-organizes.

The second study addresses the synonymous suffix pair *–ic* and *–ical*, which we analyze in greater detail. The overall goal in studying such pairs is to discover why a language would systematize synonymous productive affixes. English exhibits a large number of doublets containing both rival suffixes, e.g. *geographic* and *geographical*; but with many pairs one member is strongly preferred over the other: *statistical* is much more common than *statistic*, while *heuristic* is much more common than *heuristical*. First we ask whether both suffixes are in fact productive and whether one suffix is more productive than the other overall. In this study, we measure productivity as the total number of Google hits for every word ending in each suffix: for every word, we do a Google search on the exact word and list the number of hits, which provides a much larger sample than if we measured frequency within a preexisting corpus.

From Merriam-Webster's *Second International Dictionary*, available online, we identified 11966 stems of English words ending in either *–ic* or *–ical*. For each stem, either one or both derivatives was listed in the dictionary. We then searched for words ending in both *–ic* and *–ical* in each of the 11966 stems. For some stems, a search will record hits for both *–ic* and *–ical* words (e.g. *historic* and *historical*), while for some, only one is found (e.g. *transoceanic* vs. **transoceanical* but *pseudopsychological* vs.**pseudopsychologic*). We then determined for each pair whether *–ic* or *–ical* had more hits. The one with more hits is the 'winner' for that pair.

We then put this database of *–ic* and *–ical* pairs and associated numbers of Google hits in an Excel spreadsheet and subjected it to analysis. Overall, we identified 10613 *–ic* winners vs. 1353 *–ical* winners, with an overall ratio of 7.84 in favor of *–ic*. This demonstrates that overall *–ic* is more productive than *–ical*. Finer-grained analysis, however, reveals a subtler story. First, we sorted all the items in our database into reverse-alphabetical neighborhoods of from three to seven letters, not including final *–al*. When we sort the words in this way, the only set of words ending in *–ical* with a neighborhood >100 in size is *–ological*; for this subset only, *–ical* is the winner over *–ic* (e.g. *psychological* over *psychologic*), by a total ratio of 8.30, almost the exact reverse of the ratio of the full set (7.84 in favor of *–ic*). In other words, although overall *–ic* is more productive than *–ical*, the reverse is true for words ending in *–ological*. Another set of words for which *–ical* is more productive than expected comprises those based on nouns ending in *–ics* (e.g. *physics, physical, physic*). For these, adjectives in *–ic* still outnumber those in *–ical,* but *–ical* words are twice as common as normal, outnumbered only four to one by *–ic*, instead of the normal 8.30. Overall, and somewhat surprisingly, English derivational morphology, especially when it involves the emergence of productive affixes from sets of borrowed words (in which English is especially rich), is a fertile proving ground for the study of self-organizing systems in languages, in part because of the databases that electronic resources provide.

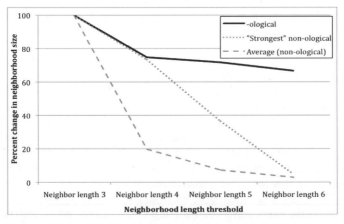

Figure 1. Percent change in neighborhood size as a function of threshold length.

BEYOND COMMUNICATION: LANGUAGE MODULATES VISUAL PROCESSING

GARY LUPYAN

Institute for Research in Cognitive Science and Center for Cognitive Neuroscience.
University of Pennsylvania. Philadelphia, PA 19104, USA

Understanding the extra-communicative functions of language (e.g., Clark, 1998) is central for constraining theories of language evolution. If, in addition to its communicative functions, language has extra-communicative functions— affecting nonverbal cognitive and perceptual processes—then an important force in the evolution of language may have been the effect language had and continues to have on such processes. Such reasoning helps to address a question central to the evolution of language: what adaptive benefits did early language users derive from rudimentary linguistic systems?

In the present work I will present an overview of the past 4 years of research in which we find that, across a range of paradigms, language exerts a rapid and automatic influence on basic visual processes. These results provide (indirect) evidence that even in rudimentary forms, language systems may have conferred basic perceptual (and non-communicative) benefits to their users.

A critical aspect of human development is the development of conceptual and perceptual categories—learning that things with feathers tend to fly, that animals possessing certain features are dogs, and that foods of a certain color and shape are edible (Rogers & McClelland, 2004; Keil, 1992; Carey, 1987). This conceptual acquisition is, in principle, separable from the acquisition of language (a child can have a conceptual category of "dog" without having a verbal label associated with the category). However, in practice the two processes appear to be intimately linked. Not only does conceptual development shape linguistic development (Snedeker & Gleitman, 2004), but linguistic development, specifically learning words for things, appears to be impact conceptual development (Gentner & Goldin-Meadow, 2003; Lupyan, Rakison, & McClelland, 2007; Waxman & Markow, 1995). The empirical findings in the present work argue that such effects of language are not limited to long-term effects on conceptual development. It is argued that language exerts a on-line modulatory role on even the most basic perceptual processes.

The data come from standard paradigms from the vision sciences: visual search, mental rotation, cued target-detection, simple detection, and picture verification. These experiments license the following broad conclusions:

1. Hearing a category label such as "chair" facilitates the visual processing of the named category compared to trials on which participants know the relevant object category but do not actually hear its name. In some instances, producing the verbal label has similar facilitatory effects (Lupyan, 2007, 2008b, under review).

2. The above effects are transient, having a characteristic temporal profile, and are heavily modulated by the typicality of the visual exemplar. Visual processing of more typical items is more facilitated by hearing their name (Lupyan, 2007; 2008b; under review).

3. Hearing a label increases the perceptual saliency of the named category, enabling people to detect objects that are otherwise invisible (Lupyan & Spivey, 2008; under review).

4. Very brief amounts of training can alter the associations between labels and object categories suggesting that, at least in adults, such linguistic modulation of perception is highly flexible (Lupyan, 2007; Lupyan, Thompson-Schill, & Swingley, in press).

Ongoing work is showing that verbal labels evoke associated perceptual representations faster and more reliably than nonverbal stimuli. For example, people activate the visual properties of a cat faster when they hear the word "cat" than when they hear a meowing sound. Specifically, it appears that verbal labels come to have a special status of being able to activate *categorical* representations.

This linguistic modulation of perception may have important consequences for higher-level cognition such as the learning of new categories (Lupyan et al., 2007), memory (Lupyan, 2008), and conceptually grouping items along a particular dimension (e.g., color) (Lupyan, 2009) as well as inference in reasoning.

Theories of language evolution have maintained an almost exclusive focus on the communicative aspects of language. The present findings show that simple word-object pairings can modulate even basic visual processes, providing support for the idea that even in its early stages, languages may have conferred cognitive and perceptual benefits on their users.

DECLARATIVES IN APES: IMPACT OF ENVIRONMENT ON PURELY INFOMATIVE COMMUNICATIONS

HEIDI LYN[a]
PATRICIA GREENFIELD[b]
SUE SAVAGE-RUMBAUGH[c]
JAMIE L. RUSSELL[d]
KRISTEN GILLESPE-LYNCH[b]
WILLIAM D. HOPKINS[a, d]

a. Department of Psychology, Agnes Scott College, 141 E. College Ave, Decatur, GA, 30030 USA

b. Department of Psychology and FPR-UCLA Center for Culture, Brain, and Development, University of California, Los Angeles CA 90095

c. Great Ape Trust of Iowa, Des Moines, IA 50320

d. Department of Psychobiology, Yerkes National Primate Research Center, Emory University, 954 Gatewood Rd. NE, Atlanta, GA 30329 USA

Recent discussions about the evolution of communication have stressed a perceived qualitative distinction between humans and our closest evolutionary relatives, the great apes, wherein human nature is described as uniquely cooperative relative to the more competitive great apes (e.g. Tomasello, 2007). One major argument at the root of this cooperative hypothesis of the origin of language is the relative lack of declarative as opposed to imperative (request-driven) communication demonstrated by apes. For instance, it has been reported in multiple studies that apes cannot, as a rule, glean information from a human's declarative cue in a cooperative paradigm, although other, arguably more cooperative species can do so (see Lyn & Hopkins, 2009 for a review).

We recently tested apes reared in different environments on a declarative comprehension object choice task (Lyn, Russell, & Hopkins, in press). Significantly higher scores on the task were obtained from the two groups of apes that were reared in a socio-linguistically complex environment (as part of a language project at the Language Research Center, Atlanta, GA (LRC) compared to the two standard-reared groups (F(3, 57) = 6.54, p<.01). This

445

rearing difference was seen in both proximal and distal pointing tasks. The results further showed that bonobos, an allegedly more cooperative species, did not outperform chimpanzees (t(59) = 1.78, p>.05). Our results demonstrated that environmental factors, specifically access to a socio-linguistically rich environment, directly influence apes' ability to comprehend declarative signals.

To determine the ability of great apes to produce declaratives, we compared the lexigram and gesture utterances of two bonobos and one chimpanzee reared at the LRC to the verbal utterances of two normally-developing children. All three apes made declarative gestures and lexigram utterances. These utterances fell into most of the same categories as the declaratives made by the children, including declaratives about past events, future behavior, and naming concrete and nonconcrete items, among others. Apes and children did differ in the frequency of declaratives ($\chi^2(1$, n=110074) = 8315, p<.001) and the frequencies of certain declarative types (e.g. the children had more declaratives that were concrete naming ($\chi^2(1$, n=7451) = 283.8, p<.001), and the apes had more declaratives about future plans ($\chi^2(1$, n=7451) = 572.3, p<.001)).

According to our results, both chimpanzees and bonobos are capable of utilizing the environment to support declarative communication. As the end result is a distinction of quantity, we must look elsewhere for a qualitative communicative difference between ourselves and our nearest evolutionary relatives, for instance, in the formation of social structures that support these abilities.

References

Lyn, H., & Hopkins, W. D. (2009). *Declarative comprehension and production in apes.* Paper presented at the American Society of Primatologists.

Lyn, H., Russell, J. L., & Hopkins, W. D. (in press). The impact of environment on the comprehension of declarative communication in apes. *Psychological Science.*

Tomasello, M. (2007). If they're so good at grammar, then why don't they talk? Hints from apes' and humans' use of gestures. *Language Learning and Development, 3*(2), 133-156.

Acknowledgements

The authors wish to acknowledge the assistance of the staff and administration of the Language Research Center, The Yerkes National Primate Research Center, The Great Ape Trust of Iowa, and the Jacksonville Zoo and Gardens where these data were collected. Funding for this study was provided by NIH grants HD-56232 and HD-38105.

LANGUAGES AS EVOLUTIONARY AGGREGATES

LUKE MCCROHON

*Graduate School of Information Science and Technology, The University of Tokyo,
Bunkyo-Ku, Tokyo, 113-0033, Japan*

1. Introduction

In recent years Darwinian theories of evolution have started to be applied not only to the biological evolution of the language faculty, but also to the cultural evolution of languages (Croft 2000, Ritt 2004). This paper considers differences between cultural and biological evolution, with regards to their influence on the question of *"at what level is linguistic information subject to selection?"* It is shown that rather than viewing languages as jointly evolving entities, it is more appropriate to view them as *evolutionary aggregates*, comprised of a large number of independently evolving features. Moreover, it is argued that the degree of evolutionary independence of these features is far higher than that of Dawkins' (1976) selfish genes in biology. This has implications for evolutionary explanations of language changes and certain kinds of structuralist reasoning.

2. Differing Mechanisms of Inheritance and Selection

The prototypical example of biological evolution is that observed in sexually reproducing macroscopic organisms. Reproduction of any genetic material from such organisms is dependent upon the reproduction of host organisms in their entirety. In such organisms the reproductive success of individual genes is dependent on the phenotype of the whole organism, not just on those genes' specific contribution to it.

In the case of language evolution the situation is different. Linguistic information corresponding to any language feature can be reproduced in another speaker independently of the reproduction of other features. Additionally an individual's linguistic knowledge can originate from interactions with any number of other speakers. But most importantly, the reproductive success of any language feature is only dependent on its individual success in getting itself replicated by speakers (Keller 1990).

3. Languages as Evolutionary Aggregates

One consequence of these differences is that the features of a language each have separate evolutionary histories, where at each stage they have been selected based primarily on their own merits. They have no constraints forcing them to be selected/reproduce together as a group. This results in a far higher degree of independence than is observed in biology, with each separately learnable feature of a language evolving on its own, largely independent of surrounding features.

The concept of "languages" becomes more abstract, referring to collections of independently evolving, but interacting features; *evolutionary aggregates*, analogous to biological "communities". And as with communities, their internal features can potentially interact in many ways, from cooperation to competition.

4. Linguistic Evidence

In areal linguistics it has long been realized that not only can parts of languages diffuse separately, but following diffusion, those parts are often modified for integration into the destination language (Haugen 1950). Both independent diffusion and subsequent integration are used to show that linguistic information is not tied to a particular linguistic system. Sociolinguistic evidence is taken from examples of intra-language competition between features that would not be expected if it were whole languages that were being selected.

5. Linguistic Consequences

A consequence of languages being evolutionary aggregates is that we should not simply assume cooperation between all of their features. A degree of co-adaption can be expected to arise (Dawkins 1982), but only in so far as it benefits each feature individually. This has consequences for the validity of many kinds of linguistic reasoning; only those explanations that show benefit to all relevant features can be justified. This effects not only explanations of diachronic changes, but also explanations of synchronic patterns they produce.

References

Croft, W. (2000). Explaining Language Change: An Evolutionary Approach. Harlow, Essex: Longman.
Dawkins, R. (1976). The Selfish Gene. Oxford: Oxford University Press.
Dawkins, R. (1982). The Extended Phenotype. Oxford: Oxford University Press.
Keller, R. (1990). On language change: The invisible hand in language. London: Routledge.
Ritt, N. (2004). Selfish sounds. A Darwinian approach to language change. Cambridge: University Press.

3D-MORPHOMETRIC AND ACOUSTIC ANALYSIS OF CHIMPANZEE AND HUMAN VOCAL TRACTS, AND THEIR USE IN THE RECONSTRUCTION OF NEANDERTHAL VOCAL TRACTS AND THEIR ACOUSTIC POTENTIAL.

SANDRA MARTELLI

AHRC Centre for the Evolution of Cultural Diversity, Institute of Archaeology, UCL, London, UK

ANTOINE SERRURIER

Institute of Sound and Vibration Research, University of Southampton, UK

ANNA BARNEY

Institute of Sound and Vibration Research, University of Southampton, UK

JAMES STEELE

AHRC Centre for the Evolution of Cultural Diversity, Institute of Archaeology, UCL, London, UK

Although chimpanzees have an equally long evolutionary history as our own since the last common ancestor of these two species, their morphology is often taken as a closer approximation of the ancestral condition. Early chimp language training experiments failed to elicit language-like output in the vocal channel, for reasons that may relate both to neural control systems and to the morphology of the vocal tract itself. It therefore remains relevant to ask whether the geometry and muscle architecture of the chimpanzee vocal tract could enable the stable deformations required to produce a human-like phonological repertoire. If not, then it also becomes relevant to ask at what point in human evolution the hominin vocal tract evolved a shape that was consistent with such articulatory manoeuvres.

We obtained CT-scans of an ontogenetic series of chimpanzee cadavers from the Zurich Anthropology Institute collections, and isolated their vocal tracts for morphological analysis and acoustic/articulatory modelling. We analysed these vocal tracts in three dimensions, and identified a set of anatomical features that define characteristic constrictions and expansions along their lengths. Acoustic modelling of these tracts in a multi-tube configuration (which best approximated the observed morphology) enabled us to predict their passive or resting-state acoustic potential, and also enabled us to digitally perturb this resting-state configuration to explore their phonetic potential in relation to the human vowel triangle. We will compare our anatomical results with those of Nishimura (e.g. 2005), and our acoustic results with those of Lieberman, Crelin and Klatt (1972).

We also analysed this chimpanzee head-and-neck CT scan series and a sample of 20 adult human head-and-neck CT scans, to identify hard-tissue landmarks and inter-landmark relationships that constrain the position of soft tissue features of the vocal tract of each of these extant species. We then applied these relationships to predict hyoid position in Neanderthals using an additional set of 3D-scanned fossil skulls from this extinct species. We report a potential envelope of hyoid positions for adult Neanderthals based on linear regression analysis, in which we predict their hyoid positions from inter-landmark distances of skull and mandible in three dimensions (using human and chimpanzee as alternative reference models). The human models result in anatomically-viable hyoid positions for Neanderthals whereas the chimpanzee models result in less anatomically plausible Neanderthal hyoid positions. The Neanderthal hyoid bone most likely occupied similar positions in relation to skull and mandible (and the vertebral column) to those observed in modern humans, which means that it cannot be used to discount the presence of human-like speech in this species.

Acknowledgements

This study is part of HANDTOMOUTH, funded by the EUROPEAN COMMISSION (Grant No. 029065).

References

Lieberman, P., Crelin, E.S., Klatt, D.H.. (1972) Phonetic ability and related anatomy of the newborn, adult human, Neanderthal man, and the chimpanzee. *Am. Anthropol.* 74: 287–307.

Nishimura, T. (2005) Developmental changes in the shape of the supralaryngeal vocal tract in chimpanzees. *Am. J. Phys. Anthropol.* 126: 193-204.

THE CULTURAL EVOLUTION OF LANGUAGE IN A WORLD OF CONTINUOUS MEANINGS

CRISTINA MATTHEWS, SIMON KIRBY, HANNAH CORNISH

School of Philosophy, Psychology & Language Sciences, University of Edinburgh,
3 Charles St, Edinburgh, EH8 9AD, UK

The structure of language is the result of a complex interaction between biologically given prior biases, the arena of language use, and the space of meanings that language users convey (see, e.g., Hurford, 1990). Recent research has attempted to understand these interactions by focussing on the way in which languages persist over time by repeated cycles of learning and use – a process called *iterated learning* (e.g. Kirby et al., 2007).

Previous work has used a combination of artificial language learning and diffusion chain methodologies to observe the iterated learning of language in human participants in laboratory conditions (Kirby et al., 2008). The results from these studies demonstrate that compositional structure gradually emerges as an adaptation by language to various pressures placed on it during cultural transmission.

A noticeable feature of this work, however, is that the language structure that emerges is bound to reflect precisely the fixed (and finite) structure of the set of meanings that experimenters have pre-specified. In particular, the meanings used in these kinds of studies have typically been made up of a finite set of features each taking one of a fixed finite set of values.

Of course, in reality we use language to convey meanings from a set that is neither finite nor parceled neatly into features and values. Instead, the world is by-and-large characterised by continuously variable dimensions which permit a wide range of possible categorisations. Put crudely, although language is digital, the world it refers to is analogue.

If the broad conclusion of previous work on iterated learning is correct – that language structure is an adaptive consequence of being culturally transmitted – then we should expect languages to evolve whose signals reflect structure in meanings even if those meanings are drawn from a continuous space. To test this, we ran a modified form of Kirby et al.'s (2008) cultural transmission experiment in which participants were asked to try and learn strings in an "alien" language that was in fact the previous participant's output at test (with the first participant being exposed to a completely unstructured, random seed language). Whereas Kirby et al. (2008) used pictures to represent the alien meanings, which contained one of three shapes in one of three colours moving in one of three possible ways, we used pictures drawn from a continuous space of shapes that smoothly vary between triangles and rectangles (see Fig. 1).

452

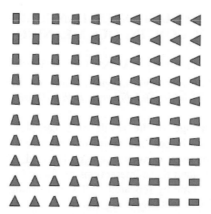

Figure 1. The meaning space used in our experiments. The "meaning" at each point in the space is a shape that is an average of the four corner shapes inversely weighted by distance to that corner. Each participant learned a language that labels points in this space and then was asked to generalise these labels to unseen shapes. Each participant's output became the training data for the next.

The results are striking: just as in the previous work, the languages adapt to become more learnable as they are passed down each of the different chains of participants in the study. The measure of learnability is determined by the transmission error in the language from one participant to the next in each chain of participants. In addition, as before, linguistic structure emerges out of the random initial state. However, in this experiment there are no clear dimensions or pre-specified category boundaries for language to adapt to. Instead, each chain of participants in the experiment gives rise to a language that supports a distinct way of conceptualising the space. That is, we find chain-specific variation in the categories that emerge in each language (e.g., some categories account for rotation, while others do not). The particular scheme a language uses emerges gradually in the experiment, often out of a competition between different ways in which similarity can be defined between shapes, and is reliably maintained after the sixth generation (of a total ten generations).

This study supports the general conclusions of the ongoing work on iterated learning, that language structure arises from the cycle of repeated learning by individuals in a population. In addition, it demonstrates that iterated learning can be used to explore the emergence not only of features like compositionality, but also of categorisation and conceptualisation.

References

Hurford, J. (1990). Nativist and functional explanations in language acquisition. In I. M. Roca, editor, *Logical Issues in Language Acquisition*. Dordrecht: Foris.

Kirby, S., Cornish, H., & Smith, K. (2008). Cumulative cultural evolution in the laboratory: An experimental approach to the origins of structure in human language. *PNAS*, 105(31):10681-10686.

Kirby, S., Dowman, M., & Griffiths, T. L. (2007). Innateness and culture in the evolution of language. *PNAS*, 104(12):5241-5245.

INVESTIGATION OF GESTURAL *VS* VOCAL ORIGINS OF LANGUAGE IN NONHUMAN PRIMATES: DISTINGUISHING COMPREHENSION AND PRODUCTION OF SIGNALS

ADRIEN MEGUERDITCHIAN[1,2] & JACQUES VAUCLAIR[1]

[1]*Research Center in Psychology of Cognition, Language & Emotion, Aix-Marseille University, Aix-en-Provence, France.* [2]*Station de Primatologie CNRS, Rousset, France.*

Human language is an extraordinary and unique means of communication involving left-hemispheric specialization for both production and comprehension, and specific properties such as intentionality, flexibility, categorization, referential properties, etc. Since nonhuman primates are very close to humans from a phylogenetic standpoint, research on their communicative systems might provide elements for inferring the features of our ancestral communicative systems. There is a considerable debate about whether precursors of language may be found either in the gestural or in the vocal communicative systems of our primate cousins within theoretical framework about the origins of language (e.g., Ghazanfar & Hauser, 1999, Corballis, 2002).

In the present paper, we propose that the advocates of gestural *vs* vocal origins of language might be reconciled if we foresee distinguishing the origins of the linguistic *perceptive* system from the human speech *production* system. In fact, it turns out that most of the arguments proposed by the proponents of the vocal hypothesis come from the findings that are specifically related to the *perception* of vocalizations, that might involves amodal processes of categorization and understanding of the external world, rather than the vocal modality itself (Meguerditchian & Vauclair, 2008). It is largely admitted that conspecific vocalizations are referential since listeners are able to extract information from vocal signals such as the identity of the caller, the nature of the social relationships among conspecifics, matrilineal kin, dominance rank. In congruence with such a potential behavioral continuity with speech *comprehension*, behavioral asymmetries and neurobiological studies showed that *perception* of vocalizations involve a left-hemispheric dominance and a cerebral circuit that might be related to Wernicke's area in humans (involved in language *comprehension*). Concerning the *production* of vocal signals, contrary to speech *production*, although a certain degree of audience's effect and of plasticity of the vocal system have been demonstrated in nonhuman primates,

(1) they fail to be dissociated from their appropriated emotional context and are related to a whole group rather than a specific recipient; (2) the vocal repertoire remains inextensible across groups of a given species and the subtle inter- or intra-group structural variations reported in some vocal signals concern only existing species-specific vocalizations of this repertoire; (3) there is no evidence that vocal *production* involves left-hemispheric specialization and homologous language's areas, but rather subcortical areas and the limbic system (related to emotions in humans). By contrast, as in human language *production*, the use of communicative gestures appears to be (1) much more flexible within a extensible gestural repertoire, (2) independent of a specific social context; (3) clearly intentional, exclusively directed to a specific recipient (Pika, 2008); (4) to involve left-hemispheric specialization and homologous of Broca's area in chimpanzees according to both behavioural asymmetries studies and neuroanatomical and neurofunctional imaging studies (Taglialatela et al., 2008). In conclusion, we suggest that the abilities in nonhuman primates for processing meaningful vocalizations are better related to their remarkable capacity to understand and categorize the external world, including vocalizations and visual events (Cheney & Seyfarth, 1990), rather than to their specific vocal *production* system. Then, such features might constitute the precursor of the representational processes involved in the *comprehension* of language in humans whereas the properties of gestural communication appear more convincing for inferring the prerequisites of the speech *production* system.

Research funded by National Research Agency ANR-08-BLAN-0011_01.

References

Corballis, M. C. (2002). *From Hand to Mouth. The Origins of Language.* Princeton, NJ: Princeton University Press.

Ghazanfar, A. A., & Hauser, M. D. (1999). The neuroethology of primate vocal communication: substrates for the evolution of speech. *Trends in Cognitive Sciences, 3*, 377-384.

Meguerditchian, A., & Vauclair, J. (2008). Vocal and gestural communication in nonhuman primates and the question of the origin of language. In L.S. Roska-Hardy & E.M. Neumann-Held (Eds.), *Learning from animals?* (pp. 61–85). London: Psychology Press.

Pika, S. (2008). Gestures of apes and pre-linguistic human children: Similar or different? *First Language, 28,* 116-140.

Taglialatela, J. P., Russell, J. L, Schaeffer, J. A., & Hopkins, W. D. (2008). Communicative signaling activates "Broca's" homologue in chimpanzees. *Current Biology, 18*, 343–348.

THE INTERACTION OF ANIMACY AND WORD ORDER IN HUMAN LANGUAGES: A STUDY OF STRATEGIES IN A NOVEL COMMUNICATION TASK

IRIT MEIR

*Department of Communication Disorders and Department of Hebrew Language,
University of Haifa, Mt. Carmel, Haifa 31905, Israel*

ADI LIFSHITZ

*Department of Learning Disabilities, University of Haifa, Mt. Carmel
Haifa 31905, Israel*

DENIZ ILKBASARAN, CAROL PADDEN

*Department of Communication and Center for Research in Language,
University of California San Diego, 9500 Gilman Dr., La Jolla, CA 92093-0503*

Introduction: The use of word order for signaling participants' roles is an important property of human languages. Yet the particular order employed may vary across languages. Indeed, all six possible orders of the components of a transitive event - the subject/actor (S), the patient/object (O) and the action (V) – appear in the worlds' languages. This fact suggests that there is no order which is cognitively or linguistically impossible. However, the distribution of these orders in languages is uneven. Of the six possible orders, two are by far more common than the others: SOV and SVO. This uneven distribution suggests the possibility that cognitive and/or communicative factors are involved in determining word order.

In evolutionary terms, several researchers have argued that SOV is the basic word order, and that other orders developed later, as a response to various processing efficiency and communicative demands. The study presented here investigates the question of what gives rise to different word orders. We suggest that different types of clauses present different communicative challenges, and that one means of coping with these different challenges is the use of differential word order. Two types of transitive clauses are considered here: canonical clauses and reversible clauses. In canonical clauses, the subject/actor (S) is animate and the object/patient inanimate. In such cases, the clause may be understood on the basis of semantics alone. In reversible clauses, both arguments are animate, and special machinery is needed to mark one argument as S and the other is O. We show that in a communication system invented on the spot, the two types of sentences give rise to two different word order patterns.

Method: Thirty three hearing subjects, native speakers of Hebrew (a SVO language) that were not previously exposed to a sign language were asked to describe by gesture alone a set of 18 short video clips, each depicting a single transitive or di-transitive event. The clips varied with respect to whether the object participant is human (e.g., *the girl pulled the man*) or inanimate (*the girl pulled the cart*). Their gesture productions were videotaped and then analyzed according to the order of the gestures representing the instigator of the action (S), the affected argument (O) and the action (V).

Results: A statistically significant distinction was found between the two types of clauses in terms of word order. In clauses with an inanimate object, SOV order is dominant (65% of responses) and SVO appeared only in 31% of the clauses. In clauses with human object the reverse pattern was found: the dominant order is SVO (64%), and SOV occurring in 31% of the responses. Furthermore, subjects invented additional devices when describing sentences with human objects, such as gesturing that there were two human participants: *'Two: man, woman, man look'*.

Discussion: The fact that SOV was the dominant order in canonical clauses supports the hypothesis that SOV is cognitively more basic. In these clauses the message can be understood based on the semantics alone. The consistent SOV order seems to serve more of a cognitive than communicative function. But this basic order is used less in reversible clauses, most likely because they are potentially ambiguous, and demand specific mechanisms to disambiguate the message. Word order, as well as other special devices (not included in the word order count), is used to cope with these challenges. Preliminary results from nine Turkish speakers who performed the same task support the suggestion that reversible clauses call for special machinery. Though SOV (the dominant order in Turkish) was dominant in both types of clauses, in clauses with inanimate object it was almost the only order (accounting for 88% of the productions), while in clauses with a human object it accounted for 64%, and another order, OSV, occurred in 28% of their responses.

Our study shows that different types of clauses pose different communicative challenges, and different word orders and other devices may emerge to cope with them. It may be, then, that a language begins with more than one word order, and conventionalizes to a particular order later in its development.

ON THE TRACK OF THE ORIGIN OF LANGUAGE: A COMPARATIVE STUDY QUANTIFYING HAND PREFERENCE IN OBJECT MANIPULATION AND GESTURAL COMMUNICATION IN NON HUMAN PRIMATES

HELENE MEUNIER & JACQUES VAUCLAIR
Department of Psychology, Research Center in Psychology of Cognition, Language & Emotion, University of Provence, Aix-en-Provence, 13621, France

Behavioural and brain asymmetries at a population level have been historically considered as unique to human evolution and exclusively associated to the emergence of speech. But the recent highlighting of similar asymmetries in numerous species of vertebrates questions the validity of this hypothesis (see Rogers & Andrews, 2002; Vallortigara & Rogers, 2005; Hopkins, 2007 for reviews) and opens new debates concerning the neurobiological origin of language. This very controversial topic opposes two basic ways of thinking: (1) the gestural origin of language (see Meguerditchian & Vauclair, 2008 for a review) and (2) the vocal origin of language (e.g. Zuberbühler, 2005). However, an increasing number of studies converge to the hypothesis according to which language is the product of the evolution of gestural communication rather than vocal communication (Corballis, 2002; Arbib, 2005). Because non human primates are phylogenetically closed to humans and show behavioural asymmetries at the population level, they appear to be an ideal model to investigate the precursors of brain hemispheric specialization in humans. Studies on great apes (Hopkins, 1995; see also Pika, Liebal, Call, & Tomasello, 2005 for a review) and other non human primates (Vauclair, Meguerditchian, & Hopkins, 2005) showed a significant hand preference at a group level for a coordinated bimanual task and, with a stronger effect, for a communicative gesture. This latter result indicates that gestural communication in those species could involve a specific cerebral system, different from the one involved in non communicative bimanual coordinated tasks. In this context, the study of hand specialization in gestural communication appears necessary to investigate the precursors of speech. Because the existence of such a specific system involving a higher degree of lateralization is still uncertain, more comparative studies between tasks and species, including similar experimental procedures are needed. The present study aims to bring such elements using an adaptation of the Bishop's Quantifying Hand Preference task (QHP, Hill & Bishop, 1998), which allows the precise and comparable measurement of the degree of handedness in different tasks. We used the QHP test with two different species of non human primates, olive baboons (*Papio Anubis*) and rhesus macaques (*Macaca mulatta*), to conduct three experiments: (1) a simple reaching task, (2) a bimanual coordinated task and (3) a gestural communication task, in which subjects have to point at an object in order to obtain it. Results from simple reaching task revealed the crucial influence of item position on handedness in both species, even from position separated of only 30° from the sagittal median plan of the subject. For this task, although numerous baboons and macaques were individually lateralized, we did not observe population-level handedness for the central position. On the other hand, preliminary results of the gestural communication task showed a population-level right handedness for the same central position. Concerning the other positions, individuals tended to use more their right hand to point than to reach an object. Data from the bimanual coordinated task are currently under analysis. This set of results will be discussed within the theoretical framework about hemispheric specialization for objects manipulations, communicative gestures and the origin of language.

Acknowledgements

This research was supported by French National Research Agency (ANR) grant ANR-08-BLAN-0011_01. Authors sincerely thank Anaïs Maugard & Margarita Briseño for helping in data collection.

References

Arbib, M. (2005). From monkey-like action recognition to human language: an evolutionary framework for neurolinguistics. *Behavioral and Brain Sciences, 28*, 105-167.

Corballis, M. C. (2002). *From Hand to Mouth. The Origins of Language.* Princeton University Press.

Hill, E. L., & Bishop, D. V. (1998). A reaching test reveals weak hand preference in specific language impairment and developmental co-ordination disorder. *Laterality, 3*, 295-310.

Hopkins, W. D. (1995). Hand preferences for a coordinated bimanual task in 110 chimpanzees: Cross-sectional analysis. *Journal of Comparative Psychology, 109*, 291-297.

Hopkins, W. D. (Ed.). (2007). *Evolution of hemispheric specialization in primates.* Academic Press.

Meguerditchian, A., & Vauclair, J. (2008). Vocal and gestural communication in nonhuman primates and the question of the origin of language. In L. S. Roska-Hardy & E. M. Neumann-Held (Eds.), *Learning from animals? Examining the nature of human uniqueness* (pp. 61–85). Psychology Press.

Pika, S., Liebal, K., Call, J., & Tomasello, M. (2005). The gestural communication of apes. *Gesture, 5,* 41-56.

Rogers, L. J., & Andrew, J. R. (2002). *Comparative vertebrate lateralization.* CUP.

Vallortigara, G., & Rogers, L. J. (2005). Survival with an asymmetrical brain: Advantages and disadvantages of cerebral lateralization. *Behavioral and Brain Sciences, 28*, 575-589.

Vauclair, J., Meguerditchian, A., & Hopkins, W. D. (2005). Hand preferences for unimanual and coordinated bimanual tasks in baboons (*Papio anubis*). *Cognitive Brain Research, 25,* 210-216.

Zuberbühler, K. (2005). The phylogenetic roots of language. Evidence from primate communication and cognition. *Psychological Science, 14,* 126-130.

A FUNCTIONAL TRANSCRANIAL DOPPLER ULTRASOUND STUDY OF BRAIN LATERALISATION IN STONE TOOL MAKING AND LANGUAGE

GEORG MEYER & SOPHIE WUERGER

School of Psychology, University of Liverpool, Liverpool, L69 7ZA, UK

NATALIE T. UOMINI

*School of Archaeology, Classics & Egyptology, University of Liverpool, L69 3GS, UK
and British Academy Project "Lucy to Language", UK*

Among the many theories of language evolution, the Gestural Origins Hypothesis (Hewes, 1973; Corballis, 2002) makes clear and testable predictions about common neural substrates for language and complex body actions. In particular, there is growing evidence that the left hemisphere is responsible for action planning (Frey, 2008). While the archaeological data are silent about language origins, they clearly show an increase in tool complexity at 1.7 million years ago with the beginning of the Acheulean industries. A co-evolution of complex language and hand actions would predict shared neural areas for language and Acheulean tool-making.

This paper will present the first ever study to directly compare cerebral blood flow lateralisation for a language task and a complex stone-tool-making task, using functional transcranial Doppler ultrasound. This non-invasive method measures relative blood flow changes between the cerebral hemispheres at all moments during task execution, allowing the study of precise temporal events (Deppe *et al.*, 2004). In addition, it is well suited to studying stone tool-making because it does not restrict participants' natural postures or movements.

According to previous studies using PET (Stout & Chaminade, 2007, 2009; Stout *et al.*, 2008), complex stone tool making (Acheulean) caused increased lateralisation to right Broca's homolog, but no activation of action planning circuits was found. However, according to Kroliczak & Frey (2009) there should be left hemisphere activation for tool-use planning. Our experiment was designed to isolate the complex planning component of Acheulean handaxe production, so that the motor execution of the task was controlled for. In the tool-making task we contrasted cerebral blood flow during handaxe production with a control condition in which hammerstones were struck together. In the language task we used the standard paradigm of silent word-generation.

We will present the results from ten subjects and discuss their implications for the Gestural Origins Hypothesis of language evolution. Our previous work on

459

body action and speech recognition (Meyer *et al.*, 2009) shows that both tasks invoke shared circuitry in the brain and is consistent with the view that complex action planning and speech may have co-evolved. Our functional transcranial Doppler ultrasound data isolate the motor planning components required for the creation of the earliest complex tools and therefore allow a direct test of whether complex action planning and speech both are left-lateralised. We show highly correlated (p<0.05) relative lateralisation changes in the target compared with the rest condition.

References

Corballis, M.C. (2002). *From hand to mouth: the gestural origins of language.* Princeton, NJ: Princeton University Press.

Deppe, M., Ringelstein, E.B., & Knecht, S. (2004). The investigation of functional brain lateralization by transcranial Doppler sonography. *NeuroImage*, 21, 1124-1146.

Frey, S.H. (2008). Tool use, communicative gesture and cerebral asymmetries in the modern human brain. *Philosophical Transactions of the Royal Society of London B*, 363, 1951-1957.

Hewes, G.W. (1973). Primate communication and the gestural origins of language. *Current Anthropology*, 14, 5-25.

Kroliczak, G., & Frey, S.H. (2009). A common network in the left cerebral hemisphere represents planning of tool use pantomimes and familiar intransitive gestures at the hand-independent level. *Cerebral Cortex*, 19, 2396-2410.

Meyer, G., Wuerger, S., & Uomini, N. (2009). Direct evidence for shared networks involved in the categorisation of speech and body actions. Paper presented at *Ways to Protolanguage*, September 2009, Toruń, Poland.

Stout, D., & Chaminade, T. (2007). The evolutionary neuroscience of tool making. *Neuropsychologia*, 45, 1091-1100.

Stout, D., Toth, N., Schick, K.D., & Chaminade, T. (2008). Neural correlates of Early Stone Age tool-making: technology, language and cognition in human evolution. *Philosophical Transactions of the Royal Society of London B*, 363, 1939-1949.

Stout, D., & Chaminade, T. (2009). Making tools and making sense: complex, intentional behaviour in human evolution. *Cambridge Archaeological Journal*, 19, 85-96.

THE EVOLUTION OF INFORMATION STRUCTURE

VANESSA MICELLI

Sony Computer Science Laboratory, 6 Rue Amyot,
Paris, 75005, France
vanessa@csl.sony.fr

One of the most prominent questions when working on dialogue is why speakers of all languages have different ways to express the same idea depending on different communicative circumstances. Research on *information structure* addresses exactly this question. This paper presents an ongoing study of the evolution of information structure through computational experiments in which autonomous communicative agents engage in a series of language games.

Information structure can formally be represented in various ways, such as through prosody, grammatical markers, order of syntactic constituents in the form of complex grammatical constructions, depending on which *language strategy* is accepted by the language community (Steels, to appear). A language strategy consists of a set of procedures helping members of a community to become and remain successful in communication. More specifically, these are procedures for acquiring or inventing new concepts, words or grammatical constructions demanded by the context. Additionally, a language strategy provides a mechanism for aligning the language systems of interacting agents.

This research presents a computational implementation of the language strategies that are needed for investigating the evolution of information structure through a case study of German, which expresses information structure through word order influenced by case, focus and determination constraints (Lenerz, 1977). Speakers of German have to establish knowledge about those constraints to produce and understand utterances correctly. Typologically speaking, German is an interesting case because its combination of syntax and focus structure does not nicely fit the cross-linguistic tendency of either having a rigid syntactic structure combined with a flexible focus structure or a rigid focus structure combined with a flexible syntax.

In the first phase of the experiments, we operationalized the German language system for expressing information structure by reverse engineering the necessary production and comprehension procedures in Fluid Construction Grammar (FCG) (De Beule & Steels, 2005). This formalization effort includes the ontology, lexicon and grammatical constructions that are necessary for handling German declarative sentences including intransitive, transitive and ditransitive verbs. In the next step, we designed a language game for studying the function of this language system in symbolic communication. We propose a Question-Answering (QA) game, in which two agents are randomly picked from the population. One agent asks a *wh*-question about a jointly observed scene. Joint attention between the agents is required and assumed. The other agent has to respond to the question accordingly.

The next set of experiments investigates the learning mechanisms which are necessary for agents to acquire information structure in communication. The population includes 'tutor agents' and 'learning agents', not possessing the same grammatical proficiency. Interlocutor-1 (I-1) chooses one of the observed events and picks a topic, which corresponds to one of the event participants. I-1 produces a question by using the FCG rules and expects an appropriate answer from Interlocutor-2. All agents can always play both interlocutor roles. The experiments use local measures for steering linguistic behavior: communicative success and cognitive effort. The results show that even though explicit focus-marking is not necessary for reaching communicative success, learners acquire the correct rules for emphasizing the participant asked for in order to reduce cognitive effort. Cognitive effort is measured by calculating the number of processes that are needed for retrieving the topic of the question (e.g. case comparison). As argued by e.g. Selkirk (1986), questions allow control over which syntactic constituent in the answer has to be emphasized. In the current scenario this means that it has to be focus-marked by using a grammatical rule.

The final set of experiments investigates the emergence of information structure, by allowing the agents to innovate if they experience too much processing effort or if they want to avoid ambiguity. It is shown that given the right language strategy agents can develop language systems for conventionalizing the position of the topic in an utterance, on top of existing determination and case systems.

The current set-up only involves one language strategy, but future research includes how multiple strategies, such as fronting, intonation and word order, compete with each other in a single population, and how this might lead to different kinds of language systems for expressing information structure.

References

De Beule, J., & Steels, L. (2005). Hierarchy in Fluid Construction Grammar. In U. Furbach (Ed.), *Proceedings of ki-2005* (Vol. 3698, p. 1-15). Berlin: Springer-Verlag.

Lenerz, J. (1977). *Zur Abfolge nominaler Satzglieder im Deutschen.* Tübingen: Narr.

Selkirk, E. O. (1986). *Phonology and Syntax: The Relation between Sound and Structure.* MIT Press.

Steels, L. (to appear). Can Evolutionary Linguistics Become a Science. *Journal of Evolutionary Linguistics, 1.*

A MISSING LINK IN THE CULTURAL EVOLUTION OF LANGUAGE: CONNECTING SEQUENTIAL LEARNING AND LANGUAGE EMPIRICALLY

JENNIFER B. MISYAK & MORTEN H. CHRISTIANSEN

Psychology Department, Cornell University, Uris Hall
Ithaca, NY, 14853, USA

J. BRUCE TOMBLIN

Department of Communication Sciences and Disorders, University of Iowa
Iowa City, IA, 52242, USA

Within the growing perspective of cultural transmission as a pivotal component to language evolution (e.g., Kirby, Christiansen & Chater, 2009; Tomasello, 2008), it has been proposed that language has been substantially shaped by the human brain—constrained in its evolution by socio-pragmatic, perceptuo-motor, cognitive and other nonlinguistically-specific factors defining the nature of human learning and processing biases (Christiansen & Chater, 2008). As one such factor, pre-existing learning mechanisms for the processing of sequential structure may have played a substantial role in the evolution of human language. This hypothesis is supported from artificial grammar/language learning studies and computational simulations examining the relationship between sequential learning biases and the structure of evolved languages (see, e.g., Kirby et al., 2009), but few studies exist that directly test within individuals for an empirical link between such learning and language.

A clear prediction of the above theoretical view would be that observed variation in language processing performance should be associated with variation in sequential learning abilities. We investigated this hypothesis, using a within-subjects design in which 50 monolingual native English speakers were assessed on both sequence learning and on-line language processing. In our sequence-learning task, an artificial language (Gómez, 2002) was instantiated within an adapted serial reaction time (SRT) task, thereby providing continuous reaction-time (RT) measures of learning as it unfolded. The group learning trajectory revealed a gradually emerging sensitivity to nonadjacent dependencies in the artificial language. Learning was further confirmed by an offline standard grammaticality judgment post-test in which scores were significantly above chance. Crucial to our study aim, we calculated a learning score for each

464

participant by subtracting their RT performance in the initial training block of string-trials from that in the final training block, with resulting scores reflecting substantial individual differences in pattern-specific sequential learning.

To determine whether good sequential learners are also good at tracking the long-distance dependencies characteristic of natural language, the same participants completed a word-by-word self-paced reading task involving sentences with center-embedded subject- (SR) and object-relative (OR) clauses. Individual differences in processing these sentences are well documented, with ORs eliciting longer reading times, especially at the main verb (King & Just, 1991). We found a positive relationship between continuous individual differences in sequential learning and better processing performance for the relative clauses at the main verb. Additionally, when classifying learners as "good"/"poor" based on scores from the sequence learning task, good learners displayed reading patterns characteristic of more proficient language processors, with less difficulty at the OR main verb and less of a divergence in processing patterns for the two clause-types.

These findings thus provide an empirical association between individuals' on-line sequential learning of nonadjacencies and their on-line processing of complex, long-distance dependencies in natural language. These results further dovetail with recent molecular genetics findings implicating the involvement of *FOXP2* in sequential learning on a SRT task. Common allelic variation in *FOXP2* was associated with differences in sequential learning patterns, which in turn were linked to variation in grammatical abilities (Tomblin et al., 2007). This suggests that *FOXP2* may have served as a pre-adaptation for human sequential learning mechanisms, while providing further evidence for a key role of such abilities in the cultural transmission of language. By empirically connecting sequential learning and language, these studies thus offer a heretofore missing link in the cultural evolution of language.

References

Christiansen, M.H. & Chater, N. (2008). Language as shaped by the brain. *Behavioral and Brain Sciences, 31*, 489-509.

Gómez, R. (2002). Variability and detection of invariant structure. *Psychological Science, 13*, 431-436.

King, J., & Just, M.A. (1991). Individual differences in syntactic processing: The role of working memory. *Journal of Memory and Language, 30*, 580-602.

Kirby, S., Christiansen, M.H. & Chater, N. (2009). Syntax as an adaptation to the learner. In D. Bickerton & E. Szathmáry (Eds.), *Biological foundations and origin of syntax. Strüngmann Forum Reports, Vol. 3* (pp. 325-343). Cambridge, MA: MIT Press.

Tomasello, M. (2008). *Origins of human communication*. Cambridge, MA: MIT Press.

Tomblin, J.B., Christiansen, M.H., Bjork, J.B., Iyengar, S.K. & Murray, J.C. (2007). *Association of FOXP2 genetic markers with procedural learning and language*. Poster presented at the 57th Annual Meeting of the American Society of Human Genetics, San Diego, CA.

BALANCING ARBITRARINESS AND SYSTEMATICITY IN LANGUAGE EVOLUTION

PADRAIC MONAGHAN

Department of Psychology, Lancaster University, Lancaster, LA1 4YF, UK

MORTEN H. CHRISTIANSEN

Department of Psychology, Cornell University, Ithaca, NY 14853, USA

STANKA FITNEVA

Department of Psychology, Queen's University, Kingston, K7L 3N6, Canada

In 1866, the Société de Linguistique of Paris met to issue a moratorium on papers concerning language evolution. Less well known is that the same meeting also prohibited papers discussing universal languages. These universal language studies were speculative attempts to rediscover the pre-Babel tongue, and several proposed that the arbitrariness of the mapping between the spoken form and the meaning of words was an indication of imperfection in human communication. If one could describe a perfectly systematic language in terms of form-meaning mappings then one could rediscover the universal language (see Eco, 1995, for a review). This ideology led to artificially constructed languages such as Wilkins' "Analytical Language" (1668), in which similar concepts had orthographically similar referents. However, systematicity results in confusions because similar sounding words are being used in similar contexts, with survival: "edible plants could be confused with poisonous ones, and animals that attack be confused with benign ones" (Corballis, 2002, p.186).

We contend, instead, that the cultural evolution of language has resulted in a crucial balance between arbitrariness and systematicity (see also Tamariz, 2008). Though arbitrariness may be advantageous for individuating referents, it impairs recognition of similarities among words. Indeed, form-*syntactic category* mappings demonstrate a high degree of systematicity in natural language (Monaghan et al., 2007). In a series of computational simulations and experiments we tested the extent to which arbitrariness benefits individuation and systematicity benefits categorization in a language learning task.

In two simulations, we trained a feedforward connectionist model to learn mappings between form and meaning representations for 12 words referring to 6 actions and 6 objects. The representations were either correlated (systematic) or uncorrelated (arbitrary). The second simulation had additional contextual information as a part of the model's input by indicating whether the word was an action or an object, more realistically representing the multiple contextual cues available in the language learner's environment. In two experiments, we trained undergraduate participants on the same 12 words and pictures of actions and objects, either with or without contextual information in the form of distinct words preceding either the object or the action word. We tested performance at four points in training in terms of learning to: (1) individuate the meanings of the words and (2) categorise the words into objects or actions.

Without context, for both the simulation and the experiment, there was a systematic advantage for individuation and categorisation. Learners exploited the generalizations in the systematic relationships. With context, for the categorization task there was a systematic advantage for both the simulation and the experiment. However, for individuation, there was a significant *interaction* between training time and systematic/arbitrary condition – an initial systematic advantage became an arbitrary advantage later in training.

Our studies illustrate the importance of *both* arbitrariness and systematicity, and indicate how each contributes to learning different aspects of language, interacting in complex ways with contextual information in the environment. We suggest that because word-learning involves not only discovering its form-meaning mapping but also how to use it in syntactic contexts, language has evolved to balance arbitrariness and systematicity.

References

Corballis, M.C. (2002). *From hand to mouth: The origins of language.* Princeton, NJ: Princeton University Press.

Eco, U. (1995). *The search for the perfect language.* London: Blackwell.

Monaghan, P., Christiansen, M. H., & Chater, N. (2007). The Phonological Distributional Coherence Hypothesis: Cross-linguisitic evidence in language acquisition. *Cognitive Psychology, 55,* 259-305.

Tamariz, M. (2008). Exploring systematicity between phonological and context-cooccurrence representations of the mental lexicon. *The Mental Lexicon, 3,* 259-278.

Wilkins, J. (1668). *An essay towards a real character and a philosophical language.* London: Sa. Gellibrand.

SPEAKER-INDEPENDENT PERCEPTION OF HUMAN SPEECH BY ZEBRA FINCHES

VERENA R. OHMS

Behavioural Biology, Institute of Biology Leiden (IBL), Leiden University
Sylvius Laboratory, Sylviusweg 72, Leiden, 2333BE, The Netherlands,
Email: v.r.ohms@biology.leidenuniv.nl

CAROLINE A. A. VAN HEIJNINGEN, ARIKE GILL

Behavioural Biology, Institute of Biology Leiden (IBL), Leiden University
Sylvius Laboratory, Sylviusweg 72, Leiden, 2333BE, The Netherlands

GABRIEL J. L. BECKERS

Behavioural Neurobiology, Max-Planck-Institute for Ornithology,
Eberhard-Gwinner Strasse, Seewiesen, 82319, Germany

CAREL TEN CATE

Behavioural Biology, Institute of Biology Leiden (IBL), Leiden University
Sylvius Laboratory, Sylviusweg 72, Leiden, 2333BE, The Netherlands and Leiden
Institute for Brain and Cognition (LIBC), PO Box 9600, 2300 RA Leiden, The
Netherlands

Human speech is a hierarchically organized coding system in which meaningless sounds, called phonemes, are combined into larger meaningful units: words. An important role in the coding process is played by formants - vocal tract resonances that can be altered rapidly by changing the geometry of the vocal tract using different articulators such as tongue and lips. Changing the formant pattern of an articulation results in a different vowel produced. Although human voices differ in acoustic parameters such as fundamental frequency and spectral distribution the relative formant frequencies of an utterance enable intelligibility of speech regardless of individual variation across speakers. Although it has been argued originally that speech is special and uniquely human (Lieberman 1975), several studies have shown that some aspects of speech perception also apply to other species. Chinchillas for example show the same phonetic boundary effect as humans do when discriminating between /d/ and /t/

consonant-vowel syllables (Kuhl & Miller, 1975). Nevertheless, there is still an ongoing debate about which characteristics of speech production and perception are unique to humans and which are shared with other species (Hauser *et al.*, 2002; Trout, 2003; Pinker & Jackendoff, 2005). In this study (Ohms *et al.*, 2010) we addressed the question whether birds (zebra finches) are able to distinguish between spoken words with a minimal difference in acoustic features, and, if so, which cues they might use to do so. We trained 8 zebra finches on a go/no-go operant conditioning task to discriminate between the Dutch words *wit* (wIt) and *wet* (wɛt) which differ in their vowels only and which were recorded from several native speakers. The results show that zebra finches when trained to discriminate a single minimal pair can transfer this discrimination to unfamiliar voices of the same and even to the other sex. When confronted with new voices the discrimination performance was immediately clearly above chance level. However, our data also revealed a learning process since performance increased constantly. This suggests that both intrinsic and extrinsic speaker normalization are involved in discriminating between the two words. These results indicate that formant normalization and the capability of normalizing formant patterns across different speakers and sexes is a perceptual trait that not only occurs in humans but also in songbirds.

References

Hauser, M. D., Chomsky, N. & Fitch, W. T. (2002). The faculty of language: what is it, who has it and how did it evolve? *Science, 298*, 1569-1579.

Kuhl, P. K. & Miller, J. D. (1975). Speech perception by the chinchilla: voiced-voiceless distinction in alveolar plosive consonants. *Science, 190*, 69-72.

Lieberman, P. (1975). *On the origins of language. An introduction to the evolution of human speech.* New York, NY: Macmillan.

Ohms, V. R., Gill, A., van Heijningen, C. A. A., Beckers, G. J. L. & ten Cate, C. (2010). Zebra finches exhibit speaker-independent phonetic perception of human speech. *Proceedings of the Royal Society Series B,* doi: 10.1098/rspb.2009.1788

Pinker, S. & Jackendoff, R. (2005). The faculty of language: what's special about it? *Cognition, 95,* 201-236.

Trout, J. D. (2003). Biological specializations for speech: what can the animals tell us? *Current Directions in Psychological Science, 12,* 155-159.

AN AVIAN MODEL FOR LANGUAGE EVOLUTION

IRENE PEPPERBERG

Department of Psychology, Harvard University, Wm James Hall, Cambridge, MA 02138, USA

Most language evolution research focuses on primates, positing a hominid transitional link with the beginnings of learned vocal communication. Interest in primate models of language evolution increased after apes, humans' closest genetic relatives—although incapable of acquiring full, complex human language—learned elements of human communication systems. But how vocal language, and vocal learning, developed from what was likely a precursor gestural communication system is still a matter of speculation. Other species, however, phylogenetically distant from primates, notably Grey parrots (*Psittacus erithacus*) and cetaceans, acquire human-like communication skills comparable to those of great apes (Hillix & Rumbaugh, 2003), and, unlike present-day nonhuman primates, engage in vocal learning. Many studies have also demonstrated striking parallels between both the ontogeny and the neurological underpinnings of vocal communication in birds and humans (e.g., Jarvis et al. 2005). Recently, an avian species, once thought to be incapable of vocal learning, has shown elements of such acquisition (Kroodsma, 2005; Saranathan et al. 2007), suggesting that it might be a living avian model for the transitional link between our nonvocal-learning and vocal-learning hominid ancestors. This paper explores the data supporting use of such an avian model for language evolution.

References

Hillix, W.A. & Rumbaugh, D.M. (2003). Animal bodies, human minds: Ape, dolphin, and parrot language skills. New York: Springer.

Kroodsma, D.E. (2005). The singing life of birds. New York: Houghton Mifflin.

Jarvis, J.D., Güntürkün, O., Bruce, L., Csillag, A., Karten, H., Kuenzel, W. et al. (2005). Avian brains and a new understanding of vertebrate evolution. Nature Reviews Neuroscience, 6, 151-159.

Saranathan, V., Hamilton, D., Powell, G.V.N., Kroodsma, D.E. & Prum, R.O. (2007). Genetic evidence supports song-learning in te three-wattled bellbird Procnias trucarunculata (Cotingidae). Molecular Ecology, 16, 3689-3702.

GROOMING GESTURES OF CHIMPANZEES IN THE WILD: FIRST INSIGHTS INTO MEANING AND FUNCTION

SIMONE PIKA

School of Psychological Sciences, University of Manchester, Coupland 1 Building, Oxford Road, Manchester, M13 9PL, United Kingdom

CHRIS KNIGHT

Comenius University, Fakulta sociálnych vied, Odbojárov 10/A, 820 05 Bratislava, Slovakia

Chimpanzees vocalizations are referential, but only functionally (Mitani & Brandt, 1994; Slocombe & Zuberbühler, 2006). Contrary to human linguistic signs – which are used to influence what others know, think, believe, or desire (Grice, 1957) – they don't intentionally provide conspecifics with information(Seyfarth & Cheney, 2003). On the other hand, research on gestural abilities of human-reared or language-trained great apes showed that signalers use gestures in intentional and referential ways (Gardner et al., 1989; Savage-Rumbaugh et al., 1986). Furthermore, Pika and Mitani (2006) recently described a distinct gesture, the 'directed scratch', used by adult chimpanzee males in the wild to indicate just where on their bodies they wished to be groomed.

The present study aims to provide further insight on the meaning and function of 'directed scratches' and other related grooming gestures by distinguishing between the perspectives of signalers and receivers (Smith, 1965). Analyses are based on behavioral observations of ~100 grooming sessions between twenty adult male chimpanzees, collected during June and July 2008 at the Ngogo community, Kibale National Park, Uganda.

The results reveal that chimpanzee signalers use their grooming gestures in flexible, manifold ways to request an intended meaning, which is understood by chimpanzee recipients. "Answers" to these request however vary in relation to rank, age and strength of social bonds between signalers and recipients. These results will be discussed with a special focus on recent theories of gesture acquisition, signal evolution, and cooperation.

472

References:

Gardner, R.A., Gardner, B., & Van Cantford, T.E. (1989). *Teaching sign language to chimpanzees*. Albany: State University of New York Press.

Grice, H.P. (1957). Meaning. *The Philosophical Review, 66*, 377-388.

Mitani, J.C., & Brandt, K.L. (1994). Social factors influence the acoustic variability in the long-distance calls of male chimpanzees. *Ethology, 96*, 233-252.

Pika, S., & Mitani, J.C. (2006). Referential gesturing in wild chimpanzees (Pan troglodytes). *Current Biology, 16*, 191-192.

Savage-Rumbaugh, E.S., McDonald, K., Sevcic, R.A., Hopkins, W.D., & Rupert, E. (1986). Spontaneous symbol acquisition and communicative use by pygmy chimpanzees (*Pan paniscus*). *Journal of Experimental Psychology: General, 115*, 211-235.

Seyfarth, R.M., & Cheney, D.L. (2003). Signalers and receivers in animal communication. *Annual Review of Psychology, 54*, 145-173.

Slocombe, K.E., & Zuberbühler, K. (2006). Food-associated calls in chimpanzees: Responses to food types or reative food value? *Animal Behaviour*.

Smith, W.J. (1965). Message, meaning, and context in ethology. *American Naturalist, 908*, 405-409.

THE RELEVANCE OF THE DEVELOPMENTAL STRESS HYPOTHESIS TO THE EVOLUTION OF LANGUAGE

ANNE PRITCHARD

Linguistics and English Language, The University of Edinburgh, 3 Charles street, Edinburgh, EH89AD, Scotland

The crucial component uniting contemporary theories that posit a role for sexual selection in language evolution is the postulation that language, or some aspect of it, served as an honest indicator of an individual's genetic or phenotypic quality. Okanoya (2002) and Mithen (2005) have proposed the existence of an ancestral 'protolanguage' constituting elaborately structured vocalisations and body movements that was driven in part by sexual selection.

An interesting question that follows from this hypothesis concerns the nature of the relationship between such a protolanguage and underlying genetic quality. The answer may lie in the developmental stress hypothesis (DSH) which has been formulated as a result of findings from experimental studies involving observations or manipulations of early stress conditions in avian species. Environmental stress affects the development of forebrain structures necessary for the production of song features shown to be important to females when selecting mates, and also affects other aspects of male phenotypic quality (Nowicki *et al.* 1998). There is also some evidence that certain genotypes fare better than others in conferring resistance to developmental stressors (see Buchanan *et al.* 2004). Given the striking similarities between birdsong and human language, it is important that the DSH is acknowledged, investigated, and applied to understanding language evolution. As Ritchie, Kirby & Hawkey (2008) suggest, the DSH may provide an explanation for the evolutionary maintenance of vocal learning in both songbirds and humans. Perhaps at some stage in language evolution, the ability to learn and produce structurally complex vocalisations served as an indicator of an individual's ability to cope with the costs involved in the growth of neural substrates underlying fine motor control in the face of environmental stress.

A concomitant issue concerns whether developmental stress influences language development in contemporary humans. One hypothesis that can be investigated empirically is that individuals use linguistic adeptness to evaluate the developmental stability of potential mates or in maximizing indirect benefits by choosing mates who possess high quality genotypes or those that confer resistance to environmental stressors. The first main prediction to be tested is that developmental stress affects brain development and linguistic competence. The second is that developmental stress affects the ability to produce linguistic parameters important in mate choice. A recent developmental study following a natural disaster provides support for the former (Laplante *et al*. 2008). The longitudinal extension of studies such as this is encouraged to determine whether linguistic deficits persist in later life, and it may be fruitful to involve subjects in studies of human mating preferences that focus on linguistic parameters in order to investigate the latter prediction. Moreover, the close examination of individual differences in groups exposed to similar levels of stress may reveal whether certain genotypes cope better with environmental stress than others. This may help to ascertain whether linguistic competence functions as a marker of developmental stability or if it is intrinsically related to underlying genetic quality. These large-scale studies can be complemented by experiments investigating possible relationships between linguistic ability and proposed morphological measures of developmental stability.

References

Buchanan, K. L. *et al*. (2004) Developmental stress selectively affects the song control nucleus HVC in the zebra finch. *Proc. R. Soc. Lond. B*. 271, 2381-238.

Laplante, D. P. *et al*. (2008) Project Ice Storm: prenatal maternal stress affects cognitive and linguistic functioning in 5 1/2 year-old children. *J Am Acad Child Adolesc Psychiatry*, 1062-1072.

Mithen, S. (2005) The Singing Neanderthals: The Origins of Music, Language, Mind and Body. Kent: Phoenix Paperback.

Nowicki, S. *et al*. (1998). Song learning, early nutrition and sexual selection in songbirds. *Amer. Zool. 38*, 179-190.

Okanoya, K. (2002) 'Sexual display as a Syntactical Vehicle: The Evolution of Syntax in Birdsong and Human Language through Sexual Selection'. In: Wray, A (ed.) (2002) *The Transition to Language*. Oxford: Oxford University Press.pp.47-63.

Ritchie, G. R. S., Kirby, S. and Hawkey, D. J.C. (2008) Song learning as an indicator mechanism: Modelling the developmental stress hypothesis. *Journal of Theoretical Biology* 251, 570-583.

CO-EVOLUTION OF LANGUAGE AND SOCIAL NETWORK STRUCTURE THROUGH CULTURAL TRANSMISSION

JUSTIN QUILLINAN AND SIMON KIRBY

Language Evolution and Computation Research Unit, University of Edinburgh, UK
justin@ling.ed.ac.uk, simon@ling.ed.ac.uk

KENNY SMITH

Department of Psychology, Northumbria University, UK
kenny.smith@northumbria.ac.uk

Human populations are organised in social networks, which are structurally distinct from other types of network (Newman & Park, 2003). Social structure provides a constraint on the transmission of language, such that language is influenced by the structure of the population over which it is transmitted (Chambers, 2003), a relationship which is often ignored in models of language evolution. Furthermore, social networks and languages might co-evolve: human social networks may have the form they do in part due to the transmission of language over those networks. We present a model of the co-evolution of social network structure and language by means of learning and interaction among agents in a dynamic population. This study models network growth and language evolution using a plausible mechanism, namely homophily, the tendency of individuals to establish and maintain social bonds based on similarity (McPherson et al., 2001).

Boguñá et al. (2004) have shown that the presence of communities in a social space is sufficient to trigger social structure when the agents show a preference for similarity. However, they treat communities as predefined static entities. Centola et al. (2007) demonstrate the influence of homophily in the co-evolution of both network structure and cultural diversity.

We define a model of cultural transmission over a dynamic network using homophily and cultural learning. The model consists of a population of agents. Each agent is randomly assigned a position in the social space, represented by a vector of continuous real numbers. This is analogous to a number of linguistic traits that an individual possesses. The social distance between two agents is defined as the sum of the difference between each trait. The population is represented by an unweighted, undirected network of vertices. It is initially unconnected and evolves by three methods – attachment to similar vertices, detachment from dissimilar vertices, and learning from adjacent vertices. These correspond to mechanisms of homophily and cultural learning events such as language learning.

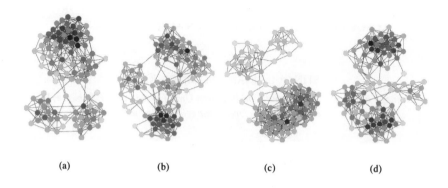

Figure 1. Typical evolved networks. The language is represented by the vertex's shade.

Evolved networks (Fig. 1) possess the characteristic measures of social networks: assortativity, transitivity and community structure (Newman & Park, 2003). Social distance shows a positive correlation with network distance, displaying emergent social clusters of similar languages. This shows that individuals communicative success decreases with social distance. The rate of learning affects the size, density and linguistic diversity of the communities that form. The model demonstrates that the existence of a learnable language and a preference for establishing and maintaining connections with similar individuals can lead naturally to social structure. The co-evolutionary dynamic of homophily and learning influences both the topology of the resulting network and the type and distribution of the emergent languages.

References

Boguñá, M., Pastor-Satorras, R., Díaz-Guilera, A., & Arenas, A. (2004). Models of social networks based on social distance attachment. *Phys. Rev. E*, *70*(5), 056122.

Centola, D., González-Avella, J. C., Eguíluz, V. M., & San Miguel, M. (2007). Homophily, cultural drift, and the co-evolution of cultural groups. *Journal of Conflict Resolution*, *51*(6), 905–929.

Chambers, J. K. (2003). *Sociolinguistic theory: linguistic variation and its social significance*. Oxford: Blackwell.

McPherson, M., Smith-Lovin, L., & Cook, J. M. (2001). Birds of a feather: Homophily in social networks. *Annual Review of Sociology*, *27*, 415-444.

Newman, M. E. J., & Park, J. (2003). Why social networks are different from other types of networks. *Phys. Rev. E*, *68*(3), 036122.

THE ORIGINS OF SOCIOLINGUISTIC MARKING AND ITS ROLE IN LANGUAGE DIVERGENCE: AN EXPERIMENTAL STUDY

GARETH ROBERTS

Language Evolution and Computation Research Unit, University of Edinburgh
gareth@ling.ed.ac.uk

Social markers appear to originate, at least partly, in the need to protect cooperative networks from outsiders (Nettle & Dunbar, 1997). Simulations suggest that the use of language as a source of such markers introduces a selective pressure—social selection—to language evolution, which contributes significantly to the development of linguistic diversity (Nettle & Dunbar, 1997; Nettle, 1999). Other simulations, however, have challenged these findings (Livingstone, 2002), suggesting that a high level of diversity can emerge through variation in the frequency of interaction, without the need for social selection. Similar disagreements exist in sociolinguistics (e.g. Labov, 2001; Trudgill, 2008; Baxter et al., 2009).

To investigate this question experimentally, a study was carried out in which participants played an economic game that involved negotiating anonymously, on an instant-messenger-style program, to exchange resources. The experiment involved 80 participants and had a 2 × 2 design, with five games of four players each in every condition (see Table 1). Each game consisted of a series of rounds in which every player was partnered with one of the other three players; no two players were paired up for more than two rounds in a row. Each player began the game with 28 points of resources and, during each round, negotiated to exchange resources by typing messages to their partner in an artificial 'alien language' of twenty randomly generated words (e.g. *seduki, kago*). All four players were trained on the same language. After negotiation, players could give resources away to their partners; any resource given was worth double to the receiver. In the cooperative conditions, all four players in a game belonged to one team, and the object was to accumulate resources for the team. In the competitive conditions, players were divided into two teams of two, and the object was to acquire more resources for one's own team than the opposing team. It was thus advantageous to give gifts to team-mates, but not to opponents. Except in the first round, however, players were not told whether they were negotiating with a team-mate or opponent until the end of the round. Since the alien language contained only twenty basic lexical items (e.g. *I, want, meat, thanks* etc.), there was little scope for developing explicit strategies, and players had to rely on linguistic cues to identify team-mates.

The frequency with which players were paired was also manipulated (see Table 1); players were not made aware of the frequency or order of pairings.

Table 1.   Summary of conditions

	High-frequency	Low-frequency
Competitive	2 teams.	2 teams.
	Paired half the time with team-mate,	Paired third of time
	quarter of time with each opponent.	with every other player.
Cooperative	1 team.	1 team.
	Paired half the time with one player,	Paired third of time
	quarter the time with each of the others.	with every other player.

Players in the high-frequency competitive condition did significantly better than chance at recognising when they were paired with team-mates ($S = 75$ incorrect guesses out of 285; $p < .001$). In addition, the alien language diverged significantly into team 'dialects' in this condition only ($p < .001$), based on how often different players used different variant forms in the alien language (new variants having arisen chiefly through error). This suggests that a combination of frequent interaction and a pressure to mark identity can lead to divergence over a short time period. Neither factor, however, was sufficient on its own.

Acknowledgements

The author would like to thank the ESRC for financial support, April McMahon and Andrew Smith for academic support, and Justin Quillinan for technical assistance.

References

Baxter, G., Blythe, R., Croft, W., & McKane, A. J. (2009). Modeling language change: an evaluation of Trudgill's theory of the emergence of New Zealand English. *Language Variation and Change*, *21*(2), 257–96.

Labov, W. (2001). *Principles of linguistic change. volume 2: Social factors.* Malden, MA/Oxford: Blackwell.

Livingstone, D. (2002). The evolution of dialect diversity. In A. Cangelosi & D. Parisi (Eds.), *Simulating the evolution of language* (pp. 99–117). London: Springer Verlag.

Nettle, D. (1999). *Linguistic diversity.* Oxford: Oxford University Press.

Nettle, D., & Dunbar, R. (1997). Social markers and the evolution of cooperative exchange. *Current Anthropology*, *38*(1), 93–9.

Trudgill, P. (2008). Colonial dialect contact in the history of European languages: On the irrelevance of identity to new-dialect formation. *Language in Society*, *37*(2), 241–54.

CONSIDERING LANGUAGE EVOLUTION FROM BIRDSONG DEVELOPMENT

KAZUTOSHI SASAHARA[1], MIKI TAKAHASI[1], KENTA SUZUKI[1], OLGA FÉHER[2], OFER TCHERNICHOVSKI[2], AND KAZUO OKANOYA[1]

[1]*Laboratory for Biolinguistics, RIKEN Brain Science Institute, Saitama 351-0198, Japan*
[2]*Department of Biology, City College, City University of New York, NY 10031, USA*
kazutoshi.sasahara@gmail.com

Language is considered as the great divide between the cognitive and social ability of humans and those of other animals. How did language emerge and evolve into such a complex system? A promising approach to this is to compare and contrast language with animal signal systems, which involve key substrates for language. We focus on birdsong development from the aspect that language is a learned vocal behavior. Although birdsong is different from language in many ways, they share biological foundations for vocal learning. So far birdsong study has yielded significant implications for language evolution; for example, a cultural evolution of birdsong (Fehér, Wang, Saar, Mitra, & Tchernichovski, 2009).

Here we study the development of phonology and syntax in Bengalese finch song. Adults sing complex song that consists of a number of chunks, which in turn consist of a few patterned notes (Okanoya, 2004). Juveniles learn individually distinct song by imitating adult males. To track the entire song development, 24-hour recording was conducted for 16 juveniles every 4 to 5 days after hatching. When recording, each juvenile was kept in a soundproof box with a microphone, and all singing activities were recorded. From all the recordings, we computed six acoustic features of notes, such as note duration, mean pitch, and mean Wiener entropy. Figure 1 shows (a) a phonological development in the acoustic feature space, and (b) a syntactic development. At day 50, every note was acoustically similar to each other. At day 60, notes with longer duration emerged abruptly, and then ones with harmonics diverged from the residuals, which gradually differentiated with development. Finally, eight types of notes emerged from a single acoustic stem-cluster. The recorded songs were converted to texts by annotating letters to identical note types, and then a grammatical inference method (Kakishita, Sasahara, Nishino, Takahasi, & Okanoya, 2009) was applied. Before day 70, it was not able to extract a syntax due to the transitional instability of notes. Song notes stabilized with development, becoming some patterned chunks, and the transitions also gradually stabilized. After day 100, the song syntax was crystallized.

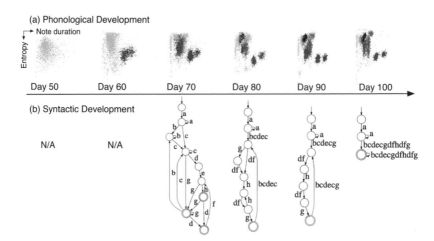

Figure 1. (a) Each point shows a note and each cluster shows a note type in the acoustic feature space. (b) Letters denote note types, and the song syntax is represented as a finite automaton.

The results demonstrated a co-developmental process of phonology and syntax in birdsong; exposed in a social environment, juveniles developed note types and sequential and sub-sequential structures as well. While the striking parallels between birdsong and language in development, there is a significant difference. It is known that human infants develop words with the aid of contextual semantic cues. Thus words develop based not only on phonological rules but also on semantic constraints. Song chunks look similar to words in form, but they develop without any atomic meanings. Birdsong therefore lacks 'double articulation,' by which small meaningless sound units combine into large meaningful units. These suggest that a precursor of syntax, like song syntax, could emerge from a learned vocal behavior, evolving relatively independent of semantics; however, to become syntax with double articulation, semantic constraints are indispensable in development. What adaptation mechanism is required for the syntax-semantics entanglement to become exist? Our findings raise further questions to be solved.

References

Fehér, O., Wang, H., Saar, S., Mitra, P. P., & Tchernichovski, O. (2009). De novo establishment of wild-type song culture in the zebra finch. *Nature, 459,* 564–8.

Kakishita, Y., Sasahara, K., Nishino, T., Takahasi, M., & Okanoya, K. (2009). Ethological data mining: an automata-based approach to extract behavioral units and rules. *Data Mining and Knowledge Discovery, 18,* 446–471.

Okanoya, K. (2004). Song syntax in bengalese finches: proximate and ultimate analyses. *Advances in the Study of Behavior, 34,* 297–346.

SEMANTIC BOOTSTRAPPING OF GRAMMAR IN EMBODIED ROBOTS

YO SATO

Adaptive Systems Group, University of Hertfordshire
College Lane, Hatfield, AL10 9AB, U.K.
y.sato@herts.ac.uk

JOE SAUNDERS

Adaptive Systems Group, University of Hertfordshire
College Lane, Hatfield, AL10 9AB, U.K.
j.l.saunders@herts.ac.uk

1. Situated grammar learning from partially word-detected string

The concept of semantic bootstrapping of grammar, though tracing back at least to Pinker (1984), has not been explored fully in applied computational linguistics as a grammar learning algorithm. Experimental methods with embodied robots may however open up the possibility to exploit their fine sensori-motor capabilities to examine the feasibility of such an algorithm. We report one such attempt.

In view of the difficulty of word segmentation from audio stream, we start from the stage where only *some* of the constituent words have been detected in an utterance, marking a departure from most grammar induction methods, semantically oriented or not, which presuppose the full set of terminal symbols.

Such partially word-detected strings are obtained from the human-robot interaction experiments, in which the human participant is asked to explain simple objects verbally to the robot. The recorded speech is first converted with a speech recogniser to phoneme strings. We then create a small vocabulary of the frequently ocurring words and convert only those phoneme sequences that have a match in this vocabulary into words, creating what we call a phoneme-word list (PWL). For example, if our vocabulary list is $\langle$sɜːkl ('*circle*'), rɛd ('*red*'), siː ('*see*'), juː ('*you*')$\rangle$, then the phoneme string $\langle$juːsiːðætrɛdstaːʃeɪp$\rangle$ ('You see that red star shape') is converted into $\langle$[*you*], [*see*], ðæt, [*red*], staːʃeɪp$\rangle$, where the elements in square brackets represent 'detected' words.

Another crucial piece of data is a possible meaning relevant to a given situation, i.e. meaning hypothesis. Thus, the proposal amounts to the learning of syntax from the pairs of a meaning hypothesis and a PWL, e.g.:

$$see'(r, o) \land red'(o) \land star'(o) \quad : \quad \langle [you], [see], \text{ðæt}, [red], \text{staːʃeɪp} \rangle$$

where r and o represent the individual constants for the robot learner and the object talked about. Notice that the semantics is not fully spelt out: the predicate corresponding to *shape* is missing. We build consistent *grammar* hypotheses such an underspecified hypothesis in a manner to be described below.

2. Grammar learning as lexical type induction

Taking inspiration from Fulop's (2004) type-logical work on samantic grammar induction in a lexicalist but broadly Montagovian framework (Montague, 1973), we characterise grammar learning as the induction of syntactic behaviour of words from their *semantic types* that could compose a meaning hypothesis. However we employ a typed-feature structure (TFS) grammar in a manner of HPSG (Pollard & Sag, 1994), taking advantage of its underspecifiability inherent in unification, so that the intermediate stages of learning can be represented succinctly. Our PWL can be characterised as a list of underspecified TFSs, as below:

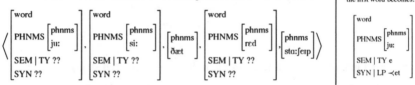

This PWL can be taken as a compact representation of *any* string that satisfies the given constraints. The grammar induction, then, boils down to populating the as yet empty features (with '??') for the SEM(ANTICS) and SYN(TAX) features.

As semantic bootstrapping, the immediate target of learning is the semantic TY(PE) feature. If, for example, the TY value of the first word, *you*, is hypothesised to the type e (individual) (see the right hand side in the above figure), then the hypothesising on the TY feature of the other words as well as the SYN feature can start: given the assumption that the utterance is a truth-value bearing type, t, one can predict that one of the following words is part of the et type, and that our present word, *you*, may be hypothesised to linearly precede the et type.

3. Preliminary results and future tasks

The preliminary evaluations of the initial experiment indicate that the size of the hypothesis space may be problematic. For a relatively quick convergence of hypotheses, it would need to be reduced. Possible methods include cognitively plausible biases and, perhaps more contentiously, corrective feedback from humans.

References

Fulop, S. A. (2004). Semantic bootstrapping of type-logical grammar. *Journal of Logic, Language and Information*, *14*, 49-86.

Montague, R. (1973). The proper treatment of quantification in ordinary English. In Hintikka (Ed.), *Approaches to natural language*.

Pinker, S. (1984). *Language learnability and language development*. Harvard UP.

Pollard, C., & Sag, I. (1994). *Head-Driven Phrase Structure Grammar*. CSLI.

WHY DO WILD CHIMPANZEES PRODUCE FOOD-ASSOCIATED CALLS: A CASE OF VOCAL GROOMING?

ANNE SCHEL

Department of Psychology, University of York, York, YO105DD, England

KLAUS ZUBERBÜHLER

School of Psychology, University of St Andrews, St Andrews, KY16 9JP, Scotland

KATIE E SLOCOMBE

Department of Psychology, University of York, York, YO105DD, England

Chimpanzees, like many other species, produce specific vocalisations when they encounter food (Goodall, 1986). In chimpanzees these are called rough grunts. Listening individuals often approach the caller and share the food source, imposing a cost on the caller. In order to for such a seemingly altruistic behaviour to be an evolutionary stable strategy, the caller must accrue some benefits to offset these costs. Chimpanzees, unlike many other smaller bodied species, do not benefit from a reduction in predation risk or vigilance costs when attracting others to a food source. Instead, we propose that in chimpanzees this vocal behaviour fulfils a similar social function to grooming: the benefits are in terms of increasing affiliative relationships with socially significant individuals.

Manual grooming serves to establish and maintain strong affiliative social relationships between individuals, but it is time consuming and can only be conducted during rest periods. It has been proposed that as group size increases it becomes increasingly difficult to satisfactorily service all relationships with grooming (Dunbar 1996). It is suggested that in evolution when humans reached such a critically large group size, our own species supplemented physical grooming with 'vocal grooming', to maintain social cohesion (Dunbar 1996). The production of such affiliative social vocal signals, that functioned to increase social bonds between individuals, may have been one of the earliest driving forces behind the evolution of language (Dunbar 1996). In order to test the hypothesis that chimpanzee food-associated calls function as 'vocal grooming' signals we conducted a systematic study of the factors that determine whether chimpanzees produce food-associated calls or not. We predicted that chimpanzees should be sensitive to the composition of their audience and preferentially produce calls in the presence of socially significant others, such as grooming partners.

We collected data on 9 free ranging adult male chimpanzees of the Budongo Forest, Uganda for 9 months. We collected ecological data about the food source, including an estimate of patch quality (cumulative feeding time of all chimps present). We also recorded the arrival and departure of all individuals to the focal individual's feeding tree and the timing of all food-associated calls along with the identity of the callers. In addition we recorded social data on the focal individual, including all grooming interactions.

We found that chimpanzees only produce calls in just over half of all feeding bouts, indicating that calls are not simply an involuntary emotional reaction to food. Instead, in line with our predictions, we found that chimpanzees were more likely to produce food-associated calls when individuals they choose to groom were present, rather than absent. The presence of such a grooming partner was the factor that accounted for most variance in whether rough grunts were produced or not. The quality of the food patch also influenced the likelihood of call production, with higher quality patches eliciting more grunts, however this explained less variance than the social factor. The presence of oestrus females and the number of individuals in the party did not influence calling behaviour.

These findings show that chimpanzees are selectively producing food-associated calls in the presence of individuals they groom. Basic factors such as the number of individuals in the vicinity did not influence calling behaviour, indicating that simple mechanisms such as social facilitation can not explain our results. Feeding takes up a considerable proportion of a wild chimpanzee's day (Goodall, 1986) and during this time they cannot engage in grooming, the primary mechanism we know of for strengthening social bonds between individuals. Our data suggests that rough grunts may represent a kind of 'vocal grooming' that allows individuals to maintain positive relationships with important others in the feeding context. This may represent an empirical example of vocal signals functioning to maintain relationships, that Dunbar (1996) argues could be one of the driving forces behind the evolution of human language.

References

Dunbar, R. (1996) Grooming, gossip and the evolution of language. London: Faber and Faber

Goodall, J. 1986. The chimpanzees of Gombe: patterns of behavior. Cambridge: Harvard University Press.

THE IMPORTANCE OF EXPLORING NON-LINGUISTIC FUNCTIONS OF HUMAN BRAIN LANGUAGE AREAS FOR EXPLAINING LANGUAGE EVOLUTION

P. THOMAS SCHOENEMANN

Department of Anthropology, Indiana University, 701 E. Kirkwood Avenue
Bloomington, Indiana 47405, USA

The evolution of language is a special case of the evolution of behavior. Evolutionary biologists have long recognized that behavioral change drives biological change, rather than the other way around (Mayr 1978). This has recently been highlighted specifically with respect to language evolution (e.g., Christiansen and Chater 2008).

In the context of human evolution, this means that cultural evolution will, to a large extent, drive biological evolution. The transition from quadrupedalism to bipedalism, for example, was driven by behavioral changes (Hunt 1994). We didn't evolve bipedal anatomy first, only to stumble upon its usefulness later. The spread of agriculture lead to selection for sickle-cell alleles (Livingstone 1958). The domestication of dairying animals lead to selection for continued lactase production (Durham 1991).

Applying this logic to language evolution, for every generation in which greater facility at communication was adaptive, individuals would have used pre-existing cognitive abilities to communicate as best they could. Genetic changes would have therefore been strongly biased towards those that modified pre-existing abilities, rather than entirely new neural circuits devoted exclusively to language. This also means that we should *expect* homologs of human language circuits in non-human primate brains (Schoenemann 1999).

Homologs of Broca's and Wernicke's areas have in fact been located in primates (Striedter 2005), and finding out what they use them for is critical to understanding the coevolutionary process that lead to language in humans. One fruitful approach is to identify non-language abilities that are also processed in human language areas. Broca's area in humans has been implicated in non-linguistic sequential processing (Christiansen and Ellefson 2002; Petersson et al.

2004), hand/tool manipulation (e.g., Binkofski et al. 2000; Higuchi et al. 2009), and non-verbal auditory processing (e.g., Muller et al. 2001). Because these are non-linguistic, their functional localization can also be explored in non-human primates. If they also activate Broca's area homologs, this would support the view that language adapted to pre-existing cognitive architectures, rather than requiring the creation of completely new, language-specific brain areas.

References

Binkofski F, Amunts K, Stephan KM, Posse S, Schormann T, Freund H-J, Zilles K, and Seitz RJ. 2000. Broca's region subserves imagery of motion: A combined cytoarchitectonic and fMRI study. *Human Brain Mapping* 11(4):273-285.

Christiansen MH, and Chater N. 2008. Language as shaped by the brain. *Behavioral and Brain Sciences* 31:489-509.

Christiansen MH, and Ellefson MR. 2002. Linguistic Adaptation Without Linguistic Constraints: The Role of Sequential Learning in Language Evolution. In: Wray A, editor. *The Transition to Language*. Oxford: Oxford University Press. p 335-358.

Durham WH. 1991. *Coevolution : genes, culture, and human diversity*. Stanford, Calif.: Stanford University Press.

Higuchi S, Chaminade T, Imamizu H, and Kawato M. 2009. Shared neural correlates for language and tool use in Broca's area. *Neuroreport*.

Hunt KD. 1994. The evolution of human bipedality: ecology and functional morphology. *Journal of Human Evolution* 26(3):183-202.

Livingstone FB. 1958. Anthropological implications of sickle cell gene distribution in West Africa. *American Anthropologist* 60:533-562.

Mayr E. 1978. Evolution. *Scientific American* 239:47-55.

Muller RA, Kleinhans N, and Courchesne E. 2001. Broca's area and the discrimination of frequency transitions: a functional MRI study. *Brain and Language* 76(1):70-76.

Petersson KM, Forkstam C, and Ingvarc M. 2004. Artificial syntactic violations activate Broca's region. *Cognitive Science* 28:383–407.

Schoenemann PT. 1999. Syntax as an emergent characteristic of the evolution of semantic complexity. *Minds and Machines* 9:309-346.

Striedter GF. 2005. *Principles of Brain Evolution*. Sunderland, MA: Sinauer Associates.

LANGUAGE EVOLUTION: THE VIEW FROM ADULT SECOND LANGUAGE LEARNERS

MARIEKE SCHOUWSTRA

*UiL OTS, Utrecht University, Janskerkhof 13,
3512 BL, Utrecht, The Netherlands
Marieke.Schouwstra@phil.uu.nl*

In the process of acquiring a second language outside the classroom, adult learners go through a stage that has been characterized as being (1) determined by a small number of organizational principles, (2) largely independent of the source or target language of the learner and (3) simple but successful for communication (Klein & Perdue, 1997). This stage is called the Basic Variety (henceforth BV). In the BV, a speaker constructs relatively short sentences and a striking characteristic of these sentences is that there is no inflection. Some examples of organizational principles of this variety are FocusLast ('put the information that is in focus, new information, in the end of the sentence') and AgentFirst ('the NP referent with the highest control comes first'). The BV is thus not seen as an imperfect version of the target language, but as an independent linguistic system.

In the talk I focus on the expression of *temporal displacement* (reference to past and future) in the BV. Languages generally have sophisticated ways to express temporal structure (tense and aspect), quite often through inflection on the verb. In the BV, verbs are used but usually not inflected. Still, people refer to past and future, and the way they do it seems a very effective and robust strategy, as in the following example from Starren (2001):

(1) 'Gisteren ik bergen gaan naar' (p. 149)
Yesterday I mountains go to
Yesterday, I went to the mountains

In this example a temporal adverb is fronted to indicate that the event described took place in the past. This strategy is observed in learners of different languages (even when it is highly marked or ungrammatical), as well as speakers of homesign (Benazzo, 2009).

The fact that strategies like the above are structurally found in the BV, and that they are largely independent from source and target language, plus the observation that there are similarities between the BV and other 'restricted linguistic systems' like homesign and pidgin, makes it interesting for the debate about the emergence and evolution of language. Evolutionary claims have been made on the basis of observations from the BV. E.g., Jackendoff (2002) hypothesises that the principles that govern the BV are fossil principles from *protolanguage*.

Data from the BV would be very welcome as a source of evidence in the language evolution debate, especially because a lot of data is available from learners of different source and target languages (Perdue, 1993). But to avoid mere speculations, we need to formulate precisely *what* the structures in the BV tell us about *which* aspects of the evolution of language, and *why*. Unfortunately, not many people have concentrated on these questions, although a general framework is sketched in Botha (2005). In the presentation, I concentrate on the hypothesis that data from the BV reveals information about early human language forms, and justify this hypothesis on the basis of two strategies that seem implicitly present in recent literature on restricted linguistic systems.

One strategy is to claim that the sentence structures found in BV utterances are direct reflections of cognitive biases, and that these biases were already present in our evolutionary ancestors. If we were to choose this strategy, we would have to explain why the cognitive structures that were relevant in our evolutionary ancestors are still relevant in speakers of the BV.

Another strategy becomes relevant once we take the claim seriously that utterances in the BV are shaped by communicative needs. The structure of the utterances in the BV might not be simply a reflection of the cognitive structures of their speakers, but be shaped indirectly by their usage of the structures in communication, and whether they reach communicative success.

I argue that, in order to arrive at a good justification for evolutionary claims on the basis of BV utterances, both strategies need to be taken into account, and I sketch a way to combine the two, by taking the second strategy as a basis, and showing that the role of cognitive biases can be incorporated in this approach.

References

Benazzo, S. (2009). The emergence of temporality. In R. Botha & H. de Swart (Eds.), *Language evolution: the view from restricted linguistic systems*. LOT.

Botha, R. (2005). On the Windows Approach to language evolution. *Language and Communication, 25.*

Jackendoff, R. (2002). *Foundations of language: Brain, meaning, grammar, evolution.* Oxford University Press.

Klein, W., & Perdue, C. (1997). The Basic Variety (or: couldn't natural languages be much simpler?). *Second Language Research, 13,* 301–347.

Perdue, C. (1993). *Adult language acquisition: Cross-linguistic perspectives.* Cambridge University Press.

Starren, M. (2001). *The second time. the acquisition of temporality in Dutch and French as a second language.* LOT.

THE EVOLUTION OF COMMUNICATION AND RELEVANCE

THOMAS C. SCOTT-PHILLIPS

School of Philosophy, Psychology and Language Sciences, University of Edinburgh
3 Charles Street, Edinburgh, EH8 9AD

Ambiguity is commonplace and indeed inevitable in everyday language; an utterance produced in one context can have a quite different meaning in another context. Despite this, listeners almost always converge upon the speaker's intended meaning. How is the achieved? Grice's cooperative principle (Grice, 1975) provides a still widely accepted answer. It comprises four maxims of conversation: quality (tell the truth), quantity (do not say too much or too little), relation (be relevant) and manner (be clear and concise). It is, according to Grice, because listeners assume that speakers follow these maxims that they are able to interpret utterances in a contextually sensible way.

Since Grice's seminal contribution, numerous refinements, additions and extensions to his work have been proposed (e.g. Horn, 1984; Levinson, 1983). The Gricean foundation, however, remains widely accepted. This acceptance means that the neo-Gricean framework has also been influential in several related disciplines, including psycholinguistics (Clark, 1996), the philosophy of language (Lycan, 2008), and indeed language evolution (Cheney & Seyfarth, 2005; Gärdenfors, 2006; Haiman, 1996; Hurford, 2007). One alternative is *Relevance Theory* (Sperber & Wilson, 1995), which supplants the four maxims with a single notion of relevance, which is claimed to be more basic than the Gricean maxims. As such, Relevance Theory constitutes "an ambitious bid for a paradigm-change in pragmatics" (Levinson, 1989, p.469).

One way in which we can choose between competing theories in linguistics is to use evolutionary considerations (Kinsella, 2009). This presentation (which is based upon Scott-Phillips, in press) will describe a very basic and simple evolutionary game-theoretic model of the evolution of communication. It assumes only that listeners maximise their payoffs, and that speakers do the same, given that listeners will do this. Two entirely general statements about the evolution of communication are generated. These are functional descriptions

490

that will apply to all evolved communication systems. It is then asked what they imply for linguistic communication in particular.

The answer is that they predict, quite precisely, the two principles of relevance that lie at the heart of Relevance Theory: that listeners will seek to maximise relevance, and that the very production of an utterance brings with it a guarantee of relevance. This suggests that something like Relevance Theory, and the cognitive mechanisms that it posits, must be correct; and hence that Relevance Theory, rather than the Gricean paradigm, should be the default framework for pragmatics.

References

Cheney, D. L., & Seyfarth, R. M. (2005). Constraints and preadaptations in the earliest stages of language evolution. *The Linguistic Review, 22*, 135-159.

Clark, H. H. (1996). *Using Language.* Cambridge: Cambridge University Press.

Gärdenfors, P. (2006). *How Home Became Sapiens: On the Evolution of Thinking.* Oxford: Oxford University Press.

Grice, H. P. (1975). Logic and conversation. In P. Cole & J. Morgan (Eds.), *Syntax and Semantics III: Speech Acts* (pp. 41-58). New York: Academic Press.

Haiman, J. (1996). *Talk is Cheap: Sarcasm, Alienation, and the Evolution of Language.* Oxford: Oxford University Press.

Horn, L. R. (1984). Towards a new taxonomy for pragmatic inference: Q-based and R-based implicature. In D. Schiffrin (Ed.), *Meaning, Form, and its Use in Context: Linguistic Applications* (pp. 11-42). Washington, DC: Georgetown University Press.

Hurford, J. R. (2007). *Origins of Meaning.* Oxford: Oxford University Press.

Kinsella, A. R. (2009). *Language Evolution and Syntactic Theory.* Cambridge: Cambridge University Press.

Levinson, S. C. (1983). *Pragmatics.* Cambridge: Cambridge University Press.

Levinson, S. C. (1989). A review of Relevance. *Journal of Linguistics, 25*, 455-472.

Lycan, W. (2008). *The Philosophy of Language: A Contemporary Introduction.* New York, NY: Routledge.

Scott-Phillips, T. C. (in press). The evolution of relevance. *Cognitive Science*

Sperber, D., & Wilson, D. (1995). *Relevance: Communication and Cognition* (2nd. ed.). Oxford: Blackwell.

PRAGMATICS NOT SEMANTICS AS THE BASIS FOR CLAUSE STRUCTURE

THOM SCOTT-PHILLIPS, JAMES R. HURFORD, GARETH ROBERTS, SEAN ROBERTS

LEC, School of Philosophy, Psychology and Language Sciences, The University of Edinburgh, Dugald Stewart Building, Edinburgh, EH8 9AD, UK
jim@ling.ed.ac.uk

1. Hypothesis

Our hypothesis is that the bipartite organization of clauses stems from a central communicative function of language, namely (1) to identify what you are talking about, and (2) to give new information about what you are talking about. We label this the **pragmatic** hypothesis. It contrasts with a **semantic** hypothesis, which is that humans instinctively encode the difference between actions and objects into major syntactic categories, which become the basis of the bipartite organization. According to this semantic hypothesis, an innate template for sentence organization determines the two main parts of a sentence, and items denoting objects (i.e. nouns) occupy the Subject part, and items denoting actions (i.e. verbs) occupy the Predicate part.

Our pragmatic hypothesis is that speakers identify what is **constant** in a changing world, and assume that a hearer will be aware of this constancy. The speaker then uses a term identifying the constant factor to indicate what he is talking about. The speaker also identifies what is **changeable** in the world he is communicating about, and assumes that the hearer does not know of the change that the speaker has observed. The speaker uses a term identifying the changing element in the world. Thus the bipartite organization of sentences reflects, we claim, a distinction between constant and changing, and not between objects and actions.

2. Experiment

Our experiment aims to tease these distinctions apart, by presenting people with an untypical world in which what is constant is the motion of an object, and what is changeable is the sortal type of an object. Translating our broad hypothesis into narrower experimental terms, we hypothesize that people attempting to communicate about this abnormal world will segregate their utterances into two parts, one identifying what is constant, i.e. the action/motion type (spin, bounce, wave), and the other part identifying the changing sortal type of the constantly moving object (cow, cat, pig). For interpretation of our results, we rely on the fact that, almost universally, the Topics of sentences are placed in initial position, with the Comment portion following. We think it comes naturally to identify what you are talking about before you go on to say anything about it. Further, given that our experimental subjects are English speakers, we also rely on the fact that verbal morphology (e.g. the suffix -*ing*) identifies changing states. Put simply, we predict that our experimental subjects, confronted with the task of communicating successfully about this abnormal world, will come up with expressions like *bounce cowing* (as opposed to *cow bouncing*, more to be expected in a normal world), or *spin pigging* (as opposed to *pig spinning*).

The experimental stimuli and protocols are complete, and we have run a pilot study to fine-tune details of the experimental procedures.

3. Results

The pilot study suggests that in the experimental condition, subjects do change their communicative behaviour from the 'normal'. Results at present are too few to interpret sensibly. By April 2010, we will have run many more trials with many more subjects, and can present our full results.

Acknowledgements

Three of the authors are supported by the UK Economic and Social Research Council [Scott-Phillips,ES/G030936/1; G.Roberts, PTA-031-2006-00425; S.Roberts, ES/G010277/1].

PRODUCTION OF THE VOWELS /a i u/ BASED ON AN ARTICULATORY MODEL OF FEEDING

ANTOINE SERRURIER AND ANNA BARNEY

Institute of Sound and Vibration Research
University of Southampton, UK

1. Introduction

Both ontogenetically and phylogenetically feeding tasks precede speaking tasks, two of the major functions of the human vocal tract (VT). Researchers have therefore suggested that speech cyclicity, in particular tongue movements, derives from feeding cyclicity (MacNeilage, 1998; Hiiemae and Palmer 2003). Our study explores this hypothesis using articulatory modelling to determine if the tongue movements in speech are a subset of those in feeding. In a previous study (Serrurier *et al.*, 2008) we used ElectroMagnetic Articulography, however this is an invasive technique that further gives no VT boundaries. To overcome these limitations we here use Digital VideoFluoroscopy (DVF). We wish to explore if we can extract from the raw data and from an articulatory model based on the data, articulations which are geometrically and acoustically close to the quantal vowels /a i u/. Their typical F1-F2 values and their typical geometric shape constitute respectively our *acoustic* and *articulatory targets*.

2. Method and results

Two swallows of pourable custard were recorded with DVF on a single female subject. Each image was manually segmented to extract the tongue contour. Following Serrurier *et al.* (2008), a mid-sagittal articulatory model of the tongue was built. Three tongue articulations optimally approaching our two targets simultaneously were extracted from the raw data and also reconstructed from the model. The articulatory model has the advantage over the raw data of encompassing all task-derivable articulations theoretically producible by the tongue. The six articulations were placed in a fixed, midsagittal VT outline; the area functions in 3D were derived; the planar acoustic wave propagation was

493

simulated and F1-F2 (see Figure 1) values were extracted. For the articulations extracted from the data, none of the F1-F2 points are inside the target ellipses; those computed from the model fall on the border or just inside.

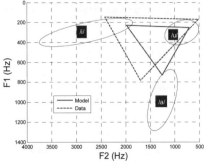

Figure 1. Position in the F1-F2 plane of the six articulations extracted in the study (data = dashed line; model = solid line). The ellipses for the vowels are adapted from Peterson and Barney (1952).

3. Conclusion

The recorded feeding movements allow articulation of tongue shapes close to typical midsagittal patterns found for /a i u/ with predicted F1-F2 just touching the corresponding ellipses. It seems thus just reasonable to claim that speech movements are a subset of feeding movements based on this data set. This study complements our previous study with a new recording technique and further subject and supports its general conclusion, that speech movements could have evolved from feeding movements, with the caveat that we have neglected any control considerations. A similar approach using ape data had been considered but could not been carried out due to the lack of data.

Acknowledgements

The authors wish to acknowledge the help of A. Matos, R. Santos, Dr M. Collins and Dr P. Badin. This work is part of the HandtoMouth project (EC NEST initiative).

References

Hiiemae, K. M. & Palmer, J. B. (2003). Tongue Movements in feeding and speech. *Crit. Rev. Oral Biol. M.*, *14(6)*, 413-429.

MacNeilage, P. F. (1998). The frame/content theory of evolution of speech production. *Behav. Brain Sci.*, *21*, 499-546.

Peterson, G. E. & Barney, H. L. (1952). Control methods used in a study of the vowels. *J. Acoust. Soc. Am.*, *24*, 175-184.

Serrurier, A., Barney, A., Badin, P., Boë, L.-J. & Savariaux, C. (2008). Comparative articulatory modelling of the tongue in speech and feeding. *Proc. 8th ISSP*, 325-328.

VOCAL OR GESTURAL? WHAT EMPIRICAL COMPARATIVE EVIDENCE CAN AND CANNOT CURRENTLY TELL US ABOUT LANGUAGE EVOLUTION

KATIE E SLOCOMBE

Department of Psychology, University of York, York, YO105DD, England

BRIDGET WALLER

Department of Psychology, University of Portsmouth, Portsmouth, PO1 2DY, England

KATJA LIEBAL

Faculty of Psychology, Freie Universität Berlin, Habelschwerdter Allee 45, 14195 Berlin, Germany

Theoretical accounts of language evolution usually argue exclusively for a vocal or gestural origin of language. Such theories draw heavily on comparative evidence of the communicative competencies of extant primates. Similarities between language and primate communication, in terms of gestures being flexible, intentional and generative and vocalisations being referential and following simple combinatorial rules, are often highlighted by the respective theories. Currently many theories also place significant weight on the comparison of primate abilities across the vocal and gestural modalities (e.g. Tomasello 2008; Corballis 2002). Arguments directly comparing the evidence from the two modalities, and using the absence of a certain facet in the opposing modality as evidence in favour of the other, are common. Does the evidence warrant such comparisons?

We present a systematic review of comparative communication studies that have been published in peer review journals between 1960 and 2008. We suggest that cross-modal comparisons are problematic due to inherent biases in the methodological approach, study species and focus of unimodal research. For instance ¾ of gestural studies focus on great apes, compared to just 1 in 10 of the vocal studies. The relative number of studies conducted with wild and captive primates also shows considerable divergence depending on the modality being studied. The proportion of experimental and observational studies in each modalities is also inconsistent. Finally, partly due to methodological constraints, vocal and gestural researchers have tended to focus on communication in different contexts (evolutionarily urgent vs relaxed social). The review demonstrates that 95% of studies focus on only one modality. Given the stark differences in the profile of the research in each modality it seems many direct cross-modal comparisons are problematic. In particular it is important to be aware of the relative lack of vocal research on apes, gestural work conducted in the wild and with monkeys and facial research conducted in the wild and of an experimental nature, making direct comparisons problematic.

We question the validity of the arguments favouring one modality over the other in terms of language evolution that are based on such an incomplete comparative dataset. We argue therefore that absence of evidence for a certain competence in a particular modality cannot be cited as absence of ability: it may simply reflect the inherent biases in methodological approaches of studying each modality. We propose the way forward is firstly to focus research effort into filling in the critical gaps in our knowledge. Secondly, as a complement to unimodal research, integrated multimodal research should be encouraged. This could offer a number of advantages: First, by studying modalities side by side we will use comparable methods and contexts for each modality, which is vital for the generation of data for the purpose of direct comparison. The second reason to focus on multi-modal communication in primates is that as human language is customarily exchanged in a multi-modal format, this may be the appropriate comparison to language. Communication is important not simply to transfer information about the external environment, but also to learn about others' emotion and motivation. By examining how vocal, gestural and facial communication interact we may be able to enhance our understanding of emotional and cognitive integration in communication and consequently better understand the phylogenetic pre-cursors to human language.

In conclusion we urge proponents of unimodal theories of language origin to consider the validity of critically comparing the competencies of primates in different modalities without consideration of the inherent biases and gaps in our present understanding of each modality. We propose that empirical primate research should focus on addressing the gaps in our knowledge and integrated multi modal research should be encouraged.

References

Corballis, M.C. (2002) From Hand to Mouth: the Origins of Language, Princeton University Press
Tomasello, M. (2008). Origins of Human Communication. MIT Press.

REGULARISATION OF UNPREDICTABLE VARIATION THROUGH ITERTATED LEARNING

KENNY SMITH

Department of Psychology, Northumbria University

ELIZABETH WONNACOTT

Department of Experimental Psychology, University of Oxford

Natural languages do not differ arbitrarily, but are constrained so that certain properties recur across the languages of the world. These constraints presumably arise, at least in part, from the nature of the human brain, but the nature of the mapping from brain to language structure is unclear. One theory argues that strong (or even absolute) constraints are built into the language faculty and imposed by individual learners (Chomsky, 1965). An alternative suggestion (e.g. Kirby, Dowman & Griffiths, 2007) is that the same typological distributions could arise given only weak biases in individual learners, as a consequence of cultural transmission within populations. This debate has profound implications for theories of the origins and evolution of language, because the culturally-mediated mapping between learner biases and language structure complicates the biological evolution of the language faculty (see e.g. Smith & Kirby, 2008).

A test-case for the relationship between cognitive biases of individuals and structural properties of language is *linguistic variation*. Variation in language tends to be predictable: in general, no two linguistic forms will occur in precisely the same environments and perform precisely the same functions. Instead, usage of alternate forms is conditioned in accordance with phonological, semantic, pragmatic or sociolinguistic criteria. Experimental studies (e.g. Hudson Kam & Newport, 2005) show that, given a language in which two forms are in free variation, adult learners tend to *probability match* (i.e. produce each variant according to its frequency in the input), whereas children are more likely to regularize, suggesting that unpredictable variation is absent from natural languages simply because it cannot be acquired by children.

We show here that iterated learning can produce linguistically-conditioned stable variability (see also Reali & Griffiths, 2009). 25 adult participants were trained on an artificial language exhibiting unpredictable variation (plurality could be marked using two forms, which alternated freely). These participants showed no evidence of having eliminated this variability, i.e. they appeared to probability match. Ten of these participants were then used as the first generation for ten independent iterated learning chains, with the language produced by the first generation on test being used to train the second generation, and so on. Variability was preserved across five generations in seven of the ten chains. However, the predictability of that variability gradually increased, until nine of ten chains exhibited entirely predictable plural marking: the choice of marker became conditioned on the noun being marked. This demonstrates that adult learners have a relatively weak bias against unpredictable variation (not detectable in a sample of 25 individual learners), which nonetheless becomes apparent through iterated learning. The predictability of variation in natural language might therefore be explained as a consequence of either strong learner biases against unpredictability (in children), or the repeated application of far weaker biases (in adults, or children, or both).

Cultural transmission may act to amplify weak biases, and therefore obscure the relationship between learner biases and linguistic consequences of those biases. This implies that we cannot simply read off the biases of learners from population-level behaviour, nor extrapolate with confidence from individual-based experiments to population-level phenomena. Furthermore, evolutionary pressures acting on the language faculty face a similarly opaque mapping between the structure of the languages (over which selection presumably acts) and the cognitive traits that produce those linguistic structures

References

Chomsky, N. (1965). *Aspects of the theory of syntax*. Cambridge: MIT Press.

Hudson Kam, C., & Newport, E. L. (2005). Regularizing unpredictable variation: The roles of adult and child learners in language formation and change. *Language Learning and Development, 1*, 151–195.

Kirby, S., Dowman, M., & Griffiths, T. L. (2007). Innateness and culture in the evolution of language. *PNAS, 104*, 5241–5245.

Reali, F., & Griffiths, T. L. (2009). The evolution of frequency distributions: Relating regularization to inductive biases through iterated learning. *Cognition, 111*, 317-328.

Smith, K., & Kirby, S. (2008). Cultural evolution: implications for understanding the human language faculty and its evolution. *Philosophical Transactions of the Royal Society B, 363*, 3591- 3603.

IMPLAUSIBLY COOPERATIVE ROBOTS MEET THEIR SELFISH GENE COUNTERPARTS

LUC STEELS

Vrije Universiteit Brussel. AI lab. 10G-725. Pleinlaan 2, B-1050 Brussels Belgium

CHRIS KNIGHT

Comenius University, Fakulta sociálnych vied, Odbojárov 10/A, 820 05 Bratislava, Slovakia

The use and testing of computational models has become a core methodology for formalising, operationalising and testing theories across the natural sciences. Applied to language origins research, such methods can make explicit the assumptions needed to make a particular theory work, leading to conclusions potentially useful to evolutionary linguists, psychologists, archaeologists and anthropologists.

A frequent objection to the computational models and experiments developed by Steels and his team (e.g. Steels 2009) is that they are biologically implausible. Steels' robotic agents spontaneously evolving lexicons and grammars as they repeatedly interact are not Darwinian organisms. Lacking selfish genes, they don't fight or deploy their signalling capacities for purposes of deception. Since their signals need not demonstrate honesty or reliability, the strategic costs of producing an effective signal in the animal world (Maynard Smith & Harper 2003) are absent by experimental design. Many of the problems likely to have been encountered by ancestral humans attempting to establish linguistic communication are consequently not represented.

Steels' work is useful to the extent that it differentiates problems already solved from those which cry out to be addressed using other methods and assumptions. Symbolic communication by its very nature presupposes intentional honesty and communal coherence. Speakers might occasionally cheat once a linguistic code is in place, but a shared code cannot be established unless honesty is the default. It is not difficult to release robots into a community free of competition or conflict. Signallers may then communicate on the basis of infinite trust. In fact, levels of trust beyond anything biologically plausible have been shown to be optimal for linguistic self-organization across a community (Steels 2009). This is an interesting result, confronting Darwinians with a theoretical challenge. Can natural selection design minds to expect 'infinite trust'?

What if Steels' robots could be designated male and female, each male seeking out fertile females and calculating whether to invest in his current partner's offspring or abandon her in favour of mating opportunities elsewhere? Female robots seeking to attract investment for their offspring would develop strategies aimed at maximizing the costs of philanderering. The *Female Cosmetic Coalitions* (FCC) model (Power 2009) sets out from assumptions in Darwinian behavioural ecology. Instead of invoking principles such as kin selection or reciprocal altrusim in the abstract, it accounts for distinctively human ultrasociality under specified conditions, distinguishing female fitness-enhancing strategies from male ones, differentiating between adjacent generations and connecting the logic at all stages to palaoanthropological and archaeological data. It posits costly communal ritual as the mechanism capable of enforcing cooperation across whole communities, and explains why such ritual should be focused on initiation, especially female initiation timed to coincide with first menstruation. It explains how the experience of initiation transposes language-ready minds from 'brute' reality into 'virtual' or 'institutional' reality – a world of patent fictions collectively taken on trust. It makes fine-grained predictions testable in the light of archaeological data – predictions recently vindicated by finds of Middle Stone Age ochre pigments at Blombos Cave and comparable South African sites. Until a rival hypothesis emerges, FCC seems the most promising way of connecting Steels' experiments and findings with the available archaeological and other empirical data.

References

Maynard Smith, J. & D. Harper (2003). *Animal Signals.* Oxford: Oxford University Press.

Power, C. (2009). Sexual selection models for the emergence of symbolic communication: why they should be reversed. In R. Botha & C. Knight (eds), *The Cradle of Language.* Oxford: Oxford Universioty Press, pp. 257-280.

Steels, L. (2009). Is sociality a crucial prerequisite for the emergence of language? In R. Botha & C. Knight (eds), 2009. *The Prehistory of language.* Oxford: Oxford University Press, pp. 36-57.

IDENTIFYING SELECTIVE PRESSURES IN LANGUAGE EVOLUTION: PÓLYA URNS AND THE PRICE EQUATION

MÓNICA TAMARIZ

Language Evolution and Computation, PPLS, The University of Edinburgh, 3 Charles Street, Edinburgh EH8, UK. monica@ling.ed.ac.uk.

Different models of language change and evolution place emphasis on different factors driving evolution. Croft (2000), for instance, highlights the effects of social prestige as a selective pressure behind language change. This paper outlines a new methodology to quantitatively assess whether a proposed factor exerts selective pressure on the evolution of linguistic variants, or whether evolution is neutral with respect to that factor. The method involves running simulations of the spread of linguistic variants (using Pólya urn dynamics, see below) and then applying the Price equation, a tool from evolutionary biology (Price, 1970) recently applied to models of language evolution (Jaeger, 2008), to the simulation outcomes. A Pólya urn contains a number of tokens of different variant types. At each time step a token is *drawn* at random and then it is returned to the urn and n tokens of the same type are *added* to the urn. Urns represent agents and the tokens are exemplars of cultural variants. Drawing a token stands for production of an exemplar and addition of new tokens represents storage of perceived exemplars. The variant population evolves as the relative proportions of the types change.

The price equation (Eqn. 1) quantifies the respective contribution of selection (the covariance term in Eqn. 1) and transmission error (the expectation term in Eqn. 1) to change in a quantifiable feature z of the tokens (Δz in Eqn. 1). In this paper we focus on selection: if we find that the covariance term is different from zero, we can infer that the feature constitutes a selective pressure. The proposed methodology is illustrated by examining whether the factor "variant prestige" exerts selective pressure on variant evolution in the Pólya urn simulations or not. In a simulation with variant prestige in place, when a high-prestige variant is selected, three tokens of that type are added to the urn (modeling production of a high-prestige variant having a high impact on hearers); conversely, when a low-prestige variant is drawn, only one token of that type is added to the urn. In the "no prestige" condition, one token is added regardless of which type is drawn.

$$(1) \quad \Delta \bar{z} = Cov\left(\frac{w_i}{\bar{w}}, z_i\right) + E\left(\frac{w_i}{\bar{w}} \Delta z_i\right)$$

The Price equation is applied at every timestep in the simulation by comparing the state of the urn at the current and the previous timestep. Fig. 1 shows the average covariance values with and without prestige. Positive covariance on the right-hand plot indicates that prestige level covaries with fitness, therefore prestige poses positive selective pressure on variant evolution.

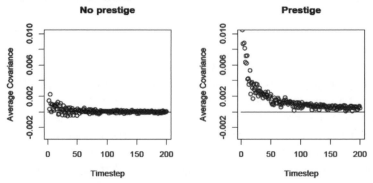

Figure 1. Covariance term of the Price equation calculated at each timestep of a Pólya urn simulation (values averaged for each timestep over 1000 simulation runs). Decreasing values over time reflect the fact that adding one or two tokens has diminishing impact on the increasing population of tokens that accumulates in the urn.

This is a simple illustration of a methodology that can be extended in multiple ways: by examining the second term of the Price equation, transmission error can be investigated; the Pólya urn simulation can be extended to include social network structure, learning algorithms, generation turnover, random or directed mutation, etc.; the feature of interest can be not only social prestige, but also novelty value, resilience to noise, ease of production etc.

Acknowledgements

Monica Tamariz is funded by ESRC Grant RES-062-23-1537 and AHRC Grant AH/F017677/1. Thanks to W. Zuidema and G. Jaeger.

References

Croft, W. (2000). *Explaining language change*. Harlow: Longman.
Jaeger, G. (2008). Language evolution and George Price's "General theory of selection", in R. Cooper & R. Kempson (eds.), *Language in Flux: Dialogue Coordination, Language Variation, Change and Evolution*, College Publications, 53-82.
Price, G.R. (1970). Selection and covariance. *Nature*, 227, 520-521.

WHAT ARE THE ANALOGUES OF GENOTYPE AND PHENOTYPE IN THE CULTURAL EVOLUTION OF LANGUAGE?

MÓNICA TAMARIZ

Language Evolution and Computation, PPLS, The University of Edinburgh, 3 Charles Street, Edinburgh EH8, UK. monica@ling.ed.ac.uk.

Inspired by the assumption that all evolutionary systems are instantiations of the same process of random variation and differential retention of variants (Hull, 1988), a number of scholars have based their models of language change and evolution on evolutionary biology. The convention in evolutionary anthropology and archaeology tends to be that knowledge, skills and values residing in people's brains constitute the cultural genotype, while artifacts and behaviours constitute the phenotype (e.g. Boyd & Richerson, 1995). Some models of language evolution also see the genotype in mental entities such as rules (Kirby, 1999) or information in neural assemblies (Ritt, 2004). Others, however, define mental phenotypes: grammars, or sets of learned rules (Croft, 2000; Mufwene, 2008) and public, behavioural genotypes residing in usage data (utterances). This paper offers theoretical support and evidence for the latter option.

The relationship between phenotype and genotype is an asymmetric one: the central dogma of molecular biology (Crick, 1970) states that information cannot flow back from protein to gene. Generalising, phenotypic features, acquired during development, cannot be encoded in the genotype and therefore cannot be inherited. Genotypic information acquired during replication or mutation, on the other hand, is indeed heritable.

Let us consider two examples from language change: First, the ongoing collapse of a three-gender into a two-gender system in Dutch. Dutch masculine and feminine nouns take the definite article *de* (while neuter nouns take the article *het*), and speakers in some communities can't tell the gender of etymologically masculine or feminine words. When prompted to produce an utterance where a *de*-noun requires a (gendered) possessive, some speakers will apply the feminine possessive and others the masculine. This is evidence that, from the same usage data, some learners induce the masculine rule for a given noun while others induce the feminine rule. If the rules are the genotype, which replicate when speakers induce rules from data, and the data is the phenotype, we have here a case where genotypic information is not being faithfully replicated from generation to generation: different people have different rules in their grammars, but this is not noticed during communication because *de*-nouns seldom have gendered modifiers. However, if the data is the genotype and the rules are the phenotype that develops from the interaction between the data and the learner's brain, the different rules induced by different learners are simply phenotypes with different developmental trajectories. These different rules, as expected, are nevertheless faithfully replicate the genotypic information (*de* followed by noun) in the data they produce.

Second, during the process of degemination where a double consonant becomes a single consonant (e.g. Latin *cuppa* becomes Spanish *copa*), speakers before the change had a rule that distinguished between double and single consonants. After the change, speakers have a new rule for pronouncing the consonants that does not include such distinction. During the transition, speakers with the distinction rule produced data where double and single consonants were barely distinguishable; learners exposed to such data must have induced the no-distinction rule. If the rule is the genotype and the data is the phenotype that develops from the interaction between the rule and the social communicative environment, the loss of distinction between double and single consonants is acquired during development of the phenotype (production of data). The central dogma would not allow that information from being encoded into the genotype (the learners' rule); yet here phenotypic information does precisely that and continues to be inherited over subsequent generations. This is why it has been proposed that cultural evolution is Lamarckian, as it allows inheritance of acquired characters. A solution to this problem that does not require appealing to Lamarckism is to take the data to be the genotype and the rule to be the phenotype that develops from the interaction between the data and the brain during social communication. Now, the loss of distinction is an error in replication of the genotype (a mutation), which is, as expected, heritable.

References

Croft, W. (2000). *Explaining language change*. Harlow: Longman.

Boyd R. & Richerson, P. (1995). *Culture and the evolutionary process*. U. of Chicago Press.

Mufwene, S.S. (2008). *Language evolution: Contact, competition and change*. London: Continuum.

Hull, D.L. (1988). *Science as process*. U. of Chicago Press.

Ritt, N. (2004). *Selfish sounds and linguistic evolution*. Cambridge U. Press.

Kirby, S. (1999). *Function, selection and innateness*. Oxford U. Press.

Crick, F. (1970): Central Dogma of Molecular Biology. *Nature* 227, 561-563.

ACOUSTIC POTENTIAL FOR REFERENCE-LIKE COMMUNICATION IN WILD INDRIS

VALERIA TORTI[1], VIVIANA SORRENTINO[1], CRISTINA GIACOMA[1], MARCO GAMBA[1]

(1) Department of Animal and Human Biology, University of Turin, Via Accademia Albertina 13, 10123 Torino, Italy.

1. Introduction

In nonhuman Primates there is evidence that some vocalizations can be combined according to structural rules to form complex utterances (Zuberbühler, 2002). This combinatory ability, which resembles human language, is sometimes linked with changes in vocalizations meaning in relation to the context in which the vocal signal is emitted. Long-distance calls are relatively common among primates, including lemurs. However, indri (*Indri indri*) represents a unique case because of its impressive howling cries, known as "the song of the indri" (Sorrentino et al., 2010). The song is a complex sequence of vocalizations emitted by group members in a coordinated manner. The song informs neighbouring groups about the occupation of a territory and also may serve a cohesion function for the group members (Pollock, 1986). Within this study, we analyzed the acoustic features of indri's songs given in two different contexts: when the group members are in visual contact (Territorial songs, hereafter TS) and when indris are dispersed in their territory (Cohesion, hereafter CS). We aimed to investigate to what extent songs given in the two contexts showed acoustic differences that could show a potential for reference-like communication in these lemurs.

2. Materials and Methods

For the purpose of this work we studied 59 songs of 11 groups from different populations of indris (*Indri indri*) in Eastern Madagascar. We audio-recorded 31 individuals, both males and females, both adults and sub-adults. We recognized individual contribution to the song. For each song we measured: the number of notes, song duration, the percentage of individual contribution and the number of signallers. Statistical analyses were performed using SPSS 17.0 for Mac.

3. Results

We observed that while the group members usually did not show specific movements after TS, movements towards the direction of one of the emitters always followed the emission of CS. Analyzing the timing of each individual contribution we have found out that TS showed longer duration (127.4 s ± 74.8 s) than CS (74.6 s ± 24.8 s; t-test, N = 59, t = 2.918, p = 0.005). TS showed a higher number of notes uttered (70 ± 37), on average twice the number of the notes given in CS (35 ± 18; t-test, N = 59, t = 3.752, p < 0.001). Even if indris have shown that they do generally produce more calls during TS, the percentage of individual contribution is greater in CS (t-test, N = 59, t = -2.378, p = 0.021). Notes emitted during TS and CS showed differences in Fundamental frequency modulation in relation to the sex of the emitters.

4. Discussion and conclusion

This study provides evidence that the acoustic potential for functionally referential communication is present in the loud vocalizations of free-ranging strepsirrhines. Our results showed that songs given by the indris differ in timing of sound production and duration of the individual song depending on the context of emission (territorial vs. cohesion) and on the sex of signallers.

These differences are in agreement with the prediction that utterances serving different functions show characteristic acoustic cues (Clarke et al., 2006), even if, in the indris' song, they are mainly related to temporal parameters.

References

Clarke, E., Reichart, U. H., & Zuberbühler, K. (2006). The Syntax and Meaning of Wild Gibbon Songs. *PlosOne, 1,* 73.

Pollock, J. I. (1986). The song of Indris (*Indri indri*; Primates, Lemuroidea): Natural history, form and function. *International Journal of Primatology, 7,* 225-267.

Sorrentino, V., Gamba, M. & Giacoma, C. (2010). A quantitative description of the vocal types emitted in the indri's song. In J.C. Masters, M. Gamba and F. Genin (Eds.), *Leaping Ahead: Advances in Prosimian Biology.* New York: Springer Science + Business Media.

Zuberbühler, K. (2002). A syntactic rule in forest monkey communication. *Animal Behaviour, 63,* 293-299.

SIMPLE RULES CAN EXPLAIN DISCRIMINATION OF PUTATIVE RECURSIVE SYNTACTIC STRUCTURES BY SONGBIRDS: A CASE STUDY ON ZEBRA FINCHES

CAROLINE A.A. VAN HEIJNINGEN
Behavioural Biology, IBL Leiden University
Leiden, P.O. Box 9505, 2300 RA, the Netherlands
Leiden Institute for Brain and Cognition, Leiden University
Leiden, Postzone 2c-S, P.O. Box 9600, 2300RC, the Netherlands
c.a.a.van.heijningen@biology.leidenuniv.nl

JOS DE VISSER
Behavioural Biology, IBL Leiden University
Leiden, P.O. Box 9505, 2300 RA, the Netherlands

WILLEM ZUIDEMA
Institute for Logic, Language and Computation, University of Amsterdam
Amsterdam, P.O. Box 94242, 1090 GE, the Netherlands

CAREL TEN CATE
Behavioural Biology, IBL Leiden University
Leiden, P.O. Box 9505, 2300 RA, the Netherlands
Leiden Institute for Brain and Cognition, Leiden University
Leiden, Postzone 2c-S, P.O. Box 9600, 2300 RC, the Netherlands

According to a controversial hypothesis, a characteristic unique to human language is recursion (Hauser, Chomsky and Fitch, 2002). Contradicting this hypothesis, it has been claimed that the starling, one of the two animal species tested for this ability to date, is able to distinguish between acoustic stimuli based on the presence or absence of an abstract, center-embedded recursive structure i.e. they did distinguish between song fragments (A, B, etc) structured as AABB (recursive) and ABAB (non-recursive) (Gentner et al, 2006). In our experiment (van Heijningen et al, 2009) we show that another songbird species, the zebra finch, can also discriminate between artificial song stimuli with these structures. Zebra finches are able to generalize this to new songs constructed using novel elements belonging to the same categories, similar to starlings, i.e. new A and B type exemplars. However, to demonstrate that this is based on the ability to detect the putative recursive structure it is critical to test whether the birds can also distinguish songs with the same structure consisting of elements belonging to novel, unfamiliar categories, in this case C's and D's. We performed this test and show that seven out of eight zebra finches failed it. This suggests that the acquired discrimination was based on phonetic rather than syntactic generalization. The eighth bird, however, must have used more abstract, structural, cues. Nevertheless, further probe testing showed that the results of this bird, as well as those of others, could be explained by simpler rules than recursive ones. The eight bird for instance, used 'recency xx', meaning that he seemed to respond to structures ending with a repeated element and so made the distinction between AABB and ABAB instead of using all elements. Although our study casts doubts on whether the rules used by starlings and zebra finches really provide evidence for the ability to detect recursion as present in 'context-free' syntax, it does provide clear evidence for abstract learning of vocal structure in a songbird.

References

Gentner, TQ, Fenn KM, Margoliash D, Nusbaum HC (2006). Recursive syntactic pattern learning by songbirds. *Nature* 440:1204-1207.

Hauser MD, Chomsky N and Fitch WT (2002). The faculty of language: What is it, who has it and how did it evolve? *Science*, 298:1569-1579.

van Heijningen CAA, de Visser J, Zuidema W, ten Cate C (2009). Simple rules can explain discrimination of putative recursive syntactic structures by a songbird species. *Proc. Nat. Ac. Sci. USA*. 106 (48): 20538-20543.

THE CRITICAL PERIOD AND PRESERVATION OF EMERGED VOWEL SYSTEMS

TESSA VERHOEF & BART DE BOER

Amsterdam Center for Language and Communication, University of Amsterdam
Spuistraat 210, 1012 VT Amsterdam, the Netherlands
t.verhoef@uva.nl, b.g.deboer@uva.nl

The critical period for language acquisition is often assumed to be nothing more than a by-product of development. However, evolutionary computer simulations show that it can be explained as a result of biological evolution (Hurford, 1991). In the present study the aim is not to explain how and why this age sensitivity evolved but to investigate the consequences of this individual-level disadvantage on a culturally evolving vowel system as a whole. Using two different agent-based computer models it will be argued that a difference in learning ability between children and adults can improve the stabilization and preservation of complexity of vowel systems in a changing population.

The first model is a re-implementation of the one described by de Boer and Vogt (1999), which consists of a population of agents that interact through imitation games using realistic mechanisms for production and perception of vowels. The agents have a vowel memory in which they store learned prototypes of vowels and in response to their interactions with other agents they update their memory and learn new sounds. Analogous to the results of de Boer and Vogt (1999) the model shows that a population in which new members are born and old members die, a critical period stabilizes vowel systems over the generations. In this case the adults provide the learners with a stable target facilitating the acquisition process. Figure 1 shows the difference in the changes of the vowel system after transmission in a population with and without age structure.

The second model is a variation on the first which integrates the linguistic paradigm of Optimality Theory (OT). In this version of the model, the agents imitate each other using their own bidirectional stochastic OT grammar (Boersma & Hamann, 2008) consisting of a ranked set of articulatory and cue constraints. To produce or perceive a speech signal, a set of possible candidate forms is evaluated by the grammar. The candidate that violates the fewest highly ranked constraints is selected. In response to their interactions with other agents they learn by adjusting

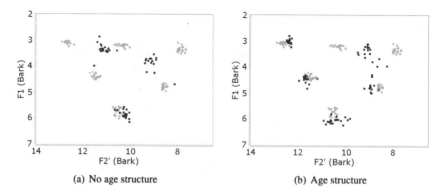

(a) No age structure   (b) Age structure

Figure 1.   Emerged vowel systems in the first model. Initial vowel system in grey.

the ranking values in their grammar. This new approach replicates the stabilizing effects on the emerged vowel systems.

The results suggest that the critical period might be more than just an unfortunate consequence of development since its influence can be beneficial at the population level. If complexity can be more faithfully transmitted from one generation to the next, there is less need for new agents to reinvent structures that were already present. A cultural behavior can lead to biological adaptations for this behavior (the Baldwin effect). However, in language, one of the obstacles involved in this process is change (Christiansen & Chater, 2008). Biological evolution takes a long time to evolve adaptations, so the more stable the linguistic environment, the higher the expected role of the Baldwin effect. We propose that the age structure plays a role in the evolution of adaptations for functional features of language. It may provide the stability needed for the evolution of learning biases that favor the acquisition of more complex speech (and language).

Acknowledgement

The research is part of the NWO vidi project *Modelling the Evolution of Speech*.

References

Boersma, P., & Hamann, S. (2008). The evolution of auditory dispersion in bidirectional constraint grammars. *Phonology*, *25*(02), 217–270.

Christiansen, M., & Chater, N. (2008). Language as shaped by the brain. *Behavioral and Brain Sciences*, *31*(05), 489–509.

de Boer, B., & Vogt, P. (1999). Emergence of speech sounds in changing populations. In D. Floreano, J. D. Nicoud, & F. Mondada (Eds.), *Advances in artificial life* (pp. 664–673). Berlin Springer Verlag.

Hurford, J. R. (1991). The evolution of the critical period for language acquisition. *Cognition*, *40*(3), 159–201.

SIMULATIONS OF SOCIO-LINGUISTIC CHANGE: IMPLICATIONS FOR UNIDIRECTIONALITY

MAARTEN VERSTEEGH

Centre for Language Studies, Radboud University,
Erasmusplein 1, 6525 HT Nijmegen, The Netherlands
m.versteegh@let.ru.nl

FEDERICO SANGATI & WILLEM ZUIDEMA

Institute for Logic, Language and Computation, University of Amsterdam,
Science Park 904, 1098 XH Amsterdam, The Netherlands
f.sangati@uva.nl, zuidema@uva.nl

1. Unidirectionality in linguistic change

The study of language change is relevant for theories of language evolution in various ways. One important connection emerging from grammaticalization theory is the unidirectionality hypothesis (Hopper & Traugott, 2003): the idea that language change is a directed rather than a cyclical process. While not without its critics, (cf. Fischer (2000), Newmeyer (2006)), unidirectionality allows for the reconstruction of earlier language states, including, at least in principle, the earliest stage of human language (Heine & Kuteva, 2002). The aim of this paper is to study the plausibility of unidirectionality and the possibility of cyclical processes from the perspective of social factors in language change, using computer models of cultural transmission.

2. A simulation of socio-linguistic change

We present a number of high-level computer models simulating the social factors involved in language change. The models all build on the concept of a *linguistic community*, consisting of interacting agents that adapt their use of linguistic items to their peers. Linguistic items are treated as cultural traits: pieces of information that are transmitted through the population by social learning.

We study the effects of different transmission models, inspired by Nettle's (1999) adaptation of Social Impact Theory. We simulate language learning, where the linguistic items acquired by an individual are a function of the community's linguistic behaviour. This function incorporates differences in social status, proximity of agents to each other and the number of individuals carrying different traits. The result is a high-level description of a heterogeneous linguistic community that allows us to efficiently study processes involved in language change, while considering different community structures, learning algorithms and language structures. We incorporate insights from socio-linguistic theories on the transmission of linguistic forms; in particular, we model William Labov's (2001) investigations into probability matching in variant use by formalizing the social pressures on language users in a game-theoretic framework.

3. Results

The results of our simulations show that, due to the social factors we included in our models, language change frequently shows reversals, where two states of the language alternate. Moreover, we find that the direction of change, even in a small community, is often unpredictable. To the best of our knowledge, ours is the first model to show ongoing linguistic change, where the process neither settles in a fixed point nor continues to drift driven by stochasticity alone. Our findings imply that language change does not necessarily proceed unidirectionally, and thus call into question attempts to reconstruct early language states by backward application of general trends observed in diachronic change. This means that the results from historical linguistics need to be treated with caution when applied to the study of language evolution.

References

Fischer, O. (2000). Grammaticalisation: uni-directional, non-reversible? In O. Fischer, A. Rosenbach, & D. Stein (Eds.), *Pathways of change* (pp. 149–169). Benjamins.

Heine, B., & Kuteva, T. (2002). On the evolution of grammatical forms. In A. Wray (Ed.), *The transition to language* (pp. 376–397). Oxford: Oxford University Press.

Hopper, P., & Traugott, E. (2003). *Grammaticalization.* Cambridge: Cambridge University Press.

Labov, W. (2001). *Principles of linguistic change: social factors.* Malden, Massachusetts: Blackwell Publisher.

Nettle, D. (1999). Using Social Impact Theory to simulate language change. *Lingua, 108,* 95–117.

Newmeyer, F. (2006). What can grammaticalization tell us about the origins of language? In A. Cangelosi, A. Smith, & K. Smith (Eds.), *The evolution of language* (pp. 434–435). World Scientific.

LESSONS FOR EVOLUTION FROM FIRST LANGUAGE DEVELOPMENT

MARILYN VIHMAN

Language and Linguistic Science, University of York, Heslington, York, England, UK

To gain insight into possible scenarios for evolution from what we know about the development of language it is useful to distinguish what is 'old' from what is 'new' in the species. I take just two properties of human language to be critically 'new': the wide diversity of sound patterns made possible by our uniquely flexible speech production mechanism – whereas the corresponding perceptual apparatus, widely shared by other mammals, is evolutionarily ancient (Hauser, 1996) and our capacity for declarative memory, which makes it possible to rapidly retain arbitrary sound-meaning pairings and thus to encode symbolic meaning (Deacon, 1997) – whereas the slow mechanisms of procedural memory are broadly characteristic of biological species (O'Reilly & Norman, 2002).

To understand ontogenetic development from (i) the production of speech-like or 'canonical' syllables, which emerge quite suddenly in the middle of the first year of life, through (ii) interpersonal discourse, which supports the construction of meaning, to (iii) symbolic word use and the beginnings of phonological systematicity in the second year, just two more characteristics of human brain function must be added: the Mirror Neuron response (di Pellegrino et al., 1992), which makes the actions of others salient sources of imitative behavior once a child's own repertoire includes those actions (Vihman, 2002), and the rhythmic underpinning of emergent motor skills (Thelen, 1981), including canonical babbling (Oller, 2000). One key element in this developmental profile cannot be projected back to evolutionary time – namely, 'interpersonal discourse'. However, Knight (2000) argued persuasively that vocal exploration in the safety of the mother-child relationship, with instinctive turn-taking and mutual imitation, is a highly plausible source for the 'discovery' of the potential of distinctive sound patterns for carrying referential meaning.

The first vocal symbols take on meaning from their use in consistent situational or affective contexts, whether learned from adults or, in the case of 'protowords', 'invented' as a response to the expressive impulse (Vihman, 1996). The next step is the formation of categories of prosodic shapes or 'templates' based on distributional learning over the early vocal forms (or exemplars), as is found in both first and second language learning (Ellis, 2005; Vihman & Croft, 2007). Here the principles of rhythm, alliteration, assonance, etc. which underlie adult poetic practice (and which serve a mnemonic as well as an aesthetic function) must be at work. Since subtle templatic patterns have been identified in both Semitic (McCarthy & Prince, 1995) and non-Semitic adult languages (Scheer, 2004), this patterning in the service of memory, which we see as the origins of system in the child, could have arisen in a similar way in prehistory, through cycles of declarative and procedural learning – once vocal exploration had led to the first symbolic expression.

References

Deacon, T. (1997). *The Symbolic Species.* New York: W. W. Norton.

di Pellegrino, G., Fadiga, L., Fogassi, L., Gallese, V. & Rizzolatti, G. (1992). Understanding motor events. *Experimental Brain Research, 91,* 176-180.

Ellis, N. C. (2005). At the interface: Dynamic interactions of explicit and implicit language knowledge. *Studies in Second Language Acquisition, 27,* 305-352.

Hauser, M. D. (1996). *The Evolution of Communication.* Cambridge, MA: MIT Press.

Knight, C. (2000). Play as precursor of phonology and syntax. In C. Knight, M. Studdert-Kennedy & J. Hurford (eds.), *The Evolutionary Emergence of Language.* Cambridge: CUP.

McCarthy, J. & Prince, A. (1995). Prosodic morphology. In J. Goldsmith (ed.) *The Handbook of Phonological Theory.* Cambridge, MA: Blackwell.

Oller, D. K. (2000). *The Emergence of the Speech Capacity.* Mahwah, NJ: Lawrence Erlbaum.

O'Reilly, R. C. & Norman, K. A. (2002). Hippocampal and neocortical contributions to memory. *Trends in Cognitive Sciences, 6,* 505-510.

Scheer T. (2004), *A Lateral Theory of Phonology, vol. I,* Berlin, Mouton de Gruyter.

Thelen, E. (1981). Rhythmical behavior in infancy: An ethological perspective. *Developmental Psychology, 17,* 237-257.

Vihman, M. M. (1996). *Phonological Development.* Oxford: Blackwell.

Vihman, M. M. (2002). The role of mirror neurons in the ontogeny of speech. In M. Stamenov & V. Gallese (eds.), *Mirror Neurons and the Evolution of Brain and Language.* Amsterdam: John Benjamins.

Vihman, M. M. & Croft, W. (2007). Phonological development: Toward a 'radical' templatic phonology. *Linguistics, 45,* 683-725.

THE RELEVANCE OF BODY LANGUAGE TO EVOLUTION OF LANGUAGE RESEARCH

SŁAWOMIR WACEWICZ & PRZEMYSŁAW ŻYWICZYŃSKI

Department of English, Nicolaus Copernicus University, Fosa Staromiejska 3
Toruń, 87-100, Poland

The heterogeneous category of phenomena covered by the term *body language* (roughly equivalent to nonverbal communication, NVC), although essential to human day-to-day communication, is also largely dissociable from human verbal behaviour. As such, it has received little attention in the area of evolution of language research. In this paper we point to an important factor – signal reliability (honesty) as an elementary constraint on communication as an evolutionarily stable strategy (ESS) – which shows promise of restoring the relevance of broadly construed *body language* to the evolution of language.

Contemporary research on the emergence of language-like communication has tended to target the language-related cognitive capacities, with relatively less focus on the fundamental game-theoretic constraints as dictated by evolutionary logic. Communication, in order to remain an ESS, must be *honest*, i.e. signals must be reliably correlated with those aspects of the environment for which they are shorthand[1]. Despite suggestions at possible mechanisms (e.g. Scott-Phillips 2008), the origin of honest, cooperative signalling in human phylogeny remains among the least understood aspects of the evolution of language.

It has been compellingly argued that the evolution of communication in nonhuman animals is reception-driven, i.e. it is the receivers that are selected to "acquire information from signalers who do not, in the human sense, intend to provide it" (Seyfarth & Cheney 2003: 168). Body language is characterised by similar properties, that is the transfer of information not intentionally provided by the signaller. Crucially, it is this last property that makes body language resistant to manipulation, and thus endows it with relatively high signal reliability (honesty). At the same time, in *mimetic* (Donald 1991) creatures, body

---

[1] The full argument, principally an extension of the reasoning already extremely well established in evolutionary literature, is made in Wacewicz & Żywiczyński (2008), section 2.

language can be brought under limited voluntary control by the signaller, with its elements selected as self-contained individual communicative segments. Consequently, although lacking continuity in most other respects, in this respect body language becomes continuous with language-like communication. This fact is most clearly reflected in gesture studies where gesticulations are placed on a continuum, through pantomime and emblems, to linguistic signs (McNeill 2005).

We argue that the set of phenomena subsumed under the term 'body language' is very likely to have played an essential role at the critical bootstrapping stages of (proto)language evolution by attenuating its initial fragility. At a minimum, body language could have provided a reliable frame of reference to check against during exchanges of first language-like messages (e.g. Laver & Hutcheson 1972 for examples from modern human communication). More boldly, however, it can be proposed that microbehaviours originating in body language could have themselves become taken over and employed as segments in a qualitatively new communicative system. This possibility is relevant to increasingly popular 'gesture-first' theories (e.g. Corballis 2002), and still more relevant to 'gesture-together-with-speech' theories (e.g. McNeill 2005), providing a noteworthy alternative to the assumption that the first signs had their origins, through ritualisation or otherwise, in instrumental action. We offer this last suggestion merely as an interesting conjecture, which nevertheless has the merit of pointing to a yet unexplored research area.

References

Corballis, M. C. (2002). *From hand to mouth: The origins of language.* Princeton, NJ: Princeton University Press.

Donald, M. (1991). *Origins of the modern mind.* Harvard: Harvard University Press.

Laver, J. & Hutcheson, S. (1972). *Communication in Face to Face Interaction.* Harmondsworth: Penguin Books.

McNeill, D. (2005). *Gesture and Thought.* Chicago: Chicago University Press.

Scott-Phillips, T. (2008). On the correct application of animal signalling theory to human communication. In A. D. M. Smith and K. Smith and R. Ferrer-i-Cancho (eds.), *Proceedings of the 7th International Conference on the Evolution of Language* (pp. 275-282). World Scientific.

Seyfarth, R. & Cheney, D. (2003). Signalers and receivers in animal communication. *Annual Review of Psychology, 54*, 145-173.

Wacewicz, S. & Żywiczyński, P. (2008). Broadcast Transmission, Signal Secrecy and Gestural Primacy Hypothesis. In A. D. M. Smith and K. Smith and R. Ferrer-i-Cancho (eds.), *Proceedings of the 7th International Conference on the Evolution of Language* (pp. 354-361). World Scientific.

VOCAL AND FACIAL PRODUCTIONS IN NONHUMAN PRIMATES: DO THEY EXPRESS EMOTIONS OR LANGUAGE RELATED TREATMENTS?

CATHERINE WALLEZ & JACQUES VAUCLAIR

Center for Research in the Psychology Cognition, Language & Emotion, Department of Psychology, University of Provence, 13621 Aix-en-Provence, France.

In humans, facial expressions, associated or not with speech, constitute a mean of communication in itself. By contrast, facial and vocal productions in nonhuman primate are essential communicative signals that form an integral part of inter-individual social interactions. The measures of asymmetrical facial expressions in humans show a right hemi-face bias when speaking and a left side bias for expressing facial emotions (Graves & Landis, 1990). These findings demonstrate the right hemispheric dominance theory for the control of emotions whatever the emotional valence (i.e., Borod et al., 1997). However, Davidson et al. (1990) have formulated a hypothesis named the valence theory for which negative emotions are controlled by the right cerebral hemisphere and positive ones by the left cerebral hemisphere. Few studies have investigated hemispheric lateralization for vocal and facial productions in nonhuman primates. In chimpanzees and in rhesus monkeys, a significant leftward bias (hence right hemisphere dominance) for emotional expressions was found, whereas a significant left bias for positive emotions and a right bias for the negative ones was reported in marmosets (for a review, see Hopkins & Fernandez-Carriba, 2002). Reynold Losin et al. (2008) have found a right hemi-face bias for producing learned vocal signals (atypical sounds intentionally produced by captive chimpanzees). In view of these few studies, one of our primary interests is to study the presence of asymmetrical oro-facial productions in baboons in order to determinate if these communicative signals reflect cerebral control that are related to homologues of the language area, or by contrast are of a purely emotional nature. According to the emotional hemispheric dominance theory, it is expected that the left side of the baboon's face, and thus the right hemisphere, would be more involved in the production of vocal and facial expressions whatever the emotional valence. However, in compliance with the valence

518

theory, we should observe an involvement of the right hemisphere for negative emotions and a left hemisphere specialization for positive emotions. Still images of full expressions from videos were obtained on a sample of 73 captive baboons (*Papio anubis*) concerning affiliative (lipsmack, copulation calls) and agonistic behaviors (screeching, eyebrow rising). To analyze still pictures, a line is drawn between the inner corners of the eyes and compared to the horizontal lines on a fixed grid in order to rotate the face into a vertical position. A perpendicular vertical line is drawn at the midpoint of the line between the inner corners of the eyes that split the face into two halves. To measure the hemi-mouth's area, a freehand line on the inner side of each hemi-mouth is drawn and the surface (in pixels) is calculated for the two hemi-mouths. A Facial Asymmetry Index (FAI) is calculated by subtracting the left hemi-mouth area from the right hemi-mouth area and divided by the sum of right and left measures. The results are still under analysis. However some interesting findings are already available. Thus, for screeching, an agonistic behavior, a significant leftward bias appeared ($t(48) = -0.07$, $p = <.01$). The results will be discussed in the light of the available literature concerning asymmetrical facial and vocal emotional productions in nonhuman primates and hypotheses regarding language evolution from the perspective of our primate heritage.

This research was supported by a French National Research Agency (ANR) grant reference ANR-08-BLAN-0011_01.

References

Borod, J. C., Haywood, C. S., & Koff, E. (1997). Neuropsychological aspects of facial asymmetry during emotional expression: a review of the normal adult literature. *Neuropsychology Review, 7,* 41-60.

Davidson, R. J., Eckman, P., Saron, C. D., Senulis, J.A., & Friesen, W.V. (1990). Approach-withdrawal and cerebral asymmetry: emotional expression and brain physiology. *Journal of Personality and social Psychology, 58,* 330-341.

Graves, R., & Landis, T. (1990). Asymmetry in mouth opening during different speech tasks. *International Journal of Psychology, 25,* 179-189.

Hopkins, W. D., & Fernandez-Carriba, S. (2002). Laterality of communicative behaviours in nonhuman primates : a critical analysis. In L. J. Rogers & R. J. Andrew (Eds.), *Cerebral vertebrate lateralization* (pp. 445-479). New-York: Cambridge University Press.

Reynolds Losin, E. A., Russel, J. L., Freeman, H., Merguerditchian, A., & Hopkins, W. D. (2008). Left hemisphere specialization for oro-facial movements of learned vocal signals by captive chimpanzees. *PLoS ONE, 3,* 1-7.

LANGUAGE AS EXTENDED PHENOTYPE?

DENNIS P WATERS
GenomeWeb LLC, 125 Maiden Lane
New York, NY, 10038, USA

Several insights of evolutionary biologist Richard Dawkins have contributed to the study of language evolution. One often cited is the *meme* – a culturally-transmitted replicator (Dawkins, 1976). In addition, the work of Krebs and Dawkins (1984) on animal signaling is widely referenced. One less-cited Dawkins concept is the *extended phenotype* (Dawkins, 1982). Kirby observed that language is "part of our *extended phenotype*" (1998, emphasis his), and Levinson and Evans state that humans have "a very highly developed 'extended phenotype'" (2009), but how might this apply to language evolution?

It is the view of Dawkins that the somatic phenotype is incomplete, that the effects of genes can also constitute an extended phenotype (*"EP"*) in the form of artifacts or effects on the behavior of others. This concept was introduced as part of his larger project of developing a "gene-centric" view of evolution, so his book on the topic (Dawkins, 1982) does not discuss language as such.

For example, consider the spider's web. Although an artifact, the web is as much a part of her phenotype as her legs or eyes, "a huge extension of the effective catchment area of her predatory organs" (Dawkins, 1982). The work of beavers is a related artifactual example, although there is a key difference. The web is transient; its functional value disappears with the death of the spider. A dam, on the other hand, can outlive the beaver(s) that built it and continue to function for future populations.

Dawkins also considers phenotypes extended not by *construction* but by *instruction*. Many examples can be found in the somewhat gruesome world of animal parasites. At some stage in their often complex life cycles, many parasites use chemical signals to control the behavior of their intermediate hosts, often to the hosts' detriment (Moore, 2002). This is a different sort of EP, not *artifactual* but *behavioral*.

A more complex behavioral example is the alarm system of vervet monkeys

(Cheney & Seyfarth, 1990). They use three calls – one for each of three predator classes and each yielding a specific evasive behavior. When one monkey sees a predator, it emits the characteristic alarm and nearby monkeys engage in the appropriate behavior. The "lookout" is part of the EP of every other monkey, but the others also are part of the lookout's EP. The monkeys appear to share a *common, socially-constructed* EP, but their audible behavioral controls work only in the present time and in the local environment.

Do these examples clarify whether the EP is relevant to language evolution? Two thoughts come to mind. First, language is an artifact like a spider's web or a beaver's dam. It persists as long as new speakers come into being, and its functionality outlives its creators. But it is also an artifact that can continue to influence the behavior of others – not only a *construction*, but a construction that embodies *instruction*. Through language, the human phenotype can extend without limit spatially and temporally.

One constraint is that the EP is limited to the effects of language on others' behavior, and while these effects contribute raw material to natural selection (Waddington, 1972), they are not the entire story. Also, it is debatable whether a strict "gene-centric" reading of Dawkins includes artifacts and influences that are not under direct genetic control. Perhaps when Kirby and others speak of the EP, they are speaking metaphorically. But metaphor or not, the EP appears worthy of further analysis for thinking about language evolution.

References

Cheney, D., & Seyfarth, R. (1990). *How Monkeys See the World: Inside the Mind of Another Species*. Chicago: University of Chicago Press.

Dawkins, R. (1982). *The Extended Phenotype*. San Francisco: W.H. Freeman.

Dawkins, R. (1976). *The Selfish Gene*. Oxford: Oxford University Press.

Kirby, S. (1998). Fitness and the selective adaptation of language. In J. Hurford, M. Studdert-Kennedy, & C. Knight, (Eds.). *Approaches to the Evolution of Language* (pp. 359-383). Cambridge, UK: Cambridge University Press.

Krebs, J. & Dawkins, R. (1984). Animal signals: mind reading and manipulation. In J. Krebs & N. Davies (Eds.). *Behavioural Ecology: An evolutionary approach, Second Edition* (pp. 380-402). Oxford: Blackwell.

Levinson, N. & Evans, S.C. (2009). With diversity in mind: freeing the language sciences from universal grammar. *Behavioral & Brain Sciences* 32:472-484.

Moore, J. (2002). *Parasites and the Behavior of Animals*. New York: Oxford University Press.

Waddington, C.H. (1972). Epilogue. In C.H. Waddington (Ed.). *Towards a Theoretical Biology 4: Essays* (pp. 283-289). Chicago: Aldine.

RECONSIDERING THE CODE MODEL OF COMMUNICATION FOR SIMULATIONS OF LANGUAGE EVOLUTION

MATTHIJS WESTERA

Graduate School of Natural Sciences, Utrecht University,
Leuvenlaan 4, 3584 CE Utrecht, The Netherlands
Matthijs.Westera@phil.uu.nl

In all human languages, the link between forms and meanings is highly *systematic*. Particular forms correspond to particular meanings, and particular compositions of forms correspond to particular compositions of meanings (*compositionality*). The conditions under which compositional languages may evolve have been extensively studied, often employing computational models (Briscoe, 2002). Such conditions are for instance the presence of a *learning bottleneck* (Kirby, 2002) and the presence of certain innate or acquired *learning biases* (Smith, 2003).

Smith (2003) developed a model to investigate which learning biases are required for a compositional language to evolve in a population of agents. In the model, each agent is modelled as an association network linking signals to meanings. The algorithms for signal production and signal interpretation strongly resemble encoding and decoding. For instance, interpreting a signal amounts to retrieving the meaning to which the signal is most strongly associated.

Smith (2003) concluded that two learning biases are necessary for the emergence of a highly compositional language. First, the agents in the population need a bias in favour of one-to-one mappings between signals and meanings. Second, the agents need a bias in favour of decomposing signals and meanings into smaller parts. In a population of agents lacking one or both of these biases, a compositional language cannot be maintained through a learning bottleneck.

This conclusion holds, at least, when the agents involved do not possess any inferential capabilities. The model in (Smith, 2003) is based on the *code model of communication*, which assumes that signal production and interpretation can be fully described as a matter of encoding and decoding (Shannon & Weaver, 1949). The central position of the code model in many computational models of language evolution has been food for discussion during previous editions of the Evolang conference. What will happen to the necessity of certain learning biases, as proposed by Smith (2003), if the assumptions underlying the code model of communication are dropped?

I will present a re-implementation of the model by Smith (2003) that addresses this question in two ways. First, following Langacker (1987) the model attempts to embed linguistic knowledge into the more general framework of conceptual knowledge. Utterance production and interpretation are regarded as the same cognitive process, rather than the antagonistic encoding and decoding. Additionally, following Hoefler (2009) the (cognitive) distinction between signals and meanings is entirely dropped.

Second, the model incorporates the *inferential account of communication* as formulated within Relevance Theory (Sperber & Wilson, 1995). The inferential account of communication describes utterance interpretation as an inferential process, rather than a mere decoding. Relevance Theory grounds inference in the fundamental principle that all cognitive processes tend to the maximisation of relevance, i.e. obtaining the highest effect, which is context-dependent, with the least effort. Context, finally, is modelled using the notions of *ignorable* and *inferable* information as introduced by Hoefler (2009).

Abandoning the code model as such has resulted in a synthesis of the model developed by Smith (2003) to simulate learning biases and the model developed by Hoefler (2009) to simulate the role of context. The results obtained with this synthesis confirm the findings of Smith (2003) and Hoefler (2009) individually. However, exploring the parameter space further, by combining different learning biases with different kinds of contexts, has so far revealed an interesting and complex interplay of language learning and language use.

I will explain how the learning bottleneck, learning biases and inference may together determine the evolution of systematic languages. Based on the results obtained, I will discuss the validity of the code model of communication for simulations of language evolution.

References

Briscoe, E. J. (2002). *Linguistic evolution through language acquisition: Formal and computational models.* Cambridge: Cambridge University Press.

Hoefler, S. H. (2009). *Modelling the role of pragmatic plasticity in the evolution of linguistic communication.* Edinburgh: Edinburgh University Press.

Kirby, S. (2002). Learning, bottlenecks and the evolution of recursive syntax. In E. J. Briscoe (Ed.), *Linguistic evolution through language acquisition: Formal and computational models.* Cambridge: Cambridge University Press.

Langacker, R. W. (1987). *Foundations of cognitive grammar: Theoretical prerequisites* (Vol. 1). Stanford, California: Stanford University Press.

Shannon, C. E., & Weaver, W. (1949). *A mathermatical model of communication.* Urbana, IL: University of Illinois Press.

Smith, K. (2003). *The transmission of language: models of biological and cultural evolution.* Edinburgh: Edinburgh University Press.

Sperber, D., & Wilson, D. (1995). *Relevance: Communication and cognition.* Oxford: Blackwell.

CULTURAL EVOLUTION OF BIRD SONG AND GENETIC DEGRADATION OF LEARNING BIAS

HAJIME YAMAUCHI*

TERRANCE W. DEACON**

KAZUO OKANOYA*

* *Laboratory for Biolinguistics, RIKEN Brain Science Institute (BSI), Japan*
hoplite/okanoya@brain.riken.jp

** *Department of Anthropology, University California, USA*
deacon@berkeley.edu

Over the last decade, the potential explanatory power of cultural evolution has been widely promoted in the field of language evolution. However, a recent study reports an intriguing case of cultural evolution (Fehér, Wang, Saar, Mitra, & Tchernichovski, 2009). Birds reared in a deprived, unexposed environment consisting of singing males acquire different types of songs to the wild-type. Interestingly, if their offspring of the captive birds are exclusively exposed to songs in this lineage, within a few generations, their songs converge back to the wild-type. This suggests that cultural evolution may not complexify a cognitive system if it is strongly genetically biased.

Deacon (2003) has proposed that the complexification of a cognitive system is often triggered by the degradation of genetic biases. Masked from natural selection, a given cognitive system would be unharnessed from its genetic biases: it would accept a novel information flow from various neural modules, and synergistically exhibit a new property. He termed this "*genetic redistribution*." Given this, Deacon hypothesizes that the perplexing case of the song evolution of the Bengalese finch (Okanoya, 2004) is due to the degradation of the genetic bias of song learning. He proposes that the domestication of the species allows novel neural modules to affect its song learning, and consequently complexifies the song pattern of the finch compared to that of its feral ancestor.

We model this hypothesis within the Iterated Learning Framework. Agents are represented as Jordan recurrent neural networks (Figure.1). The network is specifically chosen as it can naturally model sequential song production based on auditory feedback. During the learning period, a learning agent receives song inputs from an adult. Before the experiment begins, a neural network is trained to master a simple, linear song, and its weight configuration is then transferred to the

524

first agent as the genetic bias. Although this bias is inherited by the agent's descendants in order to model a masked situation, no selection is introduced. Thus, mutations gradually erode the original weight configuration over the generations, and degrade the genetic bias. Finally, to model the redistributional nature of the masking process an extra set of input nodes is designed to provide an additional source of information flow and random noises are constantly added to the nodes. In the early generations, inputs from these nodes may be ignored as the network is trained to focus only on inputs fed back from the output layer in order to acquire the simple song provided during the training mode.

Our result demonstrates that as the genetic bias degrades over the generations, agents start to acquire more complex songs. This tendency is further strengthened by the iteration of learning, as later generations receive the deformed songs as their inputs. By and large, the result is on a par with (Ritchie & Kirby, 2005). However, we find that as noise is removed from the network, the birdsong tends to increase in single note repetition, and hence decreases in its complexity. The result supports Deacon's hypothesis.

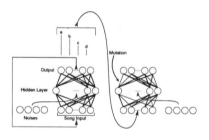

Figure 1.   A schematized figure of the model.

References

Deacon, T. W. (2003). Multilevel selection in a complex adaptive system: The problem of language origins. In B. H. Weber & D. J. Depew (Eds.), *Evolution and learning* (p. 81-106). Cambridge, MA: The MIT Press.

Fehér, O., Wang, H., Saar, S., Mitra, P. P., & Tchernichovski, O. (2009). De novo establishment of wild-type song culture in the zebra finch. *Nature*, *459*(7246), 564–568.

Okanoya, K. (2004). The bengalese finch: A window on the behavioral neurobiology of birdsong syntax. *Annals of the New York Academy of Science*, *1016*, 724-735.

Ritchie, G., & Kirby, S. (2005). Selection, domestication, and the emergence of learned communication systems. In *Second international symposium on the emergence and evolution of linguistic communication.*

OPTIMALITY AND TELEOMATIC CAUSES IN THE FACULTY OF LANGUAGE

HAJIME YAMAUCHI

KAZUO OKANOYA

Laboratory for Biolinguistics, RIKEN Brain Science Institute (BSI), Japan
okanoya@brain.riken.jp

In the mid 1990's, Chomsky started a new research program called "the Minimalist program". He abductively infers that the kernel of the language faculty (the faculty of language in the narrow sense, FLN) would be perfect in an ontological sense: one which is similarly found in physical systems such as snow flakes or soap films (Chomsky, 2004). These physical entities can spontaneously optimize their states against restrictions acting as their boundary conditions. Along the same line, Chomsky writes that the peculiar property of FLN is mostly described as the result of its spontaneous reaction to constraints imposed by other neural modules where FLN is inserted. Using its strongest thesis, Minimalism postulates that FLN is completely comparable with physical, non-adaptive principles.

One of the secondary effects of this thesis is its implications for language evolution: If it is really proven, Chomsky claims, a teleonomic explanation of the ontological emergence of FLN becomes unnecessary (Chomsky, 2004). Instead, one can consider the emergence of FLN as a result of non-organismal processes in living organisms. Mayr (1974) has pointed out that apparently end-directed processes also exist in physical systems (such as the fact that a pendulum always stopping at the plumb line). He called such a propensity in physics "*teleomatic*", although he did not himself believe that teleomatic properties have a causal power in evolution. Yet, this line of thinking has been elaborated on recently. For instance, Kauffman (1989) assumes that self-organization, a teleomatic process in non-equilibrium systems, would be utilized a number of times during the history of biological evolution. Minimalism follows this avenue, and this is partly why self-organization has become one of the key terms in the program.

We believe, however, that this derived conclusion seems to be a little farfetched. For example, while approving his creative contribution to evolutionary biology, Gould (Gould, 1971) refuted D'Arcy Thompson's view of physicomathematical regularities in living organisms. Thompson indicated that such regularities found in various forms of organisms are traces of physical principles working on them, and there is no need to invoke adaptive explanations. However, this does not necessarily mean that there is no teleonomic cause involve. Consider the case of honeycomb, one of the most cited examples of perfect physico-mathematical regularities found in living organisms. If its ontological emergence is purely teleomatic, how do we explain its obvious function as a nest (e.g., structural strength, minimal usage of resources, and/or maximized capacity with minimized surface occupation)? If these functions are not teleofunctional, they must be somehow exapted. However, this claim is implausible as it suggests that the ancestral honeybees had somehow started to create honeycomb (with the perfect form) for nothing, and then began to use it as a nest.

We identify as a problem with the program that it vests teleomatic processes with too much explanatory power. The strong minimalist thesis seems like an attempt to expel all possible teleonomic factors from the kernel of the language faculty. To rectify this view (and while allowing for the possibility of optimality in FLN), we hypothesize that FLN has taken advantage of teleomatic properties at various stages in its evolution. In other words, teleomatic processes are subsumed within teleonomic processes in evolution. Adaptive evolution is an optimization process of a number of parameters distributed on a higher-order space. As Kauffman (1989) has eloquently expressed, teleomatic processes enable organisms to establish orders *for free*. Together with the fact that breaking physical stabilities would be a costly option, evolution may sometimes leave organisms under local minima in adaptation (This is somewhat similar to the fact that historical contingencies often interfere optimizing adaptation), but carve physico-mathematical traces on their forms. This is why, we believe, parts of the language faculty appears as though they are defying potential adaptive values of the system. We also assume that cultural evolution is a part of this synergy of teleonomic and teleomatic processes: by cascading information through learning, the parasitic knowledge of language becomes self-organized to take constraints imposed by the brain. Therefore, boundary conditions mostly hold in the acquisition process, as, for example, in the poverty of the stimulus.

References

Chomsky, N. (2004). *The generative grammar enterprise revisited.* Berlin, Germany: Mouton de Gruyter.

Gould, S. J. (1971). D'arcy thompson and the science of form. *New Literary History, 2,* 229–258.

Kauffman, S. A. (1989). Adaptation on rugged fitness landscapes. In D. L. Stein (Ed.), *Lectures in the sciences of complexity* (Vol. I, p. 527-618). Redwood City, CA: Addison Wesley.

Mayr, E. (1974). Teleological and teleonomic: A new analysis. *Boston Studies in the Philosophy of Science, 14,* 91–117.

FROM BODY – TO MOUTH AND BODY

JORDAN ZLATEV[1], MERLIN DONALD[2] & GÖRAN SONESSON[1]

[1]*Centre for Cognitive Semiotics, SOL, Lund University, Sweden*
[2]*Department of Psychology, Queen's University, Ontario, Canada*

We aim to add some clarity to the ongoing debate between gesture-primacy and speech-primacy theories of language evolution by addressing the questions: (1) What is meant by "gestural primacy"? (2) What kind of evidence can be adduced for (or against) it? With respect to (1), we must distinguish between theories of (1a) an evolutionary stage of gestural language (Corballis 2002), (1b) gestural protolanguage ("protosign") (Arbib 2005) and (1c) gestural, and more generally mimetic prerequisites for (proto)language (Donald 1991, 1999; Zlatev 2003, 2008).

Concerning (2), a wealth of convergent evidence in favor of gestural primacy has been presented over the past decade: (2a) the ubiquity and universality of gesticulation (which differs from signed languages by not being fully conventional), in both speakers and signers; (2b) the overlap between the cortical regions involved in action, gesture and speech, with BA 45 standing out as a late specialization for the latter; (2c) the fact that human non-verbal communication is multi-modal, involving the whole body, and largely preserved in aphasia; (2d) the primacy of iconic and pointing gestures (and joint attention) with respect to speech in ontogenetic development; (2e) paleontological and archeological evidence showing adaptations in early Homo for tool use, but not for anatomical structures that have been associated specifically with speech, such as an enlarged hypoglossal canal and the canal down to the thorax: evidence for improved motor control of the tongue and breathing, respectively; (2f) the greater flexibility (of a limited range) of gestures in non-human apes compared to vocalizations.

While all of these can be (and have been) debated, when taken together they constitute a strong case for early Homo communication being carried out with the whole body, serving as a basis for the gradual recruiting of voluntary vocal signs (i.e. speech) overlying bodily communication as the main channel of language in hearing people – without replacing it, i.e. for theories of the type (1c).

If speech had evolved first, as a specific adaptation similar to birdsong, there would be no rationale for the late evolution of a multi-modal communication system. If a purely manual signed language (1a), or even protolanguage (1b), had evolved first, the evolution of speech remains problematic, as the constant recurrence of the counter-argument "why then don't we all use signed languages?" testifies. If speech and gesture evolved simultaneously and constitute an inseparable "single system", evidence of the type (2b-2f), and especially the preservation of whole body communication in speech breakdown becomes extremely difficult to account for.

The remaining alternative is that of the title: not "from hand to mouth" (Corballis 2002), but from whole-body communication, supported by species-specific adaptation(s) for bodily mimesis, to the multi-modal system of linguistic communication which we use today, involving both speech and "gesture", in a wide sense of the term (Zlatev and Andrén 2009).

References

Arbib, M. (2005). From monkey-like action recognition to human language: An evolutionary framework for neurolinguistics. *Behavioral and Brain Sciences* 28/2: 105-124.

Corballis, M. C. (2002). *From Hand to Mouth: The Origins of Language.* Princeton: Princeton University Press.

Donald, M. (1991). *Origins of the Modern Mind: Three stages in the Evolution of Culture and Cognition.* Harvard: Harvard University Press.

Donald, M. (1999). Preconditions for the evolution of protolanguages. In M. C. Corballis & I. Lea. (Eds.) *The Descent of Mind* (pp. 355-365). Oxford: Oxford University Press.

Zlatev, J. (2003). Meaning = Life (+ Culture). An outline of a unified biocultural theory of meaning. *Evolution of Communication,* 4/2: 253-296.

Zlatev, J. (2008). From proto-mimesis to language: Evidence from primatology and social neuroscience. *Journal of Physiology – Paris* 102: 137-152.

Zlatev, J., & Andrén, M. (2009). Stages and transitions in children's semiotic development. In J. Zlatev, M. Andrén, M. Johansson-Falck, & C. Lundmark (Eds.) *Studies in Language and Cognition,* 380-401. Newcaslte, UK: Cambridge Scholars Publishing.

Author Index